THE SOUL
and Graves
of
YUGOSLAVIA
1941 - 1946
A National Tragedy

Part 2

THE PROLOGUE TO THE TRAGEDY

MARKO PIVAC

Copyright © 2014 by Marko Pivac

All rights reserved

No part of this book may be reproduced or utilized in any form or by any means, mechanical or electronic, through photocopying, or by any other storage and retrieval system, without prior written permission by the author or his designated beneficiary. Inquiries should be addressed to Mrs. Kathleen Olsen, kwolsen@gmail.com.

Library of Congress Cataloguing-in-Publication Data

Pivac, Marko
The Soul and Graves of Yugoslavia, 1941-1946 A National Tragedy:
Part 2   The Prologue to the Tragedy/
Marko Pivac – 1st ed.

Cover design: Kathy Olsen

1. Activities of Section D of the Secret Intelligence Service and of the Special Operations Executive
2. "Subsidies" to domestic "contacts" and planning the "post-occupational resistance"
3. Aggressive overt and covert propaganda aimed at stimulating the Serb public opinion
4. Participation of British services in the preparation and timing of the coup of 27 March 1941
5. Misleading negotiations of support by the Soviet Union
6. Deceptions in the execution of the *coup d'état*
7. Formation and activities of the new government
8. Hitler's decision and crushing operations to destroy Yugoslavia as a national state
9. "Rifles against tanks", and the government hurriedly leaving the country
10. Dismemberment of Yugoslavia, annexations to Italy and Germany, occupations, formation of the Independent State of Croatia, prisoners of war
11. Seeds for the Yugoslavian national tragedy

Printed in the United States of America
ISBN-13 978-0-9720246-2-4

First edition 2014

IN MEMORY

OF THE VICTIMS

OF

THE SECOND WORLD WAR

Table of Contents

Acknowledgements xiii

Notes on the structure of the text.. xiv
   Notes on the pronunciation of the South-Slavic (Yugo-Slav) names............................ xiv

Shapers of events xv

Introduction 1

Chapter 1.. 2
   British secret services: SIS, MI(R), Section D, Electra House, and SOE 2
   Formation of Section D 2
   Belgrade: the center of Section D and its activities in the Balkans............................... 3
      • Widely connected Jakob Altmaier 4
      • Section D's man from Hungary 5
      • The "D" center in Cairo – for the Balkan section 5

Chapter 2.. 6
   Blockade of the Danube – an early Section D operation.. 6
      • The London Foreign Office – Section D conference, April 1940 6
      • Unsuccessful attempts of blocking the Danube 6
      • Germany's security units in Rumania.. 7
      • Hanau and Bailey withdrawn from Yugoslavia 7
   The end of Lawrence Grand's time in Section D 7
   Formation of the Special Operations Executive (SOE)... 8
      • Leadership of SOE, London 8
   Joint Section D / SOE operations in Yugoslavia 9
   Subversion – "an essential element in any large scale offensive action" 9
   Thomas Masterson's leadership of SOE Belgrade 10
   8 January 1941: "Interference with German Oil Supplies"... 10

Chapter 3.. 12
   Some Section D/SOE and military services' "contacts" in Belgrade............................ 12
      • Bailey – Mihailović – Birčanin – Žarko Popović – SOE 14
      • Popović - Mirković cooperation with the British before August 1940 17
      • Mirković – Mapplebeck intimate contacts... 17
      • Mirković – Mapplebeck – Žika Krstić connection 18
      • British contacts with officers 18
      • All British worked together 19
   Was General Mirković a British agent?.. 19
   Gen. Simović was activated after meeting Col. Donovan 20
   Work, and play …where gypsies strummed their violins 21

Chapter 4.. 23
   British "subsidies" to "contacts" in Yugoslavia 23
   Money from the secret vote 23
   Financing widespread activities 23
   "Operating through local organizations".. 25
   Subsidizing the Serbian Peasant Party 26
   Intention to bribe the Yugoslav General Staff 31
   Subsidizing Narodna Odbrana (The Defense League).. 31

After Thomas Masterson came to Belgrade *32*
Subsidizing the Democratic Party and the Independent Democrats *32*

Chapter 5 33

"Plastic and such, a few toys" – "Toys and chocolate" *33*
The "toys" for Hungary *33*
The "toys and chocolate" for the Middle East and Yugoslavia *34*

Chapter 6 36

George Taylor's mission in Belgrade: *36*
- *Taylor's report to SOE London, 26 February 1941* *37*

Chapter 7 39

Exploiting aggressive propaganda *39*
"... distributing clandestine printed propaganda and rumors ..." *39*
"... subsidies were given to certain Yugoslav newspapers." *39*
Britanova News Agency *40*
Magazine Britannia and biweeklies Balkan Herald and South Slav Herald *40*
Creating climate of opinion in favor of a coup *41*
Preparing Serb political and public opinion *41*
Pro-British Serb public opinion – SOE's best hope; British full-court-press on Prince Paul *41*
Simović: "Germany's penetration across the Danube ... should not have been allowed..." *43*
Agitation vociferous particularly from early March onwards *43*
- *Simović's praise of agitation and of his own role* *45*

Moscow's instructions to Lebedev and Tito *45*
American broadcasts in Serbo-Croat – in strong terms *46*
BBC's appeal to the Serbs: heavenly kingdom *47*
Stimulating the will of the Serbs to "resist" *47*
"... urging the necessity of action for a coup d'état" *49*

Chapter 8 50

Coup-wishers' diverse motivations and goals *50*
Motivation and goals of the Serbian Peasant Party *50*
Aims of Đonović – Trifunović-Birčanin and their friends *51*
- *Yugoslavia's joining the Tripartite Pact was not the initial motivation for the coup* *51*
- *Standing up to Germans – even at the cost of defeat* *52*
- *Disregarding Hitler's readiness to aid Italy in Albania* *52*

The coup: advantage for Britain, not for Yugoslavia *53*
London's reaction to the coup suggestion: premature at present, but keep in touch *53*
Agenda of the Democratic Party *54*
General Bora Mirković's motivation and objectives *54*
- *Writing memoirs with post-coup experience, March – November 1941* *54*
- *First take power in Belgrade by force ...* *55*
- *... then give the power to the Generals Simović and Ilić, ...* *55*
- *... and expect the victory* *55*

General Dušan Simović's motives and goals *56*
- *" ... my heart replied without meditation ... "* *56*
- *As stated in Simović's memoirs of 1 January 1944* *58*

Motivation of the Knežević brothers *59*
- *The Kneževićs expected a short war with Germany* *59*

The Putschists: Participants in victory *60*
Diversity of motivations and goals *60*
Simović missed a chance to harm the Axis' war effort *60*

Chapter 9 63
Preparing for the coup d'état of 27 March 1941 63
a reminder of the flow of major events: 63
An unrealistic political program, 11 March 1941 64

Chapter 10 67
SUNDAY, 23 MARCH 1941 67
Campbell's use of SOE 67
Đonović – Trifunović-Birčanin – Simović – Mirković connection 67
Mirković – Macdonald meeting, afternoon of the 23rd March 68
Did Gen. Mirković agree to put all troops in Belgrade under Major Živan Knežević's command? 68
Prince Paul – Minister Lane meeting, the evening of the 23rd March 70
Simović's meeting with Prince Paul, the evening of the 23rd March 70
- As Simović described the meeting 71
- This Simović's idea about guerrilla warfare in the mountains 71
- Maček's recollection of the meeting 72
- Mirković claimed: he had not known about Simović's audience with Prince Paul 73

Britain was not interested in a new Salonika Front 73

Chapter 11 74
MONDAY, 24 MARCH 1941 74
The meeting of the Commandants of the Belgrade garrison: Simović was informed of the secret clauses in the Pact 74
- Simović's account of the meeting 74
- General Pandurović's account of the meeting 75

Gen. Mirković threatened the Court Minister Milan Antić 77
Campbell's question to Eden on the desired timing of the coup 78
Eden authorized the coup d'état in Belgrade 78
Vojvoda Trifunović – General Mirković daily contact, 24 – 27 March 1841 78
Mirković – Vojvoda Trifunović-Birčanin cooperation, according to Mirković 79
More on Trifunović-Birčanin's daily contacts with Mirković, 24-27 March 80

Chapter 12 81
TUESDAY, 25 MARCH 1941 81
Živan Knežević's account: Two meetings with Mirković 81
Mirković - Mapplebeck meeting on 25 Mach 81
Mirković – Macdonald meeting, afternoon of the 25th March 82
Suggestion from London: Blow up the train with Ministers 83

Chapter 13 84
WEDNESDAY, 26 MARCH 1941 84
an early morning Macdonald – Simović secret meeting. 84
Notes 1 and 2 of the Tripartite Pact Protocol were published. 86
Activities on 26 March 1941 leading to the coup 86
- Živan Knežević's partial account – meeting with Mirković 87
- Before 10 a.m., the morning of the 26^{th,} : Simović – Mirković's 1st meeting 87
- Noon, 26 March – Simović: HE issued the order for the execution of the Putsch 87
- Živan Knežević: About noon, Mirković decided to act, but … 87
- Mirković's claim: after 1 p.m. on 26 March HE decided for the coup 88
- At 3:00 p.m.: Brothers Knežević – Mirković meeting 88
- Between 3:00 p.m and 5:00 p.m. – Mirković looked for Simović 89
- At 4:30 p.m., 26 March: Simović's instructions to a relative 89

Transfer of bombers to Zemun airport 89
- From Mirković's memoirs of 1 December 1941 89
- Mirković's letter to "The Evening News" (4 November 1960) has a different story 89

About 5 p.m. on 26 March, Simović – Mirković's 2nd meeting 90
- Mirković's version of the 2nd meeting 90
- Simović's version – written in exile 91
- Simović's version – written in 1951 91
- Simović's version – written in January 1956 91

Simović's letter to Churchill about Živan Knežević, 20 January 1956 93
Between 5 p.m. and 6 p.m. on 26 March, Macdonald – Simović's 2nd meeting 94
- Simović's version – written in exile 94
- Simović's version – written in 1951 95

Tupanjanin's pressure on Simović 95
In the evening of the 26th March: Simović – Mirković's 3rd meeting 96
According to Trifunović-Birčanin – Decision for the Putsch: between 7 and 9 p.m. 96
Gen. Mirković and Vojvoda Ilija Trifunović-Birčanin 96
On 26 March, after 9 p.m. – plan to blow up his train, seize Prince Paul 97
Preparation of the Royal Proclamation 98
- General Mirković's recollections of Radoje Knežević's role 98
- Živan Knežević's version 99
- What Simović said about the proclamation 100

Civilians aware of the preparations for the coup 100
- According to Mirković 100
- According to Simović 101

What was Radoje Knežević's coup-related role? 102
- First in R. Knežević's own words 102
- As stated by Simović on 28 March 1941, in 1944, and in 1951 107
- As stated by Dragiša Ristić in 1955 and 1966 108

Did Simović want to be "the leader of the state" like General Antonescu in Rumania? 110

Chapter 14 112

THURSDAY, 27 MARCH 1941 – the day of the military coup 112
Very early on 27 March, Mirković was assigning important missions; "...the King and people are in danger" 112
Execution of the coup – in the name of the young King 113
The deception of the diaspora 114
The deception of high Commanders 114
The formation of the new Government 115
- As stated by Gen. Simović on 28 March 1941: 115
- As described by the brothers Knežević 116
- "A painful scene" between the General and the Professor 116
- The Brothers Knežević's description of the Government's formation continues 117
- Developments as described by General Bora Mirković in 1941 118
- The formation of the new Government – Professor Mirko Kosić's version 119
- The formation of the new Government - a reported version of Vice Premier Slobodan Jovanović 120
- The formation of the new Government - Dragiša Ristić's version 121

Simović – Maček negotiations, 27 March 1941 122
The role of the Croats, Slovenes, and Bosnian Muslims in the new Government 122
- As explained by Simović on 28 March 1941 122
- And Simović added in 1951 123
- Not so, claimed Simović's second Vice Premier 123
- Actual reasons for the presence of the Croats, Slovenes, and Muslims in Simović's Government – according to Živan Knežević 124

Ordering Prince Paul to return to Belgrade 125
The story of the Royal Proclamation continues 126
- As described by Živan Knežević 126

Deception of the nation: Announcement of the Royal Proclamation on Radio Belgrade 127
- As Živan Knežević wrote about it: 127

- Simović, on 28 March: King's signature on the Proclamation was not important 128
"Full exploitation of the Royal Proclamation" *128*
    - Again, in Živan Knežević's words: 128
The effect of the Proclamation *129*
"The most moving and heartfelt demonstration of pure joy …" *129*
The Soviet Union's wishful effects of the coup *130*
… and falsification by the Communist " Scribe of the Revolution" *131*

Chapter 15 132

THURSDAY, 27 MARCH - Activities of the new government 132
German Minister's contact with Simović and Ninčić 132
Suggested: replacement of Valona for Salonika 132
Washington's message to the new Government 132
Simović maintained contact with Macdonald after the coup 132
BBC was pushing Yugoslavia into the war 133
Providing vague, encouraging information 134
Von Heeren's visit to Simović 134
Forced abdications of the Regents, Prince Paul's departure into exile 134
    - First, as told by Gen. Dušan Simović on 28 March 1941: 135
    - Second, from the letter of Capt. Božidar Delibašić[#] to Capt. Miodrag C. Urošević, 1961 135
"… without a plan, thoughtlessly, adventurously" *135*

Chapter 16 136

28 – 31 MARCH 1941 .... *136*
    - Friday, 28 March 1941 136
Hitler to Mussolini: protect passes from Yugoslavia to Albania 136
Early information on Hitler's decision to destroy Yugoslavia, while Churchill's hope was high ... 136
Simović spoke on 28 March 1941 136
Immediate task of the new Government – "peace-loving intent" 137
The Tripartite Pact Protocol was valid and in force 137
Replacement of Valona for Salonika rejected 137
Apologies for hostile behavior of the public 138
Simović – Lane meeting, the evening of 28 March 138
    - Saturday, 29 March 1941 139
Simović's conversation with the Italian Minister in Belgrade 139
Ninčić – Lane meeting; Eden's statement to the American Ambassador in Athens 139
Radoje Knežević … Minister of the Royal Court 139
(C)   Comintern's letter to Tito 140
(U)   Pavelić's debt to Mussolini: Dalmatia 140
    - Sunday, 30 March 1941 141
The new Government formally accepted the Tripartite Pact and disallowed Eden's visit 141
"This was their Roman holiday." *141*
Post-demonstrations worries *141*
Simović's oral offer of a mutual assistance pact with the Soviets 142
On the armaments of the Yugoslav army 142
(U) Details of Pavelić's group returning to Croatia were worked out 143
    - Monday, 31 March 1941 143
Macdonald confirmed: Mirković had informed him of planning the coup 143

Chapter 17 145

1 – 5 APRIL 1941 .... *145*
    - Tuesday, 1 April 1941 145
Three messages foretelling trouble for Yugoslavia 145
Government's attempt at mediation with Hitler (1 – 5 April 1941) 145
    - According to Vice Premier Slobodan Jovanović: 145
    - According to Dragiša Ristić 145

Ninčić "was simply and solely a supporter of the Protocol (Tripartite Pact), which was signed in Vienna." 146
General Dill's secret and unsuccessful visit to Belgrade 31 March – 1 April 1941 146
- Wednesday, 2 April 1941 147
Vauhnik sent warning to Belgrade 147
Campbell – Mirković, and Macdonald – Mirković meetings, 2 April 148
- Thursday, 3 April 1941 149
The British were dissatisfied with the attempts of mediation 149
Belgrade did not trust Vauhnik's telegrams 150
"... blocking the Danube ... the decisive factor for England ..." 151
State of affairs always hard, but nevertheless not critical 151
Acceptance of the Tripartite Pact Protocol confirmed 151
The British – Yugoslav conference in Greece, 3-4 April 1941 151
- Friday, 4 April 1941 152
Maček – Simović brief meeting 152
Belgrade, Zagreb and Ljubljana were declared open cities 152
Campbell: Simović considered the German attack almost unavoidable 152
Churchill about Germany's onslaught on Yugoslavia 152
- Saturday, 5 April 1941 153
British warning of the forthcoming German attack 153
Government's last peacetime session and Simović's "fiery speech" 154
- Jovanović 154
- Živan Knežević 154
- Maček 155
- Ristić 155

Chapter 18 157

SUNDAY, 6 APRIL 1941, in Moscow, Belgrade 157
The Soviet – Yugoslav treaty negotiations, 1941 157
- General Simović's claim to the initiative for the establishment of relations 157
- Milan Gavrilović's information on the subject 158
- Timetable of the Soviet-Yugoslav agreement negotiations 158
- Colonel Žarko Popović, Military Attaché in Moscow 159
- Clandestine talks in Paris, September 1940, and a shopping list 159
- The Soviets wanted to avoid a collision with Germany 159
- Offer of armament 159
- Stalin suspected Yugoslavia's proposals for cooperation 160
- Stalin was informed of Hitler's plan to attack the Soviet Union 160
- Gavrilović's report to Cincar Marković, 14 March 1941 160
- Soviet Politburo approved negotiations for a Soviet-Yugoslav treaty 160
- Negotiations with Vishinsky 161
- The neutrality clause in the Soviet-Yugoslav agreement 161
- Prince Paul's information of Hitler's intention to attack the Soviet Union was known to Simović and others 162
- Reports on forthcoming attack on Yugoslavia 163
- Negotiations in Moscow on 4 April, between Vishinsky and Gavrilović 163
- Molotov informed the German Ambassador of Yugoslavia's proposal 164
- A pact of Soviet-Yugoslav assistance ... incongruous with Soviet aims 164
- Negotiations in Moscow continued on 5 and 6 April 164
- Signing of the agreement in Moscow, on 6 April 164
- Banquet in Moscow ... while bombs were being loaded into German aircraft to "punish" Belgrade 166
- "A rather romanticized myth" 166
- Soviet withdrawal of the recognition of Yugoslavia's Government 167

During Germany's war against Yugoslavia and Greece, the Soviet Union was supplying Germany with resources 167

- Sunday, 6 April 1941, in Belgrade ... 168
"Unmerciful harshness and military destruction" ... 168
Danube blocked for a few weeks ... 169

Chapter 19 ... 170

6 APRIL – 17 JUNE 1941, from Belgrade to London ... 170
"British troops were said to have landed ... on the Yugoslav coast" ... 170
Mission accomplished – retreat ... 170
Evacuation of important figures and local SOE-cooperators ... 170
Under bombs, SOE-men were safeguarding their "toys" ... 171
- Diplomatic immunity extended to the British non-Legation personnel ... 172

Chapter 20 ... 173

6–18 APRIL 1941... from Simović's "fiery speech" to "unconditional capitulation" ... 173
- Sunday, 6 April 1941 – From Belgrade to Užice and Banja Koviljača ... 173
- Monday, 7 April ... 173
- Tuesday, 8 April – In Sevojno; Maribor, Skoplje and Prilep fell ... 174
- Wednesday, 9 April – Niš and Monastir (Bitolj) fell; the Germans in Salonika ... 175
- Thursday, 10 April - German troops in Zagreb; ... 176

(U) Independent State of Croatia proclaimed ... 176
- Friday, 11 April – From Sevojno to Pale; the Germans in Osijek ... 177

(U) Pavelić agrees to hand Dalmatia over to Italy ... 178
"The treachery of the Croats" ... 178
(C) "Disorganize the resistance of the Yugoslav Army" ... 180
- Saturday, 12 April – Conference in Pale; the King to Foča, Nikšić; German platoon enters Belgrade ... 180
- Sunday, 13 April – Situation very difficult but not hopeless ... 181

Churchill's greetings to the people of Yugoslavia ... 183
Churchill: "... Yugoslavs have given us no chance to help them" ... 184
(U) Pavelić to S. Kvaternik - disinformation: no commitments to Italy ... 185
- Monday, 14 April – Gen. Kalafatović in Pale; the King flown to Greece; the Government in Nikšić ... 185

(U) Pavelić recognizes Italian rights in Dalmatia ... 189
- Tuesday, 15 April 1941 ... 189

(U) Pavelić in Zagreb ... 190
(U) Precursor of the Treaties of Rome of 18 May 1941 ... 190
- (A) Wednesday, 16 April – Terms of complete capitulation; Simović in Athens ... 190
- (A) Thursday, 17 April - Armistice agreement signed ... 192
- (A) Friday, 18 April – Unconditional surrender was in effect ... 193

"... insufficiency of our forces for a decisive battle" ... 193

Chapter 21 ... 195

18 APRIL – END OF JUNE 1941 ... 195
"... terrible error of sending anything beyond a small token force to Greece." ... 195
"... numerous warnings of a German attack upon Russia" ... 196
George Taylor back in London ... 196
"The Jug collapse seems to have been catastrophic" ... 197
Closing George Taylor's mission ... 197

Chapter 22 ... 199

Sowing the seeds of tragedy ... 199
(C) Comintern in 1925: "Yugoslavia must be made to disintegrate" ... 199
(C) Tito, in September 1934: Seven states – but no Yugoslavia ... 199
(C) Forming the CP of Slovenia, and CP of Croatia ... an indication of the reorganization of "Tito's" Communist Yugoslavia ... 199
(C) In 1939, the Communists still supported the Ustaše ... 200

- (C) In 1940, "... a world revolution ... of which the Soviet Union is our glorious model" 200
  - (C) • CPY – an obedient member of the Communist International 201
  - (C) • Sabotaging an imperialist war 201
  - (C) • Not the Fatherland, but the world revolution 201
  - (C) • Keep Yugoslavia out of the capitalist war... 201
- (C) 22 March 1941 – Comintern's instructions to the CPY 202
- (C) Tito's secret directive in the wake of the Putsch 202
- (U) Pavelić and "Legal decrees ..." ("Zakonske odredbe ...") 203
- (U) From "collection" and "emigration" camps to concentration camps, Jasenovac 203
- (C) the Soviet Union withdraws recognition of the Putschist Government, ... 204
- (C)... but on 9 May 1941 the Comintern issued Directives for Future Work to the CPY 204
- 12 May 1941 – Colonel Dragoljub Mihailović comes to Western Serbia 205
- (U) 18 May 1941 – Treaties of Rome between Italy and the ISC 206
- (C) 22 June 1941: Germany invades the Soviet Union; the Comintern's instruction to the CPY . 206
- (C) ... but there was no explicit call to arms by the CPY 206
  - (C) • After 22 June, "Moscow ordered us " 207
- (C) 4 July CPY had no elaborate plan, did not talk of any uprising 207
- (C) The Comintern orders the start of Partisan actions in Yugoslavia 207
- (C) 7 July Killing two domestic gendarmes, not the German occupiers 208
  - (C) • "... paralysis of the machinery of local government and food requisitioning" 208
- (C) "At the end of the war, they [the Germans] will leave the country." 209

"Unexpected consequences" 210

The Putsch of 27 March 1941 did not help the British expedition in Greece 210
... but the Putschists turned out to be the builders of Communist-ruled Yugoslavia 210

Appendix G 212

Section D of the Secret Intelligence Service 212

Appendix H 213

Notes on George Taylor, Bill Bailey, Bill Hudson 213

Appendix I 214

Formation of Special Operations Executive 214

Appendix J 216

"High explosives, the usual S.O. 2 devices," 216

Appendix K 218

Report on SOE organization and plans in the Balkans, 26 February 1941 218

Appendix L 220

Calls to arms 220

Appendix M 221

About the Putsch, Putschists, and their Government 221
Slobodan Jovanović's remarks 221
Mirković's role in the coup 222
- According to his memoirs, 1941 222
- In 1948 224
- In 1955 224

Mirković's role in the coup ... according to Dr. Miloš Sekulić 225
The coup ... "one of the most unrealistic ... defiance" ... "Britain simply did not have the resources." 226
- Military historian John Keegan, in 1989 226
- Alexander Glen, in 1975 and 2002 226

- Captain (later Major) Dragiša Ristić 227
  The Putschists and Churchill's memoirs 227

Appendix N 228
  Leaving the country 228

Sources 229
- Notes regarding General Simović's and General Mirković's documents 229

Sources and selected bibliography 231

Selected Chronology of Events 237

Index 263

Acknowledgements

I am very grateful to Ivan Jakić, late Borivoje M. Karapandžić, and Paul Taylor for providing me valuable sources of information which are widely used in this book.

To show a more complete and truthful story of the military coup of 27 March 1941 and its consequences for the people and former state of Yugoslavia, relevant sources of information were eagerly sought and used, with sincere appreciation for and gratitude to their authors.

A special gratitude is felt to late Stephen Clissold, a very knowledgeable participant in Yugoslavia's wartime events, for his revelations of documents of the Communist organizations' provenance.

Copy editing and helpful suggestions by Mihailo – Miša Kostić are truly appreciated.

My deepest gratitude is expressed to Kathleen – Kathy Olsen for all encouragement, assistance and support she had given me over years of work on this book, and for her help in the preparation of this book.

Information and quotations from The Hoover Institution Archives, Stanford University, USA, and The National Archives at Kew, Richmond, Great Britain, appear with the permission of their respective authorities.

Notes on the structure of the text

For the sake of documentation, and to relay to the reader information as found in the sources, lengthier excerpts are often quoted - very respectfully and gratefully to the authors - rather than paraphrased or summarized.

Except in the case of short sentences, translated text is not put in quotation marks "...".

The reason: *Translation* is not an exact process, and text translated from the original may vary from one translator to another.

Therefore, the translated text is put into double parentheses marks ((...)).

Geographical names are written as found in the sources; personal Slavic names likewise, but are also given in their Slavic spelling.

This story is generally presented chronologically. However, some themes and parts of the overall story are described in the Appendices.

(A) is inserted to mark the armistice negotiations between the German and Yugoslav military,
(C) for the activities of the Communists, and
(U) for the events related to the Independent State of Croatia.

Notes on the pronunciation of the South-Slavic (Yugo-Slav) names

In this book, the Latin alphabet ("Latinica") is used in what is now "politically correctly" called the "Bosnian / Croatian / Montenegrin / Serbian" language(s).

Latinica alphabet letters:	Pronounced as in the English word:
a, A	**a**rt
c, C	**tsets**e fly
č, Č	**ch**urch
ć, Ć	soft **ch**, as in future, (or Italian ciao)
dž, DŽ	**j**am
đ, Đ	soft **j**, as in job
e, E	p**e**t
I, I	it **is**
j, J	**y**ou
lj, LJ	wi**ll y**ou
nj, NJ	**kn**ew
o, O	**o**ld
š, Š	**sh**e
u, U	f**oo**d
ž. Ž	vi**s**ion

In Slovenian, pronunciation is identical to the other South-Slav language(s).

In the course of the war, military personnel advanced in ranks and so many persons mentioned in this story were - after the war - honored for their services, decorated, knighted... It was not easy, and it was not essential, to follow promotions and to use correct ranks, as they applied at the given times. Therefore, with all due respect to each individual, ranks and titles used are as found in the identified sources.

Shapers of events

Germany :
Dr. Jacob ALTMAIER - Journalist (code-name A/H 9)
Viktor von HEEREN - Minister in Belgrade
Adolf HITLER - Leader of the National Socialist German Workers' Party (the Nazi Party), the Chancellor after 30 January 1933, *Der Führer* after 19 August 1934
Joachim von RIBBENTROP - Foreign Minister

Great Britain :
Julian AMERY - Son of Leopold (Leo) Amery, Secretary for India. Section D / SOE agent (code-name A/HA); Assistant Press Attaché in Belgrade
W. S. (Bill) BAILEY - A metallurgist at the Trepča mine. Section D / SOE agent; later Liaison officer with General Dragoljub-Draža Mihailović.
John BENNETT - Section D /SOE agent. One of Taylor's "chief lieutenants in Yugoslavia", who "discovered" Trifunović Birčanin.
Peter BOUGHEY - Section D / SOE agent (code-name D/H 70)
Sir Alexander CADOGAN - Permanent Under-Secretary at the Foreign Office
Ronald Ian CAMPBELL - Minister in Belgrade
Winston Spenser CHURCHILL - Prime Minister and Secretary of State for Defence (10 May 1940 - 26 July 1945)
Colonel Charles S. CLARKE - Military Attaché in Belgrade
Dr. Hugh DALTON - Minister of Economic Warfare ((MEW), 15 May 1940 – 22 February 1942), in charge of the Special Operations Executive (SOE), from 22 July 1940 to 22 February 1942 (code-name, SO)
General Sir John DILL - Chief of Imperial General Staff (CIGS)
Anthony EDEN - Secretary of State for War (10 May - 22 December 1940); Secretary of State for Foreign Affairs (22 December 1940 - 26 July 1945)
Alexander GLEN - Arctic explorer; Section D / SOE agent (code name A/H 10); Assistant Naval Attaché in Belgrade
Julius HANAU - Businessman. Section D agent (code-name *Caesar*). He originally "picked winner in Tupanjanin".
Duane T. (Bill) HUDSON - A mining engineer. Section D agent – (code-names D/HZ). ; later the first British officer sent to Yugoslavia (known as Fred Smith, Marko)
Gladwyn JEBB - Chief Executive Officer of SOE, formerly Private Secretary to Sir Alexander Cadogan
Hugh H. MACDONALD - Wing Commander, Air Attaché in Belgrade
Thomas G. MAPPLEBECK - Businessman. Honorary Air Attaché in Belgrade
Thomas MASTERSON - Businessman connected with oil companies. The head of SOE in Belgrade from November 1940 (code-name DHY). Another of Taylor's "chief lieutenants in Yugoslavia".
Sir Frank NELSON - Businessman in India and Britain, and former Conservative Member of Parliament. Executive Director of SOE, from July 1940 to May 1942 (code-name CD)
Terence C. RAPP - General Consul in Zagreb
Roundell Palmer, 3rd Earl of SELBORNE - Minister of Economic Warfare, in charge of SOE (22 February 1942 – 23 May 1945)
Hugh SETON-WATSON - Section D / SOE agent (code-name D-H 72)
Terence A. SHONE - Former Secretary of the British Legation in Belgrade
George Francis TAYLOR - A businessman from Australia. Chief of Staff of the Executive Director of SOE (code-name, AD)
General Sir Archibald WAVELL - Commander-in-Chief, Middle East

Greece :
Alexandros KORYZIS - Prime Minister (after 29 January 1941)
General Ioannis METAXAS - Prime Minister and Minister for Foreign Affairs (until 29 Jan. 1941)

General Alexandros PAPAGOS - Commander-in-Chief of the Greek Army
………. PAPPAS - journalist and propagandist in Belgrade, March 1941

Italy :
Galeazzo CIANO - Foreign Minister
Benito MUSSOLINI - Leader of the National Fascist Party; Prime Minister (31 October 1922 – 25 July 1943); *Il Duce* since 1925; "His Excellency Benito Mussolini, Head of Government, Duce of Fascism, and Founder of the Empire" after the victorious war against Abyssinia in 1936

The Soviet Union :
Vyacheslav Mikhailovich MOLOTOV - the Commissar for Foreign Affairs of the Soviet Union
Joseph Vissarionovich Dzhugashvili STALIN - a leader of the Bolshevik October Revolution in 1917, the first General Secretary of the Central Committee of the Communist Party of the Soviet Union (1922 - 1953), the Premier of the Soviet Union (6 May 1941 - 5 March 1953)
Andrei Yanuarievich VYSHINSKY - the Deputy Commissar for Foreign Affairs

Turkey :
Ismet INÖNÜ - President of Turkey
Sükrü SARACOGLU - Foreign Minister

USA :
Colonel William J. "Wild Bill" DONOVAN - Special emissary for the President
Arthur Bliss LANE - Minister in Belgrade
Franklin Delano ROOSEVELT - The President (4 March 1933 - 12 April 1945)

Yugoslavia :
Aleksandar CINCAR-MARKOVIĆ - Minister for Foreign Affairs (until 27 March 1941)
Dragiša CVETKOVIĆ - The Premier (until 27 March 1941)
Jovan ĐONOVIĆ - Former Minister in Tirana, Albania (Code-name "Monkey")
Dr. Milan GAVRILOVIĆ - President of *Zemljoradnička stranka,* the Agrarian Party; Ambassador in Moscow from August 1940
Ilija JUKIĆ - Assistant Foreign Minister
Knez Pavle KARAĐORĐEVIĆ (Prince Paul) - The Regent (9 October 1934 - 27 March 1941) (Code-name "F")
Major Živan-Žika KNEŽEVIĆ - Battalion Commander, Royal Guards
Radoje KNEŽEVIĆ - member of the Main Committee of the Democratic Party
Dr. Fran KULOVEC - Slovenian representative, Minister without portfolio (until 27 March 1941)
Dr. Vladko MAČEK - The Vice-Premier in Cvetković and Simović Government; President of *Hrvatska seljačka stranka* (the Croatian Peasant Party)
Brigadier General Borivoje-Bora MIRKOVIĆ - Assistant to the Commander of the Air Force before the coup
Momčilo NINČIĆ - Foreign Minister in Simović's Government
General Petar PEŠIĆ - the war Minister
Dr. Svetislav-Sveta PETROVIĆ - radio broadcaster
Colonel Žarko POPOVIĆ - Military Attaché in Moscow
Captain Dragiša RISTIĆ - General Simović's *aide-de-camp*
Army General Dušan SIMOVIĆ - The Commander of the Air Force; the Premier after 27 March 1941
Vojvoda Ilija TRIFUNOVIĆ-BIRČANIN - President of *Narodna odbrana* (The National Defense League). (*Vojvoda* - Highest military rank, obtained in war). (Code-name "Daddy")
Dr. Miloš TUPANJANIN - Deputy President of the Serbian Peasant Party (Code-name "Uncle")
Colonel Vladimir VAUHNIK - Military Attaché in Berlin
Zemljoradnička stranka - The Agrarian Party, usually called the Serbian Peasant Party (SPP)

Introduction

Part One of this book examines reasons and British initiatives for drawing Yugoslavia into the Second World War. **Part Two** deals with activities of the British and their domestic "friends" and "contacts" in implementing the British goals. The official diplomatic personnel of the British Legation in Belgrade were not the only ones who patriotically responded to the directions of His Majesty's Government to "encourage" the Yugoslav Government to "resist" the Axis; most other British residents, and specifically agents of the British secret services, faithfully cooperated.

Of these services only the Secret Intelligence Service (SIS) was commonly known to exist and operate in Yugoslavia and elsewhere in the Balkans. The existence and activities of other services operating in Yugoslavia in the 1939-1941 periods were well-guarded secrets not only in Yugoslavia, but also in Great Britain herself. Two of these were the most important: Section D of the SIS, and the Special Operations Executive (SOE), the successor to Section D. Yet the agents of these services, collaborating with disgruntled domestic opposition to the Regent Prince Paul, to the existing Government and to their policies, were instrumental in implementing the directions of the British Government to draw Yugoslavia into the war.

Before proceeding, however, the following remark should be illustrative and informative: major participants in the preparation and the execution of the coup, *the Putsch* - known as *the Putschists* - who later wrote about the Putsch, omitted to write about the "contacts" of the "opposition" with the British, and about the role and influence of the British on the execution of the Putsch.

General Borivoje-Bora Mirković, the chief executor of the coup, made partial exception. In his memoirs, dated 1 December 1941 in Cairo, he confirmed the cooperation with the British Air and Army Attaché, A.H.H. Macdonald and C.S. Clarke, respectively, resolutely claiming that he had not been an agent of the SIS. However, he did not write about his meeting with the honorary Air Attaché, Tom Mapplebeck, who on 25 March 1941 strongly urged the General to launch the coup as soon as possible. (Stafford(cp), 415)

As much as could be seen from the sources researched for this book, General Simović did not reveal his **first,** secret meeting with the Air Attaché Macdonald in the morning of the 26th March. **If** he did elsewhere, it was a proper thing to do. He wrote about their **second** meeting in the late afternoon of the 26th March, but gave two different explanations of the purpose of that meeting.

In exile, and outside the government, but seeing himself in a historic context and approval, Simović considered the coup of 27 March 1941 to have been ((a decisive moment, fateful not only for our country, but perhaps for the entire world)) - "odsudan moment, sudbonosan ne samo po našu Otadžbinu, nego možda i za ceo svet.". (Simović(44), 1) In reality, the coup was not fateful for the entire world, but it was decisively fateful for the citizens of Yugoslavia: it acted as a switch on a railroad track, taking them form a coexisting historic path - through the devastation of a war and truly bloody civil wars - into tragedy, the consequences of which will be felt for a long, long time to come.

Simović's adjutant Dragiša Ristić and brothers Knežević, likewise, wanted to present - and get credit for - the coup as purely Yugoslav, i.e., Serbian affair, in which the British had no role at all.

Chapter 1

"Ja nisam bio agent Intelidžens Servisa" ("I was not an agent of the Intelligence Service"), wrote General Borivoje Mirković at the conclusion of his memoirs, dated 1 December 1941 in Cairo. (Bosnić(ed), 35) He may not have known that his daily advisor from 24 to 27 March 1941, "Daddy" Ilija Trifunović-Birčanin (Knežević, 112-13n2) – the man who during those days served as a two-way channel between Mirković and the Secret Operations Executive (Williams, 31) – was a favorite "contact" of another, newer super-secret British service, the SOE. While it was a common knowledge that the older, established Secret Intelligence Service (SIS) was active in Yugoslavia, activities of other British agencies were carefully kept secret. But other agencies also did exist and were active, and therefore are briefly mentioned here to provide a broader understanding of British activities in the pre-war Yugoslavia.

British secret services: SIS, MI(R), Section D, Electra House, and SOE

Organized in October 1909, the Secret Intelligence Service was headed by Commander Mansfield George Smith-Cumming, who was soon referred to simply as 'C'. (West (6), 6-7) Upon his death [14 June 1923] the next 'C', Admiral Sir Hugh P. Sinclair, [June 1923 – 4 November 1939] led SIS through a very turbulent and fateful period of European history including: Germany's reoccupation of Rheinland, on 7 March 1936, in violation of the Versailles Treaty; Germany's annexation (*Anschluss*) of Austria on 12 March 1938; the Munich crisis and infamous Agreement of 29 September 1938; and Germany's occupation of Prague on 15 March 1939.

Shortly after the annexation of Austria, the British formed three main clandestine organizations of a subversive character:

- Section of the General Staff at the War Office, known as GS(R) and later as MI(R) [Military Intelligence, Research]. Its purpose: to study techniques of irregular warfare. Headed by a sapper, Colonel John (Joe) Holland, MI(R) was intended not only to develop guerrilla warfare techniques, but also to circulate pamphlets on the subject. (West(sw), 14) Holland sent his people all over the world, just in case. They were very active in the Balkans. (Sweet-Escott, 28)
- Section D [for "Destruction"] of SIS, "to investigate every possibility of attacking potential enemies by means other than the operations of military forces".
- Department of Propaganda, known as EH, after **Electra House**, its London headquarters, to specialize in *"black", i.e. un-attributable propaganda* in Europe. (Stafford(so), 19-20. Italics added.)

Formation of Section D

(More details are outlined in **Appendix G.**)

The Berlin-Rome Axis was formalized with the Pact of Steel between Germany and Italy, signed on 22 May 1939. From Great Britain's point of view, the logic of *attacking potential enemies by means other than the operations of military forces* led to a conclusion: that Yugoslavia – bordering with Germany and Italy – should be one of the bases from which such potential attacks could be covertly waged. Therefore, organizing covert operatives in Yugoslavia became self-evident need. The presence of mining tycoon Chester Beatty's operations and interest in Yugoslavia alleviated the existence and activities of such organization.

As is shown in **Appendix G**, the mining magnate Chester Beatty not only greatly assisted in financing initial operations of Section D, but provided services of "a number of his staff to 'D' Section while keeping them on his payroll." (Amery, 160)

Among reliable men with a knowledge of the Balkans, whom Beatty recommended to Major Laurence Grand, was George Taylor, "a ruthless Australian businessman, who had supervised the establishment of Section D's principal office at 2 Caxton Street, ..." (West(sw), 9) Taylor became the head of the Balkan section of the "D", (West(sw), 11, 13) He had a singular role in Yugoslavia in the winter-spring of 1941.

Other men recommended to Grand were two of Beatty's senior staff, "who were to play important roles in Section D and then SOE: a metallurgist, S.W. (Bill) Bailey, and a South African mining engineer, Duane

T. (Bill) Hudson." (West(sw), 11) (Later, during the war, they both were sent to Yugoslavia with specific and important missions.)

Because of relevance of all three Beatty's protégées, their brief biographical notes are provided in **Appendix H.**

Belgrade: the center of Section D and its activities in the Balkans

Although the idea of drawing Yugoslavia into the war has been firmed up **after** Italy's attack on Greece in October 1940, British agents were operating in Yugoslavia **before** Italy's attack, executing the assignments given to them by their Government. Same operatives were used under evolving circumstances. Political activities and contacts with local individuals and/or political groups were being developed before the idea of the Balkan Front, and some British financial "subsidies" given to "contacts" likewise. With the intention of forming a Balkan Front (Turkey, Greece, and Yugoslavia), the assignments to British operatives changed.

*****

Knowing exactly what he wanted, **George Taylor** operated on the principle that in each of the neutral countries Section D should recruit a number of reliable British residents who, in turn, would build up contacts with local elements friendly to the Allied cause. "It was these elements he hoped to use to do the work of subversion and sabotage which was our [Section D's] aim in life." (Sweet-Escott, 22) This principle was indeed applied in finding reliable British residents in Belgrade who subsequently linked with the Yugoslav Government-opposing elements in the implementation of Section D aims in the Balkans.

Julius Hanau "Caesar" - "somewhat sinister but Balkans streetwise" (Glen(B), 32) - had been recruited into Section D by Lawrence Grand in June 1938. He was later told that blocking the Danube, in the event of war, was a major British interest. (Barker, 37) It was the most important project of Section D at the time. Thus in June 1939 he became the main "D" man in Belgrade. (His real name was Hannon.) "Hanau was a South African Jew, who had held a British commission in the war of 1914-18, had finished up in Yugoslavia after fighting on the Salonika front, and had remained in Belgrade, where he had become a successful businessman, ... He possessed a thorough knowledge of Yugoslavia and of the seamy side of Yugoslav affairs; ..." (Mackenzie, 15, 24-5)

> Our chief and prophet in Belgrade was Julius Hanau, an arms dealer of wide and varied experience, steeped in the culture of France and Germany, learned in history and endowed with all the power of his race to compel imagination. The Balkans held few secrets for him; and it was in his hands that the threads of our network throughout the peninsula came together. (Amery(A), 26)

"Hanau ... knew more about the Balkans than any living Englishman." (Amery, 223) He was Vickers representative in Belgrade, had close connections with Beatty (West(sw), 9), a host of contacts with local people, and a large party of "D" agents under his control. (Sweet-Escott, 22) Members of that large party were **Julian Amery** and **Alexander-Sandy Glen.**

Amery - only a few months over 20 years old - came to Belgrade on 5 September 1939, with a letter of recommendation to Minister Campbell from his father, Leopold Stennett "Leo", the Secretary of State for India. Three days later he lunched with the Minister who "seemed genuinely interested in what I told him and especially in the strength of pro-Allied sentiment I had met everywhere on the journey and indeed since I had come to Belgrade." (Amery, 135, 138)

The Second World War was just eight days old. It is worth remembering what Amery wrote next because it reflected the British policy toward Yugoslavia at that time – the policy which evolved into the opposite direction as the war spread.

> Then, to my surprise, he [Campbell] said that pro-Allied sentiment among the Serbs was the thing that worried him most. *There was no question of the British and French opening a new Salonika front.* It was, therefore, important to check any signs of war fever in Yugoslavia. We must try to prevent the Yugoslavs provoking the Germans and keep them on ice *until we could use them to best advantage.* Starting from this premise, Campbell deprecated the attitude of the Opposition leaders in Belgrade and said *they were simply trying to ride back to power on a wave of pro-Allied sentiment.* The only wise course was to work closely with Prince Paul and his ministers. They were our friends and would help us as much as they safely could. (Amery, 138. Italics added.)

After the lunch with the Minister, young Julian was quickly added to the Diplomatic Corps list as the deputy Press Attaché (to Stephen Childs). (Amery, 139) In April 1940 he joined Section D, in which he was active for some months, but was still paid by the Legation. (Amery, 135-9, 160, 184)

When Amery became a "D-man", he promptly recruited *The Times* correspondent **Ralph Parker.** "He was a trained observer and had had some experience of underground work in Prague, where he had helped to rescue Czechs from the Gestapo." (Amery, 162)

In January 1940, Admiral J.H. Godfrey, Director of Naval Intelligence, sent **Alexander Glen** to Belgrade as Assistant to the Naval Attaché, explaining: "Captain [Max] Despard is Naval Attaché with rather wide duties; spend a few days in the section and find out which country is which [Yugoslavia and Rumania]. *The Danube is our interest."* (Glen, 43-4. Italics added.) " 'Assistant to the Naval Attaché' was quickly altered to 'Assistant Naval Attaché', providing diplomatic cover for these additional duties." (Glen[B], 5) "Section D was to be my second boss in London, agreed with the Director of Naval Intelligence and accepted by Despard so that I had a formal D identification." (Glen(B), 36) The identification was A/H 10. (Vodušek Starič, 430)

When Hanau and Glen met, probably in late January 1940 - Glen wrote much later - Hanau "made it clear that I was intended for duties other than I had thought. It was also clear that there was a professional, highly disciplined with no illusions and Balkans-wise after his long years as a Vickers agent in Yugoslavia." (Glen[B], 36)

"Glen was short, prematurely bald, with small eyes glinting behind powerful spectacles. He had been to Baliol, had explored the Arctic and had worked as a banker. ... We soon became friends and, presently, decided to pool our resources and take a spacious flat with a view of enlarging our circle of Yugoslav acquaintances." (Amery, 158) The flat was just around the corner from the Legation; later **Peter Boughey** and **Archie Dunlop Mackenzie** joined them. (Glen, 53)

In the spring of 1940 Section D sent to Belgrade a young lawyer called **John Bennett.** "He was a wild man, gaunt, loose limbed and prematurely bold." (Amery, 161) He played " a significant part in the events leading up to the military *coup d'état* which ranged Yugoslavia on the side of the Allies. (Amery(A), 26)

Thus - according to Nigel West - in early 1940, Section D in Belgrade had eleven agents, while in twelve other capitals of Europe and the Middle East a total of just fourteen. Operating from Belgrade were:

Julian Amery, William "Bill" Bailey, John Bennett, Peter Boughey, Alexander Glen, Julius Hanau, Duane T. "Bill" Hudson, Archie Lyall, Michael Mason, Ralph Parker, and Hugh Seton-Watson. (West(sa), 10)

In Slovenia, Section D's representative was **A.C. Lawreson**, and his deputy was **Frodsham**. (Mackenzie, 28) Alec Lawreson was " very active in his anti-Axis work, being involved, for example, in the sabotage of rolling stock ... In due course he was given the protective diplomatic cover of a vice-consul's appointment, as well as an assistant, GS Fordham." (Some personalities in SIS operations in Yugoslavia http://www.oocities.org/sebrit/personalities2.html 9/18/12)

"**John Lloyd- Evans** was officially a press officer at the British consulate in Zagreb. But in fact he worked for SIS with **James Miller** and **Bill Stuart**. He had formerly run the SIS "Z" network in Prague, after which he worked in Rumania." (Some personalities in SIS operations in Yugoslavia http://www.oocities.org/sebrit/personalities2.html 9/18/12)

- **Widely connected Jakob Altmaier**

However, in addition to "D"-men, there was another man who operated in Belgrade as more-than-a-contact between the British, the Opposition to the Government, and the Government-overthrow-wishers: **Jakob Altmaier**. Julian Amery became close to him and in his book left a partial record of Altmaier's activities.

A search on Internet of his early years showed that Altmaier was born in 1889 in Flörsheim am Main, Germany; joined the Socialist Party in 1913; volunteered in First World War and was decorated with the Iron Cross; in 1918 participated in the Revolution in Frankfurt am Main, Germany; in the Weimar Republic worked as a journalist; as a Jew he had to flee Germany in 1933, first to Paris and later to the Balkans and Africa; in exile he worked also as a journalist; during the Spanish Civil War he was a correspondent from Spain of a Socialist newspaper; in 1945 he returned to Germany.

It would be interesting to know whether Altmaier, while working as a correspondent in Spain, met any of the Communist from Yugoslavia who fought in the International Brigades, and whether he ever met Josip Broz Tito or heard about his activities related to the Spanish civil war.

- **Section D's man from Hungary**

In January 1940, when 27-year-old Alexander Glen was sent to Yugoslavia, 25-year-old **Basil Davidson** went to the neighboring Danubian country, Hungary. In due time Davidson would have significant assignment related to Yugoslavia, and for that reason some of his Section D/SOE activities in Hungary are mentioned here.

Located in large part on the Pannonian Plains, Hungary did not possess physical features needed for an effective Danube blockade, which were available in Yugoslavia, and therefore was not as important for Section D sabotages as was Yugoslavia. The Section D organizational chart shows two agents in Budapest and 12 in Belgrade. (West(sa), 10)

The Hungary's much lesser importance to Section D is also reflected in funds made available for its operations. As Davidson wrote:

> D's man in Hungary, …, had two immediate tasks. The first was to found and operate a legal and above-board news agency for the distribution of British news to the Hungarian press and radio. …
> … Obtained from D by way of a diplomatic contact in the British legation, money proved to be no problem. …
> The second task, below board and illegal, was less exhilarating. This was "to promote resistance". …
> "There is," said my legation contact, a few weeks after my arrival, "this parcel of money for you." This contained a hundred crisp fivers of the large white kind of those days. The decoded instructions said that I was to use them for bribing politicians. (Davidson, 55)

So, money was no problem to illegally promote resistance, to bribe Hungarian politicians - a total of five hundred sterling pounds. To "subsidize" politicians in Yugoslavia, however – several thousands pounds per month! That was a true measure of the importance of the SOE co-operatives in Yugoslavia for the British goals in the Balkans.

*****

As in other European countries, the SIS was active also in Yugoslavia through its Passport Control (PC) office. To avoid compromising the Foreign Office, the department's officials were employed by the Foreign Office, but did not enjoy diplomatic status. (West(6), 21) The heads of the PC station in Belgrade were: Buckland, Captain Clement Hope [in 1939], and [Robert F.] St. George Lethbridge [in 1940]. (West[6], xix)

- **The "D" center in Cairo – for the Balkan section**

As expected, Italy's entry into the war "on the wrong side" would close the Mediterranean to the British and Section D. Lines of supply would have to go round the Cape, and "the conception of directing the section's operations in the Balkans from London would have to be abandoned." Therefore at the end of May 1940 it was decided that **George Taylor** and most of the staff of the Balkan section in London should set themselves up in Cairo, leaving Sweet-Escott and Hilton Nixon to be their link in London. (Sweet-Escott, 30)

> Two of my companions on the flight in May 1940 to Cairo had been George Taylor and Ian Pirie, destined for Belgrade and Athens respectively, to see what could be done to organize resistance to anticipated Nazi/Fascist aggression. (Dodds-Parker, 188)

Taylor returned to London early in August 1940, (Sweet-Escott, 39) During the May-August period, some political opponents of the Yugoslav Government's policies suggested a *coup d'état* against the Prince Regent. **(Appendix D, Part One)** Remembering that May 1940 trip to Cairo forty four years later, Dodds-Parker wrote: "George Taylor [was] on his way to Cairo to set up a D-Section Office, and then round the Balkans, and to Yugoslavia to make the first proposals for the coup which, a year later, was to support King Peter against the defeatists and traitors." (Dodds-Parker, 46)

"Defeatists and traitors" – from the self-serving point of view of the British.

Chapter 2

Blockade of the Danube – an early Section D operation

According to the "D"-man Bickham Sweet-Escott, if Section D had a charter, "it would have covered a wide range of activities, of which *sabotage, political subversion, and underground propaganda* were the most important." These were "un-acknowledgeable activities", meant to keep the government's operations blameless. (Sweet-Escott, 20. Italics added.) While the activities in the field of political subversion and underground propaganda took place at a later stage, the sabotage of German supplies via the Danube river comprised an early activity of Section D.

> The agents have been active in the Balkans since 1938, and after September 1939 [beginning of the Second World War] the area became vital to the economic war, especially with regard to denying Rumanian oil and grain to the Third Reich. (Williams, 9)

> ... the British establishment believed that economic stranglehold would bring the inherent weaknesses of the Reich to the fore and it would collapse from within, with the minimum of material expenditure by Britain. (Onslow, 9)

- **The London Foreign Office – Section D conference, April 1940**

At the end of April 1940, Lord Halifax, the Foreign Secretary, summoned to London the British diplomatic missions in the Balkans, to inform them about the government's policy. That was important because, whatever the "D"-men had to do in the Balkans, it could be done only through local organizations, including political parties. "Laurence Grand and George Taylor described our scope and our proposed activities to the assembled diplomats. But the meeting did not result in the issue of a clear directive to Section D. ..." (Sweet-Escott, 25) "When British diplomatic representatives met in London in April 1940 they were told that 'considerable success' had attended 'the special propaganda effort' launched in Yugoslavia, largely due to the cooperation built up between the Press Attaché and Section D." (Barker, 44)

Grand's exposition at the conference was received with sympathy. However, Germany's victory in the West - which followed shortly thereafter - increased pressure on the Balkan governments. "Nothing was to be gained by frontal opposition until the situation had improved, and British policy was cautious until in the autumn the Italians compromised Axis prestige by their defeats in Greece and in Libya." (Mackenzie, 29)

- **Unsuccessful attempts of blocking the Danube**

The conferees discussed the importance of blocking the Danube. "Immense weight was still attached to economic warfare, and the belief seemed to be seriously entertained that Germany would be crippled if we could interfere materially with the transport of Rumanian oil." (Sweet-Escott, 26)

One way to do this would be to interfere with the oil barges and pilots. The Goeland Shipping Company was to be created, to buy oil barges and thus to deny them to the Germans, and to bribe the Danube pilots not to work for the Germans. (Sweet-Escott, 26)

The second way to blockade the Danube involved Julius Hanau, "Caesar". When he joined Section D in June 1939, he was entrusted with plans to block the Danube transports to Germany. Three points were suggested for an attack: the Greben narrows, the Kazan defile, and the Iron Gates [Đerdapska klisura]. (Mackenzie, 25)

At the Greben narrows, inside Yugoslav territory, the river was constricted by a retaining wall; the destruction of the wall was expected to make navigation impossible. After a charge was duly laid against the wall - according to William Mackenzie, an SOE historian - "an enthusiastic Yugoslav ... could not resist touching it off in November 1939 when a German tug with four oil barges was passing. Two of the barges were sunk, and some inconvenience was caused to navigation." However, the plan failed and the opportunity to carry it out again never came. (Mackenzie, 25)

At the Kazan defile the Danube is very deep, but not wide, and high cliffs on the Yugoslav side overhang it. It was planned to detonate a huge quantity of explosives, placed in the cliffs; it was expected that the detonation would throw a vast mass of rocks into the river, which would make the navigation impossible. The British Minister, Sir Ronald Hugh Campbell, was skeptical, the action was prohibited, but Hanau began quarrying operations above the defile, on the pretext of searching for minerals. In December 1939 the Germans detected the operation. An investigation by Yugoslav officials was inevitable. The Yugoslav General Staff could not assume responsibility, and the detonation was never executed. (Mackenzie, 25-6)

The Iron Gates plan had a political background. According to the original concept: some barges, controlled by the British, should be filled with cement and sunk in the narrow. The line of railway track - used for towing at this point - would then be destroyed and the locomotives flung into the river. Early in October 1939, French General [Maurice Gustave] Gamelin began to press for action along these lines. Colonel Grand, the head of "D", diverted the approach to diplomatic circles and the Foreign Office argued powerfully against violent action. On 15 May 1940 the British decided that: "No action must be taken which was likely to precipitate the armed occupation of the river or an early invasion of the Balkan States by Germany."; British action should be limited to impressing the Rumanian and Yugoslav Governments about the need for their destruction. The plan was not implemented. (Mackenzie, 26-7)

- **Germany's security units in Rumania**

However, while the British plans for the blockade were being worked on, in September 1939 the Germans organized "the Brandenberg Regiment's special security units in plain clothes to be in key positions along the Danube, especially around the Iron Gates cataracts and the huge Giurgiu terminal and marshalling yards, as well as in the Ploesti oil fields themselves." "This security operation and its deployment of large specialist forces by Germany which so frustrated British plans, *was not known to London at the time* or, indeed, for some time after the war." (Glen(B), 14. Italics added.)

As the plan for blowing up the Iron Gates had been abandoned because of Germany's activities in Rumania, "it was decided that we should start work on a scheme for sinking a large steamer in the middle of the narrows. ... Our man was to have an active time. ... but a need for a charter and a directive was still unfilled." (Sweet-Escott, 26)

*****

As Sir Alexander Glen pointed out, Britain enjoyed personal relations with so many influential Rumanian families, "as well as the large British contingents in the Romanian oil companies." Captain Max Despard DSC, RN, the British Naval Attaché to Belgrade and Bucharest – to whom Glen had been assigned – "had his fingers in many pies ... " (Glen(B), 11) For instance, he bribed Rumanian personnel to encourage their cooperation. (Seaman(ed), 131)

For an illustration of good family relations, one can mention the connection of Hugh Seton-Watson's family with Iuliu Maniu, president of the National Peasant Party. "This party is a main basis of S.O.2 work in Rumania," George Taylor reported to Nelson on 26 February 1941, adding that the Maniu's Party had been funded by SOE. (Report pp. 1, 3) "Maniu was given funds and a radio transmitter." (Seaman(ed), 134)

- **Hanau and Bailey withdrawn from Yugoslavia**

Exposed by his activities, Hanau was withdrawn from Yugoslavia in June 1940. His assistants, Bill Bailey and Major G.H. Head, were expelled in July, and "D's agent in Skoplje [Ralph Parker] in August. (Mackenzie, 29) **Sandy Glen** temporarily replaced Bailey. Eventually, **Thomas Masterson** - a person long connected with Rumanian oil companies - was moved from Rumania to Yugoslavia in November 1940, and from December 1940 to April 1941 was the head of the SOE team in Belgrade.

The end of Lawrence Grand's time in Section D

In the words of the prominent Section D's "Baker Street Irregular" – Bickham Sweet-Escott:

> Laurence Grand had done a magnificent job in convincing our superiors that this kind of warfare was worthwhile. ... The swiftness of events from April to July 1940 had prevented us from building up the right sort of organization or recruiting the right sort of man. ... There were a few successful operations to our credit, but certainly not many; and we had something, which could be called an organization on the ground in the Balkans. But even there we had failed to do anything spectacular. The oil of Rumania continued to arrive in Germany punctually and without much in the way of let or hindrance, and our

essays in Balkan subversion had succeeded only in making the Foreign Office jumpy. As for Western Europe, ... we did not possess one single agent between the Balkans and the English Channel. It is not surprising that the new Churchill government [since 10 May 1940] should have decided upon a drastic reorganization. ... we were due for a new broom. (Sweet-Escott, 39)

A man "suitable to write SOE's history" - Professor William James Millar Mackenzie - concluded about the Section D's operations: great energy and ingenuity spread thinly over an immense field; could not produce visible results; demonstrable achievements were few; minor achievements included some railway sabotage in the Balkans, some propaganda distributed in Germany, and certain contacts with political groups of the Left Center in various parts of Europe; but "D Section and all its work were a nuisance to the Foreign Office, the Secret Intelligence Service, and the War Office alike". (Mackenzie, 36-7)

However, Section D did have an organization in the Balkans, and most of its agents were transferred to the "new broom" – SOE. In Yugoslavia, "Definitely the best of our organisations", there were 9 British and 3 Serb agents; In Rumania 7 British; in Greece 7; in Turkey, "HQ of Balkan Organisation", 6 . (Mackenzie, 89)

These three Serb agents were not identified.

Formation of the Special Operations Executive (SOE)

Foreseeing Germany's victories in the Low Countries, and the collapse of France on 19 May 1940, made the British Chiefs of Staff to meet and discuss a paper entitled "British strategy in a certain eventuality". The paper recommended immediate measures against 'fifth column', and economic pressures that could eventually defeat Germany. These would include a blockade and a bombing offensive on economic targets; a consequent stimulation of discontent in the occupied territories would bring about a situation of revolt.

> In circumstances envisaged we regard this form of activity as of the very highest importance. A special organisation will be required and plans to put these operations into effect should be proceeded with the matter of urgency."

On 27 May the War Cabinet concurred with these recommendations. (Stafford(so), 23)

> Almost from the start, Churchill had great hopes of turning European discontent under Nazi occupation into outright revolt. In May 1940, he had appointed Dr. Hugh Dalton, a well-off socialist, to be minister for economic warfare and supervise the creation of the Special Operations Executive. Dalton was not popular in the Labour Party, but as an anti-appeaser he had done much in the late 1930s to move it away from its pacific position. He had long been a great admirer of Churchill, although the prime minister did not reciprocate his feeling. He could not 'stand his booming voice and shifty eyes' ... (Beevor, 419)

SOE was formed on 22 July 1940 – as described in **Appendix I**.

- **Leadership of SOE, London**

SO	Hugh Dalton	Chairman	22 July 1040 – 22 February 1942
	Gladwyn Jebb	CEO	August 1940 – March 1942
CD	Sir Frank Nelson	Executive Director	28 August 1940 – May 1942
AD	George Taylor	Chief of Staff to CD	August 1940 -15 January 1946
SO	Lord Selborne		22 February 1942 – 1 January 1946
CD	Charles Hambro		May 1942 – March 1943
CD	Colin Gubbins		March 1943 – 15 January 1946

Thus, the SOE leaders and major shapers of events - from the SOE's set-up until Germany's attack on Yugoslavia on Sunday, 6 April 1941 - were **Dalton, Jebb, Nelson**, and **Taylor.**

Gladwyn Jebb was "a powerful personality at work behind the scenes. His was one of the main directing characters in the earliest and in some ways the most formative months of SOE's development, when that body was working out the main guidelines along which it hoped resistance would develop in turn." **George Taylor** "was in effect Jebb's chief of staff, and worked with him closely." (Foot(R), 77-8)

Sir Frank Nelson – head of the sabotage branch of the new body, a former conservative MP, a businessman, ... an SIS man in Basle for Z network. Nelson "seemed to have no family life, and was in the office seven days a week ... He was completely single-minded, and expected his staff to follow his example, and of course to be on the job when he was on the job...." (Sweet-Escott, 56)

Most of "D"-men in Yugoslavia were transferred to SOE. This SOE network "was deemed to be the most promising in the Balkans, and which appeared to offer the advantages of a substantial base for subversive activities in neighbouring countries. (Onslow, 17) For all practical purposes, the offices of the British Consulate, in Zrinjskoga St. No. 14, in Zagreb, served as headquarters of SOE. (Vodušič Starič, 28)

Joint Section D / SOE operations in Yugoslavia

When SOE replaced Section D, the activities started by "D" were not terminated with its merger into SOE. As the changing situation and policies required, the activities of "D" were continued and expanded by SOE. Therefore, they are examined here as one continuing effort, with the understanding that the operations through July 1940 should be attributed to "D", and those thereafter to SOE. Anyway, many operations were directed and performed by the same personnel who were transferred from "D" to SOE.

Subversion – "an essential element in any large scale offensive action"

On 21 August 1940 the Vice Chiefs of Staff discussed Dalton's paper of 19 August, "The Fourth Arm", which presented his views on Subversion – in addition to questions of organization and liaison of SOE with three Fighting Services. As subversion was to be a significant part of SOE's activities in Yugoslavia, here are some of Dalton's views of it:

> Subversion, I suggest, is an essential element in any large-scale offensive action; ... if we are to win the war, we must, at some stage, pass to the offensive on the Continent of Europe. ... My last conclusion (which is really elementary) is that no one of the Fighting Services is in a better position than another to run "Subversion". It seems to follow from this that Subversion should be clearly recognised by all three Fighting Services as another and independent service. (Mackenzie, 84-5)

*****

"Passing to the offensive on the Continent of Europe", at some stage – was also the view of American Colonel W. Donovan at a conference on 20 February 1941, but for him the "stage" to do so was early 1941: "It is quite certain that Germany will never tolerate Great Britain getting on to the Continent, either now or in the future. Therefore it is best to leap in now while the going is good." (Danchev(ed), 60)

*****

On 12 November 1940 - two weeks after Italy's attack on Greece - Frank Nelson, the Executive Director of SOE, attended a meeting of the Chiefs of Staff and reviewed the situation of SOE. "The Chiefs of Staff express rather unwonted enthusiasm for subversion." (Mackenze, 91) Out of that meeting arose their first directive to SOE, "Subversive activities in Relation to Strategy", dated 25 November 1940 – just a few days after Hungary and Rumania joined the Tripartite Pact. "This paper has been prepared with a view to guiding the Special Operations Executive as to the direction in which the subversive activities can best assist our Strategy." (Stafford(so), 219) The following directions related to Hungary, Yugoslavia, Rumania and Bulgaria:

> In any neutral countries from which the enemy draws supplies, our activities should be directed towards causing the maximum interference with such supplies. In particular, immediate destruction of communications by rail and road, especially of oil to Germany, in Roumania, would be of great assistance.
> Preparation for destruction of communications between Germany and Italy and the south and east through Yugoslavia, Hungary and Bulgaria should also be made in case of further Axis moves to the south-east and arrangements subsequently to create economic disorganisation so as to hinder the enemy from exploiting the resources of the occupied areas. (Stafford(so), 222)

Priority:
> Against this background, we consider that the following requirements are all of *first priority*:

(d) Interference with communications by rail and river from Roumania to Germany and Italy, particularly of oil.
(f) Preparation for destruction of communications in Yugoslavia and Bulgaria. (Stafford(so), 223-4. Italics in the source.)

Thomas Masterson's leadership of SOE Belgrade

This directive set the disruption of enemy communications as the main target for SOE. "That same month SOE work in the Balkans was put on a new footing with the despatch [from Bucharest] to Belgrade of Tom Masterson to head the SOE mission there, ..." (Stafford[so], 49) **Thomas S. Masterson**, "a very competent representative ... was sent to Belgrade in November 1940". "... a businessman with oil interests in Roumania and an intimate knowledge of the Balkans" reached Belgrade early in December. (Mackenzie, 30, 105)

Masterson was given cover as the First Secretary of the Legation. He was "a wise and most impressive old man ... of about sixty, but he was still full of vitality. He had won a D.S.O. in World War I for helping to destroy the Rumanian oil wells before the German occupation in 1916. He was well known in the Balkans, and we hoped that his appointment to Belgrade would do something to restore the confidence of the legation, which had been shaken by some of the wilder spirits who had been led by Caesar [Hanau], and by the row which followed the discovery by the Yugoslavs of our plan to blow up the Iron Gates." (Sweet-Escott, 52)

Upon Masterson's arrival, SOE activities became more disciplined, better organized and enlarged.

> The activity was greatest in Belgrade, where Tom Masterson had now surrounded himself with Hugh Seton-Watson, Julian Amery, John Bennett and a host of others. As we had hoped, Tom Masterson had evidently succeeded in obtaining the confidence of our minister, in spite of his distrust of easy philosophies. ... But our main hopes in Belgrade were pinned on the Serb Peasant party. Tom Masterson had established the closest of contacts with Tupanjanin, one of its principal leaders. Our Minister, Sir Ronald [Ian] Campbell, encouraged us to do all we possibly could, and this included what was referred to as financial support, to induce the party to persist in defying the pro-German attitude of the Cvetkovic government. (Sweet-Escott, 62)

8 January 1941: "Interference with German Oil Supplies"

In addition to current "funding" of propaganda and sabotages, and "subsidizing" political parties and patriotic organizations, in January 1941 the British hoped to complete the blocking of the Danube, mostly by bribery. On 8 January 1941, SOE issued a memorandum, 'Interference with German Oil Supplies'. (COS(41)3(0) in *CAB 80/56*) The paper was based on certain "assumptions regarding the assistance which would be given to SOE" by other departments of His Majesty's Government.

Among assorted assistances required, SOE stated: "3. We would require very large funds to be placed at our disposal." (Stafford[so], 226) In a summary of possible schemes of attack, the Memorandum stated:

> E. Blocking the Danube at Kazan and possibly the Iron Gate as well. This is our business. Detailed plans have been prepared by S.O.2, but those for Kazan are in the hands of the Yugoslav General Staff who will clearly not take action in advance of a German invasion of Yugoslavia. It would be the function of S.O.2 to secure the final completion of the preparations and then, by a large and judicious expenditure to ensure that, irrespective of the wishes of the Yugoslav government, the charges were fired at a moment suitable to us. (Stafford(so), 229-30)

Of all the schemes, in SOE's view,

> Scheme E is the only one which, if successful, would be likely to deal the Germans a really crippling blow. It is unfortunately, also hardest to bring off. We recommend, nevertheless, that no expense or effort should be spared to achieve it, ... (Stafford[so], 230)

According to the Memorandum, plans for blocking the Iron Gate "were well on the way to completion by the middle of December 1939", while those for the Kazan defile had existed since September 1940. However, the Yugoslav government "intervened, stopped the work, and took over the mines which had already been laid." (Stafford(so), 231)

In January 1941, the Memorandum continued, the blocking of the Danube could be done in two phases. In phase one, "With diplomatic pressure from the Minister, plus bribery by us, there is a fair chance that we can get the work proceeded with and finished before the river again becomes navigable." (Stafford(so), 231-2)

> (ii) The second phase is for us to try to arrange to fire the charges at the appropriate moment without the knowledge of the Yugoslav government. This would have to be done almost entirely by bribery.
>
> C. The assistance required would be:
> (i) Foreign office decision and explicit instructions to the Minister to co-operate in our plans.
> (ii) *Finance for the bribing operations.* We cannot give an estimate of how much would be required, as this would need a careful review of the personalities concerned, by our representatives in the field. We would, of course, have to spend a lot of money. (Stafford(so), 232. Italics added.)

As stated by W. Mackenzie, neither the Kazan nor the Iron Gates demolition plan was implemented. "The estimates and directives from the Chiefs of Staff in London, ... , were often unrealistic." (Dodds-Parker, 54) When George Taylor came to the Balkans, he was well aware of the situation, and in his Report of 26 February 1941 informed Nelson that attempts of blocking the Danube had not been satisfactory. The secret operations on the Kazan defile, commenced in September 1939, were discovered in December.

> Every effort has been made in the last two months, and particularly in the last three weeks, to induce the Yugoslav General Staff to complete the work with the idea that we would be able, probably through Daddy [Ilija Trifunović-Birčanin], to have charges fired at the right moment *regardless of the attitude of Belgrade.* (Report, page 15. Italics added.)

Then Taylor added: "We are continuing our efforts both by argument and *political pressure on the Prince Regent,* and if necessary by the *offer of large bribes,* to have the work on the Kasarn [Kazan] scheme renewed." And finally Taylor was relying "on the influence of Daddy with the local military commander to ensure that the final action is taken." (Report p. 16. Italics added.)

It was not.

Chapter 3

Some Section D/SOE and military services' "contacts" in Belgrade

George Taylor reported to Dalton on 27 March 1941, that Julius Hanau *originally picked the winner in* Dr. Miloš Tupanjanin of the Serbian Peasant Party, and that John Bennett had *"discovered"* Trifunović-Birčanin of *Narodna Odbrana*. (Great Britain, Special Operations Executive, 91087-10V, Hoover Institution Archives) In his description of the initial coup proposal (presented in **Appendix D, Part One**) Julian Amery gave details of his contacts with Jovan Đonović – Trifunović-Birčanin, and with Jacob Altmaier. Alexander Glen wrote about the contacts among the military, including his and Amery's meetings with Colonel Draža Mihailović. Initiated at various times, the contacts existed throughout the Section D and SOE times.

> ... the UK did not suffer from lack of information about Yugoslavia; she possessed sound intelligence and good links with ruling circles and the Yugoslav service departments. The Section D/SOE networks were more extensive that historians have charted. (Onslow, 7) Britain viewed Yugoslavia as part of the Balkan jigsaw, through the lens of British regional strategic imperatives. (Onslow, 8)

Once the decision was made to form the Balkan Front,

> The British government demanded not neutrality but alliance and dangled hints of the arrival of shipments of arms and invasion forces to encourage the Yugoslavs and Turks. Such efforts were not merely pointless. As some British official and semiofficial historians have recently suggested, to have "egged on" these small countries by promises of assistance that could not be fulfilled while encouraging them to oppose Nazi Germany with her "military record" and her "vastly superior armaments" was simply irresponsible. In light of the horror that an extended occupation and civil and guerrilla war would bring to the region in the following four years, London's pressure on the Balkan governments to become overt enemies of Nazi Germany in the spring of 1941 is one of the heavier ethical burdens that has weighed on Britain's official postwar conscience. (Smith, 46)

By the nature of things, the Legation personnel had to work as a team, under the direction of Minister Campbell. That applied to the SOE agents as well, directed by Tom Masterson until George Taylor arrived in Belgrade to take over. Since his arrival on 27 February 1941, the two teams operated as one. At the all-British meeting on 19 March the roles were defined and assigned, and information shared as required by the ultimate goal: the overthrow of Prince Paul's Government and formation of a new one which would comply with the British objectives. (**Part One, 108-10**)

In those circumstances, the duty of British operatives was to *"egg on"* people in Yugoslavia *by promises of assistance that could not be fulfilled while encouraging them to oppose Nazi Germany with her "military record" and her "vastly superior armaments"*. That kind of "encouragement" was done through the regular diplomatic channels, and even more so through the Section D / SOE "contacts". Following is the information about some of these "contacts".

As already described, the mining tycoon Chester Beatty recommended George Taylor, S.W. (Bill) Bailey, and Duane T. (Bill) Hudson to Section D. As Bailey and Hudson worked in Yugoslavia for some time, and Bailey used to carry and distribute explosives, it must be assumed that they had some "contacts" with certain domestic people.

George Taylor was working on the principle that in each of the neutral countries the British should recruit a number of reliable British residents who in turn would build contacts with friendly local elements. In Belgrade, "there was a large party of people under the control of a British business man called Julius Hanau. ... Bill Bailey, who ... had acquired a noteworthy grasp of Balkan politics, assisted him. Julius Hanau ... had good friends among some of the political parties in opposition ... especially the Serb Peasant Party and the Slovenes." (Sweet-Escott, 22)

So: Sweet-Escott also confirmed that Hanau had established British contact with the Serbian Peasant Party (SPP), i.e, its leaders, Dr. Milan Gavrilović, Dr. Miloš Tupanjanin, and Dr. Branko Čubrilović.

- Alexander Glen added more information: "… we had made our contact through Bill Bailey with the Serbian Peasant Party, …" (Glen, 53-4) Until told to leave the country, Bailey also was influencing SPP.

- Thomas G. Mapplebeck was another reliable British resident in Belgrade. "He first went to Yugoslavia as part of a British economic mission after the [First World] war and settled down as a commercial agent." "As Assistant Air Attaché in Belgrade, [he] *played a crucial role in 1941 coup,* … A fluent speaker of Serbo-Croat, he had refused to join MI(R) in Belgrade because he felt he would have to spy on old friends but nevertheless agreed to pass on any valuable information to the intelligence agencies. It helped, too, that his brother-in-law was chief of police in Zagreb." (Glen(B), 189. Italics added.) "The Briton, who claimed to be closest to the makers of the coup, and the most in the know, was not a member of SOE, but Tom Mapplebeck, an honorary air attaché. …." (Williams, 32; 254n28)

- "Tom Masterson had established the closest of contacts with Tupanjanin, …" (Sweet-Escott, 62)

- On 2 March 1941, at a meeting at Chequers, Dalton informed Churchill that SOE undercover agents in Belgrade "were in contact with dissident senior Royal Yugoslav Air Force officers and secret subsidies were being fed to anti-government newspapers and politicians." (Stafford(C), 211-12) (**Part One, 85-6**)

- John Bennett "discovered" Ilija Trifunović-Birčanin – and thus with him *Narodna Odbrana* and all the organizations connected with it. Trifunović - "Daddy" - was able to mediate between the coup-plotters and SOE because he also had close ties with former and active military personnel, including General Borivoje-Bora Mirković – the chief executor of the coup. Mirković wrote about ties with Trifunović-Birčanin in his accounts of the coup; they were together during its execution. Jovan Đonović wrote that Trifunović was politically advising Mirković every day from the 24th to the night of the 26th of March. (Knežević, 112-13n2)

- Amery also confirmed: "Birchanin was in direct contact with S.O.E." (Amery, 228)

On 27 March 1941, Taylor reported to Dalton: "Trifunovich had kept us informed of conspiracy under strictest promise of silence. He had promised to give us 12 hours' notice so that we could advise you about coup". (Great Britain, Special Operations Executive, 91087-10V, Hoover Institution Archives) This established the fact of direct, two-way communication between SOE and Trifunović.

- Jacob Altmaier [code-name A/H 9] took Julian Amery to see M. Gavrilović, and to meet Tupanjanin. (Amery, 148, 173) Altmaier - who was hiding, for some time, under a false name, at Gavrilović's residence in Belgrade - also established Amery's contact with Jovan Đonović. (Vodušek Starič, 56) Đonović, then, connected Amery with *Vojvoda* Ilija Trifunović-Birčanin. (Amery, 175/6)

So: *Vojvoda* Birčanin was connected at least with Bennett and Amery; as George Taylor put it: *Vojvoda* had "close personal relationship" with SOE.

- British Military Attaché, Lt.-Col. Charles S. Clarke, was in contact with Col. Dragoljub-Draža Mihailović since the summer of 1940. Mihailović connected Clarke with Col. Žarko Popović, Yugoslav director of military intelligence, and other officers. They had meetings in Clarke's residence at Vračar in Belgrade, and on the Topčider Hill, in the residence of one of the British Legation members. (Vodušek Starič, 70) "I had known Mihailovitch as Director of Operations on the General Staff in Belgrade, and along with Sandy Glen had often discussed guerrilla warfare with him." (Amery, 244) In September 1941, Peter Boughey was SOE's liaison officer with the Yugoslav Government in Exile. He "felt that sending him to Yugoslavia was probably the best solution as he was friendly with Mihailović. (Williams, 55)

So: Attaché Clarke and SOE-men Masterson, Glen, Amery and Boughey had contacts with Mihailović (code-named A/H 31) and Žarko Popović.

"There was growing contact between the plotters and British agents including the military and air attachés", Charles S. Clarke and A.H.H. Macdonald. (Sulzberger, 100) Clarke "had extremely close relations with Colonel Žarko Popović, the chief of Yugoslav military intelligence. Their relationship went beyond strictly intelligence matters, to consideration of post occupational planning, with which the SOE was also involved. Clarke and Popović met regularly, and it was through Clarke that Glen, for example, first met Draža Mihailović in the late summer of 1940. Masterson, the head of SOE in Belgrade, was later also in touch with Mihailović.» (Stafford(cp), 413)

Clarke was getting information from Col. Žarko Popović. When Popović was sent to Moscow as military attaché, in August 1940, Gen. Mirković replaced him in supplying information to Clarke via Major Dušan Babić, the Intelligence Chief of the Air Force Staff, and via reserve Captain Živojin Krstić. Mirković was personally giving information to Macdonald even before he had met Clarke. (Bosnić(ed), 33-4)

Thus: there was a connection among Popović – Mirković – Clarke – Macdonald – Mapplebeck.

- **Bailey – Mihailović – Birčanin – Žarko Popović – SOE**

"Bill Bailey was personally acquainted with Mihailović, and was aware of his strongly pro-British and anti-German sentiments." (Howarth, 77)

"Private talks between Charlie Clark and Hugh Macdonald with their Yugoslav army and air force colleagues became increasingly frank and we talked seriously too with a certain Colonel Draza Mihailović, who by then was responsible for planning against post-occupational contingencies." (Glen, 61)

British officers in Belgrade, representing all three services, were getting to know members of the Yugoslav General Staff, "and examining with them the increasing likelihood that Yugoslavia would be dragged into the war. In the summer of 1940, Colonel Clark, the head of the British military mission, and the junior Naval Attaché, Alexander Glen, were told that in the event of an occupation of Yugoslavia, the planning of internal resistance was being entrusted to staff-officer, Colonel Draža Mihailović. (Beloff, 62)

Colonel Dragoljub-Draža Mihailović was then Chief of the Operations Bureau of the General Staff responsible for the organization of resistance in the event of occupation, and as such known as an expert on guerrilla warfare. Glen described the Colonel as "quiet, rather academic", "whom ... we had got to know quite well" "through the Director of Military Intelligence, the extrovert and passionately anti-German Jarko [Žarko] Popović," (Glen, 124) Mihailović's section "worked closely with certain patriotic groups, particularly the Narodna Odbrana (the National Patriotic League) under Ilya Birchanin [Ilija Birčanin], which had some quarter of a million members all over the land," (Glen, 124)

Amery wrote about Mihailović:

> We [Glen and Amery] had consulted him more than once on Albania; and he was now coming to dinner, for the specific purpose of telling us something about his plans for fighting a guerrilla war, if the Germans should overrun Yugoslavia. Mihailovitch was usually self-controlled and rather professional in his bearing, but his mood that night was violent and bitter. When we asked him how his plans for guerrilla warfare were going, he replied acidly that they all depend on fighting a regular campaign first. As things were going, the country seemed to be heading not for resistance, but for capitulation. Sandy and I judged that Mihailovitch was probably too disciplined an officer to lead a military coup, but we had no doubt which side he would be on, if one was made, though we were far from guessing the role he was destined to play. (Amery, 179-80)

In an interview in London in November 1984, Sir Alexander Glen told the author Nora Beloff that he had "invited Mihailović to several private dinners." Glen wrote about Mihailović with respect. "A man I am proud to have known; a man of honour; serious, well informed, a good listener, articulate when he spoke, and I found him broad in his understanding with loyalty to the whole of Yugoslavia and not to a narrow Serb hegemony." (Beloff, 62; 268n11)

Amery did not provide the dates of the meetings with Mihailović, but it is clear from his book that the meetings were taking place in the summer of 1940, after Jovan Đonović first brought up the idea of a coup.

> After the war Amery still had the opinion that much more could have been achieved if Dzonović had been supported in his plans to overthrow Prince Paul a year earlier. (Howarth, 61)

- "So that late summer and autumn of 1940 we [SOE] mixed with a wide range of politicians and army officers, including the then colonel Draza Mihailovic, who had been charged with preparing post-occupation operations. These were the establishment, those running the country, almost all Serb." (Glen(B), 42) "Julian Amery, Alexander Glen and George Taylor had had personal contact with Col. Dragoljub Mihajlović, already known as an expert on guerilla warfare, at one stage concerned with planning post-occupational activities; but no joint plans had been made with him." (Barker, 154)

- Clarke and Macdonald "were frequent visitors" at the Reserve Officers Club. (Stafford(cp), 413n53) "In 1940 and 1941 the majority of active members of this club were air force reserve officers. In them, the British Military attaché, Lt. Col, C.S. Clarke, and the Air Attaché, Wing Commander A.H.H. MacDonald, found a receptive audience." (Hoptner, 254)

- "Both Macdonald and Clarke had built close links with the Yugoslav Air Staff and General Staff respectively." (Glen(B), 35)

- "Reuter correspondent Peter Brown ... had very useful contacts with the Yugoslav left wing. The Communist Party was banned in Yugoslavia but it remained influential in the universities and capitalised on the traditionally pro-Russian and Slav sympathies of the average Serb and Montenegrin." (Amery, 142)
  Julian Amery and Peter Brown were in contact with Professor Dragoljub Jovanović, "the leader of the left-wing Serbian Agrarian Party, a break-away from Milan Gavrilovitch's Peasant Party. ... In Belgrade he [Dragoljub Jovanović] was widely regarded as a secret Communist. Green was the Peasant Party colour, and he was often compared to a water melon, green on the outside but red inside." (Amery, 152)

- There were ... some S.O.E. members who had Communist friends in Belgrade, and who knew how strong was the sympathy for both the Soviet Russia and for social revolution among young educated Serbs. (G.H.N. Seton-Watson, "Afterword: Thirty Years After", in Authy & Cloog(ed), p. 286)

"... Julian Amery succeeded in getting at least a glimpse of what young Communists might amount to." (Glen, 56) He had established contact "with a few young [Communist] Party members in Belgrade University, specifically with Olga Nincic [Ninčić] and her brother Djura [Đura], unlikely Communist Party children of Momcilo Nincic, [Momčilo Ninčić] (#), veteran politician of the extreme right. (Glen(B), 43)
  (#) Minister for Foreign Affairs in the new Putschist Government.

(In August 1944, Olga Ninčić was interpreter for Josip Broz Tito – the Secretary General of the Communist Party of Yugoslavia - in his talks with Prime Minister Churchill, in Italy.)

"Belgrade University had been both the main recruiting ground and the training centre except when, as was frequent, Party members were in prison and the prisons themselves became universities of revolution." (Glen, 138)

*****

In SOE's dealings with their local "contacts" in the Balkans, "Few UK personnel were needed: the collusion of the key members of the local population, directed by British operatives, was the means to further British strategic planning." (Onslow, 17)

In her study of Britain and the Belgrade coup, Dr. Sue Onslow pointed out to the following contacts:

> ... the focus of British political activity and attention, both SOE and Legation, was primarily on Belgrade. (Onslow, 22)

> Beyond the Prince, the Legation enjoyed excellent links with a small circle within the Yugoslav governing elite. The Ambassador drew upon three or four sources; the Legation as a whole regularly cited information from approximately ten. ... The Shadow missions enjoyed good links with the Yugoslav General Staff, Army and Air Force. (Onslow, 15)

> SIS also established excellent networks of information and intelligence gathering throughout the country, using vice-consular and pro-consular cover in Zagreb, Split, Dubrovnik, Susak [Sušak], Ljubljana and Skoplje. (Onslow, 15-16)

Based on Alexander Glen's report of 17 November 1941: "German pressure on the Yugoslav Government curtailed Alexander Glen's weekly contacts with the Yugoslav military in the autumn of 1940." (Onslow, 15n35)

> Stephen Clissold [an SIS agent (Williams, 42)] papers at the Bodleian Library show that in Yugoslavia at least there was remarkable co-operation and concord between SOE and SIS before April 1941. (Onslow 16)

> ... the prime focus of the organisation's [SOE] activity came to rest on a small element within the Serbian political spectrum ... (Onslow, 17)

> The leader of the Croatian Independent Democrats, Dr. Srdjan Budisavljevic, was a firm friend of Alexander Glen, and his party also received British subsidy from January 1941. (Onslow, 20) No record survives of the start date of this financial support, nor of the sums involved. (Onslow, 20n48)

> SOE also had links with 'odd groups of communists in Croatia and Slovenia'; ... however, 'SO2 never discovered the names of the leaders'. Julian Amery had put out feelers to the proscribed Yugoslav Communist Party, which was well organised with 'apparently large following in the schools and universities'. (Onslow, 20-21)

> Terence Glanville (the SOE officer based in the Consulate in Zagreb) also developed links with the United Jugoslavs, an influential organisation of businessmen that formed the commercial and financial backbone of the country. Its members included a considerable number of Jews and many Christians. Its youth organisation, the Organisation of United Jugoslav Students, printed and circulated propaganda for SOE. SOE specifically made use of Shell Company, Cunard White Star and Canadian Pacific. (Onslow, 21)

> In view of Glanville, the CPP [Croatian Peasant Party] was 'the only well-organised and statesmanlike political party in Yugoslavia'. ... However, the focus of British political activity and attention, both SOE and Legation, was primarily on Belgrade. (Onslow, 22)

> Glen knew Milan Gavrilovic [leader of the subsidized Serbian Peasant Party] well, and regularly spent one afternoon a week visiting his wife and family in Belgrade after Gavrilovic's departure to Moscow as Yugoslavia's first Ambassador in the Soviet Union. From July 1940 until the German invasion [6 April 1941] Glen was 'at least in daily contact with Tupanjanin [Gavrilović's deputy] and also in frequent touch with many of the leading politicians in the Serbian Peasant Party'. (Onslow, 29-30)

> By March 1941 SOE had also developed close links with the leaders of the Radical (Momcilo Nincic) and Democrat Parties (Dr. [Milan] Grol, Boka Vlaic and Radjoe Knesevic [Radoje Knežević]. (Onslow, 30)

> Also SOE established contact, originated originally by Julian Amery, with [Jovan] Djonovic and the Yugoslav Nationalist Party... (Onslow, 30)

> ... SOE's contacts with the Serb community extended to the nationalist organisations' leader, Ilija Trifunovic, well known as 'a leader of men ... and with great influence in all sections of Yugoslav life'. This represented potentially a very influential network throughout Serbia, some 200,000 strong, with association in every Serbian town. (Onslow, 31)
> The nationalist organisations comprised the *Narodna Odbrana*, the Chetniks, the Veterans Associations, the Order of White Eagle with Swords, and other World War I resistance associations... (Onslow, 31n86)

> ... under Tupajanin's leadership, the Serbian Peasant party was also preparing for action in secret – another attraction as far as SOE was concerned (hence their advocacy of a subsidy from the UK in July 1940.) (Onslow, 31)

> Throughout the second half of 1940 SOE worked to build up a Serbian front among the Serbian opposition, with the Serbian Peasant Party the spearhead of their attack. (Onslow, 38)

In his study of the SOE and British involvement in the Belgrade coup, Dr. David A.T. Stafford wrote about widespread British contacts with the domestic military and civilians:

> ... in the context of Yugoslavia's move toward signature of the [Tripartite] Pact, subversive activities by the SOE assumed great significance. As the SOE representatives in Belgrade saw it, their special function was to act in areas closed to the official mission. They particularly wanted to maintain intimate contacts with elements in opposition to the Yugoslav government, which included most of Serb politicians who were excluded from power by the regent, in alliance with Maček, the Croat leader. While the official mission in Belgrade concentrated on influencing Prince Paul's government against signature of the Tripartite Pact, the SOE strategy was to mobilize and direct the major Serb elements in Yugoslavia with the object of reversing or influencing the policy of the government. (Stafford(cp), 410)

There were three major political instruments available for the SOE's purpose: the Serb Peasant Party; the Radical, Democratic, and Nationalist opposition parties; and the national associations such as the *Narodna Odbrana* (subsidized by the SOE), the Chetniks, the Veterans associations, the Order of White Eagles with swords, and other groups mostly associated with Serb resistance in World War I. (Stafford[cp], 410. Italics in the source.)

These organizations, with the SOE's encouragement, flooded the government with petitions against signature of the Pact in the days immediately preceding the coup. (Stafford(cp), 411)

- **Popović - Mirković cooperation with the British before August 1940**

Cyrus Leo Sulzberger, *The New York Time's* foreign correspondent at the time, wrote in 1969 that "it was an open secret that an air force general, Borivoje Mirković, was conspiring with Serb officers, above all General Dušan Simović, air commander, to prepare a possible *coup d'état*". Then Sulzberger added more light on the subject:

There was growing contact between the plotters and British agents including the military and air attachés, Lieutenant Colonel C. S. Clarke and Wing Commander A.H.H. MacDonald, a lean temerarious Scot. Clarke had started his assignment clumsily; he attempted to bribe Colonel Žarko Popović, Jugoslav director of military intelligence, with a generous sum of dollars. Popović ignored this *faux pas* with bitter serenity and agreed to give Clarke names of Axis agents if he would exchange results. (Sulzberger, 100)

This is what Mirković wrote about the contact with the Military Attaché Clarke:

Intelligence Director of the Yugoslav General Staff, Colonel Žarko Popović, was regularly passing on the information on the German and Italian troops to the British Military Attaché in Belgrade, Col. Clarke. When Popović was assigned to Moscow, in August 1940, as the Military Attaché, Clarke was wondering who would continue providing the information. Popović assured him: he did not know any greater friend of Great Britain than General Mirković, and he was the only one who could provide the needed information. (Bosnić(ed), 33-4)

Indeed, Mirković was supplying the most confidential information on the movement of German and Italian troops to the British Air Attaché, Macdonald, **even before he met Clarke in August 1940.** The information was forwarded through Major Dušan Babić and reserve Captain Živojin [Žika] Krstić. (Bosnić(ed), 34)

In spite of the presence of the Secret Intelligence Service agents in Yugoslavia, none of them could get this information except Col. Clarke from Popović, and Macdonald from Mirković. (Bosnić(ed), 34)

- **Mirković – Mapplebeck intimate contacts**

Regarding his cooperation with Mapplebeck, Mirković stated: *"In the entire 1940 and 1941 year, Mapplebeck had never entered into the Air Force Command, and even less into his office."* Whether they were meeting in Mirković's office or elsewhere, Prof. D. Stafford concluded:

Mapplebeck was in many ways much better situated than MacDonald to have intimate contacts with members of the Yugoslav Air Force. An expatriate Englishman, who had flown with the Royal Flying Corps in France in World War I, and had spent two years in a German prisoner of war camp, Mapplebeck had live continuously in Belgrade since 1923. In addition to developing his own business interests, he also acted as agent for the Hawker Aircraft and Rolls-Royce companies, played an important part in negotiations for the purchase of British military aircraft by the Royal Yugoslav Air Force in the 1930s, and as a consequence developed close contacts with individuals such as Simović and Mirković. He certainly passed on information which came his way to the Air Ministry in London, but more important than that, he had also developed a very close relationship with Mirković. In the spring of 1940, before the collapse of France, Mirković began passing onto Mapplebeck the weekly intelligence summaries of the Yugoslav General Staff, copies of which Mapplebeck duly passed on to MacDonald. It was because of this activity that Mapplebeck, in 1940, was appointed honorary attaché at the legation, … (Stafford(cp), 415)

In 1951 Simović claimed that he personally had no contact at all with the representatives of the US, Great Britain and the USSR. …

However, Simović confirms that Gen. Mirković had official contacts with the British Air Attaché, Colonel Macdonald, and the representative of the «Bristol Co.», Mapplebeck. Simović also claims that he did not know whether they exerted any influence on Mirković, and he thought that other participants in the coup of 27 March 1941 did not have any contact with foreign representatives. (Simović(51), 12)

- **Mirković – Mapplebeck – Žika Krstić connection**

From 20 July through 20 August 1960, the Belgrade daily *Večernje novosti (The Evening News)* published a feuilleton by Nikola Milovanović, «Vojni puč i 27. mart 1941. godine» ("The Military Putsch and March 27[th,] 1941").
General Mirković thought that the author had described ((this important historic event in a way that many events had been incorrectly presented.))
((Having been, in these events, the principal organizer, and having managed the execution of the Coup d'état of 27 March 1941, I considered it my duty to present before the Yugoslav public the facts, and thereby to correct at least the principal inaccuracies)), wrote Mirković, and sent a letter to the paper, dated in London, 4 November 1960. - Translated excerpts follow.

> ((Krstić – Mapplebeck – Mirković. It is an ordinary and shameless lie that Krstić allegedly "connected" me with Mapplebeck for some ostensible work with the Intelligence Service or something like that. I met Mapplebeck before I did Krstić. Therefore there was no need for Krstić to introduce me to Mapplebeck, nor to link me with him for some conspiratorial work. Not even in Cairo did Krstić belong to my group, because he did not consent to enter into wires [the camp], into which was put Mirković with 420 officers and non-commissioned officers, by a directive of a clique and a government, that clique and that government who had liquidated the Dynasty and the Kingdom of Yugoslavia. ...)) (Karapandžić(AB), 146)

> ((... It is completely inaccurate and fictitious that Krstić used to be present to my conversations [about the preparations for the coup, with very trustworthy people] or that he was recruiting for me officers for the Coup d'état. In the entire 1940 and 1941 year, Mapplebeck had never entered into the Air Force Command, and even less into my office. Only the Air Attaché, Lt.-Col. MacDonald, personally, was coming to see me. If I had some information about movements of the Nazi troops to report, I was reporting it only to him personally....
> ((Not only that the British Legation was not in a position to give us some "directives", but materially they were so poorly off, or they pretended to be, that they did not have even a liter of gasoline to give us, let alone some aid in materiel or manpower, in case of war. On the contrary, they would occasionally ask stuff from us, and they never gave us anything, or made us any offers, because they themselves did not have everything they needed.)) (Karapandžić(AB), 147)

> ((The truth is, however, just the opposite, namely that the "putschist" General Mirković, at the request of the Air Attaché of Great Britain, gave from his command three light trucks for moving their offices and things on 4 April 1941. ... Furthermore, as they [the British] had no contact with London and Greece, I gave them to use one mobile radio station with a long range.)) (Karapandžić(AB), 147-8)

> *((Whether certain political people were receiving huge sums from British agents, that comes into another line of writing, not here. The main thing is that those men were absolutely not known to me. As I learned later, in exile, those politicians - British agents had received an unconditional order, as every mercenary gets, to remain with the people after the departure of the British legation and to stir insurrection, especially among the peasants, whose representatives they also were.))* (Karapandžić(AB), 148. Italics in the source.)

Actually, Mirković knew at least one man who was "subsidized" by the British – *Vojvoda* Trifunović-Birčanin – although it is possible that the General did not know about the "subsidy".

- **British contacts with officers**

Clarke introduced SOE agent Alexander Glen to Col. Dragoljub-Draža Mihailović in the late summer of 1940. Thomas Masterson, the head of the SOE in Belgrade [since December 1940] was also in touch with Mihailović. (Stafford(cp), 413)

> That Mihailović was in contact with the military attaché and Masterson over matters relating to post occupational planning prior to the coup has been confirmed to the author by Sir Alexander Glen, who was at least formally, assistant naval attaché in Belgrade. (Stafford(cp), 413n52)

More likely sources for army information about a coup would come from Clarke's contacts with the Reserve Officers' Club, to which he and MacDonald were frequent visitors. (Stafford(cp), 413n53)

(Mirković partially described contacts with MacDonald in his story of the coup, presented below.)

- **All British worked together**

    The SOE, of course, was not the only service or agency involved on the British side. Apart from the regular diplomatic staff, three services, represented by the attachés, and the SIS were all working in one way or another on the various problems associated with the efforts to stiffen the resolve of the Yugoslavs. (Stafford(cp), 413)

On the basis of evidence presented above - without a claim of being complete - it is clear that the British were linked with both military men and civilians. A diagram of these contacts would make it easier to visualize interconnections and relations. Even without it, though, it is evident that the ties were widespread. Operating together, the British and their "contacts" influenced and shaped events in Yugoslavia. Financial "subsidies" and outright bribes were given to some "contacts"- not to all – for implementation and advancement of British specific goals.

Was General Mirković a British agent?

According to Campbell, the former British Minister in Belgrade, the Yugoslav Foreign Minister in the Putschist Government, Momčilo Ninčić, told him in 1942 that

   Mirković had stated before a number of people in Egypt that while still in Belgrade before the coup d'état he had already been an agent of the British. ... If he was indeed an 'agent' I [Campbell] did not know it; I knew he was in confidential contact with the Air Attaché and told him that a coup d'état was being planned but he never furnished details or dates, ... (Stafford(cp), 415n58)

Campbell's statement, that *Mirković never furnished Macdonald details and dates,* agrees with Mirković's claims that he made the decision about the Putsch *in the afternoon of 26 March* **(Chapter 13).** Mirković wrote that he had meetings with Macdonald on the 23rd and 25th March - but that was **before** his decision was made, so he could not inform Macdonald about it. From the 24th through the 26th March Mirković was "advised" by the SOE-contact, *Vojvoda* Trifunović-Birčanin - who was so admired by George Taylor, the SOE chief in Belgrade at that time.
   As noted in Chapter 1, Mirković stated in bold letters: "**Ja nisam bio agent Inteliđens Servisa**" **((I was not an agent of the Intelligence Service.))** (Bosnić(ed), 35)
   However, in addition to the British Secret Intelligence Service (SIS), in the pre-war Yugoslavia operated also other British services, such as the Special Operations Executive (SOE), Military Intelligence, etc., generally unknown to the local population. By claiming not to be an agent of the SIS, perhaps Mirković meant not to be an agent of any British service?
   Ninčić's information on Mirković's alleged admission was given to Campbell in 1942, during the so-called "Cairo Affair" - a bitter dissension between Mirković and other military in Egypt, and the Government of Slobodan Jovanović in London, who replaced Simović's on 11 January 1942.
   In his *Zapisi ... (Notes ...),* Jovanović presented the Government's view of the Affair. Regarding the coup of 27 March 1941, Jovanović wrote that one ought to distinguish between two groups of officers who had executed it: 1 – the younger ones, who wanted to prevent the tying of Yugoslavia to the Axis at any price, and 2 – the other ones – among whom Mirković had been in the first place – who stood in tight connection with the British agents, and were instigated and encouraged by them.

   ((That link between Mirković and English agents was unknown to many until the Cairo Affair. Only then, when not only the English command Middle East, but also the English diplomacy, began actively interest themselves for the fate of Mirković, our eyes began to open.))
   "Ta veza između Mirkovića i engleskih agenata bila je mnogima nepoznata sve do Kairske afere. Tek onda kad se ne samo Engleska komada na Srednnjem Istoku, nego i engleska diplomatija stala živo interesovati za Mirkovićevu sudbinu, nama su se stale otvarati oči." (Jovanović, 30)

On Thursday, 21 May 1942, S. Jovanović, Ninčić, Gavrilović, and Radoje Knežević discussed the steps to be taken about Mirković. The following day R. Knežević talked about them with his Democratic Party president, Milan Grol, giving him the following information:

A report from Cairo by [Ilija] Smiljanić established that B. Mirković stated, in presence of the British, that he had been in agreement with them ("*s njima u sporazumu*") before 27 March [1941]; now it is established here in London that General *Shea* was coming to Belgrade a year before 27 March, ((and already then arranged the action with Bora Mirković about the overthrow of the regime.)) "I tada već uglavio akciju sa Borom Mirkovićem o obaranju režima" (Grol, 137-8)

On 4 June 1943, Grol wrote that Mirković *'se u Kairu hvalio da je bio "agent" [britanski]'* ((in Cairo boasted that he had been the "agent" [British].)) (Grol, 359)

Whether General John Shea was in Belgrade "a year before" the coup, i.e. in March 1940, or not, in December 1939 he "conducted an extensive survey into the capabilities and requirements of the Yugoslav Army" (Onslow, 11) That was some six months before Germany invaded France and other western countries, some seven months before the first suggestions were made to the British about the coup, some eleven months before Italy invaded Greece. In December 1939, His Majesty's Government was quite satisfied with policies of the Yugoslav Government, and the British Government was not contemplating the overthrow of Prince Paul's regime. Therefore, Radoje Knežević's information about the Mirković-Shea plot should be doubted until proven true.

Because of the adversarial attitudes between the exile groups in London and Cairo, one would have to definitely establish the veracity of information about Mirković's reported statements, given to Campbell by Ninčić and to Grol by R. Knežević – before concluding that Mirković indeed had been **an agent** of the British. He himself acknowledged **cooperation** with them, but that is not the same as being **an agent**. "I should doubt that he [Mirković] ever received pay from any of our intelligence or other services", wrote Campbell to Orme Sargent of the Foreign Office on 1 July 1942. (Staffor(cp), 415n58) Campbell had to know because he was the one who was approving payments. It is very probable that other officers-putschists likewise were receiving no payments. However, that was not true for some important and influential civilian British "contacts".

In a private letter, dated 3 July 1953, Mirković wrote that, after coming to England, being a heavy invalid, he was forced to ask The National Assistance Board for assistance. Initially he was getting 38 shillings a week, which was later raised to three pounds sterling a week. (Karapandžić(AB), 127) Some persons who kept contact with the General in London stated that he had died as a poor man.

S. Jovanović wrote that Mirković's link with the British was unknown to many until the Cairo Affair. One wonders did Jovanović know about the link between SOE's Tom Masterson and Radoje Knežević, about whom Jovanović had a high opinion? R. Knežević edited Jovanović's *Zapisi …* after the author's death. Unlike Mirković, Knežević's Democratic Party was receiving British pay for a while, which was approved by Campbell. (Vodušek Starič, 214-15)

Gen. Simović was activated after meeting Col. Donovan

In the sources describing the one-hour meeting of Simović and Donovan on 24 January 1941, researched for this book, there is no evidence that the American guest detailed to Simović the purposes of his second mission for President Roosevelt (6 December 1940 to 18 March 1941) and Prime minister Churchhill. There was no reason for Donovan to reveal them. Therefore, it seems probable that Simović did not know that:

the President wanted Donovan to visit Gibraltar, Egypt, Palestine and Greece (Danchev(ed), 19; 229n1) – not Bulgaria and Yugoslavia;

but Prime Minister Churchill requested Donovan to visit Bulgaria and Yugoslavia (Ford, 100) – not Roosevelt;

on his Mediterranean tour Donovan was flying in Biritish bombers, used British facilities, and for all effects and purposes became Churchill's as well as Roosevelt's confidential agent. (Dunlap, 243)

Consequently, it is probable that Simović assumed that President Roosevelt sent Donovan to Belgrade with a mission related specifically to Yugoslavia. That gave the mission an extra significance that influenced Simović's subsequent activities. To put them in perspective, one ought to keep in mind that by 24 January 1941, many events which the coup-plotters-executioners used later as jusifications for their acts had not ocurred yet. Thus, for instance:

there was no Eden-Dill mission to Greece;

there was no George Taylor's mission to Yugoslavia;

Bulgaria had no Pact with the Axis, German troops were still in Rumania, and not crossing the Danube into Bulgaria;

the decision was not made to send the British troops to Greece;

the decision was not made by the Yugoslav Government to adhere to the Tripartite Pact;

the decision was not made at Chequers [2 March] and at the all-British meeting in Belgrade [19 March] to overthrow Prince Paul;

Prince Paul met Hitler 39 days **after** 24 January;

the British troops were not landing into Greece;

a petitions campagn to influence the Regent against the Tripartite Pact was to be organized later, in March;

Churchill's order to draw Yugoslavia into the war by any means whatever was yet to come, almost two months later.

Nevertheless - as Simović wrote in his memoirs before returning to Belgrade - **by the end of January 1941,** he had started preparing actions which were to be taken if his attempts failed in convincing the authorities of needed resistance and defense of the honor and the future of the people – as he put it. Why? A plausible answer is found in his statement to Donovan about the fidelity to the «Allies», and in his vision of sharing the victory with Great Britain.

*****

Before continuing with the examination of political activities of the young British secret operatives and their "contacts", let it be noted that assignments of these young men were not only the hard work without play. They did have quite a bit of fun, and here is just a brief glance at it.

Work, and play ...where gypsies strummed their violins ...

Devoted to the cause of their country, young D/SOE-men concentrated their attention first and foremost on accomplishing their given assignments the best they could. However, they had plenty of time available for themselves, their personal activities and pursuits – until the defining all-British conference on 19 March 1941.

Living conditions and style in then still-neutral Yugoslavia and Hungary were different than in the war-fighting Britain, and taking advantage of the still "normal" way-of-life was understamable. A few words about that "personal time" are written here not as a criticism, but just as an illustration.

Sir Alexander Glen died on 6 March 2004, and three days later TIMESONLINE carried his obituary from *The Times*. Two sentences read: "In 1940 he was sent by Admiral Godfrey, the Director of Naval Intelligence, to Belgrade as assistant naval attaché. There, he shared a flat with Julian Amery, and *they partied every night*." (Italics added.) The sentences echoed Sir Alexander's own words:

The first weeks in Belgrade Glen saw little of Captain Max Despard, and was left rather to his own resources, "partying most nights with the Americans, Belgians and Greeks, and with new Yugoslav friends." (Glen(B), 34-5)

Belgrade was a heady place for a young man in 1940, particularly for a young Calvinist Scott, ... Yugoslavs enjoy themselves; they enjoy good food, good drinking; they enjoy parties and they love discussion. ... The girls were lovely and extremely elegant, entrancingly and distractingly different from the more demure ones at home, while the men were outgoing and welcoming.

Café life was a fascinating revelation to one who had no knowledge of Vienna or Budapest. ...

... life was then lived in Belgrade to the full every moment. Julian Amery and I shared a flat just around the corner from the Legation, ... Scarcely a night passed without a party, after which we would go on to one or other of the night places like Russki Czar or the Casbek, sometimes to a *tsigane cafana* [gipsy café] outside town. We would dance the night away, captured by those sad, haunting songs like 'Tako Dalaika' ('My heart is far away') **, and often end for breakfast by Max Despard's swimming pool in his lovely home at Dedine. (Glen, 52-3)

** Probably "Tamo daleko..." ("Over there, so far away ...", a WWI Serb army favorite song.)

> In my own case, it was the Serbian Peasant Party that enabled me to enter local village life, at Party meetings, local marriages and funerals. (Glen(B), 43)

> We did not spend our time only in Belgrade. Particularly after we had made our contact through Bill Bailey with the Serbian Peasant Party, there were frequent visits to villages in Sumadija or Morava. Weddings or christenings were usually the reasons. We feasted out of doors off *caymak* and superbly roasted suckling pigs. ... (Glen, 53-4)

> Visiting much of Serbia in my Packard saloon, ... , helped me to form my own perceptions of the country. I was accompanied often by Shems Mardin, secretary of the Turkish Legation, ... , and sometimes by the Greek minister, Rosetti, with whom at first light we would hunt wildfowl on the Danube, fortified with sacher tortes, their caramelised exteriors hiding the most delectable centers, washed down with good local wines as the sun rose slowly. (Glen(B), 43)
>
> Unlike Bosnia, the valleys of Serbia are rich, lavish with fields of maize and grain, the blue plums and fat apricots weighing down the trees along the lanes and tracks. Village occasions revolved around the suckling pigs and baby lambs turning slowly on the spit outside, basted with good beer. Afterwards, the *kola* was danced in long weaving lines over the fields and hills. (Glen(B), 43)
>
> In the smallest taverns you ate well, the local dishes with a wealth of character as in Leskovac, while in towns and cities, restaurants like Dva Ribara [Two Fishermen] or Magestic in Belgrade gave the best of Hungarian and old Turkish cooking, none of the nonsense of some television chefs of today. (Glen(B), 43)

Julian Amery, Glen's colleague in Section D, also remembered good times they had in Belgrade.

> My work there kept me busy, but I still found time for discovering and enjoying Belgrade. Until the snow came I used to ride, most mornings, with a group of young Yugoslav officers. I also took lessons in Serbo-Croat from a Croat official in the Foreign Office and met a number of his friends. There was a good deal of entertaining within the diplomatic corps, and I explored the restaurants and night life of Belgrade with Yugoslav and British pressmen. Sometimes our high spirits got the better of us and led me to depart from the traditional decorum of diplomacy. (Amery, 144)

With or without *kajmak* - a type of Serbian cream cheese - or superbly roasted suckling pigs, Basil Davidson had his own merry-go-round in Budapest:

> So you might well think me fortunate: my own news agency, links with the "underground", plenty to eat and drink and money in my purse, safe job if ever that existed: or safe at any rate for as long as one survived, ... All this I had, and more: for magically the shores of love now lost their splintering disaster. Here they were changed to gentler scenarios, transported to the hot-spring bathing pools of Buda ringed deliciously with snow as long winter lasted, or in summer carried to the tilting lake-lapped beaches of Balaton and soothed in the winds of weekend walks through woods and meadows of the Dunantul, hand in hand, or bejazzed and befumed in the dives and clubs of Pest, carried further in the candle-lit cellars of Harom Csiri Kocza, that blessed Three Billed Duck, and other dining joints where gypsies from the Alföld strummed their violins and sang their purple songs, till brought at last to happy ending in the waiting beds of Buda. Could anyone want more, or half as much? (Davidson, 56)

How could one blame them for having some good time while doing their duty?

Chapter 4

British "subsidies" to "contacts" in Yugoslavia

Subsidizing political parties provided the British some potential for favorable political influence. In Slovenia, "D" man A.C. Lawrenson "was on excellent terms with local Slovene leaders. The most promising field was in those groups which were both nationalist and progressive, or at least anti-conservative. There were various Slovene organisations which felt strongly enough about the position of Slovenes in Austria and Italy to undertake minor sabotage of railway vehicles en route to Germany, even against the policy of their own government. (Mackenzie, 28) The political atmosphere in Croatia was different and not nearly as favorable for British activities. The greatest attention was paid to potential impact in Serbia.

On Thursday, 27 March 1941, Dalton recorded in his diary: " ... 'There was a *coup d'état* early this morning at Belgrade.' .... The money we spent on the *Serb Peasant Party and other Opposition Parties has given wonderful value. ...*" (Pimlot(ed), 176-7. Italics added.)

On 28 March Dalton sent to Churchill a letter about the SOE's special operations in the Balkans. "To continue the work, *already well in hand, of encouraging the Yugoslav opposition parties to bring pressure to bear on the Government in a sense favourable to this country,*" concerned him the most at that moment, and he informed the Prime Minister:

> Since I took over the SOE, we have spent in Yugoslavia no less than £100,000. This has mainly gone to financing the Serb Peasant Party and to bribery of various sorts, including payment for recurrent acts of minor sabotage. We also succeeded in creating an emergency reserve of 16 million Dinars to be used if remittances from London should become impossible. I think we have had good value for this expenditure!
> (Great Britain, Special Operations Executive – 91087-10.V
> Hoover Institution Archives)

It would be interesting to know how that entire sum was spent, but the information is not available. Even incomplete information will suffice to illustrate how some money was used in Yugoslavia and for which purposes. For the nine month period (July 1940 – March 1941) it seems that SPP received £36,000. As the sabotage was "minor", it is likely that only a minor share of the remaining sum (no less than £64,000) was used for that purpose, and a larger one for *bribery of various sorts*. A few notes on the money and its use follow.

Money from the secret vote

Professor M.R.D. Foot observed that "SOE was a secret service". Its Charter "laid down that it would be 'very undesirable' for questions about it to be asked, let alone answered in the House of Commons. Parliament was to have no say in how it was run, what it did or did not do. Money for it - ... – was to come from the secret vote, into which, by longstanding convention, the Commons do not inquire, and which the Lords by statute cannot touch because it forms part of a money bill." (Foot(S), 34) "SOE got all the money it needed from secret funds." (Foot(S), 30) "The purpose of S.O.E. was to exploit every means of making the enemy uncomfortable: strikes, propaganda, terrorism, riots, boycott and bribery." (Dilks(ed), 313)

British operations in Yugoslavia before World War Two were multifaceted. In addition to the ones mentioned above, there was systematic nurturing of domestic contacts – cultural, political, military, etc. – and of their activities. In the course of the preceding story it was shown that certain "contacts" were "subsidized". It is hard to imagine that those "subsidized" would refuse to comply when "suggestions" were made to them.

Financing widespread activities

Revisiting the Belgrade Putsch of 27 March 1941, Professor Sue Onslow noted that a lot had been written about

> sabotage of Axis economic interests and strategic communications [in Yugoslavia], through ambitious schemes to block Danube river traffic, thus denying the German war economy precious shipments of Romanian oil and wheat; and post-occupational planning for resistance and wireless networks. SOE's contacts and activities in Yugoslavia went beyond this, and were more wide ranging than has been appreciated hitherto. (Onslow, 16-17)

In the eyes of SOE, this underground resistance had already proved its worth in small-scale acts of sabotage (such as destruction of rail freight and transports, attacks on warehouses and factories) as well as distributing British-produced propaganda against German influence in Yugoslavia itself.(Onslow, 17)

... Prior to the enemy occupation of Yugoslavia and the departure of the Yugoslav government, there was widespread subversive activity in the country undertaken by SOE or by its predecessor, Section D of SIS. Officers were entering the country on a weekly basis with large consignments of explosives both by land and sea, initially building up a strong underground network ... They also supported the Serb Peasant Party and the Slovene underground organizations. ...
(Special Operations Executive, 1940-1946: Subversion and Sabotage ...
http://www.ampltf.co.uk/collections_az/SOE-2-1.description.aspx 6/22/07)

Although it is probable that most of these SOE *sodelavci* (collaborators – as Professor Vodušek Starič called them) operated out of a patriotic sense of duty toward their country and out of the resentment toward neighboring Germany and Italy, their operating expenses had to be covered. In addition, they also had to be "encouraged" – rewarded or outright bribed – and thus enabled by their British *sodelavci* for further, post-occupational tasks the British war leaders had planned.

Based mostly on the documents in the Public Record Office, Vodušek Starič presented in details many activities of the "Slovene underground organizations", their relations with the Section D/SOE operatives in the period 1938-1942, and the British funding of some of the activities, not only in Slovenia. A few of her findings/observations are summarized below:

- M.R.D. Foot, the SOE historian, wrote that SOE has had deep pocket to cover needs of the personnel in the field and many activities behind the enemy lines. The Slovenian *SOE sodelavci* reported many times that the British agents have had a lot of money. (Vodušek Starič, 28)
- In Belgrade, the British subsidized two bi-weeklies published by Terence Atherton, the *Balkan Herald* and the *South Slav Herald*. (Vodušek Starič, 59)
- In Zagreb, the British Consulate financially supported Većeslav Vilder's *Nova riječ,* Slavko Vereš's *Alarm*, as well as *Slobodni Balkan* and *Novi red.* (Vodušek Starič, 90)
- The Consul in Zagreb was pointing directions to and financing the student organization YMCA [Young Men Christian Association] at the University of Ljubljana. (Vodušek Starič, 143-4)
- The British Council in Zagreb supported the English Club in Ljubljana. (Vodušek Starič, 145)
- SOE Zagreb financed the Slovenes in Maribor with a "war chest", giving them the codes for communications, other things needed to establish communications, presses, as well as plans for demolitions, evacuation, and distribution of funds. (Vodušek Starič, 224)
- To execute plans for demolitions of some bridges, viaducts, and dams in Slovenia, SOE provided 50,000 *dinars* [worth $1,000] to pay the accomplices, to buy groceries for hideouts, etc. (Vodušek Starič, 190)
- As the war in Yugoslavia started, various sabotages were done in the Maribor-Dravograd area of Slovenia. The Consulate in Zagreb gave to the leaders 29,000 *dinars* and a large supply of drinks for briberies. (Vodušek Starič, 181)
- Stephen Clissold, Zagreb Consulate's press attaché, financed propaganda and intelligence activities in Slovenia. Trevor Glanville "Nero" - operating under cover of the Vice-consul in Zagreb - covered all travel expenses of one *SOE sodelavec,* and gave him a monthly salary between 1,500 and 2,000 *dinars.* (Vodušek Starič, 201-2)
- Money was also paid for information obtained from Trieste [Trst]. (Vodušek Starič, 202)
- A Slovenian Chetnik organization, some 500 members strong, was provided with a "war chest" for sustenance of an under-ground activity during the occupation of the country, and for preparation of hide-outs in the Kamnik mountains, well-supplied with food-stuff. (Vodušek Starič, 204-5)
- At the end of January 1941, Tom Masterson requested more money from London for the Zagreb Consulate's propaganda. (Vodušek Starič, 215)
- In February 1941, George Taylor informed London that groups of future guerrillas were supplied with "war chests" and money. (Vodušek Starič, 221)
- SOE Zagreb supplied their Slovenian collaborators with communication systems, and plans for printing and distribution of propaganda, dispensing of money, demolitions, and evacuation. (Vodušek Starič, 224)
- SOE itself illegally printed and distributed pamphlets to inflame the public. (Vodušek Starič, 232)
- An important Slovenian "*SOE sodelavec*", when evacuated to Cairo, was paid £100 per month. (Vodušek Starič, 225-6)

Professor Onslow noted that British funds were used to finance a Slovenian group's attempt to spread anthrax in cattle shipments to Germany and Austria and – on at least one occasion, with Dr. A. Becker (A/H 2) – to infect Yugoslav livestock bound for Germany with hoof and mouth. (Onslow, 19) " In November 1940 a memorandum entitled 'Functions and organisation of D Section of Yugoslavia' effectively condoned such activity, as it noted:

> [P]oisoning water supplies, spreading bacteria and similar sabotage is ruled out, but introduction of foot and mouth disease, potato pest etc, are encouraged and naturally any attacks on communications, power stations or centres of production of important manufacturers." (Onslow, 20)

The Croatian Trade Unions, comprised of employees of private enterprises in Croatia, "as well as its newspaper, *Pravica,* was funded by SO2." (Onslow, 21-2)

"Operating through local organizations"

> … for large-scale subversive operations, for widespread sabotage or for political subversion – in other words for the kind of work 'D' was supposed to be doing - it was essential for us [Section D] to operate through local organizations, such as one or other local trade unions or political parties. In the Balkans the only possible organizations that could be used for such purposes were political. And if we were to work through such bodies *it was necessary first of all to convince them that a British victory would help them to achieve their political objectives*. This almost certainly meant that we would be required to give some political commitment to the group we wished to use, for instance for Slovenes or for the Serb Peasant party, a problem which was by no means confined to the Balkans. Here was a point of possible conflict with the Foreign Office.
> It meant also that *we would often be required to help them with propaganda that would assist groups to achieve their political aims*. (Sweet-Escott, 28-9. Italics added.)

For some political parties and organizations in Yugoslavia not much convincing was necessary that *a British victory would help them to achieve their political objectives.*

The initial proposal to overthrow the government of Prince Paul, made to Julian Amery in June 1940 by Jovan Đonović, has been described above. According to Baron J. Amery, Đonović "wanted no material support from Britain for what was to be done in Yugoslavia. But he needed our moral support and wanted to know that we should treat the Revolutionary Government as friends." (Amery, 177) However, he did want the British help to achieve his - and his associates' - broad political objectives. He played "a leading part in preparing the ground for the revolt against Prince Paul in which Yugoslavia 'found her soul'." (Amery(A), 28)

> The right course for the Serbs, he went on, was to stand up to the Germans even if this meant war. In a war they could give a good account of themselves and, though military defeat might follow, *they would have a place of honor at the Conference Table and would share in the fruits of victory.* Little Serbia had suffered heavier casualties in the First World War than the British Empire. The whole country had been occupied. But at the end of the day, Serbia's sacrifices had proved to be the title deeds of the new Yugoslavia. No one could read the future, but if Yugoslavia stood up to Germans now, she might be able at the next Peace Conference to extend her frontiers to include Bulgaria in a federation of all the South Slavs." (Amery, 175. Italics added.)

To achieve his broad objectives, "He [Đonović] could do little to organize the Opposition in Sofia while they were still in Opposition themselves. This, like the preparation of the revolt in Albania, would be a task for Britain." (Amery 177)

> SOE secretly subsidised anti-German Balkan politicians and plotted sabotage against German economic interests. The most significant was oil, extracted from the Romanian oil fields at Ploesti and transported to Germany by rail through the Balkans or on oil barges up the Danube. (Stafford(C), 211)

> Serbian political parties were not above bribery – both the Independent Democratic Party and the powerful Serb Peasant Party were subsidized by SOE. (Balfour-Mackay, 253)

The leader of Independent Democrats, Dr. Srđan Budisavljević, «was a firm friend of Alexander Glen, and this Party also received a British subsidy from January 1941." (Onslow, 20)

SOE had chosen to subsidize Narodna Odbrana [People's Defense or Defense League]. It was the most active of organizations and its leader, Ilija Trifunović-Birčanin was president of all the National Associations and a man of considerable influence. (Balfour-Mackay, 253)

Subsidizing the Serbian Peasant Party

The Serb Peasant Party was the most useful of SOE's political allies since it was actually part of the government, having made a tactical alliance with Paul. Its line of foreign policy was anti-German while its pro-Allied propaganda had been subsidised by SOE since July 1940, (Williams, 28)

According to the SOE historian William Mackenzie: the chief Section D man in Belgrade, Julius Hanau "Caesar", was working with the leaders of the (Serbian) Agrarian Party – generally called the Serbian Peasant Party (SPP), (principally with Dr. Milan Gavrilović and Mikić), since the spring of 1940. Described as "a small and purely Serbian organisation with some progressive aspirations", "their organisation appears to have been used for minor sabotage of German interests before there was any question of paying them or instigating a coup d'état; large ideas were not broached until the spring of 1940, when a subsidy of £5,000 a month was proposed by Hanau." For his conspicuous activities "Hanau was finally withdrawn from Yugoslavia in June [1940]". (Mackenzie, 27, 29) However, Gavrilović, who "had had extremely close links both with Section D and with the British Legation" (Balfour and Mackay, 253), continued broaching the idea of subsidy with Julian Amery – who had closely cooperated with Hanau before he had to leave Yugoslavia. (Amery, 160-1)

> The Serbian Peasant Party, felt by the British Legation to be the most likely long-term supporters of resistance, should German occupation occur, and it was they, under Milan Gavrilovic, and later Tupanjanin, whom we British supported with arms and finance, although we also maintained relations with the Democrats. (Glen(B), 41-2)

As the basic information on this subject is provided by Baron Julian Amery, it seems appropriate to examine in some details his link with Gavrilović and the SPP.

Julian arrived in Belgrade on 5 September 1939. Some of the Opposition Parties' leaders having been friends of his family, he decided to meet them. The first he met was Dr. Momčilo Ninčić, Foreign Minister from 1918 to 1923. (Amery, 146) Later on a journalist, Jakob Altmaier, took Amery to see Gavrilović. (Amery, 148) After the dinner, serious conversation and an enjoyable good time, Amery "was invited once more to dine with the Gavrilovitchs and then told that there would be no more invitations." He was to come whenever he wanted to, but they expected him to come at least once a week. (Amery, 149) That way young Amery had an opportunity to become acquainted with the leader of the SPP and get to know his political aims.

> Milan Gavrilovitch, ... , aimed to set up a federation of the four South Slav peoples - Serbs, Croats, Slovenes and Bulgars - based on peasant co-operatives. He was a strong Serb patriot but soon persuaded me that I must visit Croatia and Bulgaria if I was really to understand the South Slav problem. He was in close touch with the powerful Peasant Parties in both countries and promised to recommend me to their leaders. (Amery, 149)

*****

As shown above, before making the final decision to serve as the Yugoslav Ambassador in Moscow, Gavrilović wanted to know whether London would approve it. London did, and Amery met Gavrilović two days later to inform him so.

> Gavrilovitch now asked whether we could help him build up the necessary organisation. He would need wireless sets to communicate with the British after occupation and clandestine presses to print propaganda. He might also need our help to build up caches of arms and explosives. If I was interested, and I assured him I was, he would arrange for me to meet his deputy, Milosh Tupanyanin, who would be in charge of the Party after he had gone to Moscow. Tupanyanin and I, he suggested, might draw up a plan and then we could all meet to settle details before he left for Moscow. (Amery, 173)

Baron Amery did not provide dates of his meetings with the SPP leaders so exact dates are not available. As the announcement of the establishment of Soviet-Yugoslav relations was made on 24 June 1940, it is likely that the conversation described above happened shortly after the 24th.

A day or two later, Amery went - with Jakob Altmaier –
- to meet Tupanjanin.

> ... Between us we drew a plan. This was in two phases. Phase One aimed at expanding the Peasant Party's activities while Yugoslavia was still neutral. It was directed to stiffening the Government's resistance to German demands and to creating a climate of opinion hostile to capitulation. Phase Two was concerned with the organisation of propaganda, sabotage and guerrilla warfare in the event of German occupation. (Amery, 173)
>
> Bailey [another D/SOE agent] and I agreed [to] a final version of this plan with Gavrilovitch and Tupanyanin two days before Gavrilovitch left for Moscow. But we had still to negotiate it with London. (Amery, 174) Gavrilović left Belgrade on 2 July, and arrived in Moscow at the beginning of August 1940. (Jukić, 34)

*****

Because Altmaier – neither a British nor a Yugoslav – participated in drawing the plan that would affect not only a political party but also the state of Yugoslavia, it is proper to register Amery's relation with Jakob Altmaier [who had the SOE code name A/H 9]. (Vodušek Starič, 425)]

> ... my chief mentor in Yugoslav politics was Jakob Altmaier. Altmaier was a German Jew from Frankfurt. He had been a non-commissioned officer in the First War and had seized power for the Socialist in Frankfurt after the 1918 armistice. For ten days he had been 'boss' of Frankfurt. One day ... he took train to Berlin ... Altmaier later turned to journalism and was for many years correspondent of the *Frankfurter Zeitung* and of the *Manchester Guardian* in Belgrade and Sofia. He left the Balkans in 1936 to play an active part in the Spanish Civil War [17 July 1936 – 1 April 1939]. (Amery, 147)

One such "active part" which Amery mentioned was Altmaier's negotiation – in the autumn of 1938, at the time of the Munich agreement – on behalf of Indalecio Prieto, the head of the Spanish Socialist Party, "with an Austrian Monarchist leader who was in turn in touch with [Juan] Yague", a General in the Nationalist forces. "This was the Republic's last chance of staving off the defeat. ... and the talks came to nothing." (Amery, 108-9)

(It would be interesting to know whether Altmaier – while in Spain or at any other time – knew about or met Tito or some other Communists from Yugoslavia who were fighting in the International Brigades.)

Amery continued: "But after the fall of the Spanish Republic, [Altmaier] came back to Belgrade and was staying with Milan Gavrilovitch, the leader of the Serbian Peasant Party." (Amery, 147) For some time Altmaier was staying with Gavrilović under a false name; he established a link between Amery and Gavrilović, Tupanjanin and Đonović. (Vodušek Starič, 56) About his first contact with Altmaier, Amery recounted:

> ... I first met him when Childs [British Press Attaché in Belgrade] sent him over to my office to discuss some proposals he had made about British propaganda to Yugoslavia. ... I was impressed by the depth as well as originality of his ideas, ... From the time of this first meeting I saw him almost daily for the next six months. (Amery, 147)
>
> Altmaier knew everyone in Belgrade and opened every door to me. But he did much more than that. Until then the main formative influences on my political thinking had come from the right wing in politics: from my father and his friends, from mainly Conservative school teachers and dons, and from friends in Nationalist Spain. I was now, for the first time, brouht into daily touch with a brilliant and experienced colleague whose political roots were Marxist. Altmaier taught me to distinguish between the truth in Marxism and the errors. More important, he accustomed me to apply the Marxist social and economic method of analysis to current political problems. (Amery, 147-8)
>
> At an early stage in our acquaintance, Altmaier took me to see Milan Gavrilovitch. ... (Amery, 148)

That was the beginning. Afterwards, Altmaier introduced Amery to other important and influential men in Serbia. - But now back to the process of financing SPP.

*****

Bailey, Amery, Gavrilović and Tupanjanin agreed to a two-phased plan, but they still had to negotiate it with London. "After some weeks of telegraphic discussion, phase one was finally authorized. This was something to start with. (Amery, 174)

However, it seems that the funding for the plan could not be done without the knowledge and approval of Minister Campbell. Professor Sue Onslow remarked on the subject:

> Galvanised by the possibility of being inadvertently but actively involved in the overthrow of what he deemed to be the legitimate government – if necessary by violence – Campbell was stung into declaring that, while he would support a subsidy of up to 5,000 [pound sterling] per month, he could not condone a *coup d'état*. In a flurry of telegrams, Campbell begged London to put an end to such behaviour: 'the whole thing [is] clumsy and amateurish', and described Section D operatives as a collection of 'bomb happy parvenus', compromising official diplomatic channels with Prince Paul and the UK Government's express policy of preserving 'peaceful conditions' in Yugoslavia. This reflected Campbell's fears that any such action by Britain 'might definitely provoke Germany to overrun Yugoslavia'. (Onslow, 33-4)

Professor Heather Williams expressed a similar view: "Campbell was also concerned about subsidies paid by SOE to the Serb Peasant Party which were tied in with a possibility of a coup, something which definitely infringed the rules of diplomatic relations." (Williams, 24)

*****

When the D-men on the spot "had failed to persuade the ministry's local representative that what the D section wanted was the right thing to do", they would ask their superiors in London for positive intervention. Thus it happened that after Milan Gavrilović – in June/July 1940 – asked Julian Amery for British help, the D/SOE Belgrade contacted D/SOE London. Sweet-Escott got "a telegram from Belgrade telling me to get authority in London for us to pay a subsidy amounting to several thousand pounds sterling a month to the Serb Peasant Party. This led to a great deal of meetings and minute-writing, but the project was turned down on the strength of 'Z's' [Secret Intelligence Service, (SIS)] opinion that it would be a 'sheer waste of money'." (Sweet-Escott, 34-5)

Actually, on 23 July 1940, the D/SOE-man code-named D/SH, in London, sent telegram No. 903 to the D/SOE-man code-named A/GH in Belgrade [Alexander Glen, who was at the moment in charge of Belgrade SOE]:

> A. Foreign office have at last sanctioned grant of £5000 repeat £5000 per month to Serb peasant party provided that funds do not repeat not reach party through anyone connected with Legation.
> B. For first payment you should consult commercial secretary unofficially repeat unofficially as to local persons who can advance dinars to equivalent of £5000 repeat £5000 to party and you should wire us name of London banks to which remittance of sterling counterpart must be made.
> C. For future payments I am consulting Chester Beatty who may shortly be able to effect remittances through new neutral mining concern. (TNA HS 5   872   C325542)

On 31 July Glen replied to D/HS in telegram No. 862:

> A. On discussion of your paragraph B. with Legation, I was instructed to delay making payment until Minister [Ronald Ian Campbell] had time to consider matter.
> B. Minister now says he has no confirmation from Foreign Office that this monthly subsidy should be paid.
> C. It is essential that payment be paid at once in order that shadow organisations be established by Peasant Party for our use in event Yugoslavia engaged in war. Therefore request you arrange at once for Foreign Office to confirm their approval to Minister. (TNA HS 5   872   C325542)

On 30 August 1940, in the Most Secret telegram (No. 625) to Campbell, Mr. Hopkinson cautioned, *inter alia*:

> 4. If, however, it is decided to give subsidy, I consider that £5,000 per month is far too much in the present circumstances though the full amount might be required later. It would therefore be satisfactory to spend up to £5,000 monthly although only part of this would actually be spent at first. The [Section] D representative here agrees. (TNA HS 5   872   C325542)

Therefore, in spite of the objection of SIS, the subsidy was ultimately approved. "...payments of £4,000 a month were started through the agency of a bogus company floated for the purpose with Mr. Chester Beatty's assistance." (Mackenzie, 104-5) "We have subsidised this party since last July and they are definitely at our disposal for underground propaganda, sabotage and guerilla warfare once Yugoslavia is involved in war" – George Taylor informed his superior in a Report dated 26 February 1941 (page 8). The authorization of the subsidy was made

> with the stipulation that funds did not reach the SPP 'through anyone connected with Legation'. The consciences of the opponents at the British Legation and in London who opposed the notion of supporting a *coup* against Prince Paul, were soothed by SOE's view that Tupanjanin and the Serbian Peasant Party 'had nothing whatever to do with the larger scheme'. (Onslow, 35)

Yet Julian Amery, under cover of an Assistant to the Press Attaché, "was making payments to the adherents of [Albania's] King Zog ... on the premises of the British Legation." (Williams, 25))

*****

How large was the sum of 4,000 *a month*? In Britain, in 1945, the Members of Parliament were paid £600 *a year*. (Dodds-Parker, 213-14) After returning from Belgrade to London in the spring of 1939, Cecil Parrott, the former tutor to King Peter II, was hired in the Ministry of Information with a salary of "three hundred and fifty pounds a year, which, taken all together, represented a considerable drop" of what he had been getting in Yugoslavia. (Parrott, 117)

In Yugoslavia, the exchange rates in 1940-41 were: one pound for slightly over four US dollars, and one dollar for 50 Yugoslav *dinars* – or more than 200 *dinars* per pound. The Majors in the Yugoslav army were paid 2,300 *dinars* a month, and entry level of college graduates 1,200 dinars. (Kosić(N), 83-4) More than 800,000 *dinars* per months was a huge sum in non-industrialized, agrarian Yugoslavia at that time: it would cover the monthly salaries of some 350 army Majors, or close to 670 recent college graduates.

*****

While *telegraphic discussion* about the Section D–SPP Phase One plan was proceeding, the Special Operations Executive (SOE) was formed in London on 22 July 1940 to "*set Europe ablaze*" - in Churchill's commanding directive - but not the German-occupied British Channel Islands. ... Therefore, the discussions of financing SPP appear to have been going on at the time when Section D still existed, but the decision was being made to establish SOE. The payments started for July, and it is irrelevant whether during the "D" or "SOE" period, because SOE continued the operations that had been initiated by "D".

*****

Then, after the coup in Belgrade on 27 March 1941, Sweet-Escott had second thoughts about the value of financing SPP.

> I spent some time wondering whether the proposal of the summer before, that we should subsidize the Serb Peasant Party, really would have been a 'sheer waste of money'. But of course the change came too late. Within a day or two of the *coup d'état* we were evacuating our female staff to Athens, including - though I did not know it till weeks later - my sister. Ten days later the campaign had begun with the bombardment of Belgrade by the Luftwaffe. (Sweet-Escott, 63)

(Before leaving Belgrade, Sweet-Escott's sister was helping to burn the Legation archives. "A year later she was to help in burning the S.O.E. records in Cairo, and must hold the record for this kind of things.") (Sweet-Escott, 73))

****

A very important decision at this meeting related to the Putsch was its timing: *if and **when** the Tripartite Pact was signed, not **before** the signing.* As described elsewhere, the conspirators had plenty of time to do it *before the signing* – but they did not. **It was done only when the British determined the timing.**

*****

From the information presented above it follows that, in addition of financing some Slovenian underground organizations and individuals, the British had financed, at least: the Serbian Peasant Party (Srpska Zemljoradnička Stranka) **(##)**; the Independent Democratic Party (Samostalna Demokratska Stranka); the Democratic Party (Demokratska Stranka); Narodna Odbrana (Defense

League*)* and other patriotic associations; various newspapers, editors and journalists; some students' and English clubs.

(##) of Dr. Milan Gavrilović, not the splinter party led by Professor Dragoljub Jovanović.

*****

According to Prof. Dragoljub Jovanović, the British "subsidy" to the SPP was not a secret in Belgrade. In his *Political Memoirs* he wrote that:
* they considered Tupanjanin to be a British agent;
* the first to speak about Gavrilović as being a British man was Branko Lazarević, a writer and an old diplomat. He told Dr. Sveta Živković that - in Gavrilović's home at the Topčider Hill, in the presence of Gavrilović himself - Lazarević was saying that some were getting [French] Francs, others Dollars, [German] Marks or [Italian] Lira, and Gavrilović [British] Pounds, while he and a friend, then present with him in the home, were getting no foreign currency. Gavrilović did not respond to that at all, and was not angry. (Petranović & Žutić, 486n1)

*****

If it is ever possible, someone with access to all of the pertinent documents might be able to compute all the expenses Great Britain paid for the prewar Section D/ SOE and other British operations that involved Yugoslavia in the war against Germany. How much money was given to political parties, patriotic associations and other non-military groups/entities for political activities, agitation and propaganda? How much to the military or others for other types of activities? Information presented above is just a pale, incomplete silhouette. The costs of "toys and chocolates" - sent from Britain and Greece – for demolition, sabotage, armaments for future "resistance" - once Yugoslavia would be occupied, etc., should be included.

It would be informative to know the total war-time costs to the Allies of the scant supplies that went to Mihailović first, and of the huge volume of supplies and all kinds of services to Tito later; as well as the costs of the destruction of cities and other targets in Yugoslavia in 1944 - mostly in Serbia and Montenegro - by Allied bombing, reportedly in support of the Partisan war "contribution" to the Allied victory. In light of such figures – and the post-war inclusion of Yugoslavia into the Soviet Bloc of states – it would be interesting to revisit Dalton's statement of 27 March 1941: *"The money we have spent on the Serb Peasant Party and other Opposition Parties has given wonderful value."* (Pimlott(ed), 176) A *wonderful value* to Great Britain – is what he meant.

The cost in human lives to the people in Yugoslavia is, of course, another matter. To the British – they were expendable. To the people in Yugoslavia, their *value* was incalculable and never compensable.

*****

The use of bribery to achieve Britain's specific goals was not applied only to Yugoslavia. Another country was Spain, "guardian of the western Mediterranean".

At the end of May 1940, Churchill charged Captain Alan Hillgarth to keep Spain out of the war by means of bribery and corruption, for which $10 million was deposited in an account of the Swiss Bank Corporation in New York. (Stafford(C), 202)

> By late June 1940 the scheme was already showing results. Of the $10 million, at least $2 million went to General Antonio Aranda Mata, Commander of the Spanish War College who was expected to head the Spanish armed forces if [General Francisco] Franco were toppled. (Stafford(C), 203)

The scheme to maintain pressure on Franco, to remain neutral, was boosted with additional British funds in 1941. (Stafford(C), 229)

Bribery in Spain to keep her neutral – but "subsidies" in Yugoslavia to "resist" the Axis. For example, by attacking the Italians in Albania, as suggested by Churchill and Eden.

Intention to bribe the Yugoslav General Staff

In a letter dated 15 November 1940, Orme Sargent [Deputy Under-Secretary, Foreign Office] complained to Gladwyn Jebb, SOE's chief executive officer, that

> it seemed from Campbell's reports that the Yugoslav General Staff were in greater need of their resolve being stiffened than Prince Paul. While he felt that the subsidy being paid to the Serb Peasant Party was 'no doubt doing us good' he continued 'but could we not spend at least some of the money on the General Staff? Rumor has it that several Yugoslav Generals have built themselves villas with money supplied by the Germans. Perhaps we could help them to add wings?' (Williams, 27)
>
> In reply to this suggestion it was pointed out [by Jebb] that subsidies to the Serb Peasant Party and other political and patriotic organizations were not out and out bribery, but meant to fund resistance to the Axis if the British were forced out of the Balkans. Hoping to avoid that eventuality, funds were also provided to establish an alternative government or nucleus of men who would resist Axis demands. (Williams, 27) (The subject of alternative government is discussed elsewhere.)

As for Jebb's disclaim of out and out bribery: "... there appears no awareness or assessment in the British files of the extent to which the SPP were using British political encouragement and financial aid for their own ends. Nor was SOE apparently aware that Tupanjanin was also on the Soviet NKVD [People's Commissariat for Internal Affairs] payroll." (Onslow, 55) This information was taken from Professor Gabriel Gorodetsky's book (p. 139), who wrote extensively about Yugoslavia's futile attempt to get Soviet military support.

*****

The usefulness of the SPP to the goals of the SOE plans was widespread, and was acknowledged particularly on March 20 1941, when they unsuccessfully attempted, in tandem, to bring down the government of the Prince Regent.

SOE was publishing a large volume of pamphlets, "designed to arouse public opinion." (Williams, 29) The pamphlets had the same theme as the many petitions sent to Prince Paul by the patriotic associations which were funded by SOE.

Subsidizing *Narodna Odbrana* (The Defense League)

On 26 February 1941, George Taylor reported to SOE London: "The second of these [main organisations in Serbia and Bosnia] is virtually presented by our close personal relationship with Ilya Trifunovic, hereafter known as Daddy, who is a head of all National Associations in Yugoslavia, such as Narodna Odbrana, the Chetniks, and various other ex service-men's groups" (TNA HS5 /166, p.8) On the subject of financing, Taylor reported: "All the organisations described above have been provided by us with a war chest to enable them to carry on financially after we leave the country." (*Ibid*, 11)

The first main organization was the Serbian Peasant Party. (*Ibid*, 8) Their financing was not to be used only for activities after the British left Yugoslavia. Thus, for instance, the war chest was used also for transporting and distributing high explosives and other SOE devices in February 1941:

> Daddy [Ilija Trifunović-Birčanin of *Narodna Odbrana*] and Uncle [Dr. Miloš Tupanjanin of the Serbian Peasant Party] are making arrangements ... to enable us to consign trucks to addresses in Northern Yugoslavia, with the idea that these trucks will be "lost" en route, and their contents taken out and distributed by our friends. .... the necessary arrangements have been made for three truckloads to be sent [from Greece], and the first should leave within a couple of days. (*Ibid*, 11-12)

On 28 March 1941, SOE's head, Dr. Dalton, confirmed to the Prime Minister that *Narodna Odbrana* was "in our pay" – like the Serb Peasant party – "the principal instrument of our policy". (Great Britain, Special Operations Executive, 91087-10.V, Hoover Institution Archives)

"Subsidies" by the British were not used to buy explosives and arms, because the British themselves - as shown below, supplied them to their domestic co-operatives.

After Thomas Masterson came to Belgrade …

The SOE had been helping to subsidize the [Serbian] Peasant Party since July 1940. The leader of the party, Milan Gavrilović, was the official Yugoslav representative in Moscow, but [Tom] Masterson was in close touch with Miloš Tupanjanin, the temporary party leader within the country. (Stafford(cp), 411)

Masterson and his associates had operated very quietly among the opposition politicians; so quietly, in fact, that General Bora Mirković, the man who led the revolt, learned only later, as a refugee, that the British intelligence service had distributed funds with the aim of supporting national uprising. … They had concentrated on a few individuals who would shape policies of the new government born of revolution. Their assurances of success and promises of power had carried more weight in political warfare than had simple bribery. (Hoptner, 243) Even if it was so, bribery was still offered and taken.

Subsidizing the Democratic Party and the Independent Democrats

Around 20 January 1941, in a long conversation, Dr. Milan Grol, president of the Democratic Party, told Tom Masterson that they would be inclined to active resistance in case of an attack by the Axis forces against Yugoslavia. He thought that it would be good to preventively attack Bulgaria, if she would allow passage of German troops through her territory.

After the talk, Masterson proposed SOE financial support for the Democratic Party. The Party's help would enlarge the range of propaganda, and in the public mind it would fortify awareness of the danger of German penetration into Bulgaria. Campbell consented with the proposal of 1,000-pound sterling per month. (Vodušek Starič, 214-15)

Confirmation of this "subsidy" is found in Tom Masterson's communication to SOE London, dated 27 March 1941. (**Chapter 13**)

*****

Subsidies were also given to Budisavljević's Independent Democrats starting in January, 1941.

During 1940 Section D and then S.O.E. had been cultivating political leaders in Belgrade and subsidising the Serb Peasant Party, the Independent Democrat Party and Narodna Odbrana. Through these contacts, it was known that there were elements which were dissatisfied with the pro-Axis leaning of the existing regime and were contemplating a *coup d'etat*. (Pimlott(ed), 138)

Chapter 5

"Plastic and such, a few toys" – "Toys and chocolate"

Section D's immediate purpose, throughout the Balkans, was to carry out "the maximum interference by unacknowledgeable means with the movement of supplies to Germany." The "D" supplies to interfere included: explosives, detonators, specially constructed time fuses, weapons, and some devices invented for the purpose. One of these was called a limpet. It looked like a steel helmet, but really contained a lump of explosive which could be attached to the side of a ship by magnets inside the helmet. However, a supply of money to "encourage our friends and swell their numbers by suitable propaganda" was needed above all. "As the Balkans at the time were neutral, this propaganda also had to be disseminated by secret methods." All these supplies had to be sent from England by clandestine means. (Sweet-Escott, 22-3) "... at home, radio sets and codes and signals were being developed as well as explosives, delay fuses and 'toys' of many ingenious types; ... " (Dodds-Parker, 78) Among other ingenious types were "sink bombes, itching powder and other unacknowledgeable 'toys'." (Dodds-Parker, 131)

As SOE became better organized, it started designing and producing its own tools, weapons and "toys" – wireless sets, "rifles, ammunition, revolvers, explosive this and explosive that, incendiary this and incendiary that", "sleeve gun", "fake vegetables", "all sorts of nasty things", "some of science fiction variety." "Some of the things we did could be termed atrocities. They couldn't be termed warfare – not blowing up people with torches" – as described by a technician involved. (Bailey(fv), 65-73)

The "toys" for Hungary

From December 1939 the "D" (and later SOE) man in Budapest was twenty-five year old Basil Davidson, a former reporter for the London *Economist* in Paris. In April 1941 he fled to Belgrade and later became influential in Cairo SOE's dealing with Yugoslavia – where he had lived some time before. His activities in Budapest being similar to those of his colleagues in Belgrade, his own account is therefore illustrative of D / SOE activities in Yugoslavia as well.

A storeroom on the fourth floor of Section D quarters in London was full of 'toys'. Once they were assembled and packed, they were given to young gentlemen "who had been furnished with return tickets complete with Wagon-Lits reservations to Budapest; taxis, sometime two or three if these were a heavy load, were summoned, the bags were loaded, and off the party went to Victoria station. They did I think have ex-Scotland Yard detectives as guards, but not always." (Sweet-Escott, 23-4)

Joined by a "D" colleague, Ian Pirie, at the end of 1939 Davidson went by train to his assignment in Budapest: via Milan, Italy, and the northern plains of Yugoslavia. Approaching the Yugoslav-Hungarian border, the oher man pointed to the rack above Davidson's head: "Those blue sacks. We can't have them inspected. You'll make a diversion. Throw a fit, threaten to jump out of the window, almost anything may do. I've got diplomatic immunity, so don't worry about me." Money passed, so there was no inspection. (Davidson, 54; Bailey(fv), 10-11)

What was in the sacks? "Plastic and such, a few toys. The sort of thing, you know, that D goes in for." Loaded in a taxi, the sacks were taken to the British Legation building and deposited in rarely visited cellars. (Davidson, 54-5)

"The blue sacks continued to arrive, every now and then, and their contents went discretely into the cellars of the legation." The plastic was a conveniently malleable form of high explosive. Some were packed inside small metal containers, "limpets", which were magnetized, and thus could be attached to the outside of hulls. Time-delayed detonators would set them off. "These limpet "toys" were said to work quite well." (Davidson, 58)

Davidson's second task in Budapest – which he considered to be "below board and illegal", was "to promote resistance": although Hungary's passing into the Axis camp might not be avoidable, it might be delayed. (Davidson, 55) Accordingly, London's order was: to distribute the smuggled "toys" to Hungarian volunteers who would use them against German shipping on the Danube as when the local "balloon went up", and when no further diplomatic considerations were involved. This was a part of an overall plan of economic warfare against Germany – centered in Yugoslavia: a blockade of supplies on the Danube. Davidson and "a colleague in another secret branch", made some progress "in finding appropriate volunteers to stick them ["toys"] on [river barges], but the time for hand-out had still to come." (Davidson, 58)

However, the handout time never did come. The British Minister in Budapest, apparently not enthusiastic about the *"below board and illegal"* activities, ordered his Military Attaché to throw all the "toys" into the Danube. Threatening to do the same with any additional supplies, the Minister told Davidson that he would denounce him to the Hungarian police if he continued to act in this manner. (Davidson, 59)

The *"toys and chocolate"* for the Middle East and Yugoslavia

Germany's invasion of the Low Countries and France in May 1940, and the expectation of Italy's coming into the war on "the wrong side", meant that the Mediterranean would be closed to the British. That, in turn, would mean that the British lines of supplies to the Balkans would have to go round the Cape, and that directing Section D's operations from London would have to be abandoned. Thus, on 29 May, George Taylor and most of the staff in the Balkan section of "D", flew off to Alexandria to set up an office in Cairo. (Sweet-Escott, 30)

"The first and absolutely overriding priority" for Taylor's assistant, B. Sweet-Escott - who remained in London - "was to ship to Alexandria the greatest amount of stores in the shortest possible time." (Sweet-Escott, 30)

On 30 May 1940, a large consignment of supplies was due to be shipped by the Simplon-Orient to Belgrade, with two "D" couriers. The stuff was urgently needed. All went well until they arrived in Milan, Italy, but the Simplon-Orient would not go any farther. A train, however, would go to Ljubljana, Yugoslavia – but not until the following day. Thus the "D" party "had to sit on Milan station watching thirty-five parcels full of dangerous explosives and time-fuses, and hoping that the Italians would not declare war against us till they were inside Yugoslav territory. They made it and no questions were asked, …" (Sweet-Escott, 31)

Thirty-five parcels – a lot of "toys", then, were to be distributed for many *"below board and illegal"* activities in a neutral Yugoslavia. As Hanau was just about to be withdrawn [in June 1940] because of his activities, the explosives and such were not to be handled by the "D" men, but rather by local contacts established by Hanau and his colleagues in Serbia and Slovenia. "… there were gangs at work in Slovenia putting sand and other abrasives in the axle-boxes of railway vehicles bound for Germany. Even if no major operation could yet take place, Caesar [Hanau] seemed to be responsible for a constant succession of minor pinpricks." (Sweet-Escott, 22)

The May-1940 shipment followed many earlier ones. Thus, in February 1940, "a one-eyed courier with a black patch over the other", brought to the Belgrade station, via Orient Express, two large suitcases. When Section D-men, Bill Bailey and Sandy Glen - who were waiting for him - offered to help, he waved them aside: "These have to be delivered immediately and directly to Major Hanau," he said. Within minutes after the delivery, Hanau's "Serb colleagues were on the floor, opening the suitcases and examining and identifying the contents, enjoying themselves hugely as one seized this and another that, exclaiming at the time: 'No, not that way, detonators go here,' and 'That's wrong, come on let me do it.'" (Glen(B), 36-7)

> A routine of Diplomatic Bags from London was now a regular early-morning affair with the Belgrade porters. 'Never mind the big ones,' they said, slinging them unto a pile, 'it's the small ones that have the detonators, the ones you have to watch for.' (Glen(B), 37)

> Regular consignments of detonators, explosives, fuses, limpets, wicks, knuckledusters, rifles, and grenades were sent to Belgrade by courier from London and, from late 1940, from the British Military Mission in Athens. These "toys and chocolate", as they were coyly referred to in the telegrams, were stored in Masterson's office in the Legation annex, before being distributed to Serb contacts and buried in arms caches in the hills. (Onslow, 36) General Wavell, Commander-in-Chief, Middle East, took great interest in these plans, which he wished to supplement British intervention in Greece. (Onslow, 36n101)

Unless the supplies to the Balkans could be moved through the Mediterranean before Italy entered the war, they would have to be shipped via the Cape route. To save time, some of the supplies could go by air, if the aircraft were available. On 31st May Sweet-Escott was informed that a load could be sent directly to Cairo. Thus, three tons of supplies – explosives, fuses and weapons – went at that time, and two further loads were flown in Sunderlands to Egypt between 31st May and 10th June 1940. (Sweet-Escott, 32)

Within that time period one of the Section D operatives, a former MIR-officer, Douglas Dodds-Parker, was assigned to transport 'toys' to Egypt: "My final task was to load six tons of 'toys' from the Magazine in Hyde Park for transport by flying boat to Egypt. There they were to prove their worth." (Dodds-Parker, 45)

"They proved their worth" by being later shipped and used in Yugoslavia and Greece.

George Taylor described in detail how the SOE "toys" were - and would be - used in Yugoslavia. Some excerpts from his 26 February Report to Nelson are cited in **Appendix J.**

Smuggling "toys and chocolates" across the border, or moving them through a consular service channel, was an illegal operation. Breaking laws of a sovereign and neutral country did not bother SOE, which was considered to be *"a new instrument of war"*, formed to conduct *"ungentlemanly warfare".*

Ultimately, what were the results of all this SOE planning and smuggling, training and "subsidizing", preparing for *"post-occupational resistance"*? No demolitions took place when the Germans invaded to slow or stop them. No bands were left behind to carry on sabotage raids and terrorist work against the occupiers, no Central Station to communicate with the British War Station in Istanbul ... Of the major SOE domestic cooperatives only Daddy, Ilija Trifunović-Birčanin, remained in the country, probably because of poor health. The others fled Yugoslavia in a hurry, just like Taylor and his SOE-team ... and the Putschists, too.

One wonders: How would the British authorities react to such breaking of Britain's laws, illegal smuggling, distribution and use of arms in their own country?

Chapter 6

George Taylor's mission in Belgrade:

"to prepare the way for a coup against the country rulers."

The British broke the German Air Force code on 22 May 1940.

George Taylor informed E. Barker that, from deciphered German communications and other sources, Churchill became convinced - at the end of 1940 - that Hitler was going to drive south into the Balkans. In December 1940, Churchill told Dalton that the Balkan situation was "the acid test for SOE", and to prepare SOE for action in Yugoslavia. (Barker, 87; 281n53) "For Dalton, this was manna from heaven! After the first difficult six months of the SOE existence, the organisation had been notching up evidence of its potential, ... So one can imagine the relief for Dalton in January 1941 when Churchill, acting on the by then positive evidence of German movements against Greece, charged him to respond." (Glen[B], 57)

Dalton responded by sending George Taylor on a mission to the Balkans. Here is a brief inside backgound information about the mission.

By the New Year, 1941 - i.e., before the decision was made to send the British Expeditionary Force to Greece - "it was obvious that there was going to be a campaign in the Balkans." (Sweet-Escott, 55) "Now that a campaign in the Balkans was impending, it was George Taylor's main task *to draw all the strings together* so that the best possible use might be made of our contacts by those who were to direct it. A firm hand was certainly needed." (Sweet-Escott, 60. Italics added.)

"Drawing all strings together" involved four tasks which Dalton described in a letter to Churchill on 28 March 1941: to implement the plans for the Danube blockade, to prepare for a revolt In Rumania, to organize post-occupational operations, and to continue pressure on the Yugoslav Government "in a sense favourable to this country [Great Britain]".

> The second part of George's task was to prepare for the worst. If the whole of the Balkan Peninsula were to be overrun by the axis, we would first have to make sure that any demolitions not carried out by the regular troops in their retreat were carried out by our friends or ourselves, and then prepare for the return of the allies. This now began to be known in our progress reports as post-occupational work. Post-occupational work meant evacuating and maintaining in friendly territory the people who were likely to be of most use to us either for propaganda and political subversion or for infiltration at a later date. This in turn meant the assembling of teams of likely propagandists, which was already in hand under Bill Bailey and others in Istanbul. Here the remnants of our organizations in Rumania and Bulgaria were concentrating, for diplomatic relations with these two countries had been broken off in February and March respectively. There were grounds for optimism about work in these two countries from Turkey, for we had been told by Bill Stephenson in New York that an important American named Col. William Donovan, who was touring the Balkans at the time with a British staff officer called Vivian Dykes, might be able to arrange communications for us through American diplomatic channels. (Sweet-Escott, 60-61)

On 13 January 1941, Dalton convinced the Cabinet's Defence Committee to approve Taylor's mission. (Stafford(so), 51) Then having the rank of a Major, Taylor would go on the assigned mission with the local rank of full Colonel and Counsellor in the Foreign Office. (Mackenzie, 106) The whole SOE existence in London would be disrupted by the decision to send Taylor "out there to organize our part in it."

> The preparations for George's departure were long and elaborate. ... He had to be accredited to all our embassies and legations in the area. And long before he left we started to plan what should happen to our organizations [SOE] if the Balkan campaign should fail. We decided that we must arrange to leave parties behind which could take to the mountains and organize resistance from behind the enemy lines. To do this we would have to have a stock of wireless sets, which might work to Cairo or Istanbul, or wherever our base might be. We had no trained operators to leave behind, ... Secret wireless communications was a monopoly of 'Z'. [Secret Intelligence Service] We hoped that 'Z' would let us have the sets we needed and would arrange to pick up our messages. (#) We hoped that we might find competent operators among the Greek or Yugoslav forces ... whatever the reason, we were to find that no more than seven sets could be spared for our operations throughout the Balkans, and even these were not immediately available. None of us could see how we could carry on if the whole of the Balkans were overrun and we had no wireless sets to leave behind. However, it was plainly right that George, who at any rate knew what he wanted to get done, should go off and try to do it, and off he went. (Sweet-Escott, 55)

(#) "Under an agreement reached in September 1940, all SOE's W/T traffic was to be handled through SIS, which was given the right to accept or reject it. This dependence lasted until March 1942, ..." (Seaman(ed), 53)

"George Taylor was very much the spokesman for the SOE's efforts ..." (Glen(B), 42) His knowledgeable agent and co-worker, Sandy Glen - the head of the Section D / SOE team in Belgrade in the summer and autumn of 1940 - wrote about Taylor's mission: "In January 1941 he was sent to take over operations in Belgrade **to prepare the way for a coup against the country rulers.**" (Glen(B), 187. Emphasis added.) In Athens "he was to spend rather a longer time than intended in discussions with the British Military Mission and with Ian Pirie **(##)** and the Greek SOE team." (Glen(B), 58)

(##) "An old Section D hand ... He arrived in Greece in the guise of a specialist on air raid precaution for the British Community but was, in fact, No. 2 in the subversive cell which included various British Lloyd's agents and engineers." (Glen(B), 188 n1)

Off Taylor went to prepare for a coup and other activities. "... more and more of the effort was being aimed at the future, *at a post-occupational resistance and in public relations* throughout the country". (Glen(B), 42. Italics added.)

"The post-occupational resistance" presumed that the British expected Yugoslavia would be occupied by Germany. As an occupation follows a war, it means that the British first expected - and worked for - a war in which Yugoslavia would be defeated and occupied.

*****

As for his activities in the public relations field, "... Taylor assessed pro-British Serb public opinion as SOE's best hope of influencing the Yugoslav government's policy" – Professor H. Williams observed. (Williams, 28-9) No efforts were spared to influence the public opinion, especially of the Serbs.

- **Taylor's report to SOE London, 26 February 1941**

On February 8 1941, Taylor arrived in Istanbul, four days before the Eden – Dill team left England on their mission to the Middle East. Two days later he reported to London from Istanbul. (Mackenzie, 107n2) "By the time I arrived in Istanbul the dominating fact of the whole situation was the evident intention of the Germans to move down at an early date and the only possible policy for S. O. was to get as much laid on as we could in the short time left" - wrote Taylor to Sir Frank Nelson in a letter dated 26 February 1941 which accompanied his lengthy Report to Nelson.

> This in turn meant that we all had to get out in the field dividing the work between us – roughly D.H.13 taking Rumania, G.H.2 Bulgaria and myself J.S. [Yugoslavia] and Greece. These latter countries, in the light of the approaching German occupation of Bulgaraia and of the decision taken here the other day, become the vital points for the whole Balkans – added Taylor in his letter.

That is: between the 10th and the 26$^{th\,of}$ February his agent DH13 went to Rumania and DH2 to Bulgaria before Great Britain broke diplomatic relations with these countries; Taylor went to Yugoslavia and returned to Athens – *where a decision was taken the other day.*

That decision was the one taken at the Tatoi conference between the British representatives, the Eden-Dill team, and the Greek representatives on 22/23 February after which Eden reported to Churchill:

> In full agreement with the Greek Government the following detailed decisions were reached:
> a. In view of the importance of the Yugoslav attitude as affecting the redeployment of troops in Greece, it was agreed that I should make a further effort to attempt *to persuade the Yugoslav Government to play their part.* (Carlton, 175-6. Italics added.)

Because of the Tatoi conference decision, Taylor added in his letter to Nelson that his Report was "written from the angle of what help we [SOE] can be to Wavell", stating that he was sure that Nelson would agree that "in the present situation and with the recent decision" that was "the only possible point of view to take." **(Part One, 74-7)**

Thus, in the changing situation, Taylor's principal task became *to persuade the Yugoslav Government to play their part* - as His Majesty's Government decided what that part should be and how it should be played.

*****

'... I am working against the clock. The bag has really closed and I am only getting this [his Report] on the plane by "influence".' – wrote Taylor to Sir Frank. That implies that Taylor's Report probably reached London and Dr. Dalton - the head of SOE - by the time Dalton visited Churchill at Checkers, on 2 March. (**Part One, 85-6**) At that meeting the Prime Minister thoroughly approved Dalton's secret plan for the coup in Belgrade.

That decision defined Taylor's and SOE's subsequent activities in Yugoslavia - regardless of how his plans were laid out in his Report to Nelson - which is summarized in **Appendix K.** Glen's conclusion that Taylor was sent to Belgrade "to prepare the way for a coup against the country rulers" is justified. After all, Dalton himself acknowledged that Taylor was the chief organizer of the coup of 27 March 1941. (Pimlott(ed), 178)

*****

Six days after Eden and Dill had "found a changed and disturbing situation" in Greece (**Part One, 90-91**), on 11 March, 1941, Taylor sent another report from Athens to SOE London. (Mackenzie, 107n2) By that time the British war leaders knew that Turkey was not going to join Greece and Yugoslavia in the proposed Balkan Front. That caused them to increase their pressure on Prince Paul and the Yugoslav Government.

Chapter 7

Exploiting aggressive propaganda

"... in foreign affairs the Government announces events and actions in the manner it wishes them to be understood." – Sir Robert Bruce Lockhart, Director General of the Political Warfare Executive

"... The SOE strategy was to mobilize and direct the major Serb element in Yugoslavia with the object of reversing or influencing the policy of the government." (Stafford(cp), 410) "The SOE's basic plan was to *encourage Serb political and public opinion* to exert pressure on Prince Paul." (Stafford(cp), 411. Italics added.)

Encouraging Serb political and public opinion was the basic plan not only of SOE, but also of Section D. One of the projected Section D's activities was underground, i.e., un-acknowledgeable propaganda. (Sweet-Escott, 20). So propaganda became a means to influence and form the public opinion from the very start of Section D operations. The Section's head, Laurence Grand, was "desirous of exploiting propaganda potential. He made plans for aggressive propaganda against Germany using neutral countries as the notional point of origin in order to mask material's connection with Britain. He was similarly interested in the potential of 'black' wireless broadcasting and funded the Joint Broadcasting Committee of his own secret vote." (Seaman(ed), 10)

Along with Section D, the Department of Propaganda, known as EH (for Electra House), was also specializing in un-attributable propaganda. (Stafford(so), 20) When the SOE was formed in July 1940, its section SO1 was charged with propaganda activities, directly answerable to Dr. H. Dalton. However, in August 1941 the Political Warfare Executive (PWE) took over the functions of SO1, including black propaganda. (Seaman(ed), 201)

"... distributing clandestine printed propaganda and rumors ..."

Department D/Q was originally formed as a part of Section D. "To this very day their official title is still a state secret and blanked out in official documents but were later known as the 'Press Propaganda Department'. Despite the bulk of SOE's surviving documents being released for public inspection at least half of Department D/Q's work remains classified. However what we do know is that they were responsible for distributing clandestine printed propaganda and rumors, 'secret journalism' to manipulate the world's press - partly through their own News Agencies - and had a hand in Britain's legendary deception operations, amongst other things. The department was staffed with journalists and was originally headed by Colonel Leslie Sheridan. Prior to the war he was on the staff of the *Daily Mirror."* Sheridan later moved up the chain of command, and the head of Department D/Q became Lionel Hale. "Department D/Q remained a small but seemly effective section of SOE, the history of their spin-doctoring would make compelling, if a little unnerving, reading when, or if, it is ever fully revealed." (Whispers of War – The British World War II rumor campaign... http://www.psywar.org/sibs.php 6/11/11)

As for 'their own News Agencies': "D/Q formed and operated a news agency in New York which Leslie Sheridan christened *Britanova*. ... British Embassy and Legation staff abroad also had their whisper officers who received their sib lists, called *Venom* telegrams, via Foreign Office cipher."
(Whispers of War – The British World War II rumor campaign... http://www.psywar.org/sibs.php 6/11/11)

> ... the British secret service was operating an anti-Paul local radio station and both helped to create the false impression that an anti-German rising could produce positive result. (Beloff, 64)

For the purpose of this book, however, the information on the British propaganda in Yugoslavia - and particularly in Belgrade - is treated as a common effort of British agencies, regardless of which particular agency was generating it.

"... subsidies were given to certain Yugoslav newspapers."

For the first few weeks after his arrival in Belgrade, Julian Amery, as the deputy Press Attaché, had the task of listening to BBC broadcasts twice daily, preparing short news bulletin based on the broadcasts, and - guided telegraphically from London - composing suitable commentary. The bulletins were then distributed to a score of the leading people in Belgrade. "... my bulletins soon became quite influential. It was surprising how quickly the contents of a score of bulletins spread round Belgrade." (Amery, 130)

Amery also delivered copies of the bulletins personally to the editors of three Belgrade's newspapers, *Politika, Vreme,* and *Pravda. Politika's* proprietor and editor, Vlada Ribnikar, "… later proved to have been a secret Communist." *Vreme's* editor, [Danilo] Gregorić, favored the Germans. *Pravda* was owned by seven Sokić brothers. "The Sokitch brothers were voracious trenchermen and no less greedy for money. They were genuinely pro-Allied but had no scruple in seeking to capitalise their sentiments. One day, lunching alone with the six of them, I was asked for a subsidy of a million dinars, about £20,000, from the British Government." (Amery, 139-40)

Amery did not explain the outcome of this financial request, but Elisabeth Barker stated that "In the propaganda field, subsidies were given to certain Yugoslav newspapers." (Barker, 44) It is to be understood that the British would not subsidize newspapers which would not propagate British points of view and their interpretations of political affairs.

Britanova News Agency

According to J. Amery's account: the great majority of Yugoslav journalists had pro-Allied sympathies, and wanted to show to their editors - and the Government - that news and views they published had reached them from a reliable source. To provide them with news or views *"from a responsible source"*, Amery suggested to his Press Attaché, Stephen Childs, that they might start a news agency. "This would be *on the lines of Reuters but more propagandist*. It would issue its bulletins through a commercial office in Belgrade selling them to the newspapers at a nominal rate. The bulletins themselves could be prepared in the Legation with the help of friendly Yugoslav journalists. The Ministry of Information might also supply material." (Amery, 141. Italics added.)

The Ministry of Information "bought" the idea, and sent to Belgrade an energetic journalist, Donald Mallet, to help set up the agency. "A news agency, Britanova, owned by the British Government and supplied it information through British official channels, was started in December 1939, with its headquarters in Belgrade and branches in Budapest, Bucharest, Sofia, Athens and Istanbul. (Barker, 44) The Agency was set up in a couple of rooms "where [Gradimir-Mirko] Kozomaritch, a former editor of *Vreme,* concocted bulletins based on B.B.C., the British Press and material supplied from the Legation. … Kozomaritch was reputed to be pro-German. This gave the whole operation an appearance of impartiality and made it easier for the Yugoslav Government to turn a blind eye to *Britanova's* activities." (Amery, 141) (Kozomarić later died in a German concentration camp. (Barker, 44))

"Julian Amery was actively involved, with one foot in the press Attaché's office and another in Section D." (Barker, 44) "[Section D/SOE] Agents there [in the Balkans] included a number of journalists, whose profession gave them good cover for being in the region while they fed pro-British propaganda to the indigenous press through the 'Britanova' press agency, and engineers who were useful for their sabotage potential." (Williams, 9) "In Hungary, Britanova was run by the journalist and writer, Basil Davidson". (Barker, 44) (In the course of the war Davidson - a Section D/SOE agent - became heavily involved in Yugoslavia's affairs.)

Magazine Britannia and biweeklies Balkan Herald and South Slav Herald

A magazine called *Britannia* supplemented propaganda through the *Britanova* Agency. Planned as a fortnightly, the magazine contained articles ostensibly written "by such eminent contributors as Churchill and Lloyd George."

> They did not, of course, write the articles themselves but allowed us to pirate articles they had already written and even, with the help of scissors and paste, to concoct the new articles from their speeches and writings The first number led off with a strongly pro-Allied editorial and was quickly sold out. We doubled the circulation for the second number and again for the third. The German Legation, of course, protested. The editor was fined, and the magazine closed down. We paid the fine, appointed a new editor, and produced further numbers under another name. (Amery, 141)

Amery's additional duties at that time included briefing Yugoslav journalists on their way to London and helping the British correspondents in Belgrade. Among the latter group were Patrick Maitland, the Balkan correspondent of *The Times,* Lovat Edwards of Beaverbrook Press, and Reuter's Peter Brown. Brown had "very useful contacts with the Yugoslav left wing". (Amery, 141-2)

Drafting dispatches for Press Attaché Childs and Minister Campbell "on the attitude of the Belgrade Press and the state of Yugoslav public opinion" expanded Amery's activities at that time. Lloyd

George, then chairman of the British Council, was so impressed with the operations of the Belgrade Legation's press office that he described it as "the only good one *for propaganda in the Balkans*". (Amery, 143-4. Italics added.)

Another British journalist who helped develop propaganda was Terence Atherton, correspondent for the London *Daily Mail.* Living in Yugoslavia almost ten years, he spoke Serbo-Croatian fluently, married a Muslim lady from Bosnia, and knew the country well. Subsidized by Britain, he was publishing two biweeklies, the *Balkan Herald* and *South Slav Herald.* (Vodušek Starič, 59, 286) He was also a Section D agent in pre-war Belgrade. (Williams, 65)

Jacob Altmaier, Julian Amery's "chief mentor in Yugoslav politics", "was for many years correspondent of the *Frankfurter Zeitung* and of the *Manchester Guardian* in Belgrade and Sofia." Amery actually met him when he came to the British Legation to discuss his proposals about British propaganda to Yugoslavia. (Amery, 147)

Creating climate of opinion in favor of a coup

On the subject of propaganda and briberies, Professor Onslow remarked:

> A considerable amount has already been written on Section D/SOE in Yugoslavia before 1941, pointing to its propaganda work (the establishment and financial support of the *Britanova* news agency, and the *Britannia* publication), as well as the systematic bribery of newspaper editors and political subversion;" (Onslow, 16)

Creating a *climate of opinion* in favor of a coup had begun to be nurtured already in the summer of 1940. Julian Amery, later Baron of Lustleigh, wrote in 1973:

> " ... S.O.E.'s co-operation with the Djonovich-Birchanin group and with Gavrilovitch's Peasant Party undoubtedly strengthened both these and *helped them to create climate of opinion in which the coup became inevitable.* " (Amery, 227-8. Italics added.)

Preparing Serb political and public opinion

Influencing the Yugoslav (and particularly the Serb) public opinion *in the sense desired,* became, especially in 1941, the principal goal of British propaganda. Special attention was paid to political parties and patriotic organizations.

> "... S.O.E.'s contacts with Serb political parties and patriotic organisations were very useful *for purposes of agitation and propaganda, ...* (Barker, 92. Italics added.)

Thus, for example, in January 1941 Masterson had a long conversation with Dr Milan Grol, president of the Democratic Party, about enlarging the Party's range of propaganda. This was followed be a meeting of Masterson with Radoje Knežević, a member of the party's Main Committee, in the middle of February, to discuss the possibility of developing propaganda. (On 27 March 1941 Masterson reported to SOE London about this meeting, but Radoje's younger brother, Živan, did not even mentioned it in his book: it fitted their claim that there had been no foreign influence on the execution of the coup of 27 March 1941.)

Pro-British Serb public opinion – SOE's best hope; British full-court-press on Prince Paul

While the opposition in Belgrade was busy with their schemes, **on 24 February 1941** Churchill cabled to Eden, "Full speed ahead" with the British Expedition Forces (BEF) in Greece. The participation of Yugoslavia in the war on the British side was badly needed. Consequently, a full-court-press on Prince Paul had to be applied by all British personnel in Yugoslavia and by their domestic co-operatives. **On 27 February** George Taylor arrived in Belgrade. Bulgaria joined the Tripartite Pact unconditionally on 1 March, and German troops began moving from Rumania into Bulgaria. Taylor took over the direction of pressuring the Yugoslav Government with the approval and oversight by Minister Campbell.

Drawing on his personal experience from earlier secret visits to Belgrade, and on information by his SOE agents and other British institutions and individuals in Belgrade, Taylor assessed the situation and best opportunities for implementing SOE plans.

> On his arrival Taylor assessed pro-British Serb public opinion as SOE's best hope of influencing the Yugoslav government's policy: ... SOE hoped to counteract German threats by convincing Prince Paul that submission to these would not be tolerated by the Serb people and would result in the overthrow of his government, and possibly the end of the Karadjordjević dynasty ... (Williams, 28)

In addition to the contacts with the groups "subsidized" by the British, whom Taylor identified in his Report to Nelson, "SOE's political contacts also included the opposition parties - Radicals, Democrats and the Yugoslav National Party - which had many influential members who held sway over Serb public opinion." "SOE was almost in daily contacts" with them. (Williams, 28-9) "Taylor regarded SOE's influence with the party leaders as 'undoubtedly effective in preventing this good material being led astray'." (Williams, 29)

To direct that "good material" in a desired direction, full attention was given to propaganda generated not only by British sources - such as the news agencies, BBC, etc. - but also by the "subsidized" domestic sources. *Narodna odbrana* and other Serb patriotic organizations

> were particularly influential with the Serbian public and they submitted many petitions to Prince Paul, setting out Serb objections to giving way to German threats, while SOE published a large volume of pamphlets on the same theme, designed to arouse public opinion. In short, all possible means of bringing pressure on Prince Paul not to sign the Tripartite Pact were utilized by SOE. (Williams, 29)

> ... early in 1941, S.O.E. had stepped up their activities, aiming, first, *by means of political agitation and propaganda* to deter Prince Paul from signing the pact, ... Agitation against the pact became vociferous *from early March on*. (Barker, 91. Italics added.)

> Through February and the early part of March 1941, Masterson and Taylor made full use of this network of [political] contacts in the hope that Prince Paul would respond to the pressure of public opinion. Encouraged by S.O.E., the National Associations flooded Belgrade with pro-British and anti-German leaflets and, as a telegram on 15th March from Campbell reported, neither Paul nor the government were spared: '48 patriotic societies have presented a petition to the Prince Regent urging resistance to German demands. ... Letters and telegrams urging a firm attitude are reaching the Yugoslav Government in some numbers.' (Balfour & Mackay, 253-4)

*****

Taylor planned not only for the pre-occupation, but for the post-occupation propaganda as well. His report to Sir Frank Nelson on the organization and plans of SOE in the Balkans, dated 26 February 1941 in Athens, contained a plan for Slovenia and Croatia, but concentrated mostly on Serbia and Bosnia.

> In the event either of capitulation by Belgrade, or German occupation, underground propaganda will immediately be commenced on a wide scale by Uncle's organsation [Serbian Peasant Party]. Adequate finance has been provided and his organisation possesses the necessary facilities for the secret printing and distribution of this material. (Report p. 13)

*****

According to Bill Bailey, former head of SOE in Belgrade, "the necessary preliminary conditions were established largely through the work of the S.O.2 [S.O.E.] staff in Belgrade during the past six months." [since Italy's attack on Greece]. However, "the action immediately preceding the coup d'état may have been directed by others." (Barker, 151; 289n14) Those others were the Legation personnel. Sandy Glen confirmed that they had "encouraged" the events of 27 March:

> There has been considerable speculation in Yugoslavia recently [in the 1970s] as to how much the events of 27 March were influenced and encouraged by the British. The answer as regards the latter must be a considerable amount, as Hugh Macdonald and Charlie Clark [Air and Military Attaché, respectively] were too close to the organizers for this to have been otherwise. (Glen, 63)

The historian who wrote about «SOE and British Involvement in the Belgrade Coup d'Etat of March 1941», stated that

> Their [SOE] links with the air force conspirators, led by [General Borivoje] Bora Mirković, were only indirect – through Trifunović and Radoje Knežević on the Yugoslav side, and through the air attaché's contact with Mirković on the British side. Nevertheless, they were kept relatively well informed of developments. (Staffor(cp), 412)

Mirković himself acknowledged contact with Macdonald and other Legation personnel. At the same time, Masterson also had considerable contacts with both active and reserve officers, who in turn maintained liaison with Mirković, Trifunović-Birčanin, and other coup-wishers-and-plotters.

Simović: "Germany's penetration across the Danube ... should not have been allowed..."

Following the unconditional adhesion of Bulgaria to the Tripartite Pact on 1 March 1941, German troops began crossing the Danube from Rumania into Bulgaria. Reflecting on those events more than two years later, Gen. Simović still insisted:

> ((Germany's penetration across the Danube into Bulgaria, towards our eastern flank and our connections with Salonika and our Allies should not have ben allowed even at a price of getting into the war.))
> "Prodiranje Nemačke preko Dunava u Bugarsku, prema našem istočnom boku i našim vezama sa Solunom i Saveznicima nije se smelo dozvolti ni po cenu stupanja u rat." (Simović(44), 31)

By 1 March 1941, Yugoslavia's former Allies were defeated or controlled by Germany. Yugoslavia had no pact of alliance with Great Britain, and a new Salonika Front was not favored by Britain. Even after a bitter experience of defeat in a 12-day war against Germany in April of 1941, Simović still maintained that getting into the war in March of 1941 was the correct historical act to do, without bothering to show how would that have stopped or slowed Germany's penetration towards Greece. That shows once again that he wanted to lead Yugoslavia into the war on the side of "our Allies" no matter what, whatever the consequences – fully aware of Germany's military superiority. That stand paralleled the war-mongering wave pushed by the "Oppositionists" to the Government's policy.

Agitation vociferous particularly from early March onwards

By the end of February 1941, Eden and General Dill knew that Turkey was refusing to join the Balkan Front. That prompted Churchill, on 1 March, to instruct Eden: "Your main appeal should now be made to Yugoslavia." (Churchill(GA), 97) On 2 March the Prime Minister *"thoroughly approved"* SOE's secret plan to deal with Price Paul, including support for a *coup d'état*. (Stafford (C), 211-12) On 5 March Eden and General Dill found *"changed and disturbing situation"* in Greece ... as the British troops were already sailing from Egypt to Greece.

> "On 5 March ... General Papagos ... offered only sixteen to twenty-three battalions for the defence of the Aliakmon line, instead of the thirty-five that we had been led to expect; and he was no longer prepared to order any withdrawals from the Albanian front. ... " (Ismay, 199)

> Thereafter, British policy became a desperate race [to] prevent Yugoslavia's signature of the Tripartite Pact to protect Britain's exposed flank in Greece, compromising Commonwealth troops (from Australia and New Zealand, which was politically very sensitive in itself, given the theatre of war.) (Onslow, 43)

So, how to appeal to Yugoslavia in the changing and disturbing situation? Propaganda was one way. Landing British troops in Greece offered a potent argument. Robert St. John, the Associated Press correspondent in Belgrade, described how the Greek journalist Pappas spread untraceable, "black" propaganda to selected people in Belgrade. (**Appendix B**) After having been confidentially contacted by Pappas, St. John explained:

> ... then I went to the British Legation and asked them flatly how about these landings of British troops in Greece? Officially, they said, they were obliged to deny it. Categorically, in fact. But unofficially ... well ... and they hesitated and smiled. Who gave me the information? Pappas? Well, Pappas was a very reputable man, all right, and he had just come from Athens, and he ought to know what was going on down in Greece. (St. John, 22)

And how did St. John respond to these assurances? By engaging himself in propaganda.

> So I sent the story about a hundred thousand British troops in Greece, with planes and tanks and munitions. Then I sent a story about the blue Mediterranean being black with British ships. Later I boosted the number to two hundred thousand and eventually to three hundred thousand, all on the say-so of the Greek Pappas and the unofficial confirmation (but official denial) of the British Legation in Belgrade. (St. John, 22)

In March 1941 "Belgrade was full of British and American newspapermen" covering the Balkan countries. Competing for timely deliveries of news to their papers and/or agencies, they also collaborated, shared newest information, and engaged in straight reporting and/or advocacy journalism for their cause(s). After the Putsch of 27 March, "waiting for war" to break out, some exchanged their views on the current situation and guesses on future developments. One of them was Robert St. John, whose story on the propaganda activities of the Greek journalist Pappas was presented above. He identified the following American and British colleagues:

Terence Atherton	of the London *Daily Mail*
Ralph W. Barnes	American War Correspondent, who died in Podgorica, Montenegro, on 18 November 1940
Sam Brewer	of *The* Chicago *Tribune*
Ray Brock	of *The New York Times*
Cecil Brown	of Columbia Broadcasting
Michael Chinigo	of The International News Service
Lovat Edwards	an English correspondent, who had a Serbian wife
Max Harrelson	of The Associated Press
Russell Hill	of The New York *Herald Tribune*
Leon Kay	of The United Press
Cy Sulzberger	of *The New York Times*
Paul Vajda	of The Associated Press
Dave Walker	of Reuter's and the London *Daly Mail*
Leigh White	of Columbia Broadcasting

And what were the total effects of a kind of St. John's reporting ... a Great Power coming so mightily to help the threatened and small but heroic peoples? A congregate effect of all these journalists' reporting and commentaries had to be in favor of Great Britain and against evil-minded Hitler and his policies. The newspapermen reported their stories to their papers or agencies. The readers formed their opinions on the basis of the reports from these locations and the given commentaries. Some of those stories then reached the public back in Yugoslavia, to be mostly accepted at face value: it must be so when the American press reported it. That way the news-circle was closed, and the news became believable.

Most of the top-flight American correspondents were "passionate anti-Axis crusaders who had converged upon the Yugoslav capital in the expectation that the Balkans were about to become a major theater of war. These men had been fighting the Axis long before Roosevelt decided to place the United States on the side of the British. They represented the 'Fourth Estate', the most influential single force in American politics, reflecting as well as forging the public opinion." (Petrov, 146)

> How seriously General Simovich himself took the Pappas reports and how much these reports inspired his *coup d'état* and his defiance of Hitler no one will never know definitely, but weeks later some of his little circle of advisors, ministers, and army officers told me they had believed every word of the reports and had been convinced that at least fifteen British divisions and hundreds of British planes would rush to Yugoslavia's aid when the zero hour came. (St. John, 22)

While Pappas was spreading his black propaganda, Serb patriotic oganizations, SOE and their contacts, the "oppositionist", etc, joined in a petitions-and-pamphlets-campaign by some non-Serbian authors, as described above.

- **Simović's praise of agitation and of his own role**

From the beginning or middle of March – Simović wrote in his memoirs – petitions, appeals, even threats were pouring in to Prince Paul, the members of the Government, the Chief of the General Staff, and other influential military and civilian individuals. Various delegations from the common people and patriotic organizations were visiting some Ministers and military men, including his Air Force Command. In all this "bitterness of the people" - which he understood, hailed, and which touched him deeply - he wrote,

> ((men began turning to me and looking at me, expecting from me the situation of the country not to be let totally loose. I felt a mighty responsibility before the people and the history for events which were to occur as a consequence of the fatefull decision by the Government. At the same time – it is perhaps immodest for me to say it, but I must say – in those historic moments I felt the call of the entire people, (#) to fulfill my duty toward the Fatherland and the people to the end, not shrinking from taking them the way of Golgotha and sufferings in the defense of the people's honor and future, which were awaiting us and of which I was fully aware.))
> (#) He probably meant the people in Serbia, not in the entire Yugoslavia.

> "Osećao sam silnu odgovornost i pred narodom i pred istorijom za događaje koji su imali nastupiti kao posledica sudbonosne vladine odluke. U isto vreme, - možda je neskromno od mene, ali moram reći, - u tim istoriskim momentima osećao sam poziv celokupnog naroda, da svoju dužnost prema Otadžbini i narodu ispunim do kraja, ne prezajući da ga u odbranu narodne časti i budućnosti povedem putem Golgote i stradanja, koja su nss u tome slučaju očekivala i kojih sam ja bio potpuno svestan."
> (Simović(44), 32-33)

Yet in the morning of 26 March - fully aware that the Pact had been signed - Simović told the British Air Attaché that Britain had to wait a few more days for the coup. Given all the normal contacts of the British service Attachés with their Yugoslav counterparts, British contacts with the patriotic organizations, political parties, etc., it is hard to assume that Simović had no inkling of the British participation in the agitation and petitions campaign against the Prince and his Government.

Moscow's instructions to Lebedev and Tito

Agitation and propaganda were not limited only to the British and their domestic "contacts". Following their own objectives, the Soviets were involved as well.

> As in the Bulgarian case, Soviet efforts were directed towards the mobilization of popular support in Belgrade; this was done both through the diplomatic channels and through the Comintern. Lebedev, the Soviet ambassador in Yugoslavia, was charged with exposing the insincerity of the Yugoslav government's overtures to Russia, which concealed the German-Yugoslav activities 'behind the scene'. (Gorodetsky 140; 355n21)

> Tito, the leader of the Yugoslav Communist Party, was instructed 'to mobilize the Party against the capitulation to the Germans. Support the movement for a mass opposition to the incursion of the German military into Yugoslavia. Demand friendship with the Soviet Union.' (Gorodetsky, 140)

(C) On 15 March 1941, the Central Committee of the Communist Party of Yugoslavia (CC CPY) issued a resolution, "Against Capitulation – In Favor of a Pact of Mutual Assistance with the Soviet Union".

> Public opinion was moulded in Belgrade to press the government to make concrete propositions [to the Soviets].
> Concurrently, Tupanjanin, following instructions from Moscow, leaked information on the forthcoming negotiations with the military. (Gorodetsky, 140)

The CPY membership in the entire country was estimated to be around 12,000, and therefore less than that in Serbia. Compared to the membership of the Serb patriotic organizations and Opposition - "subsidized" or not by the British - the Communist membership was a tiny fraction. Although more disciplined and active, by their numbers and organization the Communists could not be so widely effective in their propaganda as the "pro-British" side was in forming and maintaining the Serb public opinion – which was considered to be the main leverage against the Government's policy.

American broadcasts in Serbo-Croat – in strong terms

As stated above, on 20 March Campbell telegraphed to Eden that "It would be well, too, if American broadcast in Serbo-Croat should voice the feelings of Yugoslavs in the United States in strong terms." (PRO, Premier 3 / 570/11)

There was, indeed, a short-wave American radio station that did broadcast in Serbo-Croat: WRUL [World Radio University Listeners] studios of the World Wide Broadcasting Foundation, in Boston, and a broadcaster who claimed to voice the feelings of the Yugoslavs in the USA – Dr. Svetislav-Sveta Petrović. He was a former Paris correspondent of Belgrade's daily *Pravda,* Julian Amery's favorite newspaper.

Rockefeller, Sloan and Carnegie cash and listeners' contribution since 1935 sponsored the WRUL studios. "Among those who have needled the Führer over its facilities have been Dorothy Thompson, Hendrik Willem von Loon, Norway's Carl J. Hambro. But none has packed the wallop of cultured, graying, 46-year old Dr. Svetislav-Sveta Petrovitch, author of last fortnight's appeals to the Yugoslavs. (Short-Wave Paul Revere – TIME   http://www.time.com/time/agazine/article/0.9171.932243.00.html 9/1/08)

"... Boston's WRUL also had a special place in the US war effort. ... WRUL's anti-German broadcasts in Serbo-Croat by former Paris correspondent of the Belgrade *Pravda,* Dr. Svetislav-Sveta Petrovich, were a powerful incentive for Yugoslavia to fight the Germans." (Jerome S. Borg, *On the Short Waves, 1923-1945,* pp. 214-15)

"British Security Coordination, a covert organization that by the British Secret Intelligence Service [MI6] [had] established in New York City [in May 1940], operated the broadcast service." (WNYW (shortwave) http://en.wikipeda.org/wiki/WNYW_(shortwave)   6/8/11)

William Boyd described the British Security Cooperation (BSC) in the *Guardian* in 2006:

> BSC was set up by a Canadian entrepreneur called William Stephenson, working on behalf of the British Secret Intelligence Service (SIS). An office was opened in the Rockefeller Centre in Manhattan ... What actually occurred as 1940 became 1941 was that BSC became a huge secret agency of nationwide news manipulation and black propaganda. Pro-British and Anti-German stories were planted in American newspapers and broadcast on American radio stations, ...
>
> BSC's media reach was extensive: ... BSC effectively ran its own radio station, WRUL., and a press agency, the Overseas News Agency (ONA), feeding stories to the media as they required from foreign datelines to disguise their provenance. WRUL would broadcast a story from ONA and it thus became a US "source" suitable for further dissemination, even though it had arrived there via BSC agents. It would then be legitimately picked up by other radio stations and newspapers, and relayed to listeners and readers as fact. The story would spread exponentially and nobody suspected this was emanating from three floors of the Rockefeller Centre. BSC took enormous pains to ensure its propaganda was circulated and consumed as bona fide news reporting. ... (British Security Coordination Powerbase http://www.powerbase.info/index.php?title=British_Security_C... 6/10/11)

(According to J. Amery's description, *Britanova* News Agency in Belgrade operated in similar fashion.)

Not referring to St. John's reports, Petrović quoted extensively from the reports by Ray Brock, who shared the on-duty-time and news with St. John during the night of the coup, 26/27 March 1941. Petrović wrote:

> ... Much earlier [before March 1941] I started my campaign against the dictators and their intentions from Paris. In 750 consecutive radiobroadcasts from there I gave the truth to my people. ... In December 1940, I was given the opportunity to talk to my people from the center of liberty through the facilities of WRUL and WRUW short-wave radio stations at Boston. (Petrovitch, 238, 236)

Upon arriving in the USA, Petrović was broadcasting twice a day, but the subjects of his broadcasts were not described in his book, *Free Yugoslavia Calling,* published in the autumn of 1941. He revealed more information about his broadcasts made after the all-British conference in Belgrade on 19 March 1941, when he was given the opportunity to broadcast three times daily. Short notes on his activities at that time are shown in **Appendix L, Calls to arms**. Petrović knew that his broadcasts were heard clearly in Yugoslavia, that many people listened to them, therefore he "began to call upon the people to rise and expel the Cvetkovitch government". (Petrovitch, 243)

This was also the scope of Campbell's suggestion to Eden on 20 March 1941 about the American broadcast. The BBC Serbo-Croat broadcasts likewise complied with Campbell' suggestion. (**Part One, 129**)

BBC's appeal to the Serbs: heavenly kingdom

"B.B.C. Serb-Croat broadcasts should now adopt stronger line, *working on the feelings of Serbs in particular ensuring vehement reaction in Serbia.*", requested Minister Campbell on 20 March.

> While the BBC blared forth its radio appeals against the pact and British agents worked covertly to prepare the ground, the tension mounted. Leaflets were widely distributed in Belgrade, reminding the Serbs of their glorious past, long-forgotten battles and victories against the Turks were again evoked. One such leaflet circulated throughout Belgrade reflects emotional climate of dark suspicions, perfidy and apprehensions of treason. (Hehn, 382)

On 24 March Campbell informed the Foreign Office of the content of this leaflet. Here are some excerpts:

> Serbs, Belgradians [*sic*], the Government is preparing capitulation. In a day or two the tripartite pact is to be signed which means certain shameful death to the country, freedom and the people. For the first time in our history we must bow our knee to tyrants and perish in dishonor and slavery. ...

> Serbs, Belgradians, let us show ourselves worthy of our forbears. We dare not be worse than the heroes of Kosovo, the Karageorge rebels or the famous heroes of Kumanovo, Bregalnica, Suvobor, Mojkovac, and Kajmakčalan. (Hehn, 382-3; 462n74)

The response from BBC to Campbell's suggestion came six days later, in the evening of 26 March, after the Notes 1 and 2 to the Protocol of adhesion to the Tripartite Pact had been published in the morning of the 26th March.

"... On March 26th Leopold Amery, ... , appealed to Yugoslavia in a radio message over the BBC. Actually he addressed his remarks *not so much to all Yugoslavs as to the Serbs alone. ...* , he asked why the Serbs should now leave all the glory to the Greeks ... He reminded them *of the tradition of Kosovo and the heroic King Lazar*," ... (Hoptner, 241-2. Italics added.) "... it [the speech] was heard by some of the officers who were preparing the coup ... They afterward told me that they took it as a public sign of British support ..." (Amery, 227)

As shown in **Part One, pages 142-3,** on 28 March 1941 Dalton sent to Churchill a letter about the SOE's special operations in the Balkans. Referring to Yugoslavia, Dalton informed the Prime Minister that, by expenditure of money "our agents were able to maintain the friendship of the principal anti-Axis Yugoslavs (such as TUPANJANIN of the Serb Peasant Party, and TRIFUNOVICH of the Narodna Odbrana) *and our secret propaganda agencies constantly stimulated the national will to resist."* (Great Britain, Special Operations Executive, 91087-10V, Hoover Institution Archives. Italics added.)

Stimulating the will of the Serbs to "resist"

Constantly stimulating the Serb public will to resist ... the British indeed did. Here are some abbreviated statements of some of Dalton's agents, themselves the shapers of events, which have been already quoted in **Part One:**

John H. Bennett wrote about SOE propaganda to the head of SOE:

> "... I am also certain that *the propaganda emanating from SO2 in Belgrade was largely responsible for the spirit maintained until their final entry into the war on the side of the Allies."*

(Great Britain, Special Operations Executive, 91087-10V, Hoover Institution Archives. Italics added)

"... S.O.E. could fairly claim that they had done a great deal to *prepare Serb political and popular opinion,* so that the coup was accepted in Serbia with enormous enthusiasm." (Barker, 93. Italics added.)

Trevor J. Glanville "Nero" concluded that, "one can honestly attribute some measure of the *popular feeling* which endorsed it [the coup], and made possible the formation of the new Government, to our [SOE's] activities and that one can regard it as the fruit of 18 months of hard work by all concerned." (Great Britain, Special Operations Executive, 91087-10V, Hoover Institution Archives. Italics added.)

W.S. "Bill"" Bailey felt "very strongly that ... the necessary preliminary conditions [for the coup] were established largely through the work of the S.O.2 [S.O.E.] staff in Belgrade during the past six months. (Barker, 151; 289n14)

Professor Ben Pimlott, the editor of Dalton's diaries, commented:

" ... S.O.E. agents had given every encouragement and *had done much to prepare Serb opinion for the event.* Hence Dalton was delighted by what seemed like a tangible triumph for his organisation."   (Pimlott(ed), 175. Italics added.)

The British-subsidized national organizations, presided over by Trifunović-Birčanin, "with the SOE's encouragement, flooded the government with petitions against signature of the Pact in the days immediately preceding the coup." (Stafford(cp), 410-11)

Tupanjanin and the subsidized Serb Peasant Party were "valuable in publicizing the issues involved and arousing Serb public opinion, ..." (Stafford(cp), 412)

The Democratic Party's *help would enlarge the range of propaganda ...*

early in 1941, S.O.E. had stepped up their activities *by means of political agitation and propaganda. ...* Agitation against the pact became vociferous *from early March on.* (Barker, 91. Italics added.)

*****

When one puts all these statements together, the following picture emerges:

As early as December 1939 the British were feeding the press and influential individuals with concocted articles and stories of war *"from a reliable source".* The opposition political parties and patriotic organizations - especially the "subsidized" ones - were useful in spreading propaganda and agitation, tailored to constantly stimulate the will - especially of the Serbs - to "oppose" the Germans. In simple language that meant to oppose with arms ... that Yugoslavia did not have and Great Britain could not supply.

As the Government was not willing to go to war under those conditions, SOE abundantly helped the opposition groups to create *"climate of opinion in which the coup became inevitable" ...* in hope that the new government would "resist" the Germans ... even for a brief period. Propaganda in this sense was strengthened after SOE's George Taylor arrived in Belgrade on 27 February 1941, and assessed that stimulating pro-British Serb public opinion would give SOE the best chance to positively influence the policies of the Regent, Prince Paul. When this did not succeed, then massive propaganda was exerted by the opposition forces – along the lines agitated by the British, and assisted from the USA: national honor, glorious Serb past and heroism, freedom, love of the country ... while at the same time the British knew that the "resistance" to Germany would be short-lived ... so they were simultaneously preparing for the "post-occupational" resistance.

This concentrated propaganda was successful, as witnessed after the *coup d'état* by the explosion of enthusiasm and the demonstrations in Belgrade and other predominately Serb cities – but not in the entire country.

However, the events in Belgrade between the outbreak of the Second World War and the coup of 27 March 1941 "were seen as, and interpreted as, a remarkable propaganda victory for the British cause. The coup proved a tremendous, if ephemeral, boost to British morale,..." (Onslow, 2)

An ephemeral boost to British morale, and a lasting tragedy for the people of Yugoslavia.

(How an orchestrated propaganda campaign can galvanize public opinion in a desired sense, was demonstrated in the United States of America, when the supposed existence of the "weapons of mass destruction" in Iraq in 2003 was presented to the people as the reality – which they were not.)

"… urging the necessity of action for a coup d'état"

British diplomatic personnel, secret operatives, propagandists, etc., performed their various patriotic duties in Yugoslavia as their Government asked them to do, overtly and/or covertly, as situations demanded. Crossing of the Danube by German troops, from Rumania into Bulgaria, the first days of March 1941, with the plan of attacking Greece, caused the British to strengthen their pressure on the Yugoslav Government not only to not adhere to the Tripartite Pact, but to actually "resist" Germany militarily.

- George Taylor, reporting to Sir Frank Nelson on 26 February, stated that his report was *written rather from the angle of what help SOE can be to Wavell (and in the present situation and with the present decision Nelson would agree, Taylor was sure, that this was the only possible point of view to take)*. (The decision was the Anglo-Greek Tatoi agreement of 22/23 February.) (TNA HS5/166)

- Within instructions from Dalton related to the coup, approved at Chequers on 2 March, on 18 March George Taylor decided to act:

    " The work of SOE during these days therefore was essentially that of urging the necessity of action for a coup d'état upon all our friends and everyone with whom we had contact ", as Taylor put it, (Williams, 30-31. Italics added.)

- Churchill *greatly admired all Minister Campbell had done,* but asked him *to not neglect any alternative to which the British may have to resort if they find present Government have gone beyond recall.* (Dilks(ed), 366)

Briefly: individuals and/or groups involved in the coup - directly or indirectly - were the Legation personnel, the SOE operatives and their domestic "friends" with whom SOE had "contacts". Some of these "friends" and "contacts" were subsidized, engaged in sabotage, diversions, and/or propaganda activities – as shown here. Secret Intelligence Service (SIS) agents who were providing contacts between the SOE and local civilians and military, should also be included. The number of officials of the Consulate in Belgrade was raised from 12 to 60. (Vodušek Starič, 28) Adding the personnel to other British agencies, British business and press people, etc. - who were patriotically duty-bound to support the British cause - the number of supporters of the British policies was imposing. Their contributions to *desperate British efforts* were multi-faceted, but all focused on pressuring Prince Paul and his Government *in the sense desired*. While all people involved and their contributions were influential, for purposes of this analysis a special attention is focused on the Service Attachés, SOE agents, their domestic co-operatives, and their activities.

Chapter 8

As pointed out in Chapter 1, in September 1939, the British Minister in Belgrade "deprecated the attitude of the Opposition leaders in Belgrade and said that they were simply trying to ride back to power on a wave of pro-Allied sentiment." (Amery, 138) That was thirteen months before Italy attacked Greece from Albania, when "there was no question of the British and French opening a new Salonika front", and some fifteen months before Churchill decided to form a Balkan front with Turkey, Greece and Yugoslavia. During that period the Opposition leaders persisted in removing the existing Government and the Regency, but without a common, unifying goal for a hoped-for post-Regent era. Here is some information on this subject.

Coup-wishers' diverse motivations and goals

While the coup-wishers-planners-makers were united in a desire to overthrow Prince Paul's regime, they were not united in their motivations and political purposes. Individuals, the political Opposition Parties, the veterans, the Serb national organizations, etc. – they harbored different motives for the coup and different objectives to be achieved after it. The views of the major domestic coup-wishers are examined below and presented as found in their own accounts, and in the accounts by the British participants in the events.

First, about the civilian coup-wishers.

Motivation and goals of the Serbian Peasant Party

As shown in **Part One, Appendix D, the** President of the SPP, Milan Gavrilović, contacted Julian Amery toward the end of June 1940, to find out what the British Government would think of his accepting the post as Yugoslavia's Ambassador in Moscow. Two days later, as Amery relayed a positive answer from London, Gavrilović told Amery that he would prefer war and occupation to capitulation without war. (Amery, 173) Why? As Amery explained:

> … Of the two, he favoured war but knew that defeat was inevitable. The real struggle would begin after the occupation had taken place, and it would be waged by the peasants. The Germans would find it easy enough to keep down townsmen whether workers or middle class. But the peasants would be a much tougher proposition. They are scattered. They could feed themselves. The woods and mountains would protect them from pursuit. Above all, they had a long tradition of guerrilla resistance against the Turks and Austrians. Serbia, he went on, would be the natural centre of Resistance for all the Balkans, and his Peasant Party, with its links with Bulgaria and Croatia, would be the natural spearhead. (Amery, 173)

Then Gavrilović asked for material support and his party started receiving £4,000 per month.

*****

On 17 April 1956, Dragiša Ristić visited Gavrilović in Washington, D.C.. In a lengthy and friendly conversation Gavrilović told his guest:

In his opinion, a strong alliance of the Balkan countries would have meant a sure resistance and a guarantee against endangerment from the East or the West. He tried to promote this view, but without success. He was still firmly convinced that in no way the Germans should have been allowed to move their troops across the Danube [i.e. from Rumania into Bulgaria, on 2 March 1941], and that this had been the right moment for the *coup d'état* in Yugoslavia. (Box 2, folder 2.18, Hoover Institutions archives)

*****

As seen from his conversation with J. Amery, what Gavrilović had in mind was the central role of his Peasant Party, tied with similar parties in Bulgaria and Croatia – regardless of the consequences of an *inevitable defeat*.

As for the right moment for the Putsch, London had a different time-table. Besides, how would the coup have stopped German troops from crossing the Danube – Gavrilović offered no ideas.

Aims of Đonović – Trifunović-Birčanin and their friends

Julian Amery's first contact with Jovan Đonović, the former Yugoslav Ambassador in Albania, also occurred in the summer of 1940 - long before the first negotiation between Germany and Yugoslavia took place. At their first meeting Đonović assumed that "the Germans were bound to carve Yugoslavia up to meet the claims of Italy, Bulgaria and Hungary." If the Yugoslavs surrendered without fighting, "the soul of the nation would die". ... "Honour was the soul of the nation. Serbia had survived five hundred years of Turkish domination because she had never given in." (Amery, 174-5) Then Đonović went on:

> The right course for the Serbs was to stand up to the Germans *even if this meant war*. In a war they could give a good account of themselves and, *though military defeat might follow*, they would have a place of honour at the Conference Table and *would share in the fruits of victory*. ... (Amery, 175. Italics added.)

> No-one could read the future, but if Yugoslavia stood up to the Germans now, she might be able at the next Peace Conference *to extend her frontiers to include Bulgaria in a federation of all the South Slavs.* (Amery, 175. Italics added.)

> Djonovitch now told me that he had been in consultation with Birchanin for several days. They had examined every possible course of action and had come to a solemn but radical conclusion. The only way to save their country from capitulation to Hitler was to overthrow Prince Paul's regime by a military coup d'état. Birchanin had taken sounding among his friends in the Army and was satisfied that the job could be done. Several senior officers, indeed, were already pressing him to give a lead. (Amery, 176)

*****

Đonović asked Amery if he knew his friend *Vojvoda* [guerrilla highest rank] Ilija Trifunović- Birčanin. Amery had never met him but "knew him by reputation as the greatest of the Serb guerrilla leaders in the Balkan and First World Wars. He was then President of the *Narodna Odbrana* or National Defence League, a powerful patriotic society, some two hundred thousand strong with branches in every town and big village where there were Serbs." (Amery, 175) The following day Amery met Birčanin and three decades later wrote about the meeting:

> ... An empty sleeve stuck in his pocket showed that he had lost an arm. He addressed me for about twenty minutes ... His people, he said, were for freedom and against the hereditary German enemy. They were for the old Allies of Salonika days and for the Russians. They had a long tradition of war. *They would soon see off the Italians.* As for the Bulgars, he had fought with them and against them, but basically they were brothers. They too wanted a great South Slav State, stretching from the Black Sea to the Adriatic. ... Now was the time for action. He and his friends are ready to do the job and put *a true Serb* at the head of the Government. All they wanted was to know that, in our hearts, whatever we might say officially, we were with them. (Amery, 177-8. Italics added.)

Clearly, for Birčanin and his friends, Prince Paul was not *a true Serb*. Calling him a White Russian Prince, Đonović told Amery that "Paul was no hero and no leader. He had no following among the people." The British were wrong to put their faith in him. "The Prince is already an unconscious agent of the Germans. You will soon find him a conscious one." (Amery, 175)

*****

While, reportedly, *several senior Army officers* were pressing Birčanin to lead a military coup, "Djonovitch, for his own part, had also discussed his analysis of the situation, *though not his conclusions*, with the chief men in the Opposition parties. *They shared his views* and would all be prepared to serve in a Government of National Unity. Bishop Nikolai Velimirovitch, the most dynamic of the Serbian Orthodox priests, would probably be the most acceptable figure to head this Government either as Prime Minister or as Regent to King Peter." (Amery, 176. Italics added.)

- **Yugoslavia's joining the Tripartite Pact was not the initial motivation for the coup**

The first proposal suggested to the British was to overthrow Prince Paul's regime. Because this solicited a British response, it seem appropriate to briefly analyze the proposal and its background.

The proposal was made at the end of June or beginning of July 1940. The Rome-Berlin Axis was formed in October 1936. The Tripartite Pact was concluded on 27 September 1940, i.e. a few months after the coup-proposal. Yugoslavia's neighbor Hungary joined the Pact on 20 November, and Rumania on the 23rd. Hitler conferred with the Yugoslav Foreign Minister *after* these adhesions, on 28 November, when he suggested a non-aggression pact, not the Tripartite Pact. Therefore, Yugoslavia joining the Tripartite Pact could not be Đonović's and his friends' motivation for the coup at that time – although some used the Pact later on as the justification for their opposition.

Đonović started with the assumption of Germany's intention to carve up Yugoslavia. There was no evidence of such intention at that time. Actually, Hitler issued such a directive on 27 March 1941 – the day of the coup; it was a direct consequence of the coup.

Đonović talked of the Honor of the nation – a natural and self-evident feeling. But he was also motivated by specific political goals: victory at the end of the war, the place of honor at the Conference Table which would make possible the formation of a South Slavic Federation – as he and Trifunović-Birčanin had envisioned it.

Leaders of the Opposition parties, with whom Đonović talked, shared his views on the situation. However, because he did not talk with them about his conclusion - *the need for a military coup* – these leaders were not aware of his conclusion and therefore could not approve or disapprove it. They were *prepared to serve in a Government of National Unity*, but not necessarily to go to war. This is a very important point because all the leaders were not in favor of a war – as Đonović and Trifunović were – which will be shown during the formation of the new *putschist* Government in early hours of 27 March 1941. Also, all the Opposition parties were not receiving the British "subsidies", either – as the SPP and Trifunović's *Narodna Odbrana*.

- **Standing up to Germans – even at the cost of defeat**

According to Amery, Đonović told him that standing up to the Germans was the right course for the Serbs to take even if that meant war with a possible military defeat. First, the Serbs were not the only citizens of Yugoslavia – and not taking that into account, when planning for a possible war, was a capital misjudgment. Then, a war would result in loss of human lives and people's material goods, and the probable defeat would be followed by an oppressive occupation. If he, and his like-minded friends reasoned about it, and still persisted, then it should be concluded that they had been willing to expose the country to the consequences of war in order to achieve a political objective to fit their views. This is implied by another train of thought attributed to Birčanin and Đonović.

Reportedly, Birčanin told Amery that his people *would soon see off the Italians.* Đonović was more specific, as Amery stated:

> If the coup succeeded they must expect a strong reaction from the Germans. But they had some good cards to play. The Yugoslav Army could hardly expect to resist a German attack for very long. But they were more than a match for the Italians. If the Germans began to mass troops against them, they could at once attack the Italians in Albania and throw them into the Adriatic. (Amery, 176)

- **Disregarding Hitler's readiness to aid Italy in Albania**

Expecting a strong German attack, against which Yugoslavia's resistance would be brief – meant a defeat, even if the Italians were to be thrown into the Adriatic. However, according to Amery, Birčanin and Đonović were willing to accept a defeat.

Even without the coup, it is probable that Hitler would have come to Mussolini's aid if Yugoslavia were to attack the Italian troops in Albania. On 11 March 1938, after ordering the invasion of Austria at 8:45 p.m., at 10:25 p.m. Hitler received a telephone message from Rome: Mussolini sent his best greetings – "Austria did not interest him at all." Emotionally relieved, Hitler bubbled: "Tell Mussolini I will never forget this. ... Never, never, never, whatever happens. ... I will never forget, whatever may happen. ... If he should ever need any help or be in any danger, he can be convinced that I shall stick to him, whatever may happen, even if the whole world be against him." (Taylor, 145) To this the British historian A.J.P. Taylor added: "This was one promise which Hitler kept." Military historian Robin Higham observed:

> The Churchillian suggestion that an attack on Albania would create a disaster for the enemy naively overlooked the realities of Axis politics; Hitler simply would not allow Mussolini to be demolished, especially if it resulted in the establishment of a British-led bloc based on Greece, as in the First World War. The English are a gambling nation and Churchill was no exception, but he was an ill-informed

amateur at guessing the odds in the Balkans. The Yugoslavs had been notified by the Bulgarians of their adherence to the Axis, and warned that German troops would be moving through Bulgaria to the Greek border. And when Prince Paul visited Hitler at Berchtesgaden on 4 March the regent emerged from the five-hour confrontation with a sinking heart, knowing where Yugoslavia really stood. (Higham, 138-39; 251n196)

*****

Another point in Amery's conversations is worth noting. Birčanin told Amery that his people were *for the Russians.* Đonović similarly told Amery that the Serbian people "were pro-Russian and, in their hearts, still looked on the Russians as the protectors of the Slavs." Indeed, many Serbs - and not only the Serbs - did not distinguish *the Soviets* from *the Russians,* nor the new *Soviet Union* from the old *"Mother Russia."* Such misidentification was skillfully used by the Communists, abusing deeply rooted sympathies of the people toward national *"Mother Russia"* to promote policies and interests of the internationalist *" land of Socialism".*

The coup: advantage for Britain, not for Yugoslavia

Exposed to Đonović's views, what did Amery think of the merits of the coup proposal? "...the more I looked at it, the more attractive it seemed. I could, indeed, see objections from a Yugoslav point of view.
… But *from a British point of view*, I could see only advantage. If Yugoslavia stood up to Germany, some, at least, of the pressure on Britain must be relieved and there was just a chance that Russia might be drawn into the war. At the very worst, it meant that the Germans would have to fight for the Balkans, instead of picking them up for nothing; and war has a way of leading to unexpected consequences. (Amery, 177. Italics added.)

Seeing only the advantage for Britain, Amery discussed the proposal with his Section D colleagues Sandy Glen and John Bennett; judging it sound, they informed Minister Campbell about it. (Amery, 178)

At the same time, Amery was in discussions with Gavrilović and Tupanjanin of the Serbian Peasant Party which were likewise reported to Campbell. So, in July 1940 Campbell reported to the Foreign Office that

> he had learnt (presumably from Section D) that there were elements, particularly in Serbia, 'who are thinking of utilizing the discontent which is felt at the pro-Axis policy of the present government to attempt a coup d'état and simultaneously to declare common cause with Great Britain'. Behind the plan were patriotic organisations, such as the Narodna Odbrana, the Orthodox Church, important sections of the army, and, particularly, 'the peasants'. There would be a simultaneous coup in Bulgaria by the Bulgarian Agrarians. The Yugoslav Regent would be removed 'if necessary by violence' but the dynasty would be maintained under the young King; the Bulgarian king would be removed 'by violence' as a step on the way to Yugoslav-Bulgarian federation. The Yugoslavs would attack Albania to promote revolution and provoke Italy. The coup organisers would declare common cause with Britain and try to get Soviet support. If the Germans invaded, the Yugoslavs would offer 'maximum military resistance' and carry out 'maximum sabotage'. Britain would be expected to recognise the new government immediately and offer an alliance. (Barker, 85)

London's reaction to the coup suggestion: premature at present, but keep in touch
…

Based on the input by Amery, this letter contained more details than he had revealed in his autobiography. On 27 July, 1940, John Nicholls of the FO minuted that Lord Halifax, the Foreign Minister, thought it would be premature to encourage the movement *at present*, but later on it "might be of the first class importance to H.M.G. [His Majesty's Government]". Hugh Dalton, as Minister responsible for SOE, minuted: "We cannot afford to neglect any chance, however slight of improving our prospect of victory within a tolerable time". The Chiefs of Staff agreed that a slightly more encouraging reply should be sent to Belgrade. (Barker, 86)

Amery noted that the Foreign Office "suggested that we should keep in touch with the conspirators and, while *discouraging immediate action,* try to form our own assessment of how much support Djonovitch and his friends could rely on." (Amery, 178. Italics added.) In the end, however, "it was agreed that we should keep in touch with Djonovitch and our other friends in the Yugoslav and Bulgarian Opposition and give them discreet support as a reinsurance against the possible defection of Prince Paul or King Boris." (Amery, 212)

"The Djonovitch proposals for overthrowing Prince Paul and King Boris and replacing them with men committed against the Germans" became actual when Mussolini attacked Greece [on 28 October 1940]. (Amery 198)

Agenda of the Democratic Party

As examined above, the President of the Party, Milan Grol, preferred to preventively attack Bulgaria in the case of German troops passing through her, and was ready to resist the Axis' forces if they attacked Yugoslavia. His Party also was "subsidized" by the British since January 1941. (Vodušek Starič, 214-15) However, during the formation of the Putschist Government on 27 March 1941, Grol declared in favor of peace, not war.

Next, here is what the major military coup-wishers wrote about themselves.

General Bora Mirković's motivation and objectives

By mid-April 1941, Yugoslavia's leading Putsch-organizers were fleeing their country, hurriedly and ingloriously, while the country was being mercilessly defeated and dismembered by Germany and her allies. Brigadier General Borivoje-Bora Mirković was among the last to leave. After having been seriously injured in a crash-landing in Greece, he was moved to Egypt. Subsequently, he wrote his memoirs which were signed and dated in Cairo on 1 December 1941.

- **Writing memoirs with post-coup experience, March – November 1941**

The motives and goals of the **civilian coup-wishers**, presented above, were expressed before the coup and without impact of the post-coup events on the wishers. By 1 December 1941, events in Yugoslavia had already determined the future war-time developments:
   • the genocidal persecutions of the Serbs, Jews and Gypsies in the Independent State of Croatia, caused existentially-motivated reactions of the persecuted;
   • the Comintern's directives from Moscow to the Communist Parties in Yugoslavia to assist the German-invaded Soviet Union, the "fortress of World Communism" and the "leading socialist country", resulted in the formation of the Communist-led-and-controlled Partisans;
   • the politically-motivated reactions of the Serbs in occupied Serbia generated the formation of the Četnik forces, with the intention of restoring the defeated state and the previous social order;
   • the formation of the Soviet-style Republic of Užice in occupied Serbia, with the intention of implementing Communist-revolutionary goals, was covered under an appealing call for "national liberation";
   • Germany's pacification of occupied Serbia produced the bloodiest reprisals in the whole of occupied Europe;
   • the un-compromising, un-reconcilable civil wars, the outcome of which was more important to each side than their contribution to the Western Allies' causes, marked the beginning of tremendous loss of human lives, the memory of which may live for centuries;
   • the British war leaders initiated resistance policies to fit their short-term military goals, regardless of the objectives of the disunited Yugoslav Government in exile and the "resistance movements" within the country. Former Section D operative Duane T. Hudson was sent to Yugoslavia on 20 September 1941 (Mission *Bullseye*). He met both Tito and Mihailović, who met twice, before Mirković signed his memoirs.

How much was Mirković aware of all those events and of their significance? What were his reactions to them, and to what extent did they affect his writing? It is not clear from the memoirs. It can be reasonably assumed that he wanted to explain and justify his own activities related to the coup of 27 March 1941. (The memoirs were later edited by Petar Bosnić, in Belgrade, in 1996.)

Some of Mirković's assertions were critically commented, derided, and/or contradicted by Simović after his return to Belgrade in 1945. An analysis of their personal relations is outside the scope of this book. However, quite relevant are Mirković's motivations and objectives, and his pre-coup contacts with the British in Belgrade. Although he revealed some of these contacts, he did not offer details about them. While he was claiming a need for "the Putsch of people's liberation", his British contacts had quite a different goal in mind.

- **First take power in Belgrade by force ...**

Summarized here are the General's motivations and objectives, as he described them in his memoirs of 1941.

He was convinced that sick ambitions of the Prince Regent [Paul Karađorđević] and his wife [Princess Olga] were going against the people's vital interests and that they – not shrinking from anything – were even conspiring against the head of the young King Peter. (Bosnić(ed), 14)

In order to achieve a real liberation of the people from all evil which, as some monster, had been oppressing the life of the people, it was necessary first to take power in Belgrade by force, to overturn the regime, and to bring in new people who would create a new, better and safer order in the land. (Bosnić(ed), 15)

> ((Everything that was dragging the land into the mud for a decade had to be – according to my notion – drowned in blood, mercilessly, to the last culprit, even if it involved up to a million of them.))
> «Sve ono što je vuklo zemlju u blato desetinu godina trebalo je, po mojoj zamisli, da se utopi u krvi, bespoštedno i do poslednjeg krivca, pa makar to išlo i do miliona.» (Bosnić(ed), 15)

- **... then give the power to the Generals Simović and Ilić, ...**

However, as Mirković put it, he was thinking and deliberating for many years who were the individuals in the military - he did not know politicians - who could be considered for the salvation of the country. Two men were attracting his attention: Generals Dušan Simović – his superior in the Air Force, and Bogoljub Ilić. At that time there were no more illustrious names and greater characters. He firmly believed that these two men, in whom he believed endlessly, could in critical times take over the guidance of the affairs of the state. Therefore he was elevating their names to the Himalayan heights and was placing them along the deities of Olympus. (Bosnić(ed), 19-20)

Mirković, himself, did not want to assume power on 27 March 1941 under any circumstances; he desired his effort to benefit the people but remain absolutely anonymous. (Bosnić(ed), 20)

(Yet he wrote the memoirs so his deeds could be known by posterity!)

So, to achieve a real 'liberation of the people', it was necessary first to take over power in Belgrade by force, to overturn the regime, and to bring in new people who would create a new, better and safer order in the land. (Bosnić(ed), 15)

- **... and expect the victory**

Later, in 1960, in a letter to the Belgrade's *Evening News*, Mirković forgot *everything that was dragging the land into the mud for a decade,* and stated his political motivation:

> ((My conviction at that time was that our destiny in that war had to be tied to the destiny of the Great western powers, not to the destiny of Hitler's Nazi Germany, because I was foreseeing that the final victory in the war would belong to the Western Powers.))
> «Moje je uverenje tada bilo da se naša sudbina u ondašnjem ratu morala da veže za sudbinu Velikih zapadnih sila, a ne za sudbinu nacističke Hitlerove Nemačke, jer sam predviđao da će krajnja pobeda u ratu pripasti Zapadnim silama.» (Karapandžić(AB), 146)

Thus, like other coup-plotters, Mirković was also ready to expose the country to the war in the expectation of a final victory.

*****

While Mirković characterized the Coup of the 27th of March as "the Putsch of people's liberation", in 1941 he also stated his view on the relation between the Coup and the «German new order»:

> ((The 27th March is our people's necessity and that day ought to have been a turning point between the sick people's organism and its definitive healing.
> ((Had the German new order allowed us to make that possible and accomplished, perhaps that would have been better for both the German race and the German policy.))
> «27 mart je naša narodna nužda i taj dan trebao je da bude prekretnica između bolesnog narodnog organizma i njegovog definitivnog isceljenja.
> «Da nam je nemački novi poredak dozvolio da to omogućimo i sprovedemo, možda bi to bilo bolje i za nemačku rasu i za nemačku politiku.» (Bosnić(ed), 20)

How would have the German new order allow the healing of the Yugoslavia's sick organism by tying Yugoslavia to the Great Western powers, who were going to win the war – perhaps only Mirković had figured out, but did not describe it.

General Dušan Simović's motives and goals

- " ... my heart replied without meditation ... "

Referring to their meeting on 24 January 1941, Simović recollected – some ten years later - a question posed by Donovan and his answer:

> (("And on which side will Yugoslavia fight in the case of war?" I did not expect this question and was surprised, but my heart replied without meditation: "I do not know what those higher in authority think, but I can tell you only one [thing]: that our people will never betray our friends and allies from the past war."))... (Simović(51), 6-7. Bold type in the source.)

So, firmly set not to *betray our friends and allies* from the First World War, Simović went out to contact *eminent, important* people to convince them of Prince Paul's treacherous policies. If the Prince would not change them, his Government ought to be toppled – even by force, if necessary. So Simović first went to see the Patriarch, then other eminent people – whose names he did not mention in his speech on 28 March 1941. Reportedly, they all agreed *in principle* with his recommendations, including a coup by the military: *in principle* only - which means that they made no actual commitment, and that no time for the coup was discussed or set. Somebody else - not those eminent, important people - made the decision and determined the date. In his speech on 28 March Simović revealed some details on who did what; some other participants in the coup did likewise.

Simović's trusted former aide-de-camp, Captain Dragiša N. Ristić, stated that Simović had *"started giving thought to revolution"* in January 1941. (Ristić, 84) That coincides with the General's meeting with Donovan. Simović himself wrote that he had begun preparing his action *since the end of January*. (Simović(44), 33) That was two months *before* Yugoslavia signed the Tripartite Pact in Vienna.

Simović's claim *after the coup* that he did not denounce the Pact, because he wanted to gain time for full mobilization of the army, implied his thinking that the mobilization would have been helpful. This argument sounded hollow in light of his own frequent admission that Yugoslavia was militarily quite inferior to Germany, and could not resist her successfully. Thus, for example, he claimed to have been talking with Bill Donovan, on 24 January 1941, about *the dangers of Yugoslavia's situation and the insufficiency of the Yugoslav forces for a decisive defense*. (Simović(51), 6) Aware of all that in January - and not receiving any arms from Britain and America in the meantime - how did he expect to defend the country in March – even if he had time for a full mobilization? (More on this subject was written by Živan Knežević, and presented below.)

The Putschists - fully aware of Germany's tremendous military superiority over Yugoslavia - knew that the coup, and siding with Britain, *at that time and under those conditions,* meant war. Simović himself acknowledged that in later conversations with the British and a later to Churchill.

((The overthrow will mean the thwarting of Hitler's plans, and it is likely that Hitler will attack us ...))   (Knežević, 88)

The fundamental cause of the ensuing tragedy was the fact that the Putschists exposed the country to the war - notwithstanding their knowledge of Yugoslavia's military inferiority. Their vision of a victory at the end of the war disabled their reasoned analysis of the situation: Great Britain had no treaty of alliance with Yugoslavia, and therefore no obligation toward her, and could not provide badly needed military assistance. Donovan's making a list of arms needed by Yugoslavia was no guarantee of their availability for Yugoslavia, nor of a timely delivery, if at all.

*****

On 22 March 1941, Minister Campbell reported from Belgrade to the Foreign Secretary Eden that General Simović was the only military man capable of leading the opposition movement against Prince Paul's government. (PRO, PREMIER 3, 570-11)

In the evening of 23 March 1941, Simović had a lengthy conversation with Prince Paul at the Palace.

After 7 p.m. on 26 March - Simović wrote - he told Col. Dragutin Savić, his Chief of Staff:
((We have to be aware that, starting with tomorrow, our entire people are actually stepping on their new Golgotha, and that we'll have to expect at least three years of exile in our prolonged fight against the enemy.)) (Simović(44), 40)

On 27 March 1941, he became the head of the new Government.

On 11 January 1942, Simović's Putschist government fell for a variety of reasons (which are not part of the subject of this book).

On 9 July 1942, General Simović wrote to Churchill, putting himself at the Prime Minister's disposal: "I would like to offer you my services with the ardent wish to help the common cause to my utmost ability." Probably alluding to Churchill's statement after the coup on 27 March 1941 that *the Yugoslav nation found its soul*, the General wrote that he had been passionately fond of his military profession, and added: "I assumed a political position on the memorial March 27th 1941, to *save the soul* and honour of my country, ... I took on the grave responsibility for the military defeat *which was to be foreseen and inevitable* but which I was convinced would be of the utmost valued for the allied cause, ..." (Simović - Churchill correspondence, 1942-1956, Box 2, Hoover Institution Archives. Italics added.)

"To save the soul and honor of the country", Simović wrote that he wanted to be of the "*utmost value for the allied cause"* – although Yugoslavia had no alliance with Britain. The British Prime Minister, a realist, was not sentimental toward *allies from the past war,* nor toward the *men who gave "Hitler a bloody nose"* in the new one. Not being useful any more, Simović was dropped – his contribution in heading the Putsch notwithstanding. Thus on 25 August, 1942, Churchill coolly declined the General's offer. Given Simović's devotion to the supposed 'great Allies', this refusal from Churchill probably was a bitter pill for him to swallow.

Thus the General found himself without a specific assignment, responsibility or authority, while strategic political changes related to Yugoslavia were taking shape. In the fall of 1943, the once-glorified resistance fighter, General Draža Mihailović (who was inadequately supplied by the British, incapable and unwilling to execute every British assignment which was designed to promote British short-range military goals, regardless of the detrimental consequences for the people in Yugoslavia) was replaced in the British strategic policies by the leader of the Communist Party of Yugoslavia, Josip Broz Tito, and the Communist-led Partisans.

The most important British missions to Tito were headed by Bill Deakin (on 27 May 1943), and Brigadier Fitzroy Maclean (on 18 September 1943). Support of Tito was formally approved at the Teheran Conference (28 November -1 December 1943).)

So, by the time Simović completed writing his memoirs while still in exile, he was much better and more completely informed about the events that affected Yugoslavia since the coup of the 27th March, 1941, than was Mirković, when he wrote his memoirs. Probably only Simović knew whether or not the changes in Churchill's policy toward Yugoslavia had colored his own thinking and writing of the memoirs.

- **As stated in Simović's memoirs of 1 January 1944**

The memoirs written in exile contain, among other topics, the General's description of the conversation with the Prince Regent on 23 March 1941, which shows his motivations and goals. Here are some excerpts on this theme:

> ((... In the sole desire to serve, at that moment, as usefully as possible to my people, from whom I hailed and, to my beloved Fatherland, which is to me above everything else, and ready to gladly sacrifice even my life for them; and without any personal ambitions and pretensions - without any vacillation I have gone even farther towards the goal which corresponded to the feeling and aspiration of the people, assuming full responsibility before the people and history for the ensuing consequences. I considered that, in that way, I was only doing my duty! ...))
> " ... ... U jedinoj želji da u tome trenutku što korisnije poslužim svome narodu iz koga sam ponikao i svojoj ljubljenoj Otadžbini, koja mi je iznad svega, i spreman da i svoj život rado žrtvujem za njih; a bez ikakvih ličnih ambicija i pretenzija, - ja sam bez ikakvog kolebanja pošao i dalje ka cilju koji je odgovarao osećanju i težnji naroda, preduzimajući na sebe punu odgovornost pred narodom i istorijom za dalje posledice. Smatrao sam da time samo vršim svoju dužnost! ..." (Simović(44), 32-3)

However, behind these high-principled motivations there was a purely political calculation for his *taking the people on the road to Golgotha and suffering.* He told Prince Paul, on the evening of 23 March, that he was ((convinced that the final victory was England's. England loses all battles except the last one.)) "... ubedjen sam da će krajna pobeda biti Engleska. Engleska gubi sve bitke sem poslednje." (Simović(44), 15)

To the Prince's remark that Yugoslavia was weak and unprepared to withstand Hitler, and that her campaign had no chance of success, Simović replied:

> ((Without doubt, the German military might is so strong today that we can not resist it with a chance of success, no matter how ready we are. Not even France, much stronger than we, well armed and protected by the mightily fortified Maginot Line, could withstand the German assault. We have to deal with that fact. Therefore, our material strength can not play a decisive role; it can influence only the duration of our organized resistance within the country. *Our strength is in the victory of our great Allies* and in the great morale force of our people to endure in this struggle. There is nothing left for us but to form the Salonika Front again, and for the people and those forces that are left within the country, to withdraw into the mountains and to continue the campaign by a guerrilla warfare which is ... very suitable for the defender with high morale and determined to continue the struggle.)) (Smović(44), 18. Italics added.)

As he wrote to Churchill, Simović had been aware in March 1941 that the military defeat of Yugoslavia was *foreseen and inevitable,* yet he opted for the war anyway, because *"England loses all bottles except the last one. Our strength is in the victory of our great Allies."* (*"Naša jačina leži u pobedi naših velikih Saveznika...."*) Like some civilian "oppositionists", Simović also was willing to expose the people and the country to the devastation of war, calculating that all losses and sacrifices would be remedied by the victory at the end.

*****

Simović's ideas of guerrilla warfare in the occupied Yugoslavia, expressed to Prince Paul on 23 March 1941, had a lot in common with the SOE's plans for the *post-occupational resistance,* promoted by George Taylor.

These post-occupational guerrilla plans could not to be realized. Taylor's expectations of such resistance, envisioned in his Report to Sir Frank Nelson of 26 February 1941, were quickly dispersed as the people who were expected to organize it hurriedly left the country. SOE's Sandy Glen had foreseen a failure of armed resistance already on 2 August 1940, in a letter to his superior, Bill Bailey:

> As you well know, lack of anti-aircraft and anti-tank guns places the Yugoslav army in no position to offer opposition to a German attack. Some talk of resistance from the hills of old Serbia, involving gallant memories of a war that is past. That resistance too, I am convinced would be quickly broken for Yugoslavia has no air force to oppose what would be the systematic low level bombing and machine-gunning of every village and every road.(Great Britain, Special Operations Executive, 91087-10V. Hoover Institution Archives) **(Part One, Appendix E.)**

Motivation of the Knežević brothers

At the very beginning of his book, Živan Knežević placed himself and his friends at the center of events:

> ((It is not possible to establish with confidence on what day *the idea was conceived with my friends and me* to prevent Yugoslavia's crossing over to the camp of Germany and Italy by an intervention of the army.
> ((In any case, it could not have been long before the end of 1940. Until than nobody was thinking that Prince Paul, ... , could stand at the side of Hitler and Mussolini in their clash with the Western Powers.))

> "Nije mogućno utvrditi s pouzdanjem koga se dana, *kod mojih prijatelja i mene*, začela misao da intervencijom vojske sprečimo prelazak Jugoslavije u tabor Nemačke i talije.
> "U svakom slučaju to nije moglo biti mnogo pre kraja 1940. godine. Dotle nije nikome dolazilo na um da bi knez Pavle, ... , mogao stati uz bok Hitleru I Musoliniju u njihovom sukobu sa Zapadnim Silama." (Knežević, 13. Italics added.)

As shown above, he was wrong: Đonović and others discussed such plan with Julian Amery in June 1940 before the German-Yugoslav negotiations even began. Amery detailed the topic in his book, published six years **before** Živan's. But Živan was not eager to find out and present many such facts. Throughout his book and other writings he was consistent in the unwarranted promotion of himself and his brother, "Professor" Radoje.

According to Živan's writing at an unspecified time long **after** the war:
In the beginning of 1941, Hitler had 240 "unemployed" divisions, 186 of which were of first-class quality, excellently armed, equipped and even better trained. Morale was at a level hardly ever seen in history.
Yugoslavia had 29 poorly armed infantry divisions, 3 cavalry divisions, 17 infantry detachments and 2 cavalry brigades, 100 old-fashioned, light, 12-ton tanks from the First world war; 200 modern aircraft. A 3,000 kilometer-long front was to be defended by only 400 anti-armor weapons. Thus,

> ((the second conclusion that we the conspirators accepted was: Yugoslavia will be broken in the shortest time, but that such a short resistance will make *us to be on the victorious side after the war.*))
> "drugi zaključak koji smo mi zaverenici prihvatili bio je: da će Jugoslavija biti slomljena za najkraće vreme, ali da će tako kratak otpor učiniti *da budemo na pobeničkoj strani posle rata."* (Milunović(ed), 39. Italics added.)

- **The Kneževićs expected a short war with Germany**

When, in early summer of 1940, Jovan Đonović first suggested the overthrow of Prince Paul's Government (**Part One, Appendix D**), he told Julian Amery that *the Serbs would give good account of themselves in a war.* (**Chapter 4**)

Giving good account of oneself in a war, that *might be lost* - but *might* also be won - implies a war of some duration. In a short war one might not have enough time and opportunity to give a good account of himself.

According to Živan, as stated above, the conspirators expected that *a short resistance* to Germany would make them the victors at the end of the war. (Milunović(ed), 39) Perhaps some of them did expect only a short war, or after the war they pretended so, in order to avoid the accountability for the consequences of the war. They did not factor into their expectations the centrifugal tendencies in the country that were so visible and so active for some time, and some of them were supported from abroad.
Once again: they were willing to expose the people and the country to a war with tremendously superior enemy, in order to share the spoils of victory. They had *"unconditionally believed in the victory of the Allies".* (Milunović(ed), 39)

The Putschists: Participants in victory ...

To "*share in the fruits of victory*" did not motivate only Mirković, Simović, SPP, Đonović –Trifunović & friends. In the late 1980s journalist Milo Gligorijević had the following exchange with one of the known putschists, Major Nikola Kosić (translated):

MG: ((Were you, the putschists, foreseeing the consequences? Were you expecting the war?))
NK: ((We were. You will see that in my diary, that is written also in Živan's [Knežević's] book. We were thinking that the Western Powers would help us. We knew: *if you wish to be a participant in the victory, you must take part in the war.*))
MG: ((Did you know how much the country was weakened by intra-national and political friction?))
NK: ((We did know, of course. We knew what was happening in Croatia. ... I saw Zagreb covered with paroles LLAP: Long Live Ante Pavelić! ...)) (Kosić(N), 81. Italics added.)

Suggested conclusion: because the Major did not see an Englishman, and neither did the Professor, so the Putschists were not British marionettes! However, the Professor **did** work as a propagandist with an Englishman, Thomas Masterson.

If Major Kosić did not know in 1941 of the British role in the coup, by the late 1970s a lot of relevant information could be found in British sources, like the books by Hugh Dalton, Bickham Sweet-Escott , Julian Amery, Alexander Glen – instigators of the coup. It seems that Major N. Kosić did not want to find that out ... or admit it, just like the brothers Knežević.

If not as marionettes, the Putschists did serve the British purposes. *Sharing in an expected victory* was one of their basic motivations. The British understood that well and behaved accordingly:

> And if we were to work through such bodies it was necessary first of all to convince them that *a British victory would help them to achieve their political objectives.*" (Sweet-Escott, 29. Italics added.)

Diversity of motivations and goals

The above brief analysis shows clearly that - although they all expected to partake in the victory at the end of the war - specific plans and future goals of the principal coup-wishers-planners were diverse. Lacking unifying goals could not produce a unified common objective for the new Government. Retaining the Croatian, Slovenian, and Muslim representatives from the previous Government - as duly elected representatives of the people - served the purpose of claiming democratic character for the new concentration Government. However, those duly elected representatives were known to be in favor of the acceptance of the Tripartite Pact which did not contain "military clauses" and which guaranteed the sovereignty and territorial integrity of Yugoslavia. (The Protocol of Adhesion to the pact, **Part One, pages 124-6**) Thus from the very day of the Putsch there was lack of the clarity and unity of the purpose and of further proceedings of the new Government. While most Ministers wanted peace, Simović wanted to side with Britain – which meant war. He was persistent: *"England loses all bottles except the last one. Our strength is in the victory of our great Allies."* With that in mind, he took the country into the war knowing that the defeat was *foreseen and inevitable* – as he confessed to Churchill.

He was so committed to the British plans of the moment, that - based on his own statements -

Simović missed a chance to harm the Axis' war effort .

In his memoirs written in London, Simović devoted several pages to his conversation with Col. William Donovan on 24 January 1941. *"It is my conviction"* - he wrote *inter alia*:

> ((That Hitler will attack Soviet Russia as his principal enemy during the course of this year; that the attack must begin at the earliest, at the latest in the month of May, so he would have time to complete the anticipated operations before the onset of winter in Russia; ...))
> "Da će Hitler u toku ove godine napasti Sovjetsku Rusiju, kao svog glavnog neprijatelja; da taj napad mora otpočeti što pre, najdalje meseca maja, kako bi imao vremena da predviđene operacije završi pre nastupanja zime u Rusiji; ... " (Simović(44), 8)

Back in Belgrade, responding to the questions posed to Gen. Simović by *Institut za istorijska pitanja (The Institute for Historical Questions)* on 14 June 1951, relating to his conversation with Col. William Donovan in January 1941, the General described - quite lengthily - his foresight about Hitler's grandiose plan for subduing the world. Thus he pointed out

> ((the inevitability of [Hitler's] attack on the Soviet Russia)), and ((the peril of our position and the insufficiency of our forces for a resolute defense)).
> "neminovnost [Hitlerovog] napada na Sovjetsku Rusiju" and "opasnost našeg položaja i nedovoljnost naših snaga za odlučnu odbranu", (Simović(51), 6)

Answering the Institute's questions about Prince Paul, the General said that, **about the middle of March,** the Prince had invited him twice to the Palace. On both occasions the General was outlining to the Prince Hitler's probable intentions, and a possible flow of events, the way he was describing them to Col. Donovan,

> ((and I was reassuring him [the Prince] that Hitler would attack the Soviet Russia, that he would collapse there and that 'England loses all battles except the last one')).
> "i uveravao ga [Princa] da će Hitler napasti Sovjetsku Rusiju, da će tamo propasti i da 'Engleska gubi sve bitke sem poslednje' ", (Simović(51), 9)

It is noteworthy that in the statement given in Belgrade Simović did not specify the month of May as the time of Hitler's attack. However, whether in May or some other time, the essence of his reported warning was that Germany's attack would happen in the near future. Convinced of that – and, in his own words, aware of the perilous position of Yugoslavia and of the insufficiency of her military strength, why did Simović not wait for the overwhelmingly superior German war machine to get engaged in the war, and then execute the coup – if he thought that the overthrow of the Government had been the best thing for Yugoslavia and the Allies? Insufficiency of Yugoslavia's military power meant a sure defeat - he knew that (and wrote to Churchill about it on 9 July 1942) - but, like other coup-wishers-plotters, he too was committed to the British plans and policies.

As shown in **Part One, page 102,** Hitler stated at the conference preceding the formulation of *Directive No. 25* that *if the overthrow of the [Yugoslav] government would have happened during the Barbarossa-action* [invasion of the Soviet Union], *the consequences for us would have been considerably more serious.* (The Avalon Project. Nazi Conspiracy and Aggression – Document No. 1746. Italics added; Churchill(GA), 163)

Thus, based on his own reported foresight, Simović missed to cause *considerably more serious consequences* to Germany's war efforts.

*****

In his memoirs written in exile, (Simović(44), Simović did not mention the two audiences with the Prince "about the middle of March". In this account, (Simović(51), he noted precisely the date of 23 March of his meeting with the Prince, but provided no dates for the middle-March meetings. However, Simović's claimed prediction of Hitler's forthcoming attack on the Soviet Union was no news to the Prince. On 30 March 1941, the American Minister in Belgrade reported to the State Department that he had been informed by a reliable source "that Hitler said to Prince ... Yugoslavia must sign Tripartite Pact in own interest as in June or July he was going to attack Russia." The British Minister in Belgrade had the same information. (FRUS1, 973) **(Part One, 87)**

In 1951 the General also stated that Prince Paul

> ((Personally he held more secret meetings with Hitler, Göring and Ribbentrop, at which talks were conducted about Yugoslavia's joining the Tripartite Pact. ... Information about those talks and decisions are not known, but it is certain that some specific personal promises were being made to Prince Paul. ...))
> "Lično je održao više tajnih sastanaka s Hitlerom, Geringom i Ribentropom, na kojima su vođeni razgovori o pristupanju Jugoslavije Trojnom sporazumu ... Podaci o tim razgovorima i odlukama nisu poznati, ali je sigurno da su Knezu Pavlu činjena naročita lična obećanja. ..."
> (Simović(51), 9)

The claims of mutiple meetings were not substantiated, and "personal promises" allegations were used also by Gen. Mirković in his attack on Prince Paul, but not proven.

Chapter 9

Preparing for the *coup d'état* of 27 March 1941

When Baron Julian Amery visited Yugoslavia half a century after the Belgrade coup, he commented that there was "stuff in the British archives that would make your hair stand on end ". (Onslow, 17) There is no chance of that happening any more, because a lot of the original SOE archives - relating to Yugoslavia as well - have been lost. It is estimated that between 85% - 87% of the material was lost because of various reasons. (Onslow, 17n40) Lacking are certain key files, including SOE's financial records and the North African records; some had been "weeded" out, some deliberately destroyed, "and others had perished in the mysterious fire which had engulfed SOE's Baker Street headquarters in January 1946." (West(sw), 4) "By the 1970s, no less than 87 per cent of the original [SOE] archives had been lost to the posterity." (Neville Wylie)

Consequently, **the whole story** of Britain's *desperate efforts* in Yugoslavia cannot be fully documented.

The whole, true, unbiased story of the roles of domestic "friends" of Britain in these *British desperate efforts* is not revealed in their own accounts and memoirs. The Putschists: Simović, Mirković, brothers Knežević, Dragiša Ristić - among others - spoke or wrote about their actions at various times after the Putsch. For diverse reasons, the Putschists disagreed among themselves on some important specifics about the events and their personal roles in them. Simović saw himself in the leading, starring role – and saw Mirković in a supporting one. Mirković did just the opposite. The Knežević brothers claimed the roles and importance which the Simović-Mirković camp persistently denied. None of their accounts can be considered unbiased and all-inclusive.

Hopefully, additional information - **if** and when available - would make the story more complete and informative, which would be most welcome.

What follows is a partially documented story based on the information contained in the sources identified in this book. The path from the initial proposal to the execution of the coup was traced, in general lines, in **Part One**. Before going into a more detailed examination, here is

a reminder of the flow of major events:

Initial proposal for the coup was made to the British **in June-July 1940**, in Belgrade, by the opponents of Prince Paul's regime and policies. The British Government preserved the offer for a more opportune time.

In July 1940, the British began financing the Serbian Peasant Party and afterwards other opposition parties and organizations. This proved to be instrumental in promoting and implementing British plans and policies.

On October 28, Italy attacked Greece from Albania, thus creating a new situation in the Balkans.

In November, the British Cabinet came up with the "Balkan Front" plan to induce Turkey and Yugoslavia in a common front with Greece against Germany.

In December 1940, Churchill told Dalton that the Balkan situation "was the acid test for SOE". That resulted in the decision to send George Taylor to the Balkans to direct SOE's activities there. One of Taylor's tasks was, "to continue the work, *already well in hand, of encouraging the Yugoslav opposition parties to bring pressure to bear on the Government in a sense favourable to this country.*"

On 24 January 1941, American Colonel William Donovan had an influential meeting with General Simović.

On 19 February 1941, Foreign Secretary, Anthony Eden, and the Chief of the Imperial General Staff, General Sir John Dill, arrived in Cairo with the mission of organizing the Balkan Front.

After the conference with the Greeks at Tatoi palace **on 22/23 February**, Eden reported to Churchill that he would attempt "to persuade the Yugoslav Government *to play their part.*" (Carlton, 175-6. Italics added.)

On 24 February Prince Paul agreed to visit Hitler. (van Creveld, 127) Churchill cabled to Eden 'while being under no illusion, we all send you order "Full steam ahead".' (Rhodes James, 251)

Failure of Eden's first mission to Turkey, **26 February – 1 March. (Part One, 81)**

On 27 February, George Taylor arrived in Belgrade and took over SOE operations in Yugoslavia, with a resolute "attempt to persuade the Yugoslav Government *to play their part.*"

"*On his arrival Taylor assessed pro-British Serb public opinion as SOE's best hope of influencing the Yugoslav government's policy.*" So, influencing Serb public opinion was the name of the game. The propaganda and "subsidies" were the means to play it. SOE aimed to deter Prince Paul from signing the Tripartite Pact by means of political agitation and propaganda; if that failed, then stage a coup against him. These efforts were analyzed in preceding chapters. The examination of the flow of the coup-related events, and who did what among the coup-plotters and executors, is continued here.

In Ankara, **26 February - 1 March**, Eden unsuccessfully attempted to induce Turkey to join the Balkan Front.

On 1 March Churchill instructed Eden: "Your main appeal should now be made to Yugoslavia."

On 2 March the German troops crossed the Danube from Rumania into Bulgaria on their way to attack Greece. Yugoslavia was totally encircled by the Tripartite Pact troops. **The same day** Churchill thoroughly approved an SOE plan to support the coup against Prince Paul, *if and when the Pact is signed*. Hugh Dalton, responsible for SOE operations, was duty-bound to order his head man in Belgrade, George Taylor, to do so.

> ...the hazards of getting the expeditionary force to Greece were great enough: the transport of 68,000 troops required the use of fifty ships **from 4 March to 24 April. (#)** With the Suez Canal blocked by German mines all sorts of cargo was delayed, including coal for the Greek railways, fuel oil for the Fleet, and war material for Greece and Turkey. Several projects were proposed to bypass the Canal, create new ports, and construct railway routes, but they all required time, which [General] Wavell did not have. (Higham, 153)
>
> **(#)** Six merchantmen ships and the light cruiser *Bonaventure* would be lost.

On 4 March the British Anti Aircraft and administrative units arrived in Greece. (Higham, 146) Prince Paul met Hitler.

In London **on 5 March,** Cabinet members heard that Eden admitted now that "the situation in Greece had deteriorated considerably. ..." (Higham, 155) **(Part One, 90)**

9-12 March, Major Milisav Perišić's had an unsuccessful mission in Athens. **(Part One, 96-7)**

"Agitation against the pact became vociferous from early March on." (Barker, 91)

An unrealistic political program, 11 March 1941

As shown in **Chapter 13,** below, in mid-February 1941 the SOE's head-man in Belgrade, Thomas Masterson, and Radoje Knežević discussed the possibility of developing propaganda – as the British wanted it, of course. (Radoje later clamed that in Yugoslavia he had not seen an Englishman at all, and had not known the name of any. **(Chapter 13)**) Never mentioning this Radoje's cooperation with the SOE, Živan Knežević wrote some thirty eight years later:

On 10 March 1941, [i.e. about four weeks after Radoje's meeting with Masterson] in Radoje's home, the brothers Knežević discussed a political program until dawn.

That night they concluded that a fundamental change had been needed. In their view, intervention of the military has to signify not only a different orientation in foreign policy, but also a return to normal democratic order. The military has to overthrow the present government and hand power to the true representatives of the people. Radoje formulated these concepts into the following proposal:

1. The regency is abolished and the King is proclaimed of age.
2. His mother, Queen Mary, should return back to the country [from England].
3. Prince Paul and his family are immediately expelled from the country.
4. The government is to be formed by the men delegated by the chiefs of the political parties.
5. Retain the Croats and the Slovenes [from the present government], in order to give the new Government a wide national basis.
6. General Simović will immediately address a proclamation to the people (the content of which should be agreed upon). It should state that the country will be governed by a concentration Government until the people representatives are elected.

7. The first decree of the new Government should be the decree about the general mobilization, so that "the probable German attack would not find us unprepared". (Knežević,87-89)

As Živan stated, the brothers expected that ((The overthrow [of the existing Government] will mean the thwarting of Hitler's plans, and it is likely that Hitler will attack us ...)) "Prevrat će značiti osujećenje Hitlerovih planova, i verovatno je da će nas Hitler napasti, ..." As for the timing of the coup, the preparations should start immediately when the agreement is reached, but the overthrow should be executed at the time of "the conclusion of the military alliance with the Powers of the Tripartite Pact." (Knežević, 88) That corresponds to the order from London:

"If and when the Regent signed a deal with Hitler, SOE undercover agents in Belgrade would support a *coup d'état",* (Stafford(C), 211-12) - was Hugh Dalton's order to SOE Belgrade after his meeting with Churchill at Chequers on 2 March 1941. (**Part One, 85-86**)

The brothers agreed that Živan would take this proposal to the Air Force Command the next day. He did so and showed it to Gen. Mirković. He, in turn, showed it to Gen. Simović, and then informed Živan that Simović accepted the proposal as written. (Knežević, 89)

For Mirković personally, however, it was important to overthrow the government, and everything else was secondary. (Knežević, 193n2)

IF the brothers indeed proposed this plan, *and expected Hitler's attack,* how could they assume to have enough time for an effective mobilization and to "turn to normal democratic order" through an election of the representatives?

(It will be shown subsequently that Gen. Mirković had described Radoje's role in the preparation of the Putsch differently.)

Now back to the flow of major events.

On 17 March Hitler "decided to occupy the whole of Greece in order to eject them [the British] (Hinsley *et al*, 364) **Also on 17 March**, Yugoslav Foreign Minister, "told the German Minister [in Belgrade] that the Crown Council had decided in principle to join the Tripartite Pact". (Eden, 225)

By 18 March "S.O.E. had come to the conclusion that it would almost certainly be necessary to bring down the Cvetković government." (Barker, 91-2; 282n86)

18 March – Eden's unsuccessful talks with the Turks on Cyprus. (**Part One, 106**)

At the all-British round-table meeting **on 19 March** it was decided:
- SOE to continue with preparation for the coup working primarily through Tupanjanin ["Uncle"] and Serbian Peasant Party, to organize politico-military movement;
- but also to coordinate the action with Trifunović-Birčanin ["Daddy"];
- the Service Attachés to work with the military elements.

For us [the British], it was quite simple: there was work to be done. Air Attaché Hugh Macdonald and his assistant Tom Mapplebeck virtually disappeared; Charlie Clark [Military Attaché] scarcely left the Yugoslav General Staff; while the rest of what were now 24-hour working days were spent with Tupanjanin and his friends. (Glen(B), 59)

The first stage of the plan was to encourage resignation of as many Ministers as possible to force a government crisis. ... (Stafford(cp), 411) (**Part One, 108-10**)

On 20 March, three Ministers resigned. The resignation "was the work of SOE in close co-ordination with Tupanjanin." (Onslow, 45; Eden, 226)

The resignation **on the 20th March** failed to cause the fall of the Yugoslav Government. All coup-plotters, military and civilians, were fully aware of this failure. When the resignation failed, SOE concluded that "the only possible course was to bring off a *coup d'état."* (Stafford(cp), 411-12)

So the *firm hand* of George Taylor began *drawing all the strings together so that the best possible use might be made of SOE's contacts by those who were to direct it* - as Sweet-Escott described it. The Legation personnel, SOE-men, *and everyone with whom SOE had contact,* had been urged for the coup.

Hugh Dalton wrote in his *Memoirs*: **on March 20th**. *"We sent a wire to our friends to use all means to raise a revolution."* (Dalton, 373. Emphasis added.)

In a conversation with Prince Paul and Princess Olga **during the evening of 20 March,** American Minister Arthur Bliss Lane used whatever argument he could think of to convince the Prince to refuse to sign the Pact and the **next day** reported their conversation to the State Department. The Prince argued that in the event of German invasion, Hungary, Bulgaria and Italy would partition the country with Germany. (FRUS1, 962-3)

On 21 March Campbell asked Eden. "If the German attack on Greece was not imminent, *would it be preferable to delay a coup* so as not to precipitate such an attack." (Stafford[cp], 403. Italics added.) Campbell could not dare to ask his Foreign Secretary that question unless he was capable of delaying the coup.

In his *Memoirs* Eden confirmed this:

On March 21st, Campbell telegraphed to ask me whether he should threaten to break off relations with Yugoslavia if the Government signed the Tripartite Pact, and so encourage the opposition to *overthrow the Government* and annul their signature. If I agreed the Ambassador wanted to know *when would it suit me*, from a military point of view, *for this to be done*. (Eden, 226. Italics added.)

At once, on 21 March, Eden replied "I agree that upon present information suggested *coup* would have to be staged at the moment of reaction caused by signature and this may be very soon." (Eden, 226)

Also on 21 March, Campbell "recommended that Serbo-Croatian broadcasts should adopt a stronger line, working on the feelings of the Serbs in particular, in order to (1) increase popular opposition to the signature, and (2) if the signature occurred, to ensure a 'vehement reaction'." (Stafford(cp), 402n12)

According to his account, **on 22 March, about 10 a.m.,** Simović intervened with Premier Cvetković against the adherence to the Tripartite Pact. (Simović[44], 11) **In the afternoon, the same day,** he talked with Dr. [Dragomir] Ikonić, " who, by joining the Government, had to hinder the signing of the Pact." (Simović(44), 14)

From London, **also on 22 March,** Prime Minister Churchill instructed Foreign Minister Eden "to get Yugoslavia in to the war anyhow". (PREM 3/510/11, no. 369) The instruction had to be taken most seriously by Eden, his Minister Campbell and all British personnel under his authority.

The same day Eden gave Campbell "authority to act on his own if he had no time" to consult Eden.

Chapter 10

SUNDAY, 23 MARCH 1941

One month after Eden (reporting to Churchill on the Tatoi conference with the Greeks) stated that he " should make a further effort to attempt to persuade the Yugoslav Government *to play their part.*" (Carlton, 175-6. Italics added.); and one day after the Prime Minister directed his Foreign Minister "to get Yugoslavia in to the war anyhow", (PREM 3/510/11, no. 369) – **the 23rd March 1941**, Belgrade was filled with considerable activities *attempting to persuade the Yugoslav Government to do what the British Government wanted them to do.* The most remarkable activities were those of Gen. Simović, the Jovan Đonović-Ilija Trifunović group, Gen. Mirković, and the British Air Force Attaché Macdonald. Theirs and related activities are examined below in order to provide a more complete accont of these events.

Campbell's use of SOE

On 23 March 1941, George Taylor assured London SOE "that Minister [Campbell] has made fullest use of SO2 and particularly of MASTERSON personally throughout the crisis." He added that "SO2 has undoubtedly made important contribution to the struggle to prevent signature [of the Pact] both as source of information and contacts, above all by work through TUPANJANIN, who has been heart and soul of the resistance." (Great Britain, Special Operation Executive, 91087 – 10.V, Hoover Institution Archives)

Đonović – Trifunović-Birčanin – Simović – Mirković connection

As shown in **Chapter 8**, when Julian Amery established a contact with Jovan Đonović in early summer of 1940, Đonović directed him to *Vojvoda* Trifunović-Birčanin. Đonović, a political figure, was staying in the background, while the *Vojvoda* was dealing with military men, especially in Serbia. In his report to Sir Frank Nelson on 26 February 1941, George Taylor provided evidence that *Vojvoda's* contact with high-ranking military personnel, reserve officers and Četniks, was a firm and on-going affair all along. After all, *Vojvoda* was the president of *Narodna Odbrana, (National Defence League).* His ties with the military were self-understood, and Đonović wrote about them in an article published in *Kanadski Srbobran* of 29 April 1952 (Knežević, 112-13n2)

Using information contained in this article and some reportedly given to him personally, Ž. Knežević reconstructed the following sequence of events:

• Probably on Friday, 21 March, Simović visited former Minister Božidar Maksimović and talked with him about the Tripartite Pact and the overthrow of the Government.

The Minister's maid, a Slovenian girl - who was eavesdropping the conversation - informed her parish priest about the conversation.

• The priest forwarded that information to Miha Krek, the Minister of Education, a Slovenian.

• Krek wrote a letter to Milan Antić, the Minister of the Court, informing him of Simović's intention to overthrow the Government and seizing the power.

The wife of Lt. Vojislav Perišić - a high-school teacher working the in cabinet of the Ministry of Education - informed her husband about Krek's letter.

• On Saturday, 22 March, Lt. Perišić revealed the information to Major Živan Knežević, who sent him, by taxi, to Zemun, to inform Gen. Mirković.

• On Sunday, 23 March, Minister Maksimović visited his friend Jovan Đonović – who in 1952 wrote about the visit in an article identified above. (Knežević, 102, 112-13n2)

According to that article:

Božidar Maksimović - who was informed about the preparations for the coup (Simović(51), 10) - visited his friend Đonović on 23rd March 1941, and told his friend that he had been informed that Air Force officers were preparing a coup; the visitor asked Đonović whether he knew General Simović. Informed that Đonović did not, the Minister asked him whether he could send a man of confidence to go to Simović and get more information.

Đonović responded affirmatively, and when the Minister left, he called *Vojvoda* Trifunović-Birčanin, who came in right away. Informing him of the preceding conversation, Đonović asked him to go to Simović and to relay to him Đonović's advice, which was:

> to explain to the Germans in advance that whatever happens was our internal affair, not pointed against Germany, and to ask the British how they could help if Hitler attacked us.

The *Vojvoda* called Simović to set an appointment. When the General confirmed to him that indeed the overthrow of the regime was being prepared, the *Vojvoda* relayed to Simović Đonović's advice. The General listened and then directed the *Vojvoda* to go to the Air Force Command [in Zemun], and to talk about all of that with General Mirković, who had been entrusted with the execution of the conspiracy.

From the 24th to the evening of 26th March *Vojvoda* went to Zemun every day and kept telling Mirković what should be done politically before the signal for the execution is given. The very first day, and than every day, when they talked about it, Mirković would reply: "Don't worry, *Vojvoda*, all that has been done." (Knežević, 112-13n2) **(#)**

Đonović did not specify the time of day of Maksimović's visit **on the 23rd**, nor the time of the day of the *Vojvoda's* talk with Simović. It is important to note that the talk about the preparation for the coup took place **four days after the all-British conference in Belgrade** complied with Dalton's direction when to foment a coup – which was approved by Churchill in their meeting at Chequers on 2 March - when the British in Belgrade began hastily working to achieve that goal. Eden's order on the 24th March had to invigorate the Đonović-Birčanin group's activities to side with the British without any reserve, because that was what Đonović and the *Vojvoda* had asked of the British in the summer of 1940. **(Part One, Appendix D)**

(#) An important point is that Đonović publicly stated that Vojvoda was with Mirković *every day from the 24th to the evening of the 26th,* counseling the General politically.

The account of daily contacts between Trifunović and Mirković is described in **Chapter 11**.

Mirković – Macdonald meeting, afternoon of the 23rd March

As stated in **Part One, pp. 118-19, in the afternoon of 23rd March** - one day before "Daddy" began visiting Mirković in Zemun - Military Attaché Macdonald informed Gen. Mirković that Cvetković and Cincar-Marković would go the next day to Germany to sign the Pact. (Bosnić(ed), 34) Was that the only topic of their conversation?

While writing about Macdonald's visits, Mirković omitted to write about contacts he frequently used to have with Macdonald's assistant, Tom Mapplebeck – whether directly or indirectly. According to Professor D. Stafford, those contacts existed – because Mirković was "passing on to Mapplebeck the weekly intelligence summaries of the Yugoslav General Staff, copies of which Mapplebeck duly passed on to MacDonald." (Stafford(cp), 415) **(Williams, 32; 254n28; Chapter 3)**

Did Gen. Mirković agree to put all troops in Belgrade under Major Živan Knežević's command?

According to the Major: On 23 March, after 1 p.m., he showed Mirković his sketch for the disposition of troops. The General did not want to look at it. *"You're a clever man. I know it's good."* The Major insisted to see the General Plan, and the General told him: *"You give a thought about the General Plan as well."*

> ((It ended up that I should take responsibility for all the troops in Belgrade, that is, to put under my command everybody who wanted to participate in the action, and that in the execution of the coup I use my own judgment. ... Therefore I begged General Mirković to set apart some detachments from the Air Force who would seize the Prefecture of the city of Belgrade, the Main Post building, and the radio stations. He consented without a word.))
>
> "Ostalo je na tome, da ja uzmem na dušu sve trupe u Beogradu, to jest da stavim pod svoju komandu sve što htedne da učestvuje u akciji, i da u izvođenju udara postupam po svojoj uviđavnosti. ... Stoga sam zamolio đenerala Mirkovića da on odvoji iz vazduhoplovstva nekoliko odreda koji bi zauzeli Upravu grada Beograda, Glavnu poštu i radio stanice. Pristao je bez reči." (Knežević, 101-2)

This account – written after the death of both Generals, Simović and Mirković – is consistent with the information Radoje Knežević gave to Tom Masterson on 27 March, after the new Government had been formed:

> Radne KNJEVICH has a younger brother, one Jika KNJEVICH, to whom he spoke *after his agreement with General MERKOVICH*. Young Jika, who is a major, then spoke to a number of captains, majors and lieutenant-colonels. With the exception of 2 or 3, they all agreed to play. *Jika was then asked to take command of the coup d'état, made the plan and divided the roles. ...*
> (Report of the coup by Masterson. Great Britain, Special Operations Executive – 91087-10v Hoover Institution Archives. Italics added.) **(Part One, 139-41)**

Persistently presenting himself as the central figure in the execution of the Putsch, it will be shown (in Chapter 14) how Major Živan claimed that the reports of the successful coup had been sent to **him** (not to Mirković), and then **he** informed Mirković and **the Professor** about them. (Knežević, 242)

*****

On the subject of a written plan of deployment of troops, reportedly prepared by Živan, Mirković wrote:

> ((Just that morning [the 26th of March] I was building the last plan for the execution of the coup in my head. I did not dare to write down anything, in order not to eventually compromise the matter. I am mentioning that this plan had been already made earlier in my head, and I was just going over it and reaffirming it.))
> "Baš toga jutra ja sam u svojoj glavi izgrađivao poslednji plan za izvršenje udara. Ništa nisam smeo da napišem, da se stvar eventualno ne bi kompromitovala. Napominjem, da je ovaj plan već ranije bio izrađen u mojoj glavi, samo sam ga obnavljao i utvrđivao. (Bosnić(ed), 17)

Mirković's statement contradicts Živan Knežević's claim that on 23 March the General had agreed, *without a word,* to put all the troops in Belgrade under the Major's command and to allow the Major to prepare a General Plan of action. **(Chapter 10)** Ristić confirmed Mirković's description of **verbal** assignment of tasks to individual officers very early on 27 March, thus contradicting Živan's claim of **his** assigning the units' deployment in the morning of 26 March, **before the meeting with Mirković**, as directed in **written** plans **signed** personally by the Major. **(Chapter 14)**

*****

The Putschist Dragiša Ristić also described events differently than Ž. Knežević. In his book, published 13 years before Živan's, i.e. when he could not know what Živan would later write, Ristić wrote that Major Knežević "was called to the general's [Simović's] office on the morning of 24 March. The major accepted a part in the coup and agreed to recruit some of his fellow officers." (Ristić, 87).

About the capture of the Prefecture of the city of Belgrade and other objects, Ristić wrote:

> Sometime after midnight [of 26 March, i.e., very early on 27 March] the author found [Colonel Stjepan] Burazović (a Croat) who was somewhat grumpy and sleepy. When he received his orders from the assistant commander [General Mirković], however, the colonel immediately showed himself more than willing to lead Lt.-Col. Miodrag Lozić and 120 airmen to capture [the Prefecture]. (Ristić, 90)

At the same time Mirković ordered Capt. Vladimir Simić to capture the Main Post Office building in Belgrade, and other officers to seize the post office in Zemun and radio station in Makiš. Within short time afterward, these officers reported to the Headquarters in Zemun – i.e. to Gen Mirković, not to Major Knežević, who was on the streets of Belgrade – that their missions had been accomplished. (Ristić, 91)

In his memoirs of 1941, Mirković described in detail the assignments he gave to the above mentioned officers very early on 27 March, and reports received from them. (Bosnić(ed), 25-27) **(More in Chapter 14)** He particularly emphasized the role of Col. Burazović.

On the basis of Mirković's and Ristić's detailed description of these operations and the officers involved - many of them of higher rank than Živan's - and of Simović's accounts, one has to conclude that Živan's claim of his command over all the troops in Belgrade is not true. Radoje's information to Tom Masterson on 27 March 1941 also is false and misleading.

Prince Paul – Minister Lane meeting, the evening of the 23rd March

At 8 p.m. Lane telegraphed to the State Department a *résimé* of his talk with Prince Paul. Some extracts follow:

- He [Prince Paul] had just received telegram from Churchill urging Yugoslavia to attack Italians in Albania.
- I ... emphasized *possible aid* we could give to Yugoslavia provided Yugoslavia remains free and independent. I said, however, *it will be for us* not for Cvetkovic or Hitler to decide what constitutes independence.
- ... I said reports from Meily [John J. Meily, American Consul at Zagreb] indicated Croatian people do not favor signature. He said, "Let him speak to Maček".
- When he repeated argument of being only a trustee for 5 more months and therefore unable to take steps leading country into war I said King will undoubtedly lean on him for advice later. He emphatically replied he would leave policy entirely to King who undoubtedly would be influenced by others. He said he would give advice to King only if latter asked for it.
- I believe he considers effect of decision as virtually ending his own influence for on my departure he presented me with his photograph usually done only on termination of mission. (FRUS1, 966-7)

Although Lane talked of *possible aid* USA could give to Yugoslavia, the Secretary of State, Cordell Hull, had been repeatedly informing him that the USA's primary concern was to meet *Britain's* requirements; at that time there was no USA aid that could be sent to Yugoslavia that could be expected to arrive before Germany's attack, two weeks later.

At 7 p.m. the next day Lane supplemented his telegram of the day before: "I have never seen Prince so upset and unless he is an excellent actor almost without self control; he said, "I am out of my head; I wish I were dead". (FRUS1, 967)

Simović's meeting with Prince Paul, the evening of the 23rd March

In the evening of 23rd March Gen. Simović had an audience with Prince Paul, after the Prince's talk with the American Minister Lane. Who requested the audience?

Major Knežević contended: **about 5:30 p.m.** Prince Paul ordered his adjutant, Col. Miodrag Rakić, to urgently call Simović. Although that was an unexpected call for the General, he arrived quickly and he was immediately ushered into the Prince's office. (Knežević, 102-3)

In his, memoirs written in exile, Simović described the story differently: **on 22 March** he "undertook measures" to be once again received by Prince Paul. Uncertain of the audience, **in the afternoon of Sunday, 23 March,** he considered an idea of going **the next day** to the Commandant of Belgrade to request a conference of the highest Commandants of the Belgrade garrison to discuss the situation in Yugoslavia and consequences of the Government's adhesion to the Tripartite Pact. Then, the entire body to go to the Minister of the Army and Navy, Gen. Petar Pešić, to request of him - in the name of the armed forces - not to sign the Pact.

Thinking about it, **around 8:20 p.m.** he received a telephone call from Prince Paul's adjutant, informing him that he should come immediately to the White Palace: the Prince was expecting him. Simović arrived at the Palace **at 8:30 p.m.**, and prince Paul immediately received him in his office. (Simović(44), 14-15)

Dragiša N. Ristić wrote: "... **(about 8:10 P.M.)**, General Simović, *who had requested an audience earlier*, received a telephone call from the aide-de-camp on duty at Beli Dvor summoning him to the palace. As the general waited for his car, the phone rang again, and the aide-de-camp urged him to hurry. Simović arrived at the palace in Dedinje **at 8:30** and was immediately received by the Prince in his office." (Ristić, 74. Italics added.)

In a document prepared after his return from London to Belgrade, Simović wrote that he had attended a meeting in the White Palace **in the evening of 23rd March** "at the invitation by Prince Paul" (Simović(51), 10) – omitting the fact that he himself had previously asked for an audience.

Knežević's account of the Prince urgently inviting Simović is not credible.

- **As Simović described the meeting**

Convinced of British victory, he expressed his views of future developments basically along the lines he - reportedly - told Col. Donovan on 24 January: Russia, together with the USA and the British Empire, will defeat Hitler by the same means by which he is now winning – tanks and airplanes. (Simović(44), 15-16)

The Prince pointed out differences of opinion held by the Minister of the Army and Navy, the Chief of the General Staff, and the Commandant of Belgrade. Simović dismissed their arguments stating - among other things - that they were too old and inadequate to the present situation. To the Prince's question, who could be the Minister of the Army and Navy, Simović told him to take a younger man, for example Gen. Bogoljub Ilić or Gen. Bora Mirković. (Simović(44), 16)

To Simović's lengthy description of his vision of direst consequences for her people if Yugoslavia does not side with the future victors - Russia, Britain and the USA - Prince Paul pointed to military weaknesses and the un-readiness of Yugoslavia to successfully resist Germany. (Simović[44], 18)

Simović then argued that Yugoslavia's power lay in the victory of her great Allies and in a great moral strength of her people to endure in this fight.

((There is nothing left for us but to form the Salonika front again, and the people and the forces that are to be left in the country, to retreat to the mountains and to continue the fight by guerrilla warfare ...))
"Nama ne ostaje ništa drugo, nego ponovno obrazovanje Solunskog fronta, a narod i one snage koje budu ostavljene u zemlji, imaju da se povuku u planine i da produže borbu gerilskim ratovanjem ..." (Simović(44), 18)

- **This Simović's idea about guerrilla warfare in the mountains**

necessitates a side-line again.

"Perhaps the most delicate part of his [George Taylor's] allotted task was to organize post-occupational planning and make preparations for guerrilla resistance if - or when - the Balkan Peninsula was overrun." (Williams, 28)

As for the idea *to retreat to the mountains and to continue the fight by guerrilla warfare* – Alexander Glen realistically commented in his letter to Bill Bailey on 2 August 1940. **(Chapter 8)** (How unrealistic was Simović's idea, and how realistic Glen's assessment, is shown in **Chapter 20**.)

(Although in the evening of **23 March 1941** Simović was recommending guerilla warfare in the mountains, when he was Commander-in-Chief, he was the author of a plan to defend Yugoslavia's frontiers. (Barker, 83))

*****

Now back again to the meeting of Prince Paul with Simović, as described by Simović.

In a continued advocacy of his views, Simović informed the Regent of the planned meeting - the next day - with the highest-ranking Commandants of the Belgrade garrison and their intended visit to the Minister of the Army and Navy. Prince Paul then asked Simović to go to the Minister right away and inform the Minister of his, Simović's, views. (Simović(44), 19-20)

Simović went, and when he told Gen. Petar Pešić of the conversation, the Minister protested: why did the Regent invite Simović for consultation and not him. Therefore, he submitted, verbally, his resignation and ordered Simović to convey it to Prince Paul. (Simović(44), 20-21)

When Simović returned to *Beli Dvor* - **about 9:30 p.m.** – he was immediately invited into the Prince's study, and found there Premier Cvetković. Upon hearing of Gen. Pešić's resignation, Prince Paul asked Simović who could replace him. He suggested Gen. Ilić or Mirković. (Simović(44), 21)

At that moment General Petar Kosić, the Chief of the General Staff, and Milan Antić **(##)**, the Minister of the Royal Court, entered the study. At Antić's request for an explanation of the difference in his views about the situation in the country and those of Simović, Kosić disagreed with Simović: the Commandants of the Armies reported that the situation was normal, without a sign of dissatisfaction. Simović persisted in his judgment that the signature of the Pact with Germany would cause a revolution in the country and a revolt among the military. In an ensuing discussion, Kosić stressed the un-readiness of Yugoslavia for war and foresaw Germany's victory. Simović expected the victory by Great Britain, the need to "save the honor and moral strength of our people and the future of our Fatherland", emphasizing "fateful consequences of the signature of the Pact". To Antić's observation that the tanks and airplanes now play the essential role and not the morale, Simović took Greece as the proof that morale is more important: un-prepared little Greece - but with strong morale - was fighting successfully against incomparably stronger and better armed Italy. (Simović(44), 22)

Then Simović advocated: the concentration of as strong as possible a force in the region of the Third Army [in southern Serbia], the establishment of a link with the Allies, and the pulling out of the Yugoslav army towards Salonika, with the intent of organizing a new Salonika front [as in the First World War]; the continuation of the fight in the country in the form of the guerrilla warfare – after the troops had been pulled out of Yugoslavia into Greece; and an urgent attack at the flank and in the rear of the Italian troops in Albania. Capturing the Italian troops Yugoslavia would secure her flank and rear, would achieve a great moral success, would gain a huge quantity or arms, and would liberate a considerable Greek force for a common defense against the Germans. (Simović(44), 22-3)

(##) As shown above, Živan Knežević wrote that, on 21 March, Miha Krek wrote a letter to Milan Antić informing him of Simović's intention to overthrow the Government and seizing the power. During the audience with Prince Paul on 23 March Simović discussed his views with Antić. While Simović described their opposing stands, he did not suggest that Antić hinted at the General's intention to overthrow the Government. (Simović(51), 11)

Now back again to the evening of the 23rd March 1941.

The discussion in the Prince's study – **on the 23rd** – ended **about 10 p.m.** Simović went to the home of Minister Pešić to inform him of the talks. At that moment the Minister was also invited to the Palace. Simović drove him there, Pešić joined Ministers Maček, Šutej and Konstantinović at the dinner hosted by the Regent's wife, Princess Olga. (Simović(44), 23-4)

General Simović went straight to his home, where he arrived **about 11 p.m.**. (Simović(44), 24)

- **Maček's recollection of the meeting**

    At 9 P.M. that Sunday [23 March 1941] I was with Šutej in Cvetković's office, awaiting the Premier's return from an audience with Prince Paul, when [Professor Mihailo] Konstantinović burst in on us. He threw himself into an easy chair and, taking his head between his hands, he moaned: "Catastrophe, catastrophe!" We urged him to tell us what had happened. He explained that a plot was in the making in certain officers' circles which aimed at a *coup d'état*. He went into other details but was interrupted by a phone call from Cvetković, who asked us all to hasten to Court without delay.

    On our arrival, the Prince, visibly nervous, told us that General Dušan Simović of the Air Force had just left him, after declaring that, if the Pact were signed, he would no longer be able to restrain his officers from bombing the Royal Court and the Government buildings before flying off to Greece. Cvetković and I told the Prince that he should place Simović under arrest at once. We advised Prince Paul to summon the Defense Minister Pešić to the Court as quickly as possible. General Pešić came and, upon hearing the story, reproached Prince Paul for having received officers like Simović over his head; this implied that the Prince had no confidence in him, and he would, therefore, tender his resignation. I interrupted and reminded Pešić that the situation was too serious to play the game of resignation. If his conscience allowed him to accept a responsible position in ordinary circumstances, he should also be prepared, as was his duty, to stay at his post in hard times. Pešić let himself be convinced and then minimized the danger by dismissing the whole story as irresponsible gossip. He said he knew Simović as un unbalanced but completely harmless type, and he, Pešić, was the man to answer for the Army's doings. This ended the affair. (Maček, 214-15)

That night he was to be arrested, claimed Simović, because the Government had issued an order for his arrest. He was not arrested because the police, who was tailing him, had established that from the Court (around 11 p.m.) he went straight to his home. (Simović(51), 12)

However, from Maček's account it appears that his and Cvetković's suggestion for Simović's arrest was not followed through, possibly because Minister Pešić's intervention and comments about Simović.

The next morning Simović continued his campaign.

- **Mirković claimed: he had not known about Simović's audience with Prince Paul**

In the letter to Belgrade's *Evening News* (4 November 1960) Mirković stated that he had not have any knowledge that Gen. Simović used to go to Prince Paul in an attempt to stop him from signing the Tripartite Pact. ((Had that meeting taken place, I believe I would have known about it.)) "Da je do toga sastanka došlo verujem da bih ja o tome znao." (Karapandžić(AB), 153)
   Not necessarily so.

Britain was not interested in a new Salonika Front

Simović's plan of moving the Yugoslav army towards Salonika neglected the reality of the moment. As described in **Part One, page 43,** in November 1940 the Foreign Office was asked whether Britain would be able to supply "at least part of shipping required and organize supply of local shipping" for the evacuation of a force of 300,000 men, probably through Salonika or Kavalla. (Barker, 84; 281n39) The Foreign Office replied on 23 November that Campbell should urge "a spirit of resistance without too much thought of withdrawal." (Barker 84; 281n40) In simple language: No.
   On 21 February 1941 - just before conferring with the Greek leaders at Tatoi residence - Eden sent a telegram to Churchill explaining his and Gen. Dill's interim conclusions about the situation. One passage read:

> ... We should all have liked to approach Greeks tomorrow with a suggestion that we should join with them in holding a line to defend Salonika, but both [Air Chief Marshal Sir Arthur] Longmore and [Admiral Sir Andrew] Cunningham are convinced that our present air resources will not allow us to do this. (Eden, 196) Simply: the British could not defend Salonika, and a Salonika front - as visualized by Simović - was not a part of Britain's strategy.

The same night General Sir John Dill sent a message to his deputy, General [Sir Robert] Hining, including this passage on Salonika:

> It is not yet possible to see what line we should aim at holding in Greece, but I doubt very much whether Salonika could be covered. If this proves to be so after our discussion with Greeks tomorrow we may still be able to hold a line covering northern Greece and giving Yugoslavia a bolt-hole through the Monastir Gap. (Eden, 198)

After the Tatoi Conference, in Athens, on 3rd March, 1941, Eden gave Campbell a letter for Prince Paul. **(Part One, 86)** Some twenty years later Eden wrote:

> I instructed Campbell to give the Prince Regent an outline of our plans to help the Greeks, including the fact that we were going to deploy our forces west of Salonika, which would be only temporarily covered by the Greek army; *the successful defence of Salonika must therefore depend largely on Yugoslavia*. I did not ask Prince Paul to commit himself blindly, but time was short. We would have been glad to discuss plans with the Yugoslavs if they had sent a staff officer to Athens at once. (Eden, 216. Italics added.)

As described in **Part One, pages 96-8**, the Yugoslav military sent Major Milisav Perišić – "who traveled on a British passport under the name L.R. (Last Ray) Hope". (Barker, 88) Whether Simović was or was not aware of the unsatisfactory results of the Major's visit, it can be assumed that he was not aware of the messages Eden and Dill sent to London on 21 February. However, on 23 March Simović advocated an attack on the Italians in Albania and the creation of a Salonika front. Three and a half days later he became the head of the new Government. At its formation, most Ministers declared for peace. As shown below, Simović declared himself *for peace, if possible*, but already had been determined to side with Britain.
   But peace was not possible. Although Simović repeated some political moves made by Prince Paul – as shown in **Part One, pages 151-3,** and herein below – the Putsch set in motion events that caused the tragedy for the people in Yugoslavia that ultimately took more than a million human lives.

Chapter 11

MONDAY, 24 MARCH 1941

Had he been aware of all the details of the negotiations [of the Tripartite Pact], even General Simović could scarcely have objected to the actual terms although he would have still opposed signing the pact. (Ristić, 82-3) Simović **was** informed of the actual terms, as is shown below.

As stated in **Chapter 8**, at the beginning of the war Campbell did not have a high opinion of the Opposition politicians in Belgrade: "they were simply trying to ride back to power on a wave of pro-Allied sentiment." (Amery, 138) But in March 1941, Campbell had confidence in Gen. Dušan Simović. **(Part One, 120-21)** In his memoirs Simović stated that his activities had started by the end of January 1941 - which was after his meeting with Col. Bill Donovan - and had continued ever since. Those activities generated Campbell's confidence, which resulted in Macdonald's **secret** meeting with Simović in the morning of 26 March 1941.

The meeting of the Commandants of the Belgrade garrison: Simović was informed of the secret clauses in the Pact

After failing to change Prince Paul's policy on Sunday evening, 23 March, **on the morning of the 24th March** Gen. Simović called to his office Major Živan Knežević, who had once served under Simović. "The major accepted a part in the coup and agreed to recruit some of his fellow officers." (Ristić, 87)

As he intended on the 23rd, **on 24 March** - probably after talking with Major Knežević - Simović went to the Commandant of Belgrade, to ask him to convene a meeting of the highest-ranking Commandants of Belgrade's garrison, hoping to get their support. Here are two accounts of this meeting: by Simović and by General Dragiša Pandurović.

- **Simović's account of the meeting**

On the 24th of March, about 8:30 a.m., Simović went to the Belgrade Command, and on his request the Commandant, General Milorad Petrović, called the highest Commandants of the Belgrade region to a conference. ((After some extended length of time, lost in waiting for all persons to gather in the Belgrade Command, the conference began.)) "Posle dosta dugog vremena, izgubljenog u čekanju da se sve ličnosti prikupe u Kommandi Beograda, otpočela je konferencija."

When the invited Commandants arrived, Petrović informed them that they had been invited at Simoviić's request to survey the attitude in the armed forces and to consult each other about the situation. (Simović(44), 26)

Then Simović presented his views in terms similar to those he had the previous evening expressed to Prince Paul: bitterness of the people because of the Government's giving in to Hitler's demands, which is turning against the military; the duty of the highest Commandants to inform the authorities about the true sentiment of the people and the military, in order to influence the responsible leaders to make right decision in the spirit of the feelings of the people and the mood of the military; that would result in the best protection of the interests and the future of the country. (Simović(44), 26)

The attendees of the meeting expressed various views of the situation in the country. ((I was disappointed by stated opinions of some gents and by a some reserved attitude of the majority.)) "Bio sam razočaran iznetim mišljenjima izvesne gospode i dosta rezervisanim stavom većine." (Simović(44), 27)

*****

[At this point of Simović's account, the description of the two scenes are out of sequence. He first wrote of his invitation by the Minister of the Army, going to him and the conversation with him, and then that he was at the conference with other Commandant which preceded the visit to the Minister. When he asked the Minister to receive them all.]

*****

The first scene:

Simović's further participation in the conference was interrupted by a telephone call to report immediately to the Minister of the Army, General Petar Pešić. ((*Upon coming into the office of the Minister of the Army General Pešić, he received me immediately ...*)) "*Došav u kabinet Ministra vojske đenerala Pešića, ovaj me je odmah primio, ...*" The Minister then informed Simović that the Premier and the Foreign Minster would leave that afternoon for Vienna to sign the Pact, explaining to "začuđen" (amazed) Simović that there was no other way out, and that the government had to make that decision. (Simović(44), 27. Italics added.)

The second scene:

((*Then I told him that I was in the Belgrade Command at the conference of the Commandants ...*)) "*Potom sam mu ja rekao, da se nalazim u Komandi Beograda na konferenciji Kommandanata ...*" The Minister at first refused Simović's plea to receive the entire group to hear their opinions, but then agreed to it. Not hearing out to the end their explications, the Minister repeated to them what he had earlier told to Simović.

After that, Simović went to the Air Force Command [in Zemun]. (Simović(44), 27-8. Italics added.)

- **General Pandurović's account of the meeting**

General Dragiša D. Pandurović, Commandant of the Danube Division region, became a prisoner of war. In a POW camp in Osnabrück, Germany, he wrote his account of the events, dated and signed it on 18 December 1941 – just 17 days after Gen. Mirković dated his memoirs in Cairo. Neither one could know what the other was writing.

They met briefly in the early morning of 27 March 1941, after the military coup, in the building of the Ministry of the Army. Mirković was ebullient, bragging about his role in the coup – which he called "the coup of people's liberation". Pandurović was worried and concerned about the effect of the coup. Relevant passages of Pandurović's account, given below in translation, provide more details about the coup-related events that, in his opinion, led Yugoslavia into "the April catastrophe". (Pandurović, 1)

*****

About 10 a.m. on 25 March [it was actually **on 24 March**], the Commandant of Belgrade - Army General Milorad Petrović ("Lord") - invited General Pandurović to his office. Pandurović came and found there General Simović. "Lord" informed Pandurović that Simović wanted a consultation about the mood among officers and state of readiness of the army.

Then Simović explained: the officers were very agitated ... One feels like something were boiling with discontent, so he came to consult with them about cautionary measures. One should not be kidding oneself by apparent calm of men, because unpleasant events may be caused by younger officers. For that reason he visited Prince Paul and the Minister of the Army and Navy, General Petar Pešić [last night]. Now he finds it necessary to assemble all higher commandants in Belgrade and to consult with them, because the matter was serious. (Pandurović, 4)

Following Simović's presentation, "Lord" expressed his views, which differed from Simović's. Here is an excerpt:

((You see - continues Lord and turns to Simović who anyway is swallowing his every word - to tell you candidly, for a few days now I feel personally very agitated, disturbed and fairly wavered, indeed unsure – am I on the right track having my personal conviction: that in the present situation the pact must be accepted, and that other solution would be catastrophic for us. To calm myself down a little and to get some moral support, I went last night to the former Minister of the Army General Milutin Nedić, my classmate, one unquestionably intelligent man and patriot who, in addition, is excellently cognizant of our defense situation. For almost an hour and a half Mića was informing me about the situation in general, and about our in particular, with deep insight and logic specific to his intelligence, concluding clearly and distinctly: that we must not resist the signing of the pact; that we are compelled by the circumstances to submit to this woe because of the military position of Yugoslavia which, by the entry of German troops into Bulgaria and by the attitude of Turkey and Russia, is made impossible to resist. In addition, one has to bear in mind – that this pact of "ours" is specifically fitted to our national sensitivity and it does not contain that sharp edge as it does in the case with Hungary, Rumania and Bulgaria. ...)) **(#)** (Pandurović, 5)

(#) The "sharpness" of the Tripartite Pact with Hungary, Rumania and Bulgaria refers to the obligatory military clauses in their pacts, of which Yugoslavia was excepted.

*****

In his account, Simović did not mention "Lord's" explanation and opinion; he considered them a loss of time while waiting for the other invitees to arrive.

*****

Six Generals were invited to the conference and five came, the Commandant of the Royal Guards could not.

((Throughout Lord's entire explanation Simović was sat motionless, like a statue, facing Lord's desk, and when he turned around at the opening of the door, his face was exceedingly pale and the forehead wrinkled.)) (Pandurović, 5)

Various assessments of the situation were expressed and opinions about how to treat them differed.
At this point Pandurović described the sequence of scenes as follows: the telephone rang, and Simović was informed that Minister General Pešić wanted to see him.

((Then, gentlemen, this way ... said Simović. I will now tell the Minister that you are all here assembled, as well as our desire to receive us immediately, to hear us out, and simultaneously to inform us about everything the government intends [to do], so we would know how to behave ... You wait here, I will phone you ...

((Not long after his leaving, the telephone rang again, and the chief of the Minister's Cabinet invited us all to the Minister.)) (Pandurović, 5)

They entered into the Minister's large office **about 11 a.m.** After having been greeted and seated, the Minister began to tell them:

((You see, gentlemen, the essence of the pact is in this: to guaranty to Yugoslavia the independence and sovereignty of her territory, that through our state no troops or any materiel will be transported; *that no kind of participation is demanded of us in the operations against enemies of the Axis,* with a prospect of Yugoslavia getting a territorial access to the Aegean Sea, meaning Salonika. That, gentlemen, is contained in a secret addendum to this pact. Something else, which is significant for us: we are not obliged in any way to disband our army which is - as you know - activated to a high degree of wartime readiness, and the "activation" will even be expanded to other units, and just a moment ago I have signed one such decision. There is, gentlemen, nothing in that pact humiliating for Yugoslavia as an independent state; we stand and remain in a posture of an armed power, and should Germany demand something besides the pact - there we stand in defense of our rights, there we are to perish honorably and gloriously like Tzar Lazar at Kosovo. ... Until then, this status ought to be accepted, as an inevitability, as something that must be tolerated, with a heavy heart, truly, but in the interest of the people and state; we must reconcile with it because we do not have another solution, we are cornered by the situation...)) (Pandurović, 6. Italics added.)

All listened carefully, especially Simović. Someone raised questions about a possibility of the defense of the country.

((That is exactly the matter, gentlemen – said the Minister – which was of decisive influence to accept the Pact. ... Our armament is insufficient, our defensive power weak in relation to the Axis Powers'. We were requesting and taking armament wherever we could, but that was inadequate, particularly with respect to air force materiel, as you, Simović, know well. ... Furthermore, the level of ammunition is very important ... We have the ammunition for only two months of war – and after that? Can we endure that period, or the link with Salonika can be denied to us after a few days by the German troops from Bulgaria ... And then what?)) (Pandurović, 7)

And about the support from Russia?

> ((Out of Russia, gentlemen, we have nothing, not even a hope, because the gents from there act deaf to all our wishes and requests. Our military attaché reports that we cannot hope for anything, not even moral support. ... They do not hear us as if we do not exist for them.)) (Pandurović, 7)

And Turkey?

> ((She guards her own skin, and nothing more.)) (Pandurović, 7)

Pandurović found it characteristic that during the conference Simović spoke the least of all. He was visibly dissatisfied with the result of the conferences.

The Generals left the Minister's office **at noon**. Only Simović stayed, some business to attend. (Pandurović, 8) The Minister's explanation of the features of the Pact did not change his mind. He remained very busy the rest of the day.

*****

In his own account, the "začuđen" (amazed) Simović recorded only the Minister's statement that there was no other way out of the Pact, and that the government had to make that decision. He left out the Minister's statements ((that no kind of participation is demanded of us in the operations against enemies of the Axis, with a prospect of Yugoslavia getting a territorial access to the Aegean Sea, meaning Salonika. That, gentlemen, is contained in a secret addendum to this pact.)

By omitting first Gen. Petrović's information and then Minister Pešić's explicit statements about the Pact, Simović could pretend not to know of those secret clauses that exempted Yugoslavia from any military obligations towards the Axis.

Živan Knežević, who perused Gen. Pandurović's account in preparing his own book, similarly omitted both Gen. Petrović's and Minister Pešić's explanations – just as Simović did. Dr. Hoptner correctly stated:

> The conspirators did not act in ignorance. *They had full knowledge of the reservations accompanying the Tripartite Pact, reservations which vitiated it as a military, economic, and political instrument.* (Hoptner, 259. Italics added.)

Admitting that he knew that Yugoslavia had **not** been required to go to war with the Axis against the Allies, Simović would have been hard pressed to justify the coup. As his trusted adjutant, Capt. Ristić, implied, Simović wanted Yugoslavia to go to war on the side of Great Britain, because he believed that *" England loses all battles except the last one."*

Gen. Mirković threatened the Court Minister Milan Antić

After these conferences with Gen. Pavlović and Ministar Pešić, **about 5 p.m.** Simović met with Mirković and lawyer Bora Marković, at the home of Simović's brother. They discussed the current events, especially what was going on in Prince Paul's surroundings, and when Ministers Cvetković and Cincar-Marković would leave for Vienna to sign the Pact. To the telephone inquiry by lawyer Marković, Antić replied that there had been no change, and that the two Ministers would leave that very day [the 24th].

Mirković then asked Antić: ((Aren't you afraid of people's rage?", and upon hearing the answer, added: "I am only telling you, you'll be in for it!)) "Ja ti samo kažem, da bereš kožu na šiljak."   (Simović(44), 28-9)

Then - Simović continued his story - he heard Mirković talking about blowing up the train with Cvetković and Cincar-Marković, and **he** stopped them (as described in **Part One, page 123**). Simović's claim is questionable because, as George Taylor stated, on the 24th March Trifunović was informing the SOE of the progress of the preparations, and "To take such a drastic action [blowing up the train] at this juncture would mean the introduction of martial law which would upset plans." (Williams, 31)

In any event, Macdonald had informed Mirković a day earlier that the Ministers would be going to Vienna on the 24th. (Bosnić(ed), 34) Did they discuss the idea of the blowing up the train at that meeting, among other things?

*****

While Simović and Mirković's activities in Belgrade were important, the British made critical decisions on the 24th March. The most important one was Eden's authorization of the *coup d'état.* It came at the most favorable time for the coup wishers and plotters, the day *Vojvoda* Trifunović-Birčanin established his daily contact with Mirković. That opened a channel through which the British, and particularly George Taylor of SOE, could be informed of the preparations for the coup and – through Trifunović – could influence those preparations.

Campbell's question to Eden on the desired timing of the coup

Why would Campbell ask Eden, on 21 March, *when would it suit him*, from a military point of view, *for the overthrow of Government to be done* (Eden, 226) – if he were not able to determine the timing? He would not dare to mislead his Foreign Minster on such an important matter.

Sir Alexander Glen wrote that "Air Attaché Hugh Macdonald and his assistant Tom Mapplebeck virtually disappeared [after the all-British conference on 19 March]; Charlie Clark scarcely left the Yugoslav General Staff; while the rest of what were now 24-hour working days were spent with Tupanjanin and his friends." (Glen[B], 59) Glen knew what was going on, because he was one of the British who was working with Tupanjanin and his friends. What did **he** ask them to do?

Eden acknowledged that Campbell "did everything in his power to encourage the more robust among the politicians and the military through his many useful contacts." (Eden, 229) And Campbell indicated clearly in his telegrams of March 25 that the *legation was in touch with army and political figures*. (Stafford(cp), 408) Why? What did the British tell to those figures, and what did the British want them to do and when?

Eden authorized the *coup d'état* in Belgrade

On 24 March – while the most trusted "Daddy" began politically advising Mirković – Eden authorized Campbell to inform the prospective Putschists secretly of British support:

> Any new Government formed as a result of these events and prepared to resist German demands would have our full support. You may *secretly* so inform any prospective leaders in whom you have confidence. (Eden, 227. Italics added.)

This was the signal that the principal coup-seekers-and-plotters were waiting for. Among the prospective leaders were *Vojvoda* Trifunović-Birčanin, Jovan Đonović and their associates – among others – who had proposed the coup back in the summer of 1940 in the first place. Now they got the decision of His Majesty's Government's that they had wanted. They were going to do whatever they could to achieve their goal.

Campbell was duty-bound to implement Eden's order. As directed, Campbell had to do it **secretly.** No public announcement or written instructions – just secret oral communication, through a most effective channel. He could secretly inform any prospective leaders – including Generals Mirković and Simovič – via the Legation personnel, SOE agents, or others.

Who, how and when informed any prospective leaders – military and civilian – of Eden's promise?

Why and how was Ilija Trifunović-Birčanin able to inform SOE on Monday 24 March that the coup was 99 per cent certain and preparations were making good progress? (Williams, 31) What instructions did SOE give him at that moment?

Vojvoda Trifunović – General Mirković daily contact, 24 – 27 March 1841

SOE operative John Bennett also recorded his views and the views of Taylor and Masterson "that the grounds for eventual Coup d'etat were laid by Tupanjanin…" "I think that Trifunovich and Djonovich played an important part in the actual Coup. *It was they* who pushed and planned how the Coup should take place. …" (Great Britain, Special Operations Executive, 91087-10V, Hoover Institution archives. Italics added.)

That "important part in the actual coup" manifested itself with the Simović – Maksimović – Đonović – *Vojvoda* Trifunović – Mirković contact on 23 March, as described in **Chapter 10**. Here is an additional detail related to that contact.

In a post-war conversation of Ristić with the former Minister Božidar Maksimović in Washington, DC, the Minister stated that his pre-coup talk with Simović was of a conspiratorial character. Simović did not directly reveal a plan and details, but it was clear to the Minister that something would happen, such as the overthrow of the government. Maksimović also confirmed that Simović had not intended to form a government composed of bureaucrats – as the brothers Knežević later claimed – but of representatives of the political parties. (Dragiša Ristić Collection – Correspondence and Interview, Box 2, Folder 2.26, Hoover Institution Archives)

(After that conversation with Simović, Maksimović went to see Đonović. It would be interesting to know whether they spread the news to other people, in addition to Trifunović-Birčanin.)

Keeping in mind the distribution of tasks assigned at the all-British conference on 19 March to ["Uncle"] Tupanjanin, ["Daddy"] Trifunović-Birčanin, and Macdonald **(Part One, 108-9)**, it is also reasonable to conclude that during the three-day period of 24-26 March "Daddy" was advising Mirković as instructed by SOE, primarily by Taylor, who was described by Dalton as *his Chief Organiser* of the coup. (Pimlott[ed], 178) In his report of 26 February Taylor informed Nelson about "Daddy's" high standing on the national scene and about his reliability. **(Chapter 4; Appendix K)**

Being very reliable, having "very close personal relationship" with SOE, and personally advocating a need for the coup since the summer of 1940, it is evident what kind of advice Daddy was giving to Mirković.

Being in daily contact with General Mirković, "Daddy" was able to observe the General's activities and the progress of the preparations, and thus was in good position to keep SOE informed about them. Dalton had very good reasons to inform Churchill on 28 March that *"the coup d'état itself was largely the work of TRIFUNOVICH, while the real political backing without which it could hardly have been made, lay outside the old Cabinet and in the Serb Peasant Party – the principal instrument of our policy and (like Narodna Odbrana) in our pay."* (Great Britain, Special Operations Executive, 91087-10V, Hoover Institution Archives. Italics added.)

Mirković – *Vojvoda* Trifunović-Birčanin cooperation, according to Mirković

In his memoirs of 1941 Mirković confirmed that *Vojvoda* was one of the civilians "invited" into the Air Force Command on 26 March, and stayed there with him throughout the night of 26th-27th. The reason for the invitation, as Mirković explained: as the President of *Narodna Odbrana*, Trifunović-Birčanin had under arms 500-600 Četniks, placed in certain homes in Belgrade; in case of a need, they would join the action where he, Mirković, would order them to act. (Bosnić(ed), 21)

However, in the letter to Belgrade *Večernje novosti,* dated 4 November 1960, Mirković had a different explanation of the *Vojvoda's* presence:

• he brought the *Vojvoda* to the Air Force Command **about 8 p.m. on the 26th March,** where he met him for the first time and they became acquainted;

• the *Vojvoda* did not have any plan, was preparing no action;

• the invitation was a measure of precaution, resulting from an earlier information to Mirković that *Vojvoda* had been preparing some action;

• so Mirković wanted to avoid a potential conflict between the army and the Četniks, which could have happened through the lack of information;

• when the *Vojvoda* came to Zemun that evening, and told Mirković that he was not preparing any action, Mirković kept him in the Command. (Karapandžić(AB), 151-2.)

Mirković's claim of meeting the *Vojvoda* for the first time **at about 8 o'clock in the evening of the 26th March** contradicts Đonović's assertion of the *Vojvoda's* seeing the General every day from the 24th through the 26th. However, the General's contradictory explanations of his contact with the *Vojvoda* and the role of his Četniks, puts a question mark on the credibility of the General's statement. In addition, the *Vojvoda's* ability on 24 March to relay to SOE the inside-information on the status of the coup-preparations (Williams, 31), ads to the General's lack of credibility, and confirms the veracity of Đonović's article.

More on Trifunović-Birčanin's daily contacts with Mirković, 24-27 March

Julian Amery wrote that the cup had been the work of three men: Mirković, Major Knežević, and *Vojvoda* Birčanin. "Of these only Birchanin was in direct contact with S.O.E." (Amery, 228) The *"direct contact"* enabled Birčanin to inform the SOE of the preparations, and to receive the SOE's "advice" "in the sense desired".

*****

SOE was not the only service or agency involved on the British side. "Apart from the regular diplomatic staff, three services, represented by the attachés, and the SIS were all working in one way or another on the various problems associated with the effort to stiffen the resolve of the Yugoslavs." (Stafford[cp], 412) As for the SOE-Legation cooperation, "Both Taylor and Masterson met daily with Campbell and Armand Dew, counselor at the legation, to exchange information. Furthermore, Taylor and Dew would usually draft a report reviewing the situation in the light of all intelligence, which the minister could use in reporting to London." (Stafford(cp), 412)

Also on 24 March, "a telegram was sent to the SOE in Belgrade telling them 'to put full steam on to assist after consulting the Minister'." "Later that day, the certainty of Yugoslav signature was confirmed by Campbell, and the War Cabinet was informed accordingly." (Stafford[ed], 405)

Chapter 12

TUESDAY, 25 MARCH 1941

When examining events in greater detail, one would expect that information generated while an event was taking place, or very shortly thereafter, is usually "un-edited", more descriptive and truthful than the information generated after the passing of time, when it could be "edited for posterity". Unfortunately, this is not necessarily so. The information generated by the domestic coup-wishers-and-plotters in Yugoslavia was "edited", to various degrees, immediately after the coup and especially after the unintended but, nevertheless, dreadful consequences of the coup became more fully known.

As a consequence, there are significant discrepancies in the accounts about the preparations and execution of the coup, and particularly about the personal roles in it and "merits" for it. Detailed review of these discrepancies is outside the scope of this book. Only major roles are examined.

Živan Knežević's account: Two meetings with Mirković

On the morning of the 24th March, Major Živan Knežević consented to Gen. Simović's call to participate in the coup. (Ristić, 87) Throughout his life later on he wrote profusely about his role. The following is one of his accounts.

During the night of 24th / 25th of March, he prepared a military plan for the coup.
Around 9 a.m. on Tuesday, the 25th, he was at the Air Force Command, in Zemun, and informed Gen. Mirković about the plan. The General was satisfied. (Knežević, 169)
During this meeting Živan also pleaded with Mirković for a meeting between his brother Radoje and Gen. Simović, in order to coordinate activities related to the coup. Such meeting was being postponed from day to day, for two weeks, for various reasons. Mirković was excusing Simović as being very busy.
Mirković himself was irresolute about the date of the coup. (Knežević 170)

In the afternoon of the 25th, Živan first visited his brother. Radoje informed him that the Association of the Retired Officers and Warriors, and some other organizations, wanted to organize massive street demonstrations against the Pact. Fearing a possibility of unfavorable consequences, Radojje was against such approach, and asked Živan to seek Gen. Mirković's support against the demonstrations.
Živan did so in his second meeting that day with Mirković. The General was reluctant to intervene, but finally promised to revoke the intended demonstrations. (Knežević, 170-71)
However, in his memoirs of 1941 Mirković wrote nothing about these allegedly planned demonstrations nor of his alleged intervention.

Mirković - Mapplebeck meeting on 25 Mach

Živan did not specify the time of the second meeting with Mirković. Similarly, the time of Mirković's meeting that day with Mapplebeck was not stated, so it is not known whether it preceded or followed the meeting with Macdonald the same day.

> Mapplebeck, because of his longstanding relationship and personal friendship with Mirković, was undoubtedly in a stronger position to be acquainted with Mirković's plans for the coup than MacDonald, even though MacDonald saw a great deal of Mirković for professional reasons. **On March 25,** ... , a meeting took place between Mirković and Mapplebeck. **Mapplebeck strongly urged Mirković to launch a coup as soon as possible,** and Mirković replied by assuring him that one could be expected shortly. Mirković apparently did not seek any specific guarantees of supplies from Britain, such as Campbell had indicated were necessary. (Stafford(cp), 416. Emphasis added.)

In his memoirs of 1 December 1941 Mirković did not mention his meeting with Mapplebeck on the 25th of March.

Mirković – Macdonald meeting, afternoon of the 25th March

However, in these memoirs Mirković acknowledged that he had been supplying Macdonald with information about movements of the German and Italian armies well before August 1940.
In the afternoon of 25 March Macdonald visited Mirković and informed him that the Pact had been signed. He, at once terribly offended and angered, exclaimed:

((That Pact must fall. ... It must be knocked down. ... It must not remain in force. ... The Serbian people cannot tolerate such a shame!))
"Taj pakt mora da padne ... On mora da bude oboren ... On ne sme da ostane na snazi ...Tu sramotu srpski narod ne može da podnese!"

When Macdonald asked him, what he could do now, Mirković replied:
((The thing I had set my mind on! The pact must fall!))
"Ono što sam naumio! Pakt mora da padne!"

And who could do that now, asked Macdonald. Again revolted, Mirković exclaimed:
((I will overthrow it!))
"Ja ću ga oboriti!" (Bosnić(ed), 34)

Then, he explained:

((Lt.-Col. Macdonald may have understood this in two ways: either as my personal revolt, which will remain futile as soon as my temper calmed, or as a revolt of a man who has in his hands an organization and a plan prepared and ready to be executed,))
"Potpukovnik Makdonald mogao je ovo da shvati dvojako, ili kao moj lični revolt, koji će ostati bez uticaja čim se smirim, ili kao revolt čoveka, koji u svojim rukama ima gotovu organizaciju i gotov plan za izvršenje." (Bosnić(ed), 34)

((His sentiment pulled him to this second possibility and it appears that he informed his Minister in Belgrade, who informed the appropriate authorities in London, because only that way can one interpret the opinion of some statesmen of Great Britain who maintain that they, too, had some influence on the 27 March [coup].))
"Njegovo osećanje vuklo ga je na ovu drugu mogućnost i izgleda, da je on o tome obavestio njegovog Ministra u Beogradu, a ovaj nadležne u Lodonu, jer samo se tako može tumačiti mišljenje pojedinih državnika Velike Britanije, koji tvrde, da su i oni imali neke uticaje na 27. mart." (Bosnić(ed), 35)

((Neither Lt.-Col. Macdonald, nor Colonel Clarke, nor Campbell the English Minister in Belgrade, nor any other Englishman had any other information about preparation for the 27 March [coup].))
"Nikakve druge podatke o pripremama za 27. mart nisu imali ni potpukovnik Makdonald, ni pukovnik Klark, ni Kembel engleski Ministar u Beogradu, niti ma ko drugi od Engleza." (Bosnić(ed), 35)

The British did not need *any other information about preparation for the 27.* Mirković himself confirmed to Macdonald on the 25th what the SOE-contact-operative, "Daddy" Trifunović-Birčanin, had told them on the 24th March, *that the cup was 99 per cent certain.*

100 per cent certainty was assured in the afternoon of the next day, the 26th March – according to Mirković's and Simović's writings.

*****

Without stating whether it was before or after he had been informed by Macdonald that the Pact had been signed, for Mirković, "Kada je 25. marta potpisan Pakt, pala je kocka." ((When on 25 March the Pact had been signed, the dice was cast.)) (Bosnić(ed), 17) In the meantime – he continued:

((...I consulted with General Simović and informed him *of my decision*. He accepted it in principle, believing that something ought to be done, but that one should wait some more.))
"...konsultovao sam đenerala Simovića i saopštio mu *moju odluku*. On je u načelu stvar prihvatio, verujući da treba nešto da se radi, ali da treba još čekati." (Bosnić(ed), 17. Italics added.)

Suggestion from London: Blow up the train with Ministers

As already stated, **on March 24**, "Daddy" assured SOE that the plans for a coup had a 99 percent chance of success. But there still remained a question how to proceed.

> ... the SOE, on March 25, turned down a suggestion from London, in response to the news of the signing of the pact, that the train bringing the Yugoslav ministers back from Vienna should be blown up. The SOE feared that such action would lead to the introduction of martial law and the disruption of the conspirators' plans. (Stafford(cp), 412)

On 25 March, Campbell indicated clearly "that the *legation was in touch with army and political figures,...* ". (Stafford(cp), 408. Italics added.) They were in touch not only on March 25th but since the all-British meeting on 19 March, as described in **Chapter 9.** In a letter of June 1942, Campbell stated: "I knew he [Gen. Mirković] was in confidential contact with the Air Attaché and told him that a coup d'état was being planned, *but he never furnished any details or dates,* and I should doubt that he received pay from any of our intelligence or other services." (Barker, 92; 282n93. Italics added.)

Indeed, he could not furnish any details or dates because the coup was just a wishful idea until Eden's order to Campbell on 24 March. According to Mirković himself, he was planning the coup from 1937, but did nothing. The actual preparations began only **after** the Putschists were secretly informed of British support.

The above-presented information shows that on March 25th :

1 – at least Mapplebeck, Macdonald and Trifunović-Birčanin concentrated their pressure on Mirković;

2 – in his memoirs of 1 December 1941, Mirković did not reveal all of his meetings with the British.

Chapter 13

WEDNESDAY, 26 MARCH 1941

The day was full of extraordinary activities. It started with

an early morning Macdonald – Simović secret meeting.

After prodding Mirković on the **23rd and 25th of March** against the Government's signing the Tripartite Pact, **on the early morning of March 26th** Macdonald had a secret meeting with Gen. D. Simović. According to Professor David A. T. Stafford, the telegram about the meeting was sent to the Foreign Office, for the director of intelligence at the Air Ministry, at 7:40 p.m.. It arrived in the Foreign Office after the coup had begun [on March 27th, at 2:20 a.m.] This telegram, like a great number of others, was then routinely sent to President F. D. Roosevelt.

When, and how this meeting was arranged and by whom? Was it Gen. Mirković? When and where was the meeting held? Researched data provided no information. However, two days earlier Minister Campbell had written to Eden that only Gen. Simović was able to lead the movement. **(Part One, p. 121)** Anyway, Macdonald met Simović. There probably was a reason for the dispatch of the telegram to London to be delayed until after the coup had already been set in motion. The content of the telegram is very relevant and revealing, and therefore it is quoted herein in its entirety.

> At my request I was afforded an interview with General Simovitch (Chief of Yugoslav Air Force) this morning. As this officer is head of an organization intending to carry out a coup d'etat, meeting was arranged with great secrecy. The General seemed to be in very good health and had an appearance of alertness, energy and ability which I have rarely observed among senior officers in Serbian Army. He was confident in his speech but cautious in his utterances and gave the impression of sincerity, truthfulness and a belief in what he said. For the sake of simplicity in recording a *conversation which ranged over various subjects*, it is summarized as follows:
>
> (a) He stated that there was no doubt that the country felt very strongly about signing of pact with Germany and wished to repudiate both the pact and present Government. *They understood that this almost certainly meant war and they preferred this alternative to continuing on present lines.*
>
> (b) There existed an organization which was working for the overthrow of present Government. General had confidence in its success and he asked us to have confidence in it and him. **We should not have to wait more than a few days before the coup d'etat.**
>
> (c) He was anxious to know how many troops we had in Greece and *hoped that we would send a great many there and that we intended to defend Salonica.* I replied that we must consider our left flank and this depended a great deal on the Serbs.
>
> (d) He foresaw that Yugoslavia would go to war in Albania immediately after the coup d'etat. He asked if Turks would then join in, to which I replied that *it was very possible but that I had no positive assurance* regarding exact circumstances he described.
>
> (e) He then asked what could the British do to help Yugoslavia if she went to war against the Italians, Bulgarians and Germans. I replied in the sense of Secretary of State's telegram from Cairo of March 25th. **(#)** He seemed impressed by conception of a common pool for materials and asked if it included supply of food, to which I replied that, *although I spoke on this matter without precise authority, I felt sure that it did.*
>
> (f) He appeared to be disappointed that we could not promise precise numbers and quantities of war material, but agreed that they should do well out of Italian loot in Albania. He feared, however, that *types of weapons were not the same and that Italian ammunition could not therefore reinforce Yugoslav units.* Reserves of 76.5 and 75 mm. ammunition for field artillery would be required.
>
> (g) In answer to a question he replied that *the Prince Regent and even the President of the Council appeared to be very depressed over the signing of the pact.* This may indicate that the Prince Regent intends to try and remain in power in the event of the Government being overthrown. From an officer on General Simovitch's staff I hear that it is *intended to hand the Prince Regent over to the British.*
>
> The impression I gained from journalists as a whole was that the General was now committed to a course of action from which nothing could deter him. Please inform General Wavell for his own secret information, but otherwise regard as highly secret, as any leakage would compromise chance of success for the coup d'etat.

("TELEGRAM SENT BY BRITISH MINISTER IN BELGRADE TO FOREIGN OFFICE ON MARCH 26th, 1941."
www.fdrlibrary.marist.edu/psf/box35/a318x07.html 10/31/08 - Italics and emphasis added.)

(#) In this telegram Eden informed Campbell:

>As those with whom you are in touch will be aware, British forces are now in Greece. These forces include anti-tank, anti-aircraft and armoured units. Yugoslav army, if they fight with us, will thus be fighting side by side with British forces armed with equipment mentioned in your telegram.
>It would be impossible to transfer this equipment from our troops to Yugoslav troops, nor would the latter without a period of training, as suggested, make effective use of those highly specialized weapons. Furthermore *there is no other source from which we can at present supply equipment of this nature, ...* (Eden, 227-8. Italics added.)

*****

It is conspicuous and characteristic that neither in his speech on 28 March 1941, nor in the documents herein referred to as "Simović(44)", "Simović(51)", and "Simović(56)", Simović never mentioned this secret meeting with Macdonald.

Dragiša Ristić, to whom Simović *entrusted his archives,* did not write anything about the General's contacts with Macdonald. Still, Macdonald's two meetings with Simović on the 26th of March are additional evidence of the British Service Attachés contacts with the Yugoslav military in Belgrade related to the coup.

*****

Now a few comments on Macdonald's report:

This report was not the first one to mention Simović's name to the Foreign Office. Cadogan wrote in his diary for Thursday, 27 March 1941: "I threw a little cold douche, but pointed out that independent, *and previous*, reports on Simovich (from Athens and Angora) were good." (Dilks(ed), 367. Italivs added.)

While the conversation of the two men, reportedly, ranged over various subjects, Macdonald's report does not reveal its details. Were the unreported details important for a better understanding of the roles played by both sides, the British and the Yugoslav, in the preparation of the coup? Macdonald told Simović that he was speaking **without precise authority** on important matters. However, Dalton - the head of SOE - contradicted him. In his diary for the 27th March Dalton stated that **Macdonald was *authorized* to make "very vague assurances"**, as D. Stafford called them (Staford(cp), 414) Alex Danchev stated in 1990: "It is now known that British Air Attachés had a hand in the coup deposing Paul in March 1941." (Danchev(ed), 230n18)

Taken as a whole, Macdonald's misleading statements were made to *encourage* Simović to expect British support after the Putsch. For example:

While Macdonald had *no positive assurance* regarding the circumstances under which the Turks would go to war [on the side of the Allies], he still stated that this was *very possible* – although by March 26th it was definitely clear to the British that the Turks would not. Likewise, even though on the subject of inclusion of food supply into a common pool for material he spoke *without precise authority*, he *felt sure* that it would be included. While Simović hoped that the British had *a great many troops in Greece and that they intended to defend Salonica,* Macdonald avoided a straight answer.

Macdonald reported that Simović *appeared to be disappointed that we could not promise precise numbers and quantities of war material.* Campbell realized that giving military supplies to the potential coup leaders would induce them to action, and therefore wrote to Eden on March 24 about the supplies. (Stafford(cp), 405) The British could not give them any, so they asked the Yugoslav military to attack the Italians in Albania to get needed armament.

Simović's reported observation that the type of Italian weapons and ammunition could not reinforce the Yugoslav units, is a partial invalidation of Churchill's unrealistic suggestion to arm the Yugoslav forces with weapons taken from the Italians in Albania.

Still, even without a promise of precise numbers and quantities of war material, Simović assured Macdonald that the coup would be executed in *a few days* and that Yugoslavia would immediately attack Italy. In D. Stafford's words:

Simović had given the British everything they could have wished, and it is ironic that the report reached London after the coup began. Here was a virtual promise to fight against the Italians in Albania and to join in the war against Germany, *regardless of any commitment of British material_support*. The information conveyed in the telegram undoubtedly was in large part responsible for the high expectations of the Simović government and for the subsequent disappointment when it failed to live up to its promise. (Stafford(cp), 414. Italics added.)

Indeed, Simović's foreseeing Yugoslavia going to *war in Albania immediately after the coup d'état* did not happen. How *sincere* he was with Macdonald probably only he knew. The fact is that after forming his government following the coup, he did not order an attack on the Italians.

*****

"The impression [Macdonald] gained *from journalists as a whole* was that the General was now committed to a course of action from which nothing could deter him" illustrates that the preparation for the coup was on 26 March much more widely known by civilians than both Generals Simović and Mirković had admitted in their memoirs.

*****

Before the Putschists got into action on March 26, a significant event took place, but the Putschists willfully ignored it.

Notes 1 and 2 of the Tripartite Pact Protocol were published

Early in the morning of 26 March, Belgrade's daily *Politika* published the first two Notes. Although they affirmed the sovereignty and territorial integrity, and non-passage of the German troops through Yugoslavia, the Putschists ignored their meaning. However, their meaning was not lost and had an impact on the protesters in Kragujevac, for example, in the course of the day.

Five thousand had gathered near the industrial city of Kragujevac, in Serbia, to protest the Pact. (Ristić, 85) When Vice Premier Maček, at that moment the Acting Premier, was informed that a battalion of gendarmes had been sent to scatter the assembly, he ordered to stop the battalion immediately, "and instead to fill a truck with copies of "The Official Gazette" containing the Pact and the related clauses and distribute them to the gathered crowd."

> The people would read and realize for themselves what had actually been going on behind the scenes. It worked. Most of the crowd dispersed quietly after having glanced over the text of the Pact and the 'secret' clauses. Only a few hundred lingered and cheered the ringleaders as hey tore up copies of "The Official Gazette". That marked the end of the 'revolution'. (Maček, 215)

The Putschists-to-be and their civilian supporters in Belgrade may have not known about the end of this "revolution" in Kragujevac, but it is hard to assume that they had not known what *Politika* and *The Official Gazette* had published about the Pact that morning. They, and their British "contacts", made up their mind to overthrow Prince Paul and the Government, and the mere publication of the text of the Protocol would not stop them now. They proceeded to act, and their major activities are presented here.

Activities on 26 March 1941 leading to the coup

Before examining the activities of the coup-makers on March 26, one ought to recall that the scenario for the coup's timing had already been set by the British decisions:

on 2 March, Churchill and Dalton wanted the SOE to deal with Prince Paul *if and when the Regent signed a deal with Hitler;*

on 20 March, Campbell suggested a BBC broadcast *ensuring vehement reaction in Serbia if agreement is signed;*

on 21 March, Eden recommended to Campbell to stage the coup *at the moment of reaction caused by the signature.*

Thus, the British had decided the timing of the coup, and those who were *secretly informed of British support* had to work out the details. As it will be seen in the following pages, their accounts of the details differ on the time and persons issuing the order for the execution of the Putsch.

**

After the Macdonald – Simović meeting, the major coup-plotters-makers were engaged in preparations for and execution of the coup. One would expect that the major participants - who claimed to be motivated by patriotism, national and personal honor, and high personal and political morale principles - would tell the same story of the event. In the case of the Putsch in Belgrade it was not so. As time passed, and consequences of the coup developed as they did, sharp differences of views and claims among the coup-participants set in. Groups were formed. Criticism, bitterness and recriminations followed. Records of this demeaning situation are found in archives of various institutions inside and outside the former Yugoslavia, including the Hoover Institution in the USA. They throw a light on some details, the presentation of which is not given here. Generals Simović and Mirković left behind them different accounts, each one claiming the key role for himself. Others exaggerated their own roles and "merits", from their personal points of view, emphasizing their own contributions in positive ways. Following are the accounts of activities on 26 March provided by major participants.

- **Živan Knežević's partial account – meeting with Mirković**

According to Živan Knežević, **on the morning of March 26th,** he went to Zemun to see Mirković. **The General still could not tell him when they would move.** He told the Major that he wanted to talk with Simović once more, and then the decision must be made. They agreed that the Major should come back again **at 3 p.m.,** together with his brother, Professor Radoje. (Knežević , 171-2. Emphasis added.)

- **Before 10 a.m., the morning of the 26^{th,} : Simović – Mirković's 1st meeting**

    Colonel Dragutin Savić, Simović's chief of staff, was usually the first to report to the commander in the morning. ... After Savić left, Mirković entered the commander's office and pressed for the action to take place as soon as possible, but Simović did not wish to act prematurely and decided to attempt the coup following the return of Cvetković and Cincar-Marković. (Ristić, 85)

*****

As Simović wrote, it was at that time that the definitive decision was made to get into action – when the Ministers who signed the Pact returned from Vienna to Belgrade – **either during the night of 26/27 or 27/28.** ((The exact time was still not determined. General Mirković insisted on the earliest, the latest on 26/27; however, I was indecisive, ...)) "Tačno vreme još nije bilo odlučeno. Đeneral Mirković je insistirao da to bude što pre, najdalje 26-27; ali ja sam bio neodlučan, ..." (Simović(44), 36)

No wonder that Simović was indecisive. Just a short time earlier he had told Macdonald that the British *should not have to wait more than a few days before the coup d'etat* – as Macdonald reported.
*****
The two Ministers returned from Vienna at 10:00 a.m. (Ristić, 85).

- **Noon, 26 March – Simović: HE issued the order for the execution of the Putsch**

On 28 March Simović told the hierarchs of the Serbian Orthodox Church that, since the Pact had been signed on the 25th, there was nothing left for him to do but give his consent to act, and **at noon of the 26th** , to issue the order for the execution of the Putsch. (Knežević, 366. Emphasis added.)

- **Živan Knežević: About noon, Mirković decided to act, but ...**

Major Knežević contradicted Simović's claim and wrote: Mirković vacillated, and **only around noon HE** decided for the military coup that night, if necessary even without Simović – whom Mirković and the brothers Knežević wanted to be the bearer of the new order of things from the very start. (Knežević, 172. Emphasis added.)

*****

Although in his book Živan clearly stated that it was Gen. Mirković who decided on the date of the coup, in an undated essay, "Ten days till Hitler's attack", Živan put himself into the picture: "Kada *smo* doneli odluku ..." ((When *we* decided ...)) (Milunović(ed), 39. Italics added.)

Describing events of April 12, 1941, he included himself and his brother Radoje – along with Generals Simović and Mirković – as "the organizers of the 27 March." (Milunović(ed), 58)

The cited essay was not the only source for unwarranted elevation of the role of the two brothers in the preparation and execution of the coup. However, nineteen years before the publication of this essay, Gen. Simović wrote that it had not been proper to emphasize the role of the Knežević brothers above other putschists. (Simović(56), 78)

- **Mirković's claim: after 1 p.m. on 26 March HE decided for the coup**

On the morning of the 26th, he was informed that Cvetković and Cincar-Marković had returned from Vienna.

Until **1 p.m. of 26 March** – Mirković wrote – not even he himself had made a definite decision for the coup. All that which preceded March 26th was only a mental preparation, and the organization was effected with a very limited, minimum number of junior officers, his collaborators. What, when and how the coup d'état would be carried out, nobody knew until that time. He repeated, up to that point, he himself had not made a decision. (Bosnić(ed), 21)

Having considered all the pros and cons - Mirković continued - **in the afternoon of 26 March** he decided to execute the coup **during the night of 26/27 March at 2:20 a.m.** (Bosnić(ed), 27)

Immediately after that decision had been made, he invited Miloje Dinić, the Infantry Colonel of the Zemun Garrison, and Živan Knežević, the Infantry Major of the Belgrade Garrison, to come to the Air Force Headquarters in Zemun.

In the meantime, Major Dušan Babić brought into Mirković's office Major Vlastimir Rožđalovski, the Commandant of the 2nd Artillery Battalion, and the General issued him actually his first order for the coup. In order to coordinate his activities, the General ordered the Major to contact Major Knežević and [Major] Danilo Zobenica, the Commandant of the armored cars battalion. (Bosnić(ed), 18)

After Rožđalovski left, the General received Major Knežević, informed him of his decision to act early on the 27th, and ordered him to inform his collaborators of the General's decision.

The Major showed the General a sketch of the disposition of two battalions of the Royal Guards, of a company from the noncommissioned officers' school, and of a battalion of armored cars and anti-aircraft artillery. Sure that the Major conscientiously performed all preparations in his sphere of action, the General approved the planned disposition of the troops, without controlling it in detail. (Bosnić(ed), 18)

On this occasion the General told Major Knežević that it would be good to bring into the Air Force Headquarters his brother, Professor Radoje, well knowledgeable of the French language, to edit a Proclamation. (Bosnić(ed), 18-19)

In 1960 Mirković wrote this about his role:

((I, Brigadier Borivoje J. Mirković, with voluntary collaboration of officers and men of our Air Force and of all other units of the Army of the Belgrade and Zemun garrisons, *have personally organized the coup d'état the night of 26/27 March 1941, and was carrying it out.*))

((Political parties, including the Communist, had not participated whatsoever in the preparations, nor in the execution of the coup, *nor have those parties known anything about our intentions.*))
(Karapandžić(AB), 156. Italics added.)

- **At 3:00 p.m.: Brothers Knežević – Mirković meeting**

As the younger Knežević wrote, the brothers came from Belgrade to the Air Force Command in Zemun at 3 p.m.. The General and the older brother, Professor Radoje, met for the first time. Mirković was with a group of officers, excited, gesticulating, louder than usual. To the Major's inquiry about the coup, the General exclaimed:

"Noćas!" ((Tonight!)) (Knežević, 172)

- **Between 3:00 p.m and 5:00 p.m. – Mirković looked for Simović**

After Knežević left, Mirković placed a phone call to Simović's home. ((His wife answered, and I begged her to tell Gen. Simović to come urgently to my office. …)) (Bosnić(ed), 19)

> Mirković. who made all arrangements for the *Putsch,* confessed to me that he came to the final decision **soon after 2:00 P.M. on March 26.** He tried to get in touch with Simović, but found he was having his siesta. (Jukić, 61. Emphasis added.)

However, according to Simović, the afternoon of March 26 was not a *siesta*-time for him. On the contrary, it was filled with activity.

- **At 4:30 p.m., 26 March: Simović's instructions to a relative**

In 1944 Simović wrote: After Mirković's morning visit with him, Simović's brother Miloš, MD, telephoned him **around 2 p.m. of the 26th** that their close relative, Ljubomir Vučićević – sent by the people of the Šumadija region – had come to Belgrade with a message for the General. They met **at 4:30 p.m.** The relative pleaded with the General not to let the enemy take away what is most sacred to the people without a drop of blood. Deeply impressed and, taking into consideration the political situation, the General advised: should German motorized columns suddenly advance, the male population should retreat to the mountains, destroying the roads and bridges behind them.

Then the General stayed with his brother for a brief moment, instructed him to contact Mirković, or two other officers, in case he should be arrested. (Simović(44), 37-8) That done, Simović went to his office in Zemun, arriving there **about 5 p.m.,** and immediately asked Mirković to come into his office. (Simović(44), 38)

Transfer of bombers to Zemun airport

According to Simović: during their first, **morning meeting on the 26th**, Mirković suggested that a squadron of twin-engine bombers be flown from the military airport near Osijek into Zemun airport, to be in state of alert. **Simović approved** – he wrote. (Simović(44), 36-7)

- **From Mirković's memoirs of 1 December 1941**

Mirković wrote that he asked the Chief of Staff, Col. Dragutin Savić, to order Major Krsta Lozić in Bijeljina, to fly into Zemun airport, **in the afternoon of 26 March,** with a squadron of bombers (type Blenheim), and to keep another squadron in readiness at Bijeljina, prepared for action. The requested squadron flew into Zemun airport at **5 p.m.** Its assignment was, for the first moment, to strengthen the 6th fighter regiment at the Zemun airport. In case of a need, *he (Mirković)* could have controlled the entire military air force. (Bosnić(ed), 23-4. Italics added.)

Major Knežević also wrote that towards evening on 26 March one squadron was transferred from Borovo to Zemun airport, ((with pilots standing by the planes in the course of the night)), while another squadron was staying in Borovo, ready to move to Zemun any time. (Knežević, 189-90)

- **Mirković's letter to "The Evening News" (4 November 1960) has a different story**

The Blenheim bombers were flown into Zemun at his personal order. He telephoned Col. Ferdo Gradišnik, then in Borovo, ordering him to immediately send the planes to Zemun. "O tome niko tada nije ništa znao." ((At that time nobody knew anything about it.)) He intended to use that squadron only in case other units offered a serious resistance to the execution of the coup. (Karapandžić(AB), 154)

*****

Mirković presented the transfer of the bombers as purely his own decision, without any reference to Simović. If some units of the Belgrade garrison actively resisted the Pusch, he was ready to bomb them.

Interestingly, on Thursday, 27th March 1941, the SOE head, Dr Dalton, described in his diary a different purpose for the bombers: "We knew before that the Air Force would be all right, and, *if necessary, would fly away to Greece…"* (Pimlott(ed), 176-7. Italics added.) Mirković himself wrote that he could have controlled the entire Air Force.

How did Dalton know about that possibility? Who informed the SOE? Their "contact" with Mirković from the 24th through the 27th March was "Daddy", Ilija Trifunović-Birčanin. (Knežević, 113) And Miković confirmed his presence in the Command on 26-27 March. (Bosnić(ed), 24)

In his article dated 2 April 1947, presented here, Dr. Miloš Sekulić commented that Mirković had two choices: 1 – To fly to Greece with the entire air force and there to fight, or 2 – To execute the *coup d'état*, and hand over to Simović both the political and military authority.

This tends to corroborate Dalton's statement about possibly flying to Greece.

However, according to Radoje Knežević - who was also in the Air Force Command during the execution of the Putsch - the three airplanes flown into Zemun on 26 March, were in the state of readiness for Mirković, Simović and their close cooperators from the Air Force in case of failure the following morning. (Grol, 138)

About 5 p.m. on 26 March, Simović – Mirković's 2nd meeting

- **Mirković's version of the 2nd meeting**

Mirković wrote: when Gen. Simović arrived at the Air Force Headquarters, **about 5 p.m,**

> ((I told him the following: General, Sir, **I have decided** to execute **tonight** the coup for people's liberation.))
> ((He replied: But you didn't need to yet … it seems that it will be prematurely …))
> "Saopštio sam mu sledeće: Gospodine đenerale, **ja sam doneo odluku** da **noćas** izvršim udar za narodno oslobođenje."
> "On mi je dogovorio: Ama, nisi trebao još …, izgleda da će to biti prerano…"

> ((After this I told him: General, Sir, **I have decided!** You have nothing to do with the eventual failure. You stay out of this, and when the moment comes, i.e., when everything is done, I'll send an auto to bring you to the Ministry of the Army to take further management of the state's administration.))
> "Iza ovoga ja sam mu rekao: Gospodine đenerale, **ja sam doneo odluku!** Vi nemate nikakve veze s eventualnim neuspehom. Budite slobodni, a kada bude momenat t.j. kada bude sve svršeno, ja ću Vam poslati automobil da Vas doveze u ministarstvo vojske i da preuzmete dalje vođenje državne uprave." (Bosnić(ed), 19. Emphasis added.)

> ((To these words of mine General Simović replied: Well, may the Lord help you. I can not participate, but if you get caught and the thing does not succeed, I shall defend you in that case.))
> "Đeneral Simović na ove moje reči odgovorio mi je: - Pa neka ti Bog bude u pomoći. Ja ne mogu učestvovati, ali ako budete pali u ruke i stvar ne uspe, ja ću vas braniti u tom slučaju." (Bosnić(ed), 19)

> ((I [Mirković] told him: Don't you defend anything. The path on which I set out is serious one, and there one can either succeed or lose the head. There is no middle.))
> "Nemojte Vi da branite ništa. Put kojim sam pošao ozbiljan je i tamo može ili da se uspe, ili da se izgubi glava. Sredine nema." (Bosnić(ed), 19)

Then they hugged and kissed with tears in their eyes. (Bosnić(ed), 19)

In a letter to the Belgrade's *Evening News*, dated 4 November 1960, Mirković again wrote about this meeting with Simović:

> ((… **On 26 March, at 1700 hours** [5 p.m.] I was issuing orders to Major Knežević, and then I noticed that he was shaking, and his legs were trembling.)) (Karapandžić(AB), 153. Emphasis added.)

> ((**The hour of the beginning of the coup [was] 0220 [2:20 a.m.], and not 0100 [1:00 a.m.]** As I personally was handling everything else, so I personally had determined that the execution of the Coup [must] begin **at 0220 hours [2:20 a.m.] on 27 March, and it was so.** The Coup was not ordered for **0100 hours. …**)) (Karapandžić(AB), 154. Emphasis added.)

((When, **in the afternoon of 26 March**, I informed General Simović that the following night I would be carrying out the Coup d'état, I personally pleaded with General Simović to go straight to his home. Later on I learned that Simović had not gone really to his home, but had gone to his sister, who was married. He returned home only after midnight, **around 0030 hours [0:30 a.m.] on 27 March.**)) (Karapandžić[AB], 155. Emphasis added.)

- **Simović's version – written in exile**

In his memoirs dated 1 January 1944, Simović wrote about their second meeting:

((When General Mirković came in, I told him: "Boro, the time has come for our action. The decisive moment has come. We have to take up the action this evening or tomorrow evening at the latest. What do you think, when are we going to?" Mirković answered like a bullet from a rifle: "I think right this evening." I asked him: "Are all preparations complete?" – He answered: "Yes, they are. **We are only awaiting your order!**" – Then I said: "**All right, we'll undertake the action tonight.** Inform Knežević and Stanojlović about the decision! And now you get going!"))
"Kad je došao đeneral Mirković, ja sam mu rekao: "Boro, došlo je vreme za našu akciju. Otsudan je čas kucnuo. Akciji treba da pristupimo večeras ili najdalje sutra uveče. Šta ti misliš, kada ćemo?" - Mirković je odgovorio kao zapeta puška: "Ja mislim još večeras."- Upitao sam ga: "A da li su gotove sve pripreme?" – Odgovorio je: "Jesu, gotove su. **Očekujemo samo Vašu zapovest!**" – Onda sam ja rekao: "**Dobro, akciju ćemo preduzeti noćas.** Izvesti Kneževića i Stanojlovića o odluci! Idi sada na posao!" (Simović(44), 38. Emphasis added.)

As is customary, the two men kissed each other [on the cheek], and wishing Mirković success, Simović informed him that he would go home. Should his presence be necessary, he would come. Simović then told him, more as a joke: "If they arrest you tonight, I'll come to get you out." (Simović(44), 38)

*****

Ristić used his updated version of Simović's *Memoirs* to describe Simović's instruction to Mirković, adding a third name:

"Good. We will take action this evening. Tell Stanojlović [in the General Staff], Knežević [in the Royal Guard], and Matić [watching the Minister of War] about our decision." Then, embracing Mirković, "now, get down to business." (Ristić, 86)

- **Simović's version – written in 1951**

After returning from exile to Belgrade, Simović wrote twice about his activities and role on 26 March 1941, in1951 and 1956.

((The signing of the Pact in Vienna and the announced return of the Prime Minister and the Foreign Minister pointed to *a fast action. I was deciding only: to take the action the night of 26/27 March, or the next night of 27/28 March. (...)* In as much as Cvetković and Cincar-Marković had arrived in Belgrade on 26 March, and since I was informed that the police state of alert would last until the midnight 26/27 March, *in the afternoon of 26 March I have decided: the action to be taken that same night, if all necessary preparations had been completed. Therefore I called General B. Mirković* and requested information about the preparations made. As General Mirković told me that all preparations had been accomplished, **I informed him of my decision: to execute the action at one o'clock after midnight of 26/27 March. It was exactly 5 o'clock in the afternoon**. Then I called the Chief of Staff, Colonel D. Savić, and issued him necessary orders. On that occasion he informed me: that one squadron of aircraft Blenim [Blenheim] had arrived at Zemun from the Osijek area at the request of Mirković, to be in a state of readiness in Zemun – according to a later interpretation – in case of the failure of the action.
((In order not to raise any suspicion, I received subordinate officers.... Thereafter, I received the British Air Attaché, *Colonel MacDonald,* who gave me some information about delivery of material for some armament of the Air Force.
((**Around 7 o'clock in the evening**, I called General Mirković and Colonel Savić, issued to them last orders and took leave of them, telling them that I would be at my home and to send me an automobile **when the action started. ...**)) (Simović(51), 14. Emphasis added.)

- **Simović's version – written in January 1956**

Then, in 1956, in Belgrade, Simović wrote about this subject again (this time in third person):

Simović first noted ((… certain individuals are engaging in public discussions on that subject [the coup] through newspapers abroad, and they have succeeded in creating erroneous views even by the Allies' leaders, which found expression even in the Memoirs of the esteemed Sir Winston Churchill. Therefore I feel impelled to state my opinion.)) (Simović(56), 76)

On the planning and leadership of the undertaking he stated:

((General Simović stood in the center of the entire undertaking; he was carrying on negotiations and effecting influence on Prince Regent Paul, on the Prime Minister Dragiša Cvetković, on the Minister of the Army and Navy, General Petar Pešić, on the Chief of the General Staff, Gen. Petar Kosić, and on the Minister Dr. Srđan Budisavljević - to prevent the signing of the Tripartite Pact; he was carrying on negotiations with the highest religious representatives, Patriarch Gavrilo [Dožić] and bishop [Dr.] Nikolaj [Velimirović], as well as with political figures. He engaged Boža Maksimović and Dr. Drag[omir] Ikonić.)) (Simović(56), 76-7)

((He engaged, personally, his aide, Brigadier Bora Mirković, for the action, issued instructions to him to carry out the preparations, brought to him [Major] Živan Knežević as liaison with the Royal Guards, sent to him [officers] Đorđe Stanojlović, Žika Radojičić and Vasa Matić.)) (Simović(56), 77)

((In the afternoon of 26 March, General Simović **made the decision** to carry out the coup the night of 26/27, and at 1700 hours [5 p.m.] **issued the order** to Bora Mirković: the action to start at 1 o'clock after midnight of 26/27.)) (Simović(56), 77. Bold letters in the source.)

((He [Simović] followed the start and execution of the action, and as soon as the start was secured, he came to the Ministry of the Army, where he was the center and the main staff of the action, **he took into his hands the action,** which had just started, and led it to the finish.)) (Simović(56), 77. Bold letters in the source.)

((Air Force Brigadier **Borivoj Mirković**, at the directive of Gen. Simović, worked out the plan of action during the night of 26/27 March, as the deputy of General Simović and in his name, and according to his directive, accomplished one half of the action with the troops from the Zemun garrison: occupation of the bridge on the River Sava, capture of the Administration of the City of Belgrade, capture of the buildings of the Gendarmerie, Post, Telegraph and Telephone Centrale, and the radio station in Makiš.)) (Simović(56), 77. Emphasis added.)

((The Air Force Captain, **Dragiša Ristić**, the orderly officer of the Commandant of the Air Force [Gen. Simović], … , that historic night, upon the order of General Simović, stood by Bora Mirković … and was assisting Mirković in assigning the roles to the participants in the execution of the coup. This way these [participants] knew that this deed [the coup] was being carried out according to the instruction and under the direction of Gen. Simović.)) (Simović(56), 77. Emphasis added.)

On the General's whereabouts at the start of the action:

((In the night of 26 March, I did not remain in the Air Force Command, and I was not personally issuing orders to individual departments, but I entrusted this to my aide Bora Mirković, because my presence for this was not necessary. Because of that, under influence of interested people, an erroneous opinion sneaked in among the misinformed that the principal executor of the coup was Bora Mirković, although he did perform just one half of the action. However, the real facts are as follows:

((Having in mind the goal, the evening of 26 March I considered that it was better for me to be on the right bank of the River Sava (in Belgrade) – close to the Royal Palace, where the main action was being carried out, with which I wanted to be in a direct touch, and where there were all junior officers, so I could assist them in case of a need. …
((Until the midnight of the 26th, I did not sleep, as some perhaps think (and B. Mirković wrote so publicly), but I was monitoring the situation vigilantly and was waiting for the time to step on the scene.)) (Simović(56), 78. Emphasis added.)

((Because I modestly stayed quiet, and others were praising their roles, an opinion crept in that I was sitting [idle] with my arms crossed, that the others (the brothers Knežević ?) had carried out the action, and that the leader of the entire action had been Bora Mirković. Therefore, in the interest of the historic truth, I am forced to state:

1. I was only doing my duty, like all the other participants in that act of March, and I do not seek any priority ahead of those who were offering to risk heir lives in performance of the direct action.

2. The opinion that Bora Mirković was the leader of the entire action, that he made the decision to carry out the action the night of 26/27 March, and that he executed the coup d'état on 27 March 1941 – I do not recognize [as true], and I consider it erroneous to emphasize his role above the roles of the executors directly involved in the act of 27 March.

3. Emphasizing the roles of Živan Knežević and his brother Radoje above those of the others, particularly above the role of Colonel Stojan Zdravković, is not proper.))

27 January 1956
Belgrade, Puškinova 13

D. T. Simović

((N. B. Corrections of the initial text I made on 5 December 1961. This document can be published in its entirety only after my death. It is located with Ante Smith Pavelić, and its transcription with Major Dragiša Ristić – in my archive.))

D. T. Simović

(Simović(56), 78)

In both accounts written in Belgrade, Simović wrote that he had ordered the action to start **at 1.00 a.m. on the 27th**. In his report on the coup, *Vojvoda* Trifunović - who spent the night of 26-27 March in Zemun with Mirković - stated: "Orders were given that the troops begin their movements at 2 am … " (Great Britain Special Operations Executive 91087-10.V, Hoover Institution Archives) Mirković wrote that he had ordered every participant to be at their assigned object at 2:20 a.m. (Bosnić(ed), 27) On the basis of this information it seems that Mirković's account of 2:20 a.m. is more credible.

Also, Simović claimed that, *as soon as the start was secured, he came to the Ministry of the Army, … he took into his hands the action, which had just started, and led it to the finish.* That implies that he had come to the Ministry **between 1 a.m. and 2:00 a.m.**

Mirković wrote that he had been informed **about 2:30 a.m.** that the block of ministry buildings had been taken, and **then** he sent Capt. Ristić to Simović's home to bring the General [to the Ministry of the Army]. (Bosnić(ed), 29)

Major Knežević stated that Simović appeared at the ministry block **exactly at 3:40 a.m.** (Knežević, 240)

This implies that Simović's claim - of leading the action, which had just started, to the finish - is not credible.

Simović's letter to Churchill about Živan Knežević, 20 January 1956

Seven days before writing the explanation given above, Gen. Simović attempted to correct a record about an episode which took place on 27 March 1941. On 20 January 1956, from the same address, he sent the following letter to Sir Winston Churchill:

Dear Sir Winston,

In connection with my letter of 14 January 1956 I owe to you an explanation. Namely:
The "Times" of the 27th March 1942 published the article "Simovic's Story", in which I had named Major Zivan Knezevic as the leader of the second group (on the right bank of the river Sava), and not the real leader Lieut. Colonel Stoyan Zdravkovic, chief of the 1st battalion, who took command of the Royal Guard and replaced Colonel Simic, chief of the Infantry regiment of the Royal Guard. Flying from Yugoslavia to Greece, Lieut. Colonel Zdravkovic's plane vanished. But I did not know Zdravkovic's fate at that time. Anxious for his destiny and in fear that he had fallen in the hands of the enemies and perhaps might be exposed to persecutions and reprisals, I did not want to mention his name. Therefore I mentioned the name of Zivan Knezevic, who had been only one of the participators under the command of Stoyan Zdravkovic.

I am very sorry to bother you with this matter, but I must do it for the sake of truth.

Yours very sincerely,
D. T. Simović /signed/
D. T. Simovic
Army General (ret.)

(Dusan Simovic – Box 2 – Correspondence Simovic-Churchill, Hoover Institution Archives)

*****

As shown below, on 27 March Radoje Knežević informed Tom Masterson that his younger brother "Jika [Žika] was then asked to take the command of the coup d'état, made the plan and divided the roles".

In an article about the history of 27 March 1941, Živan Knežević stated, ((All commandants of the Belgrade garrison units, won over for the overthrow, ... were under my direct command.)) "Svi komandanti jedinica beogradskog garnizona pridobijeni za prevrat ... stajali su pod mojom neposrednom komandom". Dragiša Ristić wrote in 1955 that this statement had not been correct and explained:

((Živan Knežević had under his direct command only his third battalion of the Royal Guards and two armored cars, with which he controlled the intersection of the streets Miloš Veliki and Nemanja; he was under the command of Lt. Col. Stojan Zdravković, and served as a contact between the building of the Ministry of the Army and Navy – the seat of General Simović – and the troops that were besieging the Palace.)) (Dragiša N. Ristić correspondence and interview, Box 2, Folder 2.33 Hoover Institution Archives)

*****

Now back to the activities of 26 March 1941.

Between 5 p.m. and 6 p.m. on 26 March, Macdonald – Simović's 2nd meeting

In addition to their secret meeting **in the morning on 26 March,** there was at least one more meeting between them, in Simović's Headquarters in Zemun, **in the late afternoon of the 26th.** In his speech on 28 March 1941, and some documents he left behind, Simović did not mention their first meeting. However, in the documents referred to as "(Simović(44)", and "Simović(51)", the General wrote about the late afternoon meeting, but described its purpose differently.

- **Simović's version – written in exile**

After having had the second meeting with Mirković **at 5 p.m. on 26 March** - which had to last a few minutes - Simović remained in his office a little longer, and he wrote about it:

((During that time the British Air Force Attaché Macdonald visited me inquiring about *the new situation* of Yugoslavia. Not telling him anything about our decision, after a shorter conversation I took leave of him.)) "Za to vreme posetio me je britanski vazduhoplovni izaslanik, pukovnik Makdonald interesujući se za *novu situaciju* Jugoslavije. Ne govoreći mu ništa o našoj odluci, ja sam se posle kraćeg ragovora oprostio s njime." (Simović(44), 39. Italics added.)

New situation ... since their first, early-morning meeting? The new was that in the meantime two Notes to the Protocol had been published, and it was understandable for Macdonald to wonder and to find out whether they had affected Simović's attitude, whether he was still committed to the coup. Perhaps that uncertainty was the reason for Macdonald's delayed dispatching of the report about the morning meeting to London until 7:40 p.m. (Stafford)cp), 414): if Simović had changed his mind, the report would be meaningless, and therefore should not be sent.

Even **IF** Simović did not tell Macdonald about their decision - which is doubtful, because they talked about it that morning - what did they talk about? What did they tell each other? Did Macdonald inform Simović of the Prime Minister's order to Campbell, "*do not neglect any alternative to which we may have to resort if we find present Government have gone beyond recall. ... Keep it up by every means that occur to you.*" ? (Dilks[ed], 366. Italics added.)

Every means included the Putsch, which the British in Belgrade had already been ordered to support, and had been committed to execute.

- **Simović's version – written in 1951**

In 1951, back in Belgrade, Simović provided quite a different explanation of that second meeting with Macdonald:

> ((Afterwards I have received British Air Attaché Macdonald who gave me some reports related to the delivery of materiel for the air force armament.))
> "Potom sam primio britanskog vazduhoplovnog izaslanika pukovnika Makdonalda, koji mi je učinio neka saopštenja u vezi sa isporukom materijala za naoružanje vazduhoplovstva." (Simović(51), 14)

In view of British armament shortages - as revealed in the Eden-Campbell correspondence - and of the topics of Macdonald and Simović's first meeting, this explanation about the second meeting is not convincing. In their accounts about contacts with the British, neither Simović nor Mirković wrote about British deliveries of material for the Air Force. If there were some, they must have been minimal – and would have been handled routinely, through the lower chain of the purchasing department, not through the Commander himself.

*****

It is intriguing to note that D. Ristić did not mention this second meeting of Macdonald and Simović on 26 March, although "General Simović urged me to assemble all available facts in the matter and have them published", and "the general turned over his archives to me", wrote Ristić (p.15) If Ristić did not know of the first meeting, because Simović did not write about it, the second meeting was recorded in Simović's archives, and Ristić had to know about it.

Similarly, Major Knežević wrote nothing about his brother Radoje's contact with Tom Masterson of SOE. Both authors wanted to present the Putsch as solely domestic, a Serbian, affair, not "influenced" or "encouraged" by the British. That served the British well because - once the tragic consequences of the Putsch began to develop throughout Yugoslavia - the British could claim: **"See, it was not our doing."**

*****

Hugh Dalton wrote in his diary for 27 March: "It was the Air Attaché who went to Simović and finally persuaded him to act." (Pimlott(ed), 176) Did Dalton have in mind the first or the second meeting, or both ?

Tupanjanin's pressure on Simović

As decided at the all-British conference on 19 March, SOE was to continue *working primarily through Tupanjanin and Serbian Peasant Party,* but also to endeavor to coordinate action with Trifunović-Birčanin; Tupanjanin was *to attempt to organize politico-military movements.* **(Part One, pages 108-9)**

Tupanjanin really made serious attempts. First, with the resignation of three ministers, on 20 March, hoping that their resignation would cause the fall of the government. (Staffoord(cp), 411) The failure did no stop him.

> "**About 7:00 [p.m., on 26 March]** news came that the air force commander had been placed on the retired list to be published the next day by the government press." (Ristić, 86. Emphasis added.)

Simović provided more details about this "news". On the 26th, after Macdonald left the Air Force Command – Simović wrote:

> ((**About 7 p.m.** my brother Dr Miloš called me on the phone and informed me, that Tupanjanin had called him and had told him: "Have you heard that your brother and General Brašić had been retired? Might as well, he deserves it, what is he waiting for?))
> "**Oko 7 časova** pozvao me je moj brat Dr. Miloš na telefon i saopštio, da ga je Tupanjanin zvao i rekao mu: "Jeste li čuli, da su vaš brat i đeneral Brašić penzionisani? Ako, tako mu i treba, šta čeka?" (Simović(44), 39)

Dr Miloš Sekulić told Ilija Jukić several times that Dr Miloš Tupanjanin, deputy-leader of SPP, **at 2 p.m., on 26 March,** indeed informed Gen. Simović's brother, Dr. Miloš, of alleged retirement of Generals Simović, Mirković and a few others. (Jukić(65), 139)

*****

Tupanjanin's question, *what is Simović waiting for*, is an additional evidence that the Serbian Peasant Party (subsidized by the British) was not only well aware of the plan for the coup, but was forcefully urging it, especially after the all-British conference on 19 March.

> ... Miloš Tupanjanin, who was very active on behalf of the British intelligence service, managed to influence some of the *Putsch* leaders without their knowing that they were being indirectly manipulated. At about 2:00 P.M. on March 26, he planted the seeds of a rumor that Generals Simović, Mirković, and Bogoljub Ilić were about to be placed on a retired list. (Jukić, 60-61)

In London, on Thursday, 27th March, Dalton recorded in his diary: "The money we have spent on the Serb *Peasant Party and other Opposition Parties has given wonderful value.*" (Pimlott(ed), 176-7. Italics added.) Tupanjanin's SPP received the lion's share of it.

In the evening of the 26th March: Simović – Mirković's 3rd meeting

Again, according to Simović, some time after he had spoken with his brother, Gen. Simović called Gen. Mirković and Col. Dragutin Savić into his office. Mirković reported about definitive preparations for the action, scheduled to start **at 2:15 a.m.** Simović instructed Savić to remain at his command post at the airport, to take over the direction of the action in case he and Mirković should be prevented. Simović added to Savić that he would be at his home. (Simović(44), 39-40) ((Because my further presence at the Air Force Headquarters was not necessary any more, I went home.)) After going through his usual paperwork routine, he went to bed **around 11 p.m.** (Simović(44), 40-41)

*****

As presented above, in 1956 Simović wrote a different account: that he had led the coup action, as soon as it had commenced, to the full conclusion. (Simović(56), 77) In 1944, however: he had gone to bed.

According to Trifunović-Birčanin – Decision for the Putsch: between 7 and 9 p.m.

As his fellow coup-wisher Jovan Đonović wrote in 1952, *Vojvoda* **Ilija Trifunović-Birčanin** was visiting Gen. Mirković in Zemun every day from 24 through the evening of 26 March. (Knežević, 113) "... on the evening of March 26 the president of the Serbian veterans' organization, Ilija Trifunović-Birčanin, was at air force headquarters with General Mirković, ..." (Ristić, 88)

As shown in **Part One, page 141, a**fter 6 a.m. on the 27th, *Vojvoda* **Birčanin** was interviewed about the sequence of events, a report on the coup was then prepared and sent to London. In it he stated that "It was decided **between the hours of 7 and 9 last night** to carry out the Coup that had been planned if the King had not left Belgrade." That was **after the second Macdonald-Simović meeting.**
 This statement contradicts Mirković's claim of making the decision about 2 p.m., and Simović's at 5 p.m. on the 26th March. However, it is not clear if *Vojvoda* was thinking of the *decision itself,* or of *issuing instructions* to the coup-participants after the decision had been previously made. One would hope that in the future it will be possible to resolve this uncertainty.

Gen. Mirković and *Vojvoda* Ilija Trifunović-Birčanin

The night of 26-27 March Trifunović stayed with Mirković at the Air Force Headquarters in Zemun. Early on the 27th they came together to Belgrade where the new government was being formed. As a witness and participant in the event, he was then able to give an interview there, which was promptly reported to London, as mentioned above.

*****

In 1941, Mirković stated that the *Vojvoda* had under arms 500-600 Četniks in Belgrade, whom Mirković could use if needed. (Bosnić(ed), 21)

In the letter to *The Evening News*, in 1960, the General provided a different information about the *Vojvoda's* presence:

> ((**Only on 26 March, around 8 o'clock in the evening, I brought** Ilija Birčanin, president of *Narodna odbrana* to the Air Force Command, and then I met and got to know him for the first time. He had nothing planned, nor was he preparing anything. I invited him as a precaution, because I have had a report that he also was preparing something, and therefore I wanted to avoid a conflict of the troops with his Četniks, which could have arisen due to lack of information. When he came to me and told me that he was preparing nothing, I kept him that evening in the Air Force Command.
>
> ((As can be seen from the above about Ilija Bičanin, he did not participate with us in the execution of the Coup d'état, and even less "could he have joined us in the middle of March", because I met him for the first time only **around 8 o'clock in the evening, 26 March.**)) (Karapandžić(AB), 151-2. Emphasis added.)

In 1966, Ristić – who used the terms *Revolution* and *revolutionaries* for the Putsch and Putschists – provided a different explanation:

> All air force regiments were on the alert and capable of reaching the capital in a short time. And on the evening of March 26, the president of the Serbian veterans' organization, Ilija Trifunović-Birčanin, was at the air force headquarters with General Mirković, *ready to mobilize his organization to help the revolutionaries if necessary.* (Ristić, 88. Italics added.)

Clearly, Birčanin – i.e., the Četniks – did not participate in the execution of the coup.

*****

In 1979, Živan Knežević wrote about yet another use of the Četniks: in a meeting **at 3 p.m. on 26 March,** Mirković asked the Major: "Hoćeš da ti stavim na raspoloženje pet stotina četnika sa Ilijom Trifunovićem?" ((Do you want me to place at your disposal five hundred Chetniks with Ilija Trifunović?)) After thinking about potentially negative effects on the operation, the Major asked that the Chetniks be placed at a park, **at 4 a.m.**, so he could use them if necessary. (Knežević, 173)

Putting a very renowned *Vojvoda* at the disposal of a *Major,* who had failed to pass General Staff exams – a very unlikely offer. However, the Major also acknowledged that the *Vojvoda* spent the night of 26-27 March in the Air Force Command.

*****

The New York Times reporter in Belgrade wrote a different story about the Četniks' activities on 26 April.

"Toward 11:30" in the evening, Brock phoned his lead to the papers' center in Bern, Switzerland.

> "This is absolute dynamite!" [Dan] Brigham interrupted, at the reports of the Montenegrin and Kragujevach [Kragujevac] revolts. "You'll be out off that country by morning, fellow, if we send this [to *The New York Times*]."
> "Nevertheless, send it," I said.
> "You've double-checked it?"
> "More," I said. "My sources are excellent. *The Serbian peasantry, led by the Chetniks, are rising all over the country.* This is to be revolution."
> "I'd better hang another dateline on it," said Dan, cautiously.
> "The dateline is Belgrade," I said. (Brock, 148. Italics added.)

However, at 11:30 p.m. on the 26th of April – three hours before the Putsch – the Četniks were not leading the Serbian peasantry in any uprising.

On 26 March, after 9 p.m. – plan to blow up his train, seize Prince Paul

> In the evening of March 26, … the officers assigned to air force headquarters were suddenly called to duty. … After 9:00 P.M. the service company was ordered to start fortifying the building…

> While all this was going on, news reached us that Prince Paul was leaving Belgrade. The cardinal first steps of the plan were the seizure of Prince Paul and the members of the cabinet and the removal of army commanders loyal to the Regent. We were gratified, however, to learn that Paul had left his family in the palace – he suspected nothing. (Ristić, 88-9)

As described in **Part One, page 141**, "Daddy", Ilija Trifunović-Birčanin, stated that the decision for the coup was made "if the King had not left Belgrade." He explained:

> The conspirators learnt that the Prince had gone away and they were not sure if he took the King with him. They passed the word to hold up the train, giving as a pretext that the line was mined. They then ascertained that the King was at home and asleep. As soon as this was learnt, they decided to execute the plan that night. Orders were given that the troops begin their movements **at 2 am** after the telephone lines were cut. (Great Britain, Special Operations Executive, 91087-10V, Hoover Institution Archives. Emphasis added.)

Gen. Mirković provided more details:

> **About 5:30 p.m. of the 26th March** Lt.-Col. Miloje Dinić informed Mirković that security had been ordered for the passage of the Royal Palace's train between Zemun and Batajnica **at 9 p.m.** The news confused Mirković for a moment. He assumed that the coup conspiracy had been betrayed and that Prince Paul was leaving the country with his family. Therefore he ordered his friend, Stevan Bobinac, president of the Četnik association in Zemun, to blow up the train. However, after getting information that Prince Paul was going to Slovenia for a vacation and that his family was staying in Belgrade, the General countermanded the order to Bobinac. (Bosnić(ed), 22-3)

*****

However, the Americans were told a different, incorrect story: "Regent Prince Paul, warned by Palace functionaries, attempted to flee with his wife, Princes Olga of Greece, and the children. He was detained." (Brock, 172)

Preparation of the Royal Proclamation

According to the Putschists' records, once committed to the Putsch, on 26 March they began planning to compose a Proclamation, even before the final schedule of operations had been set. To be prepared in a hurry – as were many other things that day – its theme and text were not thought-through and well defined; this is reflected in different versions recorded by the Putschists. However, the Proclamation was to be a very serious political move, explaining and justifying the goal of the military coup, and therefore deserves attention.

- **General Mirković's recollections of Radoje Knežević's role**

As soon a Mirković decided to act, he told Major Knežević to bring to Zemun his brother Radoje to edit a proclamation.

> **About 5 p.m.** Professor Radoje came to the Headquarters, they met there for the first time, and the General kept him there until **3 a.m. of the 27th March**. At that time the General sent the Professor, together with Capt. Dragiša Ristić, to the home of General Simović, to bring him to the Ministry of the Army, which was in the hands of Gen. Mirković. (Bosnić(ed), 21-2)

*****

Afterwards, over a period of time, Major Knežević was publishing his account of the Putsch in Serbian immigrant papers in the US and Canada. General Mirković occasionally reacted to such accounts. Thus in a letter to the *Voice of Canadian Serbs,* dated in London, 27 March 1955, then retired Mirković explained in more details how he had engaged "the Professor" to work on a Royal Proclamation:

> Gen. Simović ordered Mirković to prepare a Proclamation, in French, which would be broadcast abroad. Inquiring among his officers who could perform that task, Major Dušan Babić informed him that a brother of Major Živan Knežević had been a teacher of French to the young King Peter. Mirković telephoned Živan, and he confirmed this information. Asking whether his brother would come to the Air Force HQ, Živan replied: "Send him an auto and he will come." The General did so, and Radoje came at **about 9 p.m.** [of 26 March]. That was the first time the General saw

Radoje, and issued him an order to prepare a Proclamation. The Professor worked on it the rest of the night. (Karapandžić(AB), 135-6)

Belgrade's daily, *Večernje novosti (The Evening News),* published a serial by Nikola Milanović, «Vojni puč i 27. mart 1941. godine» («Military coup and 27 March 1941»), in its issues from 20 July to 20 August 1960. Gen. Mirković found significant inaccuracies in Milanović's presentation, and on 4 November 1960 sent a lengthy letter to the paper, providing detailed corrections on the more important mis-statements. *Inter alia,* he wrote about his engagement of Radoje Knežević, as shown here (translated):

((I met professor Radoje Knežević **on 26 March at 8 o'clock in the evening**, and General Simović met him **only on 27 March in the morning, at 03:30 a.m.**. My acquaintance with Radoje Knežević occurred in the following way: General Simović had ordered me to prepare the King's proclamation in French, to be broadcast to foreign countries on radio. I needed somebody who knew well the French literary language, and then my Head of the Intelligence Department told me that Major Knežević had a brother who, earlier, had been the King's instructor of the French language. Thus I decided to use him to draft this proclamation. I telephoned to Živan and he directed his brother to me **at 8 o'clock in the evening,** that day [26 March]. After I had given instruction to Radoje Knežević what to write, I did not see him any more until the Coup d'état had been accomplished.)) (Karapandžić(AB), 149-50. Emphasis added.)

((When, **about 03:30 a.m., on 27 March**, the Coup had been mostly accomplished, I sent Captain Dragiša Ristić in an automobile to the home of General Simović, so Simović could come to the Ministry of the Army to assume the state's powers and to form the new government. On that occasion I sent also Radoje Knežević with Ristić to Simović, so he could take along and hand in [to Simović] the already drafted proclamation. There, that was the only role of professor Knežević in the Coup d'état on 27 March 1941. He was drafting the King's proclamation in the building of the Air Force Command while we were carrying out the coup.)) (Karapandžić(AB), 150, Emphasis added.)

*****

Thus, according to Mirković, he met Radoje Knežević, for the first time, at **5 p.m., 9 p.m., and 8 p.m. of the 26th March**. Although inconsistent on the hour they met, the General was consistent on the Knežević's role and the length of his stay in the Air Force Command.

- **Živan Knežević's version**

In 1979 Živan Knežević presented the sequence of meetings differently.

On the morning of 26 March, the Major went to Zemun to see Mirković. They agreed that the Major should come back at **3 p.m.,** together with his brother, Professor Radoje. [At that time, the title of "Professor" was given in Yugoslavia to teachers in secondary education. Radoje was a high school teacher.]

At 3 p.m. both brothers came to Zemun. The General met the Professor for the first time, they kissed [on cheeks, an old custom] and, at Mirković's suggestion, they switched to the informal way of communicating. (Knežević, 172)

Because Simović was not around, his brother Radoje left *"spremljeni proglas" (a prepared proclamation)* to Gen. Mirković, with a request to hand it over to Gen. Simović.

That Proclamation was to be addressed to the people immediately after the coup, *with Simović's signature.* It contained a harsh judgment of the existing regime, and at the same time an obligation to rule the country in the future in a democratic way.

((It was stressed that, *until the election of the Parliament,* the state affairs would be managed by Government composed by the delegated representatives of the parties with a root in the people.))
"Isticalo se da će, *do izbora Skupštine,* državne poslove voditi Vlada sastavljena od delegiranih predstavnika stranaka sa korenom u narodu." (Knežević, 173. Italics added.)

Živan continued his story: **about 9 p.m., on the 26th**, *Professor Knežević left his home in an auto provided by Mirković to bring him to Zemun.* In the General's office, the Professor found Ilija Trifunović-Birčanin, president of *Narodna odbana,* and a number of officers who were to participate in the coup. (Knežević, 210. Italics added.)

*****

So, according to Živan: Radoje came to the HQ **at 3 p.m. (not at 5 p.m.),** gave an **already prepared proclamation** to Mirković, was not kept in the HQ but went home. **At about 9 p.m.** he returned to the HQ in an auto sent for him by Mirković.

Mirković did not mention this allegedly already prepared Radoje's proclamation, but claimed that **he** had instructed Radoje what to write, and that the proclamation had to be signed by the King. It would be expected that the proclamation would contain information on the King's assumption of the royal powers and the nomination of Gen. Simović as the head of the new government. Radoje's reported proclamation was much broader and resembled his alleged political program of 11 March 1941. Again, **IF** the proclamation contained a program as claimed above – and the brothers expected Hitler's attack – how could they expect to have time for the election of Parliament?

- **What Simović said about the proclamation**

On 28 March 1941, after the Thanksgiving Service for King Peter's accession to the throne, Gen. Dušan Simović delivered his address to hierarchs of the Serbian Orthodox Church. At that moment harmony and mutual understanding and praise among the members of the new Government were needed, in order to assure the citizens that everything had now been settled and returned to normal. (**Chapter 16**) Regarding the Royal Proclamation, he informed the audience:

((As soon as the Putsch had succeeded, **about 2:30 a.m.**)), Simović's adjutant, Captain Ristić, Professor Radoje Knežević, and escorts, came to the General's home, and the Professor informed him of the success. Driving toward the General Staff Headquarters, they talked about further activities. The Professor submitted to the General his draft of the Proclamation about the King's assumption of the Royal Powers and the dismissal of the Regents. With minor corrections, the General approved the text of the Proclamation – *which the King had to sign to become valid*. (Knežević, 366. Italics added.)

*****

It is not clear whether Simović talked about the proclamation *allegedly already prepared* by Radoje Knežević, and given to Mirković for Simović at 3 p.m. on 26 March (as Živan Knežević claimed), or the one that Radoje was working on in Zemun, as instructed by Mirković, while the coup was being executed (as Mirković claimed).

Whichever it was, the text of that proclamation was not read [on Radio Belgrade, after the coup, early on 27 March]. (Karapandžić(AB), 135-6) But the story about the Royal Proclamation did not end as Simović had stated on 28 March.

Civilians aware of the preparations for the coup

- **According to Mirković**

No political figure - not one - was informed about the coup for people's liberation. Only the military were called to give their last word on March 27.

If someone of civilians were present at the Air Force Headquarters during the **afternoon of the 26th and the night of the 26th/27th March,** he was invited because of real needs. Only the following were present:

Major Vladeta Bogdanović – wounded veteran, permanent deputy president of the Association of Reserve Officers, to mobilize all reserve officers of the Belgrade garrison during the night, if required;

Ilija Trifunović-Birčanin, president of *Narodna odbrana,* who had 500-600 armed Četniks in designated homes in Belgrade, who were to get into action, if needed, **where Mirković would order them;**

[Milan] Nakić, former director of the telephone exchange in Belgrade, Mirković's friend, to take the troops to possess the telephone and telegraphs building and temporarily cut services;

Radoje Knežević, Professor, to write the Proclamation.

No other civilian was present or informed of the **preparation and execution** of the 27th March. (Bosnić(ed), 21. Emphasis added.)

*****

When Mirković wrote that no political figure was informed of the preparations for the coup, he probably meant the preparations for **the physical execution of the coup that evening** – and even that was not completely true. At least some *political figures* did know in general terms that the coup was planned – as Simović stated (below). Besides, Mirković knew that *Vojvoda* Ilija Trifunović-Birčanin was a *political figure with some clout* – even if he did not lead a Political Party. Whether the General knew it or not, *"Birchanin was in direct contact with S.O.E."* (Amery, 228. Italics added.) However, Mirković was in contact with the Legation personnel – who worked together with George Taylor and SOE – and one channel was sufficient to transmit SOE's suggestions to Mirković and other conspirators. "Mirković had not set out to enlist the cooperation of civilians, but in the sympathetic minds of the Serbian Cultural Club he found eager accessories." (Hoptner, 255) "In actual fact, it was common gossip in Belgrade that a plot was brewing." (Hoptner, 253)

*****

In **Appendix D** it is shown that *Vojvoda* Trifunović-Birčanin and Jovan Đonović proposed the Putsch to the British in the summer of 1940. Now, knowing of the coup's preparation and being with Mirković in Zemun on 26 March, it is reasonable to assume that the *Vojvoda* had – in strict confidence – informed at least his coup co-plotter Đonović; they had for so long wished it to happen. Evidence shows that he was in contact with the SOE operative(s) to whom he had given the information about the coup's preparation.

Also, Mirković could not have been **certain** that the other civilians he had named did not reveal the coup's preparation to other individuals. Therefore, his assurance to the contrary is questionable.

- **According to Simović**

Prince Paul, Prime Minister Cvetković, Minister of Armed Forces [Petar] Pešić, Chief of the Main General Staff [Petar] Košić, Minister of the [Royal] Palace [Milan] Antić, and Dr. Maček did not know about the preparations for the coup of 27 March 1941. (Simović(51), 10) The civilians aware of the preparation were:

Dr. Srđan Budisavljević, Dr. Dragomir Ikonić, Boža Maksimović, late Bora Č. Marković, a lawyer from Belgrade, Simović's late brother Dr. Miloš Simović, Radoje Knežević, who was informed by his brother, Major Živan.

A few people with whom General Bora Mirković had worked, among them: Ilija Trifunović-Birčanin, and the representatives of the Association of Reserve Officers and Warriors, Raljić and [Vladeta] Bogdanović. (Simović(51), 10)

Previously, Ikonić had joined the Cvetković Government at Simović's initiative. They had to have their man in the Government in order to maintain a contact with Dr. Maček and the representatives of the Croats, and to further hinder the signing of the Tripartite Pact. (Simović(51), 10)

Looking into the list of names given above, one could conclude that most of the leaders of the political Parties were not informed about the preparations for the coup. However, Simović could not be **certain** that some or all of the individuals he named had not spread the word. It was shown above that Boža Maksimović informed Jovan Đonović. Simović also stated that the Serbian Peasant Party "had no part at all either in the preparations or the execution of the act of 27 March 1941"; that the Party's deputy chief, Miloš Tupanjanin, was leading some separate action, "financed by the Intelligence Service, but he had no connection at all with the execution of this act." (Simović(51), 15.)

He probably meant *no connection at all* with **the physical execution of the coup** – which was done by the military – because, as Dalton wrote to Churchill on 28 March, "the real political backing" for the coup "lay outside the old Cabinet and in the *Serb Peasant Party*". (Great Britain, Special Operations Executive, 91087-10V, Hoover Institution archives. Italics added.)

in the afternoon on the 26th March, Miloš Tupanjanin pressured Gen. Simović into action, asking the General's brother *what was the General waiting for.* (Simović(44), 39) So, Tupanjanin knew as well.

After all, at the all-British meeting on 19 March it was decided:

- SOE to continue with preparation for the coup working primarily through ["Uncle"] Tupanjanin and Serbian Peasant Party, to organize politico-military movement;

- but also to coordinate the action with ["Daddy"] Trifunović-Birčanin;
- Service Attachés to work with military elements.

(George Taylor's telegram to London, dated 26 March 1941. Great Britain, Special Operations Executive, 91087-10V, Hoover Institution Archives)

Simović's and Taylor's statements indicate that more civilians were aware of the preparations for the coup in general terms – but not necessarily of detailed plans – than Mirković named in his memoirs of 1 December 1941.

*****

In 1951, in Belgade, Simović contended that Dr. Maček knew nothing about the preparations for 27 March. (Simović(51), 10) Although he did not know of actual preparations, it seems that in the evening of the 23rd March Maček had a hunch that something was brewing up. As described in **Chapter 10**, that evening Simović had a lengthy conversation with Prince Paul. Writing about it, the General noted that Ministers Maček, Šutej and Konstantinović were invited for dinner hosted by the Regent's wife, Princess Olga. (Simović(44), 23-4) Maček's suspicion is also shown in **Chapter 10**: he and Cvetković suggested to the Prince to arrest Simović at once.

(Defense Minister Pešić, also present at the dinner, was against the arrest, so Simović was not arrested.)

What was Radoje Knežević's coup-related role?

The SOE historian William J. M. Mackenzie wrote THE SECRET HISTORY OF SOE in 1945-1947, but the book was allowed to be published only in 2000. On page 111 he stated about the brothers Knežević and the coup of 27 March 1941:

> The higher officers of the Army were pessimistic and cautious, and the initiative came from the younger officers, in particular Knesević, then Minister of the Court, and General Bora Mirković, the Deputy Chief of the Air Staff. SO2 knew of the conspiracy in advance, but *they were not concerned in its details,* and *it surprised them when it exploded in the small hours of 27 March, twenty-four hours before the due date.* The effective forces were supplied only by the Air Force, a Tank brigade, and a battalion of Royal Guards commanded by Knesević's younger brother; ... (Italics added.)

A minor, understandable omission: The Minister of the Court was Radoje Knežević – but he became one after the coup, not before, and he was not an officer. SOE leaders in Belgrade **were not surprised**, because they were kept informed of developments by "Daddy" Trifunović-Birčanin. **(Part One, 138-41)**

Mackenzie did not provide evidence of Radoje Knežević's coup-related initiatives and activities. Therefore it is informative to present evidence provided by the brothers themselves and other participants in the events.

- **First in R. Knežević's own words**

(A) **In October 1950**, Radoje Knežević wrote: "I, myself, took *an active part* in the planning, as well as the carrying out the coup d'état which, on 27 March 1941, overthrew the Government of Mr. Tsvetkovitch and the dictatorial and pro-German regime of Prince Paul."

In his view, the signature of the Tripartite Pact was "the surrender of Yugoslavia's neutrality and *a formal military alliance with the Axis Powers.*"

For him, Yugoslavia's adherence to the Tripartite Pact was a "pact with the devil". (R. L. Knéjévitch, "Prince Paul, Hitler, and Salonika", *International Affairs (Royal Institute of International Affairs 1944),* Vol. 27, No. 1. (Jan., 1951), 38, 40, 44. Italics added.)

> At dawn on 27 March 1941, in Belgrade, a military coup d'état, carried out *by young officers,* swept away this regime of betrayal and dictatorship. This was not the putsch of a few adventurers avid for power, or *influenced by outside interests..." (Ibid.* 40. Italics added.)

Radoje was convinced "that the signature of the Tripartite Pact was not in reality an act of weakness, but an issue of *conspiracy planned for several years. (Ibid, 43.* Italics added.)

*****

Prince Paul surely did not endear himself to R. Knežević when he had fired the professor as the instructor of French to the young King. It is hard to assume that the reasons were the professor's teaching of the language.

> **In September 1977** issue of *Slavic Review*, Professor David A. T. Stafford stated: "In the SOE view, it was [Radoje] Knežević who took the initiative in fomenting a coup, and his were 'the brains behind the conspiracy.' The SOE considered Mirković, 'while enthusiastic and energetic, to be unfortunately entirely without political capacity.' (page 412, note 48) Being *entirely without political capacity* was Mirković's weak side, skilfully used by the British to «influence» and «encourage» him to achieve their own aims.
>
> About the SOE contacts in Belgrade, Stafford wrote: 'Their links with the air force conspirators, led by Bora Mirković, were only indirect – through Trifunović and Radoje Knežević on the Yugoslav side, and through the air attaché's contacts with Mirković on the British side. Nonetheless, they were kept relatively well informed about developments." (page 412)
>
> R. Knežević reacted to Stafford's statement. First, he pointed out: "... I was one of the organizers of the said coup d'état. Winston S. Churchill in his book *The Grand Alliance* mentions me as well as my brother Živan L. Knežević."
>
> Then he continued with his dissatisfaction with Professor Stafford's statement: "In my letter to him, dated February 28, 1978, I said that his "assertion about me conveys the impression that, in some manner, I have been in connection with the SOE people then in Belgrade." I impressed upon him that "as a matter of fact, while in Yugoslavia, I have never heard the names of SOE or SIS people. I didn't even know a single Englishman living in my native country." I asked him to let me know what prompted him to state that I had been a link between SOE people and General Mirković.
>
> Dr. Stafford replied on March 13, 1978. He said that "a normally highly reliable informant, whose name I am not at liberty to divulge, told me that Masterson saw you prior to the *coup*."

On April 8, 1978, Knežević sent to Stafford the following response: "Whoever that person may be, a He or a She, that person had told you a deliberate lie. It was certainly not someone of SOE people; ... And why would you keep Him or Her hidden in anonymity? I would ask you to reveal the name of that 'normally highly reliable informant' in order for me to deal with Him or Her in an appropriate manner. It would be in the interest of historical truth, to which we are both attached."

"I have waited for his [Stafford's] response up to this date, to no avail." – wrote R. Knežević in a letter To the Editor of *Slavic Review*, (Vol. 38, No. 2, Jan. 1979, pp. 361-362)

*****

In the interest of historic truth, here is some evidence which should be considered.

++ Young officers and the Putsch

The Putsch carried out *by young officers* **only**, without Generals Mirković and Simović? As described above by his brother Živan, it was **Mirković** who determined the day of the action, not the young officers. **Mirković** was assigning specific tasks to them – not they to him. **They** had no plans of their own.

But this line of *young-officers-carrying-out-the-coup* supports the disinformation Radoje gave to Tom Masterson on 27 March about his own and Živan's role, quoted in **Chapter 10** (and in **Part One, 139**)

++ Influence of outside interests

Radoje's assertion that *the Putsch was **not** influenced by outside interests* is a gross disinformation. By the 18th of March, "when it became increasingly clear that the signature [of the Pact] was imminent, the British mobilized their full effort to prevent it. This effort encompassed both diplomatic pressure and subversive political action, and culminated in the coup on March 27." (Stafford(cp), 401)

On the 19th of March an all-British round-table conference was held in Belgrade with the SOE, SIS and Legation staff. A decision was made to apply both, diplomatic pressure and subversive political action. The roles were assigned to the SOE operatives, service attachés, the Serbian Peasant Party, *Vojvoda* Trifunović and others. (**Part One, 108-10**)

As Hugh Dalton stated, "S.O.E. agents were in Belgrade on March 27th 1941, when the coup took place ... *This had been well prepared beforehand*. (Dalton, 375. Emphasis added.)

Radoje Knežević, "a fervent Serb nationalist and leading Democratic Party politician", "was in close touch with SOE." (Onslow, 56)
Whether he did or did not know, his Party was also "subsidized" by the British from January 1941. He himself was in contact with Masterson... but told Major Nikola Kosić that he had not seen an Englishman. Also, as shown in **Chapter 3,** Radoje was telling his Party chief, Grol - years before writing this article – that Mirković had cooperated with the British. Thus, he may not have known **the extent** of the *outside interests* on the Putsch, but he did know in 1950 that there had been British contacts with the Putschists.

++ Conspiracy planned for years

"The Professor's" conviction that, *the signature of the Tripartite Pact (on 25 March 1941) was an issue of conspiracy planned for several years,* was peculiar. Germany, Italy and Japan signed the Pact on 27 September 1940. How could anybody conspire to plan signing a non-existing plan *several years in advance?*
Italy invaded Albania on 7 April 1939, and thus created not only a second frontier with Yugoslavia, but established the control of the Adriatic Sea. Prince Paul reacted by secretly transferring three-quarters of the country's gold reserve to **England** in the first half of May 1939. (Balfour & Mackay, 173) Would he do that if he *conspiratorially planned for several years* to join "*a formal military alliance with the Axis powers*" (p.40) – what the Professor accused him of? Most certainly he would not.

++ "A formal military alliance with the Axis Powers"

The older Knežević did not explain how Yugoslavia's joining the Tripartite Pact meant "*a formal military alliance with the Axis Powers.*" His younger brother attempted to do it years later. How? By circumventing the truth.

The Putschist Ristić reached the conclusion: "*Had the Cvetković government remained in power*", i.e., had the coup not been executed, "*Yugoslavia might not have participated in the German campaign against Russia."* (p. 137)
The Putschist Živan Knežević – always reflecting his brother's opinion – maintained that ((the Pact was really pulling Yugoslavia into the conflict and really on the side of the Axis Power.)) (Milunović(ed), 45)
To provide veracity to his assertion, Živan juggled the facts: he simply referred to the **Article 3** of the Tripartite Pact between Germany, Italy, and Japan of 27 September 1940, instead to the **Note No. 3** to the Protocol of Adhesion of Yugoslavia to the Pact of 25 March 1941.

In the Statement issued by the US Secretary of State on the Tripartite Pact, September 27, 1940, the **Article 3** reads:

> Japan, Germany and Italy agree to cooperate in their efforts on the aforesaid lines. They further undertake to assist one another with all political, economic and military means when one of the three Contracting Parties is attacked by a power at present not involved in the European War or in the Sino-Japanese Conflict. (http://www.mtholyoke.edu/acad/intrel/WorldWar2/tripartite.htm   3/24/13; Balfour & Mackey, 314-15)

About the 2nd sentence Živan wrote that the signatories "se OBAVEZUJU da jedan drugom priteknu u pomoć ..." ((are OBLIGATED to rush to help each other ,,,)). (Milunović(ed), 42. Capital letters in the source.) Then he continued:

> ((And whoever signed the Pact was obligating himself to fight against America alongside the Axis. Consequently, with the Pact the Prince's regime was obligated to fight alongside the Axis,))

> "I ko god je potpisao Pakt obavezivao se da se bije protiv Amerike uz Osovinu. Prema tome, Paktom se [je] Knežev režim bio obavezan da se bori uz Osovinu." (Milunović(ed), 42)

In this essay Živan simply ignored **the Notes** attached to the Protocol of Yugoslavia's adhesion to the Tripartite Pact as non-existent, although in his book he presented them and commented on them (pp. 115-23). He stated that all three Foreign Ministers (German, Italian and Japanese) signed the Protocol, but omitted to inform that the Japanese Minister added to his name: *"Ad referendum"*, which means: *For reference: to be referred to higher authority.* (Webster's II Dictionary) (*27. Mart 1941. Sedamdeset godina kasnije, Zbornik radova - 27 March 1941, Seventy years later, A collection of works*), Beograd, 2012, 182.)

The central text related to Yugoslavia's non-military obligation was contained in **Note No. 3**, which the Putschist Ristić summarized:

> Germany and Italy, taking into account the military situation, assure the Yugoslav government that they will not, of their own accord, make any demand for military assistance, ... (Ristić, 82)

Živan also stated that the Notes attached to the Protocol **(Part One, pp. 124-6)** were signed by the German and Italian Foreign Ministers only, not by the Japanese. This implied that the Pact with Yugoslavia was related to the European region only, not the Far East. Therefore, Živan's claim that Yugoslavia was obligated to fight against the USA is not valid. Not requesting military assistance, the Pact was – for all actual purposes – not a military one, in spite of Živan's calling it "vojni savez sa Nemačkom" ((a military alliance with Germany)). (Milunović(ed), 39)

Ristić quoted German Foreign Minister, Ribbentrop, stating that the whole treaty complex was *"nothing but a lot of humbug and actually did not amount to anything."* (page 82) Note No. 3 to the Protocol was the principal reason for the Minister's dissatisfaction.

*****

In his thorough analysis of Hitler's strategy in 1940-1941, military historian Dr Martin L. Creveld concluded:

> Hitler's preparation for the invasion of Greece put Yugoslavia in a position that was both weak and strong. It was weak in that Yugoslavia saw herself surrounded on all sides by the military force of the Axis; it was strong in that her attitude would in the last resort determine whether Hitler's design for a short and 'small' war in southeastern Europe was, after all, practicable. In addition, there was the problem of the Yugoslav roads and railways, the importance of which has been grossly underestimated by historical scholarship. Hitler did not treat Yugoslavia 'like a prima donna' just for the sake of having her sign a – *worthless – Tripartite Pact*. It was the railways that he – and even more than him, his generals – were after, and it was only because Cvetkovic had been too clever for him that he had to content himself with *the empty gesture that was Yugoslavia's signature of the Tripartite Pact.* To him [Hitler] 25 March 1941 was the confirmation of failure, not the beginning of success. (van Creveld, 181-2. Italics added.)

Worthless, empty gesture – not a *military alliance* that obligated Yugoslavia to fight the USA, as Knežević claimed.

*****

One can not know whether Živan had read Ristić's book or not. But one can read, in his own book, how he sacrificed the truth in order to achieve his objectives, when he misinformed his battalion twice, early on 27 March 1941, before leading it to execute the coup:

> ((**By the order of our Supreme Commander,** His Majesty King Peter II, our battalion had received tonight a solemn and historic assignment. Everybody has to carry out only my orders...)) (Knežević, 196. Emphasis added.)

The King issued no such order; at that time he had no idea what Živan had been doing. The Major did it the third time the same morning when he purposefully misinformed a mass of officers that a Royal Declaration had been signed by the King – when it had not been. (Knežević, 257) **(Part One, pages 141-2)** His and Radoje's participation in the deceptions on 27 March 1941 are presented above.

Therefore, one can not be sure that Živan's reference to **the Article 3**, instead to **the Note No. 3**, was due to his ignorance of the Protocol of 25 March 1941, signed in Vienna.

++ Thomas Masterson didn't have any reason to misinform London about Radoje Knežević's cooperation with SOE

"As a matter of fact, while in Yugoslavia, I have never heard the names of the SOE or SIS people. I didn't even know a single Englishmen living then I my native country", wrote R. Knežević to Prof. D. Stafford on 28 February 1978.

While in Yugoslavia, i.e. until mid-April 1941, Radoje may have never *heard* the names of the SOE or SIS people, because they operated in secret and used code-designations. (Masterson's was "DHY") However, that does not necessarily mean that he did not cooperate with one possibly even without knowing his name.

Radoje did know at least one Englishman, Thomas Masterson, the SOE chief in Belgrade before George Taylor came to Belgrade, and cooperated with him. As shown in Chapter 10, on 27 March 1941, Masterson reported to London what he was told by Radoje about the role of his brother Živan [Jika] in the execution of the coup. Masterson also reported:

> The following information was given to me today in connection with the Coup d'Etat.
> Radne KNJEVICH, Professor of Belgrade, who is also a member of the Democratic Party Executive and with whom, some six weeks ago, we discussed the possibility of developing propaganda, appears to have spoken to General MERKOVICH and suggested the idea of a coup d'état. After discussing questions of detail, they agreed to ask General SIMOVICH if he would take the lead. He agreed. General MERKOVICH and Professor KNJEVICH thereupon spoke to General ILICH. He agreed. … 300 planes were made available at Zemun. 16 gun batteries were brought in in readiness together with all the tanks available in Belgrade. SIMOVICH gave the order at 2 am when all left their barracks with Jika at the head of his battalion on horseback. …
>
> At 4 am, Jika went to SIMOVICH's house, announced that everything had been completed and took him to the War Office where KNJEVICH and General MERKOVICH had already arrived. CVETKOVICH, Cinzar MERKOVICH and 3 Croat ministers were brought to the War Office when General SIMOVICH told the Croats that the revolt was not against them and that there would be no alterations in their positions.
> …
>
> General SIMOVICH produced a list of people he was going to invite to form a Cabinet. It contained a list of generals and some younger civilians. KNJEVICH was asked for advice. He replied that the matter could be solved in two ways. Either a cabinet of soldiers or of civilians. He advised that he should constitute his cabinet largely from the existing political parties. General SIMOVICH eventually agreed, tore up his list and asked KNJEVICH to form a new one on the basis of party collaboration. (Great Britain, Special Operation Executive, 91087-10.V Hoover Institutions Archives)

Masterson used the French alphabet to write the brothers' names. "The Professor" told him rightly indeed that he had been a member of the *Glavni Odbor* [Executive] of the Democratic Party, and that his younger brother, "Jika" (Žika-Živan) was a Major. When comparing this report given to Masterson with the accounts of events presented by brothers Knežević (such as *"A painful scene"* between the General and the Professor, in **Chapter 14**), it becomes evident once more that the man who gave this distorted information to Masterson was Radoje Knežević. He did it after the formation of the new government, on 27 March. Masterson had to report as he had been informed, and had no reason to misinform London.

So: Radoje *did know at least one Englishman*, and *did cooperate with the SOE*, in spite of his denials. And what did Radoje tell Masterson?
- **HE** *suggested to General Mirković the idea of a coup.*
- **HE** *and Mirković then talked Generals Simović and Ilić into accepting the idea.*
- **His brother** *was then asked to take the command of the coup.*
- *300 planes were made available at Zemun.*

His brother *went to Simović's house to inform him …*

According to Mirković's memoirs of 1 December 1941 and subsequent statements, Simović's accounts, and information provided by Julian Amery, Alexander Glen – presented here and in **Part One** - Radoje's information was not true. The idea of a coup sprang in the summer of 1940. Radoje met Gen. Mirković for the first time on 26 March 1941.

The account of *300 planes made available in Zemun* is presented differently in "Transfer of bombers to Zemun airport" in **Chapter 13,** above. His brother wrote that in the whole country Yugoslavia have had 200 modern aircrafts, (Milunović(ed), 39); forty five fighters were in Zemun. (Knežević, 52-3)

While "Radne" told Masterson on 27 March, 1941, that **HE** *had suggested the idea of a coup,* some thirty eight years later "Jika" wrote that **HE AND HIS FRIEDS** conceived the idea of *an intervention of the army* sometimes late in 1940. ("Motivation of the Knežević brothers", **Chapter 8,** above.)

Then, Masterson's report was sent to Churchill. Coming from a well known and respected man, the report's veracity would probably not be questioned. One should not be surprised if this report later influenced Churchill's identification of the brothers as co-leaders of the coup. Subsequent pleas to Churchill by Simović and Ristić, to correct inaccuracies, were ineffective. **(Part One, 139-41)**

Understandably, the brothers were always ready to refer to Churchill's identification of them as the co-leaders of the coup.

++ Was Radoje Knežević really *"planning and carrying out"* the coup?

Finally, had Radoje Knežević taken *an active part in the planning, as well as the carrying out the coup d'état,* as he claimed?

- **As stated by Simović on 28 March 1941, in 1944, and in 1951**

On 28 March 1941, in his report to the Hierarchy of the Serbian Orthodox Church, the new Prime Minister, Simović, said:

> ((Among political persons the main collaborator was Professor Radoje Knežević, ... He was particularly active within the Serbian cultural club, and Slobodan Jovanović talked to me about him most favorably. *Through Knežević I had an opportunity to get in touch with political people and intellectuals* on one side; and on the other, at the same time I also consulted political and public workers.))
>
> ((Towards evening [of 26 March] I dropped into the Air Force Command [in Zemun], where I issued the final order to General Mirković. I connected him with Professor Radoje Knežević, *who was to stand as my proxy in the execution of the Putsch,* with a task of informing me personally that the Putsch succeeded, after the act had been executed.))
>
> "Od političkih ljudi glavni saradnik bio je profesor Radoje Knežević, ... Naročito je aktivan bio u radu oko Srpskog kulturnog kluba, i o njemu mi je Slobodan Jovanović najbollje govorio. *Ja sam preko Kneževića imao priliku da se povežem sa političkim ljudima i intelektualcima* s jedne strane; a s druge strane, ja sam isto tako vršio naporedo konsutovanja sa političkim i javnim radnicima." (Knežević, 365-6. Italics added.)
> "Predveče [26. marta] sam svratio u Komandu vazduhoplovstva, gde sam izdao poslednje naređenje đeneralu Mirkoviću. Dao sam mu vezu profesora Radoja Kneževića, *koji je imao da me zastupa u izvođenju Puča,* s tim da me lično, posle izvršenog čina, obavesti da je Puč uspeo." (Knežević, 366. Italics added.)

Simović's statement that, towards the evening of 26th March, he had connected Mirković with Radoje Knežević, and *that Radoje would stand for Simović as his proxy during the execution of the coup,* lacks credibility.

First, as shown bellow, both Mirković and Živan Knežević wrote that Mirković – not Simović – requested Radoje Knežević to come to the Air Force Command to work on a Proclamation. That was Radoje's only assignment.

According to Mirković: **Around 10 p. m.** – i. e., when Radoje was in an office working on the Proclamation, to be written in Serbian and French – Mirković sent Col. Dragutin Savić to the Zemun airport to take over the command over all troops of the Zemun airport, telling him that he will get all orders for using the troops only from Mirković personally. (Bosnić(ed), 24-25)

Also, in his memoirs written in exile in 1944, after the fall of his government, Simović did not include Radoje Knežević among the important people with whom he had had contact outside the armed forces. (Simoviić(44), 4-5) In these memoirs, Simović decribed his trust in his Chief of Staff, Col. Dragutin P. Savić. Fearing a possibility that the coup preparation could be discovered, and both Simović and Mirković arrested, Simović informed Savić of the coup preparations because

> ((I was convinced that Col. Savić, at his own initiative, will proceed in our own way and will carry out what we could not have done.))
> "[ja] sam bio ubeđen, da će pukovnik Savić po sopstvenoj inicijativi poći našim putem i izvršiti ono što mi nismo mogli.)) (Simović(44), 2-4)

Therefore, if anyone *were to stand as Simović's proxy in the execution of the Putsch* it would have been Col. Savić – a military man, knowledgeable and capable of handling military operations, not a civilian, Radoje Knežević.

In 1951, identifying the civilians who had known about the preparation for the coup, Simović stated that Radoje *had been informed* ("*bio je obavešten*") by his brother, Major Živan. (Simović(51), 10)

Being informed is not the same as *being the main collaborator,* as Simović stated on 28 March 1941.

In 1979 Živan Knežević stated that, on the eve of the coup, Simović had been systematically avoiding a meeting with Radoje. (Knežević, 193n2)

- **As stated by Dragiša Ristić in 1955 and 1966**

Commenting on an article written by Živan Knežević in *Voice of Canadian Serbs* on 12 May 1955, Ristić wrote (*inter alia*):

> ((Radoje Knežević was not [involved] in conspiracy, and the least in "the leading circle". He was earlier informed by brother Živan, but he had neither any role nor influence.
> ((Radoje Knežević was just a citizen present at the [time when] commands for the beginning of the action were being issued, and then he joined me when I was sent to General Simović. On that occasion (the 27th, at 2 a.m.), personally unknown until then, he introduced himself to Simović.))
>
> "Radoje Knežević nije bio ni u zaveri, a najmanje u "rukovodnom krugu". On je bio ranije upoznat od brata Živana, ali nije imao nikakvu ulogu ili uticaj.
> "Radoje Knežević je bio samo prisutan građanin pri izdavanju naređenja za početak akcije, a potom se pridružio meni koji sam bio upućen generalu Simoviću. Tom prilkom (27og u 2 časa) on se, dotle lično nepoznat, pretstavio Simoviću." (Dragiša Ristić correspondence and interview, Box 2, Folder 2.33 Hoover Institution Archives)

According to Ristić: Simović, Mirković and Col. Dragutin Savić comprised "rukovodni krug" ("the leading circle") of the operations – not Simović-Mirković-brothers Knežević, as claimed by Živan. (*Ibid.*)

In his book, published in 1966, describing events of the early 27th March, Ristić wrote:

> All assigned missions having been quickly accomplished, the author was ordered to pick up General Simović. ... When the author was about to leave, Mirković asked him to take along a person who introduced himself as "Žika's [Major Živan Knežević's] brother". He was Radoje Knežević, a Belgrade high school teacher of French ... (Ristić, 92-3)

> The car stopped in front of the house at Gladstone 13. The maid opened the door; General Simović soon appeared and the author [Ristić] reported Cvetković's overthrow and the capture of all objectives. *Radoje introduced himself to the general* who then got into the car." (Ristić, 93. Italics added.)

Had Radoje been *the main collaborator* who connected the General with political people - as Simović said on 28 March - even when they met for the first time, it would have been natural for both to engage in a meaningful, cordial conversation related to their collaboration. But they did not.

As the two autos sped trough Belgrade's streets, Radoje Knežević, *who had no previous connection with the general,* turned to Simović and asked if he intended to proclaim himself "Chief of State like [Gen. Ion] Antonescu in Rumania." Nothing was further from his mind, Simović replied; he would call on the representatives of the political parties to form a democratic government. After this, no one said anything until the party was temporarily detained in Knez Miloš street. (Ristić, 93. Italics added.)

Thus: *not having had previous connection* - Simović met Radoje for the first time during the early morning of the 27th March. Therefore: the General's claim of 28 March, that *through Knežević he had an opportunity to get in touch with political people and intellectuals* is very questionable. Perhaps the General thought that the situation on 28 March 1941, the day after the Putsch, required such kind of a statement in order to assure the people of the unity of action and purpose of the new government. Or he might have had some other reason(s).

*****

Živan Knežević ignored the role of Mirković and Ristić in this episode, in favor of his brother – as if Mirković could not make a decision without his brother's consent. In his book, published thirteen years after Ristić's, Živan claimed that:

After **his** report of the capture of the buildings reached Air Force Command in Zemun, ((General Mirković and Professor Knežević reached an agreement: the former to remain some more time at the Command – just in case – and the second to go to get General Simović)). So the Professor left **shortly before 3 a.m.,** with the escort of two officers and some well armed soldiers.

After reaching Simović's home before **3:15 a.m.,** the doorbell had to be rung several times before a housemaid showed up. Then "The gentleman in civilian suit explained to her: 'Tell the general that Professor Knežević is waiting for him. "

No sign of life was coming from the house, no sound, not a ray of light.

So the Professor rang the doorbell again, **before 3:30 a.m.**

Finally, a bulb flashed. The General appeared in his blue air force uniform, greeted the two officers, and got acquainted with Professor Knežević. (Knežević, 242-3. Emphasis added.)

Because the Major was not present at the scene, the above information had to be given to him by his brother. It is unlikely that a civilian - who had not yet met the General - would ring the doorbell, and announce himself in a self-assertive way. It is more likely that an officer – who for so long had faithfully served under the General – would announce their arrival in a more appropriate way.

*****

Actually, Julian Amery, the SOE's most involved operative with the coup-wishers in the summer of 1940 (The Đonović-Trifunović group and the Serbian Peasant Party), did not mention Radoje Knežević's involvement at all. Neither did another knowledgeable SOE-man, Alexander Glen, who was the head of the SOE-team in Belgrade at that time. **(Part One, Appendix D)** On 2 August 1940, in a letter to Bill Bailey (the former SOE chief in Belgrade, then located in Istanbul), Glen wrote:

The two intermediaries through whom information as to the proposed coup has been transmitted are Jovan DJONOVICH and Ilija TRIFUNOVICH [the head of Narodna Odbrana - The Defense League]. ...
In addition to the Narodna Odbrana, it is known ... that the Agrarian Party [The Serb Peasant Party] are planning action along somewhat similar lines. ...
(Great Britain, Special Operations Executive-SOE, 91087-10.V, Hoover Institution Archives)

One day after the coup, on 28 March 1941, Dr Dalton, in charge of the SOE, sent a letter to the Prime Minister, Churchill, with three enclosures:
- A telegram from Taylor to London, 23 March 1941,
- A telegram from Taylor to London, 26 march 1941,
- A telegram from Taylor to London, 27 March 1941.

In his accompanying letter Dalton stated, *inter alia:* "that the coup d'état itself was largely the work of TRIFUNOVICH, while the real political backing without which it could hardly have been made, lay outside the old Cabinet and in the Serb Peasant Party ... I am proud of the result, for which I feel that great credit attaches to TAYLOR and his chief lieutenants in Yugoslavia – MASTERSON AND BENNETT. (*Ibid.*)

No mention of Radoje Knežević and his Democratic Party.

*****

Relevant to the involvement in the *planning and execution* of the coup was also the already mentioned all-British conference, held in Belgrade eight days before the coup. Radoje Knežević and/or his Democratic Party were not mentioned at all.

Thus, on the basis of the evidence presented above, one can conclude that R. Knežević's pre-coup role was limited to the development of unspecified propaganda, and to the participation in the preparation of a Royal Proclamation.

However, in the interest of historic truth, **IF** whatever else he did contribute to the coup of 27 March 1941, it should be fairly and justly acknowledged.

Did Simović want to be "the leader of the state" like General Antonescu in Rumania?

Whether it was his own or his brother's judgment, Major Knežević stated:

((Judging by everything, Simović until the end wished for himself that status and that influence in the state which General Antonescu then had in Rumania)).
"Po svemu sudeći, Simović je do kraja za sebe priželjkivao onaj položaj i onaj uticaj u državi koji je u Rumuniji tada imao đeneral Antonesku" (Knežević, 246)

While the characterization of Radoje Knežević as a promoter and defender of democratic principles against Simović's autocratic plan and tendencies was published in 1979, Gen. Mirković wrote about this contention of the Kneževićs' in 1941, 1955, and 1960, supporting Ristić's account.

In 1941 – According to Gen. Mirković, **around 2:30 a.m. on 27 March** he was informed that the Putschists had taken control of the block of Ministries' buildings, the building of the Main General Staff and of the Ministry of the Army and Navy. Upon this news he directed the escorts to Simović's home. (Bosnić, 27) The head of the escorts was Capt. Ristić.

In 1955, Mirković wrote that, after verifying that all objects were taken as planned, he sent Capt. Dragiša Ristić and Radoje Knežević to Simović's home to give him an edited proclamation in French, and he went to the Ministry of the Army to meet Gen. Simović. After the two Generals embraced, Simović asked:

((But pray, Boro, where did you find that Professor Knežević?! imagine what was he proposing to me while leaving my home, he said:
((General, Sir, I think that now is the moment to declare yourself the Administrator of the State, as General Antonescu in Rumunia.
((I was stunned by that outburst and I replied:
Well, Professor, you don't know me. All my life I was fighting against the dictatorships, despots, cliques and scoundrels, and you dare to propose to me something like that. I would never and never do it.))
"Ali molim te Boro, gde pronađe onog profesora Kneževića?! Zamisli šta mi je predlagao pri polasku od moje kuće, kaže:
'Gospodine Đenerale, ja mislim da je sada momenat, da se proglasite Upravljačem Države, kao General Antonesku u Rumuniji.'
"Zaprepašćen sam bio tim ispadom i odgovorio sam mu:
'Pa, gospodine professore, vi mene ne poznajete. Ja sam se celoga života borio protivu diktatura, despota, klika i mangupa i vi meni tako što smete da predlažete. Ja to nikada i nikad ne bih učinio.' (Karapandžić(AB), 136)

In 1960 Mirković wrote again:

((... When Major Knežević wrote about the March 27th in *Glas kanadskih Srba (Voice of Canadian Serbs)*, ... , he stated, *inter alia*, how Simović and Radoje Knežević had worked on a political plan, ... Then, how some secret meetings were held by the four of us [Simović, Mirković, Radoje and Živan Knežević] prior to the Coup d'état. I reacted to this publicly and I said that General Simović, and I, not only had not known Radoje Knežević before 26 March, but we had not even known that he existed. To this Major Knežević replied in the same newspaper: "It is true that they had not known each other, but they were conferring through me." With this [statement] Major Knežević indeed admitted that his original description of those events was fictitious, and that we were not holding meetings with his brother Radoje about some consultations related to the creation of a political plan. (Karapandžić(AB), 149)

((When General Simović arrived into the Ministry of the Army, he immediately invited me to come to see him. As soon as I came, he queried me: "For God's sake, Bora, where did you find this Professor?" I did not understand him, and told him that I did not know what he meant. Then the General related to me how Radoje Knežević, during the ride in the automobile from his home to the Ministry of the Army, had attempted to suggest that he, Simović, should proclaim himself the Governor of the state, the way General Antonescu did in Rumania. Astonished Simović replied to him: "What kind of a proposition is that, Professor? My entire life I fought against various usurpers, dictators and royal camarillas, and now you dare to propose to me something like that,"...)) (Karapandžić(AB), 150. Emphasis added.)

The Simović – Mirković side steadily refuted the Kneževićs' contention that Simović had aspirations to be another Antonescu.

*****

The claims and counter-claims, shown above, could not and did not impact the tragic meaning of the Putsch itself. However, they illustrate the sorry state of affairs from the very beginning. The coup was executed on 27 March 1941, and the new Government with many coup-wisher-and-plotters left the country and the people to merciless destruction and whims of enraged and offended Hitler. The Simović Government lasted only until 11 January 1942. The Putsch was praised by the Putschists as a historic deed of supreme importance, and political credits for it were profusely claimed and some benefits obtained. After the Putsch, there developed some unforeseeable and some foreseeable fateful events. Different and often opposing views and claims began appearing already in March 1941, and a discord among the members of the Putschist Goverment kept growing into an open antagonism. Inspired and motivated by various goals – including personal ones - the Putschists executed their Putsch hastily, without a common, well-thought out, realistic program. Their desired results could not be achieved, but their acts set the stage for the national tragedy.

Chapter 14

THURSDAY, 27 MARCH 1941 – the day of the military coup

To the question by *The Institute for Historical Inquiries* about the act of 27 March 1941, Simović answered:

> ((Thinking that in these difficult moments we ought to stand united around the *lawful Government* in order to express as strong as possible resistance to Hitler's aspirations, and anticipating potential complications in our relations with the Croats, I was striving, until the last moment, to convince those in authority of the necessity *of rejecting Hitler's dictate* and of defense of our national and state independence. However, taking into account also another eventuality, ... , I was thinking also of a need and possibility of applying other means. With that objective [in mind], in the month of August 1940 (#) - while I was the Commandant of the II Army Region in Sarajevo - I was holding talks with Brigadier Borivoje Mirković - then the Deputy Commandant of the Air Force - and with Vojislav Besarović, the secretary of the Chamber of Commerce, a prominent national activist. After my transfer to Zemun (as the Commandant of the Air Force) in the month of November 1940 - after the fall of General [Milan] Nedić and the ascension of General Petar Pešić as the Minister of the Army and Navy - I began holding talks with some prominent officers about the condition of Yugoslavia and her attitude in the case of the enemy aggression, winning them over to my opinion and creating a circle, on whom I could count in case of a need. When the question of signing the Tripartite Pact surfaced - at the beginning of March 1941 - there was no time to organize a wider movement from the officers of all troops in the Belgrade garrison, but one had to work with the most important, namely: the Air Force in Zemun, which stood under my command; the infantry regiment of the Royal Guards; the battalion of armored vehicles in Belgrade, on whose superiors (except the regiment's commandant) I could count; and the junior officers of the Ministry of the Army, and [junior officers] of the Main General Staff and of the Command of Belgrade.)) (Simović(51), 12-13. Italics added.)

(#) In August 1940 the Tripartite Pact did not yet exist, Italy had not yet invaded Greece, and the British Government was satisfied with Prince Paul's foreign policy of benevolent neutrality.

Was there *no time to organize wider movement,* or was there *no interest* for it among other officers of the Belgrade garrison?

Very early on 27 March, Mirković was assigning important missions; *"...the King and people are in danger"*

> ((The lower rank executors [of the Coup] had to be led into the action at the last moment.))
> "Niži izvršioci [Puča] imali su biti uvedeni u akciju u poslednjem momentu." (Simović(44), 35)

With Vladeta Bogdanović, Trifunović-Birčanin and a few officers, Gen. Mirković stayed in office in Zemun. Prof. Knežević was working on the Proclamation in another room. (Bosnić(ed), 24-5) **About 0:30 a.m., 27 March,** the General came down from his quarters [on the 4th floor] to Simović's office [on the 3rd floor], and began assigning roles to individual officer-leaders

Mirković personally ordered the strongest group of some 200 men, under the command of Air Force Colonel Stjepan Burazović [a Croat], the task of seizing Belgrade's police headquarters (prefecture). Upon the seizure of the building, the Colonel reported to Mirković that his order had been successfully carried out. (Bosnić(ed), 25-6) Mirković also asked the former director of telephone services, [Milan] Nakić, to come to the Air Force Command; as an expert, he was to lead a group of officers and soldiers to the Main Post building and to cut the telephone and telegraph lines. (Bosnić(ed), 21)

Mirković ordered Capt. Vladimir Simić to take and hold the main Post Office in Belgrade, with its telephone and telegraph networks. Capt. Milan Janković was then ordered to take the post office in Zemun. Major Radovan Pejić was dispatched to take the shortwave radio station in Makiš. (Ristić, 91)

> ((Before the very departure, each leader-officer was conveying to the soldiers the received assignment with a parole: - that the King and people are in danger, and that as of tonight the military are taking over the administration of the land into their hands.))
> "Pred sam polazak, svaki vođa-oficir saopštavao je vojnicima primljeni zadatak sa parolom: - da je Kralj i narod u opasnosti i da od noćas vojska preuzma upravu zemlje u svoje ruke." (Bosnić(ed), 25)

Execution of the coup required each group to be at their assigned location **at 2:20 a.m. on 27 March.** (Bosnić(ed), 27)

*****

> ((A special 'conspiratorial' organization did not really exist. About the intention and the plan of the execution was informed only a small number of the most important executors, who were to make necessary preparations with their closest collaborators. The secrecy of the entire enterprise was that way completely preserved.))
> "Naročita 'zaverenička' organizacija stvarno nije postojala. S namerom I planom izvršenja bio je upoznat mali broj najvažnijih izvršilaca, koji su sa svojim najbližim saradnicima imali preduzeti potrebne pripreme. Na taj način je sačuvana potpuna tajnost celog preduzeća." (Simović(44), 35)

According to Dragiša Ristić, there were "12 main participants in the revolution of 27 March". (Notes on his visit to Lt.-Col. Miloje Dinić in September 1955, Dragiša Nikola Ristić Collection, Box 2, Folder 2.14 Hoover Institution Archives)

In Ž. Knežević's opinion, there were "around 28 executors of the 27th March". (Milunović(ed), 60)

There was simply no time to create an organization, even if Simović and Mirković wanted to do it. Eden ordered Campbell to secretly inform the coup-plotters of the British support on the 24th of March. The *Vojvoda* Trifunović-Birčanin established daily contact with Mirković also on the 24th, and the same day reported to the SOE that "the coup was 99 per cent certain and preparations were making good progress." (Williams, 31) About that good progress, however, Mirković himself stated that he made the final decision for the coup only in the afternoon of the 26th. He was issuing assignments to the most important executors even later, very early on the 27th.

So, although the coup-plotters were thinking about a coup for quite some time, the actual execution was done hastily, *when the British wanted it,* but without a comprehensive, well-thought-out political plan for a post-coup program.

*****

Now back to the coup execution.

Not knowing the decisions of the all-British conference of 19 March, for instance – but hearing from their officers that *the King and people were in danger,* this warning had to strengthen the resolve of the soldiers to defend them. Furthermore, the misinformation was not given only to the Air Force troops. The Royal Guards were misinformed by Major Živan Knežević on a large scale, as is shown below – and the entire country as well, by the leaders of the Putsch, and by Radoje Knežević.

Execution of the coup – in the name of the young King

One of the deceivers was Major Knežević of the Royal Guards. As he stated in his book: **at 0:45 a.m. on 27 March,** he ordered that all officers and non-commissioned officers of his battalion be awakened and assembled in his office. Before explaining their assignment he asked them to quietly say, "Long live our Supreme Commander King Peter II." Then he continued in a raised voice:

> ((**By the order of our Supreme Commander,** His Majesty King Peter II, our battalion had received tonight a solemn and historic assignment. Everybody has to carry out only my orders...))
> "**Po nalogu našeg Vrhovnog komandanta**, Njegovog Veličanstva Kralja Petra II, naš bataljon dobio je noćas jedan uzvišen i istorijski zadatak. Svi imaju da izvršavaju samo moja naređenja... " (Knežević, 196. Emphasis added.)

Then **at exactly 1:40 a.m.** the Major went to the assembly field, mounted his horse, and to his battalion of the Royal Guards said – *inter alia:*

> ((My brave soldiers! **By the order of our Supreme Commander,** His Majesty King Peter II, our battalion tonight, together with the other units of the Belgrade garrison, had received the assignment to protect the

Royal Palace in the city and to take possession of the Ministries. I am asking you to follow your officers, and to carry out their orders without question, for the good of our King and our Fatherland.))

"Junaci! **Po nalogu našeg Vrhovnog komendanta**, Njegovog Veličanstva Kralja Petra II, naš bataljon noćas, u sastavu sa ostalim jedinicama Beogradskog garnizona, dobio je zadatak da obezbedi Dvor u varoši i posedne ministarstva. Pozivam vas da gledate u svoje starešine, i da njihova naređenja izvršavate bez pogovora, za dobro Kralja i naše Otadžbine." (Knežević, 197. Emphasis added.)

In an article published in the Calendar of the *American Srbobran* for 1946, Knežević was more explicit about this deception: he stated that the King had issued the said order through the Commandant of the Guards. (Petranović & Žutić, 354)

The King issued no such order. At hat time he did not even know what was being said and done in his name. The officers and men did not know that they were being deceived, so they had to believe what they were told, they acted in that belief, and spread it the next morning to inquiring citizens on the streets. The ruse succeeded.

*****

Timing of Knežević's battalion leaving their barracks was later criticized by Mirković.

((When, **at 1500 hours [3:00 p.m.] on 26 March**, I issued instruction to him [Major Živan Knežević], he trembled like a leaf. I told him to sit down. ... My further order to the executors [of the Putsch] was, to leave their residences at the time to be at the places of the objects [to be captured] **exactly at 0220 hours [2:20 a.m.]. Major Knežević left 20 minutes earlier**. ... I asked him, why had he left earlier, because that way he could have compromised the whole matter? He answered: "My nerves couldn't endure it, although I have taken eight times more bromine than was medically allowed.")) (Karapandžić(AB), 137. Emphasis added.)

The deception of the diaspora

The deception did not stop with the soldiers, and through them, with the inquiring minds among ordinary people on the streets.

About 3 a.m. of the 27th March Major Nikola Kosić entered the building of the Ministry of Forests and Mines where a short-wave radio station was located. To the guards of the building he explained that the military had taken over power in the country, General Simović had become the Premier, the King had been declared of age, and that the radio station cannot begin broadcasting without a special permission. (Knežević, 207)

At 4 a.m. Kosić dictated to the speaker, M. Marković – over the phone – the following message (translated) for an overseas transmission:

((On 27 March 1941 His Majesty King Peter II decided to assume power into his own hands, with aid from the military. The Regents and Government submitted their resignations. The military are standing firmly by the King. The formation of the Government had been entrusted to General Dušan Simović. Peace and order are reigning in the land.)) (Knežević, 207)

The deception of high Commanders

After the coup had been successfully executed, Simović called to the War Office five Generals, including Milorad Petrović (Commande de Place, Belgrade) and Pandurović (Commannder of the Danube Division) – and all regimental commanders of the Belgrade army. Simović approached them and said:

((It had to come to this; otherwise, a revolution would have erupted in the land ... This way, the King assumed the powers in his hands; the Regency resigned ... *The King entrusted me with the formation of the Government.*))

"Do ovoga je moralo doći; inače u zemlji bi iskrsla revolucija ... Ovako, Kralj je primio vlast u svoje ruke; namesništvo je dalo ostavku ... *Kralj je poverio meni sastav vlade.*" (Pandurović, page 12. Italics added.)

When Pandurović asked whether the King had agreed with this act, Mirković answered, looking him firmly in the eyes: ((Completely! Since last night ...)) "Potpuno! Još od sinoć ... " (*Pandurović,* 12)

A short time later Mirković approached Gen. M. Petrović "Lord" and told him boastfully: ((I prepared all this ... I did all this ... Had it not succeeded, I would have killed myself.))
"Lord" responded, ((Nothing else would have remained to you ...)) (Pandurović, 13)

*****

General Milutin Nikolić, the first assistant to the Chief of the Main General Staff, seated next to Pandurović, was watching the hasty goings on, spoke as though to himself but loudly enough:

((Ah, my children! Ah, children, children, what did you do? Don't you know, woe not be to you, that that what you did means – war! ... Don't you know that our borders are open and unprotected, and that since this morning the enemy can cross them without care where he wants, because "the troops for the protection of the borders" are not even mobilized! ... You have learned nothing from the basic military science even if you are general-staff officers ... Nothing, when you did that! ... One ought to give you now all commands in the army, so you yourselves ought to pick the chestnuts from the fire, not let the others do it, the innocent and not guilty ones ... Badly you did, children, badly! ...))
"E, deco moja! E, deco, deco, šta učiniste? Pa zar ne znate, jadni ne bili, da to što učiniste znači – rat! ... Pa zar ne znate, da su naše granice otvorene i nezaštićene i od jutros neprijatelj ih može serbes proći gde god hoće, jer "trupe za zaštitu granice" nisu ni mobilisane! ... Vi ništa ne naučiste od osnovne vojne nauke i ako ste đeneralštabni oficiri ... Ništa kada to učiste! ... Vama bi trebalo sada dati sve komande u vojsci, da sami vadite kestenje iz žara, a ne da to čine drugi ni krivi ni dužni ... Rđavo učiniste, deco, rđavo! ... " (Pandurović, 16)

*****

(Note – As stated in the accounts by Simović and Ž. Knežević themselves, **in the evening of 26 March** the King did not know at all what was planned and going on, nor he empowered Simović with the formation of the Government.)

The formation of the new Government

Acccording to Radoje Knežević, when he and Simović came to the office of the Minister of the Army, the officers left them alone, and the two remained silent for a few moments, thinking their own thoughts. (Knežević, 243) The new Government had to be formed, by members assembled in a hurry, without preceding consultations and a unifying consent for a post-coup program. There is more than one version of the proceedings, as shown below.

- **As stated by Gen. Simović on 28 March 1941:**

As soon as he arrived in the General Staff Headquarters, Major Knežević reported to him on the Putsch. Gen. Mirković arrived too. Simović then issued two orders: 1 – to escort, under arms, the members of the deposed Government to the Headquarters, and 2 – to stop (in Zagreb) Prince Paul's train [which was heading to Slovenia], to inform the Prince that the military had executed the overthrow of the Government, that the King had assumed the Royal Powers, and that the Prince should return to Belgrade immediately. (Knežević, 366-7) Then the formation of the government proceeded.

- *Automatic adoption of the Croats, Slovene and Bosnian Muslim from the deposed Government*

In consultation with Professor Knežević, Simović continued, he invited political representatives to come to the Headquarters in order to form a new Government. Their first thought was: the Croats, Slovenes and Bosnian Muslims - being the representatives of the people's confidence - should enter into the new Government. Šutej and other Croats [all members of the deposed Government] readily accepted the solution, and promised to talk with Maček. Simović also talked with Maček directly and at length: Maček agreed - in principle - to enter into the new Government as first Vice-President [the same post he held in the just overthrown Government]. However, Maček requested that the Pact be accepted unconditionally, and that [the Serbo-Croat] *Sporazum of 1939* be approved. Simović replied that Maček should come to Belgrade as soon as possible so they all together could take a stand, emphasizing that they do not wish the war.

The Slovenes and Muslims made no difficulties at all. (Knežević, 367)

- *Formation of the new Government and delayed signature of its decree*

When the representatives of the political parties arrived, Simović continued, he immediately informed them that the military had done their duty toward the King and fatherland "and that the King had assumed the powers into his hands "...

((I pleaded with them to select the future president of the Government among themselves, and particularly [so] the Minister of Foreign Affairs ...)). ((Without discussion they all agreed on my humble self)).

"Zamolio sam ih da iz svoje sredine izaberu budućeg predsednika Vlade, a naročito Ministra spoljnjih poslova." "Bez diskusije svi su se složili sa mojom malenkošću." (Knežević, 367)

Political and national figures among the Serbs, who joined the new Government, included [Milan] Grol, [Miloš] Trifunović, Bogoljub Jevtić, Professor Slobodan Jovanović, Army General [Bogoljub] Ilić, Srđan Budisavljević, etc.

Momčilo Ninčić became the Foreign Minister. The military, including Simović, did not intend, nor desire, to interfere in the political life of the state. (Knežević, 367-8)

Professor Knežević did not even ask for a membership in the Government, "although through his merits he had more right than the others." (Knežević 367) – So spoke Simović on 28 March 1941.

- **As described by the brothers Knežević**

First, a background information – as presented by Živan:

Before the coup, Simović had resolved to withdraw from it, and attempted to talk Mirković out of it. Mirković resisted. Simović did not spend **the night of the 26th-27th** in the Air Force Command, but at home, willing – as a man not involved – to defend the Putschists before the Prince Regent in case of the failure of the Putsch. The conversation between Simović and Mirković [in Zemun, **toward the evening of the 26th**] ended with Mirković telling Simović: if the Putsch succeeded, he would send somebody to bring Simović to the Ministry so he would ((assume further guidance of the state)) „preduzeo dalje vođenje države." (Knežević, 241-2)

When Gen. Mirković and Prof. Knežević – still in Zemun in the early hours of 27 March – received Major Knežević's report of the successful coup, they agreed that Mirković would remain there a little longer – just in case – while the Professor would go to Belgrade to get Simović. The Professor left the Air Force Command – with two officers and escort – **before 3 a.m.** (Knežević, 242) They arrived at Simović's home just **before 3:15 a.m.** After some **fifteen minutes** Simović showed up, dressed in Air Force uniform. He greeted the two officers, ((and got acquainted with Professor Knežević)), "i upoznao se s profesorom Kneževićem" (Knežević, 242)

In the meantime, on 27 March, **a few minutes after 2 a.m.** the Major arrived at the intersection of Miloševa and Nemanjina streets, dismounted from his horse, and set up his command post. He stayed there all the time except when he had to go into the building of the General Staff Headquarters to see Gen. Simović, and to the Royal Palace to get the King's signature on the Proclamation. (Knežević, 203, 208)

Exactly at 3:40 a.m. Gen. Simović and Prof. Radoje arrived at the intersection, by auto, together with Captains Zaharije Ostojić and Dragiša Ristić, and their escort. The Major reported to the General that the takeover of the city had been accomplished successfully, without a drop of blood. The group drove on to the main entrance of the Ministry of the Army, at Miloševa street. A rather large number of officers greeted them there, and the General and Professor went into the office of the Minister of the Army. (Knežević, 240)

Major Knežević was not an eyewitness of further developments; his brother informed him about it. (Knežević, 241) So, according to the Professor's information, his brother continued:

- **"A painful scene" between the General and the Professor**

While the Major was still at his post on the street, "a painful scene" (*"mučna scena"*) was playing itself out in the office of the Minister of the Army – wrote Žika. So, according to "the Professor": Simović was attempting to realize his original plan of a *Government of eminent individuals*, but Radoje did not want to deviate from the agreed-on principle that the Government should be formed from *individuals delegated by the leaders of political parties "with a root in the people"*. (Knežević, 241)

Upon arriving into the Ministry of the Army, the General and the Professor were left alone in the Minister's office. They sat quietly for a while, thinking their own thoughts. The General opened the conversation, asking the Professor what should be done next. To form the Government, replied the Professor. The General took a piece of paper out of his pocket, said that this was what he had in mind, and started reading the names:

((The Prime Minister, of course, me. The Minister of the Army, General Bogoljub Ilić...
((Simović was stringing the names: Božidar Maksimović and Mirko Kosić, with the roles *I do not remember* any more, and immediately after that:
((The Minister of Education Radoje Knežević" ...))
"Predsednik Vlade, pa da, ja. Ministar vojske, đeneral Bogoljub Ilić ...
"Simović je ređao imena: Božidar Maksimović i Mirko Kosić *sa ne sećam se više* kojim ulogama, pa odmah zatim ...
"Ministar prosvete Radoje Knežević". (Knežević, 243. Bold Italics added.)

At this point the General paused and looked at his interlocutor. Professor Knežević stood up and calmly observed:

((General, Sir, until this moment we were going together. Further on we cannot.))
((We did not agree that way! You know that well. I am sorry, but further on we can not [go] together.)) (Knežević, 243)

The General kept silent. The Professor abruptly changed his tactics, transforming his business-like tone into an appeal:

((There were many military coups in the last twenty years in which Generals were seizing power and becoming dictators. Do you want that? There is for you a much nobler ambition. Isn't it nicer and for you yourself to be the first General in postwar Europe who is seizing the power in order to return it into the hand of the people?))
"Bilo je puno vojničkih pučeva za ovih dvadeset godina gde su đenerali otimali vlast i postajali diktatori. Hoćete li vi to? Ima za vas mnogo plemenitija ambicija. Zar nije lepše i za vas samoga da budete prvi đeneral u posleratnoj Evropi koji otima vlast da bi je vratio u ruke naroda?" (Knežević, 243-4)

*****

It sounds strange that Simović, who was actively opposing Prince Paul's Government since the end of January, and was engaged in the preparation of the coup, did not know what to do after the coup, and had to ask "the Professor" what to do next when they came to the Ministry of the Army, and had to listen to a lecture in history from "the Professor".

Živan was describing this scene between the General and "the Professor" **in the third person**, except in one sentence, where he wrote "... **I do not remember any more** ..." (Knežević, 243), where it should have been, **"the Professor did not remember any more"**. This slip suggests that Živan was using Radoje's own notes and forgot to convert **"I"** into **"he"**, showing "the Professor's" calm, dignified behavior.

It is also unlikely the Major's assertion that — in the early hours of the morning, in the Air Force Command – Gen. Mirković (who assigned a minor task to "the Professor"), would consult him when to leave the Command and go to the Ministry in Belgrade. Bringing Simović to the Ministry, after the coup, was prearranged, and Mirković did not have to stay in Zemun "just in case", as Živan claims.

The brothers took great liberty in presenting their roles in the execution of the coup in their favor.

- **The Brothers Knežević's description of the Government's formation continues ...**

After that "painful scene", silence reigned. After ten, perhaps twenty seconds the General said: ((Let it be as you want.))
Then they decided who among the political leaders should be invited to come to the Ministry, as soon as possible, to form the Government. Keeping a pencil in hand, with an ironic tone in the voice, Simović said: ((Dictate, Mister Professor.)) (Knežević, 244)

"The Professor" provided further information to his brother: he and Simović composed a list of the leaders of the political parties, the true representatives of the Serbian people, who should be brought in to form the new Government –
> The Democratic Party – Milan Grol, Božidar Marković, and Božidar Vlajić;
> The Radical Party - Miloš Trifunović, Momčilo Ninčić, and Krsta Miletić;
> The Agrarian Party [Serbian Peasant Party] Miloš Tupanjanin, and Branko Čubrilović;
> The Independent Democratic Party - Srđan Budisavljević;
> The Yugoslav National Party - Petar Živković, Jovan Banjanin, and Bogoljub Jevtić.
> The only non-party name was that of the University Professor, Slobodan Jovanović.

These individuals had to be called into the Ministry. (Knežević, 244-5)

According to a previously agreed political plan, the Croats, Slovenes and Muslims – the members of Prince Paul's Government – were going to keep all portfolios they had. That way the new Government would be a *democratic concentration Government.* (Knežević, 245. Italics added.)

After considering invitations to the above-named political party leaders, Simović decided not to invite three men: Ninčić, Živković, and Jevtić. In place of Ninčić, he invited Mirko Kosić. Banjanin did not want to participate in the deliberations without the leaders of his party, so Živković and Jevtić were invited also. At the urgings of Grol and S. Jovanović, an *officer* was sent to bring in Ninčić as well. Coming from Zemun, General Mirković brought along Ilija Trifunović-Birčanin. (Knežević, 251)

*****

When the invited representatives of the Serb political parties arrived, a conference began at 5 a.m., presided over by Gen. Simović. However, before the conference started, Simović explained to the Croatian Ministers [assembled in a hurry] that the coup had not been directed against the Croats and the *Sporazum (Agreement)* [of 26 August 1939] between Cvetković and Maček, and that the participation of the Croats in the new government is expected. Similar assurances were given to the Slovenian and the Muslims Ministers. (Knežević, 251-2)

A wide discussion was held about the nomination of the Minister for Foreign Affairs. Simović preferred Gavrilović, who was also staunchly supported by Miloš Tupanjanin, Gavrilović's deputy. Grol opposed him and suggested Ninčić, the former Foreign Minister of long standing, with a reputation of cultivating good relations between Italy and Yugoslavia. Professor Jovanović supported the idea and others agreed. (Knežević, 261)

((The Government assembled on 27 March was the most representative Government Yugoslavia had had since her creation. General Simović rightly named it: "the Government of people's concord".)) "Vlada sastavljena 27. marta bila je najreprezentativnija Vlada koju je Jugoslavija imala od svoga stvaranja. Đeneral Simović ju je s pravom nazvao: "Vlada narodne sloge". The Government took the oath of allegiance **at noon on 27 March,** and in the presence of the King, in the Palace, **the next morning,** before going to the cathedral for the solemn thanksgiving service. (Knežević, 261-2)

- **Developments as described by General Bora Mirković in 1941**

Around 2:30 a. m. - after receiving information from Majors Zaharija Ostojić and Vojislav Topalović that the Ministerial block of buildings and the General Staff Headquarter had been taken - Mirković sent Professor Knežević and Capt. Dragiša Ristić to Gen. Simović's home to drive him to the Ministry of the Army to take over the administration of the state.

Immediately thereafter Mirković called in Col. D. Savić from the airport into the Headquarters, asked him to substitute for the General and to keep receiving further reports.

Then, escorted by his adjutant, Capt. Slavko Stebernjak [a Slovene], Mirković crossed from Zemun to Belgrade in an automobile, and in the Ministry of the Army found Gen. Simović, already busy with the action of assuming power and forming the Government. (Bosnić(ed), 27-8)

Convinced that his undertaking had completely succeeded, that the a-national Government of the Prince Regent and Dragiša Cetković had been forever overthrown, that the powers were completely in the hands of the military, and that the coup of the national liberation had been accomplished, ((I

handed the powers over to the Generals Dušan Simović and Bogoljub Ilić, believing that I was handing them into the safe and safest hands.)) **"predao sam vlast đeneralima** Dušanu Simoviću i Bogoljubu Iliću, verujući da je predajem u sigurne i najsigurnije ruke." (Bosnić(ed), 28. Emphasis added.)

So: in Mirković's opinion, the Putsch transferred the state powers to **him,** and **he** then handed them over to the Generals.

Mirković left the building **at 9 a.m.,** inspected some locations in Belgrade, and returned to Zemun to his regular duties.

About 10 a.m. he was invited back to the Ministry of the Army. He went there accompanied by retired Major Vladeta Bogdanović. At the entrance to the Minister's office he was met by **the British Air Attaché, Lt-Col. [A.H.H.] Macdonald, ((who, excited and evidently happy, congratulated me the lucky outcome.)),** "koji mi je uzbuđen i očigledno srećan čestitao srećan ishod.." (Bosnić(ed), 28. Emphasis added.)

*****

As Mirković stated it, helping the cause and war potential of Great Britain he was also indirectly helping his own people's cause. In doing that, **he had not been an agent of the Intelligence Service** – he wrote in bold letters.

He ended his report by courageously asserting that General Simović was thinking about this matter the same way he did. (Bosnić(ed), 35)

(As it will be examined here, it turned out that Mirković was wrong on both counts.)

Mirković wanted to remain true to his words and talks which he had had with Simović over a long number of years on the subject of the *coup d'état*, right now, at the moment when he held the destiny of the land in his hands. (Bosnić(ed), 19) – So wrote Mirković.

- **The formation of the new Government – Professor Mirko Kosić's version**

Dr. Mirko Kosić, University of Belgrade Professor and one of the leaders of the Radical Party, claimed that Simović intended to include him in the new, post-coup government. Kosić was present at the formation of the new Government. In exile, he summarized his accounts in two brochures, published in 1950 and 1951, and referred to as "Kosić(50)", and "Kosić(51)". His comments are taken from these brochures:

Simović's political talks with Prince Paul and some political people, in the beginning of 1941, were conducted in order to preserve the neutrality of Yugoslavia. He wanted to bring about a kind of "government of the people's salvation". As much as Kosić was informed of the General's intentions, a military pressure on the Prince was intended to result in the formation of a government in which Simović ("or some other military man") would be the Premier, Slobodan Jovanović and Vladko Maček were foreseen as the Vice-Premiers, [Orthodox] Bishop Nikolaj [Velimirović] and [Catholic] Bishop Akšamović as the Ministers without portfolio, Dr. Đorđe Đurić as the Minister of Finances; Dr. [Miha] Krek and Ing. Sernec would represent the Slovenes, and the Croats would provide three Ministers; the Radical, Democratic and Serbian [Agrarian] Peasant Parties would have one representative each – as Kosić understood: Miloš-Miša Trifunović, Milan Grol, and Dr. Milan Gavrilović, respectively. Marko Daković would represent Montenegro, and Mirko Kosić the Vojvodina region. (Kosić(50), 15-16)

This new government plan was communicated to Kosić discreetly, and always as a government which would keep the country out of the war. (Kosić(50), 16)

*****

At the moment of the government's formation Daković was not in Belgrade. Mirković sent an airplane to Nikšić, Montenegro, to fly him to Belgrade. Informed of the composition of the new Government, Daković

((was stunned ... Almost beside himself he said: - By God I can't ... Really, I am fighting all my life against those men and now to collaborate with them ... by God I won't!))

"je bio zapanjen ... Gotovo izbezubljeno rekao je: - Ja bogami ne mogu ... Zar ja celoga života da se borim protiv tih ljudi I sada da sarađujem sa njima ... Ja bogami neću!"

Generals Simović and Ilić used all their powers to prove to him that the new government was an expression of necessity, that it was dictated by the foreign political situation. Creation of this people's front would somehow avert the peril of war. Additionally, Simović pointed to him that this was a provisional government, likely for two months only, until things settled down.

Daković finally yielded and agreed to collaborate. (Bosnić(ed), 30-31)

*****

Noteworthy: The inclusion of Bishop Nikolaj in the Government had been suggested by J. Đonović's group to Julian Amery back in the summer of 1940. Evidently, this idea was circulating among the Prince Paul's opponents for some time, and Simović adopted it. Simović, *or some other military man,* would form a Government mainly with the representatives of the Serbian opposition parties and the Croatian representatives from the existing Government.

This account by Professor Kosić contradicts the brothers' Knežević contention about Gen. Simović's authoritarian tendencies.

*****

Dr. Kosić's account of the formation of the Putschists' Government continues:

When the deliberations about the formation of the post-coup Governmet began **about 6 a.m.** on 27 March – Kosić felt morally justified to state that the selection of the Foreign Minister ((depends on what kind of policy that Minister will have to carry out, i.e., do we want *war* or *peace.*)) (Kosić(50), 16)

Dr. Tupanjanin was pressing for Dr. Gavrilović [then Ambassador in Moscow], who was known to be closely related to the British Ambassador there. That lead to a declaration: who was for war and who for peace. Grol and Trifunović said "mir" ("peace"); Petar Živković shouted "kakav rat?! Ni pomisliti na to!" ((what war?! Don't even think about it!)); Gen. Simović: "Pa mir – ako se može ..." ((Well then, peace – if possible ...)). Then Dr. Miloš Tupanjanin (about whom many knew that he had been the main agent of the Intelligence Service among the Serbs), slammed the fist at the table shouting: ((What peace? This is a national revolution and after it comes a national war!)) , "Kakav mir? Ovo je nacionalna revolucija i posle nje dolazi nacionalni rat!" (Kosić(50), 16)

That was the first time that the word "revolution" was spoken ...

Dr. Srđan Budisavljević and Dr. [Branko] Čubrilović did not declare themselves. Kosić then stated that the majority had been "za mir" ((for peace)), and then (knowing that with that statement he was closing his entrance to the Government) said:

> ((If you want Germany to believe you that you are for peace, then keep Cincar-Marković as the Minister for Foreign Affairs – at least until the first shock is over.))
> "Ako želite da Vam Nemačka veruje da ste za mir, onda zadržite kao Ministra Spoljnih Poslova Cincar-Markovića – bar dok ne prođe prvi šok." (Kosić(50), 16-17. Italics in the source.)

Grol objected immediately: "Kakav Cincar-Marković!? Nemoguće!" ((What Cincar-Marković!? Impossible!)) After reaching a judgment that the nomination of Gavrilović as the Foreign Minister would openly mean "war", they nominated Momčilo Ninčić, who was lying in bed at home almost immobile after a gall-stone operation. He joined them half-an-hour later pale as a corpse and deaf as a cannon. (Kosić(50), 17) [Gavrilović was appointed as the Minister without portfolio.]

- **The formation of the new Government - a reported version of Vice Premier Slobodan Jovanović**

In a conversation with colleague, University Professor Dragoljub Jovanović, held on 4 April 1941, the newly appointed Vice Premier reportedly stated that he entered into the new Government because a man of his confidence, Radoje Knežević, had informed him about the whole affair. Speaking of the manner by which the new government was assembled, the VP described how the representatives of some Parties were bargaining: which Party was to get how many portfolios. One after the other they were trying to convince General Simović to accept their own formula for portfolio distribution. The most persistent was Tupanjanin. For his Serbian Peasant Party he requested two portfolios and one

Ministry without portfolio. He claimed the Ministry of Foreign Affairs for Milan Gavrilović. They so bickered for a several hours. Then Slobodan Jovanović went to Simović and told him:

> ((Mr. Simović, do not listen to these Party-people. You'll never satisfy them. You simply make up the list of Ministers and call them in to inform them. You'll see, they all will be content. With them that is more a question of vanity and Party rivalry than of personal ambition.))
> "Gospodine Simoviću, ne slušajte ove partiske ljude. S njima nikad nećete izići na kraj. Prosto sami napravite listu ministara i pozovite ih i saopštite. Videćete, svi će biti zadovoljni. Kod njih je to više pitanje sujete i partiske konkurencije nego lične ambicije."

The General did that, so the Government could be formed before 11 o'clock a.m. The newspapers immediately made known the list of Ministers, and the next day published the biographies of less known members. (Petranović & Žutić, 486n1)

Professor S. Jovanović's account contradicts the brothers' Knežević description of Radoje's central role.

- **The formation of the new Government - Dragiša Ristić's version**

> Dawn was breaking when the prospective members of the new government discussed the distribution of portfolios, ...
> ... He [Simović] then asked the representatives of the political parties about their choice for prime minister. All agreed that they wanted General Simović, and only one made a reservation: "We'll have the general now. Later we'll see."
> For foreign minister, General Simović suggested Milan Gavrilović. ... But Grol felt that Gavrilović as foreign minister would be construed in Berlin as Yugoslavia's "red cap" and proposed instead Momčilo Ninčić (foreign minister in 1927) who had maintained friendly relations with the Germans and Italians and was the president of the German Club in Belgrade. Grol hoped Ninčić's good relations with Rome and Berlin might relieve the tense situation created by the overthrow of Prince Paul, ... Although Tupanjanin ... bitterly opposed this nomination, Professor Jovanović supported it and Grol won. ... (Ristić, 109-10)

Dragiša Ristić – whose father was a friend of Ninčić, as they both belonged to the Radical Party – then chose to go in person for the former foreign minister, and brought him to Simović. (Dragiša Ristić collection, Box 2, Folder 2.4 Hover Institution Archives)

> In view of the new representatives to be taken into the cabinet, General Simović proposed that two Croatian ministers be dropped from the list. Grol, on the contrary, favored leaving all of the Croatian ministers exactly as they had been in the preceding cabinet, so as to win the cooperation of the Croatian Peasant Party. Grol's recommendation was accepted. (Ristić, 110)

> Monsignor Fran Kulovec, leader of the Slovene People's Party, had been left undisturbed in his residence during the night of the uprising. When he heard what had happened, he came to the ministry of war on his own accord and agreed to participate in the government on condition that Miho Krek, a leading member of the same party, would be included as well. All Croat and Slovene ministers in the Cvetković government were retained in the new government. Džafer Kulenović, leader of the Moslems who expressed his support for the new government, was also retained. The nonpolitical persons taken into the government were Professor Jovanović as second vice prime minister, Marko Daković, a prominent Montenegrin, as minister without portfolio, and General Bogoljub Ilić as minister of war. (Ristić, 110-11)

*****

From Dr. Kosić's and the Putschist Ristić's accounts the following becomes evident:

- All Croat, Slovene and Muslim Ministers from the previous Government were retained – and they all were in favor of accepting the Tripartite Pact without military clauses ... and this was known to the opposition;
- Dr. Budisavljević and Dr. Čubrilović – whose political parties were "subsidized" by the British – did not declare themselves for war or peace;
- a majority of the new Ministers delared themselves for peace;
- Simović: *for peace – if possible* ... implying the impossibility – while personally resolved all along to side with the British;

- Dr. Tupanjanin – whose Serbian Peasant Party was heavily "subsidized" by the British – strenuously opposed peace and opted for war;
- the Foreign Minister was selected in hope that he *might relieve the tense situation created by the overthrow of Prince Paul, ...*

It is worth repeating what Dalton wrote to Churchill on 28 March: *"that ... the Serb Peasant Party [was] – the principal instrument of our policy and (like Narodna Odbrana) in our pay."* (Great Britain, Special Operations Executive, 91087-10V, Hoover Institution Archives. Italics added.)

Although Dalton and Bennett correctly reported on the roles of Tupanjanin, Đonović and Trifunović-Birčanin, their views were expressed **before** the new Government began making decisions which affected Yugoslavia's foreign policy and, through them, British expectations. But, what happened **after** the new Government was formed?

Simović – Maček negotiations, 27 March 1941

After the end of the First World War in 1918, the Government and Supreme Command of Serbia sent Dušan Simović to Zagreb as a delegate to the National Council (*Narodno Vijeće*) of the Slovenes, Croats and Serbs.

Ante Pavelić (dentist), a Vice President of the Council, welcomed Lt.-Col. Simović to Zagreb and frequently invited the Colonel to his home. (From the letter of Ante Smith Pavelić - the dentist's son - to Dragiša Ristić, dated in Paris 7 March 1967. Ristić correspondence, Box 2, Folder 234. Hoover Institution Archives) This explains Simović's confidence in Ante Smith-Pavelić that his letter – referred herein as (Simović(56)) – would be handled as the General wished.

Simović was always showing Yugoslav aspirations. (Jovanović, 20)

*****

In the morning of 27 March 1941, Croatian Ministers Juraj Šutej, Bariša Smoljan, Ivan Andres, and Josip Torbar were brought to the Defense Ministry. **At 6:00 a.m.** Šutej called Maček, then in Zagreb, who later described the event:

> He told me that the officers under the lead of General Simović had forced the overthrow of the Government, proclaimed the 17-year old King Peter II of age and asked them to enter the Government under the new Premiership of Simović. Šutej had replied that they could not do this without consulting me and, therefore had been permitted to contact me. It was obvious that Šutej and the other ministerial colleagues had become the prisoners of the putschists. I told him that I could not make a decision before I had time to consult my political co-workers.
>
> I had scarcely had time to ask [August] Košutić and [Juraj] Krnjević to my house and get into my clothes, when Vikert, Chief of the Zagreb Police, brought news that Prince Paul had arrived in the city on the Royal train ... (Maček, 216)

About 10 a.m. Simović talked with Maček for a second time. (Knežević, 262)

The role of the Croats, Slovenes, and Bosnian Muslims in the new Government

- **As explained by Simović on 28 March 1941**

In Prince Paul's Government, *the Croats and Slovenes were duly represented by people's delegates,* but representing the Serbs were those who had no justification at all to do so, thus making it possible for the Prince to rule as he saw fit. However, since yesterday [i.e. the coup, the Putsch – of 27 March], the people can speak freely what is on their mind, they can freely decide – through their representatives – abut their own needs and about the state's policies. Therefore, the way into the future is the democratic way, the way of people's confidence and of common accord and unity on all questions, which is of crucial importance for the state. (Knežević, 362. Italics added.)

Yesterday he [Simović] was honored to become the president of the Royal Government, in complete freedom "by the will of the people, through their political representatives". Thus *he became the first president of the democratic concentration government after the Putsch,* in which *for the first time the*

Serbs, Croats and Slovenes are democratically represented in equal proportion. (Knežević 362. Italics added.)

During the organization of the new Government, Simović said on 28 March 1941:

> ((Our first thought has been: that the Croats, the Slovenians and the Bosnian Muslims should join the new Government, because they had been the representatives of the people's confidence.)) "Prva naša misao bila je: da u novu Vladu uđu Hrvati i Slovenci i bosanski Muslimani, pošto su oni bili predstavnici poverenja kod naroda." (Knežević, 367)

After Simović personally explained that the King had assumed the royal powers, and that the Government and the Regency did not exist any more, Dr. [Juraj] Šutej and other Croats accepted the new solution without any excuses. The General then asked them to talk with Maček. He also talked with Maček and explained the whole thing. After long explanation and Maček's remarks, Maček agreed in principle to enter into the Government as Vice Premier. The Slovenes and Muslims made no difficulties. (Knežević, 367)

Thus, setting aside the knowledge that these Croats, Slovenes and Bosnian Muslims were members of the just overturned government and in favor of signing the Tripartite Pact, Simović and other Putschists wanted them in their Government simply because *they were representatives of their people* ... Simović claimed.

- **And Simović added in 1951**

Replying to the questions by *The Institute for historical inquiries* in Belgrade, Simović wrote in 1951

> ((By retaining Dr. V. Maček and other representatives of the CPP [Croatian Peasant Party] in the government, my aspiration was to maintain the unity and harmony of the Serbs and Croats and to preserve the wholeness of Yugoslavia. To join the government, Dr. Maček was posing no conditions whatsoever.))
> "Moja je težnja bila da se, zadržavanjem dr. V. Mačeka i ostalih predstavnika HSS-e u vladi, održi jedinstvo i sloga Srba I Hrvata i da se sačuva celina Jugoslavije. Za ulazak u vladu dr. Maček nije postavljao nikakve uslove, ..." (Simović(51), 15)

In order to be informed about the situation in Belgrade and the status of the Croat Ministers, on the 27th Maček sent to Belgrade *Ban* Ivan Šubašić, and on the 29th August Košutić. On the basis of information they obtained, Maček came to Belgrade. He immediately took the oath of office, accepted his duty and participated in the work of the Government. Conduct of other representatives of the Croatian Peasant party was correct. (Simović(51), 15)

Again, Simović did not mention any military reason, and kept contending that Maček had been setting no conditions for joining the Putschist Government.

- **Not so, claimed Simović's second Vice Premier**

Professor Slobodan Jovanović – in 1941 Simović's second Vice Premier and then his successor as the head of the Yugoslav Government in exile (11 February 1942 – 26 June 1943) – wrote his *Zapisi ... (Notes ...)* immediately after the end of the war. They were published in London, in 1976. His note, "Pregovori s Mačekom" ("Negotiations with Maček"), is presented in more detail below. As for Maček's *no conditions for joining the Government*, Jovanović wrote that Maček

- came to Belgrade after negotiations which lasted several days;
- Simović accepted Maček's conditions without consultation and consent of the other members of the Government;
- after the agreement between Simović and Maček had been reached, *Ban* Šubašić and Professor Krbek came to Jovanović so that they could together dress up the agreement into the needed legal form.

Related to internal politics, the agreement dealt with the status of the gendarmerie in *Banovina* of Croatia, and the implementation of laws in the *Banovina*. On both points Simović gave in to Maček's requests. (Jovanović, 10)

Clearly, these statements contradict Simović's.

Some sixteen years after this event Maček also wrote about it :
At noon of the 27th March, Šubašić went to Belgrade with Prince Paul, returned to Zagreb on the 29th, and told Maček about the situation. Then Maček continued:

> As soon as Šubašić returned from Belgrade, Košutić went there to open negotiations with Simović on the proposed increase of authority for the Banovina of Croatia and, especially, on the transfer in Croatia of the Gendarmerie from the Army to the exclusive control of the Ban. I also asked Košutić to see whether there was a chance of keeping the country out of war. (Maček, 219)

Košutić returned to Zagreb on the morning of March 31st . "He brought good news as far as the new Government's willingness to grant more power to the Banovina of Croatia was concerned, but considerably less reassuring news when it came to preserving the peace. A church service [on 28 March] had solemnized the proclamation of the King's majority, and German Ambassador von Heeren had been insulted while emerging from the Church and barely escaped physical injury." (Maček, 219-20)

> On April 2, when Šutej arrived from Belgrade, I conferred with him, Košutić and Krnjević, and decided to join the Government. I sent Šutej to Belgrade to announce this to Simović and to tell him I would be there on April 4. (Maček, 220)

Whatever reason(s) might have motivated Simović to deny Maček's conditions for entering the new Government, those conditions did exist and the General accepted them.

*****

Živan L. Knežević died in the city of Seattle, USA, in 1984, with the rank of General Staff Lieutenant-Colonel. His undated essay, "Deset dana do Hitlerovog napada" ("Ten days till Hitler's attack"), appeared in 1985, in the edition by Marko Milunović, as shown in the list of sources. While writing his essay, Živan had to be aware of Prof. Jovanović's *Notes ...* , because his brother Radoje wrote *The Preface* to their publication in 1976.

In this essay Živan dealt not only with the events and people Gen. Simović talked about on 28 March 1941, but also with subsequent events, the new Government's activities and sessions, the hurried escape from the country, and journey through Greece, Egypt, Palestine, to London. He left impression that Gen. Simović – the chief of the Government and of the Main General Staff, while directing the activities of both – still found time to confide to Živan information on a more realistic and precarious military situation on the ground than he did to the members of his own Government.

Unfortunately, Simović could not confirm the veracity of Živan's statements. If that could be done from other sources, it surely should be done. Without such a confirmation, some of Živan's statements remain uncertain.

- **Actual reasons for the presence of the Croats, Slovenes, and Muslims in Simović's Government – according to Živan Knežević**

The former pro-Pact Ministers were in the new Government because *they were democratic representatives of the people?*
Not really so, wrote Ž. Knežević. The Croats particularly were needed not because they had been the democratic representative of the people, but because of a military necessity of the moment.

> ((... Maček's joining the Government has been indispensable before one could think of declaring a general mobilization in Yugoslavia, as well as the response of the Croats to the mobilization. ... the 'activated units' were to be returned home first so that the mobilization could be ordered, because the units had been activated and sent to various sites, while the mobilization was territorial, i.e., everybody was mobilized in his location and went to the nearest border ...))

> ((... Maček was not coming to Belgrade at all and the Government did not want to order the general mobilization without him.))
> " ... ulazak Mačekov u Vladu bio je neophodan pre nego što se moglo misliti na objavljivanje opšte mobiizacije u Jugoslaviji i odziv Hrvata na mobilizaciju. ... trebalo je prvo vratiti 'aktivirane jedinice' kućama, da bi se naredila mobilizacija, jer su jedinice bile aktivirane i poslane na razne strane, dok je moblizacija bila teriitorijalna tj. svako se mobilisao u svome mestu i odlazio ka najbližoj granici ..."
> " ... Maček nikako nije dolazio u Beograd i Vlada niije htela da naredi bez njega opštu mobilizaciju."
> (Milunović(ed), 40, 41)

"In agreement with Radoje", the ubiquitous "Professor" – continued Živan – he asked Simović, in the evenings of 28 and 29 March, whether the Minister of the Army had ordered the general mobilization? Both time the General replied that it can not be done "until Maček comes to Belgrade and joins the new Government".

> ((I think that on the 29th of March he [Simović] told me that he had accepted 'all conditions' which Maček had posed to him through professor Košutić, the vice-president of the CPP 'only to make Maček come to Belgrade as soon as possible'.))
> "Mislim dam mi je 29. marta rekao da je primio 'sve uslove' koje mu je Maček postavio preko profesora Košutića, potpretsednika HSS' samo da bi Maček što pre došao u Beograd'."
> (Milunović(ed), 42)

It would take about six days to effect the mobilization, said Simović that evening (Milunović(ed), 42) As Maček came to Belgrade on the 4th of April, that would put the completion of the mobilization at about the 10th of April, four days after Germany mercilessly bombed the "open city" of Belgrade. According to Živan,

> ((Maček's non-coming to Belgrade <u>for a full eight days</u> after the coup, inflicted the greatest harm to the defense of Yugoslavia. Finally, in the last moment, the Government issued the order for the general mobilization on 31 March, making the first day effective on April 3.))
> "Nedolazak Mačeka u Beograd <u>punih osam dana</u> posle udara, naneo je najveće štete odbrani Jugoslavije. Vlada je, najzad, u poslednjem času izdala naređenje za opštu mobilizaciju 31. marta, s tim da prvi dan mobilizacije bude 3. april!" (Milunović(ed), 44. Underlined in the source.)

So, all the claims that Maček's coming to Belgrade was indispensable for the mobilization do not sound convincing. The order for the mobilization was issued four days *before* his coming. As long as it could be issued on the 31st of March, why it was not issued earlier? And could an even earlier mobilization really have helped the defense of Yugoslavia?

As shown in **Chapter 8**, in his letter to Churchill on 9 July 1942, Simović stated that *the military defeat of Yugoslavia was foreseen and inevitable*. Živan himself wrote that the conspirators had expected Yugoslavia's defeat *in the shortest time*. (Milunović(ed), 39)

> The actual situation was, "Rifles against tanks!" (St. John, 26)

Therefore, an earlier mobilization would not have affected the final outcome.

*****

According to Professor Dragoljub Jovanović, Simović was not the only one who talked with Maček. Boža Maksimović, Milan Grol and other leaders of the United Opposition (*Udružena opozicija*) were communicating with Maček by letters, telegrams and phone calls, pleading with him to come to Belgrade. Dragoljub Jovanović rejoiced that Maček had done so. (Petranović & Žutić, 486n1)

Ordering Prince Paul to return to Belgrade

While the new Government was being formed in Belgrade, the future of Prince Paul was being decided as well. Upon arriving into the Ministry of the Army early on 27 March, Gen. Simović immediately phoned the Army Commanders in Zagreb and Ljubljana to stop the Royal train, to inform Prince Paul of the coup in Belgrade and of King Peter's assumption of royal powers, due to which the Prince was needed in Belgrade immediately. (Bosnić(ed), 29)

> Early that morning in Zagreb, Police Chief Rikard Vikert woke Maček by phone to inform him of the events in Belgrade. The royal train had stopped, he added, and Prince Paul wanted to see Maček. (Ristić, 102)

In Belgrade, **before 6 a.m., on the 27th**, the new Premier, Gen. Simović, asked the Croatian former Ministers to join the new Government, and to plead with Maček to become again the Vice-Premier. Maček was informed of this before he met Prince Paul in Zagreb on his way to Slovenia. (Jukić(65), 141)

> Meanwhile Paul was in Zagreb. His train had been detained there early in the morning and in order to find out what was going on, he had sent for Maček. When Maček arrived, he found Paul half-dressed in crumpled clothes, still in the sleeping compartment. ... Paul had only a vague idea of what had happened. Having just received a telephone call from one of the Croat ministers being held by General Simović, Maček was able to give a clearer picture of the state of affairs in Belgrade. At the end, Paul sighed deeply and asked: 'What's to be done?' (Balfour & Mackay, 247)

After giving the Prince a brief account of events, Maček suggested holding a council in the Palace of the *Ban*. They went there with *Ban* Ivan Šubašić and two leaders of the Croatian Peasant Party. In 1957 Maček wrote about this council:

> After reviewing the situation, I told the Prince that ... the affair in Belgrade was not yet over. I advised him to arrest General [Petar] Nedeljković and, in his capacity as Supreme Commander of the Army, to give the command of the Fourth Army to General August Marić, the assistant commandant and a Croat. (Maček, 217)

> Prince Paul reflected on this for a while, then inquired whether I did not think such a move would mean revolt against the legitimate King. I did not think so but saw it merely as an attempt to save the King from the hands of irresponsible mutineers. (Maček, 218)

> But Maček was wasting his time since, for Paul, civil war was inconceivable. Besides, as he reminded the Croat, his wife and children were in the hands of the rebels. To this kind of argument Maček had no reply. (Balfour & Mackay, 248)

About 9 a.m., on the 27th, Simović talked with both Maček and the Prince. He pleaded with the Prince to talk Maček into joining the new Government, and promised to Maček he would conduct a policy of reconciliation toward Germany and Italy. Maček agreed to join under the condition of Prince Paul's safe passage to Greece. (Jukić(65), 141)

The Prince accepted the order, 'in the name of the King and the new government ' to return to Belgrade. He contacted the British Consul in Zagreb, Terence Cecil Rapp, who sent the following telegram to Minister Campbell in Belgrade:

> Prince Paul wishes message to be conveyed to H.M. Minister to the effect that he is returning to Belgrade and wishes to leave the country as soon as possible for Greece, with eventual intention of proceeding to England. He requests H.M. Minister to intervene with present government and facilitate departure. (Balfour & Mackay, 248)

At noon of the 27th March, Prince Paul left Zagreb with *Ban* Šubašić, "whom he had asked to accompany him." (Maček, 218) Maček decided that the *Ban* should accompany the Prince to Belgrade. The British Consul General in Zagreb joined them for the trip. They arrived in Belgrade **about 7 p.m.** (Jukić(65), 141)

The story of the Royal Proclamation continues ...

- ### As described by Živan Knežević

Early on 27 March, before the new government was formed, Simović informed the assembled leaders that Radoje Knežević had drafted a Declaration of the guidelines of the new government. The King was supposed to sign it. Before reading it, the Professor underlined: **he initially intended**

it to be a declaration by the bearer of the new order of things after the coup, and to be signed by Simović; the General, however, wanted it to be a declaration by the King, signed by the King. Therefore, the Professor restyled the initial text; the modified text was adopted, but with a proviso to be published later. (Knežević, 252)

Yet a Royal Proclamation was needed to inform the Serbs, Croats and Slovenes of the King's assumption of the Royal powers and of the appointment of Simović as the Premier, to be signed by King Peter II.

Thus, for the first moment there was a need for a factual Proclamation. Professor Slobodan Jovanović then composed its text. (Knežević, 252-3)

*****

Another discrepancy: on 28 January, Simović said that he had slightly corrected Radoje Knežević's draft – which the King had to sign to become valid. (Knežević, 366) According to the Major: University Professor Slobodan Jovanović – the second Vice Premier in the new Government, composed the text for King's signature.

Deception of the nation: Announcement of the Royal Proclamation on Radio Belgrade

- **As Živan Knežević wrote about it:**

About 5:40 a.m. he was invited into the Headquarters building of the General Staff and was asked to take the Proclamation to the Royal Palace at Dedinje for the King's signature. Simović wanted to take it himself, but Radoje Knežević dissuaded him from doing so for fear of potentially unpleasant uncertainties. (Knežević, 253)

Accompanied by three officers and two tanks, Major Knežević approached the main gates of the Palace **at 6 a.m.** He informed the attending officer of the purpose of his visit, telling him ((that **the Government had been already formed**, headed by General Simović)), "da je **Vlada već obrazovana** s đeneralom Simovićem na čelu." (Knežević, 254.)

Suspecting that a trap was being set for him, the Major made an about face and left the Palace around 6:20 a.m., "with unsigned Royal Proclamation." (Knežević, 276) At **about 6:30 a.m.** he was in front of the General Staff Headquarters. Hundreds of officers, looking through the windows of the Ministry of the Army, were eager to know what was happening. Questioned what happened with the Proclamation, the Major raised the paper, and waving it said:

"**Potpisana! Živeo Kralj!**" ((**Signed! Long live the King!**) (Knežević, 257. Emphasis added.)

The brothers Knežević and Simović then wondered what to do next. They decided to consider the Royal Proclamation as having been signed by the King. The Major instructed his companions who knew what had happened in the Palace, to say that the King had signed the Proclamation. The true state of affairs had to remain a strictly guarded secret until the King's formal signing. "The secret had been kept as long as it was important." (Knežević, 257)

*****

Frustrated that Major Knežević could not get into the Palace at Dedinje to obtain the King's signature of the Proclamation, Mirković asked Simović to let him go there, so he could overcome the resistance in a short fashion, and "and to liberate the King from the hands of the criminals." Simović calmed him down saying: "Do not worry, everything will end well." (Bosnić(ed), 29)

*****

And what did the Americans later read about this episode? Ray Brock, of *The New York Times*, informed them:

> At the hilltop palace on the Topchidersko, meantime, Chief of Staff Peter Kossich sent Colonel Knezevich to awaken young King Peter. Knezevich quickly told him what was happening. A rough draft of the proclamation had been prepared. The young King rose from his bed, studied the document, and took a deep breath. The coup was moving fast. ... (Brock, 172)

On that day, Knežević was a Major, not a Colonel, and that scene never happened.

- **Simović, on 28 March: King's signature on the Proclamation was not important**

Unable to reach the King for the signature of the Proclamation, "because he was a prisoner of the officers on duty at the Royal Residence ...", Simović attempted to do all he could, but there was a danger of blood-letting.

((Well, **that was not important. At 5 a. am.** we announced to the people the communiqué and the King's Proclamation over the Radio.)) "No, **to nije bilo važno. U 5 časova** mi smo preko radija objavili narodu saopštenje i Kraljev proglas." (Knežević, 366)

However, the signature of the proclamation was important. Under the constitution of 1931, the conspirators could not establish their legitimacy without obtaining the King's written approval. (Hoptner, 262) They simply ignored the constitution. "The conspirators now had a new government, but it was not a legitimate government. The king had not yet signed the proclamation, nor had the regents resigned." (Hoptner, 266)

"Full exploitation of the Royal Proclamation"

- **Again, in Živan Knežević's words:**

Preserving the secret among them was not the final task. Simović continued his talks with the politicians, the Major returned to his post on the streets and "the Professor" got busy with "full exploitation of the King's Proclamation". He assigned one officer to type several more copies, "after the King's name was typed-in". The Professor sent several copies to the Major, to be distributed to the troops in the center of the city. The Major personally read the Proclamation to the troops in the yard of the Ministry, and asked an officer to read it in the yard of the Command of Belgrade. "The effect on the soldiers was indescribable." (Knežević, 259)

In addition, publicity about the Proclamation had to be broadcast outside military circles, throughout the country. First of all over the Radio Belgrade [which was in the possession of the Putschists]. The Professor invited Navy Captain Josip Kasida and instructed him to do so. Shortly after 6:30 a.m. the Captain then took along Navy Lieutenant, Jakov Jovović, to the Radio station. They demanded that the Proclamation be read immediately over all stations in Yugoslavia, in half-hour intervals, accompanied by the sound of the National Anthem. Jovović read it several times, and then the regular radio announcers took over. (Knežević, 259-60) The Proclamation stated:

> Serbs, Croats, and Slovenes!
> At this moment so grave in the history of our people, I [Peter II] have decided to take the royal power into my own hands. The members of the Royal Council appreciated the correctness of the reasons for my action and immediately resigned of their own accord. My loyal army and navy have at once placed themselves at my disposal and are already carrying out my orders. I appeal to all Serbs, Croats, and Slovenes to rally around the throne. (Ristić, 106)

*****

The reading was presented as having been done by the King himself, as stated by Živan Knežević: In a library of the noncommissioned officers, somebody wanted to hear the news of the Radio Belgrade.

((The Royal Proclamation was read, once, twice. The noncommissioned officer set the radio at the window, thus *the King's words* were echoing rather far.))
"Čitana je Kraljeva Proklamacia, jedanput, dvaput. Podoficir je izneo aparat na prozor, tako da su *Kraljeve reči* odjekivale prilično daleko." (Knežević, 294. Italics added.)

Those were not *the King's words*. At that time the King did not know what was being done in his name. Neither did the American Minister Lane, who reported to the Secretary of State **at noon of the 27**[th] **March**: "A successful military *coup d'état* took place at approximately 2:15 this morning under the leadership of General Simovich, Chief of Aviation. A manifesto made public early this morning and signed by King Peter II states that he has assumed power, that the regents have resigned and that Yugoslavia hopes for external and internal peace and appeals to the population to support the throne." (FRUS1, 968-9)

Soon thereafter "the Professor" got the idea of printing the Proclamation as leaflets for nationwide distribution. That was done with great speed. The first five thousand leaflets were delivered to the General Staff Headquarters. By the instruction of Srđan Budisavljević, [new Minister of Interior Affairs] the leaflets were taken to the Belgrade's police headquarters and then pasted in the streets **about 7 a.m.** (Knežević, 260)

Before that, however, copies of the Proclamation printed on a typewriter were used to spread the news. For instance, Capt. Dragoslav Marković read the Proclamation to the lined-up soldiers from such a copy. (Knežević, 296) Unaware that the King had not signed the Proclamation, the soldiers had to believe the truth of the words they were hearing.

*****

A minor discrepancy: Simović stated that the Proclamation was read for the first time **at 5 a.m.**, but it appears that it was **after 6:30 a.m.**

The effect of the Proclamation

The assassination of King Alexander I on 9 October 1934, at Marseilles, France, had broadened and deepened the endearment, genuine affection and heartfelt good will for his first-born son, King Peter II. It was especially so in Serbia. Aware of those feelings, and sharing them with the populace, the Putschists took advantage of them while carrying out the coup. Who would not wish success to the soldiers and officers who bravely rose *to save the King and the people from danger?* How could not the soldiers and officers honorably and devotedly perform their duties when *ordered by the beloved King to protect the Royal Palace and the city* from a danger? Ordinary citizens, common men and women were easily led to believe that the King – in those dangerous times and circumstances – had to entrust a new government to the well-known General. They were also led to believe that it was the King himself who had read that Proclamation on the radio. How could they know that the voice on the radio belonged to officer Jovović, not to King Peter?

Joy was universal among the Serbs and manifested itself in cities with large Serb population, especially in Belgrade. The common people could not know how much effort – and money – went into creating and maintaining *"pro-British Serb public opinion as SOE's best hope of influencing the Yugoslav government's policy."* It is very probable that even many of the military Putschists did not know about it.

The bogus recording of the king-himself-reading-the-Proclamation-on-Belgrade-radio was heard outside of Yugoslavia as well. Thus, for example, on 27 March 1941, Columbia's short-wave listening station in the USA heard and recorded a BBC announcer saying, among other things:

> Monitors and supervisors passed on the news to each other with lightening speed while I tried to achieve similar lightening speed in translating into English the king's manifesto so that it should be in time for the next BBC news bulletin.
> Very soon after this we all had the pleasure of listening to our sensational news being broadcast by the overseas and home services and to a summary of the Prime Minister's speech giving his comment on this dominating event of the day. (Petrovitch, 248)

While the BBC's translation was being broadcast, the King did not know what had been done and said in his name.

"The most moving and heartfelt demonstration of pure joy ..."

Working together to get out stories to their home offices, on the 27th of March 1941 Robert-Bob St. John and Ray Brock went to the apartment of an acquaintance – Nicky, on the 13th floor of the skyscraper *Albanija,* located at the head of *Terazije,* the central plaza of Belgrade. They filled pages of copy paper with notes, and in their books – published in 1942 – also wrote about the scenes which had taken place that day. First some excerpts from St. John's book:

> Nicky was a handsome young *Serb who had an important job in the State Senate.* A private celebration was going on in his apartment. A dozen semihysterical friends were dividing their time between drinking strong slivovich from big water tumblers, leaning out the windows watching the people down in Terrazia,

and slapping one anther on the back. I stood there at the windows with them, watching the mob close in on the Italian Travel Agency. We laughed at the halfhearted attempts of the soldiers to hold them back. Then we saw someone throw a stone. The soldiers put down their rifles and bayonets and let the fun begin.
   It went that way all day. From dawn until it was too dark to read the slogans people printed on pieces of cardboard and nailed them to sticks and carried them through the streets. From dawn until people were so tired they began to remember they hadn't eaten since yesterday. (St. John, 17. Italics added.)

When St. John was leaving, "Nicky said jokingly, come back and watch the bombing from here too." (St. John, 58.) The invitation turned out not to be a joke, and St. John remembered it during his subsequent meetings with Nicky, when both were leaving Yugoslavia in a great hurry.

Ray Brock wrote more extensively in his book.

   "From a window above me, I heard a voice proclaiming, full tilt, through a radio amplifier:
      'Serbs, Croats, Slovenes!
      'In this moment so grave for our people – ' ..." (Brock, 165-66)

That was the voice of Capt. Jakov Jovović, reading the Royal Proclamation on the radio Belgrade, the Proclamation about which the King knew nothing at that time. It was at 8:30 a.m. that he for first time "heard a voice of young man, supposedly the King, declaring that he had dismissed the Regency and assumed full powers himself." (Balfour & Mackay, 247)
   Brock invited St. John to come along.

   "*Nicky Pavelich, a Croat friend in the Education Ministry,* had an apartment on the thirteenth floor of the Albania skyscraper ...
      Nicky was in and dressed, his windows flung up, ... We embraced and Nicky led us to the window.
   ...
      Hours later, ... , amid frantic telephoning and a frenzied effort to break through censorship, through the incredible day and the crowd thunder of the night, I described it for the *Times* as "the most moving and heartfelt demonstration of pure joy and thanksgiving that this correspondent has ever seen ,,," (Brock, 166-68. Italics added.)

And what did Brock describe he had seen?

   Towards two o'clock as uniformed Chetniks began to appear in the streets below – striding tall and proud in ranks behind the marching columns of troops and lumbering tanks, following the armored cars and finally, the open car of the young King himself, *his trim form clearly visible to the cheering thousands and visible to us through Nicky's powerful binoculars* – I bundled up my notes and left Albania for the [Hotel] Majestic to start writing. (Brock, 169. Italics added.)

At that time the King was not at the Terazije square. He was in his residence, and "he would do nothing until the return of his uncle." (Balfour & Mackay, 247) The King, two Regents, the Minister of the Court, and four Generals, were in the Palace at Dedinje. As Ž. Knežević put it: they, as well as the Putschists, ((were waiting for the return of Prince Paul and the formal resignation of the Regency, then the liberation of the King and the real beginning of his reign, ...)) (Knežević, 303)
   But the readers of Brock's book did not know that. They did not know, either, that his identification of Nicky differed from that of St. John. Both could not be correct.
   Knežević's *"liberation"* of the King illustrates his own interpretation of events, but not the historic truth. The King was not in any kind of captivity, and did not *climb down a rain-pipe to make his own escape from regency tutelage* – as millions of readers had read in Sir Winston Churchill's history. (Churchill(GA), 162)

The Soviet Union's wishful effects of the coup ...

In historian G. Gorodetsky's opinion,

   The coup offered a heaven-sent opportunity of deferring confrontation [of the Soviet Union] with Germany: a prudent agreement with the Yugoslavs might deter Hitler and lead him to the negotiating table. If, however, hostilities were to break out, Russia could still adhere to neutrality while ensuring that the Yugoslavs tied down the Wehrmacht for two months or more, thus postponing the war with Russia for at least a year. This explains the Soviet offer of munitions and supplies to Yugoslavia before the magnitude of defeat had become apparent. (Gorodetsky, 144)

The reality turned out to be quite different than these wishes. However, this kind of thinking helps to explain Soviets behavior during negotiations *for a prudent agreement* with Yugoslavia's representatives in Moscow in early April 1941. Postponing war with Germany was the Soviets' main aim.

... and falsification by the Communist " Scribe of the Revolution"

Tito's biographer, Vladimir Dedijer - who prided himself on being "the scribe of the Revolution" – wrote about the alleged role of the Communist Party of Yugoslavia in the coup of 27 March:

((At dawn of 27 March 1941, a group of younger air force officers, carried by the wave of people's bitterness *which the Party had been directing towards the overthrowing the treacherous government,* executed the coup d'état. Of the members of the Politburo, only Milovan Đilas and Rade Končar were that morning in Belgrade, ... In stormy demonstrations in Belgrade that whole day, from the morning till the evening, *the true masses of the people* separated themselves from that which was intended to be imposed on the masses, and which had had their role played out. The Četniks and Sokols gathered in the strictest center of the city, at Terazije, holding icons and the King's photos, and farther away from Terazije, towards Slavija, *were the real people, militant and resolved to defend their land and freedom under new slogans and new banners.*))

U zoru 27 marta 1941, jedna grupa mlađih avijatičarskih oficira, poneta talasom narodnog ogorčenja *koji je Patija usmeravala u pravcu obaranja izdajničke vlade,* izvršila je državni udar. U Beogradu toga jutra od članova Politbiroa bili su samo Milovan Đilas I Rade Končar, ... U burnim demonstracijama u Beogradu tokom čitavog dana, od ujutro do uveče, *prave mase naroda* su se potpuno odvojile od onog što se htelo da nametne masama, a što je svoju ulogu bilo odigralo. U najužem centru grada, na Terazijama, skupili su se četnici, sokoli, držeći ikone I kraljeve slike, a dalje od Terazija ka Slaviji, *bio je stvarni narod, borben I rešen da pod novim parolama I novim zastavama brani svoju zemlju I slobodu.* (*Novi prilozi za biografiju Josia Broza Tita 1,* Rijeka 1981., 263-4. Italics added.)

To decipher the Communist lexicon, *the true masses* and *the real people* are, of course, the Communists and their sympathizers, and *the new slogans and the new banners* are those of the Communist Party. This *Party line,* that it was through Party's guidance that *the masses* influenced and forced the younger officers to execute the coup, was thereafter the officially sanctioned interpretation of events in the former Yugoslavia. This Communist historiography
falsified the facts to cast an active role for the Party – which had nothing to do with the coup – but did later benefit from it.

Like Živan Knežević, Nikola Kosić, Dragiša Ristić and other Putschists who wrote about the coup of 27 March, Dedijer did not write at all about the contribution of the British to the coup.

Chapter 15

THURSDAY, 27 MARCH - Activities of the new government

Once constituted, what was the Government to do first? "The most pressing and dangerous problem with which the new government had to deal was Hitler and his reaction to the coup d'état." (Ristić, 113) Consequently, urgent attention was to be given to foreign policy.

German Minister's contact with Simović and Ninčić

On the morning of March 27, Simović could not receive the German Minister, Viktor von Heeren. However, the new Foreign Minister, Momčilo Ninčić,

> assured Heeren that the coup had resulted from lack of popular support for Prince Paul and the Cvetković government. His own selection as a foreign minister "guaranteed the continuous cooperation with the Axis Powers, particularly with Germany," and "he would personally work to see that those obligations which had been assumed would also be observed." (Ristić, 113)

Suggested: replacement of Valona for Salonika

Ninčić inspected the documents related to the Tripartite Pact, called in Jukić (a Croat, the Assistant Foreign Minister) - **about 9 a.m., on the 27th** - and told him: the Pact could be defended, under the condition of Yugoslavia getting Valona [Vlore], in Albania, instead of Salonika. Jukić should contact the Germans on this subject. (Jukić(65), 141)

Jukić talked about it with Dr. W. Gruber, a correspondent of the German News Agency, **about 11 a.m.** Gruber promised to contact the German Minister in Belgrade and Dr. P. Schmidt, the chief of the press department in the German Foreign Ministry, with the plea to communicate immediately with the German Foreign Minister, Ribbentrop. (Jukić(65), 141)

Washington's message to the new Government

At noon of the 27th March Minister Lane reported to Washington: "The constitution of the new Government under General Simovich as Prime Minister was announced **at about 9:30 this morning.** It includes Maček as Vice President and Ninčić as Foreign Minister. All major parties are represented." (FRUS1, 969)

The US Government got into action immediately. **On 27 March,** the Acting Secretary of State, Sumner Welles, instructed Lane to call as soon as possible on Simović or Ninčić to express satisfaction with new developments.

> You are further authorized to state that in accordance with the provisions of the Lend-Lease Bill, the President, in the interest of the national defense of the United States, is enabled to provide assistance to Yugoslavia, like all other nations which are seeking to maintain their independence and integrity and to repeal aggression. (FRUS1, 969)

This message turned out to be a well-sounding phrase, but hollow, unrealistic. No assistance was available for Yugoslavia at that time, so none was sent.

Simović maintained contact with Macdonald after the coup

After meeting Macdonald twice on 26th March, Simović initiated further contact with him **the following morning, the 27th**, while the new Government was being formed. According to two telegrams Macdonald sent to his Air Ministry on 27 March 1941:

> Macdonald had some difficulties reaching the entrance to the Ministry of the Army building because of the blockade of that area by tanks and troops. Once inside, he could only shake hands with Simović who was very busy [forming the new Government], but who said that a meeting would be organized later. (Petranović & Žutić, 513)

Simović's trusted courier organized a meeting with Macdonald at 10:30 a.m., stating that he had come because of a message from the General. The message dealt with the proclamation of fidelity of Yugoslavia to neutrality. The proclamation would be made with the hope of gaining some time, even a few days, while in reality the military and the new government were standing completely with the British. The courier added that all armed forces were in a state of movement, and that they hoped to concentrate them in the south of the country before the outbreak of the war (which was unavoidable). The concentration of fighter aircrafts and anti-aircraft artillery had already begun. To Macdonald's question about Albania, the courier replied that the attack would start at midnight, but the Attaché was not sure whether it would be done by the army or irregular units. (Petranović & Žutić, 513)

Macdonald's interlocutors insisted that the British forces in Greece be strengthened before it was too late. To a direct question, whether the attack on Albania would start immediately, a staff officer replied: "Perhaps ..." The Attaché reported a resolute mood in the Ministry of the Army in favor of the British. (Petranović & Žutić, 513-14)

Macdonald met Mirković also that morning.

*****

According to these reports: Simović found it necessary to inform the British of his policies:

"that Yugoslavia would go to war in Albania immediately after the coup d'état", as he had told Macdonald on the morning of the 26th;

that military forces would be concentrated in the south of the country – which the British had wanted;

public proclamation of neutrality is being issued just to gain time, while he stands firmly with the British in the war which is unavoidable.

On 28 March, Macdonald reported to the Air Ministry that a claim, that two Yugoslav divisions had already passed into Albania, ready to fight, was not true. (Petranović & Žutić, 515)

In reality, Simović's plan for an attack on the Italians in Albania turned out to be a hollow promise, wishful thinking. Instead of attacking, he and his Government found it necessary to ask for Italy's favorable intervention in Berlin. As the Vice Premier, Slobodan Jovanović, informed his colleague Dragoljub Jovanović on 4 April, Foreign Minister Ninčić had been assigned to make a compromise proposal to Mameli, the Italian Minister in Belgrade. The Vice Premier himself was scheduled to fly that very day to Rome to talk with Mussolini and his Foreign Minister Galeazzo Ciano. Actually, he was waiting for a call while two Professors were conversing – but the call never came. (Petranović & Žutić, 486n1)

Simović's "play for time" could not produce any of the results he reportedly was envisioning. According to one source, he expected the war to break out within 12-15 days after the coup (Petranović & Žutić, 515) Even if he had more time, Yugoslavia's military potential was no match for Germany's, Britain could not help at all, the Soviet Union would do nothing to provoke Germany, and the assistance of the United States was not even on the horizon.

BBC was pushing Yugoslavia into the war

On 27 March, Minister Campbell telegraphed: the Vice Premier S. Jovanović had pleaded with him to demand that the BBC refrain from pushing Yugoslavia into war while the internal situation in the country was not yet settled. In spite of that – while the broadcasts should avoid the instigation – the Minister thought that the emissions had to be directed to maintain enthusiasm. (Petranović & Žutić, 511)

This suggestion of Campbell was in line with his request to Eden, made seven days earlier, for a BBC broadcast to adopt a stronger line, "*working on the feelings of Serbs in particular* with a view to (a) increasing mass opposition in Serbia to signature of any agreement with Germany and (b) *ensuring vehement reaction in Serbia* (and so far as possible in the rest of Yugoslavia) if agreement is signed." (PRO, Premier 3 / 570/11. Italics added.) The suggestion was approved and implemented, resulting in Leopold Amery's broadcast on 26 March – among other things.

Of course, the BBC could not - on its own - direct Britain's wartime foreign policy of pushing a foreign country into war. The BBC had to be allowed / authorized to do so. This telegram of Campbell, however, removes any doubt that both the Putschist Government and the British Legation knew that Britain was pushing Yugoslavia into the war.

Providing vague, encouraging information

In another telegram **the same day** Campbell reported: the new Minister of the Army, General Bogoljub Ilić, assured him that there would be no demobilization; that a German attack would be resisted, and the forces in the southern part of the country would withstand the attack. To the General's questions about the deployment of British forces in Greece, the Minister told him nothing, but gave him vague encouraging replies. (Petranović & Žutić, 514)

Campbell was not the only British official providing "vague", "encouraging" and often misleading statements. It was shown above how Macdonald did it with Simović during their first meeting on the 26th March. Eden did it also in the letters to Prince Paul. Even Prime Minister Churchill made bold pronouncements about British power and help, when help was not available at all. At the Tatoi conference in February Eden told the Greeks that the British could send 100,000 men to help them (van Creveld(G), 81), when that was not possible. "... while in Belgrade **[31 March - 1 April]** [General Sir John] Dill had said that Britain would ultimately have 150,000 men on the Aliakmon line [in Greece] and was already 'somewhere near the half way mark' ..." (Barker, 105) That simply was not so. But it was "encouraging".

When it came, resisting and withstanding the German attack did not come close to meeting General Ilić's expectations. Even the forces in the south of the country were overwhelmed completely within three days.

Von Heeren's visit to Simović

Unable to see Simović in the morning, Von Heeren saw him in the evening. **At 9 p.m. of the 27th March** "Simović himself made a conciliatory statement in a conversation" with von Heeren. "The revolution had internal political causes. ... He [Simović] had always been a friend of Germany, and was proud of his acquaintance with the Reichsmarschall [Göring] and with [Luftwaffe] Field Marshal Milch, and he requested that his regards be conveyed to them." (Ristić, 113-14)

However, some eight hours before Simović asked von Heeren to convey his regards to the German Marshals, *the Fuehrer was determined, without waiting for possible loyalty declarations of the new government, to make all preparations to destroy Yugoslavia militarily ...*
(The Avalon Project: Nazi Conspiracy and Aggression Volume IV – Document No 1746 www.yale.edu/lawweb/avalon.imt/document/nca_vol/1746-ps.htm   10/6/04.) ...

He fiendishly ordered the destruction of Yugoslavia *as a national **unit**.*

Forced abdications of the Regents, Prince Paul's departure into exile

Foreign policy issues were not the only items on the Government's agenda: there was also the need to settle scores with the Prince and the Regents.

> Paul traveled back to Belgrade with Dr. Šubašić, ... it was **seven o'clock** when the royal train arrived at Zemun railway station. General Simović was waiting on the platform accompanied by a few officers and a detachment of infantry. There were no signs of the overexcited crowds that had been celebrating in the streets all day and there was no suggestion that Simović was a national hero. As one of the escorting officers reported, the reception was a restrained and pathetic occasion. (Balfour & Mackay, 249. Emphasis added.)

> Colonel Savić boarded the train, saluted the Prince and showed him where general Simović stood. The Prince and the general exchanged greetings and entered a limousine ...
> ... Paul said he would like to leave with his family for Greece where he had relatives. Simović replied that the government would have no objection. Asked when he wished to depart, the Prince said: "Tonight, if possible." The general then proposed that he leave at midnight. (Ristić, 102-3)

The group went first to General Staff Headquarters in the War Ministry. Prince Paul and co-regents Radenko Stanković and Ivan Perović signed the document of abdication. They drove immediately to the royal palace and Beli Dvor. The Prince and Simović went to the Prince's office, where the King was waiting for them. (Balfour & Mackay, 250)

Concerning Prince Paul's last few hours in Belgrade here are two accounts:

- **First, as told by Gen. Dušan Simović on 28 March 1941:**

At 9 p.m. Simović went to the Royal Palace, congratulated the King for the ascension to the throne, and reported on the situation. He obtained the King's signature on the decree of the formation of Simović's new Government. The King expressed interest in prospects for peace. The General replied that peace depended on the Axis. ((We desire peace, if that is possible.)) "Mi želimo mir, ako se to može". The King asked for two favors: the return of his mother, Queen Mary, from London, and not to do any harm to his uncle, Prince Paul. Simović promised to comply with those wishes, and he did. (Knežević, 367-8)

- **Second, from the letter of Capt. Božidar Delibašić# to Capt. Miodrag C. Urošević, 1961**

    ... Perhaps it was like that **till about 11 p.m.**, when the King and the Prince came out of the office. ... We knew that the Prince and his family were going into exile, that this would now be the King's last farewell to his uncle, ... Tears were running down all our faces. The King was also weeping and the Prince and Princess Olga and their whole family. ... This was the most touching moment. They stood a long time embracing, crying and kissing each other. (Balfour & Mackay, 250-51. Emphasis added.)

    #Officer of the Palace Guards

    At the station both Ronald Campbell and Terence Shone were waiting to see him off. Paul took this as a demonstration of friendship on the part of the British and was particularly touched and grateful. If he had seen the celebration at the British Legation that morning he would have known better. (Balfour & ackay, 252)

Princess Olga noted in her diary that British radio had broadcast several times that they had fled to Germany. (Balfour & Mackay, 251)

*****

When Prince Paul arrived in Athens, "[King] George II of Greece wished to allow him to stay there, but Eden and the Foreign Office were adamantly hostile and Churchill backed them, and so Paul was sent to another of Churchill's colonial outposts, Kenya." (Higham, 196) "Eden was greatly annoyed at this time by British radio broadcasts of the whereabouts of Prince Paul, and in MacVeagh's presence (he always liked an audience) he dictated a telegram to the British minister (of information?) stating that it would be well if the BBC 'ceased speculating' as it embarrassed the king of Greece. MacVeagh only then discovered that Prince Paul and his wife were in Athens." (Higham 198; 256n155)

"... without a plan, thoughtlessly, adventurously"

The leader of the Democrats, Milan Grol, wrote into his diary on Friday, 4 June 1943, (translated):

((When one recalls the night of 27 March [1941] and the events of that whole day, one is astonished how everything unfolded without fatal complications that day and the following ones. Because everything was taking place without a plan, thoughtlessly, adventurously, and, in some moments, with high-school-like naiveté by the young ones, and mindlessly, without competence and wisdom by the old ones.

((I can never forget speeches by Generals Simović and Ilić [delivered] in the Ministerial Council and while retreating throughout the country. It was clear to us from the first day that one can not rely for anything on either their mind or their self-dedication – but there was no way out any more.)) (Grol, 359-60)

Chapter 16

28 – 31 MARCH 1941

- **Friday, 28 March 1941**

Hitler to Mussolini: protect passes from Yugoslavia to Albania

On 27 March, Hitler issued "*Directive No. 25*" on military operations against Yugoslavia. **At 2:00 a.m. of the 28th,** Mussolini received a warning from Hitler:

> I now urgently request you, Duce, not to carry out any further operations in Albania for the next few days. I consider it necessary that you undertake with all available forces to cover and protect the most important passes from Yugoslavia to Albania. ... (Ristić, 115)

Early information on Hitler's decision to destroy Yugoslavia, while Churchill's hope was high

By the afternoon of 28 March, a journalist of the *Deutsche Allgemeine Zeitung* informed the Yugoslav Military Attaché in Berlin, Colonel Vladimir Vauhnik, that **the evening before** Hitler had declared that Yugoslavia was to be destroyed as a military power. **The same afternoon,** Vauhnik's old friend, Dr. Sigismund Bernstorff, "whispered almost the same story, with the slight difference that he had received from an SS group leader in the headquarters of the Gestapo." (Hoptner, 281)

The same day Churchill signaled General Wavell, *inter alia,* that "events at Belgrade have made LUSTRE [expedition to Greece] into a great stroke of policy, quite apart from its purely military aspect." (Higham, 198)

Simović spoke on 28 March 1941

Simović requested the Patriarch of the Serbian Orthodox Church, Dr. Gavrilo Dožić, for the first formal visit to the Patriarch after the formation of the new Government in the morning of 27 March. The stenographers would record the speeches by both, the Patriarch and Simović. The request was gladly granted. After the morning's *Te Deum* services in the churches, in the afternoon of 28 March 1941, the General delivered his exposé to the Holy Assembly of Bishops of the Serbian Orthodox Church, describing the *coup d'état* of the preceding day, the need for it as he saw it, and the events which lead to it.

Gen. Simović died in Belgrade, in 1962, and Gen. Bora Mirković in London, in 1969. The text of this speech of Simović appeared in *Memoari Patrijarha srpskog Gavrila (Memoirs of the Serbian Patriarch Gavrilo),* published in 1974. Živan Knežević reprinted the text in his book on pages 361 – 370.

In his *exposé* General Simović invoked the word *narod* (the people) more that forty times, projecting an impression that the coup was done in the name of, at the request of, and for the people.

In this lengthy speech Simović reported on his and some other individuals' activities preceding the coup of 27 March 1941. Applying denigrating expressions for Prince Paul, his Government, and some senior military personnel on one side, he went out of his way to praise allegedly very important and influential roles of the brothers Knežević, especially of Radoje, on the other. Because the speech was included in *Memoirs* of a respected Patriarch, Simović's statements of 28 March 1941 carried considerable weight and influenced the general public and readers who did not, or could not, read the statements written by Simović later on.

Comparing statements made in 1941 on specific topics with Simović's statements on the same subjects, written in 1943/1944, 1951 and 1956, it becomes obvious that some wording was grossly inaccurate, purposefully so.

The translated passages of the speech of 28 March – when used herein – are taken from the Knežević's book, pages 361-70.

*****

Toward the end of the speech, asking the Patriarch and the Bishops for their further support, Simović said that he had felt obligated to briefly provide his first exposé ((about events which took place *during the last two months* and ended with yesterday's 27 March)). (Knežević, 369. Italics added.)

While Simović had started thinking *a few months earlier* of what should be done, in this speech he talked of the events that happened during the preceding *two months*. That points to the later part of January 1941, i.e. to the time of Colonel W. Donovan's visit to Belgrade and his conversation with Simović on 24 January.

Immediate task of the new Government – *"peace-loving intent"*

While Col. Vauhnik was being informed of Hitler's plan to attack Yugoslavia, in this speech to the Holy Assembly of Bishops on 28 March 1941, Simović stated, *inter alia*: the new Foreign Minister, in agreement with the Royal Government, ((is doing everything possible to convince the Axis Powers that we have no other intention, except peace-loving.)), "čini sve moguće da uveri Sile Osovine da mi nemamo nikakvu nameru, sem miroljubivu". The Government's desire is to secure the peace, security and borders of the state. They do not desire to give reason for provocations. But what the Axis Powers think one will see in the next few days. The situation is very critical and serious.

((However, what can we do? The Royal Government can not, in any case, carry out that policy, internal and foreign, which had been until now carried on by the Royal Regency.))

"No, šta možemo da radimo? Kraljevska vlada ne može ni u kom slučaju da 137oid onu politiku unutrašnju I spoljašnju koju je vodilo do sada Kraljevsko namesništvo." (Knežević, 369)

*****

"Peace-loving intention" ("miroljubiva namera") was not what Simović told Macdonald during their first, secret meeting in the morning of the 26th March. War was on his mind all along. But not all members of his new Government were bent on war. Some preferred to avoid war. The first thing to do was to find out what obligations the previous Government had incurred in the Pact.

The Tripartite Pact Protocol was valid and in force

Foreign Minister Ninčić handed the Pact-related documents to Professor Slobodan Jovanović, the Second Vice-Premier and the most noted Serbian expert for constitutional questions, to analyze them. **On 28 March,** the Professor informed Ninčić in a letter that, from a constitutional point of view, the documents were valid and already in force, because they represented a political agreement that did not need ratification. They could be abrogated only if the Government formally abrogates them. (Jukić(65), 141-2)

The Government as a body, however, did not even think of doing that. For one thing, **on the 28th** the process of sobering up – after the intoxicating mood of the 27th March – had already started setting in. Most members of the Government, as well as the people on the streets, began to ask with anxiety: what and which way now? (Jukić(65), 142)

Replacement of Valona for Salonika rejected

Von Heeren visited Jukić **from 4 to 5 p.m.** on **the 28th**. Aware of Ninčić's suggestion to replace Salonika with Valona, he explained that the switch could not be made for two reasons: 1 – Salonika would be given to Yugoslavia in order to end the centuries-old Serbo-Bulgarian quarrel about Macedonia in favor of the Serbs; 2 – Valona was already in a possession of Italy. (Jukić(65), 142)

Jukić now relayed Maček's message for von Heeren, received via Šubašić: Maček will take all measures to ensure the acceptance of the Pact with Germany by the new Government. He pleaded with von Heeren to attempt to calm Berlin on account of the changes in Belgrade. (Jukić(65), 141-2)

Von Heeren complained about the hostile behavior of the public toward him that morning, when he was driving to the Cathedral to attend the thanksgiving services for King Peter II, and other incidents involving two members of his staff. Von Heeren then went to see Simović, and Jukić to visit Ninčić. (Jukić(65), 142)

Apologies for hostile behavior of the public

Grol was with Ninčić when Jukić arrived and told them of von Heeren's complaints. Upon verifying the basis for these complaints by Dr. Budisavljević, the Minister of Internal Affairs, Ninčić and Grol asked Jukić to apologize to the German Minister in the name of the Government. Jukić did so **between 6:30 and 7 p.m.**, in the German Legation. (Jukić(65), 142)

Simović – Lane meeting, the evening of 28 March

The morning of the 28th March, probably during the *Te Deum* service for the young King, Dr. Gavrilović, Vice Director of the Political Division of the Yugoslav Foreign Office, was sent to the British and American Legations with the same message. In the American Legation he spoke with official Bonbright, and **at 4 p.m.** Minister Lane informed the Secretary of State about the conversation (telegram 257):

> The most difficult situation facing the new Government ... is of course its relations with Germany. There has been "consternation" in Berlin over the events of yesterday here and the reaction there has been very strong. As indicated in King Peter's manifesto **(#)** yesterday this country wants pact and it wishes to avoid any act of provocation. It is hoped, therefore, that in any governmental utterances which we [the USA] may make we will sympathetically bear in mind the delicacy of the Yugoslav position.
>
> He said that they had spoken to the British in the same sense.
>
> When asked directly what action the Government intended to take with respect to the Tripartite Pact he said that he was unable to make any comment. (FRUS1, 971. The copy of the document was obtained through the Freedom of Information Act.)

(#) That was **not** the King's manifesto. The declaration was composed by the new Government without the King's knowledge, as described previously.

After his lengthy speech to the leaders of the Serbian Orthodox Church on 28 March, Simović met Lane who at midnight telegraphed to the Secretary of State, *inter alia*:

> General Simović received me this evening. ...The following is strictly confidential for the Acting Secretary [Sumner Welles].
>
> Having further evidence of uneasiness as mentioned in my 257 regarding possibility of our *using pressure to force Yugoslavia to take offensive as Britain has done*, I said we had never urged on previous government such a move and my efforts had been solely to prevent Yugoslavia from *relinquishing her independence*. ...
>
> As to Tripartite pact Simović said Government wishes to avoid discussion if possible. It does not wish to denounce pact nor will it ratify it.
>
> ... Yugoslavia does not wish to provoke Germany or Italy but will resist by force any attempt to take Salonika, which is vital to national interest, nor will it tolerate move against sovereignty of country.
>
> As Meily reports lack of enthusiasm in Zagreb regarding the developments I asked him about situation in Croatia. He said he had assurances from Maček through Subasic who is now here that Croatian Peasant Party will support Government. ... (FRUS1, 971. Italics added.)

However, as Lane told Prince Paul on 23 March, it was the USA who would define what constitutes independence – not the Yugoslav Government.

*****

On 28 March Sir Alexander Cadogan remarked in his diary: "Yugo going canny. But I hope they're all right." (Dilks(ed), 367)

The British were evacuating their female staff from Yugoslavia to Athens. (Sweet-Escott, 63)

*****

(U) Also on the 28th March, Mussolini invited Ante Pavelić – the leader of the Ustaše, then residing in Florence – to visit him in Rome. (Krizman1, 368)

- **Saturday, 29 March 1941**

Simović's conversation with the Italian Minister in Belgrade

On the 29th of March, in the office of the Minister of War, Simović warned Giorgio Mameli, the Italian Minister in Belgrade, that Yugoslavia could not allow itself to be encircled. Should German troops enter Salonika – thereby cutting off Yugoslavia from the Aegean Sea – Yugoslavia would have to occupy Albania in order to secure an exit from the Adriatic. (Ristić, 115)

Ninčić – Lane meeting; Eden's statement to the American Ambassador in Athens

In the afternoon of the 29th of March, Foreign Minister Ninčić received Arthur Bliss Lane, who reported Ninčić's statements to the Secretary of State:

> Following is substance of his [Ninčić's] remarks: The Government has as yet taken no position regarding Tripartite Pact. His feeling is that it cannot be repudiated as terms of the pact provided that it would enter into effect immediately on signature. Croats Slovenes and Mussulmans (Bosnians) desire adherence to pact's terms. Refusal of Government to honor terms would not only lead to trouble with Germany but would also bring about dissolution of country as Maček in that case would not enter Government. ... Personally he is in favor of peace. ... Demonstrations of yesterday in favor of democracies and against Axis puts Yugoslavia in bad situation with Germany ... Unwise British broadcasts also embarrassing. ...
>
> He said that Yugoslavia could not count on Soviet support and the Soviet Union were in danger of being attacked by Germany. ...
>
> On leaving Minister I met Kulovec and Krek, two Slovene leaders, who said situation in Slovenia very delicate and that Government should shortly make its decision otherwise trouble might be expected. I explained to them as I had to Ninčić that our Government had never urged Yugoslavia to be the aggressor in any conflict despite rumors to the contrary. (FRUS1, 971-2)

Not to be an aggressor was one thing, but to "*resist*" aggression, take "*a positive stand*", and "*take offensive*", was quite a different one. Following his President's lead, Lane firmly supported the British in these urgings, especially after Col. Donovan's visit to Belgrade in January 1941.

*****

> On Saturday morning the twenty-ninth, Eden told Lincoln MacVeagh that he felt that the immediate implications of the Yugoslavian coup were being exaggerated in England and America, but that he had returned [to Athens] to explore the possibility of their development. He went on,
>
> "I don't care if the Yugoslavs don't actually repudiate their signature of the Tripartite Pact if only we can get together now and formulate some sort of a common policy after which we can take it to the Turks."
>
> He added that the British minister in Belgrade was to talk with the Yugoslav prime minister and would fly to Athens immediately afterwards. (Higham, 198)

Very understandable: Eden's efforts to draw the Turks into the war continued to be fruitless.

Radoje Knežević ... Minister of the Royal Court

As Radoje Knežević described it to his brother, he created the impression that he had calmly and with dignity passed over Gen. Simović's offer of the Ministry of Education, thereby revealing an idealistic motivation and disinterest in personal recognition and gains. Gen. Mirković, however, told a different story.

Mirković claimed that he had no influence whatsoever on the formation of the Government, and the Government was assembled by the will and agreement of Gen. Simović. **Two days after the coup,** Mirković did one thing, though: at the pleading and imploring by Major Živan for his brother, Radoje, to be appointed a Minister within the Presidency of the Government, Mirković suggested to Simović that he appoint Radoje to the still vacant post of Minister of the Royal Court. Simović complied. (Bosnić(ed), 31) (Karapandžić(AB), 136) On March 30 the appointment was formally announced and accepted.

It turned out, later on, that in that post Radoje Knežević had greater influence over the young King than he would have had as the Education Minister.

*****

However, this was not the only Mirković's intervention in favor of the Knežević brothers. In 1940 – he wrote - he had succeeded to place the infantry Major Živan as the Commandant of the Battalion of the Royal Guards. (Bosnić(ed), 16)

(C) Comintern's letter to Tito

After the Putsch,

> He [Stalin] remained cautious, as it was an open secret that the coup had not brought about a full reversal of Yugoslav policies. After assuming power Simović informed the King of his intention of adhering to the Axis. He was quick to assure the German ambassador that Yugoslavia stood for 'continued co-operation with the Axis Powers, particularly with Germany', and a 'return as far as possible to a policy of neutrality'. (Gorodetsky, 143; 355n38)

Without a direct dialogue with the Government in Belgrade before the Putsch, the Soviets conducted their affairs through the Communist Party.

> In the new circumstances urgent steps were taken to dampen popular enthusiasm. Dimitrov, the President of the Comintern, was promptly instructed by Molotov to call off street demonstrations which, he feared, might be 'exploited by the British as well as by the domestic reactionaries.' Tito was instructed to watch over 'the unruly British warmongers and Great Serbian chauvinists, who are pushing the country into military slaughter by their provocations.' (Gorodetsky, 143; 355n39)

(U) Pavelić's debt to Mussolini: Dalmatia

On 29 March Mussolini received Pavelić in the modest dining room of his private residence, *vila Torlonia*. That was their first meeting. Mussolini addressed him: "Adesso è il vostro momento." ("Now it's your moment.") (Krizman1, 370) Filippo Anfuso (of the Italian Foreign Ministry) was present at the conversation and later wrote about it in his memoirs. Here are some excerpts:

Pavelić reconfirms previously assumed commitments to Italy. He guarantees to implement them and dispels any doubt about loyalty. Although supported by Germany, he knows how much he owes to Italy, which until now was striving to secure for him German god-parenthood. The crux of the problem is Dalmatia. Will Pavelić be able, and how far, to restrain aspirations of his co-nationals against Italian irredentism? Pavelić is not hiding that this will be hard. (Krizman1, 368-9)

Most important for Pavelić is to get to Zagreb before there could come to some other solutions which would abandon the plan to give authority in Croatia to the Ustaše. Although that plan enjoys Hitler's support, Pavelić fears that because of some unforeseen change in German mood he could lose the throne of the *Poglavnik*. Mussolini finds himself facing the solution of the Adriatic Sea question, which for him is not coming unforeseen - because he dreamed about it for many years - but the solution is too seductive and radical, to not fear that behind the guarantees - given by Pavelić - there could be a postponement of the question of Dalmatia, or a complete transition of the "independent Croatia" under the German authority – which would make Italy's agreement made with the Croatian agitator invalid. (Krizman1, 369)

Mussolini concluded his talk with Pavelić saying that he saw no reason for Pavelić not to go to Croatia. At the end of the audience, Mussolini informed Pavelić that, as soon as he was established in Zagreb, the Italian Government would initiate negotiations to conclude the agreement confirmed in their conversation. He ended the talk telling Pavelić: "Credo che sarà guerra." ("I believe that there will be war.") (Krizman1, 370)

- **Sunday, 30 March 1941**

The new Government formally accepted the Tripartite Pact and disallowed Eden's visit

On 30 March, the Yugoslav Foreign Minister summoned von Heeren and made a formal statement on behalf of the Government:

> The Present Royal Yugoslav Government remains true to the principle of respect for international treaties which have been concluded, among which the Protocol signed on the 25th of this month at Vienna belongs. It will insist in the most determined fashion on not being drawn into the present conflict. Its chief attention will be devoted to the maintenance of good and friendly relations with the neighbors, the German Reich and the kingdom of Italy.
> The Royal Government is particularly interested in the manner of applying the Protocol mentioned, in connection with this it is mindful of safeguarding all the essential interests of the Yugoslav State and people. (Ristić, 114, 158n2)

Because of this stand, **on 30 March** the Government declined Eden's request for a visit, and approved only visit to Belgrade by General Dill, **on 31 March.** (Jukić(65), 143)

"This was their Roman holiday."

On 29 March 1941, the German Foreign Minister, Ribbentrop, ordered his Minister in Belgrade, Viktor von Heeren, to attend no official functions, nor send anyone to represent him. **The next day** von Heeren was called home "for purposes of reporting." (Ristić, 123)

The Yugoslav Foreign Minster, Ninčić, delivered his message to von Heeren in a proper diplomatic manner during the day. However, some Britons delivered a different kind of message to von Heeren in the evening. The scene: **30 March 1941,** Belgrade railway station – departure of the German Minister from Yugoslavia.

> … I stood watching from behind a convenient post. Suddenly all conversation stopped. A group of young men was approaching Von Heeren's car singing "Tipperary" and roaring with laughter. I recognized most of them as youth attached to the British Legation, many of them engaged in minor espionage and secret-service work. One of them, an assistant military or naval attaché, was going up to still neutral Hungary on some strange mission I was never able to get fully explained. He had – I wondered if it was by accident – the compartment next to Von Heeren's. His pals boosted him through the window, threw his baggage in after him, and then followed for a farewell round of drinks. They pretended not to notice Von Heeren. For nearly half an hour, until the train finally pulled out, they sang college songs and British war songs with such gusto that whatever last-minute instructions Von Heeren may have had for his assistants were lost in the din. … The British boys were having the time of their lives. This was their country now, and to hell with Von Heeren and all the other Nazis. This was their Roman holiday. … (St. John, 31)

Post-demonstrations worries

While the young Britons had a good reason to be in a holiday mood, on the third day after the Putsch the emotional effusion of Belgraders was fading.

> And even in Belgrade the emotional drunk of a few days ago was beginning to wear off. The holiday spirit had disappeared quickly. People began to look worried now. Newspapers that hadn't been allowed to speak out for months, and then under the new freedom had lashed away at the overthrown traitors and the Nazis with strong language for a few days, now restrained themselves without any government order. Hitler must not be provoked. Some of the calmer minds began to argue that it would be better for Yugoslavia, and even for Britain and Greece, if Yugoslavia maintained a benevolent neutrality and thus prevented the Germans from using the country as a corridor through which to attack Greece and wind up the Albania sideshow. (St. John, 29)

Živan Knežević wrote that by the 30th of March the inhabitants of Belgrade became considerably alarmed; the attack was expected every day. The people clogged the Belgrade railroad station in an effort to leave the city, and were hanging on steps of the wagons of the departing trains. (Milunović(ed), 49)

Like deposed Prince Paul and his government had also previously concluded, by this time Simović and his Putschists did not want to receive Eden's visit to Belgrade and thus to provoke the Germans. But it was too late. The Putschists had not wanted to accept the opinion of "calmer minds" when it might have counted.

Simović's oral offer of a mutual assistance pact with the Soviets

As evidenced by Soviet Ambassador Viktor Z. Lebedev's report to Molotov of 30 March 1941, "Simović sent the Russians an oral offer of a mutual assistance pact which was tantamount to a 'real alliance'. A stronger appeal was made the same evening by the new Defence Minister [Bogoljub Ilić] in a clandestine meeting with the Soviet ambassador which took place at his own lodgings. Ilić reiterated his intention of establishing 'full political and military co-operation with the Soviet Union'; he pledged the army's resolve to 'resist to the end' a German invasion'. (Gorodetsky, 143-4; 355n42)

"The breach between the government and the armed forces seemed to be growing," concluded Professor Gorodetsky. Indeed, even at the very constitution of the new government on 27 March, most of the Ministers declared themselves for peace and subsequently worked to find a way to secure it. On the other hand, Simović's lukewarm concurring, *"Peace, if possible",* was revealing his lack of true commitment for peace all along.

On 31 March Stalin received several reports about the possibility of war. According to Simović's diary, in the early hours of 1 April

> Lebedev arrived at Simović's apartment accompanied by Sukhonin, the military attaché, and a translator. He informed the Prime Minister that Molotov had just accepted the offer of a pact and wished a delegation to proceed swiftly to Moscow to conclude the agreement. Simović wasted no time in telephoning Ninčić, his Foreign Minister, instructing him to appoint Gavrilović as the head of the delegation so that negotiations could start even before the arrival of its other members. (Gorodetsky, 144; 356n44)

Lebedev met Ninčić in the morning of 2 April and got the impression that the Yugoslav Cabinet was split. On the one hand, they naively anticipated that Hitler would leave Yugoslavia alone if Stalin were to notify him that "the Soviet Union had immense sympathy towards the Yugoslav people". On the other hand, that the Cabinet was determined to resist British pressure to open a new front in the Balkans. (Gorodetsky, 144)

On the armaments of the Yugoslav army

> We sat in the open-faced dining room of the Srpski Kralj [hotel], watching endless columns of cavalry and artillery parade past the window on their way to the frontiers. We were full of admiration of the horses as well as the men. Sturdy men and husky little horses, their harnesses decorated with the first flowers of spring and with branches of trees that had just sprouted finger-sized leaves. The men all seemed eager for action, and even the animals looked happy about it. They were going off to battle. They were going to show Hitler. A pint-sized nation was going to speak up. Look out, Berlin, here we come! (St. John, 23)
>
> Most of these million or more soldiers who were mobilized during the last days of March and the first days of April really thought they were going places. ... But often during that week some of us who had been in Rumania and had lived with three hundred thousand German soldiers camped there for months had some dark thoughts. (St. John, 23-4)
>
> "Listen," someone would suddenly lean across the table and say in dead earnest, "you can't throw those horses and peasant carts and mountain guns like that assortment out there in the street against the steel and stuff the Nazis have got all oiled up and ready for this show!"
>
> "But Serbia's a mountainous place," someone would pipe back. "This is no blitz country. These babies will lose the plains, but wait until they get the Nazis into the mountains. The Serbs know their mountains. Remember the last war? They can retire to the mountains of southern Serbia and fight there for a year." (St. John, 24)

Then St. John continued with his own observations:

> Despite all the arguing, the prospects looked pretty dark to many of us, even if there really were three hundred thousand British soldiers in Greece with plenty of British planes and even if the Croats didn't kick

> up any trouble. I remember back a few months when I was living in Bucharest and saw divisions after divisions of those grim, gray-uniformed Nazis parading past my window. I remembered watching their twenty-ton, fifty-ton, hundred-ton monsters of steel snorting along Calei Victoriei. I remembered how they amazed Bucharest by never inquiring directions. Most of them, tens of thousands of them, have memorized the map of Bucharest, with its maze of winding streets, before they ever left Germany. ... (St. John, 24-5)

After describing the German army's complete repair machine shops on wheels, the journalist wondered:

> ... That was just one little example of the cold Nazi efficiency we saw everywhere. It was that kind of an army these poor Serbs would soon be fighting with the rifles clutched so lovingly and the horses they patted so gently. No matter how much we might have disliked the Nazis, we were impressed by their army. No matter how much we sympathized with the Serbs, we knew this was a peasant-cart army. (St. John, 25)

> It was as simple as that! I shuddered. If this was the kind of an army Simovich was planning to throw against the Nazis, God help Serbia! Tomahawks against rifles. Rifles against machine guns. Machine guns against planes. But this was worse than any of them. Rifles against tanks! (St. John, 26)

There was no other kind of army in Yugoslavia. Simović and the coup-plotters knew it very well. The consequences became evident from the very start of the war, on 6 April 1941. Caught up in a feverish, chaotic retreat within days, St. John commented:

> ... Most of us [newspapermen] had been up in Rumania while the German army was getting ready for this show. We'd seen the German military supply trains. Tremendous motor trucks. Any one truck would have held almost as much as all these oxcarts put together. And the truck would have covered in an hour the distance these oxen would cover in a whole day and night.
> Of course, in a way it had been the same story the year before in France. But why hadn't anyone learned the lesson of France? Why had the British urged or even allowed these Yugoslavs to commit suicide this way? Surely the British, with all the espionage agents and military intelligence people they had had in Yugoslavia, knew that this was an oxcart army? And there had been some British in France, and there had been plenty of British espionage agents in Rumania when the Germans were preparing for this Balkan war, so they knew that the German army was no oxcart outfit. (St. John, 84)

Why had the British urged or even allowed these Yugoslavs to commit suicide this way? One would expect that Robert St. John, the journalist who personally experienced the effects of the British "black propaganda" – and sometimes had personally spread it – would have figured that out for himself.

(U) Details of Pavelić's group returning to Croatia were worked out

On 30 March Pavelić met General [Ubaldo] Soddu, a state secretary in the Ministry of war, to work out details of the travel to Zagreb. The Ustaše would be immediately concentrated in a camp in northern Italy, where they would get uniforms and arms. Radio station Florence would be made available to them for evening broadcasting as *Radio Velebit*. An Italian officer would be assigned to serve as liaison with the Italian army. (Krizman1, 370)

- **Monday, 31 March 1941**

Macdonald confirmed: Mirković had informed him of planning the coup

On March 31st Macdonald reported to the Air Ministry that "the Chief organizer of the coup d'état was General Mirković, Chief of Air Force, with whom I was in close touch, before and during events", and that he had been "a personal friend for over two years". (Stafford(cp), 414-15)

> MacDonald also implied that he had been privy to details of the coup for some time beforehand, when he mentioned that it had been difficult for him not to "give away the show" when approached by pilots and even commanders of air force units asking his advice about leaving the country. (Stafford(cp), 415)

(In his reports to Air Ministry, MacDonald used initials **J.K.** to denote Mirković. (Stafford(cp), 416n60))

In a report to Orme Sargent of the Foreign office, dated 1 July 1942, Campbell stated that he knew that Mirković "was in confidential contact with the Air Attaché and told him that a coup d'état was being planned but he never furnished details or dates, ..." (Stafford(cp), 415n58)

The above quote is repeated because it supports Mirković's contention that he had not made up his mind until **the afternoon of 26 March. However,** by that time the coup-plotters had been informed of Eden's promise of support, and *Vojvoda* Trifunović-Birčanin was advising Mirković in favor of the coup.

*****

(U) Pavelić returned from Rome to Florence and partially informed his followers about the meeting with Mussolini. To a question by one of his most important followers, whether there was a talk about Dalmatia, Pavelić answered very convincingly that there had not been. (Krizman1, 370)

Chapter 17

1 – 5 APRIL 1941

- **Tuesday, 1 April 1941**

Three messages foretelling trouble for Yugoslavia

On April 1st, Vauhnik's mail contained two messages forecasting trouble for Yugoslavia within a week to ten days. **That evening** another warning, this time by telephone, said that the attack would come in the early hours **of Sunday, April 6th**, and that heavy air raids would turn Belgrade to ashes and rubble.

Vauhnik already knew that Greece would be attacked on April 6th. He now concluded that both Greece and Yugoslavia would be attacked on the same day. (Hoptner, 281. Emphasis added.)

*****

British Air Attaché Macdonald reported from Belgrade that the Yugoslav Government would start to mobilize on the 3rd; that would bring total strength to 1,800,000 men under arms. (Higham, 201)

Government's attempt at mediation with Hitler (1 – 5 April 1941)

- **According to Vice Premier Slobodan Jovanović:**

Soon after the formation of the Simović's government, following the instruction of his government, the Italian Minister in Belgrade [Giorgio Mameli] informed Simović that Mussolini would gladly intervene between the Yugoslav government and Hitler in order to avoid an armed conflict between the German and Yugoslav forces in the Balkans. Within that frame, Simović was invited to Rome; if he could not come, the Foreign Minister Ninčić would be welcome. Both Simović and Ninčić took seriously this Mussolini's initiative. As, however, neither Simović nor Ninčić could leave Belgrade during these first days of the new government, they informed Mameli that the Vice Premier Slobodan Jovanović would substitute for them.

Jovanović had attended only a part of their conversation with Mameli, and his impression has been that his mission to Rome would be to hear directly from Mussolini his suggestions.

Rome quickly accepted Jovanović's coming, but at the same time the character of Mussolini's intervention was fundamentally changed. He now was talking of being willing to intervene with Hitler *at the Yugoslav request*; therefore, it would be necessary to first hear Yugoslav proposals.

Due to this change, Simović, Ninčić, and Jovanović himself concluded that on this basis there was no need even to begin the talks with Rome, and the whole matter then collapsed at the very start. (Jovanović, 9)

- **According to Dragiša Ristić**

Basing his account on Simović's "Memoirs", war papers, German and Italian sources, Simović's adjutant, Dragiša Ristić, provided a somewhat different story:

> [Vladislav] Stakić, the agent of the former court minister in earlier approaches to [the Italian Foreign Minister Galeazzo] Ciano and Mussolini, called on Simović on April 1 at about 4:00 p.m., with news that Mameli wished to see him. Three hours later, as the Italian Minister arrived in the office of the minister of war ..., Simović said: "Sir, you have expressed the desire to talk with me." Mameli shrank back and retorted: "Not I. You sent for me to come." Simović, noticing the diplomatic twist, merely replied: "It does not matter; there must have been some misunderstanding." Then Mameli stated that Mussolini would attempt mediation with Hitler and extended a formal invitation for Simović to come to Rome. (Ristić, 115)
>
> The Italian *démarche* was discussed at a cabinet meeting that same evening. All ministers opposed the general's departure from the country ... They unanimously decided ... to send Ninčić and Vice Prime Minister Jovanović to Rome. On the afternoon of April 2, ... Simović communicated this decision to Mameli. ... after a short pause he [Mameli] inquired "what attitude Yugoslavia would take should German troops occupy Salonika." Simović said he was not able to give an answer, advised Mameli to see Ninčić

... On the 3rd, however, the [Italian] minister relayed a request from Ciano that the Yugoslav Government clarify its attitude on certain points before Ninčić and Jovanović arrived in Rome: (a) the Tripartite Pact, (b) invasion of Greek Thrace by Germany, and (c) occupation of Salonika by Germany. In retrospect it is clear that Mussolini was merely stalling. (Ristić, 115-16, 158n5)

Ninčić "was simply and solely a supporter of the Protocol (Tripartite Pact), which was signed in Vienna."

The Simović government's attempt to negotiate with Hitler did not end with Ciano's questions. Ristić's account continues:

> During the morning of April 3, ... , Ninčić asked the German chargé d'affaires to call (Heeren had been recalled to Berlin for "consultations"). ... the chargé offered to send a minor member of the legation staff. Ninčić refused and gave his message to the German press agency instead:
>
>> The Italians had invited him to Rome in order to discuss the situation. He considered to be more correct, however, for him to negotiate directly with Berlin. He was ready at any time to come to Berlin by the speediest possible means in order to speak with the Führer and the Reich Foreign Minister.
>
> This approach elicited no reply, and at 1:00 P.M. on April 5 the foreign minister's brother, Velizar Ninčić, appeared at the German Legation with a second message. ...
>
> An hour and a half later, the foreign minister's brother appeared again at the Legation: The entire cabinet had agreed that Ninčić should go to Berlin. Certain conversations had been undertaken with the Soviet Union, but "this had occurred in the excitement after the coup of March 27, and those concerned were already thinking differently today. Ninčić did not want an understanding with Moscow, but one with Berlin." Because of the foreign minister's recent operation and the confusion that accompanied the formation of the new government, he had been unable to assert himself vigorously – but "this would change now."
>
>> The foreign Minister had the large majority of the Cabinet behind him. It would accept what he proposed. ...
>> The Foreign Minister was simply and solely a supporter of the Protocol (Tripartite Pact), which was signed in Vienna.
>> Yugoslavia had received many suggestions from abroad, but the Foreign Minister would accept only the proposals that he might receive in Berlin.
>
> This message seems to have been the last communication of the Yugoslav Government to the German Embassy. (Ristić, 116-17, 158n6)

*****

(U) On 1 April, Pavelić ordered his followers in Italy to assemble, get ready to return, to participate in an uprising in "all Croatian lands". An independent state of the Croats will soon be established "from the Mura and Drava to the Drina [rivers], and from the Danube to the blue Adriatic Sea." (Krizman1, 370-71)

General Dill's secret and unsuccessful visit to Belgrade 31 March – 1 April 1941

Unwilling to receive Foreign Secretary Anthony Eden in Belgrade, Simović consented to a secret visit by General Sir John Dill, the Chief of the Imperial General Staff. The negotiations included proposals to coordinate activities between British and Yugoslav troops in Greece. These produced no results. **(Part One, pages 151-3).** Gen. Dill "found the Prime Minister quite unwilling to sign anything that would commit the Yugoslav Government." (Eden, 234)

While Gen. Dill was still in Belgrade, **on 1 April** Churchill sent him this message:

> A variety of details shows rapid regrouping against Yugoslavia. To gain time against Germans is to lose it against Italians. Nothing should stop Yugo developing full strength against latter at earliest. By this alone can they gain far-reaching initial success and masses of equipment in good time. (Churchill(GA), 172-3)

Unable to support Yugoslavia militarily, the Prime Minister continued pushing Yugoslavia into the war against Italy, regardless of Yugoslavia's preparedness or her own best interests.

Also **on 1 April,** Gen. Dill reported to Eden:

> I was unable to persuade President of the Council [Gen. Simović] to agree to a visit by you in the immediate future. He made it plain that the Yugoslav Governmet, mainly for fear of the effect on the internal situation, were determined to take no step which might be considered provocative to Germany. (Churchill(GA), 173)
>
> During all these conversations, Dixon's **(#)** diary-report avers, Simovich and Ilitch were adamant that they woud resist the Germans, but could not say so out loud bedause of a fear that the Croatians wuld pull out. (Higham, 200; 256n158)
>   **(#)** Pierson Dixon, Eden's staff member.

*****

While Gen. Dill was in Belgrade, Maček was still in Zagreb negotiating additional advantages for *Banovina Hrvatska* with Simović.

In early March Campbell went to Zagreb to "encourage" the Croatian leaders to "resist" Germany. Maček told the British Minister that "the Yugoslavs would never agree to the passage of German troops and material through Yugoslavia. Should the Germans try to force the passage, the Yugoslavs would resist and fight, if only with sporting rifles." But he also told Campbell that "Yugoslavia should keep out of the war in her own interest and in the interest of her Western friends." **(Part One, pages 94-5)**

Simović knew Maček's views. Therefore the General had to hide from Maček any attempt from abroad to draw Yugoslavia into the war. He needed the Croats in his new Government for military reasons: to better support British operations more than to having a "concentration government" of representatives of the people – about which he talked on 28 January. He had no illusions of some "elections for the Parliament" – like brothers Knežević claimed to have had. He realized that the war was approaching fast. So, no evidence of British interference should be permitted... *No signing of any commitments to the British* – although already firmly determined to tie Yugoslavia with Great Britain.

- **Wednesday, 2 April 1941**

Vauhnik sent warning to Belgrade

In the early morning hours of 2nd April, Vauhnik "sent code telegrams to Belgrade via three different routes containing 'the fatal news that on April 6th Yugoslavia would have to reckon with a German attack'. (Hoptner, 281-2)

The night of April 2nd Vauhnik received still another warning, this time a written note from an unimpeachable source:

> Conference ended just now. Attack on Yugoslavia definitely fixed for April 6th. Surrounding attacks from Bulgaria in the east and Hungary in the north. May God's blessing and my sincerest wishes accompany you in this terrible ordeal. (Vauhnik, 282)

The validity of this message was confirmed several times during the next few days. The information poured in at such a rate that he "had the impression that whole German population sided with the Yugoslavs". (Hoptner, 282)

*****

On 2 April, Eden informed Campbell about Dill's negotiations. It appeared that Simović still had certain problems with the Croats, but he was convinced that, in the end, he would win them over, under the condition of not giving them a reason for a doubt that there existed attempts from abroad to draw Yugoslavia into the war. (Petranović & Žutić, 533)

Campbell – Mirković, and Macdonald – Mirković meetings, 2 April

On 2 April 1941, Campbell reported to the Foreign Office - in greatest secrecy - that he had a meeting with Mirković. (Petranović & Žutić, 93) What was the topic of their conversation that required such secrecy? In his memoirs General Mirković did not mention this meeting.

That same day Macdonald informed the FO and the Director of the Intelligence Service of the Air Ministry about the meeting he had had **that morning** with Gen. Mirković:

- in strictest confidence the General informed him of a likely change related to the war;
- it would depend on the British to a great extent whether forthcoming events would be taken advantage of;
- the Soviet Foreign Minister, Molotov, personally invited a Yugoslav delegation to Moscow as soon as possible. Mirković was personally invited, but he declined and sent Colonel Savić as the representative of the Air Force. The delegation **(#)** had left already, and Savić's return was expected within a few days;
- the General was firmly convinced that the Russians were expecting some kind of pact with Yugoslavia;
- he also believed that Vice Premier Slobodan Jovanović would be a member of a three-member delegation to Italy;
- he pleaded for all the aid the British could send, especially aircraft engine type "merlin" and "mercury" , which he could use now or within a month;
- he added that the American Minister [Arthur Bliss Lane] had promised him supplies (which would be brought in by the American Navy). (Petranović & Žutić, 532-3)

(#) Colonels Dragutin Savić and Božin Simić arrived in Moscow on 2 April. (Petranović & Žutić, 567) Why would Molotov invite Mirković personally when he was not a member of the government? Or was Mirković just boastfully parading his role and importance? Did he - or the Government, send Col. Savić?

*****

The request for aircraft engines to be delivered on such a short notice, "sada ili za nekih mesec dana" ((now or within a month)), demonstrates Mirković's bad judgment of reality.

While Mirković, as reported, stated that **he** was personally invited to Moscow, Živan Knežević inserted his brother, "the Professor", into this scene.

> ((With regard to the inevitability of the war with Hitler, Gen. Simović intended – immediately after bringing down the Tripartite pact – to send to Moscow Professor Radoje L. Knežević to conclude an alliance with Soviet Russia, in a belief that that could at least delay the war until we were prepared for resistance, if it could not completely prevent the war with the Germans.))
> "S obzirom na neizbežnost rata s Hitlerom, đeneral Simović imao je nameru da odmah posle obaranja Trojnog pakta uputi u Moskvu profesora Radoja L. Kneževića da sklopi savez sa Sovjetskom Rusijom u veri, da bi to moglo, ako ne da potpuno spreči rat sa Nemcima, da ga bar odloži dok se ne spremimo za otpor." (Milunović(ed), 40)

> ((*Radoje had to become the Minister of the Court*, so Božin Simić and Col. Dragutin Savić went to Moscow ...)) "*Radoje je imao da dođe za ministra Dvora*, pa je za Moskvu otišao Božin Simić i pukovnik Dragutin Savić ..." (Milunović(ed), 42. Italics added.)

Actually – according to Gen. Mirković – Radoje had become the Minister of the Court already on the 29th of March, through Mirković's intervention, (Bosnić(ed), 31), and as such was not considered for a mission to Moscow. But brother Živan's was steadily promoting "The Professor" as an unavoidably important – if not deciding - participant in all major events.

*****

In another telegram, also **on 2 April,** to the same addressees, Macdonald relayed Mirković's information that:

Prince Paul had refused an Italian offer because he had been intriguing with the Germans, who had offered him the Yugoslav Crown in exchange for his repeated cooperation;

Mirković also said that Prince Paul had twice attempted to poison the King.

Macdonald wrote that he had been repeating these stories because, if they were true, the British have to watch the Prince carefully; if they were not, the British ought to know that the clique that is in power believed them. (Petranović & Žutić, 533)

In a telegram from Belgrade **on 3 April**, the information relayed by Macdonald was characterized as incredible and unreliable. In confidence it was stated that even the British War Ministry did not have a high opinion of Macdonald's abilities and character. As related to the report that the Prince Regent had attempted to poison the King (not once but twice), it was stated that this accusation had been so fantastic that it threw the deepest doubt on everything else Macdonald had reported. In spite of all this, it was admitted as being conceivable that the military clique now in power was ill-disposed to the Prince Regent. (Petranović & Žutić, 534)

Given the above admission, one has to speculate with how much doubt were all of Macdonald's reports received. First, according to Macdonald, the statement about the attempts to poison the King came from Mirković, not from Macdonald. Then, Mirković and Simović themselves confirmed the existence of their previous meetings with Macdonald, so the Macdonald-Mirković meeting on 2 April is not unusual. SOE operative Alexander Glen wrote about Macdonald's closeness with the coup organizers. The question is: did Macdonald objectively, correctly report on his contacts' activities and statements? Mirković himself wrote that he

> ((was convinced that the sick ambitions of the Prince Regent and his wife went against the vital interests of the people, as well that the two of them would not shrink from anything, and could even go so far as to conspire against the head of the young King.))
> "Bio sam uveren da su bolesne ambicije Kneza Namesnika i njegove žene išle protiv vitalnih narodnih interesa, kao i da njih dvoje ne prezaju ni od čega, pa čak idu i dotle, da rade o glavi mladoga Kralja." (Bosnić(ed), 14)

Mirković **signed** this statement on 1 December 1941. He could have **talked** in this sense with Macdonald on 2 April, to whom he confided on 25 March that he would overthrow the Pact. (Bosnić(ed), 34)

- **Thursday, 3 April 1941**

The British were dissatisfied with the attempts of mediation

On 3 April, Campbell informed Eden, then still in Athens, about the conversation with Simović, which had held at the General's request.

On the subject of an anticipated visit to Italy by Vice Premier Jovanović, Simović stated that, first, his Government wanted to establish the basis for talks. That move was a part of maneuvering to gain time and to convince the domestic population that the government was undertaking everything to avoid war. The Croats were reluctant because they feared the new Government's adventurous policies would provoke the Germans. They were assured that this was not the case, and that policies of peace and national security would be followed. On that basis they agreed to join the Government.

The Italian Minister in Belgrade was told that there would be no demobilization and no compromise in case of an attack on Salonika.

Regarding relations with Germany, the Government also sought to gain time, and it would be even possible for the Foreign Minister to go to Germany. Hitler had been infuriated and could send bombing aircrafts right away. It was sure, though, that the members of the Yugoslav Government would take a firm line. (Petranović & Žutić, 535)

Campbell insisted that engaging in talks with the Axis Powers would be highly dangerous, but Simović emphasized again the necessity to gain time from the military and internal point of view, to show the Croats that everything in the Government's power was being done to preserve a peace-loving policy.

Campbell asked Simović how much time would he need from a military point of view. Until 22 April, the General said.

Then the British Minister wondered whether such a prolonged delay would benefit more Germany than Yugoslavia. He also asked whether the Premier knew about the movement of the German Alpine divisions, and was he not afraid that they had perhaps been sent to Italy to be transported to Albania within a few days. This would then diminish the possibility that the Yugoslav army might annihilate the Italians there. The Premier did not know, but was of the opinion that the Yugoslav army could easily handle both the Italians and the Germans. In the meantime – he thought – the British Navy should take measures to control the transfer of Germans from Italy to Albania, and Britain should send as many aircraft as soon as Yugoslavia gets included in the war. Campbell said that he was assuming that such a scenario had been considered in talks with the British [in Belgrade, March 31 – April 1]. Simović confirmed and said that General Janković would raise that question again [in the forthcoming talks] in Florina. (Petranović & Žutić, 535-6)

Campbell reported that Simović had looked quite surprised when he said that the decision to send Jovanović to Italy and the Foreign Minister to Germany would – said most gently – surprise His Majesty's Government, and that Campbell would wish to explain Yugoslavia's reasons for such conduct. Simović repeated the need to gain in time for military and internal reasons. (Petranović & Žutić, 536)

*****

Campbell's insistence about the danger of talks with Italy and Germany, his suggestion that dragging out the negotiations would benefit Germany more than Yugoslavia, and his assertion of the British Government's displeasure with Simović's stand – all these things point to the British pressure for quick action by the new Government in favor of Britain. Nothing else mattered to the British.

Simović's hope and actions of having Yugoslavia prepared for war by 22 April turned out to be unrealistic. Hitler was getting ready a swift "punishment" for Yugoslavia. The new Government had been given adequate forewarning, but the warnings were not taken seriously.

*****

As promised, the following day, **on 4 April**, Campbell telegraphed to Eden his comments on the meeting with Simović. *Inter alia* he stated that:

Simović spoke with Campbell as if it was natural to assume that Yugoslavia – already on the British side – would probably fight with Britain;

Simović therefore takes it for granted that His Majesty's Government would understand the efforts of the Yugoslav Government to gain time, would have confidence that his Government would not stray again toward the Axis, but would resolutely repel any attack or unreasonable demand.

The best the British could do to secure a resolute stand and resistance when it became necessary, was to use propaganda with which the British would maintain the mood [of the people] which would impel the government to behave accordingly.

If [under a certain scenario] General Simović could not succeed in preserving the unity of the Government and the country - although the support by the army and air force could keep him in power – in any case there was nobody foreseen who could replace him. (Petranović & Žutić, 536)

*****

In the British Minister's opinion, Simović was already on Britain's side - notwithstanding his public declarations of neutrality, and would probably fight with Britain - although that would lead to the breakup of his Government and disunity within the country.

To prevent such a development, and to keep Simović in power – propaganda was needed to influence people's mood. That request was in line with the SOE's *modus operandi*. *"On his arrival Taylor assessed pro-British Serb public opinion as SOE's best hope of influencing the Yugoslav government's policy."* (Williams, 28-9) Then, when the people's mood is aroused, claim that it is the spontaneous will of the people, with which the British had nothing to do.

If Simović should fall, there was no one to replace him. Therefore, the failure must be prevented, and his activities accelerated by discouraging any possible attempt at mediation.

Belgrade did not trust Vauhnik's telegrams

The Colonel again dispatched telegrams to Belgrade. For the fifth day Belgrade remained silent. He unsuccessfully tried to reach the General Staff by telephone. "On April 3rd he sent his assistant, major

Pupis, to Belgrade by airplane with orders to report at once to the general staff and to repeat verbally the contents of the four most important telegrams."

Later he learned that all the telegrams had reached Belgrade safely. However, convinced that he had been taken in, the officials in Belgrade did not trust the telegrams. (Hoptner, 282)

(Col. Vauhnik informed Dr. Hoptner that his source had been Admiral Wilhelm Canaris, head of the German high command's foreign and counter-intelligence office, through Major-General Hans Oster. – Hoptner, 283n53)

"... blocking the Danube ... the decisive factor for England ..."

Two early plans of Section D to block the Danube – first by blocking the Greben narrows by destroying the retaining wall, second by mining the over-hanging cliff on the Yugoslav side – failed in the first few months of the war. A third plan, to sink cement-filled barges in the Iron Gates, also failed in April 1940, ... Despite the embarrassment caused by this incident, a further attempt was made to carry out the third plan – this time working through the Yugoslav authorities in the aftermath of the coup, and on the eve of the German invasion. At the beginning of April 1941 twelve barges were ready for action, and on the 3rd, [Sir Frank] Nelson, on Dalton's behalf, cabled to Taylor in Belgrade: 'Minister and all high authorities know you realise fully that a successful blocking of Danube before it is too late would be the decisive factor for England in this war ...' (Pimlott(ed),185-6)

State of affairs always hard, but nevertheless not critical

At the Government's session at 11 a.m. Simović reported about the general state of affairs: no particular changes, always difficult, but nevertheless not critical.

The Minister of War, Gen. Ilić, reported that the military concentration camps had been closed. The Interior Minster will act on the General's suggestion to forbid a mass exodus from Belgrade, which was causing confusion.

Minister for social policies, Dr. Milan Grol, together with Gen. Ilić, proposed to undertake necessary steps for evacuation and care of young men under the military-recruitment age from the endangered territories. A committee was formed to further analyze the issue. (Miletić(ed), 430)

Acceptance of the Tripartite Pact Protocol confirmed

On the 3rd of April the Foreign Minister Ninčić informed the Yugoslav representatives abroad of the Yugoslav Government's respect for the Protocol signed in Vienna on the 25th of March, [as he had conveyed that to the German Minster in Belgrade on the 30th of March], Živan wrote. (Milunović(ed), 42)

But for Živan, this *stereotypical circular* and Ninčić's statement to von Heeren on 30 March did not mean the acceptance of the Pact. It was just the opposite: *"odbacivanje Pakta" ("the rejection of the Pact")* His explanation:
- *"Remaining true to the principle of respect for international treaties"* was just a phrase given in similar circumstances. (Milunović(ed), 42)
- Ninčić spoke ((on his own, and not in the name of the government)), ((in his own name)). "na svoju ruku, a ne u ime vlade" , "u svoje lično ime" (Milunović(ed), 46)

As shown in **Chapter 16**, on 28 March the Second Vice Premier, Prof. Slobodan Jovanović, found the Pact Protocol valid and in force, and the Simović Government never abrogated it. An attempt of mediation with Hitler could not be even conceived had the Pact been rejected, which both brothers Knežević had later claimed.

The British – Yugoslav conference in Greece, 3-4 April 1941

Following the unproductive visit by Gen. Dill in Belgrade (31 March – 1 April), another conference was held in a railcar near Florina, in Greece, on 3-4 April. Eden, who was in the area, did not attend. "The meeting ended without any clear agreement and - to judge by the British record - left a feeling of mutual distrust." (Barker, 105) **(Part One, pages 153-55)**

- Friday, 4 April 1941

Maček – Simović brief meeting

As soon as Maček arrived in Belgrade, **on 4 April**, he went to see Simović, wondering whether the war could still be averted. Explaining that a special meeting would be held the next day to explore a possibility of Italy's positive intervention with Germany, Simović was reassuring. When Maček asked the General how much time he thought the Germans would need to prepare an attack against Yugoslavia, he replied:

> If they want to attack us well prepared, they need at least two weeks to concentrate the necessary troops in Hungary. But if they don't mind taking a chance they can start immediately as they already have a considerable number of troops stationed in Bulgaria for the invasion of Greece, which they might easily turn against Yugoslavia. (Maček, 221-2)

Former Ministers Cvetković, Cincar-Marković, and Antić – arrested on the 27th of March – were sent to prison in Brus, Serbia. (Milunović(ed), 51)

Simović told Maček "nothing about Colonel Vauhnik's repeated warnings from Berlin that German planes, flying from Rumanian and Hungarian airfields would bomb Belgrade the morning of April 6th." (Hoptner, 283)

Belgrade, Zagreb and Ljubljana were declared open cities

In case of war, Belgrade, Zagreb and Ljubljana were declared open cities. According to Živan Knežević, In order to avoid panic in Belgrade, Gen. Simović issued an "incomprehensible" order for people not to leave their own homes, ((and to get killed on the threshold of his home, if it comes to an attack)) "i da pogine na pragu svoje kuće, ako do napada dođe". According to Živan: Patriarch Gavrilo asked him (when they met at Oplenac, on the 7th of April), ((Who had advised Simović to issue that imprudent order? – when it should have been advised for all to leave the cities, and especially Belgrade!)) "Ko je savetovao Simoviću da izda tu nerazumnu naredbu? – kad je trebalo savetovati da se svi uklone iz gradova, a naročito iz Beograda!" (Milunović(ed), 49)

Zagreb and Ljubljana were not bombed, but Belgrade was.

Campbell: Simović considered the German attack almost unavoidable

On 4 April, Campbell reported to Eden that he talked with Simovć as if it were natural to assume that Yugoslavia, being already on the British side, would likely fight with the British. Yugoslavia would accept an honorable neutrality, should that be feasible, but Simović considered the German attack as unavoidable. He took it for granted that His Majesty's Government would understand the efforts of the Yugoslav Government to gain time, and that HMG would have confidence that the Yugoslavs would not veer away again toward the Axis, but would resolutely repel every attack or unreasonable demand.

Campbell was sure that Simović's Government would remain firm in the present course, but the best the British could do to secure a resolute stand and resistance would be to utilize propaganda with which the British would maintain the mood which would force the government to behave in accordance with that course.

Under some conditions, especially as regarded the Croats, Simović might not be able to preserve the unity of the Government and the country, but in any case there was nobody who could replace him. (Petranović & Žutić, 536)

*****

So: propaganda before the coup, propaganda after the coup … and then, later, claim that everything had been purely a Yugoslav, i.e. Serb affair.

Churchill about Germany's *onslaught* on Yugoslavia

Years after the events, the detached **historian Winston Churchill** wrote:

> On 4 April General Dill sent a full account of his mission to Belgrade, which shows how *utterly remote from their immediate peril* were the minds of the Yugoslav Ministers. One would have thought from their mood and outlook that they had months in which to take their decision about peace or war with Germany. Actually they had only *seventy-two hours before the onslaught fell upon them.* (Churchill(GA), 173. Italics added.)

"On 4 April the Prime minister warned the Yugoslav government that GAF [German Air Force] concentrations were arriving 'from all quarters'." (Hinsley *et al* (1), 371) Still holding to his idea of attacking the Italians in Albania,

> Churchill sent Simović a telegram in which he told him that Germans were concentrating against Yugoslavia from as far away as France, and that his only hope was to make "one supreme stroke for victory and safety" by winning "a decisive forestalling victory in Albania" and collect the "masses of equipment" that would fall into his hands – and to do this before the Germans reached Albania, while he could still fall upon the "rear of the demoralized and rotten Italians." (Higham, 205)

By the 4th of April Germany's *onslaught* was near, indeed, but it was **the Prime Minister Churchill** who on 22 March 1941 had ordered his Foreign Minister *to get Yugoslavia in to the war* **by any means whatever** – regardless of Yugoslavia's war readiness - which caused the German onslaught in the first place. (**Part One, Chapter 11,** for British praise of the coup of 27 March 1941.) Although on the 26th of March Simović told Macdonald that he would attack the Italians in Albania, after the coup he had to change his mind.

*****

Expecting Germany's attack, the British were moving their offices and equipment from the Legation using 3 small trucks which Gen. Bora Mirković supplied to them. (Karapandžić(AB), 147-8) Mirković did not specify what the British were moving and where. One wonders: were there moved also some British *"toys and chocolates"*, which were still not distributed to the local "contacts"?

*****

(U) On 4 April, the Ustaše-operated *Radio station Velebit* broadcast its first emission from radio Florence, at 11:30 p.m. (Krizman1, 372)

- **Saturday, 5 April 1941**

British warning of the forthcoming German attack

On 5 April, the former Czechoslovak military attaché in Belgrade, who operated a secret radio-station in Zemun, was informed from Prague that the Germans would attack Yugoslavia **early the next morning**. This information was relayed to the British. **(#)** They then informed Simović of these plans twice that day. Ninčić was informed too. The Czechs informed S. Budisavljević. None of them forwarded this information to Maček and Kulovec.

At noon, the Secretary of the British Legation, [Armine] Dew, informed some officials of the Yugoslav Foreign Ministry about the attack. (Jukić(65), 144)

(#) It is not clear who was informed, the British in Belgrade or in London. **On 5 April** George Taylor received a warning from London that "the balloon is expected to go up tomorrow". (Barker, 39) Since his arrival in Belgrade, Taylor had cooperated closely with Dew, who could have been informed by Taylor, the Czechoslovak attaché, or both.

According to St. John, on the 5th of April he also was forewarned of the imminence of the German attack.

> "What are you doing tonight?" somebody in the Berlin office of the AP asked.
> "I was just thinking of bed. So what? Have you got a little party on up there?"
> "Seriously, St. John, if I were you I would not go to bed tonight. So long."
> "Hey, wait a minute. Why shouldn't I go to bed?"

"I don't have any idea," came back the voice from Berlin, 'but we think up here it would be an excellent night for you to sit up listening to the music from Berlin broadcasting station." (St. John, 39-40)

Government's last peacetime session and Simović's *"fiery speech"*

At 4:00 p.m. on the 5th, Cabinet members Simović, Ninčić, Maček, Jovanović, Trifunović, Grol, Jevtić and Kulovec assembled at Ninčić's request.

"During the session the author [D. Ristić] was the only person authorized to enter the conference room, bringing Simović an occasional message." (Ristić, 118) Maček wrote about the conference in his book published in 1957. Ristić's book was published in 1966. Professor Jovanović's account was written in 1946-1947 and published in 1976. Živan Knežević's account was published posthumously, in 1985. Following are data about the conference from all four sources.

- **Jovanović**

At Ninčić's request, Simović called a conference towards evening of 5 April. Ninčić spoke first and said that, if one wanted to avoid Germany's attack due very shortly, one must contact the German Government. He was ready to go to personally confer with Hitler, but needed to know on what basis to talk with him. In a discussion that lasted quite some time, all present took part except Jevtić and Jovanović, who were to express their opinion the next day. Only Maček and Kulovec on one side, and Simović on the other, formulated their views quite clearly. Maček and Kulovec held the same view they have had as members of Cvetković's Government, and that is, *that the war should be avoided at any price*. Maček was not showing any sympathies for the Axis, but was of the opinion that *our participation in a world war had no sense at all because it could not change its outcome, but it would only bring on a great calamity to our people*. He was ready for making all concessions to the Germans, even to transport of their troops over our territory; *but we ought to fight them if they attack us*. (Jovanović, 12. Italics added.)

Simović was saying that we could not let the Germans get into Salonika and thus to cut the link between the Greeks and us. In that case we would be totally encircled by the Axis Powers and their satellites and they could impose their will on us, even without a war. If we are not ready to totally submit to the Axis, we ought to resist while there is still a chance for a serious resistance, that is, before the Germans enter Salonika. (Jovanović, 12)

Jovanović concluded his note by observing: In the evening of April 5th, the difference between Simović and Maček was so great that some members of the conference foresaw a possibility of the disintegration of the Government at the meeting scheduled for the morning of 6 April. (Jovanović, 12)

That meeting was never held. Belgrade was set ablaze by Germany's planes that morning ...

- **Živan Knežević**

Although Živan Knežević quoted the entire description of the session by Professor Slobodan Jovanović, he introduced an element – the acceptance of the Pact - which Jovanović did not mention. According to Živan:

Between 28 March and 6 April he spent all his free time in the Cabinet of Gen. Simović, so he was there during the Government's conference on the 5th of April. "A great quarrel" and "shouting was heard from the room in which this session was held" about the acceptance of the Pact. Until then nobody had told him, and there was no talk at all, about the acceptance of the Pact. He remained in the Cabinet until the end of the session in order to find out the reason for such a bitter quarrel. His brother Radoje was at home and had no Idea that the Government was resolving the question of adhering to the Pact.

Just after 10 p.m. Simović came into his office, considerably tired and pale. Then he invited Živan into his room, and almost whispering told him:

((I had scarcely succeeded to prevent the Government to accept the Tripartite Pact. Maček and Kulovec were for the acceptance. Bogoljub [General Ilić] and I were resolutely against the acceptance of the Pact. The Serb members of the Government let myself to skirmish with Mačekom.))
"Jedva sam uspeo da sprečim da Vlada primi Trojni pakt. A Maček i Kulovec su za prijem Pakta. Bogoljub i ja smo bili odlučno protiv prijema Pakta. Srpski članovi Vlade pustili su mene da se nosim sa Mačekom." (Milunović(ed), 47)

Shocked, Živan then asked the General: "The Government to accept the Pact? Why had we overthrown the Prince's Government then?"

"Everything is postponed until tomorrow. We shall see", answered Simović.

Frozen, looking the General right into the eyes, Živan then ended the conversation resignedly: "Well, hopefully we won't now overthrow this Government too after only a few days." (Milunović(ed), 47)

Then Živan hurried to inform and consult his older brother.

> ((Radoje listened to me calmly, was looking me straight in the eyes, and while I was reading anger and decisiveness from his eyes, he said: 'We shall see, Schwaben [the Germans], tomorrow. ... The Pact we shall not accept under any price.'))
>
> "Radoje me je mirno slušao, gledao pravo u oči i dok sam ja iz njegovih očiju čitao ljutnju I odlučnost, rekao: 'Videćemo, Švabo, sutra ... Pakt ni po koju cenu nećemo da primimo.' " (Milunović(ed), 47. Underlined in the source.)

- **Maček**

    Foreign Minister Ninčić reported the latest communication received from Italian Ambassador Mamelli. *The Germans were willing to respect the obligations of the Pact* on the condition that the Yugoslav Army occupy the Yugoslav-Geek border for the purpose of covering their right flank during their advance into Greece. Of course, this new condition made the Pact of March 25 less digestible, but I reflected that by accepting it Yugoslavia would not actually violate her neutrality. We would merely bar the foreign troops from crossing our territory. (Maček, 222)

    I expected Simović to oppose this stipulation, but was amazed to hear him say that he had no objection to a Yugoslav occupation of the Greek frontier. On the contrary, he went even further and proposed to occupy Salonika at the same time. *Ninčić pronounced himself neither for nor against the Italian proposal,* but stressed that a demand to take Salonika inevitably meant war. The other ministers advised using the Italian proposal as a basis for negotiation and dropping the claim on Salonika. (Maček, 222-3. Italics added.)

    Then Simović began to speak. His speech had no political content whatsoever and consisted entirely of patriotic phrases and martial slogans. It became plain that Simović wanted to enter the war at all costs. I am surprised even today that Simović as a professional soldier had no capacity to visualize the complete debacle a war would entail. ... we separated with the intention of meeting again at 8 o'clock in the morning. (Maček, 223)

- **Ristić**

    Ninčić reported that *Italy was willing to intercede on Yugoslavia's behalf,* on the condition that Yugoslav troops immediately occupy the Greek-Yugoslav border as a security belt preventing Greek and British troops from entering Yugoslavia. *Ninčić proposed that they accept the Italian offer.* (Ristić, 118. Italics added.)

    Simović agreed [with Ninčić] but insisted that Yugoslav forces also occupy Salonika. This irritated Ninčić, who retorted that Simović was talking nonsense. Salonika and its hinterland were the only passage for German troops into Greece if they were to bypass Yugoslavia. (Ristić, 118)

At about 7 p.m. Ninčić informed Mameli that the session was still going on, and asked him to come to the Foreign Ministry at noon the next day for an answer. "But when the conversation was over, Ninčić, still holding the receiver, looked at his colleagues and said: 'This means war!' ." (Ristić, 118)

> The majority of the cabinet members favored peace and were ready to vote for the Ninčić proposal. *At that moment Simović took the floor and delivered a fiery speech.* In it he recalled page after page of Serbian history. He saluted the bones of Serbia's military heroic ancestors, the battle of Kosovo, the legendary princes of early Serbia, and Serbia's epic struggle against the Turks. (Ristić, 118-19. Italics added.)

*****

One wonders: After delivering this *fiery speech,* did Simović – *tired and pale* - indeed invite Živan Knežević into his room and, almost whispering, inform *him* about the Government session the way

Živan described it some forty years later? Why would Simović do that? Did he not have more important and pressing things to do and think about? For a few days already there were warnings of an imminent German attack.

And what resulted from that warning to *the Schwaben* by calm, angry and decisive Professor Radoje?

On 18 April 1956, Ristić had an amiable conversation with Maček, in Washington, DC, recorded it in his notes, and entered this passage into his book:

> In a conversation with the author fifteen years later, Maček said he was led by the idea of what, at that moment, was best for the nation; he wanted to save the people from a destructive war. At the conclusion of Simović's speech, the Croatian leader flatly declared that if Germany's wishes were not met he would resign. "Simović insisted and entreated me not to resign, since I was needed at the moment of crisis." No decision was reached and the cabinet disbanded at 8:45 P.M. after agreeing to convene again at 8:30 the next morning. "Yet I felt that Simović wanted war," said Maček, "because he set a condition [regarding Salonika] which he knew Hitler would not accept. It became obvious to me that the war could not be avoided." (Ristić, 119)

*****

(U) • Pavelić addressed the Croats in a lengthy emission over the *Radio station Velebit.* Krizman1, 374)

*****

At midnight of the 5th of April, General Petar Kosić, former Chief of the Main General Staff - also detained on the 27th of March - was sent to Niška Banja. (Milunović(ed), 51)

Chapter 18

SUNDAY, 6 APRIL 1941, in Moscow, Belgrade

While Hitler's *Directive No. 25* was being implemented to fiendishly *punish* Belgrade, Stalin was mockingly making the sign of the cross over the face of the Yugoslav Ambassador Gavrilović. The last traces of hope for Soviet military assistance to Yugoslavia were disappearing in the atmosphere of a banquet organized by the Soviet leaders.

That brought a disappointing end to a project that had started in 1940 with expectations for success.

The Soviet – Yugoslav treaty negotiations, 1941

Diplomatic relations between Great Britain and the Union of the Soviet Socialist Republics (USSR) were established in 1924, suspended on 25 May 1927, and restored in 1929. Similar relations between the USA and USSR were made on 16 November 1933, one month after Germany had quit the League of Nations.

Relations between Yugoslavia and the USSR were formalized on 24 June 1940. The Yugoslav Ambassador in Moscow became Dr. Milan Gavrilović. His acceptance of the post was greatly conditioned upon British approval – as described later by baron Julian Amery, which is included in **Appendix D**.

A full account of the contacts and activities leading to the negotiations are not reviewed here; only some major points are examined.

- **General Simović's claim to the initiative for the establishment of relations**

Responding to questions from *the Institute for historical enquiry* in Belgrade, Simović stated that he had insisted on the establishment of the relations with both King Alexander I and Regent Prince Paul. About his recommendation to the King he wrote (translated):

> ((ad 2. Because of *Hitler's aggressive policy*, which began to manifest itself soon after his takeover of power in Germany, of his disregard for the agreements concluded, and of his hasty armament, I was of the opinion that we were in a need of support from Soviet Russia, and that diplomatic relations with the Government of the USSR ought to be established promptly. I had spoken of this even with King Alexander in June 1933 when I – substituting for the Chief of the Main General Staff, the General of the Army Milan Ž. Milovanović – on two occasions made my reports.)) (Simović(51), 5. Italics added.)

It is generally considered that *Hitler's aggressive policy* - after he became the Chancellor on 30 January 1933 - was manifested mainly by the re-occupation of Rheinland (7 March 1936), the *Anschluss* of Austria (13 March 1938), and the occupation of Prague (15 March 1939). Because all these events occurred **after** the assassination of the King on 9 October 1934, Simović could not have included these acts to the King as justification to establish diplomatic relations with the Soviet Union.

In the same reply Simović also claimed:

> ((When I became the Chief of the Main General Staff [May 1938 – April 1940], I insisted on that [diplomatic relations] to the Prince Regent. After a long hesitation, the Prince approved an attempt to establish a contact with the government of the USSR through the Soviet embassy in Ankara, with a proviso that a "quite insignificant person" (in Paul's words) be sent for this purpose, and without giving him any authorization to conclude an agreement. With the concurrence of the Minister of the Army and Navy, I proposed to send to Ankara Božin Simić, which the Prince Regent approved. Božin Simić was selected because he already knew conditions and people in the Soviet Union.)) **(#)** (Simović(51), 5)

(#) Božin Simić "had fought with the Red Army during the Civil War" [in Russia]. (Gorodetsky, 138)

- **Milan Gavrilović's information on the subject**

In a letter to Dragiša N. Ristić, dated 2 February 1957, in Washington, DC, Dr. Milan Gavrilović provided the following information:

> The Foreign Minister, Dr. Aleksandar Cincar-Marković, decided in 1939 to establish relations with the Soviet Union. Earlier, he had sent to Istanbul Božin Simić, who had been known as a sympathizer of the Soviet Union, but really has been more than that. Afterwards, everything went through the Soviet Embassy in Turkey. The trade relations were established first, and then the diplomatic ones. By the end of May or the beginning of June [1940], Prince Paul and Cincar-Marković asked Gavrilović to become the Yugoslav Ambassador in Moscow. He left Belgrade on 2 July 1940, and went to Moscow via Istanbul and Odessa. (Dragiša N. Ristić, Box 2, Folder 2.18, Hoover Institution Archives)

To what extent Simović and/or other individuals influenced Prince Paul's decision is not examined in depth here. Dr. Hoptner - among other authors - provided significant information on the subject, and some of it is presented below:

> Although by 1934 Yugoslavia had agreed, under pressure from the Czechs, not to oppose admission of the Soviet Union to the League of nations, it had continued to refuse to recognize the U.S.R.R. for more than two decades after the war. After 1935, the Yugoslavs saw that they would ultimately have to recognize the Soviet Union, but they would do so only under certain conditions. It was necessary, Prince Paul advised the government, "to procrastinate as long as possible". (Hoptner, 174)

In an undated memorandum Prince Paul wrote:

> Recognize the Soviet Union only if absolutely necessary and only when conditions in the country become completely quiet and orderly. Keep in mind that the future Soviet minister will become the nucleus for all the dissatisfied elements [including] even the opposition. He would probably attract even the broader masses of the people by his Orthodoxy and Slavism. (Hoptner, 174-5)

- **Timetable of the Soviet-Yugoslav agreement negotiations**

After the Serbo-Croat *Sporazum (Agreement)* was signed on 26 August 1939, "it seemed desirable for Yugoslavia to approach the Soviet Union. ... Because of the Russian invasion of Finland, the Yugoslavs considered it advisable to defer negotiations so as to avoid irritating the French and the English, and it was not until the end of March, 1940 ... that the government actually began to lay the groundwork." (Hoptner, 175)

On 15 April 1940, each Government appointed its delegation to pursue the economic talks.
On 21 April, the Yugoslav commercial delegation left for Moscow.
On 11 May, three documents were signed: a treaty of commerce and navigation, a protocol covering methods of payments for goods, and an agreement establishing commercial delegations in Belgrade and Moscow. "The Russians were particularly interested in metals, specifically copper, the Yugoslavs in gas and oil." (Hoptner, 176)

At the end of May 1940, the Yugoslav ambassador in Ankara received instructions to sound off the Soviet ambassador on the idea of establishing diplomatic relations.
On 10 June, Moscow expressed its approval.
On 24 June, an agreement was signed "establishing diplomatic relations between the Soviet Union and the Kingdom of Yugoslavia... (Hoptner, 176-7)

From the Soviet point of view, the agreement was beneficial. "Yugoslavia had been the only country in South-east Europe to resist recognition of the Soviet Union. The move clearly aimed at curtailing German influence in Yugoslavia while extending the Soviet spheres of interest to the region." (Gorodetsky, 28)

> For its effect on domestic politics the Yugoslav government sent as its minister to Moscow a leader of the Serbian Agrarian party and in the Opposition, Milan Gavrilović. His mission was to arouse the Soviet leaders to the dangers surrounding Yugoslavia and the Balkans, to obtain armaments, and in case of Axis aggression against Yugoslavia, to obtain the help of the Red Army. Unfortunately, the time was not right and Gavrilović was never able to complete his mission. (Hoptner, 177)

As pointed out in **Appendix D**, Gavrilović sought approval from the British before finally accepting his assignment in Moscow.

Before he went to Moscow, he also had a lengthy talk with the German Minister in Belgrade, Viktor von Heeren. *Inter alia* Gavrilović told von Heeren that his countrymen liked Russia despite the régime and because of the past. "Old Russia, he pointed out, had done a great deal for the Serbs. The people knew that. They liked the Russian people. ..." (Hoptner, 177-8)

On 23 July 1940, von Heeren reported to his Foreign Ministry that the agreement gave "a strong impetus not only to the Communists, but, above all, to the Russophile tendencies of the country. The general feeling was that the alignment with Russia would provide some protection against the Italian-German danger." (Gorodetsky, 28; 332n39)

The Communists in Yugoslavia knew as well that their countrymen liked "*Old Russia*", and they played the "*Russian*" card with the Serbs masterfully ... for the benefit of the Communist Soviet Union. "Liking the Russian people" was not the same as liking the Soviet Union and the Soviet system. Gavrilović ultimately confirmed that with his own example. For all that love of the "Old Russia", after the war he did not return to the Communist-ruled Yugoslavia. His earthly remains were entombed directly behind the church of St. Sava monastery in Libertyville, Illinois, in the USA.

- **Colonel Žarko Popović, Military Attaché in Moscow**

As stated above, Colonel Žarko Popović had connected the British Military Attaché in Belgrade, Col. Clarke, with Gen. Mirković before Popović had gone to Moscow as the Military Attaché in August 1940. Upon arriving in Moscow, "in an unprecedented move the newly appointed Yugoslav military attaché was received by Marshal Timoshenko, the Defence Minister, and the Chief of Staff General Meretskov. (Gorodetsky, 138) "Timoshenko seemed to entertain high hopes of the Yugoslavs' ability to resist a German invasion, while Stalin perceived a limited agreement as a card in his complex diplomatic game. *Maintaining Russia's neutrality and achieving recognition of her spheres of interests remained his prime aim.*" (Gorodetsky, 144. Italics added.)

In his secret talks at the Ministry of Defense, Simić favorably considered co-operation to counter the German threat. (Gorodetsky, 140)

- **Clandestine talks in Paris, September 1940, and a shopping list**

Gavrilović took his post in Moscow in the beginning of August 1940. (Jukić, 34) According to a report to [Vyacheslav] Molotov, [Commissar for Foreign Affairs], by the first secretary of the Soviet Embassy in Paris, dated 13 September 1940, Gavrilović "gradually inspired the Russians to seek the support of the Yugoslav military which disapproved of the government's veering towards Germany. Clandestine talks were indeed initiated in Paris at the end of September 1940. The Yugoslav Chief of Staff wasted little time in submitting his shopping list. (Gorodetsky, 138; 354n4)

- **The Soviets wanted to avoid a collision with Germany**

Exchange of telegrams between Molotov and [Victor] Plotnikov, the Soviet Minister in Belgrade (17 October and 29 November 1940) shows that - to avoid provocation which might lead to a collision with Germany - Molotov cautioned Soviet diplomats in Belgrade against British and German attempts to "draw them into conversation which might later give them a basis for speculation making use of the Soviet Union in their interests." (Gorodetsky, 138; 354n11)

- **Offer of armament**

On 12 November 1940, the Soviet Commissar for Foreign Affairs, Molotov, went to Berlin to clarify with Hitler and Ribbentrop territorial claims related to Hungary, Rumania, and Bulgaria. Their final discussion took place during the last hours of 13 November in an air raid shelter.

> The German plan was to direct the attention of the Soviet Union from the Balkans to the Persian Gulf and to obtain Molotov's signature on the Tripartite Pact ... Russia would not be diverted from discussing the Balkans. In fact, Molotov told Hitler that the Soviet government 'would be pleased' to learn what the Axis contemplated doing about the future of Poland and about Rumania, Greece, Yugoslavia, and Bulgaria.

> The last, he said, was a matter of primary Interest to the Soviet Union. ... The German government never replied. ... (Hoptner, 179-80)
>
> After the fiasco of Molotov's visit to Berlin, the offer of armaments assumed a more concrete form. Lieutenant-Colonel Bozhina Simic [Božin Simić], who had fought with the Red Army during the Civil War, was selected to lead a military mission to Moscow. (Gorodetsky, 138)

As the leader of a military mission, Simić joined Gavrilović in Moscow in October 1940. (Jukić, 34)

- **Stalin suspected Yugoslavia's proposals for cooperation**

> As he [Stalin] expected the Yugoslav politicians and court to yield to the pressure, he attributed the forthcoming visit to Moscow of the military delegation headed by Simic, to a British plot. ... Gavrilović's proposals for co-operation were dismissed therefore as feelers 'of an exploratory nature'; after all, his standing with the Yugoslav Government was poor while his skills in diplomacy were said to be 'confined at best to playing chess'. Within the [Yugoslav] Cabinet Tupanjanin, (#) deputy leader of the Agrarian party, himself on the NKVD's payroll, questioned the sincerity of the Yugoslav initiative, as the two countries had 'only just got on to nodding terms'. (Gorodetsky, 139)

(#) "Tupanjanin proved to be only of a partial value to the Russians as his party was also 'in receipt of a subsidy from His Majesty's Government'." (Gorodetsky, 355n17)

- **Stalin was informed of Hitler's plan to attack the Soviet Union**

After Prince Paul's meeting with Hitler on 4 March 1941, 'Sophocles', the Soviet military attaché in Belgrade, informed Stalin that a reliable source in the Palace had revealed that - in an attempt to discourage the Yugoslavs from playing the Russian card - Hitler had disclosed to the Prince his intention of abandoning plans for war against England in favor of seizing the Ukraine and Baku in April-May. (Gorodetsky, 139-40)

The Soviet Government was informed, from several sources, that Germany would attack the Soviet Union. Informing Andrej Vyshinsky about it, the British Ambassador, Sir Stafford Cripps, even gave him the dates: between 15 May and 1 June 1941. But Stalin did not want to "fall for a provocation" and to risk his alliance with Hitler, at least not until Germany weakened. The Yugoslav Military Attaché in Berlin, Colonel Vladimir Vauhnik, had learned about the planned German attack on the USSR already by the end of 1940. (Petranović & Žutić, 218n1)

- **Gavrilović's report to Cincar Marković, 14 March 1941**

> Gavrilović exerted direct pressure on Cincar Marković, pointing to the severe domestic repercussions which the failure of the negotiations [with the Soviets] might have. He tried to lure the Prime Minister [Cvetković], suggesting that if proposals made by the government were eventually rejected in Moscow the people would then blame the Russians and not the government at home. He further suggested that the government would be exonerated if the Russians would agree in principle but impose harsh conditions and drag out the negotiations. But it seems that his main objective in setting the negotiations in motion was to put the Russians to the test: to find out to what extent the manifest discontent of the Soviet military with the Germans was endorsed by the Kremlin. (Gorodetsky, 140; 355n23)

- **Soviet Politburo approved negotiations for a Soviet-Yugoslav treaty**

Before the information that Yugoslavia would adhere to the Tripartite Pact had reached Moscow, fresh news were circulating within the Soviet high military circle that the Politburo had accepted the proposals of their General Staff to negotiate a Soviet-Yugoslav treaty and Vyacheslav Molotov, the Commissar for Foreign Affairs, was instructed to open negotiations with the Yugoslav Ambassador Gavrilović. (Krylov, 61)

At the same time Marshal V. M. Shaposhnikov, the Chief of the General Staff, proposed to the Yugoslav Military Attaché, Col. Žarko Popović, that a permanent contact should be established between the Soviet and Yugoslav General Staffs in order to overthrow the Yugoslav Government as soon as its adhesion to the Pact became known. Popović accepted the proposal enthusiastically. (Krylov, 61)

- **Negotiations with Vishinsky**

As soon as the news of the Yugoslav Government's decision to join the Tripartite Pact reached the British Embassy in Moscow **in the afternoon of 22 March**, Ambassador Sir Stafford Cripps sent Gavrilović to Vyshinsky, the Soviet Assistant Foreign Commissar, with a proposal to issue a communiqué which would repudiate the common belief that the Soviet Union was "abandoning the Balkans and Yugoslavia to Germany's sphere of influence". His suggestion backfired. The Soviets saw in it a British intrigue. When Vyshinsky saw Cripps that evening in the Kremlin, he "chose this moment to produce a catalogue of supposedly hostile British acts against Moscow." (Gorodetsky, 141)

Gavrilović was recalled to the Foreign Ministry at midnight where he found Vyshinsky to be "obviously anxious and sympathetic but also afraid". He seemed to fear that the request for Soviet intervention was a trap. (Gorodetsky, 141)

On 25 March, the day the Tripartite Pact was signed in Vienna, Col. Popović reportedly said that the army would take action the following day, with consent of the Queen Mother and the young King Peter. Stafford Cripps, it was reported, had an urgent talk with Gavrilović, who had sent a cipher telegram to Belgrade. Deciphered by Soviet officials, the telegram was said to contain Cripps' promise to Gavrilović of immediate assistance if Yugoslavia changed her policy. Allegedly, the Third Secretary of the British Embassy had made a similar declaration to an official of the Soviet Commissariat for Foreign Affairs. Molotov was hesitant. He insisted that Vyshinsky should conduct the negotiations in his stead so that, if necessary, the Soviet Government could get out of it if the Germans threatened to cancel the Soviet-German non-aggression treaty as a result of the Soviets' change in attitude regarding Belgrade. (Krylov, 62)

*****

The Queen Mother and the young King not only had not given consent, they had had no knowledge of the military coup preparations.

*****

A new situation arose with the Putsch of 27th March 1941.

> To close observers it was patently clear that the coup came as a surprise to Moscow. There could hardly be a 'covert or overt' Soviet involvement in a coup orchestrated by the British Special Operations Executive. Although General Solomon Milstein, deputy director of the GRU [Soviet Military Intelligence], accompanied by a few 'illegals' had been especially sent to Belgrade, his task in the affair, if any, was confined to monitoring 'British plots'. (Gorodetsky, 142)

The Soviet Ambassador, Lebedev, got carried away with the coup, and interpreted it as a political trend not only in the Balkan states, but over the entire Continent. Similarly, in a report dated 28 March, the Soviet Director of Military Intelligence, General Filip Golikov, attributed the slogans of the local Communists – such as *"For a union with the Soviet Union"* and *"To the health of Stalin and Molotov"* - as the will of the entire population. He expected that the forty-eight Yugoslav divisions, just mobilized, were determined and competent to thwart a German invasion. (Gorodetsky, 142-3; 355n37) They let their wishes influence their judgment. Stalin was more cautious.

> In the absence of a direct dialogue with the Belgrade government prior to the coup, Russian attempts to inhibit Yugoslavia from joining the Axis were conducted through the Communist Party. In the new circumstances steps were taken to dampen popular enthusiasm. [Georgi] Dimitrov, the President of the Comintern, was promptly instructed by Molotov [on 29 March] to call off street demonstrations which, he feared might be 'exploited by the British as well as the domestic reactionaries'. Tito was instructed to watch over 'the unruly British warmongers and Great Serbian chauvinists, who are pushing the country into military slaughter by their provocations.' (Gorodetsky, 143; 355n39)

- **The neutrality clause in the Soviet-Yugoslav agreement**

On Saturday evening, 29 March, American journalist Henry Chapiro [Shapiro] told his colleagues and officials that the Soviets were going to insert a neutrality clause in their agreement with Yugoslavia, in case of a war between Germany and Yugoslavia. (Krylov, 64) Indeed they did.

On April 1st, Foreign Minister Ninčić informed Gavrilović that the Soviet chargé d'affaires had said that his Government was favorably inclined toward concluding a military and political pact with Yugoslavia. With that in mind, Ninčić said that he was sending Colonels Božin Simić and Dragutin Savić to Moscow with instructions and full authority for Gavrilović to sign the document. (Hoptner, 276) On April 2nd the Colonels arrived in Moscow with a draft of the proposed agreement.

On that Wednesday the negotiations with Gavrilović were going forward rapidly. However, he insisted categorically that the neutrality clause should not be included in the treaty. Therefore, the question would have to be brought back for discussion within the Politburo. (Krylov, 68)
   Reportedly, Marshal Shaposhnikov favored dropping the neutrality clause, the Politburo was divided, and both Stalin and Molotov were hesitant. All members of the Central Committee of the Party, then present in Moscow, were invited to the session. (Krylov, 68)

In Professor Gorodetsky's words:

> Stalin had hoped that a mere demonstration of solidarity with Yugoslavia would suffice to inhibit Hitler from attacking her. While the delegation was on its way the situation had altered dramatically. An increasing flow of ominous intelligence unveiling the offensive German deployment on their borders led the Yugoslavs to raise the stakes by seeking a full military-political alliance with Russia. (Gorodetsky, 145)

On the 3rd of April, in their first conference with Andrej Vyshinsky, he told them at once that the idea of a military pact with Yugoslavia was completely new to him, and that he would have to submit the proposal to Molotov [the Foreign Commissar]. (Hoptner, 276)

"Naturally, the proposal had to be brought before Stalin, but Vyshinsky had little doubt that 'it was scarcely expedient to sign such agreements.'" (Gorodetsky, 145) According to the record of Vyshinsky's meeting with the Yugoslav delegation on 3 April,

> It was better for the Yugoslavs to watch out for provocations, whether British or German, while displaying a show of force, as "the independence of a country was best protected by a strong army". Gavrilović insisted, however, that his government "firmly wished and expected an alliance with the Soviet Union". (Gorodetsky, 145; 356n50)

- **Prince Paul's information of Hitler's intention to attack the Soviet Union was known to Simović and others**

Also on 3 April, in Belgrade, the Soviet Ambassador Lebedev was summoned by Simović and confronted with a *fait accomplit*. According to Lebedev's report to Molotov of 3 April,

> the Yugoslav government regarded the agreement as "already in existence even if in practice it may have not yet been signed." Simović counted on Stalin to present "a strong Soviet démarche in Berlin to stop a German intervention, or in any case provide Yugoslavia with time to complete the mobilization". As the outbreak of hostilities could no longer be ruled out, the Russians were invited to place troops and munitions in Yugoslavia. To goad Stalin into action *Simović even parted with fresh information obtained from Prince Paul, who had been told by Hitler during their recent meeting [on 4 March] about his intentions of attacking Russia.* (Gorodetsky, 145; 356n51. Italics added.)

*****

Knowing that Hitler intended to attack the Soviet Union, why did not Simović-Mirković-and-other-Putschists ... and the British who egged them on ... wait and execute the Putsch *after* the German troops were engaged in the war with the Soviet Union? Hitler himself stated that *if the overthrow of the government would have happened during the Barbarossa-action, the consequences for us probably would have been considerably more serious.*
   (The Avalon Project: Nazi Conspiracy and Aggression Volume IV – Document No 1746 www.yale.edu/lawweb/avalon.imt/document/nca_vol/1746-ps.htm 10/6/04. Italics added.)
   The British war leaders had their own agenda and time-table, and the coup had to be done at the moment when it best served **their** goals. It was timed to take maximum advantage of *vehement reaction in Serbia* which was systematically being built up by propaganda.

*****

Hitler's intention of invading the Soviet Union was not known only in Belgrade. Prime Minister Churchill was also informed about it. A report from Belgrade, received in London on 30 March, and from Sumner Welles, the American Under-secretary of State, on 2 April, "confirmed news from Athens, where Prince Paul had sought refuge after the coup, that Hitler revealed to him during their meeting at Berchtesgaden on 4 March his intention to take military action against Russia." (Gorodetsky, 161)

On the initiative of the British Ambassador in Moscow, even the Soviets were informed about Hitler's intention: "Cripps had exploited the favourable climate to convey to Stalin, through Gavrilović, the information obtained from Prince Paul about his meeting with Hitler. The Yugoslav ambassador attested that it was taken seriously by the Russians." (Gorodetsky, 165)

*****

Back to Lebedev's report of 3 April to Molotov.

Inviting the Soviets to place their troops and munitions in Yugoslavia – at the time when the Soviets did not want to provoke Hitler for their own reasons – was another "wishfully minded" case. The Soviets did not want to be used by Yugoslavia; instead, at that time they wanted to use Yugoslavia for their own purposes, within their own worrisome relations with Germany.

- **Reports on forthcoming attack on Yugoslavia**

A Soviet agent in Göring's headquarters reported that the German military had taken the events in Yugoslavia "most seriously". "The Luftwaffe staff was 'conducting active preparations for actions against Yugoslavia', which he expected to occur immediately."

'Sophocles' reported from Belgrade to Moscow that the Yugoslavs were informed of Hitler's intention to "start a war with the Soviet Union in May and within 7 days reach Moscow". The Yugoslav military attaché in Berlin [Col. V. Vauhnik] sent in the information that the German offensive would be conducted by three army groups, under Field Marshals [Gerd] Rundstedt, [Wilhelm] List and [Ludwig] Beck. (Gorodetsky, 146)

- **Negotiations in Moscow on 4 April, between Vishinsky and Gavrilović**

> Negotiations with the Yugoslav mission were opened … in the early afternoon of 4 April. It was now apparent that the Russians were utterly opposed to the idea of a military alliance which the Germans were bound to perceive as a blatant provocation. They [Vyshinsky] clung to the feeble technical excuse that such an agreement required 'a serious mutual examination of the forces available for such an arrangement'. Instead, they opted for a treaty of friendship and non-aggression. (Gorodetsky, 146)

> The negotiations had become so delicate that telegrams between Moscow and Belgrade were now shown only to Stalin and Molotov personally, while Vyshinsky, in charge of the negotiations, was acquainted only with their general content. … He [Stalin] … now seriously wavered between the fear of provocation and the wish to see Yugoslavia fight. … However, the fear of provocation, …, and the suspicion that Gavrilović was acting 'under the influence of Cripps' remained overwhelming. (Gorodetsky, 147)

Vishinsky summoned Gavrilović to the second meeting, in the late afternoon. Gavrilović

> was amazed to discover that without prior warning the Russians had modified the main clause of the agreement, virtually reducing it to a statement of neutrality rather than non-aggression and friendship pact. He was not impressed by Vyshinsky's assurance that the 'mere public announcement constituted an important step toward the reinforcement of peace in the Balkans', and the meeting ended inconclusively. Gavrilović condemned the new Russian proposal as a substantially watered-down version of the original proposal of a political-military alliance. He therefore postponed the signing of the agreement set for the next day, pending further consultation with Belgrade. … Gavrilović was warned before taking his leave that time was running out and that 'what was possible today, could be impossible tomorrow'. (Gorodetsky, 147-8)

In the meantime members of the Politburo had gathered that night at Stalin's dacha and endorsed the agreement, expecting the Yugoslav Government to follow suit. (Gorodetsky, 148)

- **Molotov informed the German Ambassador of Yugoslavia's proposal**

Following Vyshinsky and Gavrilović's negotiations in the afternoon, that evening (4 April) Molotov summoned to Kremlin the German Ambassador, Werner von Schulenburg, to tell him about the negotiation. In the Very Urgent Secret telegram (No. 796) the Ambassador promptly relayed Molotov's statements to his Foreign Ministry that:

> The Yugoslav Government had proposed to the Soviet Government the negotiation of a treaty of friendship and non-aggression, and the Soviet Government had accepted the proposal. This agreement would be signed today or tomorrow. ... The Soviet-Yugoslav Agreement was directed against no one and was not aimed at any other state.... Yugoslavia had concluded a treaty with Germany regarding accession to the Three Power Pact, and the Yugoslav Envoy here, who was at the same time a member of the new Cabinet, had assured the Soviet Government that the new Yugoslav Government was observing this treaty. Under these circumstances, the Soviet Government had thought that it could, for its part, conclude an agreement with Yugoslavia that was not even as far-reaching as the German-Yugoslav Treaty.
> (http://www.ibiblio.org/pha/nsr/nsr-08.html 11/19/07)

At Schulenburg's objection that the behavior of the new Yugoslav Government actually revealed no striving toward good relations with Germany – and despite all his efforts to obtain from Molotov the promise that the Soviet Government might reconsider the matter – "Molotov repeatedly stated that the Soviet Government had reached its decision after mature deliberation. ..." *(Ibid.)*

- **A pact of Soviet-Yugoslav assistance ... incongruous with Soviet aims**

Assessing the situation at the conclusion of the April 4th negotiation, historian Gorodetsky wrote that "The next morning found Stalin confident that he had shrewdly beaten the Germans and the British at their own game. He had succeeded in establishing Soviet interests vis-à-vis Hitler without firing a single shot, avoiding pitfall of being dragged into a premature war. ... Molotov appeared 'excited and optimistic'. He made it clear that General Simović's 'dreams about a pact of mutual assistance' were incongruous with Soviet aims. The optimism, however, was short-lived ... " (Gorodetsky, 148)

- **Negotiations in Moscow continued on 5 and 6 April**

On 5 April it seemed that the question on neutrality had been settled. The Politburo and the members of the Central Committee present adopted the text of the Soviet treaty with Yugoslavia. The neutrality clause was included. (Krylov, 70)

> When the negotiations resumed [on 5 April] the Yugoslav mission [now including Gavrilović, Božin Simić and Dragutin Savić] persisted in its demands for the original friendship agreement to be reinstated. Now that Russia was not being involved directly in hostilities, Vyshinsky was prepared to concede that a supplementary agreement between Yugoslavia and Britain would be 'expedient'; it could eliminate the likelihood of a separate peace and deter the danger of a German attack on Russia [as Vishinsky suggested to Simić]. (Gorodetsky, 148; 356n62)

*****

At the same time, in Belgrade, "the Yugoslav government was little encouraged by Lebedev's noncommittal statements that 'the Soviet Union was already pursuing a struggle to secure peace for Yugoslavia, and was endeavouring to lay the necessary political foundations to consolidate such a peace in the future'. (Gorodetsky, 148)

In order to avoid war, on 5 April Ninčić was ready to go to Berlin to personally talk with Hitler. On 5 April, the German chargé d'affairs in Belgrade reported to his Foreign Ministry the Yugoslav Government's attempt to explain to him the negotiations in Moscow: they were sparked by the momentary 'excitement' of the uprising but had been opposed by the entire Cabinet, which "did not want an understanding with Moscow, but one with Berlin." (Gorodetsky, 148-9; 356n64)

- **Signing of the agreement in Moscow, on 6 April**

The signing of the agreement was originally scheduled for 10 p.m. on 5 April – but it did not happen as scheduled.

The special Soviet Ambassador in Berlin informed Stalin - by midnight - that a German invasion of Yugoslavia was imminent. It was also established that the Yugoslav mission had not received any telegrams that night. At one o'clock in the morning of 6 April Gavrilović was located in the American Embassy. "He was evasive and disinclined to co-operate, informing Vyshinsky on the phone that he did not expect the government to respond until later in the morning." Dissatisfied with this reply, Vyshinsky arranged for Gavrilović to speak directly with Simović from his own Embassy. (Gorodetsky, 149)

Suspecting that a trap was set up for him, Gavrilović did not want to talk with Simović about the agreement until he verified that he was really talking with Simović – by getting his correct home address. As they began to talk, a profound disagreement emerged very quickly. Simović, "who had had no response from the Germans and was constantly primed with intelligence of the forthcoming assault, was now desperate to conclude the agreement [with the Soviets]. (Gorodetsky, 149)

> 'Sign whatever the Russians are proposing to you.'
> 'I cannot, General. I know what is my duty and what is my job.'
> 'You have to sign.'
> 'I cannot, General, trust me.'
> 'Sign, Gavrilović.'
> 'I know what I am doing, General. I cannot sign this document.'
> 'All right. If you want an order, then I am ordering you to sign.'
> 'I know what I am doing, trust me.'

Gavrilović then slammed down the receiver. (Gorodetsky, 149-50; 356n68)

"Gavrilović ... knew perfectly well that the 'telephone conversation had undoubtedly been recorded and reported to Stalin'." When, within a minute, the head of the Eastern Department of the Soviet Foreign Ministry called him, Gavrilović explained that "he 'thought' that he had been instructed to sign the agreement, but he 'nonetheless wished that the mention of neutrality be removed'." When Vyshinsky appealed to Gavrilović, he persevered but now attributed the wish "to exclude the mention of neutrality from the agreement," to his government. (Gorodetsky, 150)

Vyshinsky then insisted that the entire delegation assemble at the Kremlin at 2:30 a.m. [6 April]. Trying to delay, Gavrilović regretted that the members of the delegation could not be located. The agents of the NKVD, however, found them promptly, and drove them to the Kremlin. (Gorodetsky, 150)

Gavrilović was ushered into Molotov's office where he found "an easy-going and cheerful Stalin". Turning to Stalin, Molotov announced that he proposed to "make an amendment by removing the word 'neutrality' throughout", and blamed Vyshinsky for the bungle.

> "They appeared so anxious to conclude the agreement that there was no time for the revised version to be translated into Serbo-Croat, and the retyped Russian one was signed around 3 a.m. on 6 April. As the main addressee was Germany, the signing was announced on the radio within an hour. Stalin insisted, however, that the date of the signing should be 5 April, so as not to suggest that it had been signed with preknowledge of or concurrently with the German invasion of Yugoslavia. (Gorodetsky, 150)

The treaty between the Soviet Union and Yugoslavia contained five items. The former American Ambassador in the USSR, Joseph E. Davies, summarized the stipulation of Item 2 in his diary under April 5, 1941:

> A treaty of friendship and nonaggression was signed between the Soviet Union and Yugoslavia. It contained this extraordinary statement: "That should one of the contracting parties be attacked by a third state, the other contracting party pledges itself to preserve its policy of friendship". ... of course the third state referred to obviously means not only Italy but Russia's ally, Germany. (Davies, 474)

Extraordinary indeed.

- **Banquet in Moscow ... while bombs were being loaded into German aircraft to "punish" Belgrade**

After the signing, the participants retired to watch a newsreel, and Molotov improvised a banquet which lasted until 7 a.m. (Gorodetsky, 150)

Captain Ivan Krylov, present at the event, wrote that "it was perhaps half-past eight in the morning when the strange banquet began." They were all seated around Stalin and Gavrilović. Stalin was in very good mood, and declared that it was a great joy for him to sign a treaty with an orthodox Slav country threatened by the Germans. Krylov quoted the following exchange between Stalin and Gavrilović:

(S) We are brothers by blood and religion. Nothing will ever be able to separate our two countries. I hope that your army will be able to hold up the Germans for a long time. You have mountains and forests where the tanks will be unable to operate. Organize guerila warfare.

(G) *We have a formal promise of assistance from London.* If British troops land on our coast what will you do?

(S) If you succeed in organizing a sufficiently strong resistance to allow the British to land and to bar the way to the Germans that would be a fine success worthy of your army. The sympathy of the people of the Soviet Union will always be with you. ... How many planes, tanks, and anti-tank guns have you? How far are your reservists ready for action?

I noticed that Gabrilovitch had difficulty in replying to these numerous questions. ... (Krylov, 72. Italics added.)

It is important to observe that Stalin did not disclose what the Soviets might do, and Gavrilović could not answer the questions about Yugoslavia's armament. But the Ambassador did say that *Yugoslavia had had a British formal promise of assistance.*

After the toasts were drunk, the party began to break up, and Krylov "saw a strange sight. Stalin went up to Gabrilovitch, shook him by the hand and then, before turning to go, made the sign of the cross in the orthodox manner from right to left which is common to both Russians and Serbians, as though he were blessing the Yugoslav minister. ... In a corner I noticed [Anastas] Mikoyan, an Armenian Catholic and a man much given to hearty laughter, hiding his face in his handkerchief. A fit of coughing seemed to be choking him." (Krylov, 73)

*****

Reacting to the German threat to Yugoslavia and the Soviet Union, after the agreement had been signed, Stalin nonchalantly boasted, "Let them come. We have strong nerves!" (Gorodetsky, 150) In Professor Gorodetsky's opinion, this remark was widely quoted but not in the right context.

> ... it was fear of invasion which had led Stalin to seek the agreement. The Russian objective was to deter Germany; now that the invasion of Yugoslavia seemed inevitable the aim was to prolong the breathing space and defer the attack on Russia by stiffening Yugoslav resistance. Stalin went out of his way to display exaggerated confidence; he described in great detail the innovations introduced into the Red Army and its ability to assist the Yugoslavs. (Gorodetsky, 150-51)

Gavrilović became greatly impressed with "the incomparable Stalin". "As the Yugoslavs were parting from Stalin in jubilant spirits, Hitler unleashed the attack on Yugoslavia in a ferocious bombardment of Belgrade which turned the city into ruins. Despite the intelligence he had received, Stalin appeared to be surprised when news of the German attack came in. (Gorodetsky, 151)

- **"A rather romanticized myth"**

In Gorodetsky's opinion:

> Stalin had gone out of his way to reject the military alliance proposed by the Yugoslav armed forces and even attempted to downgrade the friendship agreement to a neutrality pact. Throughout the conflict, the leaders of the Yugoslav coup were split on the nature of their association with Russia. They ended up by playing the German, British and Soviet cards simultaneously and seeing their political achievement crumble within a week. History, however, has applauded both sides, *presenting a rather romanticized myth* of a last-minute resolve to hold back the onslaught of Nazi Germany. (Gorodetsky, 153-4. Italics added.)

((The Soviet Union was not ready to risk a break-up with Germany, but was interested in Yugoslavia's resistance to the German aggression. Every day of resistance was delaying Germany's planned attack on the USSR. ... Intentions of the Yugoslav diplomacy for the USSR to commit herself – through a military alliance [with Yugoslavia], while the Molotov-Ribbentrop Pact was still in force – were exceeding the Soviet intentions. This is a testimony to the [Yugoslav Government's] unrealistic expectation of assistance.)) (Petranović & Žutić, 218n1)

- **Soviet withdrawal of the recognition of Yugoslavia's Government**

After the signing of the Japanese-Soviet Nonaggression Pact had been concluded on 13 April 1941, the Japanese Foreign Minister [Yōsuke] Matsuoka left Moscow by train. The German Ambassador in Moscow, von Schulenburg, sent a Very Urgent Secret report to Berlin on 13 April:

> The departure of Matsuoka was delayed for an hour and then took place with extraordinary ceremony. Apparently completely unexpectedly for both the Japanese and the Russians, both Stalin and Molotov appeared and greeted Matsuoka and the Japanese ... Then Stalin publicly asked for me, and when he found me he came up to me and threw his arms around my shoulders: *"We must remain friends and you must now do everything to that end!"* Somewhat later Stalin turned to the German Acting Military Attaché Krebs, first made sure that he was a German, and then said to him: *"We will remain friends with you in any event [auf jeden Fall]!"* (http://allworldwars.com/Nazi-Soviet Relations 1939-1941.html 9/8/11 - Italics added.)

That was Stalin, "the incomparable Stalin, oh *velikij* (great) Stalin!" – just one week after the Germans had bombed Belgrade into rabble and ruins, just one day after they entered into Belgrade. This was the same Stalin from whom Simović and some other Putschists had expected military and political support against Germany.

According to the record of Vishinsky's meeting with Gavrilović on 20 April, Krebs complained that Yugoslav officers continued to appear in Moscow in uniform. Gavrilović was promptly asked to evacuate them from Russia. Krebs was reassured that their presence in Moscow "had no political relevance as the Yugoslav army and government had now ceased to exist." (Gorodetsky, 204; 365n15)

> Stalin acted forcefully to back up his conciliatory diplomacy [with Germany]. ... On 8 May, the Norwegian and Belgian ministers in Moscow received arrogant notes that their credentials were no longer valid. They were promptly expelled from Moscow and recognition of their governments-in-exile withdrawn. The new governments were recognized by Stalin instantly. While the clandestine talks were taking place Gavrilović was unexpectedly summoned by Vyshinsky and informed of the decision to withdraw recognition of his government. Gavrilović was indeed in a 'bad mood and aggravated'. He nonetheless confessed that he 'well understood what the Soviet diplomacy was attempting to achieve'. (Gorodetsky, 217)

Although the Soviets had withdrawn the recognition of his government [on 8 May 1941], Gavrilović came unwillingly from Moscow to London to join the government in exile. (Jovanović, 69-70)

Whether Prince Paul accepted *Simović's* advice to establish diplomatic relations with the Soviet Union – as Simović claimed – *or somebody else's*, it turned out that no military or diplomatic support was obtained from the Soviets, however strong the hints had been originating from Moscow in the summer of 1940. The greatest beneficiaries of this new relations were the domestic Communists. They were now able to act more openly and boastfully in making claims about the Soviet Union as "Mother Russia", asserting Slavic ethnic and historic solidarity and common interests between *"Russia"* and Yugoslavia – particularly in Serbia and Montenegro. This created some good will for the Soviet Union and its system.

During Germany's war against Yugoslavia and Greece, the Soviet Union was supplying Germany with resources

In the spring of 1940, the British Ministry of Economic Warfare (MEW) knew that "Germany was supplying the USSR with heavy machinery, machine tools and semi-manufactured goods. ... It was known that by the time of the Russo-German trade agreement of February 1940 the Germans had formed an extensive organisation in the Far East, involving Japanese firms, to further trans-Siberian trade. The supply to Germany of oil from the USSR and Romania and of chrome from Turkey was well covered by Sigint [Signal Intelligence] and SIS sources." (Hinsley *et al*, 225)

On 10 January 1941, a German-Soviet agreement on barter trade and border matters was signed in Moscow.

> The agreement regulates the trade turnover between the U.S.S.R. and Germany until Aug. 1, 1942. It provides for an amount of mutual deliveries considerably exceeding the level of the first year of operation of the agreement ... settling all problems connected with migration ... on the state frontier of the U.S.S.R. and Germany from the River Igorka to the Baltic Sea in connection with the admission of the Lithuanian Soviet Socialist Republic into the Union of the Soviet Socialist Republics, which took place Aug. 3, 1940. (Pablo Picasso – On-line Picasso Project - Dr. Enrique Mallen http://www.tamu.edu/mocll/Picasso/tour/t41.html   2/4/04)

While the unproductive Soviet-Yugoslav negotiations were going on, on 5 April Dr. Karl Schnurre, the Head of the German Foreign Ministry's East European Economic Section, released a written "Memorandum on the present status of Soviet deliveries of raw materials to Germany". Here are some excerpts:

> 1) After the conclusion of the German-Soviet Commercial Agreement of January 10, 1941, there could be at first observed on the Soviet side a noticeable restraint to the practical carrying out of Soviet deliveries, ... In consequence, imports of raw materials from the U.S.S.R. remained relatively slight in January and February (17 million RM [Reich's Mark] and 11 million RM; including, to be sure, as the largest and most important item, 200,000 tons of Bessarabian grain).
>
> 2) ... Deliveries in March rose by leaps and bounds, especially in grains, petroleum, manganese ore, and the nonferrous and precious metals. The grain contract, ... , was closed in the amount of 1,4 million tons of grain, at relatively favorable prices, for delivery by September of this year. The Soviets have already made available 110,000 tons of grain on this contract and have promised firmly to deliver 170,000 to 200,000 tons of grain in April.
>
> 4) Transit traffic through Siberia is proceeding favorably as usual. At our request, the Soviet Government even put a special freight train for rubber at our disposal at the Manchurian border. ...
>
> To sum it up, it may be said that after an initial lag Russian deliveries at the moment are quite considerable, and the Commercial Agreement of January 10th of this year is being observed on the Russian side. (http://www.ibiblio.org/pha/nsr/nsr-08.html   11/19/07)
>
> Because of a stronger German negotiation position, German Foreign Ministry official Karl Schnurre concluded that, in economic terms, the agreement was "the greatest Germany ever concluded, going well beyond the previous year's February agreement." The agreement included Soviet commitments to 2.5 million tons of grain shipment and 1 million tons of oil shipments, as well as large amount of nonferrous and precious metals.
> (http://organi.typepad.com/sdj/2011/01/germansoviet-border-an... 2/14/12)

The Communists in Yugoslavia did not talk much about the German-Soviet trade agreements of February 1940 and January 1941.

- **Sunday, 6 April 1941, in Belgrade ...**

"Unmerciful harshness and military destruction"

On 27 March 1941, at 1 p.m., Hitler conferred with German High Command on the situation in Yugoslavia. **(Part One, pages 146-8)** According to the Nuremberg records, an extremely enraged Hitler said:

> Politically it is especially important that the blow against Yugoslavia is *carried out with unmerciful harshness* and that the military destruction is done in a lightning-like undertaking. (Churchill(GA), 163-4. Italics in the source.)

Flying in relays from airfields in Austria and Romania, 150 bombers and dive-bombers protected by heavy fighter escort participated in the attack. The initial raid was carried out at fifteen minutes. Thus the city was subjected to a rain of bombs for almost one and a half hours. The German bombardiers directed their main effort against the center of the city, where the principal government buildings were located. (Blau, 48) **(Part One, pages 157-9)**

On 6 April 1941, Germany launched its attack with ferocious air assault on undefended Belgrade, killing more than 5,000 civilians, and on the same day it invaded Greece from Bulgarian bases. Even though the Yugoslav Government *had not renounced its adherence to the Tripartite Pact*, German infantry and tanks crossed the Yugoslav borders from Austria, Hungary, Rumania and Bulgaria. Italian planes joined in the attack. (Roberts,15-16. Italics added.)

The bombing was vicious. During his trial after the war, German Field Marshal von Kleist said: "The air raid on Belgrade in 1941 had a primarily political-terrorist character and had nothing to do with the war. That air bombing was a matter of Hitler's vanity, his personal revenge."
(http://en.wikipedia.org/wiki/Bombing_of_Belgrade_in_World…   5/2/10)

But bombardment of Belgrade did have an impact on the war:

Besides the losses it caused among the civilian population of the capital it destroyed the central organization of the Yugoslav army and thus rendered communications between the widely dispersed armies even more difficult. (van Creveld, 158)

The difficulties in communication made the bad military situation even worse.

*****

One of those who was spreading propaganda of British help wrote about this "bloody Sunday in Belgrade":

What disturbed me the most was why there wasn't any opposition up there in the sky. Why were these Nazi bombers having it all their own way? Where were the Yugoslav fighters? *And how about those hundreds of British planes I had been writing about?* They should been here by now from their bases in Greece. (St. John, 48. Italics added.)

There were no hundreds of British planes in Greece.

… You remember Terazzia, … It was one of the most beautiful spots in the whole city. Now it was the ugliest spot in the whole world. (St. John, 58-9) We counted two or three hundred bodies right in Terrazia. And Terrazia isn't half as big as Times Square [in New York]. (St. John, 61)

*****

While SOE-operatives Glen and Seton-Watson were safeguarding "toys and chocolate" during the bombardment of Belgrade, some British Legation personnel were leaving in a hurry.

April 6 … Vrnjachka Banya. Hugh MacDonald's arrived. And Tom Despard [the British naval attaché]. And Tom Mapplebeck's following, with radio equipment in a second Vauxhall. … (Brock, 212)

Danube blocked for a few weeks

On 6th April some half-dozen barge were successfully sunk – but the river was only blocked for a few weeks, and there was no significant drop in Romanian oil supplies to Germany.
   News of the operation only filtered through slowly, partially because of the confusion caused by the Balkan invasions. (Pimlott(ed), 186)

Chapter 19

6 APRIL – 17 JUNE 1941, from Belgrade to London

"British troops were said to have landed ... on the Yugoslav coast"

Using "the reports of American correspondents who covered the developments of events in Yugoslavia on the spot", *The New York Times* featured daily brief summaries "of the events in Yugoslavia from February 15 through April 28, 1941, in 'The International Situation'." These summaries are contained in Section One of the Volume entitled A NATION'S FIGHT FOR SURVIVAL. THE 1941 REVOLUTION AND WAR IN YUGOSLAVIA AS REPORTED BY THE AMERICAN PRESS. This Volume is intended for REFERENCE USE ONLY. Here are the excerpts of the summary related to the alleged British landings in Yugoslavia:

> MONDAY, Aril 7, 1941. The familiar pattern of a full-scale German Blitzkrieg unfolded yesterday as Berlin bulletins asserted German troops were moving slowly but steadily into Yugoslavia and Greece despite fierce Greek resistance in the Struma valley. The Nazi air force, striking hard at Yugoslav objectives, was said to have attacked Belgrade three times, leaving large fires and serious damage. Eighty-Five Yugoslav planes were reported destroyed during the day and the government of Premier Simovitch as said to have transferred to Vranesh, in Southern Serbia.
>
> Dispatches reaching Berne said the Yugoslav Air Force had harassed German troops movement throughout the day and had protected Yugoslav engineers engaged in blocking the Iron Gate, Danube narrows, with concrete-laden barges. *British troops were said to have landed at three points on the Yugoslav coast to meet any German drive south from Hungary.*
> (http://www.archive.org/stream/nationsfightfors002758mbp/nati ...   2/27/14 Italics added.)

Protecting the blocking of the Danube - instead of the city of Belgrade, and the British troops landing in Yugoslavia - which was never even considered by His Majesty's Government ... was a pure fiction, if not a deliberate propaganda through misinformation.
Instead of sending more personnel into Yugoslavia, HMG was evacuating the existing one from her.

Mission accomplished – retreat

For the British official personnel in Yugoslavia, it was mission accomplished. As Churchill ordered on 22 March 1941, Yugoslavia *[got drawn] in to the war* [in the Balkans], the war which *was not what Hitler wanted* – as Eden stated, and which *forced Hitler to undertake an operation against Yugoslavia which he had not intended, at any rate [not] at that time* – as Elisabeth Barker concluded. **(Part One, 117, 32)** After helping their Government to achieve their goal, the most reasonable thing for the British personnel to do was to leave Yugoslavia as quickly and as safely as possible. This was particularly important for the SOE operatives.

Evacuation of important figures and local SOE-cooperators

Before describing the hurried retreat of the British from a burning Belgrade in April 1941, it is important to note their long-range post-occupational evacuation planning and preparations.

Preparations for the evacuation had already begun in the autumn of 1940. The first to be evacuated were the most compromised Britons.
Negotiations between the SOE and Foreign Office (FO) about the specific criteria and details for a general evacuation started in December 1940. (Vodušek Starič, 224)
However, it soon became clear that, along with the SOE operatives, there was a need to evacuate also the Yugoslav "*sodelvce*" (collaborators) of SOE who were in increasing danger due to a worsening situation. The British Minister in Belgrade raised this question in December 1940. SOE

London and FO agreed to prepare a list of criteria for the evacuation of the Yugoslavs, important politicians and the Allies' sympathizers. (Vodušek Starič, 225)

Then Bill Bailey got the idea that it would be well to make up a list of figures who could act as a Yugoslav committee abroad. In January 1941 London approved Bailey's request to allow SOE agents, who are evacuated from the occupied countries, to go to Palestine. Thereafter, they began to individually evacuate the most exposed Yugoslav collaborators with SOE. On 11 March 1941, George Taylor reported to London that five important "fugitives" had already been sent out, and were already in Istanbul on the way to Palestine. These were: Senator [Većeslav] Vilder, Dr. [Ivan Marija] Čok, Professor [Ivan] Rudolf, and Mrs. and Miss Gavrilović, the family of Milan Gavrilović. Preparations were going on to evacuate 50 more figures. (Vodušek Starič, 225)

In mid-March Taylor reported that the evacuation of important political friends of SOE was being routed through Athens to Palestine. At the same time he proposed that a safe area should be found for them, from which they could operate back to the occupied territory. (Vodušek Starič, 226)

At that time the British evacuated some *"sodelavci"* from Slovenia. (Vodušek Starič, 226-7)

The British flew Jovan Đonović out of the country, but the date of the flight is not clear. (Vodušek Starič, 242)

The British did not give up on the evacuation from Yugoslavia of certain selected individuals even during the war. On 18 April **[?]** a telegram was sent from London to Campbell and the British Minister in Athens about additional evacuations, if possible, stating that it would be necessary for the British influence in Yugoslavia in the future. FO sent a list of names including [the Serb Orthodox] Bishop Irinej [Đorđević] from Šibenik, Joka and Milan Čurčin, Professor [Dr. Vladimir] Ćorović, Slobodan Jovanović, Ivan Meštrović, Dr. August Košutić, Ilija Jukić, and a few more. (Vodušek Starič, 227-8)

From this information one would conclude that some officials in FO were not fully apprised of the Yugoslav Government's daily moves from one place to another, and/or were not in regular contact with the British personnel from Belgrade who were retreating south toward the Adriatic.

The retreat of correspondent Robert St. John and some of his colleagues is described in **Part One**. Here is partial information about the retreat of some SOE and British Legation personnel.

Under bombs, SOE-men were safeguarding their "toys"

While civilians were being killed and city destroyed, what were doing some of those participants in the all-British conference of 19 March, those who were propagating disinformation about huge British forces in Greece, those who - a week earlier - had *their Roman holiday* at the railroad station, enjoying the departure of the German Minister from Belgrade?

Although most of the smuggled British *"toys and chocolates"* were distributed promptly upon arrival, some were still in Belgrade on 6 April 1941. "It was near midnight on 26 March when I got to bed, to be awakened at around 4 am by a call from Zorica. 'Tanks are moving here in Dedinje, things are happening', she said urgently. They certainly were! ... " (Glen(B), 59) When the bombing of Belgrade started early that day, Sandy Glen's first job was to collect another prominent SOE operative, Hugh Seton-Watson, from his flat nearby. Then they picked up Zorica Bukovac, Glen's future wife, and went to the house of Miloš Tupanjanin, the acting head of the subsidized Serbian Peasant Party (SPP). They were to travel together in two cars with Tupanjanin's son and young Aleksandar Gavrilović, the son of Milan Gavrilović, president of the SPP - who was then the Ambassador in Moscow. "But before we could leave Belgrade we had a job to do, as there were a number of suitcases filled with plastic explosives which temporarily had been left in four or five houses prior to distribution in the country outside." So Hugh, Sandy and Zorica each lugged two heavy brown suitcases to a safer place. (Glen, 65-6) In 2002 Glen wrote again about it, in more details:

> We knew that the German attack was timed for 6 am on 6 April and at that minute the Luftwaffe attack on Zemun airfield began. ... At that minute I was picking up Hugh Seton-Watson at his flat.... by this time bombing was vicious ...
>
> ... A message from Tupanjanin reached us that his party would not be ready to leave until late evening. We had already picked up Zorica and looked in on a deserted Legation. ... Hugh then thought of the many suitcases of explosives in safe houses ...

> We beat it, the car filled with plastic explosives, out of town to beyond Dedigne. ... Our objective, unknown to him, was Tom Mapplebeck's country house, which had a massive swimming pool, the only safe place for our precious suitcases and their explosive contents. We did not know then that the future tenant would be the German Commandant of Belgrade, or we might have arranged something special. (Glen(B), 63-4)

George Taylor's close associate Sweet-Escott recorded:

> Within a day or two of the *coup d'état* we were evacuating our female staff to Athens, ... Ten days later the campaign had begun with the bombardment of Belgrade by the Luftwaffe.
> Yet from this point onwards our part in the Balkans campaign was an almost complete fiasco. (Sweet-Escott 63-4)

- **Diplomatic immunity extended to the British non-Legation personnel**

While Legation personnel were covered by diplomatic immunity, Campbell extended the same protective umbrella to SOE and SIS agents, including Robert Lethbridge and John Lloyd-Evans.

> When the Axis forces invaded Yugoslavia Lethbridge and his staff fled toward the Adriatic coast. After unsuccessful efforts to evacuate them by flying boat and submarine, they surrendered to the Italians. Italy having agreed to repatriate any British diplomatic personnel captured on foreign soil, on the strict understanding that Britain fully reciprocated, Lethbridge, his staff, and other members of the British diplomatic community were then evacuated to Italy, from where they were taken by train across Vichy France to Spain. From Spain they returned to Britain via Portugal or Gibraltar. ... Like other SIS personnel he [Lloyd-Evans] gave himself up to the Italians. (Some personalities in SIS operations in Yugoslavia   http://www.oocities.org/sebrit/personalities2.html   9/18/12)

> The rest of our [SOE] party in Belgrade joined our legation in its uncomfortable trek through southern Serbia and Montenegro to Kotor, where a few of our people were taken off to Egypt in Sunderlands. (Sweet-Escott 63-4)
> But the others were eventually captured by the Italians. The seven radio sets we had with such difficulty succeeded to extricate from "Z" [Secret Intelligence Service] had arrived in Belgrade before the *coup d'état*, but time had been too short to train the operators properly, and although the sets were distributed to our friends, they never came on the air.
> Meanwhile the legation party (#), including George Taylor, Tom Masterson and a score or so of our [SOE] people who were all lucky enough to have been given diplomatic immunity, were taken by the Italians to a comfortable hotel at Chianciano in the Apennines. They were allowed to do more or less as they liked, and if they had failed to organize anything anywhere else, they at least succeeded in organizing a couple of cricket elevens.
> After a few weeks the Rome Express came to collect and transport them to the Spanish frontier. Eventually they got back to England via Gibraltar, though not till early June. (Sweet-Escott, 64)

(#) There were a total of one hundred and four "prisoners" in the British party. (Brock, 269)

*****

(The return of George Taylor to London is described by the SOE head, Dr. Hugh Dalton, in his diary for Wednesday, 18th June – in Chapter 21.)

Chapter 20

6–18 APRIL 1941... from Simović's "fiery speech" to "unconditional capitulation"

As described previously, at the ministerial conference of the new Government that was held the evening of April 5th, Simović had delivered a "fiery speech". (Ristić, 118-19)

Maček and Kulovec held the same views they had before the coup, and that is, that the war should be avoided at any price. ... In the evening of April 5^{th,} the difference between Simović and Maček was so great, that some ministers foresaw a possibility of the disintegration of the Government at the meeting scheduled for the morning of 6 April. (Jovanović, 12).

The scheduled meeting was not held because Belgrade was bombarded and the Government fled the city ... on their way out of the country.

What follows is a very sketchy description of that unprepared and disorderly journey.

*****

In London – Dalton appraised the collapse of Yugoslavia from the British point of view: it was *catastrophic* because Yugoslavia had contributed nothing to the British expedition in Greece, and there was no organization set up in Yugoslavia for post-occupational resistance, as SOE had planned. He blamed the failures on *a number of very elderly politicians.* As pointed by authors writing about SOE and Dalton, he was very eager to prove his value and the contribution of his SOE organization to Prime Minister Churchill. He knew how to use money to achieve his goals, and bragged about these accomplishments to Churchill.

But Dalton did not share opinions of military men, like Gen. John Kennedy, Director of Military Operations. "From a purely military point of view, which was never given its proper weight, we could not afford to send a strong force to Greece. ... it was clear to all, except the wishfully-minded, that we could never have held the Germans for long in Greece. ..." (Kennedy, 138-40) Dalton ignored military realities of the moment, which made Yugoslavia's contribution to the British cause in the spring of 1941 impossible. Aware of that impossibility, but still willing to expose the country to war in the expectation of a final victory, the Putschists experienced the collapse of their plans much more rapidly than they had expected.

- **Sunday, 6 April 1941 – From Belgrade to Užice and Banja Koviljača**

According to the war assignment, Gen. Simović and the Army High Command went to Banja Koviljača [near Loznica] (Knežević, 208), and the Government to Užice.

> The cabinet ministers, who fled from Belgrade when the German bombs began to fall, met later that night in the Hotel Palas in Užice, a town in western Serbia. They would try to maintain some semblance of orderly government. ... (Hoptner, 286)

All Ministers except Simović, and Kulovec (who was killed during the bombing of Belgrade) met at 9 p.m., with Maček presiding. The King's proclamation to the people – drafted by Grol – was unanimously approved and accepted. (Miletić(ed), 465)

- **Monday, 7 April**

At 9 a.m. all Ministers, except Simović, met at Sevojno, near Užice, Maček presiding. After Gen. Ilić commemorated the death of Dr. Kulovec, the Ministers declared the state of preparedness and mobilization.

In order to expedite the government's business, they established a trimmed-down Working Cabinet, consisting of Maček, Ninčić, Šutej, Budisavljević, and Gen. Ilić.

Maček informed them of his intention to suggest the acceptance of Juraj Krnjević as Minister without portfolio, who would replace Maček in case he would not be available.

The Ministers concluded that the second Vice-Premier Jovanović and Bariša Smoljan should be permanently added to Premier Simović at the Supreme Command.

They also decided that – with the agreement by the Supreme Command – a purchase of food should be made in Great Britain and the USA as soon as possible for the needy passive regions and the military. (Miletić(ed) 492-3)

*****

Lack of food in the passive, i.e. mountainous regions - among other shortages - illustrates how unrealistic were Gen. Simović's suggestions, made to Prince Paul in the evening of 23 March, ((to form the Salonika front again, and the people and the forces that are to be left in the country, to retreat to the mountains and to continue the fight by guerrilla warfare ...))

*****

In London – Dalton was still hoping for a blockade of the Danube, and wrote in his diary:

> ... Still hopes of the River, but not perhaps, according to C.E.O. [Gladwyn Jebb], more than a 30 percent chance of anything worth while. We have one or two encouraging telegrams from A.D. [George Taylor] saying that he has been assured that action will be taken as soon as Yugoslavia is attacked, and that 'the Operation' has been prepared.
> Meanwhile, the Jugs seem to be in the muddle. Their Government has left Belgrade and is out of touch with their General Staff. Their M.F.A. [Minister of Foreign Affairs] is out of touch with senior officials who are with Campbell and the other diplomats at Vranjska Banja. It s all too reminiscent of Poland to be pleasant, although one hopes that the terrain favours our side this time. (Pimlott(ed), 183)

Sir Alexander Cadogan, Permanent Undersecretary for Foreign Affairs, recorded in his diary:

> Not much news from Balkans. Germany took a knock from the Greeks in Rupel pass (that is official). But they are apparently penetrating into Yugoslavia, and I haven't heard of a Jug firing a shot yet... (*)
> Cabinet at 5. V[ery] gloomy. Bad air attack on Pireus last night. At least 6 ships and valuable cargoes lost. Menzies [head of Secret intelligence Service, 'C'] evidently worried and rather critical. Jugs (according to 'C') seem to be very uncooperative. Shipping losses v[ery] bad. ... We ought to get a good liaison with Jugs at once. ... (Dilks(ed), 370)

> (*) Many of their aircraft were destroyed on the ground, despite Dill's [General Sir John Dill, Chief of the Imperial General Staff] urgings to disperse them; and the tactics of the Yugoslav army appear to have been ill-co-ordinated. ... (Dilks(ed), 370)

*****

Along with some of the newspapers' reporters, traveling with the British personnel, were "Basil Davidson of the Budapest Britanova office, David Shillan, the bearded director of the British propaganda department at Belgrade." (Brock, 239) The reporters were eager to send their dispatches to their papers / agencies, but had no ways to do it. Somehow they found out that the British honorary Air Attaché, Tom Mapplebeck, "somewhat contrary to the international law and custom, had a portable short-wave sending set." (St. John, 80) They, naturally, wanted to use the set for their purposes. But the availability of this radio set was important for another reason.

> ... But believe it or not, General Simovich, ..., had absolutely no means of communicating with his British and Greek allies or with his own six armies scattered in various parts of Yugoslavia, no way at all, unless Maplebeck let him use the little portable radio set for his messages. So, Maplebeck [Mapplebeck] told, his radio operator was busy twenty-four hours a day tapping out pleas to the British in Greece to hurry up with some help – with some of those three hundred thousand troops and hundreds of planes. And the little sending set was also trying to get into communication with the six Yugoslav armies, because civil phone lines were all cut and military communications hadn't yet been set up. (St. John, 80)

"The British M.A. [Military Attaché, Col. Charles Clarke] handled all the Yugoslav Army dispatches,..." (Brock, 218)

- **Tuesday, 8 April – In Sevojno; Maribor, Skoplje and Prilep fell**

The Germans occupied Maribor, (Blau, 54), Skoplje and Prilep.

Maček left Sevojno to meet Simović at Koviljača.

> Hoping to encourage resistance in Croatia, Maček explained that it was necessary for him to go to Zagreb. But Simović held that Maček's efforts would be frustrated by the Ustaše and instead that the vice prime minister would render greater service with the government. If the government were to go into exile, Maček replied, he would rather remain in Croatia, and he asked that his post be given to Krnjević. (Ristić, 128)

The council of ministers met in Sevojno at 9 a.m.. At the suggestion of the Finance Minister Šutej, the Ministers approved some salary advances and payments.
They also concluded that Božidar Vlajić should be given a task of correlating the work of the Press-biro with the Supreme Command and the Foreign Ministry. (Miletić(ed), 512)

*****

In Washington, D.C. – On 8 April President Roosevelt sent a message to King Peter II of Yugoslavia, which was recorded in the Department of State Bulletin on 12 April 1941. The message read, in part:

> As I have assured Your Majesty's Government, the United States will speedily furnish all material assistance possible in accordance with its existing statutes. I send Your Majesty my most earnest hope for a successful resistance to this criminal assault upon the independence and integrity of your country. (http://www.ibiblio.org/pha/policy/1941/410408a.html   11/12/03)

As described in **Part One, pages 189-90**, Greece never received the thirty P-40 pursuit planes they had been promised. "Greece was overrun by the Germans before this important item of American aid arrived." (Langer and Gleason, 401) By contrast, Yugoslavia had never received any promises of specific military aid. Whatever needed weapons were listed by Col. W. Donovan when he spoke with Gen. Simović on 24 January, never got any consideration at all.   Whatever US help was available, it was scheduled for Great Britain. The President sent to Yugoslavia *his most earnest hope ...* not the weapons.

On this subject military historian Professor Robin Higham wrote:

> ... the infamous German attack on Belgrade had taken place in which a reputed 17,000 died, just as Simović signed a friendship pact with the Soviet Union. ... Across the world in Washington the Yugoslav military attaché asked the American government for 100 bombers, 100 fighters, 500 reconnaissance planes, 100 medium tanks, 2,000 trucks, 1,500,000 gas masks and helmets and a large number of antitank and antiaircraft guns. As the administrator of the new Lend-Lease program put it, it was "utterly impossible to meet these modest demands," but a plan was drawn up the next day to start supplying material out of stock on hand, and by the end of April a few guns, trucks, and gas masks were actually starting to move. But by then the war in the Balkans was over, and these and the supplies which the Greeks had been pressing for more than five months were delivered to the British in the Middle East. (Higham, 213-14)

*****

On the front – "By April 8 it was clear that Yugoslav resistance in the south was breaking down and that the left flank of the Aliakhmon position would shortly be threatened." (Churchill(GA), 224) While the Prime Minister found it necessary to blame weak Yugoslav resistance for the breakdown, the British Joint Planning Staff in Cairo foresaw it before the military operations started, and concluded: "The more we examined the problem, the more unsound the venture appeared." (de Guingand, 44) **(Part One, p. 54)**

*****

> Tuesday morning we watched the British and Greek diplomats pack all of their cases and documents and their short-wave radio sets and their personal luggage into their automobiles and make off. They did it in the stage-whispered manner. They were so obvious with their secrecy that before they ever started out of town all of Vranyska Banya knew they were going. (St. John, 82)

- **Wednesday, 9 April – Niš and Monastir (Bitolj) fell; the Germans in Salonika**

2nd Panzer Division elements captured Salonika at 4 a.m.; Greek Second Army capitulated.
German troops captured Niš and Bitolj (Monastir) in Yugoslavia.

*****

In London – On 9 April Prime Minister Churchill reviewed the war before the House of Commons, and *The New York Times* published the review the next day. Here are excerpts related to Yugoslavia:

> From the beginning of December the movement of German forces through Hungary and through Rumania toward Bulgaria became apparent to all. More than two months ago, by the traitorous connivance of the Bulgarian King and government, advance parties of the German air force in plain clothes gradually took possession of Bulgarian air fields. German troops then began to pour into Bulgaria in very large numbers. One of their objectives was plainly Salonika, which I may mention they entered at 4 o'clock this morning.
>
> *It has never been our policy nor our interest to see the war carried into the Balkan Peninsula. ...*
>
> ... early in March we made a military agreement with the Greeks, and considerable movement of British and Imperial troops and supplies began. ...
>
> I ... turn to the story of Yugoslavia. This valiant steadfast people, ... , made every endeavor to placate the Nazi monster. If they had made common cause with the Greeks when the Greeks hurled back the Italian invaders, the complete destruction of the Italian armies in Albania could have been certainly and swiftly achieved long before the German forces could have reached the theatre of war.
>
> ... From a few handfuls of tourists admiring the beauties of the Bulgarian landscape in the wintry weather, the German forces grew to seven, twelve, twenty and finally to twenty-five divisions. Presently the weak and unfortunate Prince [Paul of Yugoslavia] and afterward his Ministers were summoned, like others before them, to Hitler's footstool and pact was signed which would give Germany *complete control not over the body but over the soul of the Yugoslav nation*.
> (http://www.ibiblio.org/pha/policy/1941/410409a.html   3/20/04. Italics added.)

It has never been British policy to carry war into the Balkans – said the Prime Minister when the German troops were already in Salonika. But only ten days earlier - before Germany's merciless attack on Yugoslavia and Greece - he was explaining to A.W. Fadden, the Acting Prime Minister of Australia, that the expedition to Greece was not an isolated military act, but a prime mover in a large design. (Churchill(GA), 171)

Whatever he meant on 30 March 1941 with the statement that Germany did not have *complete control over the body* of Yugoslavia, at the end of the war the Prime Minister did not care any more about *the body and the soul of the Yugoslav nation* – as seen from his conversation with Fitzroy Maclean: neither he nor Maclean were going to live in Yugoslavia, so ...
*****
In Sevojno – According to records, on 9 April the Yugoslav Government held two sessions at Sevojno: the first one at 9 a.m., and the second later on.
   Complying with the letter Premier Simović had sent to the Foreign Minister Ninčić, at the first session the Ministers approved a credit of 5 million dinars ($100,000) for a political action in Albania.
   The second session, presided over by Miša Trifunović, dealt with the evacuated administrative personnel, their employments and payments. (Miletić(ed), 521)

- **Thursday, 10 April - German troops in Zagreb;**

(U) Independent State of Croatia proclaimed

German Second Army entered Zagreb. Over the Zagreb radio station, in the name of Ante Pavelić, Slavko Kvaternik proclaimed the formation of the Independent State of Croatia (ISC).

Were the coup-wishers / executors aware of that event the same day or a day-or-two later, and what were their reactions? Did they see a cause-and-affect relation between the coup of 27 March and the formation of the ISC on 10 April 1941? What did they write later about this subject?

*****

Greek East Macedonian Army surrendered.

> By 10 April AI [Air Intelligence] estimated that 900 German aircraft were in the Balkans – that an additional 500 had arrived. In fact the number was something short of 1,000 by that date, and the Enigma and the low-grade GAF ciphers had shown that the reinforcements had been brought in from north-west Europe, Sicily and North Africa. (Hinsley *et al*, 371)

This AI estimate was not news for Eden and the British Commanders in the Middle East. Before the Tatoi Conference with the Greeks, on 21 February, Eden had entered in his diary:

> Gravest anxiety is not in respect to army but to air. There is no doubt that need to fight a German air force, instead of Italian, is creating new problem for [Air Vice-Marshal Sir Arthur] Longmore. ... We should all have liked to approach Greeks tomorrow with a suggestion that we should join with them in holding a line to defend Salonika, but both Longmore and [Admiral Sir Andrew] Cunningham are convinced that our present air resources will not allow us to do this. (Eden, 196)

> Our air force in Greece in March numbered only seven squadrons (eighty operational aircraft), ... Although some small reinforcements were sent in April, the R.A..F. were overwhelmingly outnumbered by the enemy. ... They were matched against a German air strength of over eight hundred operational aircraft. (Churchill(GA), 221) **(Part One, p. 73)**

However, while only too well aware superiority of the German air force, the British had made commitment to send an under-equipped, numerically inferior Expeditionary Force to Greece. To bolster its strength, it became necessary to "draw Yugoslavia in" - especially after the Turks had refused to become enmeshed in a Balkan Front.

*****

> Campbell in his car ... was up near the head of the parade out of Užice that morning, and there were a lot of diplomats not far behind him. Then came refugees of various nationalities, and hundreds of government cars and then the army. ... This was an army in rout. ... This was different from the flight from Belgrade, ... (St. John, 93)

- **Friday, 11 April – From Sevojno to Pale; the Germans in Osijek**

"The Hungarians started their operations between the Danube and the Tisa ... and moved forward without opposition." (Jukić, 72) The Italians began their offensive. (Krizman1, 402)

German units reached the Osijek region. (Blau, 52) They took Kragujevac and Markovac in Serbia, and Vršac and Zrenjanin in Vojvodina. (Krizman1, 402)

Simović ordered that the bridges over the Sava and Danube rivers in Belgrade be blown up. (Ristić, 129)

The Government moved from Sevojno to Pale, near Sarajevo, and held a session at 5 p.m. All Ministers were present, except Simović.

The Presiding Minister, Miša Trifunović, greeted the arrival of Juraj Krnjević and his joining the Government in place of Maček. Additional changes in the government's composition were stated and approved: Miha Krek replaced the late Minister Kulovec, Snoj replaced Krek as Minister without portfolio, and Smoljan took over the Ministry of trade, vacated by Ivan Andres.

Gen. Ilić reported about the military situation at the fronts.

Šutej informed the colleagues that Maček had remained at his home in Kupinec to share the fate of his people, but he would never disavow his comrades.

The Ministers acknowledged that, with this act, Maček was making greatest personal sacrifice for his people.

The Finance Minister reported about his activities.

Foreign Minister Ninčić informed about his talks with the British and his appeals to Roosevelt and Stalin.

The Ministers then approved several decisions, including the selection of the Sarajevo's newspaper *Narodno jedinstvo (People's unity)* as the Government's official gazette, and the invitation to Gen. Simović to come to Pale. (Miletić(ed), 564-5)

According to the minutes of this meeting - referred to above - the Ministers said nothing about the formation of the ISC.

*****

According to Živan Knežević: Although busy with war and Government business, Simović found time to call **him** in to tell him **"otprilike"** (more or less in so many words) this:

> ((We lost the war much faster than we had hoped. … the main German blow came from Bulgaria with sufficiently strong auxiliary blows from Rumania, Hungary and Austria. Without mobilized forces it was hard to offer any resistance at the border. Then came 'the treachery of the Croats' and the decline of the entire northern front. … German columns have passed over the undamaged bridges on the Sava River at Zagreb and are pushing today toward Banja Luka … The defense is completely compromised. And there is no more any chance for some serious resistance.)) (Milunović(ed), 56)

Simović intended to take the king out of the country, via the Bay of Kotor or Nikšić. (Milunović(ed), 56)

So, according to Živan, only five days after the German attack it was clear to Simović that further resistance was collapsing – yet the Prime Minister, reportedly, informed Živan about it, but not the Government.

*****

> In Sarajevo that Friday afternoon [11 April] we got reports that Skoplje had fallen. … A little later I got it fairly straight that not only had Skoplje been taken, but that the Italians in Albania and the Germans who had come through that mountain pass from Bulgaria had met. That meant the corridor from Yugoslavia south into Greece was cut off now. That meant poor Yugoslavia was now hemmed in on three sides. The necklace of steel was tightening. It also meant that he British with their three hundred thousand troops and the Greeks with all the help they were going to send to the Serbs were cut off from their new ally. And it meant that all these thousands of people in Sarajevo had only one way out now. The Adriatic! (St. John, 109)

(U) Pavelić agrees to hand Dalmatia over to Italy

On 11 April Pavelić went from Florence to Rome, first to *Palazzo Chigi* (the Foreign Ministry), then to see Mussolini in *Palazzo Venezia,* and then returned to *Chigi* at 11 a.m.

Anfuso was present at the Mussolini – Pavelić meeting and later wrote about it:

> ((Mussolini concluded the conversation saying that he did not see any reason for Pavelić not to go to Croatia. Then, again true to his principle to conclude a conversation with a certain result, toward the end of the audience he explained that – as soon as the *Poglanik* came to Zagreb - the Italian Government would begin negotiations about the agreement *inspired with this conversation* – namely, that "the Dalmatian cities with prominent Italian i.e. Venetian character come under the Italian sovereignty".)) (Krizman1, 399. Italics added.)

Mussolini approved Pavelić's request to allow his followers in Italy to join him. (Krizman1, 400)

From Rome, Pavelić sent a telegram to Hitler expressing to him gratitude and fidelity for the entry of German troops into Croatia, emphasizing that the ISC will tie "its future with the new European order" created by Hitler and Mussolini. (Jelić-Butić, 83)

After an audience with Mussolini, Pavelić and some 250 Ustaša began their trip to Croatia. (Jelić-Butić, 81) He arrived in Trieste, by train, at 11 p.m., where the Italians organized a formal welcome. (Krizman1, 400)

"The treachery of the Croats"

IF the conversation between Gen. Simović and Major Knežević indeed took place as Živan reported, then questions arise: Did Simović expect treachery before he had consented to the Putsch? Was such a treachery foreseeable? To help answer these questions one ought to go back to 24 March 1941, and the conference of the highest-ranking Commandants of the Belgrade Garrison with the Minister of the Army, Gen. Petar Pešić. Simović asked for the conference and attended it. **(Chapter 11)**

After explaining the terms of the Tripartite Pact to be signed the next day, The Minister continued:

((You see, *our army is not homogeneous,* as that one of the 1912 – 1918 years. *You know what the Croats are thinking and doing.* A few days ago I asked some authoritative Croatian gentlemen what they were thinking about the behavior of the Croats in the case of war with Germany and they answered: that depends on many facts, but in general – *it could be positive* under advantageous circumstances of the development of battles on her [Croatia's] frontiers, but under other circumstances, *especially at the withdrawal of the army, nothing can be guaranteed. ...*))

"Vidite, *naša vojska nije homogena,* kao ona od 1912 – 1918. g. *Vi znate šta Hrvati misle i rade.* Pre neki dan upitah neku merodavnu hrvatsku gospodu šta misle o državnju Hrvata za slučaj rata sa Nemačkom, pa mi odgvoriše: da to zavisi od mnogih činjenica, ali u glavnom – *može biti pozitivno* pod povoljnim okolnostima razvoja borbi na granicama njenim, ali pod drugim situacijama, *naročito pri povlačenju vojske, ne može se ništa garantovati. ...* Eto tako rekoše ti merodavni. (Pandurović, 7. Italics added.)

So, Simović knew what the Croats were thinking and doing, and he heard forewarnings of their possible behavior.

By the time of his reported conversation with Major Knežević, no battles were fought at Croatia's frontiers, and army's withdrawals were taking places. So were the foreseen consequences – "the treachery of the Croats": i. e., the desertion of many officers and units., sometimes in an ugly manner, and some switches to the other side.

Like Simović, the troops on the field - including the Croats - knew that the war was lost. So most of the Croats preferred to go home rather than to continue staying in the army and retreating farther away from home.

Minister Pešić did not identify the Croats with whom he had talked. **(##)** Their principal representative in the Government and the country was Vladko Maček, the Vice Premier and the president of the Croatian Peasant Party (CPP).

At the last peacetime session of the Yugoslav Government, held in Belgrade on 5 April 1941, he explained his reasons for favoring the adherence to the Tripartite Pact. After the war, Professor Slobodan Jovanović summarized Maček's views in his *Zapisi*. **(Chapter 17.)**

In addition to the reasons given at that session, Maček *may have had additional reasons:* the situation in his own Party. Composed of very large membership, the CPP was not disciplined and tightly controlled as were the Communist Party and the Ustaše, and ideologically homogeneous as the other two. As a consequence, some members of the CPP were influenced by the other two groups and felt not obligated to strictly implement Maček's orders as the adherents of the other two groups were to their leaders. It is very hard to assume that Maček was not conscious of these facts.

(This non-monolithic state of the CPP became evident in the course of the war. While Maček was temporarily imprisoned by the Ustaše in Jasenovac concentration camp, one group of the CPP representatives joined Pavelić's Ustaše regime, and another Tito's Partisans. At the end of the war, Maček preferred to go into exile rather than to live in a Communist-ruled Yugoslavia.)

Now back to Minister Pešić: he took the forewarnings of his Croatian interlocutors seriously; Simović did not – although aware of potentially undesired consequences, such as "the treachery" of the Croats. That "treachery" was not the cause of the collapse of the Yugoslav forces. There was no "treachery" in the southern part of the country, and the German troops were moving very fast through it anyway, reaching Salonika within three days. Simović – like all coup-wishers – was very conscious of the German military overwhelming superiority, but he still wanted to take the country to the war on Britain's side, because *Britain loses all battles except the last one.*

(##) While Minister Pešić specified neither the date nor the names of his interlocutors, he attended a meeting at which Maček was present. At 10:00 a.m. on 6 March - two days after Prince Paul's meeting with Hitler - the crown council meeting at the White Palace in Dedinje, was attended by the Prince, regents Radenko Stanković and Ivan Perović, Premier Cvetković, Vice-Premier Maček, Minister Kulovec, Foreign Minister Cincar-Marković, Minister of War General Petar Pešić, and Royal

Court Minister Milan Antić. After various opinions on the situation were heard, Maček asked Gen. Pešić for an estimate of Yugoslavia's prospects in case of war. The General calmly replied that:

    Germany would soon be in possession of the entire northern part of Yugoslavia, the plains of the Danube and the Sava, including three main cities – Ljubljana, Zagreb and Belgrade;

    withdrawn into the mountains of Bosnia-Hercegovina, the army could resist about six weeks; after that time, there would be no ammunition and no food;

    for over two years, Germany controlled the Czechoslovakia's Skoda Works, once Yugoslavia's source of arms;

    the British had said that they were not in a position to give Yugoslavia any substantial military help;

    without munitions, the army could do nothing but capitulate. (Hoptner, 219-20)

(C) "Disorganize the resistance of the Yugoslav Army"

Whether in parallel or in common with "the treachery of the Croats", there was another well planned action concentrated simultaneously on weakening the Yugoslav armed forces: it was ordered by Josip Broz Tito, the Secretary General of the Communist Party of Yugoslavia (CPY). In the wake of the Putsch of 27 March, Tito issued secret directives to the Party members – presented in **Chapter 22**. One directive was:

> ... disorganise the resistance of the Yugoslav Army by creating confusion amongst officers and men so that the defeat appears to be the result of the incompetence of the officers' corps whose authority will be destroyed once and for all; ... (Clissold, 27)

Like "the treachery", this action by itself did not cause the defeat of the Yugoslav Army, but it confirmed once again the fact of mutual support among the elements who wanted the disintegration of Yugoslavia. Their informal cooperation was well known in the country, but those willing to expose the country to the war were not stopped by considering possible consequences.

- **Saturday, 12 April – Conference in Pale; the King to Foča, Nikšić; German platoon enters Belgrade**

At 2:30 a.m. the Germans entered Sremska Mitrovica. (Blau, 52)
    "The Italians crossed the Yugoslav frontier ... at Rijeka and advanced without firing a shot" (Jukić, 72)
....through the territory of the German-and-Italian-sponsored Independent State of Croatia.
    The King left at 12:30 p.m. for Foča and on for Nikšić. (Milunović(ed), 58)

> Belgrade fell at five o'clock the afternoon of April 12th to an enterprising 1st Lieutenant Klingberg and an SS infantry platoon. About two hours later the mayor officially handed his city over to Klingberg and to a representative of the German foreign office ... (Hoptner, 288)

> I had seen signs of a general disintegration [on 12 April]. A train full of air force technicians had been standing on the same spot on the Pale-Sarajevo line for three days. The men had received no food and were threatening to go out looting. Warned by the inhabitants of this danger, we explained the situation to the military authorities, but nothing had been done about it by the time we left. One of the officers, a friend of mine, told me that the men in his battalion had been unable to get any equipment, even rifles. (Jukić, 71)

According to Živan Knežević, at midnight of 12 April he arrived in Sarajevo with instructions from his brother Radoje, now the Minister of the Court, to the Court's administrator regarding where to go with the King's possessions. Živan went on to Pale and at 4 a.m. of the 13th April arrived into the building where Simović was staying. (Milunović(ed), 58-9)

*****

> ... the [Government] council convened in Pale on April 12th for a meeting that lasted all day. General Simović, invited the day before, was not present. The ministers continued with the business of

government, ordering that the penal institutions release all prisoners sentenced under provisions of the law on the protection of the state except those convicted of espionage or treason, ... (Hoptner, 289)

In the evening, Simović arrived from Koviljača to Pale, (Ristić, 129) to join the Government.

On Saturday, April 12, 1941, in its column "The International Situation" *The New York Times* reported:

> Fascist quarters in Rome intimated that Italy would claim the region of Kossovo, north of Albania and with an approximated 1,000,000 Albanian residents, if and when Yugoslavia would be divided among the Axis powers.

- **Sunday, 13 April – Situation very difficult but not hopeless**

Military resistance ended in western Bosnia and Dalmatia. German troops crossed the Una river, took Kostajnica and Bihać, and the Italians entered Gospić and Benkovac. (Krizman1, 417)

*****

On 13 April the Government convened into the plenary session which turned out to be the last one the Government held on the territory of Yugoslavia. The original minutes of the meeting were not preserved, and several versions of the session exist. (Miletić(ed), 768n2) Because of momentous decision made at the session, here are related three versions of the proceeding:

1. The Second Vice Premier, Slobodan Jovanović, who attended the session, wrote about it a few years later (translated):

((The Ministerial session at Pale was held exactly on the Catholic Easter [13 April]. Simović reported on the military situation, which he presented as very difficult, but not as hopeless. He spoke about continuing the fight on a new Sava-Drava [rivers] front. When somebody called his attention to the German penetration at Banja Luka, he was assuring that a further advance of the enemy on that site can be halted. However, for enhanced security he was proposing that the Government move immediately to Nikšić [in Montenegro]. He stated that it would be better that in the future he does not separate himself from the Government (until then he was with the Supreme Command as the Chief of its Staff, and not with the Government). Because of that he had decided to propose that General Danilo Kalafatović take over his post as the Chief of Staff of the Supreme Command. *At that session there was no mention at all about the possibility of capitulation,* although the members of the Government considered the situation to be much more serious than Simović had been presenting it.)) (Jovanović, 13. Italics added,)

*****

On the issue of *the capitulation,* former Assistant Foreign Minister wrote:

> *The government had never deliberated the question of a surrender, and no formal decision on it had been made.* It was the Premier's personal decision, made in agreement with his closest associates. He was in such a hurry to get everything done that he even forgot to issue orders for the navy to put to sea. Slobodan Jovanović told me that the generals of the high command had openly demanded the removal of the Premier and the accession of someone who could arrange a more favorable armistice with Germany and Italy. Ninčić had been considered as a possible replacement. (Jukić, 71-2. Italics added.)

2. Capt. Dragiša Ristić, Simović's adjutant, wrote the following about the session, a quarter of a century later:

> On the morning of April 13, the government met again, and the prime minister, who had arrived in Pale the previous evening, expressed the belief that the military situation was serious but not desperate. ... Now, with the consent of the prime minister, War Minister Ilić proposed that General Danilo Kalafatović be appointed chief of the high command, but that he should take over his new position only when the prime minister indicated the appropriate moment. The cabinet accepted and empowered General Simović to issue further orders. (Ristić, 129)

3. Translated excerpts of the version written in Colonel Miletić's collection of documents of 1987:

((*General Ilić* thinks it necessary for the Government to leave for Nikšić already early the next morning.

((*The President of the Government Simović* presents a military report. ... The Germans had connected with the Italians at Struga, and are advancing towards Lerin, and our four divisions had connected with the Greeks. There is no contact with them. He is outlining the events on the North and in Croatia. The Germans had crossed the Sava river near Šabac. At many spots the bridges are not destroyed. The enemy advances towards Banja Luka. He considers that the situation, although difficult, is not critical, and that the front would stabilize, if not on the Sava, then on the Vrbas, Una and lower Drina rivers. As the President of the Government, he had nominated General Kalafatović as the Chief of the General Staff. As far as he knows, the situation in the Navy is fine.

((*Dr. Ninčić* thinks that it is necessary for the Government to go to Nikšić, so – if need be – could leave the country with the King. ...

((*The President of the Government General Simović and the Minister of the Army General Ilić* consider it necessary for the Government to move to Nikšić in order to be with the King in any case.

((It is resolved to start moving [for Nikšić] on 14 April, at the latest by 7:30 a.m. ... The Minister of the Army will leave the last ...)) (Miletić(ed), 768n2. Cursive in the source.)

*****

According to this version, *during this session* Simović informed the Ministers about Kalafatović's new nomination.

Hoptner described the occurrence differently. On the basis of information he obtained from Minister Krek, Hoptner wrote:

> Shortly after the cabinet meeting, he [Simović] saw the king and resigned as chief of general staff in favor of General Kalafatović. On the 13th, in his capacity as commander-in-chief of the Yugoslav army, and on behalf of the king, he told Kalafatović to arrange a truce with the Germans. (Hoptner, 289, 289n68)

According to Col. Miletić, Simović informed Kalafatović on the 14th of April, in a top secret letter, about the decisions the Ministers had taken at the session on the 13th (as is shown below, for the 14th of April). While Simović's order was written on the 14th, that does not exclude a possibility of Simović's informing Kalafatović verbally on the 13th. In any case, Ristić clarified a point: Simović – as a leader of the Putschist Government – could hardly expect to secure the best armistice terms. "He therefore issued a written order to Kalafatović on 14 April." (Ristić, 129)

*****

Another account of Simović's activity in Pale on 13 April 1941 was provided by Živan Knežević, more than forty years later:

Having spent a part of the preceding night in the same building where Simović resided, in the morning of 13 April [i.e., **before** the Government's session] he talked with Simović. The General gave him a detailed account of the German and Hungarian operations against Serbia, identifying all divisions and armored units which participated in the operations, and the areas of their operations.

Simović then proceeded to inform Živan how Belgrade fell and to which German units, and how a German armored division could have been held in front of Banjaluka. If it were not for a total disintegration in Croatia and Slovenia, one could still think of some resistance at the Sava—Drina rivers. Resistance in Bosnia and Herzegovina could not be long and successful, because all stores of food and ammunitions were already in the hands of the Germans. "He considered the situation hopeless." He intended to move the Government to Nikšić and farther on, according to the situation. He would hand the Supreme Command over to General Kalafatović, so he could remain only the President of the Government. (Milunović(ed), 59)

Then Živan continued:

> ((On that day, 13 April, he [Simović] did not tell me anything about "seeking the armistice", nor about his further intentions. ... Not a word about the Government leaving the country. But he still added that my two companies (the 2nd and the 4th) were taken off the train in Mostar by the Commandant of the Primorska army and were used in the fight against the revolt by the Croats around Mostar. ... He had also mentioned attempts to bring British fleet into the Adriatic in order to pull out the King and some troops, but everything without success.)) (Milunović(ed), 59)

Živan's account is questionable for the following reasons:

Simović did not have continuous communications with all his own units and was not aware of their own situations and whereabouts – but reportedly he knew all details about the enemies' units and their operations;

even **IF** Simović knew all those details he reportedly described to Živan, why would he – the highest civilian and military leader – have a need or reason to use so much of his time to inform a **Major** – who had no special assignment or involvement in the business of the Government or the Military – on a busy day, before meeting his Ministers, when so important decisions were to be made?

Identity of the German units, mentioned by Živan, and details of their operations, were described in various sources **after the war**. Given Živan's admitted deceptions **(Chapter 14)**, one can not exclude a possibility of Živan's finding those details after the war but ascribing them to Simović.

*****

Now back to the activities of the Government on 13 April.

After the Government's plenary session, in conference with the Foreign Minister Ninčić and Generals B. Ilić and B. Mirković, at 4:00 p.m. Simović ordered Capt. Ristić "to make preparations for evacuating the King." At that time the King was staying in the Ostrog monastery, near Nikšić. (Ristić, 132)

Discrepancies about the discussion of the armistice notwithstanding, it seems that the decision for it was really made on 13 April.

*****

By this time [Sunday, 13 April] I don't think the Yugoslavs had a single fighter plane left. All through that short war we never saw a real battle in the air between German and opposition planes. And we never saw a single British plane anywhere in all of Yugoslavia. Or a single British soldier either. Little Yugoslavia was taking it on the chin, all alone. (St. John, 140)

Churchill's greetings to the people of Yugoslavia

While Yugoslavia's army was collapsing and far-reaching decisions were being made in Pale, the same day Prime Minister Churchill sent from London his greetings "to the people of Yugoslavia, to the Serbs, the Croats and the Slovenes" :

You have been wantonly attacked by a ruthless and barbarous aggressor. Your capital has been bombed, your women and children brutally murdered. ... Do not regret the staunch courage which has brought on you this furious onslaught. Your courage will shine out in the pages of history and will, too, reap a more immediate reward. Whatever you may lose in the present you have saved the future.

You are making a heroic resistance against formidable odds and in doing so you are proving true to your great traditions. Serbs, we know you. You were our allies in the last war and your armies are covered with glory. Croats and Slovenes, we know your military history. For centuries you were the bulwark of Christianity. Your fame as warriors spread far and wide on the Continent. One of the finest incidents in the history of Croatia is the one when, in the 16th century, long before the French Revolution, the peasants rose to defend the rights of man, and fought for those principles which centuries later gave the world democracy.

Yugoslavs, you are fighting for those principles today. The British Empire is fighting with you, and behind us is the great democracy of the U.S.A., with its vast and ever-increasing resources. However hard the fight, our victory is assured.
(http://www.ibiblio.org/pha/policy/1941/410413c.html   3/20/04)

Just three weeks earlier, the Prime Minister instructed his Foreign Minister to draw Yugoslavia into the war. In his "Iron Curtain" speech on 5 March 1946, Sir Winston regretted that - after the "assured victory" - the capital of these "heroic resisters", including Belgrade - ended up behind the Iron Curtain.

Churchill: "... Yugoslavs have given us no chance to help them"

Also on 13 April 1941, Churchill telegraphed to Campbell, who was expected to be with the Yugoslav Government and/or High Command, but was actually in Vrnjačka Banja:

> It will not be possible at any time to send British surface warships, or British or American merchant ships or transports, up the Adriatic north of Valona. The reason for this is the air, ... The ships would be sunk, ... All the aircraft we can allot to the Yugoslav theatre is already at the service of the Yugoslav General Staff through Air Marshal D'Albianc. There are no more at present. *You must remember Yugoslavs have given us no chance to help them and refused to make a common plan, ... and you must use your own judgment how much of this bad news you impart to them.* (Churchill(GA), 223)

The Yugoslavs gave the British no chance to help them? How strange a statement. **Part One** provides evidence to the contrary: when the Yugoslavs asked for help, or inquired about, the British could not provided it. Here are some examples:

- On a visit to London in May 1940, Prince Paul's wife, Princess Olga, asked Lord Halifax, then the Foreign Minister, what would Britain do if Italy attacked Yugoslavia. He told her that "We should naturally wish to do anything in our power to help but ... we must recognize that if Italians, as .... was likely, mined the entrance of the Adriatic, the navy would presumably not be able to do too much". When she asked about the Yugoslav order for aircraft, the answer came that the British were throwing everything they could into the Western battle, and that it was very difficult to spare military aircraft which the British needed for themselves. (Barker, 78; 280n2)

    In May 1940, a Yugoslav Military Mission left London empty-handed because the British could not deliver supplies requested by Yugoslavia. (**Part One, p. 36**)

- On 23 November 1940, Campbell, British Minister in Belgrade, urged London to issue a formal communication that would strengthen the hands of Prince Paul and other staunch elements. The prime Minister's response was, *inter alia,* "... If we cannot promise any effective material aid, we can at any rate assure them that, just as we did last time, we will see their wrongs are righted in the eventual victory." (Barker, 81) The Chiefs of Staff said, 'it is not possible for us to assist Yugoslavia with land forces.' (Barker, 81) (**Part One, pages 46-7**)

In March 1941, Prince Paul sent Major Milisav Perišić to Athens, to find out what help he could expect.

> The Major was mainly interested in finding out what help the Yugoslav armed forces could get in withdrawing either through Greece to the Aegean (that is, Salonika or Kavalla) or westward to the Adriatic so that they could if necessary be evacuated from Adriatic ports. (Barker, 89)

On the questions of withdrawals, the British answered that "the naval problem was difficult"; running naval convoys up and down the Adriatic would be "onerous", although they would of course do their best if "our Allies were cut off in that sea". (Barker, 89) (**Part One, pages 96-7**) *"Doing their best"* - but omitting specifics – was very frequently used phrase in 1941 when the British could not help much.

- On 17 March, Campbell suggested that "some fairly strong reassurance on the prospect of support and supply by the Navy in the Adriatic is of great importance ... to satisfy military authorities and Croats." (Barker, 89; 282n73) (**Part One, p.104**)

On 24 March Campbell suggested to Eden what should be done to sway the Yugoslav military leaders to support the coup. *Inter alia* he wrote:

> We are however convinced that in order to secure adhesion of such leaders to the idea, the possibility of offering military supplies is necessary so they could feel that if a firm attitude to Germany produced war they would be prepared with more adequate equipment in their hands. The mere promise of a share in the common pool is far too vague and would get us nowhere. The offer would also give us something with which to approach potential leaders directly. (PRO, PREMIER 3, 570/11. Italics added.) (**Part One, pages 121-22**)

On 25 March Eden informed Campbell that it would be impossible to transfer British military equipment form Greece to Yugoslavia, and added: "Furthermore *there is no other source from which we can at present supply equipment of this nature, …* " (Eden, 227-8. Italics added.) (**Part One, 124**)

*****

Clearly, the Prime Minister's statement that *the Yugoslavs have given the British no chance to help them* is misleading. The Yugoslavs *refused to make a common plan* with the British because in the meetings with the British military in March and early April they realized that the British could not help them.

As it happened, however, some military and civilian *oppositionists* wanted to make a common plan with the British, even without British military support … and they indeed did it … regardless of the consequences for the people and state of Yugoslavia: hoping to share the fruits of victory at the end of the war. It turned out that their hopes were illusory.

On 13 April Churchill himself informed Campbell: "It will not be possible at any time to send British surface warships, or British or American merchant ships or transports, up the Adriatic north of Valona. The reason for this is the air, … The ships would be sunk, …"

Churchill's *"You must…"* to Campbell was an order that the Minister had to obey. However, by that day it was clear that the British expedition in Greece was a failure because the whole idea of a Balkan Front in early 1941 had been unrealistic, *"wishfully minded",* as General John Kennedy described it. That was not easy for the Prime Minister to swallow. It was easier to blame the Yugoslavs. But, millions did read his history books and – not knowing the details mentioned above – they had to believe the Prime Minister that the Yugoslavs indeed did not want Britain's help …

… and you [Minister Campbell] must use your own judgment how much of this bad news you impart to them [the Yugoslavs]. (Churchill(GA), 223) That was no problem for the Minister: the Yugoslav Government and General Staff were themselves fully aware of *bad news* all over.

*****

(U)   In the meantime, after leaving Trieste at 10 p.m. on the 12th, Pavelić and his group crossed the bridge on the Rječina, in Sušak, at 2:10 a.m. on the 13th of April. The streets of Sušak were totally empty. (Krizman1, 403)

They arrived in Delnice at 7 a.m. In Duga Resa Pavelić was asked to get into an automobile driven by a German officer; they arrived in Karlovac after 8 p.m. (Krizman1, 404)

(U) Pavelić to S. Kvaternik - disinformation: no commitments to Italy

Slavko Kvaternik, who three days earlier had proclaimed the formation of the ISC in the name of Pavelić, had a private talk with him, and later stated about that conversation:

> ((Appealing for his straight word of honor, I asked him whether he had any personal or political commitments towards Italy, pleading for his sincere answer, … Pavelić extended his hand to me and said that I can believe him, that he had no personal or political commitments whatsoever, and that nothing had been asked of him. … Pavelić later gave the same answer to Dr. [Edmund] Veesenmayer [a representative of the German Foreign Minister].)) (Krizman1, 405)

Pavelić also told Veesenmeyer that Croatia had been Germany's ally in the First World War, that the Croats were not of the Slavic, but of the Gothic descent, and that the Ustaša government would cooperate most loyally with the Third *Reich.* (Krizman1, 405)

- **Monday, 14 April** – **Gen. Kalafatović in Pale; the King flown to Greece; the Government in Nikšić**

As Živan Knežević recorded it : About 7:15 a.m. on 14 April he went to Simović to get informed about the situation, and found the General cool and collected.

> ((He tells me almost whispering that everything is lost and that the German forces are advancing from Serbia towards Bosnia and that Užice and Loznica are in their hands. They are crossing the Sava from the north towards Tuzla and Sarajevo. … Everything is disintegrating after the decline of the northern

front due to "the treachery of the Croats". One cannot talk about any resistance whatsoever on the Drina and Sava, and even less about some resistance in the karst, where there is no ammunitions, no food, not even enough water. He had invited General Danilo Kalafatović to Pale to hand over to him the Supreme Command and to issue the instructions to seek "armistice", because every further resistance is impossible and futile. He hoped Kalafatović would be here in the afternoon, but he will be here already at 9 a.m.. He [Simović] will go with the Government to Nikšić and asked me to come there too, so we could leave the country by planes and "continue the fight against the Germans alongside our Allies".))
(Milunović(ed), 59-60)

*****

(A) Kalafatović arrived in Pale around 9 a.m.. In capacity of the President of the Ministerial Council, Simović informed him that – by the King's decree – he was appointed the Chief of Staff of the Supreme Command, and that he should assume immediately the duty entrusted to him. (Miletić(ed), 668n1) Simović proceeded as follows:

In a top secret letter, officially and personally addressed to Kalafatović, Simović informed him, on 14 April, that the Government, at their plenary session on 13 April, had decided (translated):

1.– ((To undertake all necessary measures for the speediest receiving of the already requested aid from the Allies, specifically: in aviation, armored units, other technical materiel, needs for nutrition and supplies of our troops, and in the arrival of Allied fleet into our waters.

2.- ((To continue the resistance of our army in depth, taking advantage particularly of hardly passable and for a defense suitable mountainous terrain in southern and western Serbia, Bosnia and Herzegovina, and Montenegro. Within that objective, to undertake urgent measures for the arrangement and organization of suitable defensive lines, selected by the Supreme Command.

3.- ((Having in mind the situation in our army after first failures and particularly the delicate situation of our troops due to events in Croatia and Dalmatia, the Royal Government authorizes you to immediately ask for the armistice from the enemy, so one could gain in time and alleviate the situation of the troops.

((The Royal Government will accept your decisions in this sense as their own. Inform the Royal Government the quickest way about your decision and conditions.

((Undertake further measures in accordance with the situation.

((The Royal Government are on their way towards Boka Kotorska and about their where-about will inform you as fast as possible.))

President of the Ministerial Council,
General of the Army.
D.T. Simović

(Miletić(ed), 668 -71)

A note about the ***delicate situation of our troops due to events in Croatia and Dalmatia***, ... which Simović mentioned in his order to Kalafatović:

On 10 April 1941 – while the members of the Simović Government were moving from Užice to Pale – and the German troops were advancing on Zagreb, the Independent State of Croatia was proclaimed over radio Zagreb, under the auspices of Germany and Italy, in the presence of a German high official. In the long run that event turned out to be not only ***delicate***, but tragic. Due to the prolonged terrorist activities of centrifugal political forces in Yugoslavia, especially by the Ustaše under Dr. Ante Pavelić - including the assassination of King Alexander I in 1934 - this was a foreseeable development which the coup-wishers-and-plotters had not factored into their calculation to expose Yugoslavia to war. "We knew what was happening in Croatia" long before the coup. (Kosić(N), 81). They knew, one of the Putschists acknowledged, yet ...

The minutes of their crown council meeting that day [11 April] reflect no awareness that Zagreb had fallen to the Germans; that an independent state of Croatia had been created with Ante Pavelić, murderer of

King Aexander, as its leader, that a *panzer* corps was in forty miles of Belgrade; or that two additional German army corps had crossed the Vardar river. (Hoptner, 286)

*****

Convinced that he himself could hardly secure the best armistice terms, Simović issued a written order to Kalafatović:

His Majesty's Government, at its plenary session of April 13 in Pale, has taken the following decision: ... In view of the situation of our Army after the first setbacks, caused in particular by the events in Croatia and Dalmatia, to empower you to *sue for armistice* from the enemy so that time might be gained and the situation of the Army thereby alleviated. (Ristić, 129-30) Italics added.)

It is not clear whether before or after reading this order,

"General Kalafatović, ... , had suggested that the King remain in the country and set up a new government which would conclude an armistice. General Simović rejected this proposal, but in his order authorized Kalafatović "to make decisions in this respect in the name of the Royal Government" and to advise it immediately of the decisions and the conditions of any armistice. The new chief of the high command could also "take such other measures" as he considered necessary. "His Majesty's Government is on its way to the Bay of Kotor," concluded Simović, "and you wIll be advised as soon as possible of its whereabouts." (Ristić, 130)

An important point should be made here: Professor Slobodan Jovanović wrote that *at that session there was no mention at all about a possibility of* **the capitulation**, while Simović informed Kalafatović that *the Royal Government authorizes you to immediately ask for* **the armistice** *from the enemy.*
What Kalafatović asked for, and what he had been forced to accept, is shown below.

*****

(A) To implement Simović's order, Kalafatović immediately called for a conference with three high-ranking members of the Staff of the Supreme Command. At 9:30 a.m., on 14 April, they signed the following document (translated):

((Because of failure on all fronts, because of complete disintegration of our army in Croatia, Dalmatia and Slovenia, and as well as because we came to the conclusion – after thorough study of our political and military situation – that every further military resistance is impossible and could lead to unnecessary blood-letting without any chance of a success and, on the other side, as this war is not a desire either of our people or of their military chiefs, therefore – regardless of the last sentence in item 3, but on the basis of item 4 of this order-authorization – we decided the following:

1. ((To request immediately, while our whole territory is not occupied, the cessation of the enmity with the German and Italian troops;
2. ((To undertake everything necessary for the conclusion of an honorable armistice with the German and Italian troops in order to alleviate all consequences of this unwanted war for the army and the people;
3. ((Within this goal, to immediately issue necessary orders and to undertake necessary measures.))

The Chief of Staff of the Supreme Command,
Army General,
Dan. S. Kalafatović

The Assistant of the Chief of Staff of the Supreme Command,
Division General,
Mil. P. Nikolić

The Chief of the Operative Department
of the Staff of the Supreme Command,
Division General,
Radivoje V. Janković

The Chief of the Operative section of the

Operative Department of the Staff of the Supreme Command,
General Staff Lt.-Colonel,
Branko N. Popović

Note: Item 4, mentioned above, probably refers to the Simović's sentence: ((The Royal Government will accept your decisions ...))

(Miletić(ed), 671-72)

*****

Generals Milutin P. Nikolić and Radivoje V. Janković, and Lt. Colonel Branko Popović, were sincere when they stated that the people and their military chiefs did not desire this war: they participated in the very secret conference with the British General Sir John Dill in Belgrade, on 31 March and 1 April 1941, and knew well that Britain, at that time, could not provide needed support to the Yugoslav military. **(Part One, p. 153)** In his memoirs of the March-1941 events, General Pandurović mentioned the critical views of the Putsch by Gen. Milutin Nikolić. How did he feel now, when he and other coup-critics had "to pick the chestnuts from the fire, ... , the innocent and not guilty ones"? And how did Simović feel? Did he remember conferences of the highest ranking Commanders of the Belgrade garrison he had requested, and attended, on 24 March, described by Gen. Pandurović? He discarded the explanation and warning by Gen. Pešić that day because all along he wanted to actively side with the British, accepting the consequences of the war, whatever they might be. Now, in the position of overwhelming military inferiority, did he really expect the Germans to agree with a proposed *armistice* and not demand an *unconditional capitulation?*

*****

In Nikšić - While fateful events were occurring in Pale, Gen. B. Mirković arrived in Nikšić in the morning of 14 April. He and Ristić drove to Ostrog monastery to take the King out of the country. Radoje Knežević, now the Court Minister, met Ristić at the gate. The King was dressed in a civilian suit. "While not wishing to frighten the boy, I felt obliged to inform him of the risks and asked whether he was prepared to use a parachute if necessary. The King, who had never flown before, replied that if so many had bailed out before, he could do it too. When we arrived at the lower level of the monastery where cars were parked, King Peter went to pay his respect to Patriarch Gavrilo and Bishop Nikolaj [Velimirović] who were quartered nearby." (Ristić, 133)

> "Unwillingly but on the advice of Gavrilo, Patriarch of the Serbian Orthodox Church, Peter and his entourage had flown to Greece." (Hoptner, 290) "Exactly at noon of April 14, our plane took off." "We arrived in Athens about 5 P.M. where high officials representing the Greek government awaited us at the airport." (Ristić, 134, 136)

*****

Back to the events of 14 April.

Yugoslavia's Second and Fifth Armies asked for separate cease-fire agreement. The German Commanders turned their requests down, because only the unconditional surrender of the entire Yugoslav Army could be considered as a basis for negotiations. (Blau, 61)

Government left Pale in the morning of the 14th, arrived in Nikšić during the evening and the morning of the 15th. (Ristić, 130)

> As they [the Ministers] arrived in Nikšić on the 14th and 15th Minister of War General Illić told them that Kalafatović had already concluded the formalities of capitulation. Simović, confirming what Ilić said, added that Kalafatović had acted without authorization either from him or from the king. It was, said Simović, a "capitulation on the field of battle", a military and not a political act. (Hoptner, 289-90)

> "The party of the Croatian ministers and I arrived just before midnight." (Jukić, 71)

About 9 a.m. Živan also left for Nikšić by automobile, and arrived there on 15 April at 5 a.m.. (Milunović(ed), 60)

The first thing the Government heard, late in the night, was that the King had flown off to Greece. (Jovanović, 13)

Simović left Pale at noon on the 14th, arrived in Ostrog at about 1:00 a.m. of the 15th. (Ristić, 130)

*****

(A) Now back to the pursuit of the armistice.

On the basis of Simović's written order, the high command, now at Sarajevo under general Kalafatović, dispatched emissaries to ask for an armistice: Division General Mihailo Bodi, Colonel France Tomše, and Lt. Col. Radmilo Trojanović. (Ristić, 130)

Late on the evening of 14 April, a representative of the Yugoslav Government approached the First Panzer headquarters and asked general von Kleist for an immediate cease-fire. When the [German] Army High Command was advised of this turn of events, it designated the Second Army commander, General von Weichs, to conduct the negotiations in Belgrade. (Blau, 61)

The identity of the Yugoslav representative is not identified in this source.

(U) Pavelić recognizes Italian rights in Dalmatia

Monday, 14 April, was a hectic day for Pavelić. He was still in the city of Karlovac. He and Mussolini's special emissary Anfuso composed a telegram for Mussolini in which Pavelić, in the name of the Croatian government, requested Italy's recognition of the Independent State of Croatia. Written in Italian, the telegram contained the following phrases:

((The Croatian people express their deepest gratitude to the glorious Italian troops for the liberation of Croatia. Croatia will enter into the new European order under the auspices and protection of Fascist Italy. At the determination of the frontiers of the new state, a separate account will be taken concerning Italian rights in Dalmatia.)) (Krizman1, 409)

The German representative Veesenmeyer interfered, so the telegram was not sent to Rome that day. It was given to Mussollini the following morning.

After Anfuso left, in front of the people present in the room, Slavko Kvaternik pleaded with Pavelić: "Tell us, Ante, how do we stand *now*." Pavelić replied: "Nothing had changed from what I have told you yesterday, and in the sign that Croatia will be really independent, I nominate you the military commander of Croatia." (Krizman1, 411)

- **Tuesday, 15 April 1941**

In London, Cadogan wrote in his diary:

Telegram about 6 to say that Yugoslavs have capitulated! Sent it in to A[nthony Eden], who was seeing Greek Minister. A. went over to P.M. [Prime Minister] after. Saw him when he got back and found him quite cheerful, and he said P.M. was the same. Greeks have withdrawn their left wing to keep touch with us. (Dilks(ed), 371)

*****

In Yugoslavia, "...the advance guard of the enemy motorized division entered Sarajevo and captured the Yugoslav High Command." (Ristić, 130)

On the morning of the 15th, Gen. Kalafatović sent his last message to the Minister of War Ilić, then in Nikšić.

On the basis of this [Kalafatović's] last incomplete report and under the pressure of approaching enemy columns, the cabinet decided that the government should leave the country. General Simović was informed of this by Minister of War Ilić at 11: A.M. when the prime minister arrived at Nikšić. In the course of the next two days, the members of the government, the remnant of the Yugoslav air force personnel (approximately two hundred pilots and one hundred airmen), and a part of the Yugoslav navy were evacuated to Greece and Egypt. (Ristić, 131-2)

Prime Minister General Simović, Foreign Minister Ninčić, even General Mirković "had followed their monarch out of the country." Jovanović, Tupanjanin, Grol, [Miša] Trifunović, Ilić – "they all had flown away to Athens." (Hoptner, 290)

" ... we heard that the army's surrender had been decreed, and that in a few hours we would be on our way to Greece by air. We took off at 12:45 and arrived in Greece about 4:00 P.M." (Jukić, 71)

*****

According to Živan Knežević's story:

He arrived in Nikšić at 5 a.m. and went to the airport. At about 9 a.m., Simović came to the airport, talked with Gen. Mirković first, then approached Živan, informed him that the Government was leaving the country immediately and asked him to evacuate with the Government. Živan hesitated and wondered about the other Putschists. Of course, Simović replied, they will leave too; Gen. Mirković will see to it.

Mirković showed Živan a list of persons, written down by Simović himself, who should leave the country: the members of the Government with wives and sons (Đura Ninčić); Simović's Chief of the Cabinet, with wife; Bičanić, Martinović, Boka Vlajić and some more persons. Nowhere the officers who had executed the coup of 27 March, who had remained at Ostrog after the King left. Therefore Živan decided not to leave with the Government, but to see what could be done for those in Ostrog. (Milunović(ed), 60-61)

Živan then described in details his efforts to secure the exit of other fellow officers, and especially of those identified by the Interior Minister Budisavljević as already being on the list of people to be killed by the Germans as soon as captured. (Milunović(ed), 61)

One wonders: Why would **a General** find it necessary to show the list to **a Major** in the midst of hectic activities? How did the new Interior Minister know whom the Germans wanted to kill as soon as captured, even without first interrogating them?

*****

(U) Italy named a civilian Commissar for Dalmatia, assigned to take over the civic administration. (Jelić-Butić, 84)

(U) Pavelić in Zagreb

Escorted by his followers, Pavelić left Karlovac early on 15 April, and arrived in Zagreb at 4 a.m., "unnoticed and covered by the mantle of the night", to start his bloody reign. (Krizman1, 412) No crowds of people were on the streets to welcome him, as the Italians had hoped for.

(U) Precursor of the Treaties of Rome of 18 May 1941

Back in Rome, on 15 April, before noon, Anfuso handed Mussolini the telegram which, recognizing Italian rights, served as a basis for the Treaties of 18 May. According to Anfuso, the stated agreements contained, *inter alia,* the guarantee of Italo-Croatian cooperation, the right of passage of Italian troops in Croatia, military cooperation and commitment of Croatia not to keep a Navy, possession of Dalmatia, the cities Šibenik and Split, and the Dalmatian islands and Bay of Kotor. (Krizman1, 411)

(A) Also, during the afternoon of 15 April "von Weichs and his staff arrived in Belgrade and drew up the German conditions for an armistice based on the unconditional surrender of all Yugoslav forces." (Blau, 61)

(A) • Wednesday, 16 April – Terms of complete capitulation; Simović in Athens

"Not knowing that the high command had already been captured", Bodi and Trojanović arrived in Belgrade at 3:40 a.m. of April 16. (Ristić, 130) Why it took Bodi and Trojanović so long to get to Belgrade?

According to Ristić's information, General Bodi, Colonel Tomše, and Lt.Col. Trojanović "set out [on the way to Belgrade] at midnight of 14/15 April." (Ristić, 130), which is really on the 15th of April. While going to Belgrade, "Colonel Tomše had been mistakenly detained in a Serbian town on suspicion of being a fifth columnist – as a young officer he had served the Dual Monarchy. [Austria Hungary]". Because of that delay, Bodi and Trojanović

> arrived in Belgrade at 3:40 A.M. of April 16. ... There they were taken by the Germans to Rumania Street, where the lodgings were reserved for them, and told to appear for armistice negotiation at 7:39 A.M. at the former Czechoslovak Legation, where the Second German Army had its headquarters. (Ristić,130)

Now, because *the lodgings were reserved for them,* one has to conclude that the Germans were already informed of their coming. That confirms earlier statement that *"Late on the evening of 14 April, a representative of the Yugoslav Government* [who was not identified in the source] *approached the First Panzer headquarters and asked general von Kleist for an immediate cease-fire."*
The next morning, at 7:30 a.m. on 16 April, von Weichs received Gen. Bodi and Lt. Col. Trojanović in the conference room of the former Czechoslovak Legation, where the former Italian and Hungarian military attachés and some civilians were also present. (Ristić,130-31) Shown here are four accounts of the negotiations.

1- [On 16 April]

> ... a Yugoslav arrived in the capital, but it turned out that he did not have sufficient authority to negotiate or sign the surrender. Therefore, a draft of the agreement was handed to him with the request that competent plenipotentiaries be sent to Belgrade without delay in order to avoid unnecessary bloodshed. To expedite matters, a plane was set at his disposal. (Blau, 61-2)

2- The Document of the executive decrees for cease-fire between the German and Yugoslav armed forces was dated in Belgrade, 16 April 1941, and was to be signed by both sides at 9 a.m. It contained 13 Items. (Miletić(ed), 758-60)

"Transcript" of the Minutes ("Prepis" Zapisnika) of the negotiations, presented by Col. Miletić, quotes direct exchanges between Gen. von Weichs and the Yugoslav representative. However, that representative is identified as Gen. Kalafatović. By all other accounts, that representative was Gen. Bodi, not Kalafatović – who was then at the Yugoslav Supreme Command in the Sarajevo-Pale area. (Pages 750-52)

3- The account by Major Ristić contains major points of the negotiations, shown also by Miletić, and are quoted here:

> After a few conventional words expressing his satisfaction over the cessation of hostilities, General von Weichs asked his adjutant to read the German terms: complete capitulation of Yugoslavia's armed forces; officers were to be allowed to keep their side arms in prisoners-of-war camps. In accordance with his instructions, General Bodi, who had a fair knowledge of German, suggested occupied and unoccupied zones as in France. "The Yugoslav High Command was seeking an honorable armistice while the German terms were not an honorable armistice," he complained. General von Weichs replied that he was not authorized to alter the original conditions, but he would forward the Yugoslav proposals to his superiors. General Bodi then said that he had been assigned to carry on negotiations for an armistice and could only advise the Yugoslav High Command. (Ristić, 131)

4- ... When the Germans discovered Bodi lacked sufficient authority to negotiate or sign such a document [the one which was to be signed at 9 a.m.] they gave him a draft of the document, put a plane at his disposal, and told him to see to it that competent representatives come to Belgrade without delay. (Hoptner, 290)

Bodi and Trojanović left Belgrade in a German plane at noon, landed in Bijeljina, Bosnia, and reached the high command headquarters near Sarajevo by car at midnight on 16/17 April. (Ristić, 131)

*****

On 16 April, Simović arrived in Athens. Shortly thereafter, the British flew him, the King and his immediate entourage, important members of the cabinet and Ristić to Alexandria. (Ristić, 136)

In London, Cadogan entered into his diary:

> No confirmation of Yugoslav capitulation, but their effective resistance evidently at an end. Meanwhile it seems – from our most reliable source - that Germans yesterday broke through on our right down the [Greek] coast – which was considered by our G[eneral] S[taff] nitwits to be impossible! (Dilks(ed), 372)

John Colville, Churchill's Assistant Private Secretary, noted in his diary: "Organised resistance in Yugoslavia has ceased. In Greece the Germans are entering Volo and there is much talk of a stand in the pass of Thermopylae. (Colville, 374)

Yugoslavia's Ambassador, I[van] Subotić, informed his colleague in Ankara about his conversation with the British Foreign Minister Eden:
Upon arrival in Athens, Simović expressed impression that those Yugoslav military forces, that had remained organized, would continue fighting under the command of two *Vojvode,* who had been appointed for that purpose;
Eden hoped that the Yugoslav Government would continue fighting along with the Allies, England and Greece, that this Government was considered to be the legitimate representative of the Kingdom of Yugoslavia, and that Yugoslavia would participate in the final victory. (Miletić(ed), 745)

*****

(U) In Zagreb, in a decree about the nomination of the first Croatian state government, Pavelić described himself as the *Poglavnik Nezavisne Države Hrvatske (Head of the ISC),* assuming the post of the president and the foreign minister in the government. (Jelić-Butić, 82)

(A) • Thursday, 17 April - Armistice agreement signed

Upon arrival in Sarajevo at midnight of 16/17 April, i.e. on the 17th, Bodi and Trojanović duly reported about the meeting with Gen. von Weichs in the morning of the 16th, and their report raised the question: Who could be competent to sign the capitulation document? All responsible representatives of the Simović's Government had in the meantime left the country, but somebody had to be found to sign the capitulation document. Shown here are two answers. First, from Dragiša Ristić, a former Putschist himself:

> **The Germans** in Sarajevo **simply picked** two new plenipotentiaries from the captured Yugoslav High Command, former Foreign Minister Cincar-Marković and Division General Radivoje Janković, and **ordered** them to go to Belgrade and **sign the armistice.** These two left Sarajevo for Belgrade on the morning of the 17th and **signed the armistice** with Germany and Italy at 9:00 P.M. It went into effect at noon, April 18. (Ristić, 131. Emphasis added.)

Now Dr. Hoptner's account:

> [By 17 April] No responsible political representative of the Simović government remained on the Yugoslav soil. Who then could go to Belgrade? Someone remembered that the former Foreign Minister Cincar-Marković might be acceptable to the Germans despite the fact he not only had no official connection with the Simović government but also was interned and under guard in Brus, a village in central Serbia. They did not know that Cincar-Marković and his guards had fled from Brus when the German planes bombed Belgrade and by April 15th had managed to reach Pale. While Cincar-Marković hunted for shelter from the Germans, General Kalafatović hunted for Cincar-Marković. (Hoptner, 290-91)

At a meeting in a school-house in Pale, Kalafatović did his best to convince Cincar-Marković to help him and sign the armistice document: the war was lost, the King and Government had fled, the army had disintegrated ... there remained only one thing to prevent further bloodshed ...
At first, Cincar-Marković refused to sign, but when he was brought to Kalafatović's headquarter [in the morning of 17 April],

> There he found three Yugoslav officers and a German officer drafting the text of armistice. Already completed were the documents authorizing Cincar-Marković and General Janković, head of the operational division, to act on behalf of the supreme command and the absent Yugoslav government. By this time Cincar-Marković had accepted the necessity of signing the armistice agreement. Kalafatović, hoping that part of the country would remain unoccupied, urged Cincar-Marković to see if he could obtain

for Yugoslavia the same status France had obtained after its defeat. Cincar-Marković brought the general quickly back to reality; it was all too late for negotiations of that kind, he said. Croatia had already been declared an independent state, and they could look forward to Germany's partitioning Yugoslavia to satisfy the territorial demands of the Italians, Hungarians and Bulgarians. (Hoptner, 291-2)

*****

So: according to Hoptner, General Kalafatović found and talked Cincar-Marković into signing the document of capitulation. According to Ristić, the Germans simply picked him (and Gen. Janković) and **ordered** them to sign it. However, Ristić did not explain how the German had found the former Minister in Pale in the first place. Therefore, Hoptner's account seems to be more credible.

*****

After the meeting with Gen. Kalafatović, Cincar-Marković, Gen. Janković and the German officer left for Belgrade in a German plane. "There, in the former Czechoslovak legation, on behalf of the Kingdom of Yugoslavia, they signed the document of armistice on April 17th, the 12th day of the war. The armistice went into effect at noon the following day." (Hoptner, 292)

> The armistice was concluded and signed on 17 April. General von Weichs signed for the Germans, with the Italian military attaché in Belgrade acting on behalf of his country. The Hungarians were represented by a liaisons officer who, however, did not sign the document since Hungary was technically not at war with Yugoslavia. Foreign Minister Cincar-Marcovic and General Milojko Yankovic signed for the Yugoslavs. The armistice became effective at 1200 April 18, 1941, just twelve days after the initial German attack was launched. (Blau, 62)

*****

While Cincar-Marković and Gen. Janković were being flown to Belgrade to sign the document of capitulation, in the morning and afternoon of the 17th April the Yugoslav Government were meeting in Athens and decided: their majority should go to Egypt, but the Premier, the Vice-Premier, the War and the Foreign Minister should stay in Athens, for the time being – to support the refugees and to secure their timely evacuation. (Miletić(ed), 768-70)

In London,

> On 17th April, Dalton was informed indirectly that the Danube was blocked, but nothing more. 'There have been a few other references but all quite imprecise, in the telegrams,' he noted. 'It is most tantalizing not to know what happened. The Jugs have been so inefficient that it may well be that plans were made but never executed.' (Pimlott(ed), 186)

From Cadogan's diary: "[Greek Commandant, General Alexandros] Papagos has asked us to evacuate and we agree to try. No one knows what happened." (Dilks(ed), 372)

(A) • **Friday, 18 April – Unconditional surrender was in effect**

The unconditional surrender became effective at 12:00, noon.

*****

In London – British Foreign Minister Eden met SOE chief Dalton, who recorded in his diary:

> Eden tells me that [Ambassador Sir Miles] Lampson in Cairo wanted to ask Prince Palsy [Paul] to lunch, and telegraphed whether he might. Eden replied, 'No, such an act of hospitality would not be understood here' [in London]. (Pimlott(ed), 184)

*****

"… insufficiency of our forces for a decisive battle"

In 1951 Simović wrote that, back in January 1941, he was revealing to Col. Donovan a perilous situation of Yugoslavia and "insufficiency of our forces for a decisive battle" ("nedovoljnost naših snaga za odlučnu borbu"). Therefore, he pleaded with Donovan for a speedy help in arms, especially for the Air Force and for anti-aircraft and anti-tank weapons. (Simović(51), 6) That means that, before the coup of 27 March 1941, he was acutely aware of the insufficiency of Yugoslavia's armaments. Equally aware had to be Gen. Mirković, Col. Savić, and other Air Force officers participating in the Putsch. Minister of War Pešić underlined this insufficiency on 24 March to the assembled Commanders, including Simović. **(Chapter 11)**

In March-April 1941, Yugoslavia had 284 first-line aircraft and 80 second-line. (Ristić, 125) For years the British could not procure armaments Yugoslavia asked for even before the Second World War started. Thus Germany's air superiority in March 1941 was unquestionable. "With Germany's command of the air and Yugoslavia's poor communications,, however, a general reserve could not have been shifted about rapidly enough to be of any value." (Ristić, 127)

The Yugoslav Army had no modern *Panzer* divisions, not even enough tires needed for their trucks, not enough gasoline, no military transportation means and weapons to defend against a *Blitz-Krieg* Germany was capable of waging, as she had demonstrated against much better-armed France and Western Countries. Germany's army was rested, not engaged since June of 1940, and her air force since the middle of September 1940; so the German war machine had plenty of time to increase its potential and improve war techniques. The British could not, and did not promise, to transport an envisaged retreat of Yugoslav army from the ports of the Adriatic or Salonika to safety – as it was done in the First World War.

Then how did Simović plan to "resist" a greatly superior war machine, and why did he tell Macdonald on the 26th March that *he foresaw that Yugoslavia would go to war in Albania immediately after the coup d'état*? Did he expect Hitler not to react? If he did, he was mistaken. On 28 December 1940, Mussolini asked Hitler for support in Greece. On 11 January 1941, in *Directive No. 22* (Operation *"Alpine Violets"*), Hitler confirmed his intentions to send military support to the Italians in Albania. If Simović *did not expect* Hitler's intervention, then why did he not go to war in Albania immediately after the coup, as he told Macdonald he would? If Simović *did expect* Hitler's intervention, then why did he tell Macdonald he would – but then did not?

The un-preparedness for war and the disorganization were such that, for example, Simović – because the communications with the units were not operating – had to broadcast to the troops an appeal: "All troops must engage the enemy wherever encountered and with every means at their disposal. Don't wait for direct orders from above but act on your own and be guided by your judgment, initiative, and conscience." (Blau, 52)

The military situation was worse than Gen. Pešić expected. "During the operations on 14 and 15 April, prisoners were taken by the thousands. North of Nis [Niš] the Germans captured 7,000; in and around Uzice [Užice], 40,000: around Znorvik [Zvornik] 30,000 more; and in Doboj another 6,000. (Blau, 61)

"The Germans took some 254,000 prisoners, excluding a considerable number of Croat, German, Hungarian, and Bulgarian nationals who had been inducted into the Yugoslav Army and who were quickly released after screening." (Blau, 62) Those 254,000 were the Serbs. "As during the early campaigns in World War II, the German superiority in armor and air power led to the quick conclusion of operations. Although the German General Staff planners had been well aware of the deficiencies and weaknesses of the Yugoslav Army, they were greatly surprised that the campaign could be concluded within so short a time." (Blau, 64)

In the twelve days of combat the Germans lost: 151 killed, 392 wounded, and 15 listed as missing in action, for a total of 558 men. (Blau, 62) That certainly was not what the domestic coup-wishers-and-plotters and their British inspirers-and-encouragers were expecting from Yugoslavia's "resistance" to Germany

Chapter 21

18 APRIL – END OF JUNE 1941

(U) On 21 April, Pavelić's "minister for Dalmatia", Edo Bulat, had to surrender his authority in Split to an Italian commandant, who did not allow Bulat even to inform Pavelić about it. Similar thing took place in Šibenik, Drniš, Benkovac, Metković, Sinj and other Dalmatian cities. (Jelić-Butić, 84)

*****

Cadogan, the same day: "We had been expecting to have to decide whether to evacuate from Greece or not, but a telegram came in about 4 showing that Greeks are asking us to." (Dilks(ed), 373)

On 22nd April Dalton again wrote in his diary about the Danube:

> I see Eden about the River. The P.M. [Prime Minister] is most anxious to give the public some good news. Can we say the river is blocked? I say not yet, and we go over the skimpy evidence together. He will telegraph to Cairo to ask the Jug Minister there what they knew, and also, via Washington, at my suggestion, to the American Minister in Bucharest. (Pimlott(ed), 187

On 24th April Dalton confided to his diary the British treatment of Prince Paul:

> I am delighted to read in a Colonial Office telegram that Prince Palsy and his wife are to reside in Kenya, with the status of political prisoner, and that a senior administrative official is to live with and watch them; that H.M.G. [His Majesty's Government] will pay the rent of their house, seeing that this is in the nature of prison, but that it will be put to 'our friend' that his large assets in this country should be drawn upon for his keep and other personal expenses. I hope that Lampson in Cairo has read this telegram with profit. (Pimlott(ed), 188)

"… terrible error of sending anything beyond a small token force to Greece."

On Monday 28th April, Dalton dined with Oliver Stanley, the former Secretary of State for War, January – May 1940, and then recorded their conversation in his diary. Here are lengthy excerpts related to Greece and Yugoslavia.

> Stanley then proceeded to attack, … , the terrible error, as he judged it, of sending anything beyond a small token force to Greece. This, he said, was a crowning blunder. It was the Prime Minister's fault. The decision had been taken against all military and naval advice. It should have been seen from the start that the adventure was quite hopeless. … We had thrown away a most valuable Air Force in Greece. At least four squadrons of fighters and three squadrons of bombers had been destroyed. It was quite wrong for Eden to have gone to the Middle East and worst of all to Athens. … (Pimlott(ed), 190; 189n1)

Dalton interjected:

> … As against what he had said, I saw some force in the argument that Eden might have been able, *through the offer of substantial British help,* to bring both the Yugoslavs and Turks and a total force of seventy Divisions into an anti-German bloc in the Balkans. But for Prince Paul, who had had too many friends and dupes in this country, I still thought this would have been a possibility. Stanley replied that it was useless to count Divisions; *all that was worth counting was Armored Divisions, of which neither Turkey nor Yugoslavia had any.* (Pimlott(ed), 190. Italics added.)

In the spring of 1941, Britain simply did not have *substantial help* to give to Turkey and Yugoslavia. It was the *Armored Divisions* that counted, indeed. "Rifles against tanks!" (St. John, 26), … "It should have been seen from the start that the adventure was quite hopeless."

"Churchill was equating untrained and ill-equipped Allied divisions with well-rested, battle-hardened Germans under experienced commanders." (Higham, 133)

"The real difficulty with making any arrangement with Yugoslavia was that the country was neither militarily nor psychologically ready for war. Churchill, Eden, and Papagos were hoping to count on forces which existed only on paper and upon which no one appears to have completed thorough intelligence assessment, any more than the British had studied the Czech or the French before 1938-1939. (Higham, 200)

Cadogan's diary, 29 April:

> Evacuation [from Greece] going fairly well. That's all that we're really good at! And we anticipate that 5,000 German air-borne troops are going to wipe us out of Crete! Our soldiers are most pathetic amateurs, pitted against professionals. Dill is most unimpressive – if charming – personality I have ever come across. ... (Dilks(ed), 374)

Vitally interested in the blockade of the Danube, Dalton noted on 30th April:

> The first really good news about the Danube. A telegram from B. reporting that our No. 2 in Belgrade personally supervised an operation in the K. [Kazan] narrows (probably about 8th April) whereby the No. 2, ... , estimates that the river will be blocked for at least three months. This particular block is additional to anything due to the destruction of the two railway bridges, and, almost certainly, additional to other barge sinkings at Golubac and Dombrovica. ... (Pimlott(ed), 192)

*****

On 5th May Dalton noted in his diary "news that Taylor is, after all, still safe and sound with Campbell's staff who are being brought by the Italians to Rome and are due to be released, under Anglo-Italian convention for liberation of diplomats. This is a very good news, since I had deep fears either that Taylor was dead or worse, caught by the Gestapo. I shall not be reassured till he has emerged from enemy-dominated regions, but so far so good." (Pimlott(ed), 197-8)

"... numerous warnings of a German attack upon Russia"

Writing about events unrelated to the subject of this book, the editor of Cadogan's diaries, Professor David Dilks, included the following relevant information under the date of 12 May 1941:

> Since March the Foreign Office had been receiving numerous warnings of a German attack upon Russia. Hitler was reported to have told Prince Paul that he intended to invade on 30 June. At [the British Ambassador] Cripps' suggestion, the Yugoslav Minister in Moscow [Milan Gavrilović] spoke of this to Stalin and Molotov. Cripps delivered separate warning from Churchill. Other rumors in the same sense began to circulate freely in Moscow during April. Stalin seems to have taken little notice. (Dilks(ed), 378)

*****

From John Colville's diary, 22 May: "The navy are having a heavy task off Crete and have lost a lot of ships, including *Gloucester* and *Fiji*. ..." (Colville, 389)

In Cadogan's diary, 23 May: "Cretan news not too bad, but the Navy are suffering and finding it difficult to carry on. These Germans *are* marvelously efficient. Nothing like it has ever been seen ...." (Dilks(ed), 380. Cursive in the source.)

Cadogan, 27 May: "Awful news from Crete. We are scuppered there, and I'm afraid the moral and material effects will be serious. Certainly the Germans are past-masters in the art of war – and *great* warriors. If we beat them, we shall have worked a miracle." (Dilks(ed),381. Cursive in the source.)

Cadogan, 28 May: "Cretan news terrible – it's another disaster. Private telegram from Miles Lampson to A[nthony Eden] about lack of air support in Crete and saying this has bad effect on morale everywhere – including Anzacs [Australian and New Zealand troops]. ..." (Dilks(ed), 381)

Cadogan, 29 May: "Cabinet at 12. Horrible decision to make – whether to go on with evacuation from Crete, with all damage to the Fleet, or to abandon our men. Decided to go on – for the present." (Dilks(ed), 381)

George Taylor back in London

Based on an interview with George Taylor, the editor of Dalton's diaries wrote:

> George Taylor, who had been in Belgrade at the time of the coup, had subsequently been captured by the Italians and taken first to Albania and from there flown to Italy, where his captors, unaware of the nature of his responsibilities, treated him with friendliness and liberality. An exchange of prisoners was

arranged by the Italian Foreign Ministry, and Taylor was sent in a sealed train to Madrid, returning to England on 17th June. (Pimlott, 197n2)

On Wednesday, 18 June 1941, the SOE head, Dr. Hugh Dalton, entered the following into his diary:

> [George] Taylor arrived back yesterday by air form Lisbon, sent even in advance of the Minister (R.C.) [Ronald Hugh Campbell]. He is brought to see me this morning by Gladwyn. He looks very well and fit. He was captured by the Italians when the Jugs collapsed, near Kator [Kotor], but he and the rest of the large part, more than a hundred, of captives were treated very well by his comparatively civilised enemy. They passed some weeks at Chianciano and had quite a pleasant time waiting for all the formalities to be completed for their journey on through France and Spain. He is eager to be working again, … , and he is to return to London on Sunday night [22 June] and make me a full report of all his doing. (Pimlott(ed), 230)

Dalton considered George Taylor to have been the *Chief Organiser* of the coup. (Pimlott(ed), 178n3)

"The Jug collapse seems to have been catastrophic"

Then Dalton continued:

> The Jug collapse seems to have been catastrophic, and the government formed after the coup to have consisted of a number of elderly politicians who, though their coup was a flagrant defiance of Hitler, believed that if they sat as quiet as mice he would no longer notice them. Therefore they stated publicly that their foreign policy was unchanged, privately that they were still neutral and could enter into no staff talks with us, and never issued a general mobilisation order. The Croats, moreover welcomed with open arms both Germans and Italians, and all along the Adriatic coast there was no resistance at all. All things considered, the Slovenes had done better than either the Croats or the Serbs. (Pimlott(ed), 230)

As expected, "The report to S.O. [Dalton] from A.D. [Taylor] and D.H.Y. [Masterson] on Certain S.O.2 Activities in Yugoslavia", was prepared on 24 June. "The original report consisted of six sections. The last four, dealing with post-occupational matters (sabotage and guerrilla resistance), unfortunately, are missing;…" [from Dalton Papers at the London School of Economics and Political Science] (Stafford, 410n43) If this report had actually contained some elements of post-occupational sabotage and guerrilla resistance, their removal could be understandable. There was no sabotage and no resistance as Taylor had planned and expected them.

Except for ailing *Vojvoda* Trifunović-Birčanin, other "subsidized" "friends and contacts" - who had been expected to organize the post-occupational resistance - fled Yugoslavia in a hurry, some of them with an escort of the SOE operatives. With Gavrilović in Moscow, and Tupanjanin leaving the country, Taylor's expectations that the Serb Peasant Party would be *definitely at the British disposal for underground propaganda, sabotage and guerrilla warfare once Yugoslavia is involved in war,* and that - in the case of German occupation - this Party would *immediately commence underground propaganda on a large scale* – simply did not materialize. Money spent on SPP and other Opposition Parties had indeed *"given wonderful value"* in implementing the coup of 27 March - as Hugh Dalton observed - but not for the activities Taylor expected in the event of occupation. That was one reason Dalton considered Yugoslavia's collapse catastrophic.

Another reason: Yugoslavia did not contribute any help to the British expedition in Greece. The coup of 27 March actually made it easier for the German troops to reach Salonika more quickly because they could bypass the Metaxas Line to the west.

How catastrophic that quick collapse might be for Yugoslavia and her people – that did not enter into Dalton's mind.

Closing George Taylor's mission

On 25th June, one day after receiving Taylor's and Masterson's report on SOE's activities in Yugoslavia, Dalton noted in his diary:

> I ask Eden to dine, partly in order to keep our relations well manured - … - and partly to enable him to meet Taylor and Masterson and hear their Balkan stories. I also ask Gladwyn [Jebb], C.D. [Sir Frank Nelson] and [John] Wilmot [Parliamentary Private Secretary to Dalton 1940-44]. This makes quite a nice

little party on a hot night, though Eden is late arriving, having had to see the P.M. [Prime Minister], and has to go for a Defence Committee at 9:45. None the less, I think it did good. ... (Pimlott(ed), 235-36; 15n1)

So, the Foreign Minister saw Taylor before he set on his mission to Yugoslavia and after his return. In the meantime, Taylor failed to block the Danube and to organize the post-occupation resistance, but succeeded in implementing Eden's order to topple Prince Paul's Government – which, in turn, drew Yugoslavia into the war – as the Prime Minister had ordered it. Then, what did Eden tell Taylor and Masterson? "Doctor Dynamo" did not record it.

Chapter 22

Sowing the seeds of tragedy

Yugoslavia had home-grown and foreign-fed problems which political organizations with separatist program exploited eagerly in order to achieve their own, diverse objectives. Two major organizations were the Communist Party of Yugoslavia (CPY) and the Ustaše. The Communists were first on the scene.

(C) Comintern in 1925: "Yugoslavia must be made to disintegrate"

In 1925 a special Commission was set up by the Communist International (Comintern) to examine "the nationalities questions" of Yugoslavia. Georgi Dimitrov, Secretary General of the Comintern from 1934 on, stated during the discussion:

> No serious Communist work will be possible in the Balkans until Yugoslavia disintegrates. So Yugoslavia must be made to disintegrate by our helping the Separatist movements there. (Clissold, 101-2)

The Commission then accepted the following resolution:

> The whole Party must develop its maximum propaganda and agitation to convince the working masses in Yugoslavia that the collapse of such a state is the only way towards solving the nationalities question. (Clissold, 102)

In other words: the replacement Yugoslavia with several smaller states.

Georgi Dimitrov was born in Bulgaria. One wonders whether his *disintegrate Yugoslavia* was totally devoid of the Bulgarian interpretation of historic relations between the Bulgars and the Serbs?

*****

(U) In 1929, the leader of the Ustaša separatists, Dr. Ante Pavelić, had gone to Italy, where Mussolini welcomed and used him as an instrument of his policies related to Yugoslavia and the Balkans.

> The Communists saw the Ustashas as their natural allies in the revolutionary struggle and in the early 1930s, the underground Communist paper *Proleter* began calling on Party members to give help and support to Pavelić's followers. In 1932 Communist leaflets were sent out appealing to the whole Croat nation to support the Ustashas and also urging the workers and peasants of Serbia "to help with all their strength in the Ustasha struggle". (Beloff, 49)

(C) Tito, in September 1934: Seven states – but no Yugoslavia

In September 1934, Tito

> convened a Communist conference in the castle of Gornji Grad, just outside of Ljubljana [Slovenia]. ... The Comintern had already selected two of the younger participants, Edvard Kardelj and Boris Kidrič, for Moscow training, and these were later to rank among Tito's closest collaborators.
> Tito's anti-Yugoslav line showed itself in the banners decorating Gornji Grad hall: "Long live worker- and-peasant states in Croatia, Dalmatia, Slovenia, Serbia, Montenegro, Bosnia, Vojvodina!" – the word Yugoslavia was not mentioned. (Beloff, 49)

(C) Forming the CP of Slovenia, and CP of Croatia ... an indication of the reorganization of "Tito's" Communist Yugoslavia

The Communist Party of Slovenia was founded in April, and that of Croatia in June 1937. (Petranović and Zečević, 321, 322)

In 1937 - during the Great Purge in Moscow - the approval and support of individual local Communist leaders by Stalin and the Comintern were directly proportional to the individual's loyalty, commitment, and obedience to Stalin and the Comintern. The Party careers and powers of Tito and Edvard Kardelj were on the rise. That year Tito became the Secretary General of the CP of Yugoslavia, and Kardelj continued to remain his most trusted associate.

In the Communist parlance, "the worker-and-peasant state" is a synonym for "the Communist state". Following the established practice of naming the Party according **the state** in which it operated (i.e. CP of Italy, CP of France, etc.), the CP of Croatia was meant to operate in **the state** of Croatia, and the CP of Slovenia in **the state** of Slovenia. The CP of Yugoslavia (founded in 1919) could possibly represent the remaining regions of Yugoslavia, but that was not certain.

But in September 1934 Tito wanted several states, and did not mention Yugoslavia. Did he intend to break up the remaining CP of Yugoslavia into separate Parties, to cover the regions outside Slovenia and Croatia? Was that the basis of the decision made in Jajce, on 29 November 1943?

In 1952, the Communist Party of Yugoslavia transformed itself into the League of Communists of Yugoslavia, thus marking the final breakup.

(C) In 1939, the Communists still supported the Ustaše

By 1939, one of "the Separatist movements" that the Comintern continued to help were the Ustaše. These two separatist organizations had a common goal: to disintegrate Yugoslavia. It is, therefore, not surprising to read in the Communist organ *Class Struggle* in 1939 the following:

> The idea of an armed rising should be propagated amongst the masses and they should be instructed in the practice of street fighting in preparation for it. In the event of the rising occurring in Croatia, the peasants and workers must place themselves under the leadership of the Communist Party. They must not fire on the Ustaše but support them by declaring a general strike. (Clissold, 15)

(C) In 1940, "... a world revolution ... of which the Soviet Union is our glorious model"

The goals of the Comintern's resolution of 1925 were confirmed and expanded in 1940, at the Fifth Conference of the CPY, held in Zagreb, 19-23 October.

Among the attending delegates were Lola Ribar, from Belgrade – "with heavy rings around his eyes and wearing that prematurely aged look which seems the characteristic of the professional youth leader"; and Milovan Djilas [Đilas] – "the hefty Montenegrin student-journalist with the Mongoloid features"; and the "dark, earnest-looking Edvard Kardelj, the little lame schoolmaster and tireless polemist from Slovenia". (Clissold, 17-18)

Historians Branko Petranović and Momčilo Zečević presented a brief excerpt from the Resolution of the Conference. (*Jugoslavija 1918-1984. Zbirka dokumenata*, Beograd, 1985, 323-4)

Tito's biographer Vladimir Dedijer wrote about this Conference in two volumes of his *New Contributions for the Biography of Josip Broz Tito.* In Volume 1 (Rijeka, 1981, pp. 261-3) he described details about the preparation of the this conference, "which had *historical meaning*", but produced only six lines from the content of the Resolution of the conference.

In Volume 2 (Rijeka, 1981, pp. 365-7) Dedijer wrote about the proceedings of the conference, but nothing about Tito's report and the Resolution.

By contrast, Stephen Clissold did present important points of Tito's report. Clissold lived and worked in Yugoslavia from 1938 to April 1941. In 1944 he was a member of the British military mission to the Partisan headquarters in Yugoslavia; in 1945-1946 he was Press Attaché at the British Embassy in Belgrade. In his highly praised book, *Whirlwind,* he identified sources used to produce it:

> Above all, I have drawn upon the confidential circulars and directives of the Yugoslav Communist Party and the wartime diaries kept by such Partisan leaders as Rodoljub Čolaković, Mladen Iveković, Vladimir Nazor and, above all, Dragoljub Dudić and Vladimir Dedijer. The story which I have been able to piece together from these sources has been supplemented from personal observation, from enquiries made in the country during and after the war, and from such acquaintance as I have had with some of the chief characters in the Yugoslav drama, (Clissold, 6)

In a very long address to the Fifth Conference, the Secretary General, Josip Broz Tito, discussed Party's matters and politics, as it is customary and at such Conferences. Here are some excerpts:

(C) • **CPY – an obedient member of the Communist International**

Europe has fallen a prey to the two rival blocks of the imperialist great powers. The flames of war are already scorching the soil of Yugoslavia. We are meeting together in the hour of national danger – the hour of historic opportunity for the Party. ... (Clissold,17)

Our Party sent *seven delegates* to the Seventh Congress of the Comintern [held in Moscow in August 1935], but of these *only two came back* to Yugoslavia to see that the new party line was understood and carried out. And one of these two fell into the hands of the police and had to be expelled from the Party for his unworthy conduct under investigation. So our Party was largely kept in the dark and unable to profit from the interest taken in it by Moscow. (Clissold, 19. Italics added.)

The war in Spain meant a new challenge to the Communist movement throughout the world. It was clear that the time had come for a radical purge in the leadership of our Party. A new Central Committee was needed which could return and carry on the struggle underground in Yugoslavia. By the following year - 1938 - this new Central Committee was established once again in Yugoslavia. It had full confidence and support of the Comintern. A new era in the history of the party had begun. (Clissold, 19)

(C) • **Sabotaging an imperialist war**

Let us make no mistake about the nature of the present world war. ... *It is an imperialist war*, waged between two rival blocks of capitalist Powers. We have no desire to be dragged into it. ... Our comrades in Belgrade are already planning a students' demonstration along these lines for December 14th [1940] with the watch-word of *"Down with the Imperialist war!"* (Clissold, 21. Italics added.)

... Last year - in the autumn of 1939 - the Party had been quite justified *in sabotaging the mobilisation of the Yugoslav Army*. But these tactics, comrades, are no longer expedient. ... What is more, we may one day need a strong Yugoslav Army – *an army which may be a worthy ally of the gallant Red Army*. Today, of course, the Yugoslav Army is hopelessly weak. (Clissold, 21. Italics added.)

(C) • **Not the Fatherland, but the world revolution**

... We are not interested in the bourgeois *ideal of a Fatherland to be defended, but of a world revolution to be carried through.* Remember this. The greatest revolution of the Yugoslav state - a revolution which I am confident the mass of people will accept - will be a revolution which brings national equality to Serbs, Croats, Slovenes, Macedonians, Montenegrins. And that, comrades, will in turn make possible *the greater social revolution which we plan and of which the Soviet Union is our glorious model.* (Clissold, 21. Italics added.)

(C) • **Keep Yugoslavia out of the capitalist war...**

I must ask the congress to approve the wording of the Party Resolution. Now that the flames of war are blazing more and more fiercely, and the rivals *of both rival camps of imperialist great powers* seeking to drag Yugoslavia into *the capitalist war*, every effort must be made *to unmask the war-mongers* and keep Yugoslavia neutral. In this grave crisis, the peace-loving peoples of Yugoslavia will find their natural leaders in the Yugoslav Communist Party which is resolutely opposed to all attempts to drag the nation into this bloody conflict. ... (Clissold, 23. Italics added.)

Thus spoke the Secretary General of the CPY in October 1940, when the Soviet Union was an Ally of Nazi Germany, and supported her politically and materially in the conduct of the war against 'capitalist and imperialist' Western Europe. The Agit-prop apparatus of the CPY promptly seconded the Party line in its official publications. The Party was not interested in *defending the Fatherland*, but in *the World Revolution* and in *a social revolution in Yugoslavia,* to be organized following the glorious model of the Soviet Union.

*****

Five days after the conclusion of the Fifth Conference of the CPY in Zagreb, Italy attacked Greece, from Albania, on 28 October 1940. The situation suddenly changed in the Balkans, for the worse. Ultimately it lead to the confrontation between Great Britain and Germany, ... which drew Yugoslavia into the war, as described in **Part One.** Most horribly, not only into a brief war, but into the bloodiest, prolonged tragedy the consequences of which are still felt by the people of former Yugoslavia.

(C) 22 March 1941 – Comintern's instructions to the CPY

On the same day when Britain's Prime Minister directed his Foreign Minister to "*draw Yugoslavia in to the war anyhow*", the Comintern's Secretary General, Georgi Dimitrov, ordered his subordinate Tito:

> 'to mobilize the Party against the capitulation to the Germans. Support the movement for a mass opposition to the incursion of the German military into Yugoslavia. *Demand friendship with the Soviet Union.*' (Gorodetsky, 140; 355n22. Italics added.)

In view of Germany's military superiority over the USSR **at that time**, opposing the German military in any way would be beneficial to the Soviet Union. *Demanding friendship with the Soviet Union* was designed to primarily promote a Communist Cause – not the military strength of Yugoslavia ... as it was proven by the signing of a non-supportive pact just fifteen days later.

As a disciplined member of the Comintern, however, the CPY dutifully demanded the alliance with the USSR.

(C) Tito's secret directive in the wake of the Putsch

On Friday, 28 March 1941, the day Gen. Simović was giving his long explanation to the hierarchs of the Serbian Orthodox Church concerning the alleged requirement for, success, and benefits of the coup of 27 March, Tito came from Zagreb to Belgrade. His biographer, Vladimir Dedijer, wrote nothing of a directive Tito issued before returning to Zagreb, but Stephen Clissold did.

> The events of March 27th had caught the Yugoslav Communists off their guard. It was a move by those very elements whom they most distrusted – the young chauvinists, royalist hotheads of the officers' corps – and had aroused a great outburst of popular enthusiasm in favour of the monarchy which the Party was out to destroy. The comrades in Belgrade had made a bid to turn the outburst to their own account and had mingled with the crowds cheering King Peter and launched their own slogans in favour of an alliance with the Soviet Union. Communist spokesmen had harangued the multitude thronging Belgrade's *Slavija* Square.
>
> ... Tito had hurried to Belgrade at a few hours' notice and summoned an emergency meeting of the Party's provincial committee for Serbia in the house of Lazar Kočević, ...
>
> ... Before returning to Zagreb, Tito had set out about taking urgent measures to meet the new situation. The assistance of the Comintern had to be enlisted for accelerating the return to Yugoslavia of the volunteers who had fought in the Spanish Civil War and who had been languishing in jail. Their experience of guerilla warfare would be invaluable in the event of trouble in Yugoslavia, ... Then the Party organisation inside the country needed to be rapidly overhauled to make good the gaps likely to be caused when men were called up to the Yugoslav Army, and to give the latter clear instructions as to the work expected of them. Tito had therefore drawn up a secret directive couched in the following terms:
>
> 1. The Yugoslav Communist Party is now in a position to take an active part in overthrowing of the present monarchical régime, and to this end will render assistance to all elements, regardless of their ideological outlook and character, which are bent on the same purpose. *Yugoslavia must first be dissolved into its several component parts,* and the party will then be able to pursue its work within each of them in accordance with the directives already issued.
>
> 2. Party members who may be called up to the army will have the following tasks to perform: firstly, disorganise the resistance of the Yugoslav Army by creating confusion amongst officers and men so that defeat appears to be the result of the incompetence of the officers' corps whose authority will be destroyed once and for all; collect all arms and war equipment which may be thrown away in panic and convey them to safe hiding places for later use; thirdly, collect information regarding individual officers and men who do not belong to our movement but who may be of use to us in the event of the U.S.S.R. entering the war.

> In the performance of these tasks, full use should be made of our underground organisation on the home front who will work according to the same plan.
>
> 3. *Render any assistance necessary to the Ustaše, Macedonian, Albanian and other nationalist organisations, in so far as they may contribute towards the speedy overthrow of the present régime. Help should also be given to the Montenegrin Separatists if they adopt an anti-royalist line in Montenegro.*
>
> 4. Germany will speedily crash Yugoslav resistance and, with the help of Italy, introduce the Ustaše régime in Croatia and possible similar separatist régimes elsewhere. Steps must therefore be taken *to infiltrate our own people in the new administrations for intelligence and other purposes."* (Clissold, 26-7. Italics added.)

By implementing this directive, Tito was following the Comintern's directive of 1925 to expedite the disintegration of Yugoslavia, and his own plan of September 1934 to create separate, smaller states in her place.

(U) Pavelić and "Legal decrees ..." ("Zakonske odredbe ...")

On 17 April 1941, just two days after arriving in Zagreb from Italy, Pavelić signed "Zakonsku udredbu za obranu naroda i države" (Legal decree for the defense of the people and the state): Who in any way harms or had harmed the honor or vital interests of the Croatian people, or in any way imperiled the existence of the ISC or of the state authorities – even if the act remained just an attempt – the culprit would get the death penalty. To implement the law, "Izvanredni narodni sudovi" (special people's courts) were immediately named in Zagreb, and then in other major cities. (Krizman1, 416; Jelić-Butić,159) Court-martials were formed a month later, and mobile court-martials by the end of June 1941. (Jelić-Butić,160)

On 25 April 1941, Pavelić signed into law a Decree prohibiting the use of the Cyrillic alphabet. This directly impacted the Serbian Orthodox population in the ISC, because the rites of the church were written in Cyrillic. (http://en.wikipedia.org/wiki/Ante_Pavelic   6/3/13)

On 30 April 1941, Pavelić enacted the 'Law concerning Nationality.' This essentially made all Jews non-citizens. This was followed by further laws restricting their movement and residency.
   "From 23 May all Jews were required to wear yellow identification tags, and on 20 June Pavelić issued a decree which blamed Jews for activities against the NDH [ISC] and ordered their internment in concentration camps." These three Decrees "effectively placed the Serb, Jewish and Roma population on the NDH [ISC] outside the law and lead to their persecution and destruction."
   (http://en.wikipedia.org/wiki/Ante_Pavelic   6/3/13)

On 3 May Pavelić issued a Decree about conversion from one religion to another. (Jelić-Butić, 164)

(U) From "collection" and "emigration" camps to concentration camps, Jasenovac

In the latter part of April 1941 the first groups of Serbs and Jews, and some suspected Croats, were apprehended, and on 29 April sent into camp "Danica", near Koprivnica. During June and July 1941 the internees from "Danica" were sent to the camp Jadovno, near Gospić, which was organized in June. Jadovno became the first camp in which the mass extermination of the Serbs and Jews took place. (Jelić-Butić, 185-6)

The principal concentration camps in the ISC were in Jasenovac and Stara Gradiška. Jasenovac began to form in the summer of 1941, and continued to be enlarged throughout the year. It became the largest concentration and liquidation camp and torture place of unwanted persons, whom the regime arrested and liquidated regardless of their nationality.   The concentration camp in Stara Gradiška was of the same character. (Jelić-Butić, 186-7)

*****

4 May   Hitler announced that the Yugoslav state had ceased to exist.

*****
(U) 7 May Negotiations between Mussolini and Pavelić in Tržić entered into the final phase. Pavelić agreed to everything, confirming previous agreements. It was decided that the formal agreement should be held in Rome on 18 May 1941. (Jelić-Butić, 89)
*****
(C) 8 May Josip Broz Tito moved from Zagreb (in the ISC) to Belgrade (in occupied Serbia), and settled in V. Ribnikar's villa. The same day

(C) the Soviet Union withdraws recognition of the Putschist Government, …

Recognition of Simović's Government by the Soviet Union lasted one month. For the sake of maintaining good relations with Germany, on 8 May 1941 Ambassador Gavrilović

> was unexpectedly summoned by Vyshinsky and informed of the decision to withdraw recognition of his government. Gavrilović was indeed in a 'bad mood and aggravated'. He nonetheless confessed that he 'well understood what Soviet diplomacy was attempting to achieve'. (Gorodetsky, 217)

(C)… but on 9 May 1941 the Comintern issued *Directives for Future Work* to the CPY

On 9 May, the Executive Committee of the Comintern - one of the principal operating levers of the Soviet Government - issued *Directives for Future Work*. It was a lengthy document, and Stephen Clissold presented its translation on pages 238-41 of his book. Here are revealing passages:

1. The time has now come when decisive new steps must be taken along the path to world revolution. …
(a) The Communist world revolution must be presented as a series of measures to achieve 'true democracy', and all political and military leaders of the Communist Movement must depict their activity in this light. Up to 30 per cent of Party members may come out in the open as 'front-line fighters for democracy' in the eyes of the masses.
(b) The Government of the Soviet Union may also find it necessary to make temporary concessions…
(c) Until the seizure of power, the Communist Party … should be careful to maintain good relations with patriotic and religious circles. No discrimination should be made against the Churches; … National traditions too should be respected. … representatives of the Churches should be allowed to take part in preparing and carrying through the revolution. …
(d) The press should be used for publishing the new line amongst the masses. …
(e) Once power has been seized by the Party, foreign policy will be laid down by the diplomatic representatives of the U.S.S.R., who will receive the necessary directives from the Comintern. The representatives will maintain liaison between the Central Committee of the Communist Party of the U.S.S.R. and those in the countries where the Party has newly assumed power. …
(f) Immediately after seizing power, the Central Committee will set up a new government. …
(g) Opponents of the new administration, … , should be removed as soon as possible, but in 'democratic' fashion, i.e., by being brought to trial before a regular court or a People's Court. …

2. The country where the Central Committee has recently assumed power should not apply for inclusion in the Soviet Union until the necessary instructions to this effect have been received from the Executive Committee of the Comintern.

3. Until the inclusion of the country in the Soviet Union, at least 50 per cent of the members of the Communist Party must remain in the underground conspiratorial work and act as the administration's chief allies in the government of the country.

4. Traitors to the Party are to be liquidated without trial …

5. The frontiers of the countries geographically remote from the Soviet Union are not to be closed immediately after the revolution. Everything should rather be done to induce all refugees, exiles, etc., to return home under democratic safeguards. Only then shall the frontiers be closed. …
Considerable difficulties may be encountered in the apprehension and destruction of internal opponents and class enemies. No times should be lost, however, in placing them under restraint and bringing formal charges against them to justify their detention in the eyes of the democratic world.

6. The term 'class enemy' comprises the following categories: members of ideological movements of a nationalist or religious character, priests, members of police force, officers' corps, diplomatic and civil

services in so far as they have refused to side with the revolutionary forces, all members of the ruling dynasties, any individuals known to have actively opposed the preparation or the carrying out of the revolution.

The way these class enemies are to be removed will be determined by the general situation and the methods used will be prescribed by the delegate of the Executive Committee of the Comintern ...

7. After the seizure of power, the Party shall dispose of funds, kept separate from State funds, from the following sources: property belonging to the class enemies who have been liquidated or had their possessions confiscated by the finding of a court of law; property belonging to hostile movements and organisations; property confiscated from the Churches, from the ruling dynasty, and from war profiteers.

These detailed directives from Moscow did not request the Communists in Yugoslavia to fight the occupiers to liberate the country – and suggesting how to do it. They instructed them how to prepare and carry out a Communist revolution and seize the power in a so-called "true democratic" way... deceiving both participants and observers.
These suggestions were applied after the war when the CPY took power in Yugoslavia.

*****

(U) Mass liquidation of the Serbs in the ISC has already begun **by the end of April 1941**. A notorious and very dramatic one took place in Glina on 11/12 May. (Jelić-Butić, 166)

12 May 1941 – Colonel Dragoljub Mihailović comes to Western Serbia

Unwilling to surrender, Colonel Dragoljub-Draža Mihailović arrived at Ravna Gora – south of Valjevo, in occupied Serbia. His adjutant was Vladimir-Vlado Lenac – a Croat, lawyer from Zagreb – whose father Zdravko Lenac – also a lawyer from Zagreb – was assassinated by the Ustaše in Zagreb, before the war. Vlado's godfather was Dr. Vladko Maček, President of the Croatian Peasant Party.

He [Mihailović] had always believed in a possibility of carrying out guerrilla warfare in the event of an enemy occupation of the country. Now here he was, with twenty-six equally patriotic-minded but bewildered followers and the few odd weapons they had managed to bring with them, in the heart of Šumadija, famed for its popular risings against the Turkish oppressors of bygone days. ... He had neither resources, party, nor organisation of his own. ... For an officer with a gallant but not particularly distinguished soldier's career behind him, and a smattering of diplomatic *savoir-faire* acquired while serving as Military Attaché in Prague and Sofia, the way ahead would not be an easy one. (Clissold, 54-5)

*****

But contrast Clissold's writing with a fiction offered to the US readers in 1942-1943 by a reporter of *The New York Times:* By the end of April 1941, he wrote, the reporters "imprisoned" by the Italians together with the British personnel, were

collecting information about Chetnik activity in Dalmatia and Montenegro. Hercegnovi was ideal place for it. ... The Dalmatian village swarmed with Chetnik operatives and Serb gun-runners. Bushwhacking was already under way on the wild roadways of Hercegovina, and the Italians had been forced to discontinue night patrols in the hills. Motorcycle dispatch riders who ventured off the coast road after night fall simply disappeared, motorcycles, dispatches, carbines, and all. Intermittent firing in the night up and down the Dalmatian coast was taking a small but steady toll of Italian casualties and a heavy toll of Italian morale, already ebbing fast. In a kafana off the square I found two Serb friends from Belgrade. They greeted me warmly and we withdrew into a corner.
"[Kosta] Pavlović [reportedly the Četniks' *Vojvoda* in Belgrade] is already well established," said one of them. "It will be a period of preparation, until the summer. We will have a new leader of whom you will hear much, in time. His name is Mihajlovich."
"Draja," added the other, *Draja Mihajlovich.*" (Brock, 272-73)

By the end of April, Col. Mihailović was not yet at Ravna Gora, and there were no Četnik activities anyplace.

(U) 13 May   Bosnia and Herzegovina were included into the Independent State of Croatia (ISC).

(U) 18 May 1941 – Treaties of Rome between Italy and the ISC

On 18 May 1941, in Rome, at the head of a numerous delegation, Pavelić offered the "Crown of King Zvonimir" to the Italian king and, with Mussolini, signed three agreements:

agreement to determine the frontiers between the Kingdom of Italy and Kingdom of Croatia;

agreement about the questions of military importance, related to the Adriatic-coastal region;

agreement about the guarantee and cooperation between the Kingdom of Croatia and Kingdom of Italy. (Krizman1, 473)

The Treaties formally implemented the agreement *inspired by the conversation* held in *Palazzo Venezia* between Mussolini and Pavelić on 11 April 1941. Italy annexed most of Dalmatia, including cities with the alleged *Venetian character* (Split, Trogir and Šibenik), most of the Adriatic islands (including Krk, Rab, Korčula, Mljet), the bay of Boka Kotorska, part of the Croatian Littoral and areas of Gorski Kotar. (Krizman1, 471. Italics added.)

"King Zvonimir II" [Prince Aimone Savoy-Duke of Aosta] never stepped on the Croatian soil.

*****

(U) 7 June A Legal Decree is issued to demarcate the eastern border of the ISC with Serbia. The ISC encompassed the entire region of Bosnia-Herzegovina.

(U) 14 June The ISC signs the Tripartite Pact.

(U) "The massacres began at the end of June, continued with growing violence throughout the month of July, and reached the culmination of terror at the beginning of August." (Clissold, 99)

(C) 22 June 1941: Germany invades the Soviet Union; the Comintern's instruction to the CPY

When Germany invaded the Soviet Union on 22 June 1941, the Comintern issued the following instruction to the CPY:

> Germany's treacherous attack on the USSR is not only a blow against the land of socialism, but also against the freedom and independence of all peoples. The defence of the USSR is at the same time the defence of the countries which Germany has occupied. The peoples of Yugoslavia are now offered the possibility of developing a liberation struggle on all sides against the German oppressors.
> It is essential to take all measures to support and facilitate the rightful struggle of the Soviet people. It is essential to develop a movement with the slogan of forging a united national front and the united international front already formed, in the struggle against the German and Italian Fascist bandits and to protect the oppressed peoples against fascism – a task inseparable from the victory of the USSR. Bear in mind that, at this present stage, what you are concerned with is liberation from fascist oppression, and not socialist revolution. Acknowledge receipt of this signal. (Clissold(ed), 128)

*****

When Yugoslavia was attacked by the same *German and Italian fascist bandits,* the Comintern did not issue a similar instruction in defense of Yugoslavia. It was just the opposite: the Soviet Union supplied Germany with resources, and withdrew the recognition of Yugoslavia as a state.

(C) ... but there was no explicit call to arms by the CPY

A participant extraordinaire, Milovan Đilas – prominent as a member of the Politburo of the Communist Party of Yugoslavia, and later even more prominent as an often-jailed dissident – wrote:

> The military operations which we Communists launched were *motivated by our revolutionary ideology;* however, for the people who joined us they were but a resumption of the war which the broken and exhausted forces of the Kingdom of Yugoslavia had already lost. ... We learned of certain officers who had made off to western Serbia *and hoped to reestablish the old regime with the fall of Germany.* Our

preparations against the occupiers were therefore *preparations against the old order* as well. *A revolution was not feasible without a simultaneous struggle against the occupation forces.* (Djilas, 4. Italics added.)

... not even in the declaration of the Central Committee, which Tito wrote on the very day of the German attack on the U.S.S.R., *was there an explicit call to arms,* but only a summons to make ready for a struggle. That was understandable: we had long had radio contact with the Comintern – that is, with Moscow – and as responsible and fateful a move as an uprising and armed struggle could hardly have been undertaken without approval from above. ... we waited for Moscow's directive, and for once Moscow did not delay. ... (Djilas, 4. Italics added.)

(C) • After 22 June, "Moscow ordered us "

I no longer remember how many messages reached us from Moscow on that subject, but I am sure that *Moscow ordered us to begin diversionary and guerrilla actions*. Tito so informed us, and it became obvious that the activity of the party had to be reoriented, and that we had to speed up the stockpiling of weapons. ... (Djilas, 4. Italics added.)

*****

Those "certain officers" in Western Serbia, mentioned by Đilas, were Col. Dragoljub-Draža Mihailović and his group. Đilas was right. These officers wanted to reestablish the old order, while the Communists - motivated by revolutionary ideology - wanted a new, Communist order. They seized the fight against the occupiers as a means to reach their goal.

So: even before the first shots were fired, the goals of the two sides were clearly set, and they were mutually exclusive.

*****

For whatever activities he planned, Mihailović's decision was his own, spontaneous, not ordered or set up by anybody, from within or outside of Yugoslavia. He did have contacts with the British before the war. They had been interested in his ideas for guerrilla warfare, as was shown in **Chapter 3.** Because of this British interest in his expertise, he may have known about their plans for the "post-occupational resistance." However, he was not at all in **their** plans for that activity. Other individuals and organizations had already been chosen and prepared for it, as it is shown here.

On the other side, the CPY was a disciplined and obedient member of an international organization (the Comintern) – that was supported and directed by a foreign state (the Soviet Union) – and was obligated to implement the directives / orders of that organization. In Yugoslavia the CPY acted as a representative of the Comintern / the Soviet Union. That made the CPY their agent.

The Comintern's directives to the CPY of 9 May 1941 confirm that relationship.

(C) 4 July CPY had no elaborate plan, did not talk of any uprising

At the July 4 meeting of the Central Committee, there was not yet any talk of the "elaboration of a plan", or partisan operations in Serbia, or of the creation of a free territory in western Serbia, as stated in some documents. ...

There was no talk of any uprising either, but simply of diversionary and guerrilla operations. The Politburo recognized that the party wielded its greatest influence in Montenegro, and that there were considerable quantities of weapons there which had been seized and hidden away from the royal army when it capitulated. ... (Djilas, 8)

(B) The Comintern orders the start of Partisan actions in Yugoslavia

One of many orders Đilas mentioned above was issued in *"early July 1941",* according to Stephen Clissold, himself unsure of the exact date. The order stated:

The patriotic war being waged by the Soviet people against Hitler's bandit attack is a desperate life and death struggle, on the outcome of which hangs not only the fate of the Soviet union but the freedom of your people. The hour has struck when communists must launch an open fight by the people against the invaders. Without wasting a moment, organize Partisan detachments and start a Partisan war behind the enemy lines. Set fires to war factories, stores, fuel stocks (oil, petrol, etc), aerodromes; smash and

destroy railways, the telephone and telegraph system; do not permit the transport of troops and munitions (or any war material). Organize the peasants to hide their grain and drive their cattle into the woods. It is absolutely essential to use all possible means to terrorize the enemy and make him feel he is under siege.
Acknowledge receipt of these instructions, and notify facts to show fulfillment. (Clissold(ed), 129)

Fully implementing all these instructions would hurt the people of Yugoslavia more than the occupiers, but the Comintern did not care about that. When Hitler was occupying the countries of the Western Europe, the Soviet Union was his ally and supporter, and the Comintern dutifully "followed the party line".

(C) 7 July   Killing two domestic gendarmes, not the German occupiers

Following those instructions from the Comintern, the Communists were bound to act. Their first action took place at a traditional folk fair held on 7 July 1941 at Bela Crkva, a town in Western Serbia, then occupied by the Germans. Taking advantage of a large crowd attending the fair, they first held a propaganda rally. "People listened to them quietly, with their heads bent down." (Karapandžić, 72) Then, "Žikica Jovanović ['Španac', i.e. a veteran of the Spanish Civil War] fired two revolver shots at local gendarmes [Milan Dragović and Bogdan Lončar] and not at the [occupiers] Germans." In 1945 it was decided that this date "should be observed as the anniversary of the national uprising in Serbia."

> When I remarked to [Aleksandar-Leka] Ranković at the time that we should have picked a more significant event to mark the beginning of the uprising, he replied: "Well, you know, the Supreme Staff was located in Serbia, so it was more convenient to declare that the uprising began there." (Djilas, 100)

(C) • "... paralysis of the machinery of local government and food requisitioning"

Why kill two local gendarmes and not the German occupiers? Basing his writing on official documents, apologia, and wartime diaries – as explained above – in describing the event in Bela Crkva, Stephen Clissold relied mostly on the diary of Dragoljub Dudić, Political Commissar of the Kolubarska Company of the Valjevo Partisan Detachment.

> A raid on Bela Crkva near Valjevo on July 7th, which cost two gendarmes their lives, had given the signal for similar skirmishes throughout many parts of Serbia. ... Čiča [old man] Dudić was planning more operations of this kind to go hand in hand with the steady recruitment and *propaganda drive amongst the peasants and the paralysis of the machinery of local government and food requisitioning.* Such had been the directives which he had received from the Central Committee of the Yugoslav Communist Party.
>
> The Kolubarski Partisans' next objective was now the gendarmerie post at Mionica, a town lying some fifteen miles east of Valjevo. As they passed through the villages on the way, the Partisans summoned the peasants to assemble outside the parish hall, *where the archives, tax registers, and the schedules drawn up by the requisitioning officer were brought out and ceremonially burnt.* The Political Commissar harangued his listeners on the aim of the Partisan Movement and the need to take up arms against the Germans and their Serbian quislings, ... (Clissold, 39. Italics added.)

Political Commissar Dudić planned the attack on Mionica for 1 August and entered the following into his diary:

1. Send out patrols.
2. Warn Presidents of Parish Councils to *stop all local administration work*   as it only helps the enemy. In case of refusal, take hostages.
3. *Distribute Communist Youth leaflets.*
4. Rest of company to help in harvesting and *spread propaganda amongst the peasantry.*
5. Prepare attack on the Mionica gendarmerie station. (Clissold, 37. Italics added.)

For Dudić, "the police-spies, clerks and gendarmes" were "the people's enemies". (Clissold, 42) Paralyzing local governments, destroying archives, tax registers and other documents, spreading Communist propaganda, establishing the posts of Political Commissars, ... were measures meant to destroy the "old order" and establish the "new" one ... "*of which the Soviet Union is our glorious model.*" (Clissold, 21. Italics added.) – as Tito said at the Fifth Party Conference in October 1940. "Our preparations against the occupiers were therefore *preparations against the old order* as well. A revolution was not feasible without a simultaneous struggle against the occupation forces." (Djilas, 4. Italics added.)

For the CPY, destroying the old order was the primary goal; the fight against the occupiers – the means to achieve it.

(C) "At the end of the war, they [the Germans] will leave the country."

"The March 1943 Negotiations" between Tito's delegation and the Germans is not the subject of this book. However, one episode of the negotiations is very illustrative, and so is included here.

According to the statement of Vladimir Velebit - Tito's chief diplomatic negotiator: at the negotiations with the Germans in Zagreb, on 23 and 24 March 1943, the delegation stated:

> ((*We are of the opinion*, and that was unofficially made known to us, that the Germans do not have any territorial aspirations towards the territories of former Yugoslavia, but at present they have only strategic and economic, and eventually political interests. Consequently, *at the end of the war they will leave the country.*))
>
> "*Mi smo mišljenja*, a to nam je I nezvanično stavljeno do znanja, da Nemci nemaju nikakvih teritorijalnih aspiracija na teritorije bivše Jugoslavije, nego da u sadašnje vreme imaju samo strategijske I privredne, a eventualno I političke interese. Prema tome, *oni će po završetku rata napustiti zemlju.*" (Mišo Leković, *Martovski pregovori 1943,* Narodna knjiga, Beograd, 1985, p. 134. Italics added.)

Hitler's desired *Lebensraum* included the lands of Poland, Ukraine, and Russia, not of the Balkans. Both "resistance movements" expected the Germans to leave the country at the end of the war anyway, and therefore concentrated on achieving their own primary objectives.

*****

13 July   General rising in Montenegro against the Italian occupiers.

27 July   Armed rising of the Serbs in the ISC against their persecutions.

August   First radio news of Mihailović's resistance in Serbia reached the British at Malta.

*****

The national tragedy began to unfold.

"Unexpected consequences"

The Putsch of 27 March 1941 did not help the British expedition in Greece ...

When informed of the Putsch, *"The Prime Minister was overjoyed"*, and then he declared, *"The Yugoslav nation found its soul."* The coup was *magnificent news* for his Foreign Minister. **(Part One, Chapter 11)**

The British-instigated **"resistance"** to Germany lasted only seven days – much less than the six weeks expected by the Yugoslav Minister of War Pešić. Yugoslavia's military forces could not, and did not, provide any assistance to Greece and to the British Expeditionary Force in Greece. The Putschist Government of General Simović lasted only until 11 January 1942. Unable to **"resist"** as the British were hoping for, it was soundly criticized subsequently.

> ... the sequel [of the coup] was deplorable. The Yugoslav Government formed after the coup contained a number of very elderly politicians who, though their coup was a flagrant defiance of Hitler, believed that, if they sat as quiet as mice, he would not notice them. Therefore they stated publicly that their foreign policy was unchanged, and privately that they were still neutral and could enter into no staff talks with us. ... (Dalton, 373)

> ... the Simović government did not denounce the pact or offer to help Greece, and pursued Prince Paul's foreign policy with little change. In any case, the German invasion of Yugoslavia soon negated most of the supposed beneficial effects. (Pimlott(ed), 175)

> The new government which followed under General Simovic was bewildered and rudderless. This was not surprising. It was a makeshift combination of the former discredited parties; it lacked infusion of the new and Simovic himself had played no decisive role in the events of the previous days. *Whether any government could have made effective deployment against the earthquake that they had inherited is doubtful.* (Glen(B), 60. Italics added.)

> The attitude of the new Yugoslav government, especially with regard to military preparedness and tactical deployments, was thought highly unsatisfactory by British ministers, and caused great anxiety as to whether Britain would be able to gain full benefit from the coup. It put SOE back into virtually the same situation as in the pre-coup days, attempting to put pressure on the government through its various friends and contacts. SOE had not been too pleased with Simović heading the new government, but he was the only figurehead on whom all parties could agree. SOE's closest associates, especially Tupanjanin and Trifunović Birčanin, were equally disappointed and within a few days, *according to Taylor, were discussing the possibility of another coup.* (Williams, 33. Italics added.)

> After the events of 27 March, the Southern Department [of the Foreign Office] complained that the *coup had been hijacked,* and Campbell lamented the reappearance of yesterday's men, *but there was no appreciation of the extent to which British policy had contributed to the outcome.* (Onslow, 56. Italics added.)

... but the Putschists turned out to be *the builders of Communist-ruled Yugoslavia*

Disputing some statements made by Nikola Milovanović - the practitioner of *"the Marxist-analysis of history"* - General Bora Mirković complained, in a letter to Belgrade's *Evening News* on 4 November 1960:

> ((Today's rulers, instead of *rewarding those builders of today's Federative Peoples' Republic of Yugoslavia,* they sentenced *in absentia* in greater part precisely those who *helped them to grab the power,* as war criminals, some to 20 years of hard labor, some to 12.))

"U mesto da današnji vlastodršci *nagrade te neimare današnje FNRJ [Federativne Narodne Republike Jugoslavije]*, oni ih većim delom, baš one koji su ih *pomogli da se domognu vlasti*, osudiše "u otsustvu" kao ratne zločince, koga na 20 godina robije, koga na 12 godina." (Karapandžić(AB), 146. Italics added.)

... *neimari FNRJ* ...

Amen!

*****

While they truly did not intend for the coup of 27 March to produce a Communist-ruled Yugoslavia, the Puchists willingly exposed the country to war anyhow. However, as Baron Julian Amery aptly observed, "war has a way of leading to unexpected consequences". FNRJ was one. Josip Broz Tito understood exactly how the Putsch set in motion a sequence of events that ultimately brought his Communist Party to power in Yugoslavia. He and the CPY had good reason to value highly the Putsch of 27 March 1941.

For Yugoslavia, the war directly caused more than one million avoidable losses of human beings, their bodies left mostly in mass and unmarked graves.

R.I.P.

*****

Appendix G

Section D of the Secret Intelligence Service

"In March 1938, [Admiral Hugh 'Quex'] Sinclair [head of Special Intelligence Service] authorized the formation of a special unit, **Section D**, which would begin a detailed examination of alternative forms of warfare… " What he really had in mind were sabotage and destruction, espionage, counter-espionage, para-military and para-naval operations in the states threatened by Germany. For that purpose he chose Major Lawrence Grand – a sapper and a Cambridge graduate – to head the Section. (West[6], 60-61) His assistant was Major Monty Chidson, "an experienced SIS officer who had until the previous year been the Passport Control Officer in The Hague." (West(sw), 9) Churchill supported the formation of Section D. (Stafford(C), 186)

Intended to be a secret organization, Section D's name was never to be used outside its building. "To outsiders we were to describe ourselves as members of the Statistical Research Department of the War Office." The Section was created to assist the execution of Government policy which the Government "preferred not to acknowledge as the action of its agents." Among the projected activities, the most important were sabotage, political subversion and underground propaganda i.e., un-acknowledgeable activities. (Sweet-Escott, 19-20)

Due to the secrecy of the existence and operation of Section D, the recruiting of prospective members was done by personal recommendation. Thus lawyers tended to recommend other lawyers, bankers other bankers. "Before long we [Section D] were employing one or more representatives of most of the merchant banking houses in the City and earning the reputation of being the bankers' ramp." (Sweet-Escott, 32, 44) "Its [Section D's] ranks were filled, at this stage almost to a man, by senior businessmen and bankers or others aspiring to be such when the war was over." (Davidson, 71)

Britain not being at war in 1938, the Treasury limited Major Grand's activities to preparation of studies on the advantages of 'irregular warfare' conducted by well-organized and well-armed partisan units. (West(6), 60) When informed of these restrictions, Chester Beatty, a good friend of Grand, "had agreed to finance what was referred to as the 'Sabotage Service'. Beatty produced large cheque and promised to introduce some reliable men with a knowledge of the Balkans, Section D's target area." (West(sw), 9) Beatty's inventive mind was at the disposal of L. Grand. "Mr. Chester Beatty's contacts in the Balkans and the Middle East were of great use to us [Section D] in the early days." (Sweet-Escott, 106) "… Lawrence Grand had persuaded his friend Chester Beatty, the mining magnate, to second a number of his staff to 'D' Section while keeping them on his payroll." (Amery, 160)

Chester Beatty was an American-born mining tycoon whose company, the Selection Trust Group, "owned huge holdings in South-Eastern Europe, including the Trepca [Trepča] mine in Serbia, one of the richest mineral deposits in Europe…" (West(sw), 9, 11) His "large cheque" – made large in part by profits from Trepča – thus became one source of funds for Section D agents' covert operations in Yugoslavia from 1938 on.

Appendix H

Notes on George Taylor, Bill Bailey, Bill Hudson

George Francis Taylor, "secret service officer and banker", earlier in life "freelanced as a journalist and occasionally wrote on foreign affairs before joining the Shell Co. of Australia Ltd in 1930." "In July 1939 he was employed by Major Laurence Grand in Section D.... Early in 1940 Taylor was appointed head of its Balkan network." "A short, dark man with sharp features and methodical habits. ... He was invariably described by admirers and detractors as utterly ruthless, though his friends added 'but brilliant'." (Mark Wheeler, 'Taylor, George Francis (1903-1979', *Australian Dictionary of Biography,* Online addition; http://www.adb.online.anu.edu.au/biogs/A160440b.htm 6/21/07) Alexander Glen – a subordinate SOE agent - described Taylor as "an outstanding member of Section D." (Glen(B), 187)

Assisting Taylor in the Balkan section was **Bickham Sweet-Escott** who, for several years before the war, was doing "a little part-time work" for SIS, was employed by the British Overseas Bank until 1939, and resigned from financial sector of Courtaulds shortly before joining Section D in April 1940. (Sweet-Escott, 17, 169, 19) He had knowledge of the Balkans, especially of Hungary and Greece, and spoke German. Sweet-Escott formed an opinion of Taylor as "a brilliant but ruthless Australian", who had "a mind of limpid clarity and knew exactly what he wanted. It was certainly due more to him than to any other person that the theory and practice of what eventually became S.O.E. was in the end accepted by our [SOE] detractors and competitors, as well as our supporters." (Sweet-Escott, 21) Taylor was one of Grand's right-hand men. (Sweet-Escott, 38) It seemed that he had joined Section D at the outbreak of the war; he had been put in charge of the Balkans early in 1940, and had made several trips to the region. (Sweet-Escott, 21-2) Taylor was Grand's second in command. (Mackenzie, 16)

Bill Bailey was a young mining engineer from who had worked at the Trepča mines. Although self-educated, he had acquired a noteworthy grasp of Balkan politics. (Sweet-Escott, 22) A powerfully built metallurgist from Beatty's organization, "Bailey had a remarkable gift for languages and spoke French, German, Russian and Serbo-Croat fluently. He loved the good things of life; but in the isolation of mining camps had also read widely." (Amery, 166) Glen worked with Bailey, knew him well, and later remembered: "another old Section D hand, a gifted linguist and a saboteur with aplomb, moving explosives around the country with calm assurance. In 1942 he was dropped back into occupied Yugoslavia as a British Liaison Officer with Mihailovic and his Cetniks." (Glen(B), 185) But before that, in early 1942, in the United States and Canada he had been recruiting men of Yugoslav descent to be sent to Yugoslavia to establish contact with the Communist-led Partisans. Most of these recruits were Communists who had fought in the International Brigades in the Spanish civil war.

Duane "Bill" Hudson "had managed one of Beatty's goldmines in Yugoslavia before the war." (West[sw], 56) A. Glen wrote of him: "Mining engineer and metallurgist Bill Hudson: introduced to covert warfare by Bill Bailey and became one of the most active and successful agents in Yugoslavia, being responsible for the demolition of at least one large ship in Split Harbour. He had worked in Yugoslavia since 1937 and in that time gained a working knowledge of the country, its politics and Serbo-Croat. (Glen(B), 186)

All three dutifully carried out their assigned tasks, without any apparent concern for their effects on the people of Yugoslavia.

Appendix I

Formation of Special Operations Executive

In a series of meetings which had started on 13 June 1940, top British officials discussed "certain questions arising out of a possible collapse of France," overlapping responsibilities of separate departments assigned with the tasks of subversion of the enemy, and the need for centralized departmental, control of such tasks. (West(saw), 16-18) On 2 July 1940, **Dr. Hugh Dalton**, the Minister of Economic Warfare - appointed by Churchill in his Coalition Government with the Labour Party - wrote a letter in that sense to Lord Halifax, the Foreign Minister:

> What is needed is a new organisation to co-ordinate, inspire, control and assist the nationals of the oppressed countries who must themselves be the direct participants. We need absolute secrecy, a certain fanatical enthusiasm, willingness to work with people of different nationalities, complete political reliability. Some of these qualities are certainly to be found in some military officers and, if such men are available, they should undoubtedly be used. But the organisation should, in my view, be entirely independent of the War Office machine. (West(saw), 19)

On 11 July Halifax conferred with Churchill, who then asked Neville Chamberlain – now the Lord President of the Council – to prepare a formal plan. He did so; the plan was formally approved by the War Cabinet on 22 July, and thus it became SOE's founding charter. (West[sw], 19) The charter specified, *inter alia*:

> An organisation is being established to co-ordinate all action, by way of subversion and sabotage, against the enemy overseas. This organization will be known as the Special Operations Executive.
>
> [SOE] will be under the chairmanship of Mr. Dalton, the Minister of Economic Warfare.
>
> The departments and bodies affected which will now be coordinated by Mr. Dalton are:
>
> | Title | Alternative title | Administrative Authority |
> |---|---|---|
> | Sabotage Service | "D" | F.O. [Foreign Office] |
> | M.I.R. | - | W.O. [War Office] |
> | Department Electra House | Sir Campbell Stuart's organisation | Joint F.O. and Minister of Information |
>
> (West(sw), 19-20)

Although Churchill detested Dalton, a prominent leader in the Labour Party, Churchill had to yield to political pressure in order to keep relations sound with the Labour Party, his partners in the coalition Government. "Keep that man away from me", Churchill is reported to have ordered his aides. (Seaman(ed), 49) Dalton wrote in 1957 about his appointment:

> On July 16th, 1940, the Prime Minister called me to take charge, in addition to the Ministry of Economic Warfare, of Special Operations Executive. This was a new instrument of war and I should be responsible for shaping it. ... It would be a secret or underground organisation. There would be no public announcement of my new responsibility, and knowledge of the activities of the organization will be kept within a very restricted circle. As to its scope, "sabotage" was a simple idea. It meant smashing things up. "Subversion" was a more complex conception. It meant the weakening, by whatever "covert" means, of the enemy's will and power to make war, and strengthening of the will and power of his opponents, including, in particular, guerilla and resistance movements. It thus included many forms of propaganda. (Dalton, 366)

> I accepted the Prime Minister's invitation with great eagerness and satisfaction. "And now", he exhorted me [on 22 July], "Set Europe ablaze." M.U.W., the Ministry of Ungentlemanly Warfare, as he called it, fitted in well with M.E.W. [Ministry of Economic Warfare], ... (Dalton, 366)

... Dalton's own desire for action led him to put aside some of his enthusiasm for trade unionists and leftist revolutionaries. By December 1940, the minister wrote in his diary that "there is no place, to-day, for stupid doctrinaire prejudices against 'Fascism' as such ... we must offer, and quickly, a fair price to decent Italians who will get rid of M [Mussolini] and his gang." (Smith, 44)

*****

The propaganda side of SOE was given the name of SO1, with a separate head, directly answerable to Dalton.

Section D and MI® were amalgamated, and thereafter known as SO2.

The planning side was known as SO3, but in a few months "duly planned itself out of existence." (Sweet-Escott, 40-41)

SO1 functions were later taken over by the Political Warfare Executive (PWE). (Sweet-Escott, 97) Set up in August 1941, PWE's task was subversion, including black propaganda. (Seaman(ed), 201)

Section SO2's operational tasks included sabotage and irregular warfare. (Seaman(ed), 201)

While the SO2 designation was officially used in many operations and documents, it eventually became interchangeably used with the name of the entire organization, SOE. Hence the operations initially started in Yugoslavia by Section D and MI®, eventually were continued as the operations of SOE. "The Balkan contingent of Section D transferred more or less intact into SOE." (Williams, 9)

*****

Given the chairmanship, Dalton started immediately to set up the SOE organization. He recruited first Gladwyn Jebb, then Private Secretary to Alexander Cadogan in the Foreign Office, to be the SOE's Chief Executive Officer – under the cover of "Foreign Policy Adviser" to the Ministry of Economic Warfare. Jebb brought with him Philip Broad, also a Foreign Office official. Reginald Leper - then head of the Political Intelligence Department of the Foreign Office – was put in charge of propaganda section (SO1). Late in August 1940, Sir Frank Nelson became the Executive Director of SOE, and the former head of Section D, Laurence Grand, left the organization about the end of September. (Mackenzie, 75-6)

> To build up a new machine for sabotage and subversion, I appointed Sir Frank Nelson. He had had a business career, in India and Britain, ... He was the most capable organiser and a tireless worker. ...
> On his staff were a number of most able men. One was George Taylor, an Australian, who, in addition to his responsibility for our organisation at home, found himself on duty from time to time in some of our hottest spots abroad. He was always belligerent, persistent and ingenious. (Dalton, 369)

The hottest spots abroad were Cairo and Belgrade. After setting up the Cairo center, Taylor returned to London early in August 1940, (Sweet-Escott, 39), i.e. after the formation of Special Operations Executive (SOE). As this new organization absorbed most of the "D" agents, SOE Cairo in time became the center of operations related to Yugoslavia. George Taylor became the Chief of Staff to Sir Frank Nelson.

Appendix J

"High explosives, the usual S.O. 2 devices,"

Reporting on supplies needed for SOE operations in Yugoslavia, George Taylor wrote:

> High explosives, the usual S.O. 2 devices, land mines and grenades are needed for the actual carrying out of sabotage and demolitions.

"The usual S.O.2 devices" included "a host of specialized devices" developed for sabotage and demolition. "Perhaps the single most useful tool of sabotage" was Plastic Explosive (PE). Limpets "used magnets to attach a PE charge to the hulls of ships." "Incendiary devices were also provided to SOE agents." Stun guns, Bren guns, Mills bombs, anti-tank grenades, anti-tank detonators, railway charges – among others – were items of "the usual SOE devices". (Paul Cornish in Seaman(ed), 24 – 31)

> Arms of various kinds are needed for the protection of sabotage bands and for the carrying on of guerrilla warfare. ... Our friends ... make the strongest possible request for such arms as machine pistols and tommy-guns, none of which they can obtain internally. It can not be too strongly emphasized that the degree of success achieved by our friends, and indeed their willingness to make any serious attempt to carry out *our plans* will depend largely upon whether or not we can supply them with these weapons.
>
> They also require for the same purpose grenades which can be used very effectively on raiding parties. (Taylor's Report of 26 February 1941, p. 11. Italics added.)

On the subject of shipping and stocking supplies Taylor continued:

> High explosives and devices have been going first from England, and subsequently from our bases in Egypt, since the end of 1939. Those supplies, however, were all distributed and used in north western Yugoslavia, as they arrived for the small scale continuous sabotage which has been going on from there since that time. The building up of large stocks in various centers in Yugoslavia *against the day that the country would be occupied* and diplomatic connections severed, only commenced about two months ago. (Report, p. 11. Italics added.)

"About two months ago" was the end of December 1940 / the beginning of 1941. That was the time when the British war leaders became convinced of Germany's intention to invade Greece. The expectation that Yugoslavia would be occupied implied that she would somehow be in the war against the Axis first.

About the materials that had been already supplied, Taylor continued:

> The materials actually supplied have been mostly high explosives, and the usual S.O.2 devices. ...
> The problem of distribution inside Yugoslavia appears to present no serious difficulties. So far everything delivered at Belgrade had been very promptly taken over by our various friends, and transferred to dumps which they have created at Ljubljana, Zagreb, Dubrovnik, Nis [Niš] and Skoplje. From these dumps materials are in turn distributed to the people who actually use them. (pp. 11-12)

In addition to these dumps, "with the cooperation of the British Military Mission and the Greek Ministry of Home Security", it was planned to create at least three forward dumps on the Greco-Yugoslav frontier from which "Daddy" and "Uncle" would "smuggle materials across the frontier". SOE was also investigating the possibility of using the ports of Dubrovnik or Kotor as a base for supplies. (p. 12)

> Daddy and Uncle [Miloš Tupanjanin of the Serbian Peasant party] are making arrangements through their very wide connections in official circles, particularly in the lower ranks, to enable us to consign trucks to addresses in Northern Yugoslavia, with the idea that these trucks will be "lost" en route, and their contents taken out and distributed by our friends. We have been advised by telegram from Belgrade two days ago [24 February 1941] that the necessary arrangements have been made for three truckloads to be sent, and the first should leave within a couple of days. (p. 12)

All these high explosives and SOE devices had not been distributed outside of Belgrade by the time of the German bombing of the city on 6 April 1941. Some were safely removed from their storage places by Sandy Glen and Hugh Seton-Watson.

Appendix K

Report on SOE organization and plans in the Balkans, 26 February 1941

Taylor's "MOST SECRET REPORT ON S.O. ORGANISATION AND PLANS IN THE BALKANS. " (TNA HS5/166) deals extensively with SOE's plans for Rumania, Bulgaria and Yugoslavia. Out of 16-pages, more than nine pages contain plans related to Yugoslavia.

Taylor reported on SOE *contacts* in Slovenia and Croatia, Serbia and Bosnia, and Montenegro;
   on *communications, couriers, supplies, finances*;
   on *plans*
      for Slovenia and Croatia, which included propaganda, small scale sabotage and military demolitions;
      for Serbia and Bosnia, related to propaganda, demolition, and guerrilla warfare;
      for Montenegro; and
      for the blockade of the Danube.

While SOE's activities and plans covered the entire Yugoslavia, their most important operations by far had been taking place in Serbia (including the Danube region), and had been planned for Serbia and Bosnia.

George Taylor reported to Sir Frank Nelson on 26 February 1941, that the Slovenes – who cooperated with SOE - did not represent a very large proportion of the Slovene people, but "they are highly organised on underground lines, and very experienced in conspiratorial work ..." .... "They have now definitely agreed to carry on small scale sabotage, large scale demolition, and even guerilla warfare in the event of Yugoslavia being invaded or occupied." (Report, page 7)

> We have two main organisations in this part of the Kingdom [Serbia and Bosnia].
> The first of these is the Serbian Peasant Party, of which the nominal leader is Doctor Milan Gavrilovic, now Minister in Moscow, and the effective leader, [Dr. Miloš] Tupanjanin, hereafter known as Uncle. We have subsidised this party since last July and they are definitely at our disposal for underground propaganda, sabotage and guerilla warfare once Yugoslavia is involved in war. (p. 8)

> The second of these [organizations] is virtually represented by our close personal relation with Ilya Trifunovic [Ilija Trifunović-Birčanin], hereafter known as Daddy, who is head of all the National Associations in Yugoslavia, such as Narodna Odbrana, Chetniks, and various other ex-service men's groups. ... Daddy has a very strong personal hold on all these groups, and is, we believe, entirely reliable as far as *working for us* is concerned. ... so far in the one matter in which we have tried it [the tightness of Daddy's organization] out, namely, the distribution of our materials throughout the country, it has proved effective. (pp. 8-9. Italics added.)

Stating that a plan for a particular system of communications had been worked out with the head of the Secret Intelligence Service, Taylor reported that two central radio stations would be established to communicate with the British War Station at Istanbul. One would be established at Belgrade, the other would be mobile, "established in the hills under war conditions, moving from place to place as the occasion requires." "The two sets required for this purpose are held in Belgrade, and competent operators are being finally trained in their use." (pp. 9-10) Subsidiary stations, intended to "simply communicate their messages to the central stations," were to be distributed as follows: in Ljubljana, for the Slovenes; in Zagreb, for the Croats; in Niš, for Daddy; somewhere in Bosnia, for Uncle; and in Podgorica, for Cousin [Colonel Dušan Radović]. (p. 10)

*****

Sweet-Escott, Taylor's very close associate, disclosed the following information on these sets: "The seven radio sets we had with such difficulty succeeded in extricating from 'Z' [the Secret Intelligence Service] have arrived in Belgrade before the *coup d'état*, but time had been too short to train the operators properly, and though the sets were distributed to our friends, they never came on the air." (Sweet-Escott, 64)

*****

Taylor's plans were to use the smuggled material for demolition and guerrilla warfare. For demolition, he reported, "we rely entirely upon Daddy's organisation." (p. 13) He expected Daddy to cooperate very closely with special battalions, commanded by General Mihailo Mihailović, especially in Southern Serbia. "They have also arranged for the reception by the special battalions of the explosives and other devices to be supplied by us." (p.14) As for guerrilla warfare,

> In this matter also we are working through Daddy, who has agreed to organise, out of his Chetniks and other patriotic organisations, guerilla bands which will remain behind after the occupation and carry on sabotage and terrorist work. These bands will also work in the closest co-operation with the special battalions. We have undertaken to provide Daddy's bands with some rifles, as many tommy-guns as we can obtain, Mauser machine pistols and supplies of hand grenades. (p.14)

*****

How "entirely reliably Daddy was working for the British" – to use Taylor's description – it was evident during the preparations for and the execution of the coup of 27 March 1941. "Uncle" proved his collaboration and reliability in many ways, including urging the three Ministers to resign on 20 March, spreading false rumors, urging Gen. Simović on 26 March to topple Prince Paul's Government, and pressing the members of the new Government to declare for war, etc.

*****

About the expected operations in Montenegro, Taylor informed his Executive Director:

> Cousin proposes, in the event either of formal war or a popular rising, to establish his headquarters at Podgorica and to use his guerilla bands to carry out sabotage raids. He also believes that he can 219rganize an information service on military movements, both in Albania and Yugoslavia, transmitting the intelligence to us by wireless with which we have provided him. His main dump for materials has already been established at Podgorica, and supplies are moving in via our consulate at Dubrovnik. (Report, p.15)

According to Taylor, building a "large stock" of " " and chocolate" in Yugoslavia - and overseeing their prompt distribution – began early in January. This coincides with the British awareness of Hitler's plans to intervene in Greece.

How "large" the stock sent to Yugoslavia was, one can sense from the information given by the prominent SOE operative in Belgrade, Alexander-Sandy Glen:

> Wireless sets were distributed by SOE, one playing an important role later. Considerable amounts of arms were also distributed including a consignment of 550 tommy guns to hands which were to use them well. Railway sabotage was practiced regularly in Slovenia and also in Serbia, while Bill Hudson [another SOE agent] sank at least one German ocean-going ship loading manganese ore on the Dalmatian coast." (Glen, 56)

*****

The copy of Taylor's report contains some hand-written notes on the margins, and some deletions of the text. Thus, along the subtitle "Yugoslavia, Contacts", there is a note, "The most hopeful section & most varied contacts". (page 7) Along the section on contacts with the Serbian Peasant Party, a note, "Have done well in political pressure". (p. 8) In the section on finances in Yugoslavia, there are two deletions of the text. (p. 11)

Appendix L

Calls to arms

Three Ministers in the Yugoslav Government resigned on 20 March. Svetislav-Sveta Petrović reacted over the short-wave radio station WRUL, Boston, Massachusetts.

> With my broadcast of March 21 I began to warn my people of the consequences of an eventual capitulation by Cvetkovitch. ...
>
> ... The first ray of hope came when ministers of the Serbian Agrarian Party and of the Independent Democratic Party, the only one of the Serbian democrats represented in the Government, resigned. ... The same day I told my people over the radio how much the world respected this first gesture of defiance against Hitler who was used to dictate and be obeyed. *Three posts in the cabinet remained open ...* (Petrovitch, 236-7. Italics added.)

The posts did not remain open. They were quickly filled – but the listeners were not told about it. "The Yugoslavs in emigration, specially the Serbs, were sending cable after cable to Belgrade in an attempt to save the people from shame while there was time." (Petrovitch, 237)

On 24, 25 and 26 March, "I openly called the people to arms". (Petrovitch, 238)

On 25 March, the day of the signing of the Tripartite Pact, "with bitterness over the radio from Boston", Petrović delivered a lengthy address to the Serbs. Telling them that the American people expressed "their greatest admirations for the Serbs", he continued:

> The traitors must be executed, say the Serbian people. And no one should take lightly a sentence passed by the Serbian people. The Serbs had sentenced to death the Ottoman Empire and the Austro-Hungarian Habsburg Empire, and both empires were destroyed with the help of allies. No one should doubt that the present sentence of the Serbian people against the traitors will not be carried out. For the Serbian people have passed the sentence openly and such sentence the heroic Serbian people always carry out. Woe to the cowards. (Petrovitch, 239-40)

He concluded his warnings with threats: "Those who will stand with the people in these fateful historic days will be blessed by future generations. Those against the people will be damned by history itself. They and their children's children will be damned by the people. To arms!"

> Three times daily, on March 24, 25, and 26, I called upon the people to select the government in whom they had full confidence, to call experienced national leaders to take over the fate and future of our country and to lead it the way our forefathers had shown us. (Petrovitch, 244)

As already stated, on 24 March Eden had authorized Campbell to secretly inform the coup conspirators of British support and recognition; during the 24 to 26 March period, *Vojvoda* Trifunović – in close cooperation with SOE – was advising Gen. Mirković about the coup; at the same time, Macdonald and Mapplebeck were urging Mirković in the same sense. On 26 March Macdonald met twice with Gen. Simović.

Coming from the United States, the urgings by Petrović could not fail to influence both the military conspirators and the civilian population.

Appendix M

About the Putsch, Putschists, and their Government

When considering the Putschists and their Government, it is informative to note the opinion of Professor Slobodan Jovanović, president of the *Srpski kulturni klub (The Serbian cultural club)* – who strongly opposed Prince Paul's policies. The Professor's opinion has particular importance because he became the Second Vice-Premier in the Simović's Government on 27 March 1941, and replaced the General as the Premier of the exile Government [11 January 1942 – 26 June 1943].

Slobodan Jovanović's remarks

Simović was always manifesting Yugoslavian tendencies, wrote Jovanović. While he was fairly fit to maintain contact between the military and the politicians, deep down in his soul he had no confidence in the politicians. He associated with them under the pressure of circumstances. In exile, never ceased thinking of the reconstruction of his Government. (Jovanović, 20, 23)

Reasons for the fall of Simović's Putschist Government were many, and that analysis is outside the scope of this book. However, some of the reasons included the coup-wishers' diverse motivations and goals that existed before the Putsch was executed. Slobodan Jovanović wrote afterward about discordant relations not only between Simović, the General and Party-politicians, but about the political Parties as well.

First, some of his notes on the military men and politicians. In his opinion:

• The fall of Simović's Government broke the ties which existed between the generals and the party-chiefs on 27 March 1941.
• Although by his flexibility and superficial affability he seemed at the time suitable to maintain a link between the military and politicians, Simović ((in no way ceased to think about the reconstruction of his Government with non-party individuals, such as for example Boža Maksimović – although at the time of his fall he still did not have that reconstruction prepared.))
• The politicians had to sense that Simović had not been completely sincere with them. He had no truly friendly relation with any of them, except with Budisavljević, and with him for a short time only.
• One more thing contributed to the parting between Simović and the politicians. He saw himself exclusively as the hero of the 27th March. The politicians saw in him the man responsible for the unexpectedly swift military collapse. In their eyes, his value was not any more as great as it had been on the day of the Putsch. As civilians are generally unwilling to put up with the superiority and leadership of the military, so the politicians in the Simović's Government probably could hardly wait to break off with a military man whose star began to fade. (Jovanović, 23)

S. Jovanović made a distinction among the officers involved in the Putsch. There were two groups. The first – mostly young officers, personally motivated, convinced of a need to prevent Yugoslavia from joining the Axis *"po svaku cenu"* (*at any price*). The officers in the second group, ((among whom at the head was Mirković, they stood in close ties with English agents and were by them motivated and encouraged.)) "među kojima je bio na prvom mestu Mirković, stajali su u tesnoj vezi s engleskim agentima i bili su poglavito od njih podstaknuti i ohrabreni." (Jovanović, 30. Italics added.)

Jovanović's characterization of Mirković: ((He was not reflecting [on a subject] a lot, he was ready in a moment for everything, and one could say that he was rather unrestrained than energetic in a true sense of the word.)) "Nije mnogo premišljao, bio je začas gotov na sve, i pre bi se moglo reći da je bio neobuzdan nego energičan u pravom smislu reči." (Jovanović, 30)

As this perceptive observer viewed it, the Serbs have less national discipline than the Croats and the Bulgars. The Serb members of the Government of 27 March belonged to several political parties: the

Radicals, Democrats, Agrarians ["Serbian Peasant Party" (SPP)], Yugoslav Nationalists. (Jovanović, 69)

Now some of Jovanović's notes on the political Parties and their leaders:

- The Serb members of the Putschist Government were divided into several groups.
- Banjanin of the Yugoslav National Party, and Budisavljević of the Independent Democrats, were in agreement to such extent that for practical purposes they constituted one group.
- Two leaders of the Serbian Peasant Party were in the Government, Čubrilović and Gavrilović. On 27 March Gavrilović was the Yugoslav Ambassador in Moscow, and a few months later came to London unwillingly. From earlier times Gavrilović did not get along with Ninčić [of the Radical Party] and Grol [of the Democratic Party]. In addition, because of its heterogeneous composition, Gavrilović did not have much confidence in the heterogeneous makeup of the Government. He was not hindering the Government's activities, but he was not wholly in solidarity with them either. His reserved attitude during the Ministerial sessions created all kinds of assumptions, and many thought that he had had some secret plans against the Government. Jovanović did not share that impression. In his opinion, Gavrilović tended to accept as little responsibility for the missteps of the Government as possible. ((He was saving himself for the situation that would arise after the war.)) "On se čuvao za onu situaciju koja je imala da nastane po svršetku rata"
- The Radicals and the Democrats were very active in the Government, but both followed their own direction. The Radicals behaved as if only they understood true Serb interests, and only they defended them. On that point the Democrats observed that the Radicals were claiming for themselves the monopoly of patriotism, and that they suspected national sentiments of all those who were not in their Party.
- The Democrats behaved as if they wanted to monopolize for themselves the defense of the Yugoslav state, as if they were the true statesmen, and other Serbian politicians were just nationalistic demagogues. (Jovanović, 69-72)

*****

Hugh Seton-Watson, a brainy former SOE agent involved with Yugoslavia, in 1951 offered his opinion about the Putschist Government:

> The government that followed the *coup* was formed for the greater part not of officers but of the old politicians of the democratic opposition. Their most obvious characteristic was Serbian nationalism and distrust of the Croats. Indeed there is some ground for the suspicion that they were more interested in undoing the concessions made to the Croats by Prince Paul in 1939 than in resisting the Axis. Certainly they hastened to assure Berlin and Rome that they considered the signature of the Three Power Alliance binding. At the same time they sought closer relations with Moscow. (Seton-Watson(ER), 66)

However, **IF** the Serb politicians were mostly interested in undoing the Serbo-Croat *Sporazum (Agreement)* of August 1939, Simović did not share that with them at that time. Whether he approved of the *Sporazum,* or just needed the support of the Croats for his policies of supporting "the Allies" and sharing in their victory, he wanted Maček in his Government. Professor Jovanović asserted that:

Simović accepted Maček's conditions for joining the Government;

Simović did so on his own, without prior consultation with other members of the Government;

these conditions – related to the functions of the gendarmerie and the application of laws in Banovina Hrvatska - actually broadened the concessions granted in the *Sporazum.* (Jovanović, 10)

Mirković's role in the coup

- **According to his memoirs, 1941**

Years before Professor Slobodan Jovanović had described Gen. Mirković as the head of officers who ((stood in close ties with English agents and were motivated and encouraged by them)), the General wrote about his role in the coup.

His dissatisfaction with the situation in Yugoslavia and with her leaders dated from the early existence of the state, 1918 – 1919. He characterized the leaders of the state as devoid of leadership qualities, while "irresponsible elements" and "a-national" people were totally compromising the idea of the unification of the South Slavs. (Bosnić(ed), 13)

Sometime in 1936, when he had achieved a position from which he could gather around positive forces, he made the decision to topple, once and for all, the shameful regimes of shirkers, marauders, and vagabonds who, after the unification [in 1918], followed each other, and were preparing the nation's ruin. (Bosnić(ed), 14)

Mirković systematically worked first on gathering and spiritually preparing younger men with whom he had had official contacts, not only in the Air Force, but in the entire Belgrade garrison. (Bosnić(ed), 14)

In 1937 – during the debate about the *Concordat* between Yugoslavia and the Vatican - Mirković had the first opportunity to realize his intentions and to overturn «the most shameful regime which ever existed in our land» – the regime of Milan Stojadinović. (Bosnić(ed), 15)

In his mind Mirković had prepared everything. Only one order was needed, and everything would have been done in a flash. However, his family misfortunes prevented him from doing it. (Bosnić(ed), 15)

*****

While Mirković claimed family misfortune, Simović provided a different explanation. Affirming that he knew that Mirković had been thinking about the overthrow of the regime for several years, Simović wrote that in July 1937 - during the fight about the *Concordat* - Simović hurried to return home from a trip

> ((in order to stop the execution of the overthrow at that time which would have drawn the military into an internal political struggle. - My goal was: to preserve the land and the military from unnecessary shocks, and to use personal ambitions and energy of General Borivoje Mirković in a useful direction and at the right moment, when the essential interests of the land and legal rights of our people would be imperilled. I had in mind such a role for him.))

> «da bi zadržao izvršenje prevrata koji je bio neoportun u tome vremenu i koji bi uvukao vojsku u unutrašnju političku borbu. - Cilj mi je bio: da zemlju i vojsku sačuvam od nepotrebnih potresa i da lične ambicije i energiju đenerala Borivoja Mirkovića upotrebim u korisnom pavcu i u pravom času, kad bitni interesi zemlje i legalna prava našeg naroda budu ugroženi. Takvu sam mu ulogu i namenio.» (Simović(44), 1-2)

One has to wonder about Simović's claim that already in 1937 he had foreseen that the interests and 'legal rights' of the people would be imperilled in 1941, and that he would 'use' Mirković at that time.

Now back to Mirković.

*****

To achieve his goal successfuly, however, he needed troops. So in 1939 Mirković approached General Aleksandar Stanković, the Commandant of the Royal Guards. When he invited Stanković to execute a coup d'état together, Stanković refused. Then Mirković asked Stanković to promise him not to use the Royal Guards when he, Mirković, and other troops of the Belgrade garrison do it. Stanković promised. (Bosnić(ed), 15-16)

Then, sometime in early 1940, Mirković attempted to engage General Bogoljub Ilić to cooperate in and support his plan. Ilić responded that it was too early for such a plan. (Bosnić(ed), 16)

Not having collaborators among higher-ranking officers, Mirković had to play for time. The only hope and strength on which he could rely were younger officers. (Bosnić(ed), 16)

*****

Gen. Mirković also approached a man he did not mention in his memoirs. Professor Staniša Vlahović published several articles based on conversations about the coup in Belgrade he had had with Gen. Mirković In 1954, 1955 and 1962, in London. The following details are taken from Vlahović's article

»Bez Kosova gore od Kosova, 62. godišnjica 27. marta 1941.» («Without Kosovo worse than Kosovo»), *Iskra,* Birmingam, 1 May 2003.

The General had the idea to overthrow Prince Paul's regime also in 1938, but he needed time to find a most suitable person to take over and lead affairs of the state. Such a person had to have the best character and moral qualities, ability to lead the state, and enjoy the confidence of the people. Not having been successful in this search, he decided to find a most suitable General. In the beginning of 1940 he wanted to accelerate the search in order to act in October. However, during the great military maneuvers in August 1940 in central Yugoslavia, he met an old friend from the Salonika front of the First World War, reserve Lt.-Col. Dimitrije Ljotić, president of a political movement called «Zbor». After hearing the General's plan, Ljotić refused to participate for two reasons: 1 – the path to power should be only through the Constitution and elections, and 2 – because of the internal and internatioal situation, the *coup d'état* would lead to the collapse and dismemberment of Yugoslavia. Mirković was disappointed.

Writing about Mirković's 1941-memoirs in Belgrade's biweekly *Duga,* in 1995, journalist Nenad Stefanović supplemented his comments with information from Vlahović's article. He also added Gen. Simović's critical remarks related to Mirković's account.
    Back to Mirković again.

*****

Mirković did not write what, specifically, these 'new people' would have to do politically and/or militarily to achieve the set goal. He firmly believed that two men, Generals Ilić and Simović - whose names he had been elevating to the Himmalayan heights (Bosnić(ed), 19-20) - would do the right things.

- **In 1948**

More than six years later, on 18 April 1948, in London, Mirković provided a different explanation for the neeed for a coup. In a letter to the former Premier Cvetković, a 'friend and relative', then in Paris, the General wrote:

((All this has been a historic necessity, as if everyting was coming down from HEAVEN, because of the sins committed on all sides of the state's and social life, came also the punishment. ...))
((I am not charging you, even now I am defending you, and whatever happened the way it did, as I already said: DIVINE PROVIDENCE. One could not avoid it, and with this let us end our explanation, ...))
«Sve je ovo bila jedna istorijska nužda, i kao da je sve s NEBA dolazilo, a radi grehova počinjenih na svima stranama državnog i društvenog života, došla je i kazna. ...»
« ... ja Tebe ne teretim, ja Te i sada branim, a što se sve pa onako desi, kako Ti napred rekoh: BOŽJA PROMISAO. Nije se moglo izbeći i sa tim završimo naše objašnjenje, ...»
(Dragiša Cvetković Collection, Mirković correspondence, Box 1, Hoover Institution Archives)

For Mirković - in 1941: the reason for effecting the change were the humans, their bad behavior ... In 1948: the sins of the humans, the will of Providence !

- **In 1955**

And 14 years after the coup Mirković added yet another explanatiion for the coup of March 1941, expressed in a letter to *Glas Kanadskih Srba (Voice of Canadian Serbs)*, dated 27 March 1955 in London, (Excerpts, translated)

((Your paper, *Glas Kanadskih Srba,* on 19 January 1955, carried the article "Fragments out of a book about the March 27th", signed by Živan L. Knežević. As this one, and similar falsificates of that historic date, ... threaten to mislead the uninformed world, and particularly our public, I am forced to also request the hospitality of your esteemed paper, with one and only intention, to illuminate, truthfully and correctly, the matters, people and events in which I had participated.)) (Karapandžić(AB), 134)

((Then handing over all authority immediately to the democratic Parties, we had thought that our ship of state would – at the last moment, in that global storm, and in danger, follow the right course, steered with a strong hand and a harmonious will of all people, inside and outside [the country] - arrive, with other free peoples, into a secure port of peace and justice. But everything went over a precipice. Hitler's and Mussolini's attack, and the tempest of the Second world war which grasped us, prevented a peaceful development of our young state....)) (Karapandžić(AB), 135)

Did he expect Hitler not to react to the coup, or did he want Yugoslavia to stay out the war? As shown in **Chapter 8**, in 1960 he had written:

((My conviction at that time was that our destiny in that war had to be tied to the destiny of the Great western powers, not to the destiny of Hitler's Nazi Germany, because I was foreseeing that the final victory in the war would belong to the Western Powers.)) (Karapandžić(AB), 146)

So: Mirković did not want Yugoslavia to stay out of the war.

Mirković's role in the coup ... according to Dr. Miloš Sekulić

(In an earlier issue of his bulletin, *Seljačka Jugoslavija (Peasant Yugoslavia),* Dr. Miloš Sekulić wrote about conspiratorial meetings and talks among General Dušan Simović, Joca Jovanović Pižon, and Dr Milan Gavrilović. In the issue of 2 April 1947 Sekulić reported on the matters pertaining to the Belgrade *coup d'état* of 27 March 1941.)

Sekulić was informed, to some extent, about activities of his comrades in the Agrarian Party [i.e. the Serbian Peasant Party]. He also knew about some other groups. The group to which he belonged was meeting every Sunday, mostly at night, at General Bora Mirković's place at the Zemun airport, but sometimes also at the villa of Steva Popović, near Avala. The meetings were attended by General Mirković, Colonels Draža Mihailović and Žarko Popović, professor and writer Steva Jakovljević, Dr. Miloš Simović (brother of General D. Simović), and Sekulić. At the suggestion and invitation by Sekulić, and with accurate information about the topic, a meeting was attended also by Dr. Milan Gavrilović, two days before his departure for Moscow as Yugoslavia's Ambassador. (At this time Gavrilović was talking with Julian Amery about British political and financial support for his Serbian Peasant Party. **Appendix D.**)

The central figure at the meetings was Mirković, and topics included psychological preparation for actions, and assessments of events and individuals. Occasionally the General talked about his contacts within the military, especially the air force personnel, and their role in a *coup d'état* - under his guidance and orders. After the coup he would hand over political and military authority to General Simović.

The last time this group met was at a dinner **on 1 April 1941** – four days after the coup – at the house of Dr. Miloš Simović. Present were only Mirković, Steva Popović, and Miloš Sekulić, in addition to the host. Mihailović was on a military assignment outside Belgrade, and Žarko Popović in Moscow, as the military attaché.
    Praising Mirković for the brilliant execution of the coup, they asked him for details. He complied. Here are the points he emphasized:
    he alone, without informing anybody in the world, **made the decision to exxecute the coup**, on the day the Pact had been signed (25 March);
    he had the plan in his head ... nothing on paper;
    he was alone in the office ... and exactly **at 2 p.m. of the 26th March he made the decision ... definitive;**
    he called General Simović, who was resting, and so left a message with his wife to, please, come to see Mirković;
    when Simović came, Mirković informed him: ((General, Sir, tonight I attack and strike down the traitors.)) "Gospodine Generale, noćas napadam i obaram izdajnike."
     ((Do not, for God's sake, it is early, wait a while.)) "Nemoj, kumim te Bogom, rano je, pričekaj malo!" (said Simović).
    ((It's done, General, Sir. I am not revoking the decision, and you go to your home and wait.)) "Svršeno, Gospodine Generale. Odluku ne povlačim, a Vi idite u stan i čekajte."

Then they embraced and kissed.

The time for the execution of the coup was set for 27 March, **at 2:20 a.m.**.

Mirković had only so much connection with Dušan Simović that he consented to make him the head of the revolutionary government and to be the leader of the state's politics ... reportedly said Mirković, in the presence of Miloš Simović.

(("There, this is the truth about the 27th March ...")) "Eto, to je istina o 27 martu ..." - concluded Sekulić his article in 1947 ... when both brothers Simović were back in Communist-ruled Belgrade.

*****

Mirković claimed that **on the afternoon of the 25th** he had told Macdonald that he would overthrow the government. That implies that his decision had already been made at that time. Then again he repeatedly claimed that he had not made the final decision until **the afternoon of the 26th** - two days after Eden authorized Campbell to secretly inform the leaders Britain's support.

While Mirković was boasting about his role to admiring listeners, Col. Vladimir Vauhnik was getting precious information in Berlin about the forthcoming German attack on Yugoslavia – which the new Government did not take seriously.

The coup ... "one of the most unrealistic ... defiance" ... "Britain simply did not have the resources."

- **Military historian John Keegan, in 1989**

    The Mirković coup still appears in retrospect one of the most unrealistic, if romantic, acts of defiance in modern European history. Not only did it threaten to divide a precariously unified country; it was also bound to provoke the Germans to hostile reaction, against which the Serbs could call on no external assistance whatsoever to support them. They were surrounded by states that were wholly inert, like Albania, or as threatened as themselves, like Greece, or actively hostile, like Italy, Hungary, Romania and Bulgaria, with all of which they had bitter and long-standing territorial disputes. If Croatia, which would shortly take its own independence under Italian tutelage, is added to the roll of the Serbs' enemies, the behaviour of General Mirković and his fellow conspirators of 27 March appears a collective equivalent of Gavrilo Princip's firebrand assault on the Austro-Hungarian monarchy personified by Archduke Franz Ferdinand in June 1914. It ensured the extinction of the Serb national cause as if by reflex; it would also doom Serbia, as in 1914, to invasion, defeat and occupation and with it the peoples of Yugoslavia, of whom the Serbs had assumed leadership in 1918, to an agony of protracted civil and guerrilla warfare for the next four years. Of none of this do Mirković, Simović or any of the other Serb patriots – reserve officers, cultural stalwarts and the like – who staged the 27 March coup seem to have taken the least reckoning. ... (Keegan, 152)

    ... Diplomatically it [defiance] put Yugoslavia in the wrong; for all the popular enthusiasm displayed for the coup - crowds cheering the Allied cause in Belgrade, whose streets were bedecked with British and French flags - the new government could with some reason be denounced as illegitimate. Militarily, it provided OKH [German Army Supreme Command] with a solution of its logistic difficulties: the Yugoslav railway system, ... , connected with those of Austria, Hungary, Romania and Greece (as Bulgaria's did not) and thereby provided the Wehrmacht with a direct approach to its chosen battlefront in Macedonia. Hitler did not pause to seize the advantage he had been offered. (Keegan, 152-4)

- **Alexander Glen, in 1975 and 2002**

Aleander-Sandy Glen, an important SOE-participant in the coup-related events, in 1975 acknowledged the influence and encouragement of the British service attachés on the execution of the coup, but still wrote: «In short, 27 March 1941 was a wholly Yugoslav occasion and it shoould always have an honoured place in Yugolav history.» (Glen, 63-4)

Some sixty years after the Putsch, he assessed it differently: "On military facts, the *coup* and its consequences were foolhardy." (Glen(B), 60-61) The stark truth was that "Britain was in no position to offer material supply or effective support to any Yugoslav government. Britain simply did not have the resources." (Glen(B), 58)

Given such circumstances, *was it not the British nation that lost its soul by "getting Yugoslavia in to the war anyhow"?*

- **Captain (later Major) Dragiša Ristić**

In the "Foreword" of Ristić's book, dated 11 September 1959, Simović stated that Ristić had been his *"close collaborator", "a qualified and competent reporter of the events described in [his] book"*. In 1966, in his "Balance sheet", Ristić concluded:

> Undeniably, the overthrow of the Regency and the Cvetković government precipitated the German attack on Yugoslavia. ... Had the Cvetković government remained in power, Yugoslavia might not have participated in the German campaign against Russia, ... Admittedly, the Ustaše atrocities and the German reprisals provoked by Tito's partisans could scarcely have occurred without March 27 and the ensuing German conquest. ... (Ristić, 137-8)

The Putschists and Churchill's memoirs

Excerpts from Gen. Mirković's letter to Belgrade's *Evening News,* 4 November 1960 (translated):

> ((When, in London, Simović was overthrown as Prime Minister (on 11 January 1942), and when, sometime later, Radoje Knežević heard that data were being collected for Churchill's memoirs, which would be published after the end of the war, he succeeded - through his connections - to deliver also data about our Coup d'état. On that occasion Radoje Knežević submitted also the following: that, allegedly, on 27 March 1941, Simović had had the intention to proclaim himself the Governor of the state, on the model of Antonescu in Rumania, but that he, Radoje Knežević – as a democrat and politician – dissuaded him from [doing] that.
> ((That way an incorrect and mean information entered into the Churchill's memoirs, to the detriment of General Simović's reputation, presenting him as a man with dictatorial tendencies, and professor Knežević as a democrat.)) (Karapandžić(AB), 150-51)

Appendix N

Leaving the country

When *the emotional drunk in Belgrade began to wear off* a few days after the Putsch (to use St. John's observation), pilots and even some commanders of Air Force units started asking the British Air Force Attaché's advice about leaving the country. (Stafford(cp), 415) From Macdonald's report to the Air Ministry, dated 31 March 1941, it is not clear who the inquirers were - participants or non-participants in the Putsch or perhaps both.

According to Ž. Knežević:
    On 16 April, in Nikšić, groups leaving the country were formed for each plane. Gen. Mirković was loading another box of state's gold into each plane. Other boxes were returned to a place somewhere in Nikšić. The planes waited until 2:20 p.m.. There were five planes behind the one in which Živan left. They took off every five minutes. (Milunović(ed), 62)

Three days later Knežević found out that the following had arrived in Athens:
    all members of the Government with their wives,
    Gen. Mirković with the wife, daughter and a niece,
    Simović's Chief of Cabinet, Radoje Nikolić, with his wife,
    Božidar-Boka Vlajić with his wife,
    Gen. Simović's brother, Dr. Miloš-Miša,
    Bičanić, Krsto Miletić, Miloš Bobić, Dobra Lazarević, and Boža Maksimović.
Only the brothers Knežević did not take their wives along – as it had been previously agreed with Simović to leave the wives back home. (Milunović(ed), 62)

No claim is made here that only the above-identified persons have left Yugoslavia at that time.

Sources

- ## Notes regarding General Simović's and General Mirković's documents

A - On 28 March 1941, after *the Thanksgiving service* for the young King Peter's accession to the throne , Simović delivered a long speech before the Holy Assembly of Bishops of the Serbian Orthodox Church about the coup of 27 March 1941 and his own role in it. His speech was recorded by two stenographers, in the presence of the Chief of the Central Press Bureau, Dr. Milorad Radovanović. Patriarch Gavrilo [Dr. Dožić] included the recorded text of the speech in his Memoirs, and Živan Knežević reprinted it in his book, *27 mart 1941* (pp. 361-70).

B - Mirković himself never **published** his memoirs, which were dated and signed in Cairo on 1 December 1941. In various newspaper articles he wrote and/or debated about specific subjects and/or events, but his overall account was published in Belgrade for the first time in 1995.

The typescript, *Istina o 27. martu 1941. godine* (*The truth about the 27th March 1941*), was brought to Belgrade after the conclusion of WWII. Given to the *Military-Historic Institute of the Yugoslav National Army* in Belgrade, the script was forwarded, for comments, to Gen. Simović – who in 1945 had returned from London to Belgrade.

Mirković's text and Simović's comments were published by Nenad Stefanović in Belgrade's biweekly *Duga*, in March and April, 1995. Petar Bosnić then published the memoirs - and information on their itinerary - in a serial in Belgrade's daily *Politika*, in March and April 1996. The same year he also published them in book format. Translated data, appearing here, are taken from that book.

However, these Mirković's memoirs were circulated in Great Britain. They served - among other purposes - as a source for an article titled, "March 27th. Day of Pride. Yugoslavia Thrice-armed", reportedly written (but not signed) "by one who was present on the day". The Hon. Rowland Winn advised Guy Wisdom to send it to Frank Betts, in London, to be published on or near the first anniversary of the coup. The article contained the following exchange between Mirković and British Air Attaché A. Hugh Macdonald:

> The day the pact was signed [25 March 1941] a British Embassy official called on General Mirkovitch in his office, to inform him of the fact.
> The General replied "That pact must be killed!"
> "But what is to be done?"
> "That is my responsibility. The pact must be killed."
> "And who can do it?"
> "I can." said the General, gravely.

(Žarko Popović collection, Box 2, folder 2.21, Hoover Institution Archives)

C – Formed on that fateful day of 27 March, 1941, without a consensus political program, the Simović Government fell on 11 January 1942. As mentioned in Chapter 8, on 9 July 1942 the General offered his military services to Prime Minister Churchill. On 25 August 1942 Churchill coolly rejected that offer.

Without an official assignment, Simović turned to writing his memoirs, among other things.

In a lengthy document, dated 1 January 1944 in London-Barnet, the General described the events related to the coup in a 30-pages, single-spaced type-script with Latin letters. The account of the 27 March 1941 *coup d'état* Simović organized in three sections: Prethodni događaji; Događaji koji su prethodili 27. martu; and Pripreme za državni udar (Preceding events; Events which preceded to the 27th March; and Preparations for the *coup d'état*). Then he added one page of changes and supplements, hand-written in Cyrillic. (Dušan T. Simović, Recollection of events surrounding coup of 3/27/41, Box 1, Hoover Institution Archives)

However, his associates transcribed only the first 20 pages of the original into a 41-page document with Cyrillic type, without incorporating the requested changes and supplements.

On the first page in the upper right-hand corner of the typescript - 41 pages long, double-spaced - there is a hand-written note, in Cyrillic: "Za Dr Mišu Simovića" (For Dr Miša Simović) [the General's brother Miloš].

On the last page there is a hand-written explanation, in Serbian: ((20 March 1944, Cairo. Compared and found that the transcription is true to the original.
/signed/ Colonel S. T. Živković
Colonel Žar. R. Popović
Dr. Miloš T. Simović))

For purposes of reference, this account is entitled here "Simović(44)"

In Box 1, along with Simović's recollections there are comments on the document, addressed to the General by his devoted former adjutant, Captain Dragiša N. Ristić. Most of them suggested a need to rewrite or delete the General's phrasing of the role of Major Živan Knežević which - in Ristić's opinion - the self-promoting Major had not deserved at all. Ristić wrote that Major Knežević's influence among officers was non-existent, that the brothers Knežević were "morbidly ambitious", and that they had cashed in on the coup "to the utmost limits".

D - Ristić's book, *Yugoslavia's Revolution of 1941,* was published in 1966. In the Forward to the book, on 11 September 1959 Dušan T. Simović wrote: "I entrusted my archives to him for the sake of preservation and in order to set the record straight - the record of my endeavors and work." Ristić often quoted from *Simović's "Memoirs"* - and his own recollections and diary - but it is not clear which version of the General's recollections was he referring to: the updated ones, as suggested by Ristić, or the un-updated ones. At least in one scene - Simović's instruction to Mirković during their second meeting on 26 March - Ristić used his updated version.

E - As total British political, propaganda, and military support was behind the Communist-controlled Partisans in Yugoslavia, in March 1944 Simović also declared his support for the Partisans. In May 1945 he returned from London to Belgrade. The communist Government gave him a General's pension and the right to live in his pre-war home. Those were great benefits at the time: after all, the Putsch set in motion the events which ultimately led to Communist power in Yugoslavia. As shown in Chapter 8, on 14 June 1951, *The Institute for Historical Inquiries* asked the General to comment on some political events in Yugoslavia, including the coup of 27 March 1941. Some of his responses and comments, dated July 1951, translated, are summarized in this book and referred to as document «Simović(51)".

F - Troubled by claims and comments, published mostly abroad, about the Putsch of March 27, 1941, in 1956 General Simović wrote an explanation which he, allegedly, kept to himself for some five years, and decided - shortly before his death on 26 August 1962 - to send abroad for publication.

With an accompanying letter, dated 8 December 1961, he forwarded ((a handwritten text in which he explained the role of the participants in the coup d'état of 27 March, 1941)) to Ante Smith Pavelić. With another letter dated 22 March, 1962, Simović sent to Smith Pavelić ((some supplements and corrections of that text, with the instruction that these documents could be published in their entirety only after his death))

Smith Pavelić fulfilled Simović's wish. With a letter dated in Paris 24 September, 1962 - containing the above cited information - he sent the General's text to Jovan Kontić, the editor of *Glasnik (The Herald)* of the Serbian historical-cultural association "Njegoš", to be published. The editor did so in the issue No. 10, December 1962, under the title "Politički testament generala Dušana Simovića" ((Political testament of General Dušan Simović)), duly noting that Simović's letter was being published in its entirety. The document is here referred to as «Simović(56)".

Sources and selected bibliography

Alexander, Field Marshal, Earl of Tunis *The Alexander Memoirs 1940-1945,* Cassell, London, 1962
Amery, Julian *Approach March: a Venture in Autobiography,* Hutchinson of London, 1973
Amery[A] Amery, Julian *Sons of the Eagle ,   A study in Guerrilla War,* Hailer Publishing, St. Petersburg, Florida, 2005. (First published in 1948.)
Autty & Clogg(ed) Autty, Phyllis and Clogg, Richard (ed) *British Policy Towards Wartime Resistance in Yugoslavia and Greece* Barnes & Noble with S.S.E.E.S., 1975

Bailey, Roderick " Communist in SOE: Explaining James Klugman's Recruitment and Retention", *Intelligence and National Security,* Volume 20, Number 1, March 2005
Bailey et al   Bailey, Ronald H. et al. *Partisans and Guerrillas,* World War II Time-Life Books, Alexandria, Virginia, 1978
Bailey(fv) Bailey, Roderick   *Forgotten Voices of the Secret War,* Ebury Press, 2008
Balfour & Mackay   Balfour, Neal & Mackay, Sally   *Paul of Yugoslavia, Britain's Maligned Friend,* Hamish Hamilton, London, 1980
Barker, Elisabeth *British Policy in South-East Europe in the Second World War,* Macmillan, London, 1976
Barker(CE) Barker, Elisabeth   *Churchill and Eden at War,* St. Martins, New York, 1978
Basta, Milan *Rat je završen 7 dana kasnije* (Treće izdanje), Zagreb-Novi Sad.Priština-Mostar-Opatija-Ljubljana, 1980
Batty, Peter   *Hoodwinking Churchill: Tito's Great Confidence Trick*   London, Shepheard-Walwyn, 2011
Beevor, Antony   *The Second World War* New York, Boston, London   Little, Brown and Company, 2012
Beloff, Nora   *Tito's Flawed Legacy: Yugoslavia & the West 1939-84,* Victor Gollancz Ltd, London, 1985
Bennett, Ralph *Ultra and Mediterranean Strategy,* William Morrow and Co, New York, 1989
Blake & Louis (eds)   Blake, Robert & Louis, Roger *Churchill,*   W.W. Norton & Company, New York, London, 1993
Blau, George E. *Invasion Balkans! The German Campaign in the Balkans, Spring 1941,* Burd Street Press, Shippensburg, PA, 1997
Blum, John Morton   *From The Morgenthau Diaries, Years of Urgency 1938-1941,* Houghton Mifflin Co. , Boston, 1965
Bosnić(ed)   Mirković, Borivoje *Istina o 27. martu 1941. godine (The Truth about the 27th March 1941),* Prepared and edited by Petar Bosnić, Beograd, 1996
Boyle, Andrew   *The Climate of Treason   Five who Spied for Russia,* Hutchinson of London, 1979
Brock, Ray   *Nor Any Victory* Reynal & Hitchcock,   New York, 1942
Bruce Lockhart, R.H.   *Comes the Reckoning,* Putnam, London, 1947
Buchanan, Patrick   *Churchill, Hitler, and "The Unnecessary War" : How Britain lost its empire and the West lost the world* Three Rivers Press, New York, 2008
Buck, Tim   *Yours in the Struggle - Reminiscences of Tim Buck,* NC Press Limited, Toronto, 1977

Carlton, David   *Anthony Eden   A Biography,* Allen Lane, London, 1981
Cave Brown1   Cave Brown, Anthony   *Bodyguard of Lies* Harper & Row, New York, 1975
Cave Brown2   ---   *The Last Hero   Wild Bill Donovan* Vintage Books, Random House, New York, 1984
Charmley, John *Churchill: The End of Glory   A Political Biography,* Harcourt Brace & Co., New York, San Diego, London, 1993

Churchill, Winston S. *The Second World War:*
Churchill(GS)   ---   *The Gathering Storm,* Houghton Mifflin Company, Boston, 1948
Churchill(FH)   ---   *Their Finest Hour,* Houghton Mifflin Company, Boston, 1949
Churchill(GA)   ---   *The Grand Alliance,* Houghton Mifflin Company, Boston, 1950
Churchill(HF)   ---   *The Hinge of Fate,* Houghton Mifflin Company, Boston, 1950
Churchill(CR)   ---   *Closing the Ring,* Houghton Mifflin Company, Boston, 1951
Churchill(TT)   ---   *Triumph and Tragedy,* Houghton Mifflin Company, Boston, 1953

Clissold, Stephen   *Whirlwind : An Account of Marshal Tito's Rise to Power,* Philosophical Library, New York, 1949
Clissold(ed)   Clissold, Stephen   *Yugoslavia and the Soviet Union 1939-1973 A Documentary Survey,*   Oxford University Press, London   New York Toronto, 1975
Colville, John   *The Fringes of Power, 10 Downing Street Diaries 1939-1955,* W.W. Norton & Co., New York, 1986
Corselli & Ferrar   Corsellis, John and Ferrar, Marcus   *Slovenia 1945 Memories of Death and Survival after World War II,* I.B. Tauris & Co, New York, 2006 (First published 2005.)
Cripps Brashaw, Nicholas   *Signals Intelligence, The British and the War in Yugoslavia 1941-1945* Dissertation submitted for Degree of Doctor of Philosophy, University of Southampton, December 2001

Dalton, High   *The Fateful Years   Memoirs 1939-1945,* Frederick Muller Ltd, London, 1957
Danchev(ed), Danchev, Alex   *Establishing the Anglo-American Alliance -   The Second World War Diaries of Brigadier Vivian Dykes,* Brassey's(UK), London, 1990
Davidson, Basil   *Special Operations Europe Scenes form the Anti-Nazi War,* Readers Union Group of Books Club, Newton Abbot 1981. (First published by Victor Gollancz , 1980)
Davidson(pp) Davidson, Basil   *Partisan Picture,* Bedford Books Ltd. , Bedford, 1946
Davies, Joseph E. *Mission to Moscow,* Simon and Schuster, New York, 1941

Deakin, F.W.D. *The Embattled Mountain* Oxford University Press, 1972 (First published 1971)
Dedijer1 Dedijer, Vladimir *Novi prilozi za biografiju Josipa Broza Tita 1,* GRO "Liburnija", Rijeka, 1981
Dedijer2 --- *Novi prilozi za biografiju Josipa broza Tita 2,* GRO "Liburnija", Rijeka, 1981
De Guingand, Major General Sir Francis *Operation Victory,* Natraj Publishers, Dehra Dun, 2006 (First published in 1947)
Dilks(ed), Dilks, David *Diaries of Sir Alexander Cadogan, O.M., 1938-1945,* G. P. Putman's Sons, New York, 1972
Dilks2(ed) *Retreat from Power, Studies in Britain's Foreign Policy of the twentieth Century, Volume Two, After 1939,* M, 1981 (First published 1981 by The Macmillan Press Ltd.)
- David Dilks, "Introduction"
- David Dilks, "The Twilight War and the Fall of France: Chamberlain and Churchill in 1940"
- The Late Lord Strang, "War and Foreign Policy: 1939-45"
- Graham Ross, "Operation Bracelet: Churchill in Moscow, 1942"
- Margaret Gowing, "Britain, America and the Bomb"
- Sarvepalli Gopal, "Nehru and the Commonwealth"
- Edward Spiers, "The British Nuclear Deterrent: Problems and Possibilities"

Djilas, Milovan *Wartime,* Translated by Michael B. Petrovich, Harcourt Brace Jovanovich, New York and London, 1977
Djilas(C) Djilas, Milovan *Conversations with Stalin,* Translated by Michael B. Petrovich, Harcourt, Brace & World, New York, 1962
Djilas(T) Djilas, Milovan *TITO The Story from Inside,* Translated by Vasilije Kojić and Richard Hayes, Harcourt Brace Jovanovich, New York and London, 1980
Dodds-Parker, Douglas *Setting Europe Ablaze Some Account of Ungentlemanly Warfare,* Springwood Books, 1984 (First printing 1983.)
Dorril, Stephen *MI6 Inside the Covert World of Her Majesty's Secret Intelligence Service,* The Free Press, New York London Toronto Sydney Singapore, 2000
Dunlop, Richard *Donovan America's Master Spy,* Rand McNally & Company, Chicago New York San Francisco, 1982

Đuretić1 Đuretić, Veselin *Saveznici i jugoslovenska ratna drama - Između nacionalnih i ideoloških izazova (The Allies and the Yugoslav Wartime Drama - Betwewen national and ideological challenges)* Fourth supplemented edition, Published by the author, Braunschweig, 1987
Đuretić2 ---- *Saveznici i jugoslovenska ratna drama - Prestrojavanja u znaku kompromisa (The Allies and the Yugoslav wartime drama - Realignments in a Sign of a Compromise)* Fourth supplemented edition, Published by the author, Braunschweig, 1987

Eden, Anthony (The Earl of Avon) *Memoirs: The Reckoning,* Cassell, London, 1965
Elliott, Mark R. *Pawns of Yalta Soviet Refugees and America's Role in Their Repatriation,* University of Illinois Press, Urbana Chicago London, 1982
Encyclopaedia Britannica, Volume 23, Encyclopaedia Britannica, Inc., William Benton, Chicago London ... 1973

Fisher Book review – Fischer, Bernard J. *Albania at War, 1939-1945;* http://stonebooks.com/archives/990701.shtml
Foot(R) Foot, M.R.D. *Resistance – An analysis of European resistance to Nazism 1940-1945* Eyre Methuen, London, 1977
Foot(S) Foot, M.R.D. *SOE - An Outline History of the Special Operations Executive 1940-1946*, Pimlico, 1999. (First published in 1984.)
Ford, Corey *Donovan of OSS,* Little, Brown and Co., Boston, 1970

FRUS *Foreign Relations of the United States Diplomatic Papers,* US Government Printing Office, Washington
FRUS1 --- 1941, Volume II, Europe, 1959
FRUS2 --- 1942, Volume III, Europe, 1961
FRUS3 --- 1943, Volume II, Europe, 1964
FRUS4 --- 1944, Volume II, Europe, 1966
FRUS5 --- 1945, Volume V, Europe, 1967
FRUS6 --- 1946, Volume VI, Eastern Europe, The Soviet Union, 1969

Glasnik *Glasnik srpskog istorisko-kulturnog društva "Njegoš" (The Herald of the Serbian Historic-Cultural Society "Njegoš)*
Glen, Alexander *Footholds Against a Whirlwind* Hutchinson of London, 1975
Glen(B) Glen, Alexander with Bowen, Leighton *Target Danube, A River Not Quite Too Far* The Book Guild Ltd., Susssex, England, 2002
Gorodetsky, Gabriel *Grand Delusion Stalin and the German Invasion of Russia,* Yale University Press, New Haven and London, 1999
Grol, Milan *Londonski dnevnik 1941-1945 (London's Diary 1941-1945),* Filip Višnjić, Beograd, 1990

Hehn, Paul N. *A Low Dishonest Decade,* Continuum, New York, London, 2002
Higham, Robin *Diary of a Disaster British Aid to Greece 1940-1941,* The University Press of Kentucky, 1986
Hinsley1, Hinsley, F.H. et al. *British Intelligence in the Second World War – Its Influence on Strategy and Operations,* Volume 1, Her Majesty's Stationery Office, London, 1979

Hodgson, Lynn-Philip *Inside-Camp X,* 2000
Holmes, Richard *In the Footsteps of Churchill, A Study in Character* Basic Books, New York, 2005
Hoptner, J.B. *Yugoslavia in Crisis 1934-1941* Columbia University Press, New York and London, 1962
Howard, Michael *The Mediterranean Strategy in the Second World War*, Frederick A. Prager, New York Washington, 1968
Howarth, Patrick *Undercover The men and women of the Special Operations Executive,* Phoenix Press, London, 2000. (First published in 1980.)
Hull, Cordell *The Memoirs of Cordell Hull, Volume II* The Macmillan Co., New York, 1948

Irving, David *Churchill's War,* Avon Books, New York, 1991 (First published in 1987.)
Ismay, General Hastiings L. *The Memoirs of General Lord Ismay,* The Viking Press, New York, 1960

Janković & Lalić Janković, Miodrag and Lalić, Veljko "Ekskluzivno: Trezor kneza Pavla", ("Exclusively: The Vault of Prince Paul") , *Večernje Novosti Online (Evening News Online)* 25 December 2006 -   20 January 2007
Jebb, Gladwyn *The Memoirs of Lord Gladwyn,* Weybright and Talley, New York, 1972
Jelić-Butić, Fikreta *Ustaše i Nezavisna država Hrvatska , 1941-1945* Liber i Škplska kniiga, Zagreb, 1977
Jovanović, Slobodan *Zapisi o problemima i ljudima, 1941-1944 (Notes about problems and men, 1941-1944)*, London, 1976
Jukić, Ilija *The Fall of Yugoslavia,* Translated by Dorian Cooke, Harcourt Brace Jovanovich, New York and London, 1974
Jukić(65) Jukić, Ilija *Pogledi na prošlost, sadašnjost I budućnost hrvatskog naroda (Views on the Past, Present and Future of the Croatian People)* Hrvatska politička knjižnica, London, 1965

Karapandžić, Borivoje M. *Građanski rat u Srbiji 1941-1945 (The Civil War in Serbia 1941-1945)*, Nova Iskra, Beograd 1993. (First published in 1958.)
Karapandžić(AB) Karapandžić, Adam & Borivoje *Srbija – Zemlja prevrata, zavera, buna i pučeva (Serbia – The land of subversions, conspiracies, mutinies and putschs),* Slobodna knjiga, Beograd, 2001
Keegan, John *The Second World War,* Viking, 1989
Kennedy, Major-General Sir John *The Business of War,* Wiliam Morrow and Co., New York, 1958 (First published in Great Britain in 1957.)
Klugmann, James *From Trotsky to Tito,* Lawrence & Wishart Ltd, London, 1952. (First published in 1951.)
Knežević, Živan *27. mart 1941. (March 27, 1941),* Author's edition, New York, 1979
Kočović, Bogoljub *Žrtve Drugog svetskog rata u Jugosuaviji,* Biblioteka Naše delo, London, 1985
Koliopoulos, John S. «General Papagos and the Anglo-Greek Talks of February 1941», in the *Journal of Hellenic Diaspora,* Vol. VII, Nos. 3-4, Fall-Winter 1980, Pella Publishing Co., New York
Kosić(50) Kosić, Mirko *"Je li 27 mart 1941 plaćen?" ("Is March the 27th, 1941, Paid-Up?"),* 1950
Kosić(51) --- *Grobari Jugoslavije (The Gravediggers of Yugoslavia),* 1951
Kosić(N) Kosić, Nikola *Dnevnik 17. mart – 28. mart 1941. godine   Otadžbinsko izdanje (The Diary, 17 – 28 March 1941 The Fatherland's Edition),* "Čačanski Glas", Čačak [Serbia], 1996
Kostić, Boško N. *Za istoriju naših dana (For History of Our Days),* Lille, France, 1949
Krizman1 Krizman, Bogdan *Ante Pavelić i ustaše,* Globus, Zagreb, 1978
Krizman2 --- *Pavelić između Hitlera i Musollinija,* Globus, Zagreb, 1980
Krizman3 --- *Ustaše i Treći Reich (1),* Globus, Zagreb, 1986
Krizman4 --- *Ustaše i Treći Reich (2),* Globus, Zagreb, 1986
Krizman5 --- *Pavelić u bjekstvu,* Globus, Zagreb, 1986
Krylov, Ivan *Soviet Staff Officer,* Translated by Edward Fitzgerald, The Falcon Press, London 1951

Lamb, Richard *Churchill as War Leader,* Carroll & Graff, New York, 1991
Lamb(WI) Lamb, Richard *War in Italy 1943-1945 A Brutal Story* John Murray, London, 1993
Langer & Gleason Langer, William L. and Gleason, S. Everett, *The Undeclared War 1940-1941,* Harper and Brothers, New York, 1953
Lawlor, Sheila *Churchill and the politics of war, 1940-1941* Cambridge University Press, 1995 (First published in 1994)
Lawrence, Christie *Irregular Adventure,* Farber & Farber, London, 1947
Leary, William M. *Fueling the Fires of Resistance*, Army Air Forces Special Operations in the Balkans during World War II - Air Force History and Museums Program, 1995
Lees, Michael *The Rape of Serbia, The British Role in Tito's grab for Power 1943-1944 -* Harcourt Brace Jovanovich, San Diego   New York   London, 1990
Leković, Mišo *Martovski pregovori 1943,* Narodna knjiga, Beograd, 1985
Liddell Hart, B. H. *Defence of the West,* William Morrow & Co, New York, 1950
Liddell Hart1 --- *History of the Second World War,* Volume 1, Capricorn Books, G.P. Putnam's Sons, New York , 1972
Liddell Hart2 --- *History of the Second World War,* Volume 2, ...
Liddell Hart71 --- *Why Don't We Learn from History?* Hawthorn Books, Inc., New York, 1971 (Revised and expanded revision)
Lindsay, Franklin *Beacons in the Night – With the OSS and Tito's Partisans in Wartime Yugoslavia,* Stanford University Press, Stanford, California, 1993

Loewenheim *et al* (ed)　　　Loewenheim, Francis L., Langley, Harold D., Jonas, Manfred (eds) *Roosevelt and Churchill - Their Secret Wartime Correspondence,* Saturday Review Press / E.P. Dutton & Co, New York, 1975

Mackenzie, W.J.M.　*The Secret History of SOE: The Special Operations Executive 1940-1945,*　St. Ermin's Press,　2000
Maclean, Fitzroy　*Eastern Approaches*　TIME-LIFE Books, New York, 1964
Macmillan, Harold　*War Diaries – Politics and War in the Mediterranean, January 1943 – May 1945,*　St. Marin's Press, New York, 1984
Macmillan(BW)　　Macmillan, Harold　*The Blast of War 1939 – 1945,*　Harper & Row,　New York and Evanston,　1968
Maček, Vladko　*The Struggle for Freedom,* Translated by Elizabeth and Stjepan Gazi, The Pennsylvania State University Press, University Park and London, 1957
Magazinović, Hrvoje　*Kroz jedno mučno stoljeće* (Through a Painful Century) Split, 2002
Maloney, Dr. Sean M.　"Who has seen the Wind? An historical overview of Canadian special operations",　*Canadian Military Journal,* Autumn 2004
Marks, Leo　*Between Silk and Cyanide,　A codemaker's war 1941-1945,*　The Free Press, New York , 1998
Martin, David　*The Web of Disinformation: Churchill's Yugoslav Blunder,* Harcourt Brace Jovanovich, San Diego New York London, 1990
McClymont, W.G.　*To Greece: Official History of New Zealand in the Second World War, 1939-45,* War History Branch, Department of Internal Affairs, Wellington, New Zealand, 1959
　　　　　　(http://www.nzetc.org/tm/scholarly/tei-WH2Gree-c6-1.html　1/31/07)
Miletić(ed)　　Miletić, Colonel Antun　　*Aprilski rat 1941. (April's War 1941),* Vojnoistorijski Institut, Beograd, 1987
Milovanović, Nikola　*Vojni puč i 27 mart (Military coup and 27 March),* Prosveta, Beograd, 1960
Milunović(ed)　Milunović, Marko　*U spomen Živana L. Kneževića O njemu i od njega, (In Remembrance of Živan L. Knežević   About him and by him)* Published by "Jugosloven", 1985, No. 203/205
　　• Knežević, Živan L. "Deset dana do Hitlerovog napada" ("Ten Days till Hitler's attack"), pp. 39-66
　　• Kosić, Nikola　"Oproštajni govor" ("Farewell address"), pp. 7- 9
　　• Lewis, Dennis John　"Col. Zivan Knezevich, helped put Yugoslavia on Allies' side in war", *The Washington Times,*　　　　　　　　　　　　　　　　　　　　　　　　　Monday, January 7, 1985

Mitchell, Ian　*The Cost of a Reputation – Aldington versus Tolstoy: the causes, course and consequences of a notorious libel case,* Topical Books, Isle of Islay, PA42 7DX
Moran, Lord　*Churchill at War 1940-45*　Carroll & Graf Publishers, New York, 2003 (First published in 1966)
Murphy, Robert　*Diplomat among Warriors,*　Doubleday & Co, Garden City, New York,　1964

Nicolson, Nigel　*Long Life,*　G. P. Putnam's Sons, New York, 1998
Nikoliš, Gojko　*Korijen, Stablo, Pavetina - Memoari (Root, Tree, Climber - Memoirs)* Liber-Prosvjeta, Zagreb, 1980

nz1　　　www.nzetc.org/etexts/WH2-2Doc/c19.html　NZETC - Official History of Nea Zealand in the Second World War, 1939-1945

Onslow, Sue　"Britain and the Belgrade Coup of 27 March 1941 Revisited", *Electronic Journal of International History,* (March 2005)

Pandurović, Gen. Dragiša　*27. mart 1941. - Prilog za vojno-političku istoriju - (27th March 1941 - A controbution to the military-political history)* Oflag XIIIB, 18 December 1941
Parrott, Cecil　*The Tightrope,*　Faber and Faber, London, 1975
Pavićević, Miloš　"Kako sam video 27 mart 1941 godine" (How did I see the 27 March 1941),　　*Glasnik,* Vol. 9,　June 1962, pp. 47-56
Petranović, & Zečević　Petranović, Branko & Zečević, Momčilo　*Jugoslavija 1918 - 1984; Zbirka dokumenata,* "RAD", Beograd, 1985
Petranović & Žutić　Petranović, *Branko* & Žutić, Nikola　　*27.Mart 1941. Tematska zbirka dokumenata (A thematic collection of documents),*　NICOM, Beograd, 1990
Petrov, Vladimir　*A Study in Diplomacy: the Story of Arthur Bliss Lane,* Henry Regenry Co., Chicago, 1971
Petrovitch, Svetislav-Sveta　*Free Yugoslavia Calling,* translated and edited by Joseph Ciszek Peters. The Geystone Press, New York, 1941
Pimlott(ed)　Pimlott, Ben　*The Second World War Diary of Hugh Dalton 1940-45,*　Jonathan Cape in Association with the Lonodon School of Economics and Political Science, 1986

www.pavelicpapers.com/documents/...
　　---　　　　　　　　　　　　　　/pavelic/ap0048.html　Pavelic's Radio Address to Croatia (5 April 1941)
　　---　　　　　　　　　　　　　　/pavelic/ap0001.html　Pavelic's Telegram to Mussolini (8 April 1941)
　　---　　　　　　　　　　　　　　/pavelic/ap0039.html　Decree on the First Croatian Government (16 April 1941)
　　---　　　　　　　　　　　　　　/jasenovac/ja0001.html　Decree "On Racial Affiliation" (30 April 1941)
　　---　　　　　　　　　　　　　　/jasenovac/ja0002.html　Decree "On Protection of Arian Blood" (30 April 1941)

--- /decrees/dec0002.html Decree on the Establishment of Courts-Martial (17 May 1941)
/decrees/dec0001.html Ustase Commmand-Dubrovmik, Order No. 188-44 (21 June 1941)
--- /budak/mbu0003.html Decree on Croatian Language, Its Purity and Spelling (14 August 1941)
--- /pavelic/ap0002.thml Declaration of War on the United States and Great Britain (14 December 1941)

Rebić(AR)   Aleksandra and Rade Rebić *Dragoljub-Draža Mihailović i Drugi Svetski Rat: Istorija jedne velike izdaje (Dragoljub-Draža Mihailović and the Second World War: History of a great treason),* Srpska reč, Beograd, 2003
Rees, Laurence *World War II Behind Closed Doors Stalin, the Nazis and the West,* Pantheon Books, New York, 2008
Rhodes James, Robert *Anthony Eden A Biography,* McGraw-Hill Book Co, 1987. First published in 1986
Ristić, Dragiša N. *Yugoslavia's Revolution of 1941,* The Pennsylvania State University Press, University Park / London, 1966
Roberts, Walter R. *Tito, Mihailović and the Allies, 1941 – 1945,* Rutgers University Press, New Brunswick, New Jersey, 1973
RoC   Dokumenti o Jugoslaviji - *27 mart: "Narodni ustanak" ili Zavera protiv države (March the 27th: "Popular Rebbelion" or Conspiracy Against the State),* Paris 1951
Rothenberg, Gunther E. *The Austrian Military Border in Croatia 1522-1747,* University of Illinois Press, 1960
Rothenberg, Gunther E. *The Military Border in Croatia 1740-1881,* The University of Chicago Press, 1966

St. John, Robert *From the Land of Silent People,* Doubleday, Doran & Co., Garden City, New York, 1942
Seaman(ed)   Seaman, Mark, ed. *Special Operations Executive A new instrument of war,* Routledge, London and New York, 2006
Sekulić, Miloš "Istorijska fakta Istina o 27 martu ", *Seljačka Jugoslavija* ("Historic facts The truth about the 27th March" , *Paesant Yugoslavia)* ,   No 29, 2 April 1947 – Žarko Popović Collection, Box 2, Folder 2.21, Hoover Institutions Archives
Seton-Watson(EE) Seton-Watson, Hugh *Eastern Europe Between the Wars 1918-1941,* Harper Torchbooks,, New York, 1967 (First published in 1945.)
Seton-Watson(ER) ---   *The East European Revolution,* Frederick A. Praeger, New York, 1951
Seton-Watson(NS) ---   *Nations and States, An Enquiry into the Origins of Nations and the Politics of Nationalism ,* Westview Press, Boulder, Colorado, 1977
Shoup, Paul *Communism and the Yugoslav National Question,* Columbia University Press, New York and London, 1968

Simović(44) Simović, Gen. Dušan,   Memoari (Memoirs), Žarko Popović collection, Box 2, Folder 2.9, Hoover Institution Archives
Simović(51)   ---   "Simovićev testament" ("Simović's Testament") *Glasnik,* Vol. 21,   June 1968, pp. 4-23
Simović(56)   ---   "Politički testament generala Simovića» ("Political Testament of General Simović") *Glasnik,* Vol. 10, December 1962, pp. 76-78.

Slijepčević, Đoko *Jugoslavija uoči i za vreme Drugog svetskog rata (Yugoslavia on the Eve and During the Second World War),* Minhen, 1978
Smith, Bradley F. *The Shadow Warriors* Basic Books, Inc., New York, 1983
Smith(S) Smith, Bradley F. *Sharing Secrets with Stalin How the Allies Traded Intelligence, 1941-1945,* University Press of Kansas, 1996

Stafford(C)   Stafford, David *Churchill and Secret Service,* The Overlook Press, Woodstock & New York, 1998
Stafford(cp)   ---   "SOE and British Involvement in the Belgrade Coup d'Etat of March 1941", *Slavic Review,* Vol. 36, No. 3, September 1977
Stafford(sa)   ---   *Secret Agent The True Story of the Special Operations Executive,* BBC, 2000
Stafford(so)   ---   *Britain and European Resistance, 1940 – 1945 : A Survey of the Special Operations Executive, with Documents,* M in association with St. Anthony's College, Oxford, 1980
Stafford(X)   ---   *Camp X,* Pocket Books, a division of Simon and Schuster, Inc. (First published in 1986.)

Stenton, Michael *Radio London and Resistance in Occupied Europe, British Political Warfare 1939-1943,* Oxford University Press, 2000
Street, Brian Jeffrey *The Parachute Ward*   Lester & Orpen Dennys, 1987
Sudoplatov, Pavel *et al. Special Tasks The Memoirs of an Unwanted Witness – a Soviet Spymaster,* Little, Brown and Company, Boston New York Toronto London, 1994
Sulzberger, Cyrus Leo *A Long Row of Candles, Memoirs and Diaries [1934-1954]* , The Macmillan Company, New York, 1969
Sweet-Escott, Bickham   *Baker Street Irregular,* Methuen & Co., London, 1965

Taylor, A.J.P.   *The Origins of the Second World War*   Second edition with a reply to critics, Fawcett Premier, New York, 1961
Five authors   *Churchill: Four Faces and the Man,* The Penguin Press, London, 1969
- A.J.P. Taylor, The Statesman
- Robert Rhodes James, The Politician
- J. H. Plumb, The Historian
- Basil Liddell Hart, The Military Strategist
- Anthony Storr, The Man

Taylor, George Francis   REPORT ON S. O. ORGANISATION AND PLANS IN THE BALKANS, MOST SECRET, Athens, 26th February 1941, The National Archives, HS5/166   275583
Thomas, Gordon   *Secret Wars , One Hundred Years of British Intelligence Inside MI5 and MI6,* Thomas Bunne Books, New York, 2009
Tolstoy, Nikolai *The Minister and the Massacres*, Century Hutchinson Ltd, London Melbourne Auckland Johannesburg, 1986
Tomić, Nikola N.   *Pakt. puč i rat   (The Pact, the Putsch and the War),* Srpska misao, Melbourne, 1967
Topalović, Živko   *Draža Mihailović i engleska vojna misija (Draža Mihailović and the English Military Mission)*, Zadužbina "Dr. Živko i Milica Topalović", Paris, 1980
Trifkovic, Srdja   *Ustaša (Ustasha)   Croatian Fascism and European Politics, 1929-1945*   The Lord Byron Foundation for Balkan Studies,   Chicago-Ottawa-London,   2011
Troy, Thomas F.   *Wild Bill and Intrepid - Donovan, Stephenson and the Origin of CIA,* Yale University Press, 1996

van Creveld, Martin L.   *Hitler's Strategy 1940-1941   The Balkan Clue,* Cambridge University Press, 1973
van Creveld(G)   van Creveld, Martin L.   "Prelude to Disaster: the British Decision to Aid Greece, 1940-41",   *Journal of Contemporary History,* Vol. 9, No. 3 (Jul., 1974), pp. 65-92, Sage Publications, Ltd.
Vauhnik, Vladimir   *Nevidljivi front   Borba za očuvanje Jugoslavije (The invisible front   The struggle for the preservation of Yugoslavia),* Minhen, 1984
Vodušek Starič, Jerca *Slovenski špijoni in SOE 1938-1942 (Slovenian Spies and SOE 1938-1942),* Ljubljana, 2002
Voigt, F.A.   *Pax Britannica,* Constable & Co, London, 1949

Wedemeyer, General Albert C.   *Wedemeyer Reports!*   Henry Holt & Co., New York, 1958
West, Richard *Tito and the Rise and Fall of Yugoslavia,* Carroll & Graff, New York, 1994
West(sw) 'West, Nigel' (Rupert Allason)   *Secret War   The Story of SOE, Britain's Wartime Sabotage Organisation,*   Hodder & Stoughton,   London, 1992
West(6)   'West, Nigel' (Rupert Allason)   *MI6 British Secret Intelligence Service Operations 1909-45*, Random House, New York, 1983

Wheeler-Bennett(ed), Wheeler-Bennett, Sir John   *Action This Day , Working with Churchill,* Macmillan, 1968:
- Lord Normanbrook (Cabinet Secretariat 1941—46, Secretary to the Cabinet 1947-62)
- John Colville (Assistant Private Secretary (1940-41, 1943-45, Parliamentary Private Secretary 1951-55)
- Sir John Martin   (Private Secretary 1940-41, Principal Private Secretary 1941-45)
- Sir Ian Jacob (Lt.-Gen, Military Assistant to War Cabinet 1939-45)
- Lord Bridges   (Secretary to the Cabinet 1938-45)
- Sir Leslie Rowan   (Private Secretary 1941-45, Principal Private Secretary 1945)

Wilkinson, Peter   *Foreign Fields: The story of an SOE Operative,* I.B. Tauris Publishers, London,   New York, 2002. (First published in 1997.)
Williams, Heather   *Parachutes, Patriots, and Partisans: The Special Operations Executive and Yugoslavia, 194 –1945,* The University of Wisconsin Press, 2003
Winterbotham, F.W. *The Ultra Secret ,* Harper & Row, New York, Evanston, San Francisco, London 1974
Winterbotham(NC)   Winterbotham F.W. *The Nazi Connection,* Harper & Row, New York, Hagerstown, San Francisco, London, 1978
Wood & Seaton   Wood, Alan and Seaton Wood, Mary *Islands in Danger,* New English Library, Times Mirror, 1976. (First published in 1955.)
Woodward, Sir Llewellyn   *British Foreign Policy in the Second World War,* Volume 3, Her Majesty's Stationery Office, London, 1971

Selected Chronology of Events

ASSEMBLED FROM MULTIPLE SOURCES

1915

26 April   Secret **"Treaty of London"** is signed by Britain-France-Russia on one side, and Italy. Some Austrian and South Slavic territories, including the peninsula of Istria [Istra, in Slavic] with the city of Trieste [Trst], and a part of the Dalmatian coast and islands, are to be given to Italy as a reward for switching to the Allied side in the First World War.

1917

6 Nov.   Bolshevik revolution in Russia. (By the Julian calendar, it took place on 24 October, and therefore is also known as **"The October Revolution"**.)

1918

... Mar.   The Bolsheviks refer to themselves as the Communists, and their Party as **the Communist Party (of Bolsheviks).**

16 July   Tsar Nicholas II Romanov, Tsarina Alexandra, their four daughters and a son assassinated in the Ipatiev house, in Yekaterinburg, Russia. (By order of the Communist authorities, the Ipatiev house was demolished in 1977 so it could not become an object of pilgrimage.)

1919

2-6 Mar.   The Communist International (**Comintern**) founded in Moscow.

25 Mar.   Iosif Vissarionovich Dzhugashvili "Stalin" – of Gori, Georgia - elected member of the Politburo of the Central Committee of the Communist Party (of Bosheviks).

... April   **The Communist Party of Yugoslavia (CPY)** formed. (The Party became a member of **the Comintern**.)

1921

29 July   Adolf Hitler takes over control of the National Socialist German Workers **(Nazi)** Party.

1922

3 Apr.   Stalin becomes the Secretary General of the Central Committee of **the All-Russia Communist Party (of Bolsheviks).**

24 Oct.   Benito Mussolini directs the Fascist **"Blackshirts"** to March on Rome, Italy.

29 Oct.   Italy's King Vittorio Emmanuele III appoints Mussolini the Prime Minister.

30 Dec.   Union of the Soviet Socialist Republic **(USSR)** formed by the Russian, Byelorussian, Ukrainian and Transcaucasian Republics. On that occasion, Stalin said, *inter alia,* that Soviet power was not concerned only with its preservation, "but with developing into an important international force, capable of influencing the international situation and of modifying it in the interest of the working people"; that the new state "created the dictatorship of the proletariat, awakened peoples of the East, inspired the workers of the West, transformed **the Red Flag** from a Party banner into **a State banner**, and rallied around that banner the peoples of the Soviet republics in order to unite them into a single state, the Union of the Soviet Socialist Republics, the prototype of the future World Soviet Socialist Republic."

3 Jan.   Mussolini dismisses the Italian Parliament, begins assuming dictatorial powers.

1925

.... Georgi Dimitrov (Secretary General of the Comintern from 1934 on) states, *inter alia*: "No serious Communist work will be possible in the Balkans until Yugoslavia disintegrates. So Yugoslavia must be made to disintegrate by our helping the Separatist movements there."

1929

.... Stalin becomes the Party and State leader.

1930

.... The leader of the Croatian Ustaša separatists, Ante Pavelić, moves to Italy, residing mostly in Florence.

1933

30 Jan. President Paul von Hindenburg appoints Hitler the Chancellor of Germany.
4 Mar. Franklin Delano Roosevelt becomes the President of the United States of America.
14 July **The Nazi Party** is declared the official party of Germany; all other parties banned.

1934

19 Aug. Hitler combines the offices of the President and Chancellor and assumes the title of ***Führer***.

... Sept. Josip Broz (later Tito) speaks at a Communist conference in the castle of Gornji Grad, just outside of Ljubljana, Slovenia. "Tito's anti-Yugoslav line showed itself in the banners decorating Gornji Grad hall: "Long live worker-and-peasant states in Croatia, Dalmatia, Slovenia, Serbia, Montenegro, Bosnia, Vojvodina!." – Yugoslavia is not mentioned.

9 Oct. King Aleksandar Karađorđević I of Yugoslavia assassinated in Marseilles, France. His cousin, Prince Pavle (Paul) Karađorđević – with two additional Regents - assumes the Regency for the young King Petar II. (The regency ends when the King becomes of age, on 6 September 1941.)

1935

15 Sept. Nuremberg race laws promulgated in Germany.

1936

7 Mar. German troops reoccupy **the Rhineland**, in violation of the Versailles Treaty. (Great Britain and France do not react militarily to enforce the peace treaty.)
17 July **The Spanish Civil War** begins. Stalin supports the Republicans, Hitler and Mussolini the Nationalists. Josip Broz, an operative of the Comintern - trained and schooled in Moscow - recruits Communists from Yugoslavia for the Republicans. (Some of these "Španci" (*"Spaniards"*) later become military leaders of the Communist-led Partisans in Yugoslavia during WWII.)
1 Nov. In a speech in Milan, Mussolini refers to **the Berlin-Rome Axis**.
2 Nov. In a letter for Serbia, Tito favors **seven federal units** on the territory of Yugoslavia: Serbia, Croatia, Slovenia, Macedonia, Montenegro, Vojvodina, and Bosnia-Herzegovina.

1937

17-18 Apr. **Communist Party of Slovenia** founded in Čebine. Edvard Kardelj, who returned from Moscow, talks in favor a federative organization of Yugoslavia.
28 May Neville Chamberlain becomes the Prime Minister of Britain.
11 June Josef Stalin begins purging the Red Army.
1-2 Aug. **Communist Party of Croatia** formed in Anindol, near Samobor.
17 Aug. Tito arrives in Paris and **assumes the duty** of the Secretary of **the Communist Party of Yugoslavia (CPY).**
Summer Brigadier Bora Mirković plans change of regime in Yugoslavia and the overthrow of the Regents (according to his own later claims).

1938

12 Mar. *Anschluss* (the annexation) of Austria to Germany announced.
(Mussolini reacts favorably, and Hitler thankful for this reaction.
Hitler's annexation of Austria turned out to be the first step in the Axis' encirclement of Yugoslavia.)
... Mar. Admiral Hugh "Quex" Sinclair, Chief ("C") of the Secret Intelligence Service (SIS), forms **Section D** for sabotage and subversion in enemy territories.
... Mar. British black propaganda unit formed in **"Electra House"**, London, headed by Sir Campbell Stuart.
1 May After returning from Paris to Yugoslavia, Tito forms a Provisional leadership of the CPY.
Summer **Gen. B. Mirković** discusses potential leadership roles – after the overthrow of the Regents – with Generals Nikola Stanković, Bogoljub Ilić, and the President of the Yugoslav Popular Movement Zbor, Dimitrije Ljotić. All decline to participate.
... Aug. Tito in Moscow.
15 Sept. Chamberlain-Hitler conference held at Berchtesgaden, Germany.
29 Sept. Chamberlain, Daladier, Hitler and Mussolini sign **the Munich Pact**.
30 Sept. Chamberlain and Hitler sign the peace declaration.
1-10 Oct. German troops occupy **the Czech Sudetenland** region.
9-10 Nov. *Krsitalnacht* (the Night of Broken Glass), pogrom of the Jews in Germany.

1939

... Jan. Still in Moscow, Tito gets **a mandate** to form **the Central Committee (CC) of the CPY.**
5 Feb. Dragiša Cvetković forms the new government in Yugoslavia (replacing Milan Stojadinović).
... Mar. After returning from Moscow to Yugoslavia, **Tito forms the CC of the CPY** in Bohinjska Bistrica (Slovenia) from the members of the Provisional leadership.
15 Mar. **Germany occupies Prague.** (France and Britain do not react militarily.)
(Yugoslavia's further purchase of arms from Czechoslovakia thereby became dependent on the will of Hitler.)
28 Mar. Spanish Civil War ends. (Some Communists from Yugoslavia, participants in the war, later became military leaders of the Partisans in Yugoslavia. Some other participants settled in Canada. In 1942, a few of these were recruited by the British Special Operations Executive, trained in Camp X in Canada and in Egypt, and then parachuted to Tito's Partisans during the first half of 1943.)
... Mar. British Military Intelligence sets up a "Research" unit, **MI(R)**.
31 Mar. Chamberlain announces a British and French pledge to assist Poland "in the event of any action which clearly threatened Polish independence and which the Polish Government accordingly considered it vital to resist with their national forces..."

1939, continued

7 April — Italian troops invade Albania, making the Adriatic Sea actually an Italian lake. (This turned out to be the second Axis' move to encircle Yugoslavia. Subsequent events in Albania later influenced developments in the Serbian province of Kosovo.)

13 April — Britain and France give Rumania and Greece a pledge of assistance in case they would consider it vital to resist actions threatening their independence. (Yugoslavia does not receive such a pledge.)

14 April — Roosevelt writes to Hitler and Mussolini pleading for a 10-year guaranty of peace. (*Inter alia* he wrote: "Nothing can persuade the peoples of the earth that any governing power has any right or need to inflict the consequences of war on its own or any other people **save in the case of self evident home defense**."

12 May — Anglo-Turkish mutual aid pact announced.

20 May — Gold ingots – worth $47,000,000 – is transferred from Yugoslavia to the Bank of England.

22 May — The Berlin-Rome Axis formalized with **the Pact of Steel** between Germany and Italy.

1 June — Prince Paul's state visit to Germany.

16-21 July — Prince Paul and his wife, Princess Olga, visit London.

… July — Polish intelligence passes knowledge of the German **ENIGMA** cipher machine to French and British intelligence.

23 Aug. — **German-USSR Non-Aggression Pact** signed in Moscow. The Pact includes secret protocol related to the division of spheres of influence of the two signatories.

25 Aug. — Great Britain and Poland sign formal treaty of mutual assistance.

26 Aug. — The Serbo-Croat *Sporazum (Agreement)* signed, and the new Cvetković – Maček government formed in Yugoslavia. *Banovina Hrvatska* thereby formed, to be administered by the *Ban* (Governor), Ivan Šubašić.

1 Sept. — **German Army invades Poland** from East Prussia and Slovakia. Danzig joins Germany. The **Second World War begins.**

3 Sept. — Great Britain, France, Australia and New Zealand declare war on Germany. **Winston Spencer Churchill** becomes First Lord of the Admiralty in the new War Cabinet. The Ministry of Economic Warfare (MEW) formed in Great Britain.

5 Sept. — The United States of America declares neutrality. Yugoslavia declares strict neutrality.

6 Sept. — The Union of South Africa declares war on Germany.

10 Sept. — Canada declares war on Germany.

11 Sept. — Roosevelt writes his first letter to Churchill.

17 Sept. — **Soviet Red Army invades Poland**, in accordance with the Nazi-Soviet Pact.

18 Sept. — The Comintern issues a directive to all Communist Parties to oppose the war and expose its imperialist character.

27 Sept. — Warsaw falls to the German Army. Hitler orders plans for the western offensive.

28 Sept. — The German-USSR border and friendship pact signed and **Poland partitioned.**

16 Oct. — Germany declares her military operations in Poland completed, and annexes western Poland.

19 Oct. — Anglo-French-Turkish 15-year mutual-assistance pact signed in Ankara.

1 Nov. — Germany annexes the Polish Corridor, Posen and Upper Silesia.

… Nov. — In London, Stewart Menzies replaces Sinclair as "C".

13 Dec. — Ronald Ian Campbell succeeds Sir Ronald Hugh Campbell as the British Minister in Belgrade.

1940

17 Jan. First German Army **ENIGMA cipher message decoded** by British intelligence at Bletchley Park. (That makes possible Britain's access to German military secrets. Decoded information considered *Ultra* secret, and thus becomes known as **Ultra**.)

5 Mar. Soviet Politburo signs an order to execute more than 20,000 Poles. (**"Katyn forest Massacre"**) (See the massacre at Kočevje, Slovenia, in May 1945.)

9 April German troops invade Denmark, and attack Norway. Norway appeals for British help.

... April George Taylor (of **Section D**) secretly visits Belgrade, interested in the situation in Albania, and proceeds to Athens. (His interest in Albania led to Julian Amery's contact with Jovan Đonović and *Vojvoda* Trifunović-Birčanin.)

10 May German Army invades the Netherlands, Luxemburg, Belgium and France.
In Great Britain, **Winston Spencer Churchill is appointed the Prime Minister** and **the Minister of Defense** (and he forms a Coalition Government).

15 May Dr. Hugh Dalton, of the Labour Party, becomes the Minister for Economic Warfare.

22 May **The British break the German Air Force code.**

27 May General Archibald Wavell proposes a blockade of Rumanian oil.

27 May-4 June Evacuation of the British Expeditionary Force from Dunkirk, France.

30 May Mussolini informs Hitler that he intends to enter the war.

4 June Evacuation of troops from Dunkirk completed but almost all equipment lost.

6 June Churchill instructs the Foreign Office to encourage Yugoslavia's mobilization as a countermeasure to the threat of war from Italy.

10 June **Italy declares war on Great Britain and France.**

12 June Britain orders blockade of Italy.

14 June German troops enter Paris.

20 June France asks for armistice.
The USSR occupies Estonia and Latvia.

22 June **France capitulates**. The Franco-German armistice signed at Compiegne, France.

24 June Italy and France sign armistice agreement at villa Endusa near Rome.
Diplomatic relations established between Yugoslavia and the USSR.

... June Prince Paul asks Dr. Milan Gavrilović to be the Ambassador in Moscow. Gavrilović's mind "was pretty well made up. But he wanted to know what the British Government thought before giving the Prince his final reply."

... June Gavrilović asks for British financial support for his Party's future activities.

.... Jovan Đonović and *Vojvoda* Ilija Trifunović-Birčanin propose to the British the overthrow of Prince Paul's Government. They and their friends "were ready to do the job and put a true Serb at the head of the Government. All they wanted to know that, in our [British] hearts, whatever we might say officially, we were with them." (Julian Amery) (The British Government considers the proposal premature at that time. See the Foreign Office's response, 27 July 1940)

1 July **Germany invades the British Channel Islands.**

... July Britain approves monthly subsidy of £4,000 to Gavrilović's Serbian Peasant Party (Zemljoradnička stranka).

14 July – 4 Aug. **William "Wild Bill" Donovan's first trip to Great Britain.**

1940, continued

21 July	For the first time Hitler speaks of the possibility of a campaign against the Soviet Union.
22 July	**Special Operations Executive (SOE)** formed in London. Churchill directs Dr. Hugh Dalton, its Chairman and Minister of Economic Warfare, **'Now set Europe ablaze'**. Almost all Section D agents in Yugoslavia transfer to SOE.
27 July	In response to Đonović-Birčanin suggestion, Lord Halifax thinks it would be premature to encourage the overthrow of Prince Paul's Government at present, but **"later on it might be of first class interest to His Majesty's Government."**
31 July	Hitler orders preparations for a campaign against the Soviet Union in spring of 1941.
... July	SOE's agents Julius Hanau and Duane "Bill" Hudson are expelled from Yugoslavia.
21 Aug.	Britain's Vice Chiefs of Staff discuss Dalton's paper of 19 August, *"The Fourth Arm"*, presenting his views on Subversion – in addition to questions of organization and liaison of SOE with three British Fighting Services.
25 Aug.	Estonia, Latvia and Lithuania ratify incorporation to USSR..
2 Sept.	Britain agrees to lease some of her bases to US in return for 50 US destroyers.
7 Sept.	**Germans begin day and night air attacks on London.**
11 Sept.	**Hitler** decides to send Army and Air Force missions **into Romania**.
17 Sept.	**Hitler postpones indefinitely invasion of Britain** (*"Operation Sea Lion"*). (See Oct. 12.) (This most welcome news made known to only a few British war leaders.)
27 Sept.	Germany, Italy and Japan sign, in Berlin, a 10-year military-economic alliance - **The Tripartite Pact**.
4 Oct.	Mussolini and Hitler meet at the Brenner Pass. Mussolini 'strengthened in his determination to occupy Greece."
7 Oct.	**German troops enter Rumania** under a pretext "to reorganize the Rumanian army with all equipment necessary for modern warfare".
12 Oct.	**Hitler postpones invasion of Great Britain until 1941.**
19-23 Oct.	Fifth Country-wide Conference of the Communist Party of Yugoslavia held in Dubrava near Zagreb. Tito declares, *inter alia,* "We are not interested in the bourgeois ideal of a Fatherland to be defended, but of a world revolution to be carried through. ... revolution which we plan and of which the Soviet Union is our glorious model." (Clissold)
23 Oct.	British intelligence begins to intercept the **German Enigma traffic signals about the Balkans.**
28 Oct.	(After the Greeks reject a three-hour ultimatum) **the Italian Army invades Greece from Albania**, without informing Hitler. Hitler and Mussolini meet in Florence, Italy. Churchill promises Greece "all the help in our power". Crown Council of Yugoslavia secretly decides to help Greece with foodstuff and arms.
28 Oct.-1 Nov.	The Yugoslav Crown Council meets three times. "A partial mobilization was considered, but opinions differed: everyone agreed, however, that the Italians could not be allowed to occupy Salonika."
29 Oct.	British and New Zealand troops set sail for Crete.
31 Oct.	British forces occupy Greek Islands of Crete and Lemnos.
... Oct.	Churchill tells senior commanders that Germany will inevitably attack the Soviet Union in 1941.

1940, continued

1 Nov.	Turkey declares herself non-belligerent in the Italo-Greek war. Yugoslavia declares herself neutral.
3 Nov.	Britain's military personnel begins to arrive in Greece.
4 Nov.	Britain's Royal Air Force begins to operate from Greek airfields. Hitler orders preparations for an eventual intervention in Greece.
5-6 Nov.	Italy bombs Yugoslav town Bitolj (Monastir).
6 Nov.	Gen. Petar Pešić replaces Gen. Milan Nedić as the Minister of War.
12 Nov.	Hitler's *Directive No. 18* orders preparations **to occupy the northern Greece**. "On November 12th he [Hitler] ordered the German Army Staff to prepare for an advance through Bulgaria in order to occupy the northern Greek mainland." (Eden)
... Nov.	Thomas Masterson of SOE transfers from Rumania to Belgrade, to direct SOE activities in Yugoslavia.
18 Nov.	Italian Foreign Minister requests Germany's assistance in Greece.
20 Nov.	**Hungary joins the Tripartite Pact unconditionally**.
23 Nov.	**Rumania joins the Tripartite Pact unconditionally.** (The Axis' encirclement of Yugoslavia continues.)
25 Nov.	The British Chief's of Staff issue first directive to SOE, "*Subversive Activities in Relation to Strategy*".
26 Nov.	Churchill telegraphs Gen. Wavell (in Cairo): "It seems difficult to believe that Hitler will not be forced to come to the rescue of his partner, and obviously German plans may be far advanced for a drive through Bulgaria at Salonika." Churchill to Lord Halifax: "We want Turkey to come into the war as soon as possible. ..."
28 Nov.	Hitler confers with Yugoslav Foreign Minister, Aleksandar Cincar-Marković, and asks Yugoslavia to side with the Axis in **a non-aggression pact**. Prince Paul tells the British Minister in Belgrade that, for obvious political reasons, it is impossible to leave Croatia defenseless.
....	Churchill to Dalton: the Balkan situation is "the acid test for SOE". (That is part of the rationale for subsequent mission of George Taylor to the Balkans.)
29 Nov.	Britain's and New Zealand's troops occupy the Greek island of Crete.
5 Dec.	Army presents Hitler with plans for campaigns against Greece and the USSR. He comments: "If the Greeks do not drive out the English of their own accord, it is possible that action against them through Bulgaria will become necessary."
6 Dec.	1940 – 18. March 1941 **Donovan's second trip to Britain** includes visits to the Near East and the Balkans.
13 Dec.	Hitler's *Directive No. 20* outlines campaign against Greece (*Operation "Marita"*). "Hitler issued his orders for the attack on Greece through Bulgaria ..."
18 Dec.	Hitler's *Directive No. 21* orders preparations to begin for a campaign against the USSR (*Operation "Barbarosa"*). Churchill tells Donovan that Germany will attack the Soviet Union in May of 1941. 'Donovan kept to the instructions given to him by Franklin Roosevelt. He informed Churchill that the United States and Britain must help each other in this crisis in history in a "relationship of mutual selfishness".' (Churchill **did not** inform Donovan that Hitler had called off the invasion of Britain.)
22 Dec.	Anthony Eden replaces Lord Edward Halifax as the Foreign Secretary. He "became an eager protagonist of Balkan intervention."
24 Dec.	Great Britain's Foreign Office alerts British Ambassadors in the Mediterranean area of the forthcoming visit by US Col. William Donovan. The British "**MI** [Military Intelligence], ... , repeated the view that Germany would wish to avoid fighting on two fronts, ..." (Hensley *et all*)

1940, continued

28 Dec. **Mussolini asks Hitler for support in Greece.**
Military Intelligence "quoted approvingly AI [Air Force Intelligence's] appreciation which found GAF [German Air Force] dispositions in Romania to be consistent with defence of oilfields rather than with plans for a Balkan offensive during the winter." (Hensley *et all*)

29 Dec. Roosevelt pledges that the United States will become "the great arsenal of democracy".

1941

1 Jan. Germany begins negotiations with Bulgaria to allow German troops to use Bulgaria as a springboard for Germany's attack on Greece.

... Jan. More than 500,000 German troops deploy to Rumania.
Masterson has a long conversation with Dr. Milan Grol, president of the Democratic Party, about enlarging the Party's range of propaganda. (That contact led to a subsequent cooperation of Radoje Knežević with Masterson.)

6 Jan Eden calls Churchill's attention to the Balkans: "... Germany is pressing forward her preparations in the Balkans with a view to an ultimate descent upon Greece. ..."

7 Jan. "Wild Bill" Donovan arrives in Cairo.

8 Jan. Donovan meets Britain's General Wavell and Air Chief Marshal Longmore.
The Foreign Office informs the British Minister in Athens, that the Defence Committee has decided to send General Wavell to Athens at once to ask the Greeks to allow the British forces to move into Salonika.
SOE issues a memorandum, *Interference with German Oil Supplies*.
Dalton attends conference with the SOE's top officials at which it is decided to send George Taylor to the Balkans.

9 Jan. "A telegram was sent to Wavell to say that the support of Greece was now to take precedence of all operations in the Middle East. ..."

10 Jan. Churchill's first meeting with Harry Hopkins, Roosevelt's trusted confidant. Hopkins visits Britain for some ten days, and tells Churchill: **"The President is determined that we shall win the war together."**
In Moscow, Germany and the USSR sign agreements to barter resources and settle border claims. (In a few months, when Germany brings the full force of war to Yugoslavia, the USSR will still be actively trading with Germany.)

11 Jan. In *Directive No. 22* Hitler confirms his intentions to send military support to the Italians in Albania. (*Operation "Alpine Violets"*)

13 Jan. General Wavell and Air Vice-Marshal Arthur Longmore come to Athens to confer with the Greeks.
Hitler demands Bulgaria join the Tripartite Pact.
The British Cabinet's Defence Committee approves **George Taylor's mission.**

15 Jan. **Donovan arrives in Athens.**

16 Jan. Wavell and Longmore report, "**with obvious satisfaction**, that **the Greeks did not want** our units for fear that their arrival might provoke the Germans to attack them."

18-20 Jan. Hitler meets Mussolini and informs him of the intended German attack on Greece.

22-25 Jan. **Donovan's mission in Belgrade -** He meets Cvetković, Prince Paul, Maček, and (on 24 Jan.) General Dušan Simović. (Simović becomes energized and activated by the meeting with Donovan and writes about the meeting in his memoirs.)

29 Jan. Greek Premier, General Ioannis Metaxas, dies, and Alexandros Koryzis replaces him.

31 Jan. Churchill writes to the President of Turkey: "... we shall place Turkey in a position, once our squadrons are on the Turkish airodromes, to threaten to bombard the Rumanian oilfields if any German advance is made into Bulgaria, or if the air personnel already in Bulgaria is not speedily withdrawn. We will undertake not to take such action from Turkish airfields except by agreement with you."

8 Feb. The Yugoslav Crown Council decides to maintain neutrality.

1941, continued

George Taylor arrives in Istanbul (and soon moves to Athens).

12 Feb. Anthony Eden and General John Dill leave London on their mission to Cairo and Athens, to form **the Balkan Front**, which would include Turkey, Greece, and Yugoslavia.

14 Feb. In Berghof, Germany, Hitler begins to pressure the Yugoslav Premier and Foreign Minister to join the Tripartite Pact.

... Feb. Masterson discusses the possibility of developing propaganda with Radoje Knežević.
(In 1978, Knežević wrote, *inter alia*: "...while in Yugoslavia, **I have never heard the names** of the SOE or SIS people. I did nor know a single Englishman living in my native country." The SOE and SIS people used **coded identifications**, so it is probable that Knežević never **heard** their **names**. However, not knowing **the name** does not necessarily prove that he did **not know a single Englishman**. On 27 March 1941, Masterson clearly described his contact with R. Knežević.)

19 Feb. **Eden and Gen. Dill arrive in Cairo.**
In a brief meeting with Eden, Donovan urges British resistance to a German encroachment upon the Mediterranean.

20 Feb. In the evening Donovan has a long talk with Dill about Balkan policy, intended to stiffen the General's attitude.
Donovan reports from Cairo that the Balkans offer perhaps the only place for defeat of the German army. The British must then retain a foothold in the Balkans by inducing Yugoslavia, Greece, and Turkey to stand together with England.

22/23 Feb. Greek Premier Koryzis formally accepts Britain's offer of troops.
At **the Tatoi Palace** near Athens an **agreement** is reached between Britain and Greece for a unified action in defense of Greece from Germany's expected invasion.
It is agreed that Eden should make "a further effort to attempt **to persuade the Yugoslav Government to play their part**".

24 Feb. Churchill in favor of the plan to help Greece. "It was then approved unanimously..." Churchill cables to Eden 'while being under no illusion, we all send you order "Full steam ahead."

26 Feb. In a lengthy **Report from Athens**, George Taylor informs SOE London of plans for SOE activities in the Balkans, including the post-occupational resistance, with the purpose of assisting the Greco-British plans agreed upon at Tatoi Palace on 22/23 February; attempts to block the Danube have not been satisfactory.
Taylor adds that his Report is "written from the angle of what help we [SOE] can be to Wavell", stating that he is sure that SOE London would agree that "in the present situation and with the recent decision" that is "the only possible point of view to take."

26 Feb.–1 Mar. Eden carries out his first mission in Turkey to engage Turkey against the Axis.

27 Feb. **George Taylor arrives in Belgrade** to direct SOE operations, as they are outlined in his Report of 26 February. "On his arrival Taylor assessed pro-British Serb public opinion as SOE's best hope of influencing the Yugoslav government's policy." (Williams) (Ever thereafter the British concentrated their activities and propaganda in this sense.)

28 Feb. **Eden's first mission with the Turks is not successful.** "Telegram from A. at Angora [Ankara], which puzzles me. It is couched in jaunty and self-satisfied terms, talking of the 'frankness' and 'friendliness' and 'realism' of the Turks. The 'reality' is that they won't do a damned thing. Has he had his head turned by crowds of hand-clapping Turks? And what is he now to say to the Yugoslavs and Greeks? The former will now of course curl up, and we shall be alone with the Greeks to share their inevitable disaster. ..." (Cadogan)

1 Mar. **Bulgaria joins the Tripartite Pact unconditionally.** (The Axis' encirclement of Yugoslavia is thus completed).

1941, continued

Aware that Eden got nothing out of the Turks, Churchill instructs him: **"Your main appeal should now be made to Yugoslavia."**

2 Mar. The German Twelfth Army enters Bulgaria from Rumania on the way to attack Greece.
In a **meeting at Chequers**, Dalton informs Churchill that SOE undercover agents in Belgrade "were in contact with dissident senior Royal Yugoslav Air Force officers and secret subsidies were being fed to anti-government newspapers and politicians." **Churchill approves SOE's plan to support a *coup d'état* in Belgrade if and when** Yugoslavia joins the Tripartite Pact. (Not before.)

3 Mar. Eden authorized to support revision of the Italo-Yugoslav border (which was established with the secret London Pact of 26 April 1915). For Eden, this was **a "bait"** for the Croats and Slovenes.
Eden gives a letter to Campbell for Prince Paul, asking him to resist the Germans. He also asks the Regent to send a staff-officer to Athens at once to discuss the defense of Salonika.
Donovan returns to London.

4 Mar. In Berchtesgaden, Germany, **Hitler confers with Prince Paul, increasing pressure to join the Tripartite Pact.** "After his usual harangue about the inevitability of Germany's victory, Hitler cleverly argued that after the liquidation of the British in Greece the German troops would not stay in the Balkans indefinitely; if Yugoslavia failed to stake her claim to Salonika, the city might fall to the Bulgarians or to the Italians. 'Visibly impressed' by these remarks, Prince Paul said that, although his personal sympathies were for England, Yugoslavia had no choice but to consider the course offered by Germany. He expressed the fear that agreement on his part would lead to revolution in Yugoslavia, then took his leave." (van Creveld)
Donovan confers with Churchill.
British Anti Aircraft and administrative units arrive in Greece.
British Admiral of the Fleet warns Churchill of "the considerable naval risks" in the Mediterranean.

5 Mar. Back in Athens, Eden and Dill find "a changed and disturbing situation and the atmosphere quite different from that of our last visit" [on 22/23 March].
In London, Cabinet members hear that Eden admits now that **"the situation in Greece had deteriorated considerably. ..."**

6 Mar. The Yugoslav Crown Council decides in principle to join the Tripartite Pact, with the conditions they receive written guarantees protecting Yugoslav sovereignty and territorial integrity, no transport of troops and war material through Yugoslavia, and excluding any and all military commitments.

7 Mar. **British and the Commonwealth troops begin landing in Greece.**

Eden telegraphs Churchill, *inter alia*: "...While we are all conscious of the gravity of the decision, we can find no reason to vary our previous judgment. ..." "Whole position again fully reviewed with the Commanders-in-Chief and Smuts ...We are all agreed that the course advocated should be followed and help given to Greece."
Churchill informs Eden, who is still in Cairo: "... Cabinet decided to authorise you to proceed with the operation, *and by so doing Cabinet accepts for itself the fullest responsibility.*"
Campbell reports that *Narodna Odbrana [The Defense League]* and other leading patriotic societies in Yugoslavia had addressed petitions to Price Paul urging action **"in the sense desired"**.
In London, Donovan briefs the British directors of operations and intelligence from each of the three ministries concerning his trip.

... Mar. Campbell visits the leaders of the Croatian Peasant Party, in Zagreb, but fails to gain their support for British policies.

8-12 Mar. Major Milisav Perišić meets with the British military representatives in Athens. His visit brings little satisfaction to either side.

1941, continued

9 Mar. **Donovan has another meeting with Churchill** and talks about his Balkan and Peninsular tour. Churchill pays high tribute to Donovan's 'magnificent work' in the Balkans, telling Roosevelt that he had carried everywhere an 'animating and heart-warming flame."

12 Mar. **Germany accepts all Yugoslavia's conditions**, including the clause of not transporting troops and war materiel through Yugoslavia.
The Crown Council requests that all Axis' guarantees be published.

14 Mar. Germany agrees to publish all guarantees except one, excluding Yugoslavia from military commitments. (Such exclusion had not been granted to other signatories of the Tripartite Pact.)

15 Mar. The Central Committee of the CPY issues a resolution, "Against Capitulation – In Favor of a Pact of Mutual Assistance with the Soviet Union".

17 Mar. Eden sends a letter to Prince Paul (by Terence Shone), asking him to resist German aggression (together with Greece and Turkey), to attack the Italians in Albania, and to receive him and Gen. Dill personally.
Hitler decides to occupy the whole of Greece.
The Yugoslav Privy Council decides in principle to join the Tripartite Pact.

18 Mar. **Eden meets Turkish Foreign Minister in Cyprus.** Turkey refuses again to join the Balkan Front.
Terence Shone delivers Eden's letter of 17 March to Prince Paul.
SOE Belgrade responds to Dalton's directive of 2 March and **urges** the necessity of the coup **on all their contacts**. (George Taylor)
Bill Donovan returns to the USA, after having done "magnificent work" for the British.

19 Mar. Yugoslav Privy Council agrees that Yugoslavia should sign the Pact, on condition that Yugoslavia would not be obliged to accept the transit of German troops or the use of its railways, nor sign so-called "military clauses" of the full Pact.
British diplomatic representatives, intelligence, and SOE operatives meet in a **round-table conference in Belgrade** to discuss the plan to overthrow Prince Paul's Government and the ways to do it. Specific roles are assigned to the Legation and the SOE personnel, and to the British domestic "contacts".
(Both Mirković and Simović wrote about their contacts with the British which took place **after** this all-British conference.)

20 Mar. Three Yugoslav ministers resign in hope of toppling the Yugoslav Government. "We had for some time been supporting one of the Serb parties, which had a Minister in the Government. He had taken the lead in resigning over the Pact." (Eden) (That was the Serbian Peasant Party.)
Shone asks Ilija Jukić to inform Maček of British position, which is not to sign anything with Germany.
Dalton sends a wire to Britain's friends to use all means to raise a revolution.

Campbell recommends to Eden: "**B.B.C. Serb-Croat broadcasts** should now adopt stronger line, **working on the feelings of Serbs in particular** ensuring vehement reaction in Serbia." "It would be well, too, if **American broadcast in Serbo-Croat** should voice the feelings of Yugoslavs in the United States in strong terms."

21 Mar. Campbell asks Eden. "If the German attack on Greece was not imminent, **would it be preferable to delay a coup** so as not to precipitate such an attack."
Eden replies: "I agree that upon present information suggested *coup* would have to be staged at the moment of reaction caused by signature and this may be very soon."
Svetislav-Sveta Petrović begins broadcasting to Yugoslavia over the short-wave radio station WRUL, Boston, Massachusetts.

22 Mar. Churchill instructs Eden **"to get Yugoslavia in to the war anyhow"**. (See Roosevelt's letter to Hitler, 14 April, 1939.)

1941, continued

Campbell reports to Eden that General Simović is the only military man capable of leading the opposition movement against Prince Paul's government.
Germany issues an ultimatum to Yugoslavia to adhere to the Tripartite Pact by 26 March.
The Comintern's Secretary General orders Tito: 'to mobilize the Party against the capitulation to the Germans. Support the movement for a mass opposition to the incursion of the German military into Yugoslavia. **Demand friendship with the Soviet Union.**'

23 Mar. Macdonald informs General Mirković that the next day Cvetković and Cincar-Marković will go to Germany to sign the Pact.
The Serb Orthodox Patriarch requests Prince Paul not to join the Tripartite Pact.
In late afternoon, Prince Paul meets with the American Minister Lane and tells him that he has just received telegram from Churchill urging Yugoslavia to attack the Italians in Albania. Lane writes: "I have never seen Prince so upset and unless he is an excellent actor almost without self control; he said, "I am out of my head; I wish I were dead".
Former Minister Božidar Maksimović informs Jovan Đonović that Air Force officers are preparing a coup. Đonović relays information to *Vojvoda* Trifunović-Birčanin, and asks him to verify it with Simović. Subsequently the General confirms it, and then directs the *Vojvoda* to talk about all of that with General Mirković, who has been entrusted with the execution of the conspiracy.
George Taylor assures London SOE that Campbell had made fullest use of SOE, and particularly of Masterson. He adds that SOE has made important contribution to prevent signature of the Pact, and praises, above all, the work of Tupanjanin. (Serb Peasant Party)
In the evening, General Simović requests and is granted an audience with Prince Paul. He tells the Prince that he is "convinced that the final victory was England's. **England loses all battles except the last one.**"

24 Mar. At Simović's request, **a conference of the highest Commandants of the Belgrade garrison** is held in the morning. The Commandant of Belgrade informs the Commandants that the Pact is specifically fitted to Yugoslavia's national sensitivity, and does not contain military clauses as it does with Hungary, Rumania, and Bulgaria. The Minister of the War expands on the subject of signing the Tripartite Pact:

> You see, gentlemen, the essence of the pact is in this: to guaranty to Yugoslavia the independence and sovereignty of her territory, that through our state no troops or any materiel will be transported; *that no kind of participation is demanded of us in the operations against enemies of the Axis,* with a prospect of Yugoslavia getting a territorial access to the Aegean Sea, meaning Salonika. That, gentlemen, is contained in a secret addendum to this pact. Something else, which is significant for us: we are not obliged in any way to disband our army which is - as you know - activated to a high degree of wartime readiness, and the "activation" will even be expanded to other units, and just a moment ago I have signed one such decision. There is, gentlemen, nothing in that pact humiliating for Yugoslavia as an independent state; we stand and remain in a posture of an armed power, ... (Pandurović)

(**General Simović heard this explanation** but did not mention or include it in his memoirs.)
Five senators of the subsidized Serbian Peasant Party also resign.
Turkey and USSR promise neutrality if either should be attacked.
British-subsidized patriotic societies in Belgrade protest against Yugoslavia joining the Tripartite Pact.
Eden authorizes Campbell to take any measure to change the Government or regime in Yugoslavia, even by *coup d'état*. "**Any new Government formed as a result of these events and prepared to resist German demands would have our full support. You may secretly so inform any prospective leaders in whom you have confidence.**" (Campbell was more than duty-bound to implement his Foreign Minister's order.)

1941, continued

Vojvoda Trifunović-Birčanin informs SOE that the coup is certain.

24-27 Mar. Trifunović-Birčanin meets daily with Mirković, thus serving as a contact man between Mirković on one side, and the SOE and domestic coup-wishers on the other.

24-26 Mar. Dr. Svetislav-Sveta Petrović "**openly called the people to arms**" three times daily. On 25 March, Petrović delivers a lengthy address to the Serbs, telling them, *inter alia:*

> "The traitors must be executed, say the Serbian people. And no one should take lightly a sentence passed by the Serbian people. ... No one should doubt that the present sentence of the Serbian people against the traitors will not be carried out. For the Serbian people have passed the sentence openly and such sentence the heroic Serbian people always carry out. Woe to the cowards. ... Those who will stand with the people in these fateful historic days will be blessed by future generations. Those against the people will be damned by history itself. They and their children's children will be damned by the people. To arms!" (He did not specify when and how **the Serbian people** had pronounced that alleged sentence.)

25 Mar. In Vienna, Cvetković and Cincar-Marković sign the Tripartite Pact Protocol for Yugoslavia, Ribbentrop and Ciano for Germany and Italy, respectively. The Yugoslav delegates then receive **four separate Notes**, signed by Ribbentrop and Ciano, in compliance with Yugoslavia's non-military conditions for adhering to the Pact.

The Notes promise that Germany will respect the sovereignty and territorial integrity of Yugoslavia; that Yugoslavia will not be asked to permit the passage of German troops; that Yugoslavia will not be required to participate in the war on the Axis' side; that Yugoslavia will get Salonika - in the reorganization of the Balkans.

The German radio announces (at 5 p.m.) the signing of the protocol and reveals the content of the first two German and Italian Governments' Notes to Yugoslavia.

The honorary British Air Attaché, Tom Mapplebeck, strongly urges Mirković to launch the coup as soon as possible.

Macdonald and Mirković meet in the afternoon. Mirković vows that he will bring down the Pact.

26 Mar. **Secret early-morning meeting** is held between **Macdonald and General Simović.** "There existed an organization which was working for the overthrow of present Government. General had confidence in its success and he asked us to have confidence in it and him. *We should not have to wait more than a few days before the coup d'etat."* (Macdonald) Discussing various subjects, the General declared his intention to attack the Italians in Albania immediately after the coup.

The first two Notes to the Protocol are published in Belgrade.

Simović and Mirković meet at least twice.

(Both Mirković and Simović later claimed that the decision for the coup had been made **in the afternoon of the 26th** – i.e., **seven days after** the all-British conference, and **two days after** Eden's directive to Campbell. Each claimed for himself the commanding role for the coup and its timing.)

In the afternoon, Churchill directs Campbell: " ... **do not neglect any alternative to which we may have to resort if we find present Government have gone beyond recall. Greatly admire all you have done so far. Keep it up by every means that occur to you."**

In the evening, **Simović has another meeting with Macdonald**, and later provides two different explanations of the purpose of the meeting.

In the evening, BBC broadcasts Leopold Amery's speech to influence the Serbs' attitude against the Pact.

Maček returns from Belgrade to Zagreb.

27 Mar. The **military putsch in Belgrade**: the putschists overthrow Prince Paul's government. General Dušan Simović forms a new government that includes Croatian, Slovene and Bosnian members of the previous administration, who had been known to be in favor of the Tripartite Pact.

1941, continued

In the morning, King Peter's proclamation of assuming royal powers is faked over Radio Belgrade.
Deception of the units used in the Putsch, of the nation, and of the diaspora, is systematically applied.
Simović starts negotiating with Maček terms for his joining the new government.
The protocol of adherence to the Pact is found to be valid and in force without further ratification.
Anti-Pact demonstrations are held in Belgrade and other Serb cities.
Churchill declares: **"Early this morning the Yugoslav nation found its soul."**
Eden praises the work of Campbell, and Dalton gives credit to SOE agents.
George Taylor and Tom Masterson report to London. Taylor reports to Dalton: "Trifunovich had kept us informed of conspiracy under strictest promise of silence."

(At 2:30 p.m.) Hitler issues *Directive No. 26*, outlining *"Operation 25"*, to **destroy the State of Yugoslavia unmercifully**, and asks Hungary and Bulgaria to cooperate.
Vice Premier Slobodan Jovanović pleads with Campbell to demand that the BBC refrain from pushing Yugoslavia into war. Campbell believes that BBC emissions must continue in order to maintain enthusiasm.

Churchill tells the War Cabinet that he has authorized Campbell to tell the new government that, 'on the basis that they were determined to denounce the pact with Germany and to help in defence of Greece', Britain recognizes them as the government of Yugoslavia. He has also sent a telegram to Roosevelt urging him to encourage resistance in the Balkans. (Barker)

In the evening, the Regents are forced to resign. Prince Paul and his family leave Yugoslavia for Greece.
Masterson reports to London about his contact with Radoje Knežević and the alleged role of his brother Živan.

28 Mar. In a long speech to the Holy Assembly of Bishops of the Serbian Orthodox Church, Simović states, *inter alia,* that the Government is doing everything possible to convince the Axis Powers that the intent of the Government is only to preserve peace. The Government desires to secure the peace, security and borders of the state; they do not desire to give reason for provocations. The Foreign Minister is taking steps in that direction. (Notwithstanding these public utterances, Simović worked from the end of January 1941 to move Yugoslavia to Britain's side, and kept giving assurances to the British in that sense.)
Hitler asks Mussolini to protect mountain passes from Yugoslavia to Albania.
" ... Tito had hurried [from Zagreb] to Belgrade at a few hours' notice and summoned an emergency meeting of the Party's provincial committee for Serbia in the house of Lazar Kočević, ..."
In the evening Simović meets the American Minister Lane and tells him, *inter alia,* "As to Tripartite pact ... Government wishes to avoid discussion if possible. It does not wish to denounce pact nor will it ratify it." (No ratification is needed.)

29 Mar. In the morning, Eden tells the American Minister in Athens: "I don't care if the Yugoslavs don't actually repudiate their signature of the Tripartite Pact if only we can get together now and formulate some sort of a common policy after which we can take it to the Turks."
Mussolini receives Pavelić and tells him: "Adesso è il vostro momento." ("Now it's your moment.") Mussolini informs Pavelić that, as soon as he is established in Zagreb, the Italian Government will initiate negotiations to conclude the agreement which has been confirmed in their conversation. He ends by telling Pavelić: "**Credo che sarà guerra.**" ("I believe that there will be war.")
Conference of German Army commanders, responsible for the campaign in the Balkans, was held.

1941, continued

In the afternoon, Foreign Minister Ninčić meets Lane and tells him, *inter alia,* that «Refusal of Government to honor terms [of the Pact] would not only lead to trouble with Germany but would also bring about dissolution of country as Maček in that case would not enter Government. ... Personally he [Ninčić] is in favor of peace. ... Demonstrations of yesterday in favor of democracies and against Axis put Yugoslavia in bad situation with Germany ... Unwise British broadcasts also embarrassing. ..." Ninčić also says that Yugoslavia could not count on Soviet support and the Soviet Union are in danger of being attacked by Germany.

Dimitrov is instructed by Molotov to call off street demonstrations, and Dimitrov promptly relays Molotov's instructions to Tito.

.... Before returning to Zagreb, Tito issues secret directives to the Party. Among them: "Render any assistance necessary to the Ustaše, Macedonian, Albanian and other nationalist organisations, in so far as they may contribute towards the speedy overthrow of the present régime. Help should also be given to the Montenegrin Separatists if they adopt an anti-royalist line in Montenegro."
" ... render assistance to all elements, regardless of their ideological outlook and character, which are bent on the same purpose. *Yugoslavia must first be dissolved into its several component parts...* disorganise the resistance of the Yugoslav Army ... collect all arms and war equipment which may be thrown away in panic and convey them to safe hiding places for later use ... " (Clissold)

30 Mar. The new Government formally accepts the Tripartite Pact and disallows Eden's visit.
Simović sends the Soviets an oral offer of a mutual assistance pact that is tantamount to a 'real alliance'. The new Defense Minister, Gen. Ilić, reiterates his intention of establishing 'full political and military co-operation with the Soviet Union'; he pledges the army's resolve to "resist to the end" a German invasion'.
The American Minister in Belgrade reports to the Secretary of State: "With regards to Prince Paul's meeting with Hitler at Berchtesgaden on March 4 or 5 (not 11) I am informed by reliable source that Hitler said to Prince during 2-hour interview Yugoslavia must sign Tripartite Pact in own interest as **in June or July he was going to attack Russia**."
"British Minister says foregoing fits in with information he has." (FRUS)

31 Mar.-1 Apr. General Dill secretly visits Belgrade, but Simović declines «to sign anything that would commit the Yugoslav Government.»
"... Dill had said that Britain would ultimately have 150,000 men on the Aliakmon line ..." (Intentionally or not, the number was grossly exaggerated.)

Early spring **The German Navy code is deciphered.**

1 April In Berlin, Col. Vladimir Vauhnik receives and forwards three messages foretelling Gemany's war agaist Yugoslavia, starting on 6 April, with heavy air raids on Belgrade.
Macdonald reports to London that the Yugoslav Government will start to mobilize on the 3rd; that would bring total strength to 1,800,000 men under arms.
Churchill sends a message to Gen. Dill (still in Belgrade): "... To gain time against Germans is to lose it against Italians. Nothing should stop Yugo developing full strength against latter at earliest. By this alone can they gain far-reaching initial success and masses of equipment in good time."
From Belgrade, Dill reports to Eden that Simović will not allow Eden's visit (basically for the same reasons Prince Paul did not).

2 April Relying on a Soviet initiative, Yugoslav military representatives (Col. Dragutin Savić and Col. Božin Simić) arrive in Moscow to sign a military and political pact with the Soviet Union. (In the end, this kind of a Pact was not signed.)
Mirković has a meeting with Macdonald (in the morning), and with Campbell.
Vauhnik sends a warning to Belgrade about Germny's plan to attack Yugoslavia.

1941, continued

3 April
: The Yugoslav Foreign Minister, Ninčić, informs his missions abroad that the Tripartite Pact will be honored.

 In a meeting with Campbell, Simović states that his government's actions are actually maneuvers to gain time and to convince the domestic population that the government is undertaking everything to avoid war. The Croats are reluctant because they fear the new Government's adventurous policies will provoke the Germans. They are assured that this is not the case, and that policies of peace and national security will be followed. On that basis they agree to join the Government.

 Vauhnik sends his assistant, major Pupis, to Belgrade by airplane with orders to report at once to the general staff and to repeat verbally the contents of the four most important telegrams. (The telegrams had been received, but Belgrade had no trust in them.)

3-4 Apr.
: General Miloje Janković meets Generals Dill and Papagos near Florina, Greece, but no decision of unified operations is reached.

4 April
: Campbell telegraphs to Eden his comments on the meeting with Simović on the 3rd of April. *Inter alia* he states that: Simović speaks as if it is natural to assume that Yugoslavia – already on the British side – will probably fight with Britain.

 Maček arrives in Belgrade and joins Simović's government.

 In case of war, Belgrade, Zagreb and Ljubljana are declared open cities.

 Churchill sends Simović a telegram in which he tells the General that Germans are concentrating against Yugoslavia from as far away as France, and that his only hope is to make "one supreme stroke for victory and safety" by winning "a decisive forestalling victory in Albania" and collect the "masses of equipment" that would fall into his hands.

5 April
: The British inform Simović and some other government officials of the forthcoming German attack.

 George Taylor receives a warning from London that "the balloon is expected to go up tomorrow".

 At 4:00 p.m. Cabinet members Simović, Ninčić, Maček, Jovanović, Trifunović, Grol, Jevtić and Kulovec assemble at Ninčić's request. According to Dragiša Ristić, "The majority of the cabinet members favored peace … At that moment Simović took the floor and delivered a fiery speech. In it he recalled page after page of Serbian history. He saluted the bones of Serbia's military heroic ancestors, the battle of Kosovo, the legendary princes of early Serbia, and Serbia's epic struggle against the Turks." According to Slobodan Jovanović, the difference between Simović and Maček is so great that some members of the conference foresee a possibility of the disintegration of the Government at the meeting scheduled for the following morning (April 6).

6 April
: Early in the morning the USSR signs only a treaty of friendship and non-aggression with Yugoslavia, and back-dates it to the 5th of April. (The requested military assistance from the USSR was not obtained.)

 The German Air Force starts bombing Belgrade, that lasts three days. The German Twelfth Army invades southern Yugoslavia («*Operation Punishment*") and Greece (*"Operation Marita"*). 'Operation "Punishment" had been performed' – Churchill later noted.

 "Flying in relays from airfields in Austria and Romania, 150 bombers and dive-bombers protected by heavy fighter escort participated in the attack. The initial raid was carried out at fifteen minutes. Thus the city was subjected to a rain of bombs for almost one and a half hours. The German bombardiers directed their main effort against the center of the city, where the principal government buildings were located."

 During the bombing attack, the SOE-men in Belgrade are taking their "toys" to a safe place.

 German Second Army launches limited-objective attacks against Yugoslavia.

 Italy declares war on Yugoslavia.

 Simović's cabinet ministers flee from Belgrade to Užice, while Simović and High Command go to Banja Koviljača.

1941, continued

The British Legation personnel and secret SOE agents leave Belgrade on their way to reach Great Britain in June 1941. Diplomatic immunity is extended to the British non-Legation personnel.

7 April At 9 a.m. all Ministers, except Simović, meet at Sevojno, near Užice, Maček presiding. The death of Dr. Kulovec is commemorated. The Ministers declare the state of preparedness and mobilization. Maček suggests the acceptance of Juraj Krnjević as Minister without portfolio, who will replace Maček in case he would not be available. The ministers decide that a purchase of food should be made in Great Britain and the US as soon as possible for the needy passive regions and the military.

The German invasion of the USSR (*"Operation Barbarosa"*) is postponed to June 22.

German troops enter Skoplje in Yugoslavia, on their way to bypass the Greek *Metaxas Line* on the west.

In London, Dalton writes in his diary: "...the Jugs seem to be in the muddle. Their Government has left Belgrade and is out of touch with their General Staff. Their M.F.A. [Minister of Foreign Affairs] is out of touch with senior officials who are with Campbell and the other diplomats at Vranjska Banja."

8 April German First Panzer Group starts drive toward Belgrade.

The Germans occupy Maribor, Skoplje and Prilep.

Maček leaves Sevojno to meet Simović at Koviljača.

In Washington, D.C., President Roosevelt sends a message to King Peter II saying, *inter alia*: "... I send Your Majesty my most earnest hope for a successful resistance to this criminal assault upon the independence and integrity of your country."

9 April The German Second Panzer Division enters Salonika, trapping the Greek Second Army outside the *Metaxas Line*, forcing them to surrender unconditionally.

German troops capture Niš and Bitolj (Monastir) in Yugoslavia.

Churchill delivers a somber speech in the House of Commons and states, *inter alia*: "**It has never been our policy nor our interest to see the war carried into the Balkan Peninsula. ...**" But Eden wrote: "**A war in Balkans was not what Hitler wanted.**"

10 April (As German troops are entering Zagreb) the **Independent State of Croatia (ISC)** is proclaimed on Radio Zagreb - in the presence of a German representative - in the name of Ante Pavelić - the leader of the Ustaše. He becomes *Poglavnik* (the head man) of the new state.

Hungary invades Yugoslavia.

British forces under General Henry Maitlannd Wilson withdraw from the Aliakmon line in Greece.

XLVI Panzer Corps enters the race for Belgrade. First Panzer Group reaches point forty miles from Yugoslav capital.

The Greek East Macedonian Army surrenders.

Almost 1,000 German aircraft are in the Balkans.

11 April Italian forces push down the Yugoslav coast in order to link up with their forces in Albania.

Hungary occupies Yugoslav territory.

The Germans take Osijek.

German mountain troops cross the Vardar river.

The Yugoslav Government moves from Sevojno to Pale (near Sarajevo).

Pavelić agrees to hand Dalmatia over to Italy.

"The minutes of their crown council meeting that day [11 April] reflect no awareness that Zagreb had fallen to the Germans; that an independent state of Croatia had been created with Ante Pavelić, murderer of King Alexander, as its leader, that a *panzer* corps was in forty miles of Belgrade; or that two additional German army corps had crossed the Vardar river." (Hoptner)

12 April At 2:30 a.m. the Germans enter Sremska Mitrovica.

"The Italians cross the Yugoslav frontier... at Rijeka and advanced without firing a shot."

The Government's conference is held in Pale, without Simović.

1941, continued

The King leaves at 12:30 p.m. for Foča and on for Nikšić.
(At 5 p.m.) **Belgrade falls to German forces.**
In the evening, Simović arrives from Koviljača to Pale, to join the Government.
Greek and British forces fall back to the Mount Olympus line in Greece.

13 April **Military resistance ends in western Bosnia and Dalmatia.**
The Government convenes into plenary session that turns out to be the last one the Government will hold on the territory of Yugoslavia. "Situation very difficult but not hopeless." It is decided that General Danilo Kalafatović will take over Simović's post as the Chief of Staff of the Supreme Command.
(At 4:00 p.m.) Simović orders Capt. Ristić "to make preparations for evacuating the King" - who is staying in the Ostrog monastery, near Nikšić.
Prime Minister Churchill sends his greetings from London "to the people of Yugoslavia, to the Serbs, the Croats and the Slovenes."
Churchill also telegraphs to Campbell, who was expected to be with the Yugoslav Government and/or High Command, but is actually in Vrnjačka Banja:

"It will not be possible at any time to send British surface warships, or British or American merchant ships or transports, up the Adriatic north of Valona. The reason for this is the air, ... The ships would be sunk, ... All the aircraft we can allot to the Yugoslav theatre is already at the service of the Yugoslav General Staff through Air Marshal D'Albianc. There are no more at present. **You must remember Yugoslavs have given us no chance to help them and refused to make a common plan,** ... and you **must** use your own judgment how much of this bad news you impart to them."

The Greek First Army begins to withdraw from Albania toward the Pindus Mountain.
The Germans launch an attack against the Greek and British positions near Mt. Olympus.
Hitler issues *Directive No. 27* related to occupation policy in Greece.

14 April Gen. Kalafatović arrives in Pale around 9 a.m..
The King is flown to Greece.
Government leaves Pale in the morning, arrives in Nikšić during the evening and the morning of the 15th.
Simović issues a written order to Kalafatović:

"His Majesty's Government, at its plenary session of April 13 in Pale, has taken the following decision: ... In view of the situation of our Army after the first setbacks, caused in particular by the events in Croatia and Dalmatia, to empower you to sue for armistice from the enemy so that time might be gained and the situation of the Army thereby alleviated." (That order set in motion the Yugoslav armistice negotiations with the Germans.)

Simović leaves Pale at noon, arrives in Ostrog at about 1:00 a.m. of the 15th.
The Germans break through the new Greek frontline. The Greek Army of Epirus withdraws from Albania.
"On the basis of Simović's written order, the high command, now at Sarajevo under general Kalafatović, dispatched emissaries to ask for an armistice: Division General Mihailo Bodi, Colonel France Tomše, and Lt. Col. Radmilo Trojanović." They leave Pale at midnight.

15 April German forces enter Sarajevo and capture the Yugoslav High Command.
The Goverment leaves Yugoslavia for Greece and the Middle East.

Escorted by his followers, Pavelić leaves Karlovac early on 15 April, and arrives in Zagreb at 4 a.m., "unnoticed and covered by the mantle of the night." No crowds of people are on the streets to welcome him, as the Italians had hoped for.

16 April British troops start to retreat from Greece.
Simović arrives in Athens. (Shortly thereafter, the British fly him, the King and his immediate entourage, important members of the cabinet, and Ristić to Alexandria.)

1941, continued

In London, Cadogan enters into his diary: "No confirmation of Yugoslav capitulation, but their effective resistance evidently at an end."

17 April In Belgrade, Yugoslavia's representatives sign the unconditional surrender.

"The armistice was concluded and signed on 17 April. General von Weichs signed for the Germans, with the Italian military attaché in Belgrade acting on behalf of his country. The Hungarians were represented by a liaisons officer who, however, did not sign the document since Hungary was technically not at war with Yugoslavia. Foreign Minister Cincar-Marcovic and General Milojko Yankovic signed for the Yugoslavs."

"The Germans took some 254,000 prisoners, excluding a considerable number of Croat, German, Hungarian, and Bulgarian nationals who had been inducted into the Yugoslav Army and who were quickly released after screening." (Those 254,000 were the Serbs.)

In twelve days of combat the Germans lose: 151 killed, 392 wounded, and 15 listed as missing in action, for a total of 558 men.

In Zagreb, Pavelić signs "Legal decree for the defense of the people and the state"

18 April **The German armistice with Yugoslavia becomes effective at 1200 hour.**
Athens is placed under martial law. Greek Prime Minister Koryzis committs suicide.
In London – British Foreign Minister Eden meets SOE chief Dalton, who records in his diary: "Eden tells me that [Ambassador Sir Miles] Lampson in Cairo wanted to ask Prince Palsy [Paul] to lunch, and telegraphed whether he might. Eden replied, 'No, such an act of hospitality would not be understood here' [in London]."

19 April German Fifth Panzer Division enters Plain of Thessaly. Germany's XVIII Mountain Corps captures Larissa and takes possession of the airfield. The Greek government agrees that British forces should be evacuated.

20 April British forces in Greece retreat from Mt. Olympus.
The war ends in mainland Greece.

21 April Greek First Army offers to surrender to the 1st SS Leibstandarte Division. Its commander accepts the offer, without referring to his superiors. All Greek soldiers are allowed to return home, while officers are allowed to retain their side arms. Upon hearing this, Mussolini is furious, and makes the Greeks sign another surrender document with much harsher terms.
The Germans capture the port of Volos.
Redeployment of German troops from the Balkans starts.
The British withdraw Air Force from Greece. **General Wavell orders evacuation of British troops from Greece.**

23 April The Greek First Army signs surrender agreement with the Germans and Italians.
King George II of Greece and his Government are flown to Crete by the British Air Force.

24 April The British last stand at Thermopylae. British Expeditionary Force begins the evacuation of its troops from Greece to Egypt and Crete.
Dalton confides to his diary the British treatment of Prince Paul: "I am delighted to read in a Colonial Office telegram that Prince Palsy and his wife are to reside in Kenya, with the status of political prisoner, and that a senior administrative official is to live with and watch them; that H.M.G. [His Majesty's Government] will pay the rent of their house, seeing that this is in the nature of prison, but that it will be put to 'our friend' that his large assets in this country should be drawn upon for his keep and other personal expenses. I hope that Lampson in Cairo has read this telegram with profit."

25 April Hitler issues *Directive No. 28* to seize Crete *("Operation Merkur")*. The Germans seize the Island of Lemnos.
Pavelić signs into law a Decree prohibiting the use of the Cyrillic alphabet.

26 April German parachute troops seize the Isthmus and town of Corinth.

27 April German Panzer units entered Athens.

1941, continued

In a broadcast report on the war, Curchill says that, when the people of Yugoslavia found out where they were being taken, they "rose in one **spontaneous** surge of revolt." (On the "spontaneity" of revolt see: Churchill-Dalton meeting at Chequers, 2 March 1941; all-British conference in Belgrade on 19 March; Churchill's instruction to Eden on 22 March; Eden's directive to Campbell on 24 March; Churchill's directive to Campbell on 26 and 27 March; and Leopold Amery's speech on 26 March. See also Chapter 11 of Part One.)

28 April **The British evacuation of Greece is completed.**

29 April German forces reach south coast of the Peloponnesus.
British intelligence **'Ultra'** intercepts messages which indicate that the Germans plan to attack Crete.
Cadogan writes in his diary: "Evacuation [from Greece] going fairly well. That's all that we're really good at! And we anticipate that 5,000 German air-borne troops are going to wipe us out of Crete! Our soldiers are most pathetic amateurs, pitted against professionals...."
The first groups of Serbs and Jews, and some suspected Croats, are sent into camp "Danica", near Koprivnica.

30 April **Hostilities in Greece cease.** All of Greece is under German and Italian occupation. During the campaign, the Greeks lose 15,700 killed, the British about 2,000 killed. The Germans sufffer about 2,000 killed and missing.
Pavelić enacts the 'Law Concerning Nationality.'

Spring **The British break the German Navy code.**

3 May Pavelić issues a Decree about conversion from one religion to another.

4 May **Hitler announces that the Yugoslav State has ceased to exist.**

7 May In Tržić, Pavelić confirms previous agreements made with Mussolini. It is decided that the formal agreement will be held in Rome on 18 May 1941.

8 May Tito moves from Zagreb to Belgrade and settles in Vladislav Ribnikar's villa.
The USSR breaks diplomatic relations with Yugoslavia.

9 May The Executive Committee of the Comintern issues directive No. 18, "**Directive for future work**", which must be followed by all member Parties.

11 May German troops complete the occupation of the Greek islands in the Aegean Sea.

11-12 May Mass liquidation of Serbs takes place in Glina.

12 May Colonel Dragoljub-Draža Mihailović arrives at Ravna Gora - south of Valjevo, in occupied Serbia – with seven officers and twenty-four noncommissioned officers and men.

"Since March the Foreign Office had been receiving numerous warnings of a German attack upon Russia. Hitler was reported to have told Prince Paul that he intended to invade on 30 June. At [the British Ambassador] Cripps' suggestion, the Yugoslav Minister in Moscow spoke of this to Stalin and Molotov. Cripps delivered separate warning from Churchill. Other rumors in the same sense began to circulate freely in Moscow during April. Stalin seems to have taken little notice." (Dilks)

13 May Bosnia and Herzegovina are incorporated into the Independent State of Croatia.

16 May Last British reinforcements arrive in Crete.

18 May **"The Rome Agreement"** is signed between Italy and Croatia, permitting Italy to annex some territory of the province of Dalmatia.

20 May **German invasion of the mainland Greece ends**. Start of German airborne invasion of Crete.

21 May German mountain troops begin to land at Maleme airport in Crete.

22 May John Colville: "The navy are having a heavy task off Crete and have lost a lot of ships, including *Gloucester* and *Fiji*. ..."

1941, continued

27 May — Cania (Crete) falls to the Germans. The British decide to withdraw from Crete.
Cadogan: "Awful news from Crete. We are scuppered there, and I'm afraid the moral and material effects will be serious. Certainly the Germans are past-masters in the art of war – and *great* warriors. If we beat them, we shall have worked a miracle."

28 May — The British and Commonwealth forces withdraw to the south coast of Crete.
Cadogan: "Cretan news terrible – it's another disaster. Private telegram from Miles Lampson to A[nthony Eden] about lack of air support in Crete and saying this has bad effect on morale everywhere – including Anzacs [Australian and New Zealand troops]. ..."

31 May — **British forces in Crete surrender.**

1 June — German forces complete seizure of Crete.
Evacuation of Crete completed, with 17,000 Allied troops safe.

2 June — Hitler and Mussolini meet at the Brenner Pass on the German-Italian border.

3 June — **USSR breaks diplomatic relations with Greece.**

5 June — Germans announce 15,000 prisoners taken in Crete. British declare afterward 12,970 unaccounted for.

7 June — A Legal Decree is issued to demarcate the eastern border of the ISC with Serbia.

14 June — **Croatia signs the Tripartite Pact unconditionally.**

17 June — **George Taylor returns to London.**

18 June — Hugh Dalton enters into his diary:

"Taylor arrived back yesterday by air form Lisbon, sent even in advance of the Minister (R.C.) [Ronald Hugh Campbell]. He is brought to see me this morning by Gladwyn. He looks very well and fit. He was captured by the Italians when the Jugs collapsed, near Kator [Kotor], but he and the rest of the large party, more than a hundred, of captives were treated very well by his comparatively civilised enemy. They passed some weeks at Chianciano and had quite a pleasant time waiting for all the formalities to be completed for their journey on through France and Spain. He is eager to be working again, ..., and he is to return to London on Sunday night [22 June] and make me a full report of all his doing."

22 June — **Germany invades the Soviet Union** *("Operation Barbarosa").*
Germany, Italy, Rumania, and Bulgaria declare war on USSR. Rumanians enter Bessarabia to regain it.
Tito writes a declaration of the Central Committee of the CPY, in which there is no explicit call to arms, but only a summons to make ready for a struggle. He calls the Soviet Union "our dear socialist Fatherland, our hope, the beacon to which the eyes of the working folk throughout the world are turned in longing ..." (Clissold)
Churchill declares support for the USSR.

... June — Jadovno becomes the first camp in which the mass extermination of Serbs and Jews took place.

24 June — **"The report to S.O. [Dalton] from A.D. [Taylor] and D.H.Y. [Masterson] on Certain S.O.2 Activities in Yugoslavia",** is prepared for Dalton. "The original report consisted of six sections. The last four, dealing with post-occupational matters (sabotage and guerrilla resistance), unfortunately, are missing; ..." [from Dalton Papers at the London School of Economics and Political Science]

25 June — Eden attends a meeting with Dalton, Taylor, and Masterson. Dalton notes in his diary:

"I ask Eden to dine, partly in order to keep our relations well manured ... and partly to enable him to meet Taylor and Masterson and hear their Balkan stories. I also ask Gladwyn [Jebb], C.D. [Sir Frank Nelson] and [John] Wilmot [Parliamentary Private Secretary to Dalton 1940-44]. This makes quite a nice little party on a hot night, though Eden is late arriving, having had to see the P.M. [Prime Minister], and has to go for a Defence Committee at 9:45. None the less, I think it did good. ... "

1941, continued

…………	"I am sure that **Moscow ordered us to begin diversionary and guerrilla actions.** Tito so informed us, and it became obvious that the activity of the party had to be reoriented, and that we had to speed up the stockpiling of weapons. …" (Djilas)
1 July	**Germany invades the British Channel Islands.**
4 July	Communist Party of Yugoslavia has no elaborate plan, does not talk of any uprising.
… July	The Comintern orders the start of Partisan actions in Yugoslavia. "The hour has struck when communists must launch an open fight by the people against the invaders. Without wasting a moment, **organize Partisan detachments and start a Partisan war behind the enemy lines**.…" (Clissold)
7 July	At Bela Crkva, a town in Western Serbia, "Žikica Jovanović ['Španac', i.e. a veteran of the Spanish Civil War] kills two local gendarmes [Milan Dragović and Bogdan Lončar] - not the occupiers, the Germans."
13 July	General rising takes place in Montenegro against the Italian occupiers.
27 July	Spontaneous armed rising of Serbs in the Independent State of Croatia against their persecutions - without any contacts with the "Chetniks" and Colonel Dragoljub-Draža Mihailović in Serbia.
31 July	Planning in Germany for the **"Final Solution"**, the systematic destruction of the Jews.
… Aug.	First radio news of **Mihailović's resistance** in Serbia reaches the British at Malta.
16 Sept	Hitler sets reprisal ratios for occupied Serbia: 100 Serbs to be killed for 1 German killed, 50 for 1 wounded.
19 Sept	**First meeting of Colonel Mihailović and Josip Broz Tito** at Struganik, occupied Serbia.
20 Sept.	Capt. D.T. Hudson (of SOE) lands on the Montenegro's coast («mission Bullseye») to get information on resistance. He meets the Partisans first and stays with them for a month before proceeding to Mihailović
24 Sept.	Tito's Partisans enter Užice and form the Soviet-style «Užice Republika». (This is consistent with the program announced at the Fifth Conutry-wide Conference of the CPY, held near Zagreb, 19-23 October 1940.)
17 Oct.	A solemn joint session of the Central Committee for Serbia is held in honor of the visiting General Secretary of the Comintern, Georgij Dimitrov, Tito's old friend from the Moscow days. He congratulates the Party in the name of the Comintern.
19-20 Oct.	German reprisal massacre at Kraljevo, Serbia. (100 Serbs executed for each dead German soldier.)
21 Oct.	German reprisal massacre at Kragujevac, Serbia. (The same ratio.)
25 Oct.	Captain Bill Hudson arrives at Mihailović's Chetnik's Headquarters.
26 Oct.	**Second meeting of Mihailović and Tito**, in the village of Brajići, Serbia. Mihailović does not want Hudson - who is in an adjacent room - to attend the meeting, because this is an internal Yugoslav affair.
21-28 Nov.	Parleys on truce between the Četniks and Partisans are held at Čačak, Serbia, and are attended by Capt. Hudson.
1 Dec.	General Bora Mirković signs his Memoirs in Cairo.
7 Dec.	**Japan attacks the US naval base at Pearl Harbor**, declares war on the USA, Great Britain, Australia, Canada, New Zealand and the Union of South Africa. Japan occupies the International Settlement at Shanghai.
8 Dec.	Roosevelt delivers his **"Day of Infamy"** speech.
	German offensive is halted outside Moscow.
…….	Stalin decides to defend Moscow.
14 Dec.	**Croatia declares war on the USA.**

1942

11 Jan. Simović's government falls and Professor Slobodan Jovanović forms a new Yugoslav Government in Exile.

20 Jan **"Final Solution"** efforts are coordinated and put in place at **the Wannsee Conference**.

8 Feb. At the monastery in Ostrog, Montenegro, the Communists proclaim that the liberated territory of Montenegro constitutes an integral part of the Union of the Soviet Socialist Republics.

26 May **Anglo-Soviet Treaty** of military and political alliance signed in London by Foreign Ministers.

9 July Offering his services to Churchill, Simović writes, *inter alia,* "**I took on the grave responsibility for the military defeat which was to be foreseen and inevitable** but which I was convinced would be of the utmost value for the allied cause, ..."

25 Aug. Churchill coolly declines Simović's offer of service.

1943

22-23 Mar. Referring to the negotiations between Tito's delegates and the Germans, Tito's chief diplomatic delegate, Vladimir Velebit, states:

"We are of the opinion, and that was unofficially made known to us, that the Germans do not have any territorial aspirations towards the territories of former Yugoslavia, but at present they have only strategic and economic, and eventually political interests. Consequently, **at the end of the war they will leave the country.**" (This was a common expectation that influenced the ultimate goals of all participants in the civil wars in Yugoslavia.)

1944

Saturday, 15 April 1944 – "...448 B-17s and B-24s attack marshaling yards; B-17s hit Ploesti, Rumania and Nis, Yugoslavia; ... A special group, led by lieutenant colonel Louis A. Neveleff, flies from HQ at Bari, Italy, to Medeno Polji [Polje], Yugoslavia and from there the group proceeds to Marshal Tito's HQ at Drvar, where Colonel Neveleff confers with Tito and spends several days laying the groundwork for the evacuation of downed US airmen in Yugoslav hands. Also, much information is gathered regarding the military organization and political trend of the partisan movement. The mission returns to Italy on 2 May ... " (USAAF Chronology, Mediterranean, 1944, Part I)

Sunday, 16 April 1944 (Eastern Orthodox Easter in Belgrade) –
"432 B-17s and B-24s hit targets in Rumania and Yugoslavia; B-17s bomb the industrial area at Belgrade, Yugoslavia; ..." (*Ibid*)

Monday, 17 April 1944 – "470 B-17s and B-24s hit targets in Bulgaria and Yugoslavia; B-17s bomb the industrial area, air depot and marshalling yard at Belgrade, Yugoslavia; ...") *(Ibid.)* .) "Some 2,000 ... tons fell on Yugoslav towns **designated and specifically requested by Marshal Tito's forces as containing enemy garrisons.**" (Richard G. Davis) In these carpet bombings civilian casualties were over 1,100, and German military losses 18. (There was no specific "industrial area" in Belgrade.)

6 June **D-Day**. The American, British and Canadian forces invade France at the beaches of Normandy. (*Operation "Overlord"*)

11 Aug. Churchill arrives in Italy to see military operations and to confer with Tito.

12 Aug. In Naples, Italy, **Churchill confers with Tito.** Churchill: "... Is it not true that there is a large portion the Serb peasantry who would not be very glad to see the Communist system introduced?" Tito: "We do not intend to impose any such system. I have often stated this publicly." ... Churchill: "Will you allow individual freedom in your country after the war?" Tito: "Why, yes. That is our basic principle – democracy and freedom of the individual." (Clissold)

23 Aug. **Rumania capitulates to the Red Army.**

1944, continued

25 Aug. **Paris is liberated.**
31 Aug. The Red Army occupies Bucharest, Rumania.

6 Sept. Heaviest bombing of Leskovac, in occupied Serbia, is carried out on this day – the birthday of king Peter II. - by 50 Flying Fortresses, with a pretext of attacking retreating German units. Estimates of civilian casualties vary from over a thousand to six thousands. (Some survivors put the number at about 4,500, from the population of approximately 30,000.) Fitzroy Maclean writes, *inter alia:* "... Leskovac seemed to rise bodily in the air in a tornado of dust and smoke and debris, ... What was left of Leskovac lay enveloped in a pall of smoke; ... Even the Partisans seemed subdued." "It seemed rather like taking a sledge hammer to crack a walnut." Macleaan does not mention German casualties.
The Red Army reaches the Yugoslav border.
12 Sept. After the British Government strongly insists, King Peter II invites the Yugoslavs to join Tito to the great dismay of the royalist non-Partisans.
18 Sept. Without informing the British and American military missions and the Allied Commander for the Middle East, Tito secretly flies from Vis to Craiova, Rumania.
21 Sept. Tito continues flight to Moscow to make arrangements for the entry of the Red Army into Yugoslavia and for the cooperation of his units with the Red Army. (**This precludes any entry of the Western Allies' troops into Yugoslavia.**)
23 Sept. Tito orders that members of the British and American military missions at his headquarters will not be permitted to circulate beyond corps headquarters. (Roberts)
29 Sept. Tito and the Soviet Government conclude an agreement on the entry of the Red Army into Yugoslavia. (The Western Allies are not included.)

1 Oct. **The Red Army enters Yugoslavia.**
3 Oct. The Germans evacuate Athens.
5 Oct. British forces land in Greece (to preclude Communist takeover of the country).
6 Oct. Tito returns to Yugoslavia from Moscow.
7 Oct. The Germans decide to leave Greece.
9 Oct. Churchill and Eden arrive in Moscow for a nine-day meeting with Stalin and Molotov. **Spheres of influence** between Britain and the USSR **are established** for Eastern Europe and the Balkans. Yugoslavia – Britain 50%, USSR 50%. Greece – Britain 90%, USSR 10%. (50% to 50% for Yugoslavia has no meaning because Churchill could not send British troops into Yugoslavia anyway.)
14 Oct. **The British liberate Athens.**
15 Oct. The Red Army and the Partisans take Niš (in Serbia).
20 Oct. **The Red Army and Partisans enter Belgrade.**
27 Oct. Tito's units hold a victory parade in Belgrade.

(Massive "cleansing" of the "enemies", "Quislings", etc. in Belgrade and elsewhere is implemented by the newly established Communist authorities.)

2 Nov. Following the withdrawal of German troops, **the British enter Salonika, Greece.**

3 Dec. **A Civil War** between the Communist-led forces and their opponents erupts **in Greece.**
25-28 Dec. Churchill and Eden visit Athens for talks with Greek leaders, and to secure the British sphere of influence in Greece, as agreed with Stalin.
Dec. 1944-Jan. 1945 The British troops suppress a left-wing insurrection in Greece.

1945

11 Jan. Political truce signed in Greece.
13 Jan. German Army Group E completes withdrawal from Greece and Albania.

1945, continued

4-11 Feb.	Roosevelt, Stalin and Churchill meet at **the Yalta Conference** (*"Argonaut"*) to determine the re-organization of postwar Europe. Agreements on major issues (such as Poland and "White" Russians) are subsequently not implemented by the USSR.
8 Mar.	In Bern, Switzerland, representatives of the American Office of Strategic Services and the German High Command in Italy begin secret negotiations for an early surrender of the German forces in Italy.
30 Mar.	**The Red Army** occupies Danzing (Gdansk), Poland, and **enters Austria**. American military government is established in Frankfurt, Germany.

(Edvard Kardelj insists to US official Carl F. Norden on need for "cleansing" of the opposition. (See FRUS 1945.))

5 April	**The Red Army enters Vienna suburbs.** Tito leaves for Moscow.
9 April	**The Red Army forces enter the center of Vienna.**
11 April	Tito signs a treaty with the USSR.
12 April	**President Roosevelt dies** of stroke in Warm Springs, Georgia. **Harry S. Truman replaces him as the President.**
13 April	**The Soviet Army in Vienna.**
29 April	**The German Armies in Italy sign terms of surrender** at the Royal Palace in Caserta.
1 May	The cessation of hostilities and **surrender of all German forces in Italy** is announced. New Zealand troops enter Trieste (from the west) and make contact with Tito's Partisan forces that had also entered the city (from the east).

(Activities of the anti-Partisan units and civilians, crossing from Yugoslavia into Austria and Italy, and where they meet British troops.)

2 May	**All German forces in Italy surrender** to the Western Allies. Hostilities cease at noon GMT. **The Red Army enters Berlin.** Pavelić leaves Zagreb and the retreating military and civilians, and heads separately to Austria. Maček leaves Zagreb, heading West. **(See FRUS 1945.)**
5 May	Mihailović's radio contact with outside world ceases.
6 May	**The US Fifth Army enters Austria from Italy.**
7 May	**Germany signs unconditional surrender to the Allies at 2:41 a.m., local time, in Reims, France.** The British Eighth Army crosses the Italian-Austrian border.
8 May	**Victory in Europe – VE Day. The war in Europe ends.** British troops enter Klagenfurt [Celovec], Austria, and make contact there with Tito's units.
9 May	The German forces in the Greek islands surrender. **The Red Army enters Prague.**
12 May	The German garrison in Crete surrenders.

(Croatia's army and civilians reach the Drava River and Bleiburg (Pliberk), unsuccessfully negotiate surrender to the British, and are taken over by Tito's units.)

22 May	British military begins deceitful and forcible handover of anti-Partisan units and civilians from Austria to Tito's forces.

1945, continued

(Massive massacres are committed in Kočevje and elsewhere in Slovenia after the British hand-over of military and civilians to Tito's units.)

(US Ambassador in Italy, Alexander C. Kirk, reports on massive handovers to Tito's units.) (See FRUS 1945.)

(The British-Tito negotiations relate to the annexation of the Corintia [Austria] and Julian Alps region [Italy] to Yugoslavia, retreat of Tito's units from Austria, and Tito's units' downing of two American planes.)

15 Aug. **Victory over Japan – VJ Day. The Second World War ends.**

29 Nov. The Kingdom of Yugoslavia is abolished, and the Communist-ruled Federal Popular Republic of Yugoslavia is proclaimed.

1946

5 Mar. At Westminster College, Fulton, Missouri, USA, Churchill delivers his "The Sinews of Peace" speech. It immediately becomes known as **"The Iron Curtain" speech** because of the following passage:

"From Stettin in the Baltic to Trieste in the Adriatic, an iron curtain has descended across the Continent. Behind that line lie all the capitals of the ancient states of Central and Eastern Europe. Warsaw, Berlin, Prague, Vienna, Budapest, Belgrade, Bucharest and Sofia, all these famous cities and the populations around them lie in what I must call the Soviet sphere, and all are subject in one form or another, not only to Soviet influence but to a very high and, in many cases, increasing measure of control from Moscow."

13 Mar. Aleksandar Ranković, Tito's Minister of Internal Affairs, announces that General Mihailović has been brought to OZNA prison in Belgrade.

10 June The trial of Mihailovic begins in Belgrade (without presence of British liaison officers).

17 July Mihailović is executed. The site of the execution is not revealed.

Index

Adriatic Sea 104, 140, 146
Aegean Sea 76, 77, 139
Africa 4, 177
Agit-Prop, agitation-propaganda 201
Akšamović, Bishop 119
Alarm, newspaper 24
Albania, Albanian .... xviii, 14, 25, 29, 30, 50-53, 63, 70, 72, 73, 84-86, 104, 130, 132, 133, 136, 139, 141, 150, 153, 176, 178, 181, 194, 196, 201, 219, 226, 232
Albanija, skyscraper 129
Alexander I, King of Yugoslavia 129, 157, 186
Alexander, Field Marshal Harold 231
Alexandria 34, 191, 231
Aliakmon line, also Alikhmon line 43, 134
Allied, Allies 3, 4, 21, 30, 43, 47, 51, 54, 57-61, 71, 72, 77, 85, 92, 171, 184, 186, 192, 195, 222, 226, 232, 234, 235
Alpine Violets operation 194
Altmaier, Dr. Jakob xvii, 4, 5, 12, 13, 26, 27, 41
America or United States 48, 56, 105, 139, 232
American, the Americans 9, 20, 36, 44, 46, 47, 61, 63, 66, 70, 114, 128, 138, 139, 148, 161, 163, 165, 170, 175, 184, 185, 195, 220
Amery, Julian (later Baron of Lustleigh) .... xvii, 3, 4, 10, 12-16, 21, 22, 25, 26, 28, 29, 39-41, 46, 50, 51, 59, 60, 63, 67, 80, 107, 109, 120, 157, 211, 225
Amery, Leopold-Leo 47, 133
Andres, Ivan 122, 177
Anfuso, Filippo 140, 178, 189, 190
Ankara also Angora 64, 85, 157, 158, 192
Antić, Milan also Antic 67, 71, 72, 77, 101, 152, 180
Antonescu, Gen. Ion 109, 110, 111, 227
Anzac troops 196
Apennines 172
Aranda Mata, Gen. Antonio 30
Armistice 192
Association of the Retired Officers and Warriors 81
Athens 5, 29, 34, 37, 38, 40, 42, 44, 64, 73, 85, 135, 138, 139, 149, 163, 171, 172, 184, 188, 190, 191, 192, 193, 195, 228, 236
Atherton, Terence 24, 41, 44
Australia, Australians .... xvii, 43, 176, 213
Austria, Austrians 2, 23, 25, 52, 157, 169, 178, 191, 226

Austro-Hungarian Empire 220, 226
Autty & Clogg 231
Avalon Project, The 61, 134, 162
Axios (Vardar) River 187
Axis (Berlin-Rome) 1, 2, 6, 9, 17, 19, 21, 23, 30, 31, 32, 33, 44, 51, 52, 54, 60, 76, 77, 102, 104, 105, 132, 135, 137, 139, 140, 149, 150, 152, 154, 158, 159, 161, 172, 181, 216, 221, 222

Babić, Maj. Dušan 14, 17, 88, 98
Bailey, Colonel William .... xvii, 7, 12, 13, 14, 22, 34, 36, 42, 58, 71, 109, 171, 213
Bailey, Ronald H 231
Baku 160
Balaton Lake 22
Balfour & Mackay 42, 104, 126, 130, 134, 135, 231
Balkan Front 3, 12, 38, 43, 63, 64, 177, 185
Balkan Herald biweekly 24, 40, 41
Balkan Peninsula 36, 71, 176
Balkans or Balkan States ... 1-11, 15, 23, 25, 27, 31, 33, 34, 36, 37, 40-42, 44, 47, 50, 53, 63, 142, 145, 158, 159, 161, 163, 170, 172, 174, 175-177, 195, 199, 201, 209, 212, 213, 218, 231, 233
Baltic Sea 168
Banja Koviljača 173, 175, 181
Banja Luka or Banjaluka 178, 181, 182
Banjanin, Jovan 118, 222
Banovina Hrvatska 147, 222
Barbarossa operation 61, 162
Barker, Elisabeth ... 3, 6, 15, 36, 40-42, 48, 53, 64, 65, 71, 73, 83, 134, 152, 153, 170, 184, 231
Barnes, Ralph W. 44
Basle 9
Batajnica 98
Beatty, Chester 2, 3, 12, 28, 29, 212, 213
Beck, Marshall Ludwig 163
Becker, Dr. A. 25
Beevor, Anthony 8, 231
Bela Crkva 208
Belgians, Belgium 21
Belgrade .... xvii, xviii, 1, 3-5, 7, 10-24-30, 32-34, 36-50, 53-55, 57, 61, 63-71, 73-75, 78-80, 82, 85-104, 106, 108-110, 112-119, 121, 123-126, 128, 129, 131-137, 139-142, 145-147, 149-154, 157-164, 166-175, 177, 179, 180, 182-184, 187-193, 196, 200-202, 204, 205, 210, 215-220, 223, 224-230, 234, 235

263

Beli Dvor.................................. 70, 71, 135
Beloff, journalist Nora............ 14, 39, 199, 231
Benkovac 181, 195
Bennett, John H................xvii, 4, 10, 12, 13, 47, 53, 78, 109
Bennett, Ralph 231
Berchtesgaden....................................... 53, 163
Berlin....xviii, 27, 121, 133, 136-138, 142, 146, 152-154, 159, 160, 162-165, 167, 170, 222, 226
Bern.. 97
Bernstorff, Dr. Sigismund 136
Besarović, Vojislav 112
Bessarabia 168
Bičanić... 190, 228
Bihać 181
Bijeljina.. 89, 191
Birčanin, Ilija or Trifunović Birčanin.........xvii, 13, 14, 51-53, 80, 96, 97, 210
Bitolj (Monastir) 175
Black Sea 51
Blake & Louis 231
Blau, George E............... 169, 174, 177, 180, 188-191, 193, 194, 231
Blenheim bombers 89, 91
Blitz Krieg 194
Bobić, Miloš.. 228
Bobinac, Stevan... 98
Bodi, Gen. Mihailo............................. 189-192
Bogdanović, Vladeta 100, 101, 112, 119
Boka Kotorska..................................... 186, 206
Bonaventure cruiser 64
Bonbright... 138
Borg, Jerome S. 46
Boris III, King of Bulgaria............................ 54
Borovo 89
Bosnia (Bosna).........22, 31, 41, 42, 181, 182, 185, 186, 191, 199, 206, 218
Bosnian Muslims 115, 122, 123
Bosnić, Petar.............2, 14, 17, 19, 54-56, 68, 69, 77, 79, 82, 88, 89, 90, 93, 97, 98, 101, 107, 110, 112, 113, 118-120, 125, 127, 139, 140, 148, 149, 223, 224, 229, 231
Boston 46, 220, 231, 232, 235
Boughey, Peter .... xvii, 4, 13
Boyd, William 46
Brašić, General Ilija 95
Bregalnica 47
Brewer, Sam 44
Brigham, Dan 97
Bristol Co... 17
Britain, British or England or United Kingdom.. xvii, 1-10, 12-58, 60-68, 70, 71, 73, 77-87, 91, 94-96, 101, 103, 104, 112, 113, 119, 120-122, 126, 131, 133-135, 138-143, 145- 153, 155, 157, 159-167, 169-180, 183-185, 188, 191-197, 200, 202, 205, 207, 209, 210, 212-216, 218-220, 225, 226, 228-236
Britannia magazine............................... 40, 41
Britanova news agency 39-41, 46, 174
British Broadcasting Corporation, B.B.B.,BBC 39, 42, 47, 86, 129, 13-135, 235
British Channel Islands............................... 29
British Chiefs of Staff............ 8, 9, 11, 53, 184
British Empire, Commonwealth...........25, 43, 71, 183, 232
British Expeditionary Force (BEF) 36, 210
British Government........1, 20, 40, 50, 63, 67, 112, 150
British Legation............xvii, 1, 13, 18, 26, 29, 33, 41, 44, 134, 135, 141, 153, 169, 171
British Lloyd Co. 37
British Military Mission................... 34, 37, 216
British Security Coordination (BSC) 46
Broad, Philip 215
Brock, Ray.................44, 46, 97, 98, 127, 129, 130, 169, 172, 174, 205, 231
Brown, Cecil 44
Brown, Peter....................................... 15, 40
Broz, Josip or Tito.................5, 15, 27, 30, 45, 54, 57, 131, 140, 161, 179, 180, 199, 200, 202-204, 207-209, 211, 227, 231, 233, 235, 236
Bruce Lockhart, Sir Robert................... 39, 231
Brus 152, 192
Bucharest 7, 10, 40, 143, 195
Buckland.. 5
Budapest 5, 21, 22, 33, 34, 40, 174
Budisavljević, Dr. Srđan25, 32, 92, 101, 116, 118, 120, 121, 129, 138, 153, 173, 190, 221, 222
Bukovac, Zorica... 171
Bulat, Edo... 195
Bulgaria, Bulgars, or Bulgarians................. 9, 10, 20, 21, 25, 26, 32, 36, 37, 41, 43, 49-51, 53, 54, 64, 66, 75, 76, 147, 152, 159, 169, 176, 178, 199, 218, 221, 226
Bullseye mission... 54
Burazović, Col. Stjepan...................... 69, 112

Cadogan, Sir Alexander...................... xvii, 85, 138, 174, 189, 192, 193, 195, 196, 215, 232
Cairo..............1, 2, 5, 18, 19, 20, 24, 29, 33, 34, 36, 54, 63, 75, 84, 175, 193, 195, 215, 229
Calei Victoriei 143
Campbell, Ronald Ian (later Sir)........... xvii, 28
Campbell, Sir Ronald Hugh................. 6, 197
Canada... 98, 213
Canaris, Admiral Wilhelm 151

Cape of Good Hope 5, 34
Carlton, David 37, 63, 67, 231
Carnegie.. 46
Caxton Street 2
Central Committee of CPY..........45, 46, 180, 199, 200-202, 204-207, 209, 211
Chamberlain, Neville 214, 232
Chequers........................... 13, 21, 49, 65, 68
Chetniks or Cetniks................16, 17, 31, 97, 130, 218, 219
Chianciano 172, 197
Chicago Tribune..................................... 44
Chidson, Major Monty 212
Chief of Imperial General Staff (CIGS)....... xvii
Chiefs of Staff........................ 8, 9, 11, 53, 184
Childs, Stephen, Press Attaché 4, 27, 40
Chinigo, Michael................................... 44
Churchill, Winston S. (later Sir)......................
  xvii, 8, 13, 15, 20, 21, 23, 29, 30, 36, 37, 38, 40, 41, 43, 47, 49, 50, 52, 56, 57, 58, 60, 61, 63, 64-68, 70, 73, 79, 85, 86, 92, 93, 101, 103, 107, 109, 122, 125, 130, 134-136, 146, 147, 153, 163, 169, 170, 173, 175-177, 183-185, 192, 195, 196, 212, 214, 227, 229, 231-236
Churchill and the Balkan Front idea 38, 43, 63, 64 177, 185
Churchill and Campbell........................20, 40, 41, 47, 49, 57, 66, 67, 73, 85, 86, 134, 135, 147, 177, 184, 185, 196, 214,
Churchill and Greece............20, 21, 30, 36-38, 41, 43, 49, 50, 52, 63-66, 73, 85, 93, 134-136, 146, 169, 170, 173, 175-177, 184, 185, 192, 195, 231, 232, 234, 236
Churchill and Italy............15, 20, 23, 50, 52, 63, 66, 85, 146, 147, 192, 233
Churchill and SOE..............13, 15, 20, 23, 29, 30, 36-38, 40, 41, 43, 47, 49, 58, 63-66, 75, 79, 85, 56, 101, 103, 109, 170, 173, 214, 231, 232, 234-236
Churchill and Turkey........36, 43, 50, 63, 64, 195
Churchill and USA................................ 47, 70
Churchill and Yugoslavia.....13, 15, 20, 21, 23, 29, 30, 36, 37, 38, 40, 41, 43, 47, 49, 50, 52, 56-58, 60, 61, 63, 64, 66, 67, 70, 73, 85, 86, 93, 103, 107, 109, 122, 125, 130, 134-136, 146, 147, 153, 163, 169, 170, 173, 175-177, 183, 192, 195, 212, 227, 229, 231, 233-236
Ciano, Galeazzo................ xviii, 133, 145, 146
Cincar-Marković, Aleksandar or Cincar-Markovic or Cincar Marcovic or Cinzar Merkovich..........xviii, 68, 77, 87, 88, 91, 120, 152, 158, 180, 192, 193
Civil war(s) 4, 27, 157, 160, 202, 208, 233

Clarke, Col. Charles S...................................
  ....xvii, 1, 13-15, 17, 18, 19, 82, 159, 174
Class Struggle.. 200
Clissold, Stephen ... xv, 24, 180, 199-208, 231
Clogg, Professor Richard 231
Colville, John 192, 196, 231, 236
Columbia radio station........................... 44, 129
Comintern.............. 45, 54, 140, 161, 199-208
Communism, Communists..........xv, xvi, xviii, 5, 15, 16, 27, 40, 45, 46, 53, 54, 57, 88, 131, 140, 159, 161, 167, 168, 179, 180, 199, 200, 201, 202, 204-208, 211, 213, 230, 231, 235
Communist Party of Croatia (CPC) ... 199, 200
Communist Party of Slovenia, The (CPS) . 199
Communist Party of Yugoslavia (CPY)......45, 46, 180, 199-207, 209, 211
Concordat with Vatican 223
Cornish, Paul.. 216
coup d'état in Belgrade, the putsch, or puč...
  4, 5, 17, 19, 23, 26, 28, 29, 42-44, 48-51, 53, 63, 65, 69, 72, 78, 79, 83, 86, 88, 90, 93, 94, 102, 103, 106, 107, 109, 119, 128, 131-133, 136, 143, 144, 172, 194, 218, 225, 229
Crete.. 196
Creveld, Professor Martin, van..........63, 105, 134, 169, 236
Creveld, Professor and Greece................63, 105, 134, 169, 236
Creveld, Professor and Yugoslavia..........63, 105, 134, 169, 236
Cripps, Sir Stafford 160, 161, 163, 196, 231
Croatia, Croats...............................xvi, 16, 23, 25, 26, 42, 50, 60, 64, 101, 106, 112, 115, 118, 119, 122-124, 127, 128, 130, 138-140, 143, 146, 147, 149, 152, 156, 175, 178, 179, 180, 182-187, 189, 190, 193, 197, 199-203, 206, 218, 221, 222, 226, 234, 235
Croatian Peasant Party (CPP), *Hrvatska Seljačka Stranka*...............xviii, 16, 121, 123, 126, 138, 179, 205
Croatian Trade Union 25
Crown Council (Yugoslav)........................... 65
Cunard White Star line 16
Cunningham, Admiral Sir Andrew 73, 177
Cvetković, Dr. Dragiša or Cvetkovich, Tsvetkovich, Tsvetkovitch, Cvetkovic.. xviii, 65, 66, 68, 71, 72, 77, 87, 88, 91, 92, 101, 102, 104, 108, 118, 121, 132, 152, 154, 160, 180, 224, 227
Czech, Czechoslovak............................... 196

Čok, Prof. Rudolf....................................... 171
Čolaković, Rodoljub................................. 200

Čorović, Prof. Vladimir 171
Čubrilović, Dr. Branko 12, 118, 120, 121, 222
Čurćin, Joka 171
Čurćin, Milan 171

D'Albianc, Air Marshal John Henry 184
Daily Mail, The 41, 44
Daily Mirror, The 39
Daković, Marko 119-121
Dalmatia 140, 144, 178, 181, 186, 187, 189, 190, 195, 199, 205, 206
Dalton, Dr. Hugh, head of SOE, also "Doctor Dynamo" .... xvii, 8, 9, 12, 13, 23, 30, 31, 36, 38, 39, 47, 48, 49, 53, 60, 63-66, 68, 79, 85, 86, 89, 90, 95, 96, 101, 104, 109, 122, 151, 172, 173, 174, 193, 195, 196, 197, 210, 214, 215, 231, 234
Danchev, Alex 9, 20, 85, 231
Danica concentration camp 203
Danube River 3-7, 10, 11, 21-23, 25, 33, 34, 36, 43, 49, 50, 64, 75, 114, 146, 151, 169, 170, 174, 177, 180, 193, 195, 196, 198, 218, 232
Davidson, Basil5, 22, 33, 34, 40, 174, 212, 231
de Guingand, General Francis 175
Deakin, historian William (later Sir) 57, 232
Dedijer, Vladimir 131, 200, 202, 232
Dedinje or Dedigne 70, 127, 130, 171, 179
Defence Committee 36, 198
Delibašić, Capt. Božidar 135
Delnice 185
Democratic Party .... xviii, 20, 25, 30, 32, 41, 48, 54, 104, 106, 109, 110, 118, 220, 222
Despard, Capt. Max 4, 7, 21, 169
Despard, Tom 169
Deutsche Allgemeine Zeitung 136
Dew, Armine (Armand) 80, 153
Dilks, Professor David 23, 49, 85, 94, 138, 174, 189, 192, 193, 195, 196, 232
Dill, General Sir John .... xvii, 37, 38, 43, 63, 73, 134, 141, 146, 147, 151, 153, 174, 188, 196
Dimitrov, Georgi 140, 161, 199, 202
Dinić, Lt.-Col. Miloje 88, 98, 113
Diplomatic Corps 4, 22
Directive No. 22 (Alpine Violets) 194
Directive No. 25 .... 61, 136, 157
Directives for Future Work 204
Doboj 194
Dodds-Parker, Sir Douglas 5, 11, 29, 33, 35, 232

Dombrovica 196
Donovan, Col. William Joseph .... xviii, 9, 20, 21, 36, 56, 57, 60, 61, 63, 71, 74, 137, 139, 175, 193, 231, 232, 236
Dožić, Patriarch Dr. Gavrilo 92, 136, 229
Dragović, Milan 208
Drava River 146
Drina River 146, 182, 186
Drniš 195
Dual Monarchy 191
Dubrovnik 15, 216, 219
Dudić, Dragoljub 200, 208
Duga Resa 185
Dykes, Lt.-Col. Vivian 36, 231

Đilas, Milovan or Djilas 131, 200-209, 232
Đonović, Jovan or Djonovic or Djonovich or Djonovitch .... xviii, 16, 51, 53, 54, 78
Đorđević, Bishop Dr. Irinej 171
Đurić, Dr. Đorđe 119

Economist, The 33
Eden, Anthony (later The Earl of Avon) .... xvii, 30, 37, 38, 41, 43, 46, 47, 57, 63-68, 73, 78, 83-86, 113, 133-135, 139, 141, 142, 144, 146, 147, 149, 150-152, 170, 177, 184, 185, 189, 192, 193, 195-198, 220, 226, 231, 232, 235
Eden and Campbell 41, 46, 47, 57, 66, 67, 73, 83-86, 113, 133-135, 144, 147, 149, 150, 152, 177, 184, 185, 196, 197, 220,
Eden and Greece 37, 38, 41, 63-66, 73, 84, 85, 133-135, 141, 146, 151, 152, 170, 177, 184, 185, 189, 192, 195-197, 226, 231, 232
Eden and Turkey 38, 43, 63, 64, 195
Eden and Yugoslavia 30, 37, 38, 41, 43, 46, 47, 57, 63-67, 73, 85, 86, 133, 134, 139, 141, 142, 146, 147, 150, 152, 170, 177, 184, 185, 189, 192, 193, 197, 198, 226, 231, 235
Edwards, Lovat 40, 44
Egypt 19, 20, 34, 35, 43, 54, 124, 172, 189, 193, 216
Electra House (EH) 2, 39, 214
England 20, 33, 37, 58, 60, 61, 64, 77, 104, 126, 139, 151, 160, 172, 192, 197, 216, 232
English Channel 8
English Club 24
Enigma machine 177
Europe 2, 4, 8, 9, 29, 54, 105, 117, 158, 177, 201, 208, 212, 214, 231, 232, 235

Fadden, Arthur W. 176

Far East.. 105, 168
Fascist, Fascism......................xviii, 5, 181, 189, 206, 215, 236
Fatherland............... 45, 58, 72, 114, 201, 233
Fifth Conference of CPY 200, 201
Fiji, ship... 196
Finland.. 158
First World War...........................4, 25, 51, 52, 56, 72, 122, 185, 194, 224
Florence 144, 178
Florence radio station.............................. 143
Florina 150, 151
Flörsheim am Main... 4
Foča 180
Foot, Historian M.R.D............... 9, 23, 24, 232
Ford, Corey 20, 232
Foreign Office (FO).....................xvii, 5-8, 20, 22, 25, 28, 31, 36, 39, 47, 53, 73, 84, 85, 135, 138, 148, 170, 171, 196, 210, 214, 215
Fourth Arm, *The*... 9
Fourth Estate, *The* 44
France...3, 8, 17, 20, 34, 58, 129, 143, 153, 172, 189, 191, 193, 194, 197, 200, 214, 232, 233
Franco, Gen. Francisco............................. 30
Frankfurt am Main... 4
Frankfurter Zeitung................................ 27, 41
Frodsham, G.S... 4
FRUS1 .... 61, 66, 70, 129, 132, 138, 139, 232

GAF... 153, 177
Gamelin, Gen. Maurice Gustave................. 7
Gavrilović, Aleksandar 171
Gavrilović, Dr. Milan or Gavrilovic or Gabrilovitch......xviii, 12, 16, 26, 28, 30, 32, 50, 119, 121, 157, 158, 166, 171, 196, 218, 225
Gavrilović, Dr. (Yugoslav FO) 120, 138
General Staff (Research) (GSR) 2
General Staff HQ (Yugoslav)......7, 10, 11, 14, 15, 17, 31, 65, 68, 78, 160, 184
George II, King of Greece 135
German Air Force (GAF) or Luftwaffe....... 29, 36, 134, 153, 163, 171, 172, 177
German High Command 168
German invasion.....10, 16, 66, 142, 151, 159, 161, 165, 210
German invasion of Greece 105, 152
German invasion of Yugoslavia .. 10, 165, 210
German Legation 40, 138, 146
German new order 56
German News Agency 132
Germans, the......3, 6, 7, 10, 14, 25, 31, 35, 37, 40, 45, 46, 48, 50-54, 68, 72, 84, 121, 132, 141-143, 146, 147, 148-150, 152-155, 160-167, 173-175, 177, 178, 180, 182, 186, 188, 190-197, 202, 208, 209, 226
German-Soviet Commercial Agreement ... 168
Germany...............xvii, 2-4, 6-10, 12, 20, 23-25, 28, 30, 33, 34, 37, 39, 43, 48, 49, 51-56, 59, 61, 63, 66, 68, 70, 71, 75, 76, 84, 86, 104, 105, 120, 125, 126, 131-135, 137-140, 143, 146, 147, 149, 150, 152-154, 156, 157, 159, 160,-169, 174, 176, 179, 180, 181, 184-186, 192-194, 201-204, 206, 210, 212, 216, 225
Germany and Bulgaria........................9, 10, 20, 25, 37, 43, 49, 51, 53, 54, 66, 75, 76, 147, 152, 159, 169, 176,
Germany and Greece..................3, 6, 8, 9 20, 30, 34, 37, 43, 49, 52, 54, 63, 66, 84, 105, 126, 133-135, 143, 146, 152, 167, 169, 174, 176, 184, 185, 192, 194, 201, 216,
Germany and Rumania...............4, 7, 8, 9, 37, 43, 49, 52, 76, 143, 159, 169, 176
Germany and Yugoslavia............xvii, 2-4, 6-10, 12, 20, 23-25, 28, 30, 33, 34, 37, 39, 43, 48, 49, 51-54, 56, 59, 61, 63, 66, 70, 71, 75, 76, 84, 86, 104, 105, 125, 131-134, 137-140, 143, 146, 147, 150, 152, 153, 157, 159-161, 163-169, 174, 176, 179, 180, 181, 184-186, 192-194, 201-203, 206, 210, 212, 216, 225
German-Yugoslav negotiations 59
Gestapo....................................... 4, 136, 196
Gibraltar.. 20, 172
Giurgiu 7
Gladstone No. 13 108
Glanville, Trevor-Terence ("Nero").. 16, 24, 48
Glasnik (The Herald) 230, 232, 234, 235
Gleason, historian S. Everett............. 175, 233
Glen, Alexander........xvii, 4, 5, 7, 12-16, 18, 21, 25, 28, 34, 37, 42, 53, 58, 60, 71, 78, 107, 109, 149, 171, 213, 217, 226
Gligorijević, Milo 60
Glina 205
Godfrey, Rear Admiral John..................... 4, 21
Goeland Shipping Co. 6
Golgotha... 45, 57, 58
Golikov, Gen. Filip...................................... 161
Golubac 196
Göring (Goering), *Reichsmarschall* Herman 61, 134, 163
Gornji Grad... 199
Gorodetsky, Professor Gabriel............31, 45, 130, 131, 140, 142, 157-167, 202, 204, 232
Gorski Kotar 206
Gospić 181, 203
Gradišnik, Col. Ferdo 89

Grand Alliance, The 103, 231
Grand, Colonel Laurence 2, 3, 6, 7, 39, 103, 212, 213, 215, 231, 232
Great Britain............ xvii, 1, 2, 9, 12, 13, 17, 18, 21, 23, 30, 31, 36, 37, 43, 44, 47, 48, 53, 57, 58, 67, 69, 72, 77-79, 82, 93, 98, 101, 102, 106, 109, 119, 122, 147, 157, 174, 175, 201, 229, 233
"Great Purge" in the USSR 199
Greben narrows 6, 151
Greece, Greeks....... xvii, 3, 6, 8, 9, 18, 20, 21, 30, 31, 34-38, 41-44, 47, 49, 50, 52, 54, 63-67, 72, 73, 84, 85, 90, 93, 98, 105, 112, 124, 126, 133-136, 141, 143, 145, 146, 151, 152, 154, 155, 159, 167, 169, 170-178, 182, 184, 185, 188-190, 192, 194-197, 201, 210, 213, 216, 219, 226, 231, 232, 234, 236
Gregorić, Danilo or Gregoric 40
Grol, Dr. Milan........................ 16, 20, 32, 41, 54, 90, 104, 116, 118, 119, 120, 121, 125, 135, 138, 151, 154, 173, 190, 222, 232
GRU 161
Gruber, Dr. W. 132
Guardian, The 27, 41, 46
Gubbins, Col. Colin 8
Gypsies 21, 22, 54

H.M.G. (His Majesty's Government) or HMG....... 1, 10, 20, 38, 53, 78, 150, 152, 160, 170, 187, 195
Hague, The 212
Hale, Lionel 39
Halifax, Lord Edward 6, 53, 184, 214
Hambro, Carl J. 46
Hambro, Charles 8
Hanau, Julius "Caesar" .... xvii, 3, 4, 6, 7, 10, 12, 26, 34
Harrelson, Max 44
Hawker Aircraft 17
Head, Major G. H. 7
Heeren, Viktor von .... xvii, 124, 132, 134, 137, 138, 141, 146, 151, 159
Hehn, Professor Paul N. 47, 232
Hercegnovi 205
Hercegovina or Herzegovina 182, 186, 205, 206
Higham, Professor Robin 52, 53, 64, 135, 136, 139, 145, 147, 153, 175, 195, 196, 232
Hill, Russel 44
Hillgarth, Capt. Alan 30
Hining, Gen. Sir Robert 73
Hinsley et al 65, 153, 168, 177

Hinsley, Historian Sir Francis Harry......... 65, 153, 168, 177, 232
Hitler, Adolf, der Führer, Fuehrer....... xvii, 21, 36, 44, 51, 52, 55, 57, 58-61, 63-65, 68, 70, 71, 74, 86, 87, 100, 102, 105, 111, 112, 124, 131, 132, 136, 137, 140-142, 145, 146, 148-151, 154, 156, 157, 159, 160, 162, 163, 164, 166, 168-170, 176, 178, 179, 194, 196, 197, 203, 207-210, 219, 220, 225, 226, 231, 234, 236
Hitler and Barbarossa operation.............. 61, 162
Hitler and Bulgaria...... 21, 36, 51, 64, 159, 169, 176, 178, 226
Hitler and Greece 21, 36, 44, 52, 63-65, 105, 112, 124, 136, 141, 145, 146, 151, 159, 169, 170, 176, 178, 194, 196, 197, 210, 219, 226, 231, 234, 236
Hitler and Italy 51, 52, 59, 63, 105, 112, 137, 140, 141, 146, 148-150, 178, 196, 203, 226
Hitler and Rumania........................ 21, 36, 52, 64, 111, 142, 159, 169, 176, 178
Hitler and Yugoslavia..................... 21, 36, 44, 51, 52, 57-61, 63, 64, 70, 71, 86, 87, 102, 105, 112, 124, 131, 132, 136, 137, 140-142, 145, 146, 148, 150, 157, 159, 160, 162-164, 166, 168-170, 176, 178, 179, 194, 197, 203, 207, 208-210, 219, 225, 226, 231, 234, 236
Holland, Col. John (Joe) 2
Holmes, Historian Richard....................... 233
Hoover Institution Archives........... xv, 12, 13, 23, 31, 47, 48, 57, 58, 67, 69, 79, 93, 94, 98, 102, 108, 109, 113, 122, 158, 224, 229, 235
Hope, Capt. Clement 5
Hopkinson 28
Hoptner, Dr. Jacob......................... 15, 32, 47, 77, 101, 128, 136, 145, 147, 151, 152, 158-160, 162, 173, 180-182, 187-193, 233
House of Commons....................... 23, 176
Howard, Michael....................................... 233
Howarth, Patrick 14, 233
Hudson, Capt. Duane T .... xvii, 3, 4, 12, 54, 213, 219
Hull, Cordell 70, 233
Hungary, Hungarians.......... 5, 9, 21, 33, 40, 51, 52, 66, 76, 141, 147, 152, 159, 169, 170, 176, 177, 178, 191, 193, 213, 226
Hyde Park 35

Ikonić, Dr. Dragomir 66, 92, 101

Ilić, General Bogoljub..........55, 71, 96, 106, 117, 119-121, 134, 142, 151, 154, 173, 181-183, 188, 189, 190, 223, 224
Independent Democrats.......... 16, 25, 32, 222
Independent State of Croatia (ISC) or *Nezavisna Država Hrvatska (NDH)* ....xvi, 54, 176, 178, 180, 185, 186, 189, 192, 203-206, 209
India .... xvii, 3, 215
Inönü, Ismet, President of Turkey xviii
Institut za istorijska pitanja 61
Iron Curtain speech................................... 183
Iron Gates 6, 7, 10, 11, 151
Ismay, General Sir Hastings 43, 233
Istanbul............. 35-37, 40, 109, 158, 171, 218
Italian Travel Agency................................. 130
Italians, Italy.....................xviii, 2, 3, 5, 6, 9, 10, 15, 20, 23, 24, 30, 34, 42, 50-53, 59, 63, 66, 70, 72, 73, 84-86, 104, 105, 112, 118, 121, 126, 133, 137, 138, 140, 141, 143, 146-150, 152, 153, 155, 165, 172, 177, 178, 180-186, 189, 190, 192-194, 196, 197, 199-201, 203, 205, 206, 215, 226, 233
Italians or Italy and Germany...............xvii, 2-4, 6, 9, 10, 20, 23, 24, 30, 34, 51-53, 59, 63, 66, 70, 84, 86, 104, 105, 126, 133, 137, 138, 140, 143, 146, 147, 149, 150, 152, 153, 165, 180, 181, 184-186, 192-194, 201, 203, 206
Italians or Italy and Greece...................3, 6, 9, 20, 34, 42, 50, 52, 63, 66, 72, 73, 84, 85, 105, 112, 126, 133, 141, 143, 145, 146, 152, 155, 177, 178, 184, 185, 189, 190, 192, 194, 196, 197, 201, 226
Italians or Italy and Yugoslavia..........xviii, 2, 3, 5, 6, 9, 10, 15, 20, 23, 24, 30, 34, 42, 50-53, 59, 63, 66, 70, 72, 73, 84-86, 104, 105, 112, 118, 121, 133, 137, 138, 140, 141, 143, 146-148, 150, 152, 153, 155, 165, 172, 177, 178, 180, 181, 184-186, 189, 192-194, 197, 199-201, 203, 205, 206, 215, 226, 233
Iveković, Mladen 200

Jacob, Sir Ian 236
Jadovno concentration camp 203
Jajce... 200
Jakovljević, Steva...................................... 225
Janković, Capt. Milan................................ 112
Janković, General Miloje.................. 150, 192
Janković, General Radivoje or Jankovitch. 150, 192, 193
Japan 104
Jasenovac concentration camp......... 179, 203

Jebb, Gladwyn (later Lord)..........xvii, 8, 31, 174, 197, 215, 233
Jelić-Butić, Fikreta178, 190, 192, 195, 203, 204, 205, 233
Jevtić, Bogoljub 116, 118, 154
Jews 16, 54, 203
Joint Broadcasting Committee 39
Joint Planning Staff, Cairo (JPS)............... 175
Jovanović, Jovan "Pižon" 225
Jovanović, Professor Dragoljub..........15, 30, 120, 125, 133
Jovanović, Professor Slobodan..........19, 107, 116, 118-121, 123, 127, 133, 137, 145, 148, 151, 154, 171, 179, 181, 187, 221, 222
Jovanović, Žikica "Španac" 208
Jovović, Capt. Jakov 128, 129, 130
Jukić, Ilija... xviii, 233

Kajmakčalan, Kajmakcalan 47
Kalafatović, General Danilo....181, 182, 185-188, 189, 191-193
Kamnik Mountains...................................... 24
Karageorge (Karađorđe) 47
Karageorgevich, Prince Paul or Karađorđević xviii, 1, 3, 12, 14, 16, 20, 21, 25, 28, 29, 31, 38, 39, 41, 42, 45, 48-51, 53-59, 61-64, 66, 70-77, 86, 97, 98, 101-104, 112, 115, 117, 118-122, 124-126, 130, 132, 134-136, 138, 142, 149, 157, 158, 160, 162, 163, 167, 174, 179, 184, 195, 196, 198, 210, 219, 221, 222, 224, 233
Karapandžić, Adam........................18, 20, 55, 73, 79, 88-90, 97, 99, 100, 110, 111, 114, 139, 153, 211, 224, 225, 227, 233
Karapandžić, Borivoje 233
Kardelj, Edvard................................. 199, 200
Karlovac 185, 189, 190
Kasida, Capt. Josip 128
Kavalla... 73, 184
Kay, Leon 44
Kazan defile...................................... 6, 10, 11
Keegan, military historian John 226, 233
Kennedy, General Sir John 173, 185, 233
Kenya 135, 195
Kidrič, Boris 199
King Lazar (Knez Lazar)............................. 47
King Peter II............5, 29, 51, 55, 98, 100, 105, 113, 114, 122, 125, 127, 129, 137, 138, 161, 175, 188, 202, 229
King Zvonimir 206
Kleist, Marshal P.L.E., von 169, 189, 191
Klingberg 180
Knežević, Major Živan-Žika.........xviii, 69, 70, 74, 80, 87-90, 93, 95, 98, 99, 110, 113-116, 127, 178, 179

Knežević, Radoje or Radne Knjevich........xviii, 16, 20, 41, 43, 64, 69, 90, 94, 98-104, 106-111, 113, 115, 117, 120, 126, 127, 139, 188, 227
Kočević, Lazar.......... 202
Kočović, Bogoljub.......... 233
Koliopoulos, Ioannis 233
Kolubarska Company.......... 208
Končar, Rade 131
Konstantinović, Mihailo or Constantinovich.. .... 72, 102
Kontić, Jovan.......... 230
Koprivnica 203
Korčula 206
Koryzis, Alexandros xvii
Kosić, Dr. (Prof.) Mirko.......... 117-120
Kosić, General Petar or Kossich ... 71, 92, 156
Kosić, Major Nikola 60, 104, 114, 131
Kosovo 47, 76, 155, 224
Kostajnica.......... 181
Košutić, Dr. August 122-125, 171
Kotor.......... 172, 178, 187, 190, 197, 216
Koviljača.......... 173, 175, 181
Kozomaritch (Kozomarić) Gradimir-Mirko ... 40
Kragujevac or Kragujevach.......... 86, 97, 177
Krbek, Professor 123
Krebs, Gerhard.......... 167
Krek, Dr. Miha 67, 72, 119, 121, 139, 177, 182
Kremlin 160, 161, 164, 165
Krizman, Bogdan.......... 233
Krk.......... 206
Krnjević, Dr. Juraj 122, 124, 173, 175, 177
Krstić, Živojin-Žika.......... 14, 17, 18
Krylov, Capt. Ivan Nikitch ... 160-164, 166, 233
Kulenović, Džafer.......... 121
Kulovec, Monsignor Dr. Fran .... xviii, 121, 139, 153, 154, 155, 173, 177, 180
Kvaternik, Slavko 176, 185, 189

Labour Party, The 8, 214
Lamb, Richard.......... 233
Lampson, Sir Miles.......... 193, 195, 196
Lane, Arthur Bliss.......... xviii, 66, 70, 128, 132, 138, 139, 148, 231, 234
Langer & Gleason 175, 233
Langer, historian William Leonard.... 175, 233
Lazarević, Dobra 30, 228
Legal Decrees of the ISC 203, 206
League of Communists of Yugoslavia....... 200
Leary, William M.......... 233
Lebedev, Viktor Z. 45, 142, 161-164
Legation, British.......... xvii, 1, 13, 18, 26, 29, 33, 41, 44, 134, 135, 141, 153, 169, 171
Legation, German 40, 138, 146
Leković, Mišo 209, 233

Lenac, Vladimir-Vlado 205
Lenac, Zdravko.......... 205
Lend-Lease Bill, law 132, 175
Leper, Reginald.......... 215
Lerin 182
Lethbridge, Robert.......... 5, 172
Libertyville 159
Libya 6
Lisbon.......... 197
Lithuanian Soviet Socialist Republic 168
Ljotić, Dimitrije.......... 224
Ljubljana.......... 15, 24, 34, 125, 152, 180, 199, 216, 218, 236
Lloyd-Evans, John.......... 4
Loewenheim et al 234
Lončar, Bogdan.......... 208
London.......... 2, 4-8, 11, 12, 14, 17-20, 23, 24, 26-29, 31-34, 36-41, 44, 50, 53, 60, 64-67, 70, 73, 80, 82-84, 86, 94, 96, 98, 102, 106, 109, 123, 124, 135, 136, 153, 163, 166, 167, 170-174, 176, 183, 184, 189, 192, 193, 196, 197, 215, 222-224, 227, 229-236
Longmore, Air Vice-Marshal Sir Arthur......73, 177
Loon, Hendrik Willem, von 46
Low Countries 8, 34
Lozić, Major Krsta.......... 89
Loznica 173, 185
Lustre operation 136
Lyall, Archie.......... 4

Macdonald, Group Capt. A. Hugh H. .... xvii, 1, 13-15, 17, 19, 42, 43, 65, 67, 68, 74, 77-79, 81-87, 94, 95, 119, 132-134, 137, 143, 145, 148, 149, 153, 194, 220, 226, 228, 229
Macedonia. Macedonians 137, 226
Maček, Dr. Vladko or Macek.......... xviii, 101, 102, 119, 123, 179, 205
Mackenzie, Archie Dunlop.......... 4
Mackenzie, William J.......... 6, 11, 26, 234
Maclean, Brigadier Fitzroy.......... 57, 176, 234
MacVeagh, Lincoln.......... 135, 139
Madrid 197
Maginot line 58
Main Post building 68, 112
Maitland, Patrick.......... 40
Majestic, hotel 130
Makiš radio station 69, 92, 112
Maksimović, Božidar- Boža......67, 68, 79, 92, 101, 117, 125, 221, 228
Mallet, Donald 40
Malta.......... 209
Mameli, Giorgio 133, 139, 145, 146, 155
Manchester Guardian, The.......... 27, 41

Maniu, Iuliu 7
Mapplebeck, Thomas .... xvii, 1, 13, 14, 17, 18, 65, 68, 78, 81, 83, 169, 172, 174, 220
Mardin, Shems 22
Maribor 24, 174
Maribor-Dravograd area 24
Marić, Gen. August 126
Markovac 177
Marković, Bora Č. 77
Marković, Božidar 118
Marković, Capt. Dragoslav 129
Marković, M. 114
Marseilles 129
Marsuoka, Yösuke 167
Martin, John 236
Martinović 190
Mason, Michael 4
Masterson, Thomas .... xvii, 7, 10, 12-14, 18, 20, 24, 32, 34, 41-43, 60, 64, 67, 69, 78, 80, 94, 95, 103, 104, 106, 107, 109, 172, 197, 198
Matić, Vasa 91, 92
McClymont, historian W. G. 234
Mediterranean 5, 20, 30, 34, 44, 231, 233, 234
Meily, John J. 70, 138
Menzies, Major-General Stewart 174
Meretskov, General K.A. 159
Meštrović, Ivan 171
Metaxas Line 197
Metaxas, General Ioannis .... xvii, 197
Metković 195
MEW (Ministry of Economic Warfare) .... xvii, 167, 214, 215
Middle East ..... xvii, 4, 19, 34, 37, 175, 177, 195, 212
Mihailović, Col. Dragoljub-Draža or Mihailovitch Mihajlovich, Draja (later General) .... xvii, 12-14, 18, 30, 54, 57, 205, 207, 209, 219, 225, 235, 236
Mikić (of SPP) 26
Mikoyan, Anastas 166
Milan, Italy, city of 33, 34
Milch, Marshal Erhard 134
Miletić, Krsta 118, 151, 173-176, 178, 181, 182, 186, 188, 191-193, 228, 234
Military Intelligence (MI) 2, 14, 19, 161
Military Intelligence (Research) (MI(R)) 2
Miller, James 4
Miloševa Street 116
Milovanović, Nikola 18, 157, 210, 234
Milunović, Marko 59, 87, 88, 104, 105, 107, 113, 124, 125, 142, 148, 151, 152, 155, 156, 178, 180, 182, 183, 186, 188, 190, 228, 234

Ministry of Economic Warfare (MEW) .... xvii, 167, 214, 215
Ministry of Education 67, 139
Ministry of Information 29, 40
Ministry of the Army 75, 90, 92-94, 98, 99, 110-112, 116-119, 125, 127, 132, 133
Mionica 208
Mirković, General Borivoje-Bora or Mirkovic, Mirkovich, Merkovich .. .. xviii, 1, 13, 17, 18, 19, 54, 68, 69, 78, 79, 87, 91, 96,-98 103, 106, 107, 109, 118, 143, 148, 190, 225, 226, 229
Mljet 206
Mojkovac 47
Molotov, Vyacheslav .... xviii, 140, 142, 148, 159-167, 196
Montenegrin Separatists 203
Monastir (Bitolj) Gap 73, 175
Montenegro (Crna Gora) 30, 44, 119, 167, 172, 181, 186, 199, 203, 205, 207, 209, 218, 219
Morava, river 22
Morton, Major Desmond (later Sir) 231
Moscow .... xviii, 14, 16, 17, 26, 27, 32, 45, 50, 54, 120, 131, 142, 146, 148, 157-164, 166-168, 171, 196, 197, 199, 201, 205, 207, 218, 222, 225, 231, 232
Munich (München) 2, 27
Mura, river 146
Mussolini, Benito, *il Duce* .... xviii, 52, 54, 59, 133, 136, 138, 140, 144-146, 178, 189, 190, 194, 199, 204, 206, 215, 225, 234

Nakić, Milan 100, 112
Narodna Odbrana (The Defense League) ... xviii, 12-14, 16, 17, 26, 30-32, 42, 47, 51-53, 67, 79, 97, 100, 109, 122, 218
Narodno jedinstvo 178
Narodno Vijeće 122
National Assistance Board 20
National Peasant Party (of Rumania) 7
Nazi Germany 12, 55, 166, 201, 225
Nazis, Nazism .... xvii, 5, 8, 12, 18, 55, 61,134, 141-143, 162, 166, 167, 169, 170, 176, 201, 225, 231, 232, 235, 236
Nazor, Vladimir 200
Nedeljković, Gen. Petar 126
Nedić, General Milutin 75, 112
Nelson, Sir Frank .... xvii, 7-9, 11, 35, 37, 38, 42, 49, 58, 67, 79, 151, 197, 215, 218
Nemanjina street 116
New York City 46

New York Times, The............44, 97, 127, 170, 176, 181, 205
New Zealand, New Zealanders... 43, 196, 234
Nezavisna Država Hrvatska (NDH) or Independent State of Croatia..........xvi, 54, 76, 180, 186, 189, 206, 233
Nicholls, John... 53
Nicky 129, 130
Nikolić, General Milutin 115, 187, 188
Nikolić, Radoje 228
Nikšić or Niksic..................119, 178, 180, 181-183, 185, 186, 188, 189, 190, 228
Ninčić, Dr. Momčilo..........xviii,15, 19, 26, 116, 118, 120, 121, 132
Ninčić, Đura... 190
Ninčić, Olga... 15
Ninčić, Velizar 146
Niš or Nish or Nis 175, 194, 216, 218
Niška Banja 156
Nixon, Hilton... 5
NKVD 31, 160, 165
North Africa 63, 177
Norway 46
Nova riječ 24
Novi red 24
Nuremberg 168

Odessa.. 158
Official Gazette, The 86
Olympus Mountain 55
Onslow, Dr. Sue.........6, 9, 12, 15, 16, 20, 23-25, 28, 29, 31, 34, 41, 43, 48, 63, 65, 104, 210, 234
Onslow and the coup.....................23, 28, 29, 43, 48, 63, 65, 210
Onslow and Greece 6, 9, 20, 31, 34, 41, 43, 63, 65, 210, 234
Onslow and Yugoslavia.........6, 9, 12, 15, 16, 20, 23-25, 28, 29, 31, 34, 41, 43, 48, 63, 104, 210, 234
Opposition (parties)............................. 51, 52
Order of White Eagle with Swords 16
Organisation of United Jugoslav Students.. 16
Osijek 89, 91, 177
Oster, Major-General Hans 151
Ostojić, Capt. Zaharije............................. 116
Ostrog monastery............................. 183, 188
Ottoman Empire 220
Overseas News Agency (ONA).................. 46
Oxford University............................. 232, 235

Pact of Steel... 2
Palas Hotel 173
Palazzo Chigi 178
Palazzo Venezia 178, 206
Pale..... 177, 178, 180-183, 185-189, 192, 193

Palestine...................................... 20, 124, 171
Pandurović, General Dragiša.............. 74-77, 114, 115, 179, 188, 234
Papagos, General Alexandros.....xviii, 43, 193, 195, 233
Pappas, Greek journalist .... xviii, 43-45
Paris .. 4, 33, 46, 122, 159, 224, 230, 235, 236
Parker, Ralph 4, 7
Parliament .... xvii, 23, 29, 99, 100, 147
Parrott, Sir Cecil 29, 234
Partisans.......................54, 57, 179, 208, 213, 230, 231, 233, 236
Passport Control Officer (PCO)................ 212
Patriarch Gavrilo, Dr. Dožić.............92, 136, 152, 188, 229
Pavelić, Ante, dentist................................ 122
Pavelić, Dr. Ante, *Poglavnik* 186, 199
Pavelich, Nicky 129, 130
Pavlović, *Vojvoda* Kosta.................... 77, 205
Peace Conference (table) 25, 51
Pejić, Major Radovan 112
Perišić, Major Milisav or L.R. (Last Ray) Hope 64, 73, 184
Perišić, Vojislav 67
Perović, Ivan................................... 135, 180
Pešić, General Petar............................xviii, 70-72, 75-77, 92, 101, 102, 112, 179, 188, 194, 210
Peter II, King of Yugoslavia...29, 105, 113, 114, 122, 127, 128, 129, 137, 175
Petranović & Žutić 30, 114, 121, 133, 134, 147-150, 152, 160, 234
Petranović, historian Branko 200
Petrov, Prof. Vladimir 234
Petrović, General Milorad, "Lord".. 74, 75, 114
Petrovitch (Petrović), Dr. Svetislav-Sveta xviii, 46, 220
Pimlott, historian Ben..........................30, 32, 38, 48, 79, 90, 95, 96, 151, 169, 174, 193, 195, 196, 197, 198, 210, 234
Pireus 174
Pirie, Ian 5, 33, 37
Ploesti... 7, 25
Plotnikov, Victor...................................... 159
Podgorica 44, 218, 219
Poland 159, 174, 209
Politburo 131, 160-164, 206, 207
Political Warfare Executive (PWE) 39, 215
Politika, Belgrade's daily newspaper....40, 86, 229
Popović, Lt.-Colonel Branko..................... 188
Popović, Colonel Žarko.................xviii, 13, 14, 17, 159, 160, 225, 229, 235
Popović, Steva 225
Portugal 172

Prague.............................. 2, 4, 153, 157, 205
Pravda, Belgrade's daily 40, 46
Pravica, paper.. 25
President Franklin D Roosevelt........xviii, 20, 44, 84, 175, 177, 234
Press Propaganda Department.................... 39
Prilep 174
Prince Aimone Savoy............................... 206
Prince Paul, Regent of Yugoslavia or Prince Regent or Prince Paul, Regent of Yugoslavia or Knez Pavle Karađorđević .... xviii, 1, 3, 5, 11, 12, 14, 16, 20, 21, 25, 28, 29, 31, 38, 39, 41, 42, 45, 48-59, 61-64, 66-75, 77, 84, 86, 92, 97, 98, 101-104, 112, 115-122, 124-126, 130, 132, 134-136, 138, 142, 149, 157, 158, 160, 162, 163, 167, 174, 179, 184, 193, 195, 196, 198, 210, 219, 221, 222, 224, 233
Princess Olga.......... 55, 66, 72, 102, 135, 184
Prisoners of war (POW) 75
Proclamation, Royal................98, 100, 110, 126, 127, 128, 130
Proleter... 199
Propaganda..2, 6, 8, 10, 16, 23-27, 29, 30, 32, 33, 36, 39-49, 64, 106, 110, 143, 150, 152, 162, 169, 170, 174, 197, 199, 208, 212, 214, 215, 218, 230
Public Record Office 24
Punishment operation 150, 224
Pupis, Major... 151
Putsch (Puč, *Coup d'état*)......1, 18, 19, 23, 29, 44, 50, 55-57, 60, 63, 65, 69, 73, 85-87, 89, 90, 94-101, 103, 104, 107-109, 111, 113-116, 119, 122, 140, 141, 161, 162, 178, 180, 188, 194, 202, 210, 211, 221, 226, 228-230, 236

Queen Mary of Yugoslavia................... 64, 135

Rab.. 206
Radical Party.................... 118, 119, 121, 222
Radio Belgrade 100, 127, 128, 130
Radio Velebit............................. 143, 153, 156
Radojičić, Žika.. 92
Radović, Col. Dushan ("Cousin") 218
Rakić, Col. Miodrag.................................... 70
Raljić 101
Ranković, Aleksandar-Leka 208
Rapp, Sir Terence .... xvii, 126
Ravna Gora 205
Red Army 157-60, 166, 201
Reich, Third German................6, 141, 146, 168, 185, 233
Reserve Officers Club 15
Reuters News Agency.................... 15, 40, 44

Revolutionary Government.................. 25, 226
Rheinland 2, 157
Rhodes James, historian Robert. 63, 235, 236
Ribar, Lola 200
Ribbentrop, Joachim von............................... xvii, 61, 105, 132, 141, 159
Ribnikar, Vladimir-Vlada..................... 40, 204
Ristić, Capt. Dragiša N..................... xviii, 1, 50, 56, 63, 69, 70, 74, 77, 79, 81, 85-87, 91-100, 104, 105, 107-110, 112, 113, 116, 118, 121, 122, 126, 128, 131, 132, 134, 136, 139, 141, 145, 146, 154-156, 158, 173, 175, 177, 181-183, 187-194, 227, 230, 235
Rječina River.. 185
Roberts, Walter R........................... 169, 235
Rockefeller 46
Rockefeller Centre..................................... 46
Rolls-Royce Co. 17
Rome.................52, 121, 133, 138, 144-146, 172, 178, 181, 189, 190, 196, 204, 206, 222
Roosevelt, President Franklin D........xviii, 20, 44, 84, 175, 177, 234
Rosetti, Bibica 22
Royal Guards........................xviii, 76, 88, 92, 94, 102, 112, 113, 140, 223
Royal Palace 92, 98, 116, 127, 129, 135
Royal Proclamation.............................. 98, 100, 110, 126, 127, 128, 130
Rožđalovski, Major Vlastimir 88
Rudolf, Prof. Ivan...................................... 171
Rumania, Rumanians, or Romania, Romanian or Roumania................4, 7, 8, 9, 10, 21, 36, 37, 41, 43, 49, 50, 52, 64, 76, 109-111, 142, 143, 159, 168, 169, 176, 178, 191, 218, 226, 227
Rundstedt, Marshal Gerd 163
Rupel Pass 174
Russia or Soviet Russia or Soviet Union or U.S.S.R..............................xviii, 15, 16, 45, 53, 54, 60, 61, 71, 75, 77, 104, 130, 131, 133, 139, 142, 146, 148, 157-168, 175, 196, 200-202, 204-209, 227, 231, 232

Salonika or Salonika Front.........3, 43, 50, 51, 58, 71-73, 76, 77, 102, 132, 137-139, 146, 149, 154-156, 174-177, 179, 184, 194, 197, 224
Saracoglu, Sükrü...................................... xviii
Sarajevo........112, 177, 178, 180, 185, 189, 191, 192
Sargent, Orme............................. 20, 31, 144
Sava, River......92, 93, 159, 177, 178, 180, 182, 185

Savić, Col. Dragutin............57, 87, 89, 91, 96, 107, 108, 118, 134, 148, 162, 164, 194
Savoy, Prince Aimone................................. 206
Schmidt, Dr. Paul 132
Schnurre, Dr. Karl 168
Schulenburg, Werner, von 164, 167
Seaman, Mark............. 7, 37, 39, 214-216, 235
Seattle... 124
Secret Intelligence Service (SIS) or S.I.S. or MI6 or "Z"....................................1, 2, 4, 5, 9, 15, 19, 20, 24, 28, 29, 36, 37, 46, 49, 80, 103, 104, 106, 123, 142, 168, 172, 179, 212, 213, 218, 232, 233, 236
Secretary of State, USA...................... 70, 233
Section D of SIS.........xvii, 1-9, 12, 22, 24-26, 28-30, 32-35, 37, 39-41, 53, 54, 151, 212, 213, 215
Sekulić, Dr. Miloš 90, 96, 225, 226, 235
Selborne, Roundell Palmer 3rd Earl....... xvii, 8
Serbia,Serbs................................. 16, 22, 23, 25, 27, 30, 31, 34, 42, 45-48, 50, 51, 53, 54, 67, 86, 122, 129, 133, 142, 143, 152, 155, 162, 167, 173, 177, 182, 185, 186, 192, 199, 202, 204-209, 212, 218, 219, 226, 233
Serbian Army 84
Serbian Orthodox Church................87, 100, 107, 136, 138, 188, 202, 229
Serbian Peasant Party (SPP) or Serb Peasant Party.......................................xviii, 12, 13, 16, 17, 22-32, 42, 47-50, 52, 53, 60, 63, 65, 79, 95, 96, 101, 102, 104, 109, 118, 120, 122, 171, 197, 218, 219, 222, 225
Seton-Watson, historian Hugh.................xvii, 4, 7, 10, 15, 169, 171, 217, 222, 235
Sevojno 173, 174, 175, 176, 177
Shapiro, Henry 161
Shaposhnikov, Marshal Boris............ 160, 162
Shea, General John 20
Shell Co.. 16, 213
Sheridan, Col. Leslie 39
Shillan, David 174
Shone, Terence.................................. xvii, 135
Shoup, Paul... 235
Siberia or Siberian...................................... 168
Sigint (Signal Intelligence)......................... 168
Simić, Capt. Vladimir............................ 69, 112
Simić, Colonel Božin..............................148, 157, 158, 160, 162, 164
Simović, Dr. Miloš-Miša............................. 228
Simović, General Dušan or Simovic, Simovich, Simovitch..............xviii, 17, 44, 55, 56, 72, 74, 84, 85, 93, 94, 100, 114, 119, 122, 128, 132, 135, 143, 147, 170, 174, 210, 225, 226, 230

Sinclair, Admiral Sir Hugh 2, 212
Sinj 195
Skoda Works 180
Skoplje, Skopje................ 7, 15, 174, 178, 216
Slavija... 131, 202
Slavs, the......................... .... 25, 51, 53, 223
Slobodni Balkan 24
Slovene People's Party 121
Slovenia,Slovenes.................4, 12, 16, 23, 24, 25, 26, 34, 42, 64, 98, 115, 118, 119, 122-124, 126-128, 130, 139, 171, 182, 183, 187, 197, 199-201, 218, 219, 231
Smiljanić, Ilija.. 20
Smith, Professor Bradley F. 235
Smith-Cumming, Mansfield George 2
Smith-Pavelić, Ante.................... 93, 122, 230
Smoljan, Bariša 122, 173, 177
Snoj 177
Socialist Party.. 4, 27
Soddu, Gen. Ubaldo................................. 143
Sofia 25, 27, 40, 41, 205
Sokić brothers 40
Sokol organization.................................... 131
'Sophocles' 160, 163
South Africa.. 2, 3
South Slav Herald biweekly............. 24, 40, 41
S.O.1, propaganda section of SOE..... 39, 215
S.O.2, operational section of SOE..........7, 10, 16, 25, 42, 47, 48, 67, 102, 197, 215, 216
Southern Department of FO 210
Southern Serbia 58, 72, 142, 170, 172, 219
Soviet Bloc 30
Soviet Russia, Russia, or Soviet Union or U.S.S.R................xviii, 15, 16, 45, 53, 54, 60, 61, 71, 75, 77, 104, 130, 131, 133, 139, 142, 146, 148, 157-168, 175, 196, 200-204, 206-209, 227, 231, 232
Spain 4, 5, 27, 30, 172, 197, 201
Spanish Civil War................... 4, 27, 202, 208
Special Operation Executive (SOE) ....xvii, 1-10, 12-20, 23-33, 3-43, 45, 47-49, 53, 58, 63-65, 67, 77-80, 83, 85, 86, 89, 90, 95, 101-104, 106, 109, 113, 129, 149, 150, 170-173, 193, 197, 210, 213-220, 222, 231, 232, 234-236
Split 15, 190, 195, 206, 213, 234
Sporazum (Serbo-Croat) ...115, 118, 158, 222
Sremska Mitrovica..................................... 180
Srpski Kralj, hotel 142
St. George Lethbridge, Robert F. 5
St. John, correspondent Robert...........43, 44, 46, 125, 129, 130, 141-143, 153, 154, 169, 171, 174, 175, 177, 178, 183, 195, 228, 235
Stafford, Professor David.....................1, 2, 8-11, 13-19, 25, 30, 32, 36, 39, 43, 48, 65,

66, 68, 78, 80-86, 94, 103, 106, 143, 144, 160, 161, 197, 212, 228, 235
Stakić, Vladislav 145
Stalin, Joseph Vissarionovich...xviii, 140, 142, 157, 159, 160-167, 177, 196, 199, 232, 235
Stanković, Aleksandar............................. 223
Stanković, Radenko 135, 180
Stanley, Oliver 195
Stanojlović, Đorđe 91, 92
Stara Gradiška concentration camp 203
State Department, US 61, 66, 70
Stebernjak, Capt. Slavko 118
Stefanović, Nenad 224, 229
Stephenson, William 36, 46, 236
Stoyadinovitch, Dr. Milan or Stojadinović .. 223
Strang, Lord William 232
Struga 182
Stuart , Sir Campbell 214
Stuart, Bill 4
Subbotitch, Ivan or Subotić 192
"Subsidies", "Subsidized" 3, 13, 19, 23, 28, 30-32, 39, 40, 52, 64
Suez Canel 64
Sukhonin 142
Sulzberger, Cyrus Leo 13, 17, 44, 235
Sumadia (Sumadija) 22
Sušak, Susak 15, 185
Suvobor 47
Sweet-Escott, Bickham 2, 3, 5-10, 12, 13, 25, 28, 29, 33, 34, 36, 39, 60, 65, 138, 172, 212, 213, 215, 218, 235

Šabac 182
Šibenik 171, 190, 195, 206
Šubašić, Dr. Ivan 123, 124, 126, 134, 137
Šumadija 89, 205
Šutej, Dr. Juraj ....
72, 102, 115, 122, 123, 124, 173, 175, 177
Švaba or Schwaben 155, 156

Tatoi Conference 73, 177
Taylor, George Francis .... xvii, 2, 3, 5-9, 11-14, 19, 21, 24, 29, 31, 34-37, 41, 48, 49, 58, 63-65, 67, 71, 77, 78, 101, 102, 106, 109, 153, 171, 172, 174, 196, 197, 213, 215, 216, 218
Taylor, historian Alan John Percival (A.J.P.)52
Teheran Conference 57
Terazije, square or Terazzia 129-131
Thermopylae 192
Third Army 72
Thomas, Gordon 236
Thompson, journalist Dorothy 46
Thrace, Thracia 146
Times Square, New York 169

Times, The 4, 21, 40
Timoshenko, Marshal S. K. 159
Tito, Josip Broz 5, 15, 27, 30, 45, 54, 57, 131, 140, 161, 179, 180, 199, 200, 202-204, 207-209, 211, 227, 231, 233, 235, 236
Tomše, Col. France 189, 190
Topalović, Major Vojislav 118, 236
Topčider hill or Topchidersko 13, 30
Torbar, Josip 122
Torlonia, villa 140
"Toys" 30, 33-35, 153, 169, 171, 219
Treaties of Rome, 1941 206
Trepča mines or Trepca .... xvii, 212, 213
Trieste or Trst 24, 178, 185
Trifunović, Miloš-Miša 119
Trifunović-Birčanin, Ilija or Trifunovich, Birchanin or "Daddy" .... xviii, 2, 11, 13, 26, 31, 35, 78, 90, 96-101, 118, 216, 218
Tripartite Pact 9, 16, 21, 29, 41-43, 47, 49, 51, 56, 60, 61, 64-67, 70, 73-77, 84, 86, 92, 101-105, 112, 121, 123, 132, 137-139, 141, 146, 148, 151, 154, 159-161, 169, 179, 206, 220
Trogir 206
Trojanović, Lt.-Col. Radmilo 189-192
Troy, Professor Thomas F 236
Tržić 204
Tupanjanin, Dr. Miloš or 'Uncle" .... xvii, xviii, 10, 12, 13, 16, 26-32, 45-48, 53, 65, 67, 78, 79, 95, 96, 101, 102, 118, 120-122, 160, 171, 190, 197, 210, 216, 218, 219
Turkey, Turks .... xviii, 3, 8, 12, 36, 38, 43, 47, 50, 63-65, 75, 77, 84, 85, 139, 155, 158, 168, 177, 195
Tuzla 185

Ukraine, Ukrainians 160, 209
Una, river 181, 182
"ungentlemanly warfare" 35, 214, 232
Union of Soviet Socialist Republics (USSR) or U.S.S.R 17, 157, 160, 165, 167, 168, 202, 204, 206, 207
United Jugoslavs 16
United Kingdom (UK) or Britain ...... xvii, 6, 7, 12, 15, 21, 25, 28-30, 35, 39, 41, 43, 45, 53, 56, 57, 60, 63, 70, 71, 73, 81, 133, 134, 138, 141, 150, 164, 172, 179, 184, 185, 188, 195, 202, 210, 212, 215, 226, 231, 232, 234-236
United States of America (USA) .... xv, xviii, 46-48, 70, 71, 87, 105, 124, 129, 138, 157, 159, 174
Urošević, Capt. Miodrag 135

Ustaše, the or Ustasha...... 138, 140, 143, 175, 179, 186, 199, 200, 203, 205, 227, 233, 236
Užice 54, 173, 177, 185, 186, 194

Vajda, Paul.. 44
Valjevo 205, 208
Valjevo Partisan Detachment.................... 208
Valona 132, 137, 184, 185
Vardar (Axios) River................................. 187
Vatican 223
Vauhnik. Colonel Vladimir..................... xviii, 136, 137, 145, 147, 151, 152, 160, 163, 226, 236
Večernje novosti (The Evening News), daily 18, 79, 99, 233
Veesenmeyer, Dr. Edmund............... 185, 189
Velebit, radio station................... 143, 153, 156
Velebit, Vladimir 209
Velimirović, Bishop Dr. Nikolaj 92, 119, 188
Venom telegrams 39
Versailles.. 2
Veterans Associations.......................... 16, 17
Vichy France 172
Vienna............... 21, 56, 75, 77, 83, 87, 88, 91, 106, 141, 146, 151, 161
Vikert, Rikard................................... 122, 126
Vilder, Većeslav 24, 171
Vlahović, Professor Staniša 223, 224
Vlajić, Božidar-Boka 118, 175, 190, 228
Vodušek Starič, historian Jerca................4, 13, 20, 24, 27, 32, 41, 49, 54, 170, 171, 236
Voice of Canadian Serbs 98, 108, 110, 224
Vojvodina 119, 177, 199
Volo 192
Vračar... 13
Vranesh.. 170
Vranjska Banja or Vranyska Banya... 174, 175
Vrbas River 182
Vreme, Belgrade's daily 40
Vrnjačka Banja or Vrnjachka Banya.. 169, 184
Vršac 177
Vučićević, Ljubomir 89
Vyshinsky, Andrei...........xviii, 160-165, 167, 204

Walker, Dave.. 44
War Cabinet 8, 80, 214
War Office 2, 8, 106, 114, 212, 214
Washington, D. C.......50, 79, 132, 156, 158, 175, 195, 232, 233, 234
Wavell, General Sir Archibald or later Field Marshal Earl Wavell.......xvii, 34, 37, 49, 64, 84, 136
Wedemeyer, General Albert C. 236

Weichs, Gen Maximilian, von..... .... 189, 190,191, 192, 193
Welles, Sumner......................... 132, 138, 163
West, Nigel... 236
Western Europe 8, 201, 208
Western Powers............... 55, 56, 59, 60, 225
Wheeler-Bennett 236
White Palace 70, 179
White Russian Prince 51
White, Leigh 44
Williams, Historian Heather.....2, 6, 13, 15, 26, 28, 29, 31, 37, 40-42, 49, 68, 71, 77, 78, 79, 113, 150, 210, 215, 236
Wilmot, John... 197
Winterbotham, Frederick William 236
World Radio University listeners (WRUL) .. 46, 220
World War One or WWI............................. 21
World War Two or WWII........23, 39, 231, 233, 235
World Wide Broadcasting Foundation (WWBF).. 46
WRUL radio station 46, 220
WRUW short wave radio station 46
Wylie, Neville... 63

Yalta 232
YMCA 24
Yugoslav Air Force 13, 17, 84, 170
Yugoslav General Staff..............7, 10, 11, 14, 15, 17, 31, 65, 68, 78, 160, 184
Yugoslav High Command.......... 189, 191, 192
Yugoslav Nationalist Party 16
Yugoslavia (also Yugo-Slavia, Jugoslavia, Juggery).........xv, xvii, xviii, 1-10, 12-21, 23-54, 56-61, 63, 64, 66, 67, 70-73, 75-77, 81, 84-87, 93, 94, 95, 99, 102-107, 109, 112, 118, 119, 121-125, 128-134, 136-143, 145-148, 150, 152, 153, 155, 157-186, 188-195, 197-203, 205-213, 215, 216, 218, 219, 221-231, 233-236
Yugoslavs, the..............3, 10, 12, 19, 21, 46, 47, 51, 53, 73, 80, 131, 139, 143, 147, 152, 158-160, 162, 163, 166, 171, 183, 184, 185, 189, 193, 195, 220

"Z", M16, SIS............ 1, 2, 4, 5, 9, 15, 19, 24, 28, 29, 37, 80, 103, 104, 106, 168, 172, 212, 213
Zagreb..... xvii, 4, 9, 13, 15, 16, 24, 60, 70, 115, 122, 124-126, 138, 140, 143, 147, 152, 175, 176, 178, 180, 186, 190, 192, 200-205, 209, 216, 218, 233, 234
Zapisi............................ 19, 20, 123, 179, 233
Zdravković, Col. Stojan 93, 94

Zečević, historian Momčilo........ 199, 200, 234
Zemljoradnička Stranka or Serbian Peasant Party (SPP)......... xviii, 12, 13, 16, 22, 23, 26, 27, 29-31, 42, 50, 52, 53, 60, 63, 65, 95, 96, 101, 102, 104, 109, 118, 120, 122, 171, 197, 218, 219, 222, 225
Zemun. 67- 69, 75, 79, 81, 87-94, 96, 98-101, 106, 107, 109, 112, 116-119, 134, 153, 171, 225
Zobenica, Major Danilo 88

Zog, King of Albania 29
Zrenjanin 177
Zrinjskoga street.. 9
Zvonimir, King 206
Zvornik or Znorvik.................................... 194

Živković, Dr. Sveta 30
Živković, General Petar..................... 118, 120
Žutić,Historian Dr. Nikola.......................30, 114, 121, 125, 132, 133, 134, 147-150, 152, 160, 167, 234

www.ingramcontent.com/pod-product-compliance
Lightning Source LLC
Chambersburg PA
CBHW080239170426
43192CB00014BA/2498